the ultimate
GENERAL
KNOWLEDGE quiz book

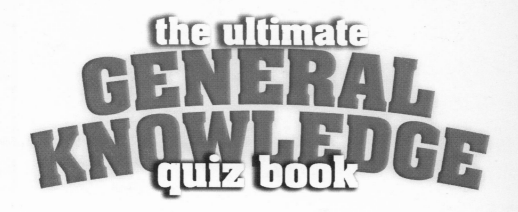

the ultimate GENERAL KNOWLEDGE quiz book

by Philip Carter & John Bray

ARCTURUS

Published by
Arcturus Publishing Limited

For Bookmart Limited
Registered Number 2372865
Desford Road
Enderby
Leicester
LE9 5AD

This edition published 2001

Printed and bound by Omnia Books limited

Cover by Communiqué
Illustrations by Peter Coupe
Design by Alex Ingr

Edited by Paula Field & Fiona Ball
Proofreader David Carr-Allinson

ISBN 1-84193-078-4

Arcturus Publishing Limited
1–7 Shand Street
London
SE1 2ES

CONTENTS

MISCELLANEOUS

Quiz 1

1   Who was the first woman to hold a seat in the British parliament?
2   Which playwright became president of Czechoslovakia in 1989?
3   What instrument was played by jazz great Coleman Hawkins?
4   Which is the most northernmost of North America's five great lakes?
5   In which country is Montego Bay?
6   At which battle did Octavian defeat the combined forces of Mark Antony and Cleopatra in 31 B.C.?
7   The name of which Jewish holiday means 'day of atonement' in Hebrew ?
8   The Ibex is a type of which animal?
9   Ice cream was first produced in which country in the 17th century?
10 What is the name of the natural process whereby the soil and rocks of the earth's crust are continuously worn away?
11 What does the letter S stand for in the poet T. S. Eliot's name?
12 Elisha Gray filed his own claim for the invention of which device only hours after the accredited inventor had done so in 1874?
13 A hussar was a light cavalryman from which country?
14 In which card game, played with a deck of 32 cards, are the jacks known as bowers?
15 Who wrote 'Waiting for Godot'?

Answers 1 Lady Nancy Astor 2 Vaclav Havel 3 Saxophone 4 Lake Superior 5 Jamaica 6 Battle of Actium 7 Yom Kippur 8 Goat 9 Italy 10 Erosion 11 Stearns 12 Telephone 13 Hungary 14 Euchre 15 Samuel Becket

MISCELLANEOUS 1

Quiz 2

1 In which country was tennis player Martina Navratilova born?

2 In which town in Israel would you find the Church of Annunciation, the Church of Saint Joseph and Saint Mary's Well?

3 Which American choreographer's work included the Academy Award winning films 'Cabaret' and 'All That Jazz'?

4 In which US city would you find the Wrigley Building?

5 Which Latin word means the water bearer?

6 What nationality was the 14/15th century astronomer Tycho Brahe?

7 What was first seriously advocated by a British builder, William Willett in his 1907 pamphlet, Waste of Daylight?

8 By the end of which period in the Earth's history had most dinosaurs become extinct?

9 *Calypso, cattleya* and *pogonia* are types of which flower?

10 What is the name of the earthenware, usually with a blue and white pattern, originally made in a town in Holland?

11 The oak is a member of which family of trees?

12 According to legend, Cleopatra committed suicide by holding which snake to her body?

13 Macbeth claimed his kingdom by murdering which Scottish king in 1040?

14 What name in Christianity is given to the Sunday before Easter?

15 Who won an Academy Award for best actor in 'One Flew Over the Cuckoo's Nest'?

Answers 1 Czechoslovakia **2** Nazareth **3** Bob Fosse **4** Chicago **5** Aquarius **6** Danish **7** Daylight Saving Time (putting the clocks forward or backward) **8** Triassic **9** Orchid **10** Delft **11** Beech **12** Asp **13** Duncan **14** Palm Sunday **15** Jack Nicholson

Quiz 3

1   What is the name given to the claw of a lobster or crab?
2   What nationality was the silent film star Sarah Bernhardt?
3   What is tacophobia the fear of?
4   Which film company produced the first talkie, 'The Jazz Singer' in 1927?
5   In psychology, what is another name for a Rorschach Test?
6   Piraeus is the port for which European capital city?
7   Anthony Babington was executed for plotting to assassinate which British monarch?
8   Henry Bessemer invented a process for the manufacture of steel in which British city?
9   What is the name of a Japanese three-line poem of seventeen syllables?
10 What kind of creature is a monitor?
11 What element has the symbol P?
12 Of what is ichthyology the study?
13 What is measured in amperes?
14 What is the surname of the father and son who were the second and sixth US presidents respectively
15 What is the world's highest navigable lake?

Answers 1 Pincer **2** French **3** Speed **4** Warner Brothers **5** Inkblot **6** Athens **7** Queen Elizabeth I **8** Sheffield **9** Haiku **10** Lizard **11** Phosphorus **12** Fish **13** Electric current **14** Adams **15** Titicaca

MISCELLANEOUS 1

Quiz 4

1 Which playwright wrote 'The Birthday Party' and 'The Caretaker'?

2 What is the highest female singing voice?

3 Adonis was slain by which creature while hunting?

4 Which republic is the third largest island in the Mediterranean Sea?

5 Which book in the Old Testament is named because the opening chapters concern a census of Israelite tribes?

6 If VHF is very high frequency, what is SHF?

7 What is the name of the forked stick used for locating underground water?

8 What breed of cat is often referred to as The Sacred Cat of Burma?

9 What type of creature is the echidna?

10 The Colossus of Rhodes was a bronze statue of which Greek god?

11 What is the largest city in Africa?

12 Who was the Hungarian-born obstetrician who was a pioneer in the field of antiseptics?

13 What number system uses only the digits 0 and 1?

14 Which sacking material is known in America as burlap?

15 What in America is the Lone Star State?

Answers 1 Harold Pinter 2 Soprano 3 A boar 4 Cyprus 5 Numbers 6 Superhigh Frequency 7 Divining Rod 8 Birman 9 Spiny anteater 10 Helios 11 Cairo 12 Ignaz Philip Semmelweiss 13 Binary 14 Hessian 15 Texas

1   Which two bodies of water are connected by the Straits of Florida?
2   What name is given to the first six books of the Bible?
3   What nationality is motor racer Mario Andretti?
4   Who famously sailed in HMS Beagle?
5   In which US state is Appomattox Court House National Park?
6   What type of song is a doxology?
7   All Souls College is part of which university?
8   Who was the wife of William the Conqueror who is said to have designed the Bayeux Tapestry?
9   What does the letter B stand for in author J.B. Priestley's name?
10   Who was the legendary son of British king Luther Pendragon?
11   The Cordillera Isabella is the highest mountain range of which Central American Republic?
12   Who succeeded Dag Hammarskjold as UN Secretary General?
13   Zanzibar is an island of which country?
14   A 'nuncio' is an ambassador of which person?
15   What word refers to the 'restructuring' of the Soviet System?

Answers 1 Atlantic Ocean and Gulf of Mexico 2 Hexateuch 3 American 4 Charles Darwin 5 Virginia 6 Hymn 7 Oxford 8 Mathilda of Flanders 9 Boynton 10 Arthur 11 Nicaragua 12 U-Thant 13 Tanzania 14 The Pope 15 Perestoika

MISCELLANEOUS 1   *Quiz 6*

1   When Armstrong and Aldrin became the first men to walk on the moon in 1969, who piloted the orbiting capsule and stayed aboard?

2   On which continent is Queen Maud Land?

3   What measurement of petroleum in the US is defined as 42 US gallons?

4   Who wrote 'Finnegan's Wake'?

5   What is another name for the grey or white wolf?

6   In which sea is Dogger Bank?

7   At the 1960 Rome Olympics who became the first American woman to win three Olympic Gold medals in running events?

8   Who was the first person to send a wireless signal across an ocean?

9   Which politician received the Nobel Peace Prize in 1990?

10   Which general commanded the Mexican troops at the Battle of the Alamo?

11   Which is the largest town in the Channel Islands?

12   Which woodwind instrument is descended from an ancient Middle Eastern folk instrument called a shawm?

13   The professional variation of which game was introduced in 1869 by the Cincinnati Red Stockings?

14   'One O'Clock Jump' was a famous recording by the big band of which jazz great?

15   Which is Scotland's biggest lake?

Answers 1 Michael Collins 2 Antarctica 3 Barrel 4 James Joyce 5 Timberwolf 6 The North Sea 7 Wilma Rudolph 8 Marconi 9 Mikhail Gorbachev 10 Santa Anna 11 St. Helier 12 Oboe 13 Baseball 14 Count Basie 15 Loch Lomond

1   The Titanic was a vessel belonging to which shipping line?

2   What do you call a phenomenally productive worker?

3   Which Agatha Christie character was created on screen by Margaret Rutherford?

4   Alexander Selkirk was the inspiration for which fictional character?

5   If A is Alpha, what is P?

6   What is the name of the French Stock Exchange?

7   RA is the international vehicle registration sign for which country?

8   What is the meaning of the Latin phrase *tempus fugit*?

9   How many glasses are served by a magnum of champagne?

10 Who was the cult leader of People's Temple who convinced hundreds of his followers to commit suicide in Guyana in 1978?

11 For which 1978 movie was the promotional line: 'Just when you thought it was safe to go back in the water'?

12 The Pieta was the only sculpture signed by which artist?

13 What lasted for just 75 seconds on April 18, 1906?

14 Who wrote the series of novels about the American private detective Lew Archer?

15 The Sex Kitten was the nickname of which actress?

Answers 1 White Star 2 Stakhanovite 3 Miss Marple 4 Robinson Crusoe 5 Papa 6 Bourse 7 Argentina 8 Time Flies 9 Twelve 10 Jim Jones 11 Jaws 2 12 Michaelangelo 13 The San Francisco Earthquake 14 F. Ross MacDonald 15 Brigette Bardot

MISCELLANEOUS 1 — Quiz 8

1 Which two planets lie between the Earth and the Sun?

2 The word Shavian refers to which writer?

3 What natural disaster struck Lisbon in Portugal in 1755?

4 What did peoples of the Ancient World refer to as 'The Pillars of Hercules'?

5 What was first discovered in February 1851 at Summerhill Creek, Australia?

6 Caroline of Brunswick was the queen of which British king?

7 Who wrote 'Die Fledermaus'?

8 In Rugby, the Calcutta Cup is competed for by which two countries?

9 Who wrote 'Auld Lang Syne'?

10 What is signalled when a ship hoists the Blue Peter flag?

11 What did Kirkpatrick MacMillan invent a type of in 1839?

12 Where does voting take place to elect a new pope?

13 At which village near Rochester in Kent was a place of imprisonment for young people founded in 1902?

14 Which metallic element was named after a Roman god?

15 In which country are the Southern Alps?

Answers 1 Mercury and Venus 2 George Bernard Shaw 3 An earthquake 4 The rocky promontories of Gibraltar on one side and Morocco on the other 5 Gold 6 George IV 7 Johann Strauss 8 England and Scotland 9 Robert Burns 10 It is about to sail 11 Bicycle 12 The Sistine Chapel 13 Borstal 14 Mercury 15 New Zealand

1   Which English king fought at the Battle of Crecy?

2   Which film actress who died in 1977 was born Lucille Fay Le Sueur?

3   Name the Icelandic explorer who, in 1000 AD, became the first European to reach America.

4   In which Middle East country are the towns of Aleppo and Latakia?

5   If A is alpha what is W?

6   What size of paper is half of A4?

7   What is the birthstone for January?

8   Victoria is the capital of which Canadian province?

9   Launched on 2 January 1959 what is the name of the first satellite to escape the Earth's gravity?

10 Whom did Madonna marry in Scotland on 22 December, 2000?

11 By what more common name is the type of rheumatic fever, chorea, known?

12 Which dancer and Dutch spy adopted a stage name meaning 'eye of the day' in Malay?

13 Joe Johnson was world champion at which sport in 1986?

14 Which note is half the length of a crotchet?

15 Hg is the symbol for which element?

MISCELLANEOUS 1 — Quiz 10

1 In which country, until 1922, was the ruler referred to as Sultan of the Ottoman Empire?

2 Built between 1928-30, one year before the Empire State Building, William van Allen was architect for which US New York skyscraper?

3 Which screen tough guy played his first gangster part in 'The Petrified Forest' in 1935?

4 What is the name of the first interballistic missile fired in 1961?

5 What part was played by Tom Hulse in the movie 'Amadeus'?

6 Which city was the venue for the 1984 Summer Olympics?

7 What was Grace Kelly's last movie before she became Princess Grace of Monaco?

8 Who was jailed for life, then acquitted, in the Dingo Baby trial?

9 Which fashion king created the H line and A line in the 1950s?

10 What does a speleologist explore?

11 What are Venetian, Egyptian and Contemporary types of?

12 Polaris is the brightest star in which constellation?

13 In which US state is Kitty Hawk where the Wright Brothers made their first plane flight?

14 Which rock singer was 'Born to Run' in 1976?

15 What colour is lapis lazuli?

Answers 1 Turkey 2 The Chrysler Building 3 Humphry Bogart 4 Minuteman 5 Mozart 6 Los Angeles 7 High Society 8 Lindy Chamberlain 9 Christian Dior 10 Caves 11 Type faces 12 Ursa Minor 13 N.Carolina 14 Bruce Springsteen 15 Blue

MISCELLANEOUS 1 *Quiz 11*

1   What pseudonym was used by two cousins Frederic Danny and Manfred B. Lee who were writers of crime fiction?

2   Who wrote the music for the 'Threepenny Opera'?

3   Which entertainer was known as the 'Last of the Red Hot Mamas'?

4   Who was Richard Nixon's vice-president when he came to power in 1968?

5   Who played Soames Forsyte in the classic 1960s TV saga?

6   Who was the actress who had an affair with Britain's Heritage Secretary David Mellor in 1992?

7   Which one of Britain's notorious gangster Kray twins died first in 1995?

8   A Zander is a type of which creature?

9   In which country is Sebastopol?

10 What is the name of the fluid portion of white blood in which blood cells are suspended?

11 The SI unit of force is named after which scientist?

12 Who is the patron saint of Russia?

13 Which cricketer, knighted in 1953, was a famous opening batsman with his partner Herbert Sutcliffe?

14 From which Spanish soccer league team was Emmanuel Petit transferred to Chelsea for £7.5 million in 2001?

15 Tralee is the administrative centre for which Irish county?

Answers 1 Ellery Queen **2** Kurt Weill **3** Sophie Tucker **4** Spiro Agnew **5** Eric Porter **6** Antonia de Sanchez **7** Ronnie **8** Fish **9** Ukraine **10** Plasma **11** Newton **12** St. Nicholas **13** Jack Hobbs **14** Barcelona **15** Kerry

MISCELLANEOUS 1 — Quiz 12

1   The composer Johann Strauss was a virtuoso on which musical instrument?

2   What are the lowest layer of clouds in the atmosphere?

3   Prior to the French Revolution what would you expect if you received a 'lettres de cachet' from the monarch?

4   Ferdinand de Lesseps masterminded which construction in the 1860s?

5   In which US state is the Mojave Desert?

6   Which former MI5 officer wrote Spycatcher?

7   Whom did Jacques Chirac succeed as French president in 1995?

8   Who played Isadora Duncan on screen in 1969?

9   About what event did Winston Churchill say: 'Never in the field of human conflict was so much owed by so many to so few'?

10 With what weapon was Leon Trotsky assassinated in Mexico in 1940?

11 Which film and stage musical was based on the poem 'Green Grow the Lilacs'?

12 Who wrote 'Uncle Vanya' and 'The Cherry Orchard'?

13 What type of creature is a cotinga?

14 What is the name of the full moon closest to the Autumn equinox?

15 Which US inventor introduced dining cars on trains?

Answers 1 Violin 2 Stratus 3 Arrest and imprisonment 4 The Suez canal 5 California 6 Peter Wright 7 Francois Mitterand 8 Vanessa Redgrave 9 The Battle of Britain 10 An ice pick 11 Oklahoma 12 Chekov 13 Bird 14 Harvest moon 15 George Pullman

MISCELLANEOUS 1 *Quiz 13*

1   In botany, pulse is a general term for what type of vegetables?
2   What is the former name of Thailand?
3   Which US state declared itself independent from Mexico in 1835?
4   On what surface would you be travelling if you were lugeing?
5   Of what is etymology the study?
6   What was invented in the 1950s by Sir Christopher Cockerell?
7   The flag of which nation is a single white cross on a red background?
8   Which international tennis team competition was first held in 1900?
9   Sn is the symbol for which element?
10 Which musical symbol raises the pitch of a note by a semitone?
11 If A is Alpha, what is N?
12 Which US State's nickname is Buckeye State?
13 In which year was the United Nations formed?
14 How many years marriage are celebrated by an emerald anniversary?
15 In the Chinese agricultural calendar what does Li Chun celebrate the start of?

Answers 1 Peas, beans and lentils 2 Siam 3 Texas 4 Snow or ice 5 Words 6 Hovercraft 7 Switzerland 8 Davis Cup 9 Tin 10 Sharp 11 November 12 Ohio 13 1945 14 55 15 Spring

MISCELLANEOUS 1

Quiz 14

1. What is a tsunami?
2. Which Irish surname means 'warlike one'?
3. What is the name given to a cross in the form of a X?
4. What is meant by the musical expression *legato*?
5. In which sport do the players wear a shaped wicker basket attached to their forearm?
6. How many bytes are there in a megabyte?
7. In the Roman Empire, how many soldiers were there in a century?
8. The ciliary body is in which part of the human body?
9. Aphrodite was the daughter of which Greek god?
10. In the 1870s in Pennsylvania, the Molly Maguires were a secret organisation of what type of workers?
11. Phenol is also called what type of acid?
12. Who said, in his 1933 book 'The Shape of Things to Come', that man will create a world state and live happily in AD2059?
13. Marion Davis was the mistress of which US press magnate?
14. What was the surname of Billie Jean King when she reached her first Wimbledon Singles final in 1962?
15. Who played Ghandi in the 1985 movie of the same name?

Answers 1 A tidal wave **2** Kelly **3** A saltire **4** Smoothly **5** Pelota **6** One million **7** 100 **8** Eye lid **9** Zeus **10** Miners **11** Carbolic **12** H.C.Wells **13** William Randolph Hearst **14** Moffitt **15** Ben Kingsley

Quiz 15

1 Of what was Maria Montessori a pioneer?

2 What, in Paris, is the Sorbonne?

3 Albion was the Greek and Roman name for which country?

4 What French word, meaning froth, is a dish of flavoured cream, whipped and frozen?

5 In which year did the British Royal family adopt the name Windsor?

6 Which East German figure skater was Olympic champion in 1984 and 1988?

7 What is the capital city of the state of Wyoming?

8 Who in Greek mythology was the muse of astronomy?

9 What in the Netherlands is polder?

10 Phoebe is the ninth natural satellite of which planet?

11 Who invented the thermos flask?

12 What is the national airline of Greece?

13 What nationality is the former gymnast Nadia Comaneci?

14 In which country is Heriot Watt University?

15 Is a sea cucumber animal, vegetable or mineral?

Answers 1 Education 2 A university 3 Britain 4 Mousse 5 1917 6 Katarina Witt 7 Cheyenne 8 Urania 9 Land reclaimed from the sea 10 Saturn 11 James Dewer 12 Olympic 13 Romanian 14 Scotland 15 Animal, it is a marine invertebrate

MISCELLANEOUS 1   *Quiz 16*

1   How many pieces are there in a set of dominoes?

2   The chrysanthemum is native to which country?

3   Which Chancellor of England fell from Royal favour when he failed to obtain papal agreement to Henry VIII's proposed divorce from Katharine of Aragon?

4   Whose nephews were Huey, Dewey and Louie?

5   Artur Rubinstein was a virtuoso on which instrument?

6   What do Americans call paraffin?

7   'Blood and Fire' is the motto of which institution?

8   Which classic story by Herman Melville features a ship called Pequod?

9   Whom did Max Hoffman describe as 'lions led by donkeys'?

10 Which television series was a spin-off from 'Dallas'?

11 Minsk is the capital of which country?

12 Which sportsman was known as the Sultan of Swat?

13 What vehicle was a Green Goddess a type of?

14 What dish containing oysters is named in honour of a famous American industrialist?

15 In the vintage TV series 'Dragnet', which character said: 'Just give me the facts, Ma'am'?

Answers 1 28 2 Japan 3 Thomas Wolsey 4 Donald Duck 5 Piano 6 Kerosene 7 Salvation Army 8 Moby Dick 9 British soldiers in World War 1 10 Knot's Landing 11 Belorus 12 Babe Ruth 13 Fire Engine 14 Oysters Rockefeller 15 Sergeant Joe Friday

24

Quiz 17

1   Which is the widest and heaviest arch bridge in the world?

2   How many members comprise the US senate?

3   Which male actor was the star of the film 'The English Patient'?

4   Who composed the opera 'Turandot'?

5   Which actor starred in the Steven Spielberg movies 'Jaws' and 'Close Encounters of the Third Kind'?

6   Which English king was the son of Edward the Black Prince?

7   Which sporting first was achieved by Sir Charles Bunbury's Diomed in 1780?

8   How many kilograms are there in a ton?

9   In the UK a billion is a million times a million. How much is it in the US?

10 What is the normal temperature of the human body?

11 What is the commonest molecular compound on earth?

12 Who was Britain's first Labour Prime Minister?

13 For which American soccer team did George Best play in the early 1960s?

14 Actress Brooke Shields was married to which tennis player?

15 Who starred opposite Mickey Rourke in the movie '9½ Weeks'?

Answers 1 The Sydney Harbour Bridge 2 100 3 Ralph Fiennes 4 Puccini 5 Richard Dreyfus 6 Richard II 7 First winner of the English Derby 8 1016 9 A thousand times a million 10 36.9°c (98.4°F) 11 Water 12 Ramsey MacDonald 13 Tampa Bay Rowdies 14 Andre Agassi 15 Kim Basinger

MISCELLANEOUS 1   Quiz 18

1   Which Canadian sprinter was stripped of his 100 metres gold medal in 1988 after failing a drug's test?

2   Who is the youngest of the 'Three Tenors'?

3   Which year did Queen Elizabeth II describe as her *annus horribilis*?

4   Born Illich Ramirez Sanchez, by what name was the one-time world's most wanted terrorist better known?

5   Who wrote 'The Female Eunuch'?

6   What was the Roman name for that area covered roughly by the Highlands of Scotland?

7   Who was the sick beggar cured of leprosy by Jesus?

8   By what name is the German Shepherd dog better known?

9   In which country is the holiday resort of Phuket?

10 Which sea lies between Egypt and Saudi Arabia?

11 'When You Wish upon a Star' is from which Disney film?

12 What is the meaning of the Latin phrase *non sequitus*?

13 What is the nickname of the South African rugby team?

14 What is the name of the coffee house where the 'friends' often meet?

15 In which ocean are the Maldive Islands?

Answers 1 Ben Johnson 2 Jose Carreras 3 1992 4 Carlos the Jackal 5 Germaine Greer 6 Caledonia 7 Lazarus 8 Alsatian 9 Thailand 10 The Red Sea 11 Pinocchio 12 It does not follow 13 The Springboks 14 Central Perk 15 Indian

1 How many times did Sean Connery play James Bond?

2 Inside Coventry Cathedral is a large tapestry by which artist?

3 Which wealthy American declared: 'The meek shall inherit the earth, but not the mineral rights'?

4 Which Egyptian president was assassinated in October 1981?

5 What is the name of the holiday celebrated in America on November 11th?

6 The Gulf of Bothnia separates which two countries?

7 Whose third symphony is known as 'Eroica'?

8 Which US actress married cable television mogul Ted Turner in 1991?

9 What is the common name for the biennial herb of the genus *Allium*?

10 Published in 1973, and later made into a movie starring Sissy Spacek, what was Stephen King's first novel?

11 What kind of insect is a viceroy?

12 Which writer created Winnie-the-Pooh?

13 Wyatt Earp and Bat Masterson were early law officers in which US city?

14 Dr Albert Sabin discovered a vaccine for which disease?

15 In which year was The Gunpowder Plot?

Answers 1 Seven **2** Graham Sutherland **3** J. Paul Getty **4** Anwar Sadat **5** Veterans Day **6** Sweden and Finland **7** Beethoven **8** Jane Fonda **9** Onion **10** Carrie **11** Butterfly **12** A.A. Milne **13** Dodge City **14** Polio **15** 1605

MISCELLANEOUS 1 — Quiz 20

1   Which Scottish heroine saved the life of Bonnie Prince Charlie after his defeat at Culloden Moor in 1746?

2   In which London thoroughfare did the Great Fire of London start in 1666?

3   Which organ of the human body produces insulin?

4   In the Bible, from which city did Goliath come?

5   In how many of his 49 professional fights did Rocky Marciano knock-out his opponent?

6   Pitcairn Island is in which ocean?

7   Which legendary Spanish warrior's full name means 'The Lord Champion'?

8   For what is WYSIWYG the acronym?

9   Which sign of the zodiac comes between Taurus and Cancer?

10 A variety of which creature is called Sally Lightfoot?

11 The name for which style of design was coined from the title of a 1925 Paris design exhibition?

12 What is another name for nacre?

13 Pecan is a species of which type of tree?

14 Which entertainer's nickname was Schnozzle?

15 What is the highest peak in the Karakorum Mountain Range?

Answers 1 Flora MacDonald 2 Pudding Lane 3 The Pancreas 4 Gath 5 43 6 Pacific 7 El Cid 8 What you see is what you get 9 Gemini 10 Crab 11 Art Deco 12 Mother-of-Pearl 13 Hickory 14 Jimmy Durante 15 K2, or Mount Godwin Austin, the world's second highest peak

1   Who was the first Christian martyr to be stoned to death for his beliefs?

2   When it is 12 noon in Los Angeles, what time is it in New York?

3   How much does each side of a baseball diamond measure?

4   What is the second order of the English peerage?

5   In which country would you find Lake Volta?

6   Which country ceded Bombay to England as part of the dowry to the consort of Charles II?

7   Buffalo is at the eastern end of which of N. America's great lakes?

8   Teal is the smallest species of which creature in Britain?

9   By what other name are Yeomen of the Guard referred to?

10 In astronomy, what is equivalent to approximately 6 million million miles?

11 In music, what is meant by the term *piano*?

12 Which is the world's largest stretch of water?

13 Which poet retold the story of the Pied Piper in verse?

14 Which former British Prime Minister collapsed and died whilst making a speech in the House of Lords?

15 What was the pen name of writer Mary Ann Evans?

Answers 1 St. Stephen **2** 3pm **3** 90 feet **4** Marquis **5** Ghana **6** Portugal **7** Erie **8** Duck **9** Beefeaters **10** A light year **11** Soft **12** The Pacific Ocean **13** Robert Browning **14** William Pitt the Elder **15** George Eliot

MISCELLANEOUS 1   *Quiz 22*

1 Originating in local taverns, to what do the P and Q refer in the saying mind your Ps and Qs?

2 After the departure of Don Revie, who became manager of Leeds United for just 44 days in 1973?

3 Who led a failed coup known as the Beer-Hall Putch in November 1923?

4 John Raitt starred opposite Doris Day in which vintage film musical?

5 Who wrote 'Of Human Bondage'?

6 In which country is the mouth of the Orinoco river?

7 Who played Rock Hudson's wife in the TV series 'Macmillan & Wife'?

8 Which fair ground attraction was first patented by Edwin Prescott in 1898?

9 Who directed the blockbuster movie 'Titanic'?

10 Who is the singer husband of Edie Gorme?

11 Which country was divided on the 38th parallel in 1945?

12 How many times did Nelson Piquet win the Formula One World Motor Racing Championship?

13 Which country singer had a 1997 smash hit with 'How Do I Live'?

14 Rosalynn Smith were the first two names of which US first lady?

15 Which cricketer was known as Fiery Fred?

Answers 1 Pints and quarts **2** Brian Clough **3** Adolf Hitler **4** The Pyjama Game **5** Somerset Maugham **6** Venezuela **7** Susan Saint James **8** The Roller Coaster **9** James Cameron **10** Steve Lawrence **11** Korea **12** 3 times (1981, 83, 87) **13** Leann Rimes **14** The wife of Jimmy Carter **15** Fred Truman

MISCELLANEOUS 1
Quiz 23

1 Gene Roddenberry was the creative force behind which cult TV series?

2 The wife of which former US vice-president is known as Tipper?

3 Complete this 1991 movie title; 'The Naked Gun 2 1/2 : . . . .'?

4 Which future US state was discovered in 1741 by Danish explorer Vitus Bering?

5 Which boxing promoter controlled the world heavyweight title from 1978-90 while Larry Holmes and Mike Tyson were both champion?

6 Robert Plant is connected with which rock group as lead singer?

7 Who wrote 'Men Are From Mars, Women Are From Venus'?

8 What did an Italian writer Vicenzo Perruggia steal in 1911?

9 What was the generic name of Oliver Cromwell's supporters in the English Civil War?

10 The Geneva Convention of 1864 for the protection of wounded in times of warfare led to the formation of which association?

11 Which sci-fi author's works include 'Fahrenheit 45' and 'Martian Chronicle'?

12 Which actress was GI Jane in the 1997 movie of the same name?

13 What was the name of Shelley Long's character in TV show 'Cheers'?

14 Who wrote 'Jane Eyre'?

15 Who was the first person to swim the English Channel?

Answers 1 Star Trek 2 Al Gore 3 The Smell of Fear 4 Alaska 5 Don King 6 Led Zeppelin 7 John Gray 8 The Mona Lisa 9 Roundheads 10 The Red Cross 11 Ray Bradbury 12 Demi Moore 13 Diane Chambers 14 Charlotte Bronte 15 Matthew Webb

31

1   Jiminy Cricket is a character in which Disney cartoon?

2   Count Danilo and Baron Zeta are characters in which Franz Lehar opera?

3   Who was the fifth man, who later called himself 'The Enigma Spy'?

4   Who plays piano player Sam in the film 'Casablanca'?

5   In which London district is Sloane Square?

6   Which sign of the Zodiac would you be if you were born on June 1?

7   Which two English towns were created Millennium cities in 2000?

8   At what would Visky Anand be competing against Alexai Shirov?

9   Who was the president of France prior to Francois Mitterand?

10 What city, in 2000, did Madonna describe as the music capital of the world?

11 Who is the virtuoso husband of the great Russian soprano Galina Vishnevskaya?

12 What was the name given in 1767 to the boundary between the north and south of America and the official border between Maryland and Pennsylvania?

13 The island of Krakatoa lies between which two other Indonesian islands?

14 Elected in 1978, which pope served just 33 days before dying of a heart attack?

15 What was first manufactured in 1830 by John Lea and William Perrins?

Answers 1 Pinocchio 2 The Merry Widow 3 John Cairncross 4 Doley Wilson 5 Knightsbridge 6 Gemini 7 Brighton & Hove and Wolverhampton 8 Chess 9 Valery Giscard-d'Estaing 10 London 11 Mistislav Rostropovich 12 The Mason-Dixon Line 13 Java and Sumatra 14 John Paul I 15 Worcester Sauce

1   Who wrote the opera 'Lohengrin'?

2   At which sport did Janet Evans win three gold medals at the 1988 Olympics and gold and silver at the 1992 Olympics?

3   Which actor/dancer starred in the 'Francis the Talking Mule' series of movies?

4   Who, in Germany, patented the first motorcycle?

5   Who played Cruella De Vil in the 1996 movie '101 Dalmations'?

6   At what sport did Briton Ben Ainslie win a gold medal at the 2000 Sydney Olympics?

7   In which European capital city was actress Ingrid Bergman born?

8   Who, in the 1980s, made the albums 'Bad', 'Captain EO' and 'Dangerous'?

9   Whom did Jack Dempsey defeat in the world heavyweight title fight in 1919?

10 Mary Ann Nichols was the first victim of which serial killer?

11 Who was Chief Prosecutor in the O. J. Simpson murder trial?

12 Who played Flint in a series of spy movies?

13 Who performed the first surgery in England under antiseptic conditions?

14 Which country music singer, and earlier rock singer of 'Rockin' Robin' fame was born Harold Lloyd Jenkins?

15 Which old-time movie actress played Lily Munster in the 'Munsters' TV series?

Answers 1 Richard Wagner 2 Swimming 3 Donald O'Connor 4 Gottlieb Daimler 5 Glenn Close 6 Yachting 7 Stockholm 8 Michael Jackson 9 Jess Willard 10 Jack the Ripper 11 Marcia Clark 12 James Coburn 13 Joseph Lister 14 Conway Twitty 15 Yvonne de Carlo

MISCELLANEOUS 1   *Quiz 26*

1 How is Louise Ciccone better known?

2 In the James Bond story, who is Goldfinger's deadly mute sidekick?

3 What in Internet terminology does ASCII stand for?

4 Which calendar was replaced by the Gregorian Calendar?

5 What does J R R stand for in J. R. R. Tolkien?

6 Who in the movies played Johnny Mnemonic?

7 Which English king was nicknamed 'The Lionheart'?

8 Ferdinand Porsche founded Porsche and which other car manufacturer?

9 Who was the first man to drive an automobile in excess of 300 mph?

10 In 1943, which island did the British eighth army use as a base for invading Italy?

11 Geronimo was a member of which tribe of N.American indians?

12 Who is the only swimmer to win gold medals in the 100 metres freestyle in three successive Olympics?

13 Which US president was assassinated by Leon Czogolz?

14 Keith Moon was the drummer with which rock group?

15 What did Harland Sanders found in 1890?

Answers 1 Madonna 2 Oddjob 3 American Standard Code for Information Interchange 4 The Julian Calendar 5 John Ronald Reuel 6 Keanu Reeves 7 Richard I 8 Volkswagen 9 Sir Malcolm Campbell 10 Sicily 11 Apache 12 Dawn Fraser 13 McKinley 14 The Who 15 Kentucky Fried Chicken

1 What is the name of the donkey in the 'Winnie-the-Pooh' stories?

2 Which actress played neighbour Ethel Mertz in the vintage TV comedy series 'I Love Lucy'?

3 Who wrote about the horse 'Black Beauty'?

4 Which British athlete emulated the feat of Mary Peters by winning the heptathlon at the 2000 Sydney Olympics?

5 Who played Det. Ken Hutchinson in 'Starsky & Hutch'?

6 What did Michaelangelo describe as eternal patience?

7 What is meant by a skewbald horse?

8 In which German city was Ludwig von Beethoven born?

9 What game was invented in Canada by James Naismith in 1891?

10 What classic Don McLean song is about the death of Buddy Holly?

11 In which year did a man last walk on the moon?

12 Which date in 1941 did Franklin D. Roosevelt say would live in infamy because of the bombing of Pearl Harbour?

13 Which is the only mammal to have four knees?

14 How is Allen Stuart Konisberg, born Brooklyn, New York in 1935, better known?

15 How many Sundays before Christmas is the first Sunday of Advent?

Answers 1 Eeyore **2** Vivian Vance **3** Anna Sewell **4** Denise Lewis **5** David Soul **6** Genius **7** White beneath any colour except black **8** Bonn **9** Basketball **10** American Pie **11** 1972 **12** 7 December **13** The elephant **14** Woody Allen **15** Four

MISCELLANEOUS 1

Quiz 28

1　In the TV series, who plays Buffy the Vampire Slayer?
2　Which British boxer won the Super-Heavyweight Gold medal at the Sydney 2000 Olympics?
3　How many British Open Golf Championships did Tom Watson win?
4　What is the name of the janitor on the 'Muppet Show' ?
5　Which French king was guillotined in the French Revolution?
6　Which Beatle was the group's rhythm guitarist?
7　Which fictional character had a manservant named Orace?
8　Whose granddaughter was Salome?
9　By what name was Gaius Caesar Augustus Germanicus better known?
10　In what type of business did the Greek multi-millionaire Aristotle Onassis make his fortune?
11　What is the Jewish New Year called?
12　What is the larva of a frog called?
13　What is a gingko a type of?
14　Who played the female lead opposite Dudley Moore in the 1981 movie 'Arthur'?
15　What in Internet terminology does FTP stand for?

Answers 1 Sarah Michelle Gellar 2 Audley Harrison 3 Five 4 George 5 Louis XVI 6 Paul McCartney 7 Simon Templar (The Saint) 8 Herod the Great 9 Caligula 10 Shipping 11 Rosh Hoshana 12 Tadpole 13 Tree 14 Liza Minnelli 15 File Transfer Protocol

MISCELLANEOUS 1 *Quiz 29*

1 Which strait separates the North and South islands of New Zealand?

2 The instrument ocarina is made of what material?

3 Who was the last British ruler of the House of Hanover?

4 The entertainer Gracie Fields was a native of which Lancashire town?

5 What do the French call La Manche?

6 In computer terminology what does the acronym ROM stand for?

7 What colour are the stars on the flag of the USA?

8 Which US actress (1918-87) was born Margarita Carmen Cansino?

9 Who, in 1987, became the first Briton to win the US Woman's Open Golf Championship?

10 Which element has the symbol Ag?

11 Which religion, which originated in ancient Persia, was centred upon the worship of the God of Light and Truth?

12 What note is half the length of a quaver?

13 What was a penny dreadful?

14 Which city is home to the soccer club Lazio?

15 Who wrote 'Our Man in Havana' and 'The Quiet American'?

Answers 1 Cook Strait 2 Terracotta 3 Queen Victoria 4 Rochdale 5 The English Channel 6 Read Only Memory 7 White 8 Rita Hayworth 9 Laura Davis 10 Silver 11 Mithraism 12 Semiquaver 13 A comic book 14 Rome 15 Graham Greene

MISCELLANEOUS 1   *Quiz 30*

1 The Maharishi Mahesh Yogi trained the Beatles in which technique?

2 Which actor died of a heart attack in 1967 shortly after completing his last film 'Guess Who's Coming to Dinner'?

3 What instrument is played by jazz great Artie Shaw?

4 In the British royal family, who is the father of David and Sarah?

5 What type of creature is a gecko?

6 Who won motor racing's Formula One Championship in 1992?

7 Who, in 1993, became America's first woman Attorney General?

8 The element 'radon' was discovered in the year 1900. By whom?

9 By what name was William Joyce known in World War II?

10 Who played the part of the heroine in the original film 'King Kong', released in 1933?

11 What in Internet terminology does LAN stand for?

12 In France, who was first president of the Fifth Republic?

13 In 1936, the American diving and tumbling champion George Nisson developed a prototype for the apparatus in which sport?

14 The Ligurian Sea is an arm of which body of water?

15 Sagas originate from which country?

Answers 1 Transcendental Meditation 2 Spencer Tracy 3 Clarinet 4 Earl of Snowdon 5 Lizard 6 Nigel Mansell 7 Janet Reno 8 The German chemist Friedrich Dorn 9 Lord Haw-Haw 10 Fay Wray 11 Local Area Network 12 Charles de Gaulle 13 Trampolining 14 The Mediterranean Sea 15 Iceland

1   In which country is the town of Fez?

2   Which comet crashed into the planet Jupiter in 1994?

3   In which European city is the Palais Du Luxembourg?

4   In what year was an American U2 spy plane shot down over the Soviet Union?

5   The parietal bone is in which part of the human body?

6   What is the value of the brown ball in snooker?

7   On the London Underground, which line is coloured yellow?

8   What in email lingo is the meaning of the acronym AFAIK?

9   What was the venue of the 1994 Winter Olympics?

10 What is the meaning of the Arabic word 'Inshallah'?

11 Where is the Ocean of Storms?

12 Which actor's daughter Cheyenne committed suicide in Tahiti in 1995?

13 What is the capital of Senegal?

14 Raymond Barre was Prime Minister of which country from 1976-81?

15 Who won the decathlon at the 1980 Moscow Olympic games?

Answers 1 Morocco 2 Shoemaker-Levy 9 3 Paris 4 1960 5 Skull 6 4 7 Circle 8 As far as I know 9 Lillehammer 10 If Allah wills it 11 On the moon 12 Marlon Brando 13 Dakar 14 France 15 Daley Thompson

MISCELLANEOUS 1   *Quiz 32*

1   Which writer was born Fingal O'Flahertie Wills?

2   Vectis is the Latin name for which English county?

3   In South America, the rivers Uruguay and Parana combine above Buenos Aires to form which river?

4   What type of animal is a whaler?

5   In the 1920s Jan Smuts became Prime Minister of which country?

6   Who painted 'Le Moulin de la Galette'?

7   What nationality was explorer Robert Peary?

8   In which country is Milford Haven?

9   Which mammal of the family *Odobenidae* resembles a sea-lion?

10 Which is the smallest woodwind instrument?

11 ...and which is the largest?

12 The top prize in which sport is the annual VFL Premiership trophy?

13 What is the penultimate letter of the Greek alphabet?

14 AZ is the code for which airline?

15 Which country is sandwiched between Austria to the West and Romania to the East?

Answers 1 Oscar Wilde 2 The Isle of Wight 3 River Plate 4 Horse 5 South Africa 6 Renoir 7 American 8 Wales 9 Walrus 10 Piccolo 11 Bassoon 12 Australian Rules Football 13 Psi 14 Alitalia 15 Hungary

MISCELLANEOUS 1 *Quiz 33*

1   What in Internet terminology does FAQ stand for?

2   Which footballing nation has won the world cup four times?

3   Who wrote the poem 'If'?

4   Which religion celebrates Navarati, or Festival of nine nights?

5   What is the birthstone for November?

6   What in the USA is the Palmetto state?

7   At which Olympic Games did Eric Liddell and Harold Abrahams win gold?

8   ...and which movie did their triumphs inspire?

9   Who was the star of the 1928 movie 'Steamboat Willie'?

10 Who wrote 'Cavallaria Rusticana'?

11 What, in the days of prohibition, was hooch?

12 Frank Baum wrote which classic children's story?

13 The moa is an extinct bird which was native to which country?

14 Who declared to the Canadian Parliament in 1941, the tide is turning?

15 What in Buddhism is the attainment of supreme bliss?

Answers 1 Frequently Asked Questions 2 Brazil 3 Rudyard Kipling 4 Hindu 5 Topaz 6 South Carolina 7 Paris 1924 8 Chariots of Fire 9 Mickey Mouse 10 Mascagni 11 Bootlegged whiskey 12 The Wizard of Oz 13 New Zealand 14 Winston Churchill 15 Nirvana

MISCELLANEOUS 1

Quiz 34

1   Which Wall Street guru was arrested in 1986 on a charge of insider trading, and obliged to pay a fine of 100 million dollars?

2   What, in China, is a pipa a type of?

3   The River Danube flows into which sea?

4   Which is the most northerly, the Shetland or the Orkney Isles?

5   Whose motto is 'be prepared'?

6   What are the names of the four vehicles which make up the US fleet of Space Shuttles?

7   ...and which one of these exploded on 26 January 1986?

8   Whom did Mike Tyson defeat in 1987 to become undisputed World Heavyweight boxing champion?

9   Who was deported from the Soviet Union to West Germany on February 13th 1974?

10 The Mau Mau were a terrorist organisation in which country?

11 Which African country lies directly south of Yemen across the Gulf of Aden?

12 What disease almost wiped out Britain's population of rabbits in the 1950s?

13 The Puerto-Rico Trench is the deepest point of which ocean?

14 Which US state is designated by the letters MO?

15 In which part of the human body is the uvula?

Answers 1 Ivan Boesky 2 Musical instrument 3 The Black Sea 4 Shetland 5 Scouts 6 Colombia, Challenger, Discovery, Atlantis 7 Challenger 8 Tony Tucker 9 Alexander Solzhenitsyn 10 Kenya 11 Somalia 12 Myxomatosis 13 Atlantic 14 Missouri 15 The mouth

MISCELLANEOUS 1 *Quiz 35*

1   Whom did Princess Margaret decide not to marry in 1955?

2   What was Cliff Richard's first hit record in 1959?

3   What does the acronym UNESCO stand for?

4   In medieval legend, which creature could only be captured by a virgin putting its head in her lap?

5   Who became US Secretary of Defense after Ronald Reagan's presidential victory in 1980?

6   Which was the first great Roman road which linked Rome with present day Capua?

7   In which conflict was the Battle of Shiloh fought?

8   Miranda and Caliban are characters in which Shakespeare play?

9   How is October 24th 1929 remembered?

10 Who, after looking at a multitude of wares exposed for sale, is reported to have said: "How many things I can do without"?

11 What in Internet terminology does SMTP stand for?

12 In Africa, which country lies squashed between Algeria to the West and Libya to the East?

13 For what offence was Christine Keeler jailed in 1963?

14 At which course is the Royal and Ancient Golf Club based?

15 Which writer was known as Plum?

Answers 1 Group Captain Peter Townsend **2** Livin' Doll **3** United Nations Educational, Scientific and Cultural Organisation **4** Unicorn **5** Casper Weinberger **6** The Appian Way **7** The American Civil War **8** The Tempest **9** As 'Black Thursday' **10** Socrates **11** Simple Mail Transfer Protocol **12** Tunisia **13** Perjury and Conspiracy to Pervert the Course of Justice **14** St. Andrews **15** P.G. Wodehouse

MISCELLANEOUS 1

Quiz 36

1 Which battle between England and Scotland in 1513 claimed the life of James IV of Scotland?

2 Which 12th century Cistercian, known as the Oracle of Christendom and the 'Mellifluous Doctor', also drew up the statutes for the Knights Templars?

3 What is the first name of actor Topol of 'Fiddler on the Roof' fame?

4 The rickshaw was invented in which country?

5 Which overseas British territory voted by almost 100% to retain British rule in 1967?

6 In 1989 in an event which signalled the end of the Berlin Wall, which eastern block country opened its borders to the West?

7 Who wrote the 'Death of a Salesman' and 'A View From The Bridge'?

8 Peter Funt was the originator of which television programme – versions of which have had successful runs in both the UK and USA?

9 Who wrote the song 'Oh! Susanna'?

10 Who, or what, were the Sassanides?

11 What in Internet terminology does OSI stand for?

12 In 1962, which record company rejected the Beatles because their experts reckoned they would never make it to the record charts?

13 What was the original name of the Hoover Dam?

14 What first in space exploration was achieved by Robert Crippen?

15 On which TV series would you find the characters Helda and Zelda?

Answers 1 Flodden 2 St. Bernard of Clairvaux 3 Chaim 4 Japan 5 Gibraltar 6 Hungary 7 Arthur Miller 8 Candid Camera 9 Stephen Foster 10 A dynasty of Persian Rulers from 226 to 625 AD 11 Open Systems Interconnection 12 Decca 13 Boulder Dam 14 He was the pilot of the first US Space Shuttle orbital flight 15 Sabrina the Teenage Witch

1 Which US track star won four gold medals at the 1936 Berlin Olympics?
2 With which country did Britain have a 'cod war' in the 1970s?
3 At which sport did Irina Rodnina win Olympic gold in 1972, 76 and 80?
4 Which ocean was discovered by Vasco Manez de Balboa when he crossed the isthmus of Panama?
5 Who wrote 'Charlie and the Chocolate Factory'?
6 Which singer, composer of 'The Christmas Song', was known as Velvet Fog?
7 Amanda tells Kyle that Taylor is pregnant and Craig holds Brook responsible for Sydney's death – this could be the story line for an episode of which US soap opera?
8 Which sport is played by the Philadelphia Eagles?
9 Which country first landed a spacecraft on the moon?
10 What is meant by the acronym OPEC?
11 In 1975, whose painting, 'The Nightwatch', was stolen in Amsterdam by an unemployed teacher with a butcher's knife?
12 Who was the first film star to appear on a postage stamp?
13 What in email lingo is the meaning of the acronym BRB?
14 What is the southernmost county of Wales?
15 Who played Caesar to Elizabeth Taylor's Cleopatra in the 1963 blockbuster movie?

NO!

---

1 What was the name of Mary Francis Crosby's character who shot JR in 'Dallas'?

2 Who discovered penicillin?

3 Henry Charles Albert David are the christian names of which British royal?

4 Which 1992 movie starring Tom Hanks, Geena Davis and Madonna tells the story of The All-American Girl's Professional League?

5 Which lake forms the boundary between Malawi and Tanzania?

6 Who discovered the Magnetic South Pole?

7 Which instrument is played by blues artist B. B. King?

8 Which TV family lived on The Ponderosa?

9 Which first was achieved by Reinhold Miessner when he climbed Mount Everest?

10 With whom did Elizabeth Barrett elope in 1846?

11 The Battle of Poitiers took place during which war?

12 Who invented the first carpet sweeper?

13 Which country was the first to grant all its women the right to vote?

14 In which US state did the first underground nuclear tests take place?

15 An earthquake killed 12,000 people in which capital city in 1985?

Answers 1 Kristin Shepard 2 Alexander Fleming 3 Prince Harry 4 A League of Their Own 5 Lake Nyasa or Lake Malawi 6 Roald Amundsen 7 Guitar 8 Cartwrights 9 The first solo ascent without using oxygen 10 Robert Browning 11 The Hundred Years War 12 Melville Bissell 13 New Zealand 14 Nevada 15 Mexico City

MISCELLANEOUS 1 *Quiz 39*

1   What is the name of a person, plant or animal which shuns the light?
2   At which event did Al Oerter win four gold medals at successive Olympic games?
3   What, in the field of optics, is biconvex?
4   What is Batman's real name?
5   Recorded in 1962, what was the Beatles first single?
6   How was Charles Edward Stuart better known in the middle of the 18th century?
7   From which Scottish shipbuilding yard was the liner Queen Elizabeth II launched?
8   For her role in which movie did Sophia Loren win best actress Oscar?
9   What was the name of the first nuclear submarine?
10 Which 'Dallas' actor played Capt. Tony Nelson in 'I Dream of Jeannie'?
11 What aid to eating ice-cream was invented by Italo Merchiony?
12 Who did Sara Jane Moore attempt to assassinate in San Francisco in 1975?
13 Which country was invaded by Iraq in 1980?
14 The New York Knickerbockers were America's first amateur team in which sport?
15 What did Johann Galle discover in 1846?

Answers 1 Lucifugous 2 Discus 3 A lens which is convex on both sides 4 Bruce Wayne 5 Love Me Do 6 Bonnie Prince Charlie 7 Clydebank 8 Two Women 9 USS Nautilus 10 Larry Hagman 11 The Cone 12 President Gerald Ford 13 Iran 14 Baseball 15 Neptune

MISCELLANEOUS 1 — Quiz 40

1. Who invented the first helicopter?

2. Which famous cowboy character was played by Clayton Moore?

3. Who directed 'The Keystone Cops'?

4. Who wrote 'The Great Gatsby'?

5. What was the nickname of country-blues folk singer Huddie Leadbetter?

6. Sue Johnson and Ricky Tomlinson who play husband and wife in 'The Royle Family', were previously husband and wife in which British soap?

7. In the US, which Nat King Cole recording was the first song, in 1948, to enter radio's The Hit Parade at the No. 1 position?

8. In 'Gone With the Wind', by what name did her father always refer to Scarlett O'Hara?

9. What is the minimum age at which someone can be elected US president?

10. At which battle in June 1942 was the first defeat inflicted on the Japanese navy since the 16th century?

11. Which is the only play in which William Shakespeare mentions America?

12. Bob Woodward and Carl Bernstein, who first broke the Watergate story were reporters with which newspaper?

13. Emil Zatopek won the Marathon Gold at the 1952 Olympics. For which event at the same Olympics did his wife Dana also win Gold?

14. In what role did muscle man Billy Welles feature in hundreds of movies?

15. What are the first words of Winnie-the-Pooh after he wakes up each morning?

Answers 1 Igor Sikorsky 2 The Lone Ranger 3 Mack Sennett 4 F.Scott Fitzgerald 5 Leadbelly 6 Brookside 7 Nature Boy 8 Katie 9 35 10 Midway 11 The Comedy of Errors 12 The Washington Post 13 Javelin 14 He struck the gong at the beginning of the J.Arthur Rank films 15 What's for breakfast?

1   What is the traditional yell of US Army paratroopers when jumping out of an airplane?

2   The song 'Getting To Know You' comes from which musical?

3   At what Jamaican retreat did Ian Fleming write his James Bond novels?

4   Who was the only American president to resign the Presidency?

5   How was painter Anna Mary Robinson better known?

6   In 1969 John Lennon officially adopted which middle name?

7   What part did Catherine Oxenberg play in 'Dynasty'?

8   What was the nickname of the German general Erwin Rommel?

9   In the early days of rock and roll who had a hit record with 'Shake, Rattle and Roll'?

10 What nationality was Isadora Duncan?

11 Which Nobel prize was won by Albert Einstein in 1955?

12 Who succeeded Winston Churchill as British Prime Minister in 1955?

13 Which American frontiersman and one time Member of Congress, was killed at the Alamo?

14 Who played King Henry VIII in 'Anne of a Thousand Days'?

15 Paradise Valley was the former name of which US city?

Answers 1 Geronimo **2** The King and I **3** Goldeneye **4** Richard Nixon **5** Grandma Moses **6** Ono **7** Amanda Carrington **8** Desert Fox **9** Bill Haley and his Comets **10** American **11** Physics **12** Anthony Eden **13** Davy Crockett **14** Richard Burton **15** Hollywood

MISCELLANEOUS 1   *Quiz 42*

1 What archaic unit of measurement was equal to 18 inches?

2 What is the name of the spicy peanut and coconut sauce served with Indonesian dishes?

3 The name of which animal is an aboriginal term meaning no water?

4 Which land animal has the biggest eyes?

5 What is the name of Elizabeth Taylor's eighth husband, whom she married in 1991?

6 Which singer was known as the Swedish Nightingale?

7 What character did Mark Hamill play in 'Star Wars'?

8 In which vessel did Sir Francis Drake sail round the world?

9 Who wrote the 'Liberty Bell March'?

10 In which year did Hong Kong revert to Chinese sovereignty?

11 Which character did Donna Douglas play in 'The Beverley Hillbillies'?

12 What was founded by Ignatius Loyola in 1540?

13 What is the stage name of 'Bat Out of Hell' singer Marvin Lee Aday?

14 Kathy Whitworth was the first lady to earn over $3,000,000 at which sport?

15 Where in England did William the Conqueror land in 1066 at the start of the Norman Conquest?

Answers 1 Cubit 2 Satay 3 Koala 4 The Horse 5 Larry Fortensky 6 Jenny Lind 7 Luke Skywalker 8 The Golden Hind 9 John Philip Sousa 10 1997 11 Elly May Clampett 12 The Jesuits (The Society of Jesus) 13 Meat Loaf 14 Golf 15 Pevensey, Sussex

1 Whom did Rocky Marciano knock out to win the World Heavyweight Boxing Championship for the first time?

2 At 5 feet 4 inches who was the shortest ever American president?

3 How many quarts are there in a peck?

4 Who wrote the opera 'The Magic Flute'?

5 Which was the first National Park to be established in England?

6 On which vessel did Charles Darwin make his voyage of discovery?

7 Whom did Johnnie Cochran defend in a famous trial in the 1990s?

8 Sting was lead soloist with which pop group?

9 The Orient Express first ran between Europe and which middle east country?

10 What was the name of The Soviet Union's first man-made satellite?

11 Which bishop won the Nobel Peace prize in 1994?

12 In which conflict did the Battle of Loos take place?

13 The bell from which ship is mounted in the underwriters room of Lloyds of London?

14 What is the name of the Linton family's estate in 'Wuthering Heights'?

15 In which South American country was Che Guevara shot and killed?

Answers 1 Jersey Joe Walcott 2 James Madison 3 Eight 4 Mozart 5 The Peak District 6 HMS Beagle 7 O.J. Simpson 8 The Police 9 Turkey 10 Sputnik 11 Desmond Tutu 12 World War I 13 Lutine 14 Thrushcross Grange 15 Bolivia

MISCELLANEOUS 1   *Quiz 44*

1 Which American president fired General Douglas McArthur?

2 Of where is Doha the capital?

3 Which creature is known as 'orange man' or 'wise man of the forest'?

4 In which country are the Sierra Madre mountains?

5 What kind of creature is a jacamar?

6 What instrument did Jack Benny take on stage with him?

7 What type of books were written by the American novelist Zane Gray?

8 Lake Erie forms most of the northern boundary of which American state?

9 A corruption of the word Bethlehem, what was the name of the first mental asylum in England?

10 Tom Dula, an American Civil War veteran hanged for murder was the subject of which folk song?

11 How many yards in a chain?

12 What is another name for the upper incisor teeth of elephants?

13 The Emperor Constantine the Great founded Constantinople on the site of which ancient city?

14 Which form of competitive skiing derives its name from a Norwegian word meaning 'sloping track'?

15 What name is given to the region of low pressure calm latitudes girdling the oceans near to the equator?

Quiz 45

1   The ocelot is a member of which family of animals?

2   Symbolising innocence, which birthstone is associated with the month of April?

3   Which cheese is traditionally grated and sprinkled on spaghetti?

4   At the start of a game of chess how many rooks are on the board in total?

5   What is measured by the Mohs Scale?

6   The ringgit is the unit of currency in which country?

7   The Akita is a breed of dog originating from which country?

8   Which songwriter wrote 'Over the Rainbow' for Judy Garland?

9   Who did Hillary Rodham marry in 1975?

10 Who was the first woman to swim the English channel?

11 Which Roman emperor died after eating poisoned mushrooms given to him by his wife Agrippina?

12 To which island was Napoleon Bonaparte exiled after his defeat at the Battle of Waterloo?

13 Who played Jessica Fletcher in 'Murder She Wrote'?

14 The border between which two countries was set at the 49th parallel in 1818?

15 Prior to being called The White House, by what name was the president's dwelling known?

Answers 1 Cat **2** Diamond **3** Parmesan **4** Four **5** The hardness of minerals **6** Malaysia **7** Japan **8** Harold Arlen **9** Bill Clinton **10** Gertrude Ederle **11** Claudius **12** St.Helena **13** Angela Lansbury **14** USA & Canada **15** Executive Mansion

MISCELLANEOUS 1 — Quiz 46

1　How many strings are there on a ukulele?

2　Who played Neddy Seagoon in 'The Goon Show'?

3　Who was the first explorer to cross the Antarctic circle?

4　What hobby was taken up by Sherlock Holmes in retirement?

5　How was Manfred von Richtofen better known in Word War I?

6　The Dance of the Sugar Plum Fairy comes from which Tchaikovsky ballet?

7　The thorax is the anatomical term for which part of the human body?

8　Who wrote the poem 'The shooting Dan McGrew'?

9　In chess, what is another name for the rook?

10　Lord Greystoke was the father of which fictional character?

11　Which country will lose its independence once there is no heir to the throne?

12　Which pop group took their name from a Dennis Wheatley novel?

13　What type of weapon is a Mills Bomb?

14　What name is given to wine that is sugared, spiced and then heated?

15　Storting is the parliament of which country?

Answers 1 Four 2 Harry Secombe 3 Captain James Cook 4 Bee-keeping 5 The Red Baron 6 The Nutcracker Suite 7 Chest 8 Robert W. Service 9 Castle 10 Tarzan 11 Monaco 12 Black Sabbath 13 A hand grenade 14 Mulled wine 15 Norway

1   What was the original name of the first Roman Emperor Augustus?

2   A firkin is equal to how many gallons?

3   What in Scotland is a skean dhu?

4   *Galanthus* is the scientific name for which garden plant?

5   What is former Liberal Democrat leader Paddy Ashdown's real first name?

6   Which famous train ran from Cincinnati to New Orleans?

7   John of Gaunt was the patron of which English writer?

8   In the soap 'Neighbours', who is played by Ian Smith?

9   What is meant by the Latin phrase *caveat emptor*?

10 Romansch is an official language of which country?

11 How many sides has an icosahedron?

12 The Black Horse is a symbol for which British bank?

13 At 69 years old who was the oldest American president to take office?

14 The Julie Christie/Donald Sutherland movie 'Don't Look Now' was based on a novel by which writer?

15 The Tigris flows through which middle eastern capital city?

Answers 1 Octavian 2 Nine 3 A dagger worn in the stockings in traditional highland dress 4 Snowdrop 5 Jeremy 6 The Chattanooga Choo Choo 7 Chaucer 8 Harold Bishop 9 Let the buyer beware 10 Switzerland 11 Twenty 12 Lloyds 13 Ronald Reagan 14 Daphne du Maurier 15 Baghdad

1. How many nautical miles is a league?

2. Thimpu is the capital of which country?

3. What is the SI unit of inductance denoted by the symbol H?

4. Edward Jenner discovered a vaccine for which disease?

5. What nationality was the composer Sibelius?

6. Who played Norm Paterson in 'Cheers'?

7. What name is given to a valved top on an inverted bottle of spirits that releases an exact tot measure when pressed?

8. Thomas Selfridge became the first fatality in a plane crash. Who was the pilot on that occasion?

9. Lieutenant Mike Stone was a character in which TV series?

10. What type of bird is a broad-breasted bronze?

11. Which English queen had an extra finger on her hand?

12. In which part of the human body is the masseter muscle?

13. Who rode a horse called Bucephalus?

14. The wine silvaner comes from which country?

15. What is the name of the very spicy Italian sausage eaten hot and cold?

Answers 1 Three **2** Bhutan **3** Henry **4** Smallpox **5** Finnish **6** George Wendt **7** Optic **8** Orville Wright **9** The Streets of San Francisco **10** Turkey **11** Anne Boleyn **12** In the head (it is used for chewing) **13** Alexander the Great **14** Germany **15** Pepperoni

1 What do the initials DH stand for in D.H. Lawrence?
2 What did the philosopher Diogenes carry round in order to find an honest man?
3 Yerevan is the capital of which country?
4 Which actor's biography was entitled 'My Wicked Wicked Ways'?
5 Which English king died from 'a surfeit of lampreys'?
6 What would someone collect if their hobby was phillumeny?
7 If you had a stamp containing the inscription Helvetia, from which country would it be from?
8 Which game consists of eight periods called chukkas?
9 What type of dog is Snoopy in the cartoon strip 'Peanuts'?
10 What is meant by the phrase splice the mainbrace?
11 Which Shakespeare character said: 'I come to bury Caesar not to praise him'?
12 Which pop star's first wife was Cynthia Powell?
13 A lactometer measures the density of which liquid?
14 Albert Einstein was offered the Presidency of which country?
15 What in America is the value of two bits?

Answers 1 David Herbert 2 A lantern 3 Armenia 4 Errol Flynn 5 Henry I 6 Matchbox labels 7 Switzerland 8 Polo 9 Beagle 10 Take a drink of alcohol 11 Mark Antony 12 John Lennon 13 Milk 14 Israel 15 25 cents

MISCELLANEOUS 1   *Quiz 50*

1   What is the name of the dog in Punch and Judy shows?

2   What kind of triangle has all its sides a different length?

3   Who was Vice-president under Dwight D. Eisenhower?

4   What is the national sport of Malaysia and Indonesia?

5   Who was the wife of King Prasutagus?

6   Whose famous last words were purported to be: 'I shall hear in heaven'?

7   In the animal kingdom what creature is otherwise known as the laughing jackass?

8   In the 'Peanuts' cartoon strip, what kind of creature is Woodstock?

9   Who is Phileas Fogg's valet in 'Around the World in 80 Days'?

10 What relation is Whitney Houston to Dionne Warwick?

11 In 'The Simpsons', who is headmaster at Bart and Lisa's school?

12 What is the common name of Beethoven's 'Piano Sonata No. 14 in C Sharp Minor'?

13 Which pop duo were originally called Tom and Jerry?

14 Point Marroqui is the most southerly point of which continent?

15 Which ventriloquist had a doll called Charlie McCarthy?

Answers 1 Toby 2 Scalene 3 Richard Nixon 4 Badminton 5 Queen Boadicea 6 Beethoven 7 Kookaburra 8 A bird 9 Passepartout 10 Cousin 11 Principal Skinner 12 Moonlight 13 Simon & Garfunkel 14 Europe (Spain) 15 Edgar Bergen

1. What would a cleric do with a mitre?
2. Which British motor racing champion was also a clay pigeon shooting champion?
3. Whose was 'the face that launched a thousand ships'?
4. Named from an arsenal near Calcutta, what type of bullet expands on impact?
5. Who was the first Holy Roman emperor?
6. What was the name of the teacher killed in the Challenger space shuttle explosion in January 1986?
7. By what nickname was mass-murderer David Berkowitz known?
8. What was the name of Thor Heyerdahl's papyrus boat on which he sailed from Africa to America, subsequent to his Kon-Tiki expedition?
9. Who is the patron saint of travellers?
10. Who in 1764 invented the spinning jenny?
11. Who wrote 'Old Possum's Book of Practical Cats'?
12. Of what is psephology the study?
13. What colour is the gem peridot?
14. Which was the last battle of the War of the Roses?
15. The Melling Road crosses which famous British racecourse?

1   What are Bora in the Adriatic, Harmatton on the African coast and Khamsin in Egypt?

2   Who, on television, did Jamie Summers become?

3   Which type of falcon shares its name with a character in Arthurian legend?

4   Which temperature is the same on both the Fahrenheit and Centigrade scales?

5   Which monk invented sparkling wine?

6   A Brough Superior, built from 1919 to 1940 was what type of vehicle?

7   Born in 1940, by what name was Edison Arantes de Nascimento better known to the world of sport?

8   In which US state is New Orleans?

9   What type of verse was popularised by Edward Lear?

10 Consisting of crystalline silica, what is the commonest of all minerals?

11 What is the name of Duncan's son who killed Macbeth?

12 Which country's flag consists of a broad yellow horizontal stripe bordered by two narrower red horizontal stripes top and bottom?

13 Ibaden is the second largest city of which African country?

14 What measure of explosive power is equal to 1000 tons of TNT?

15 What type of creature is a Portuguese man-of-war?

Answers 1 Winds 2 The Bionic Woman 3 Merlin 4 -40°C 5 Dom Perignon 6 Motorcycle 7 Pelé 8 Louisiana 9 The limerick 10 Quartz 11 Malcolm 12 Spain 13 Nigeria 14 Kiloton 15 A jellyfish

Quiz 53

1   Whose famous last words were reputedly: 'Let not poor Nellie starve'?

2   The aqueous humour and vitreous humour are in which part of the human body?

3   Which explorer discovered Victoria Falls in Africa?

4   In Greek legend, which dog guarded the entrance to the underworld?

5   Which light two or four-wheeled carriage had a collapsible hood called a calash?

6   What is the largest county in the Republic of Ireland?

7   Who was the last king of Egypt?

8   By what name is Beatrice Stella Tanner better known?

9   Holyrood House is in which British city?

10 What is the literal meaning of the word mafia?

11 What were the names of the opposing gangs in the musical 'West Side Story'?

12 The surname of which kings of England was taken from the Count of Anjou, so called because he wore a sprig of broom in his cap?

13 Which entertainer used the code name John Burrows and Dr John Carpenter when answering telephone calls?

14 1 Snoopy Place, Santa Rosa, California was the home address of which cartoonist?

15 Which war lasted sixteen years longer than its name implies?

1   Whose daughter adopted the name Lana Peters upon becoming a US citizen after defecting to the United States in 1967?

2   What was the name of the Ewing family Texas ranch in the TV series 'Dallas'?

3   Which actress was born Natasha Virpaeff?

4   What is the name of the Archangel who spoke to Joan of Arc?

5   Which fictional characters met for the first time in 1881 at the Criterion Bar in London?

6   Which word was already entered into the grid when the first crossword puzzle (called a word-cross) was published in the 'New York World' in December 1913?

7   HVJ is the radio station of which state, which began broadcasting in 1931?

8   Who wrote the novel 'Les Miserables'?

9   In the Bible, who was the first king of Israel?

10 Which 1963 musical was based on H.G. Wells' book 'Kipps'?

11 Which US president always wore a red carnation?

12 Who was the French statesman, called the Red Eminence, who totally dominated King Louis XIII?

13 Who are the two grouchy old men in "The Muppet Show' who heckle from the balcony?

14 Who succeeded Joseph Smith as head of the Mormon Church?

15 What is the largest size of champagne bottle?

Answers 1 Joseph Stalin 2 South Fork 3 Natalie Wood 4 Michael 5 Dr. Watson and Sherlock Holmes 6 Fun 7 The Vatican 8 Victor Hugo 9 Saul 10 Half a Sixpence 11 William McKinley 12 Cardinal Richelieu 13 Waldorf and Statler 14 Brigham Young 15 Nebuchadnezzar

Quiz 55

1 Which word, meaning a punched out circle of paper, became frequently used in the aftermath of the US 2000 presidential election?

2 What is the longest river in South America?

3 What was the sequel to 'Alice in Wonderland' called?

4 Who was the suffragette who died after throwing herself under the king's horse in the 1913 Derby?

5 What is the official residence of the Lord Mayor of London?

6 Which US state is the location for London Bridge?

7 Which mythical creature was part lion, part goat and part serpent?

8 Of what is silviculture the study?

9 Which Russian tsar was assassinated by his own officers in 1817?

10 What is the surname of the professor in the board game 'Cluedo'?

11 Buck and Boomer are the names for the male of which animal?

12 Who was the only survivor of the Paris car crash which killed Princess Diana?

13 Which was the first soccer team to become English soccer league first division champions three years in succession?

14 The Colorado beetle specifically damages what type of crop?

15 What in Paris is the Bois De Boulogne?

Answers 1 Chad 2 Amazon 3 Alice Through The Looking Glass 4 Emily Davidson 5 The Mansion House 6 Arizona 7 Chimaera 8 The growing and tending of trees as a branch of forestry 9 Paul I 10 Plum 11 Kangaroo 12 Trevor Rees-Jones 13 Huddersfield Town 14 Potatoes 15 A park

MISCELLANEOUS 1   *Quiz 56*

1   Which river flows through the Grand Canyon?

2   Celine Dion won the 'Eurovision Song Contest' for which country?

3   Which Shakespeare play was set in Elsinor Castle, Denmark?

4   What was the code-name for the artificial harbour used in the D-Day landings?

5   What type of food is a Bombay Duck?

6   What is the maximum number of clubs that a professional golfer is allowed to carry in his bag?

7   Who said: 'Genius is 1% inspiration and 99% perspiration'?

8   Which actress is the daughter of movie star Tippi Hedron?

9   Which pirate was knighted by Charles II and became Governor of Jamaica?

10   The Kyukyu Island chain lies between which two countries?

11   Who plays Austin Powers in the movies?

12   Which South American country has shores on both the Atlantic and Pacific oceans?

13   In 'Oliver Twist', who was Jack Dawkins otherwise known as?

14   Florence Nightingale achieved her fame during which war?

15   What are the two main ingredients of bubble and squeak?

Answers 1 Colorado 2 Switzerland 3 Hamlet 4 Mulberry 5 Fish 6 14 7 Edison 8 Melanie Griffith 9 Sir Henry Morgan 10 Japan & Taiwan 11 Mike Myers 12 Colombia 13 The Artful Dodger 14 The Crimean War 15 Cabbage and potato

1   Who was the last amateur golfer to win the British Open Championship?

2   The cardinal is the largest type of which British insect?

3   Which legendary bird cremates itself and rises from its own ashes once every 500 years?

4   What mountain range is known as the backbone of Italy?

5   Which fictional detective lived at St. Mary Mead?

6   Which character in 'Alice in Wonderland' keeps saying: 'Curiouser and curiouser'?

7   John Foster Dulles airport serves which US city?

8   Which country manufactures the Proton motor car?

9   Who in 1963 hid out at Leatherslade Farm in England?

10 Desdemona is a character in which Shakespeare play?

11 Who, after receiving bad reviews said: 'I cried all the way to the bank'?

12 Which vintage TV comedy series was set at Fort Baxter?

13 What name is given to a bell-tower that is not attached to a church?

14 What item of beachwear was made famous by Brian Hyland in the 1960s?

15 In the Bible, who was found in the bull rushes by Pharaoh's daughter?

Answers 1 Bobby Jones 2 Spider 3 Phoenix 4 Appenines 5 Miss Marple 6 Alice 7 Washington 8 Malaysia 9 The Great Train robbers 10 Othello 11 Liberace 12 The Phil Silver's Show 13 Campanile 14 An Itsy Bitsy Teeny Weeny Yellow Polka Dot Bikini 15 Moses

MISCELLANEOUS 1   *Quiz 58*

1   What kind of creature is Napoleon in George Orwell's 'Animal Farm'?

2   Which garden shrub is also known as Golden Bells?

3   In computer terminology, what is bit short for?

4   What is a triangle which has two equal sides called?

5   Who designed the bouncing bomb used by the Dambusters in World War II?

6   What, in Germany, is pumpernickel a type of?

7   What on a ship is known as a binnacle?

8   The Kodiak Bear is native to which American state?

9   What is the best-selling book which is still under copyright?

10 Which old-time screen cowboy rode a horse called Topper?

11 What is the former name of the Sellafield nuclear power plant?

12 The first department store Marshall Field was first opened in which American city?

13 Which American athlete gave his name to a particular style of high jumping?

14 What part of a horse's body is call its hock?

15 What is the main religion of Japan?

1 Which gangster gave his profession as 'Second hand furniture dealer' on his business cards?

2 Under which two American presidents did Henry Kissinger serve as Secretary of State?

3 Which Manchester City goalkeeper kept goal with a broken neck in the 1956 FA Cup Final?

4 How often does Halley's Comet visit Earth?

5 What did Dorothy Parker famously remark when told of the death of President Coolidge?

6 Who played Maddie Hayes in the TV series 'Moonlighting'?

7 How many movements are there usually in a symphony?

8 What is the name given to the official stamp on gold and other precious metals?

9 Who painted 'The Laughing Cavalier'?

10 In human anatomy what is the name of the large intestine?

11 Which Nazi committed suicide with his wife and six children in 1945?

12 Which cocktail consists of rye whiskey and sweet vermouth?

13 In the Bible, who is the father of David?

14 What was the sequel to Anita Loos' book 'Gentleman Prefer Blondes'?

15 Which British actor was born Michael Dumble-Smith?

Answers 1 Al Capone 2 Nixon & Ford 3 Bert Trautmann 4 Every 76 years 5 'How can they tell? 6 Cybil Shepherd 7 Four 8 Hallmark 9 Frans Hals 10 Colon 11 Goebbels 12 A Manhattan 13 Jesse 14 Gentleman Marry Brunettes 15 Michael Crawford

MISCELLANEOUS 1   *Quiz 60*

1   Which sport is played by the Los Angeles Lakers?

2   Sing Sing prison is in which US city?

3   Who, in a book by Anton Chekhov, are Olga, Masha and Irina?

4   Who invented jeans?

5   In Judaism what day of the week is the Sabbath?

6   What does a pomologist study?

7   Which of the world's rivers contains the most water?

8   'I'm Still Waiting' was the first No.1 hit for which singer?

9   Who wrote 'The Day of the Jackal'?

10 Princess Henrietta Maria of France was the wife of which English king?

11 Which World War I US military hero, originally a conscientious objector, was played on-screen by Gary Cooper?

12 If you travelled directly east from Cape Horn, which is the next land you would reach?

13 The Aswan Dam is on which river?

14 Who became Annie's guardian in the story of 'Little Orphan Annie'?

15 Vinho Verdi is a white wine from which country?

Answers 1 Basketball 2 New York 3 The Three Sisters 4 Levi Strauss 5 Saturday 6 Fruit growing 7 The Amazon 8 Diana Ross 9 Frederick Forsyth 10 Charles 1 11 Sergeant York 12 Cape Horn 13 Nile 14 Daddy Warbucks 15 Portugal

1. What is the nickname of American bank robber Charles Floyd?
2. Whose sailed in the 'Santa Maria'?
3. Which lord led The Charge of the Light Brigade at Balaclava?
4. Who wrote the 'Pathetique' symphony?
5. Who, in 1888, patented the pneumatic bicycle tyre?
6. On which satellite TV channel would you find Dan Rather presenting his evening news programme?
7. Which is the largest island in the Mediterranean Sea?
8. In the poem by Edward Lear, for how long did the owl and the pussycat sail for?
9. Which character was played by Ted Danson in 'Cheers'?
10. In which film does Doris Day sing 'Secret Love'?
11. What is the more common name for Hansen's Disease?
12. By what is the first bugle call of the day known?
13. What cocktail consists of vodka and tomato juice?
14. In the cartoon series, which cat chases after Tweety Pie?
15. Which was the last country in Europe, as late as 1984, to give votes to women?

Answers 1 Pretty Boy 2 Christopher Columbus 3 Lord Cardigan 4 Tchaikovsky 5 John Boyd Dunlop 6 CBS 7 Sicily 8 A year and a day 9 Sam Malone 10 Calamity Jane 11 Leprosy 12 Reveille 13 Bloody Mary 14 Sylvester 15 Liechtenstein

MISCELLANEOUS 1 — Quiz 62

1   Who was President Nixon's Attorney General who was sent to prison as a result of the Watergate scandal?

2   Which mountaineer on being asked why he wanted to climb Everest said: 'Because it's there'?

3   Who rode the Queen Mother's horse Devon Loch when it collapsed near the finishing line in the 1956 Grand National?

4   Which musical was based on a Fredrico Fellini film, 'Nights of Cabiria'?

5   Which writer was married to the archaeologist Sir Max Mallowen?

6   In economics, whose law states that: 'bad money drives out good money'?

7   Which Shakespeare character's last words are: 'The rest is silence'?

8   Who in 1849 were referred to as the 'Forty-Niners'?

9   Is the denominator the upper or lower number of a fraction?

10   The Dodgers are the baseball team of which US city?

11   What does W.E. stand for in W.E. Gladstone?

12   By what nickname was Harry Longbaugh better known?

13   Of what was ENIAC the first of its type?

14   Who made the first navigation of the globe in the vessel Victoria?

15   Walter Mondale was Vice-president to which US president?

Answers 1 John Mitchell 2 George Mallory 3 Dick Francis 4 Sweet Charity 5 Agatha Christie 6 Gresham's Law 7 Hamlet 8 Californian Gold Miners 9 Lower 10 Los Angeles 11 William Ewart 12 The Sundance Kid 13 Electronic computer 14 Magellan 15 Jimmy Carter

1   Which country was originally named Cathay?

2   What is the name of Humphrey Bogart's character in 'The Maltese Falcon'?

3   What is the central aisle of a church called?

4   What in the human body is the bone which is most frequently broken?

5   Who is the brother of Sherlock Holmes?

6   What is the name of the spear used by Zulu warriors?

7   Which countries were defeated by the forces of Napoleon at the Battle of Austerlitz?

8   In which sport do teams compete for the Dunhill Cup?

9   In which part of the human body are the metacarpals?

10   Who is the patron saint of lost causes?

11   The Sao Francisco river flows through which country?

12   In mythology, who was given ass's ears?

13   Which institution has the motto *citius, altius, fortuis* (swifter, higher, stronger)?

14   Sinhalese is a language spoken in which country?

15   Meg and Percy are the boarding house owners in which Harold Pinter story?

Answers 1 China 2 Sam Spade 3 Nave 4 Collar bone 5 Mycroft 6 Assegai 7 Austria and Russia 8 Golf 9 Hand 10 St Jude 11 Brazil 12 King Midas 13 The Olympics 14 Sri Lanka 15 The Birthday Party

MISCELLANEOUS 1   *Quiz 64*

1 The Golden Arrow was a famous train that ran from Paris to which destination?

2 Which English king died a prisoner in the Tower of London?

3 Whose mistress was Clara Petacci?

4 What is the name of the clown in Shakespeare's 'As You Like It'?

5 Which country fought on both sides in World War II?

6 Which Christian festival celebrates the purification of the Virgin Mary?

7 In which US city is Union the main train station?

8 Which market street in London is officially called Middlesex Street?

9 Which country was once called Lusitania?

10 How many human beings set sail on Noah's Ark?

11 Mrs Danvers was the housekeeper in which Daphne du Maurier novel?

12 Who in sport is known as the 'Great White Shark'?

13 In which English city was the first Boots Chemist shop opened?

14 Mount Egmont is a volcanic peak in which country?

15 What centigrade temperature is gas mark 6 equal to?

Answers 1 Monte Carlo **2** Henry VI **3** Benito Mussolini **4** Touchstone **5** Italy **6** Candlemas **7** Washington **8** Petticoat Lane **9** Portugal and parts of Spain **10** 8 **11** Rebecca **12** Greg Norman **13** Nottingham **14** New Zealand **15** 200°C

Quiz 65

1   In the game of chess, which piece is called Springer in Germany?

2   A sockeye is what type of fish?

3   What is the former name of Vanuatu, an island chain in the SW Pacific?

4   Why were the contents of Samuel Pepy's diary not revealed for 150 years after his death?

5   Native to Central Africa, what type of creature is a kob?

6   What is the meaning of the Russian word 'mir'?

7   The flag of which country contains the Star of David?

8   What is the meaning of the world 'muciferous'?

9   The word caravan originates from which language?

10 Who described foxhunting as: 'The unspeakable in pursuit of the uneatable'?

11 Which sportsman was called the Rockhampton Rocket?

12 What in a famous advertisement was 'Wadka from Warrington'?

13 Who, in World War II, were the axis forces?

14 What was the venue of the 1964 Summer Olympics?

15 'The Watch Tower' is the magazine of which organisation?

Answers 1 Knight 2 Salmon 3 New Hebrides 4 It was written in code and took so long to be deciphered 5 Antelope 6 Peace 7 Israel 8 Bearing nuts 9 Persian 10 Oscar Wilde 11 Rod Laver 12 Vladivar Vodka 13 Germany, Italy, Japan 14 Tokyo 15 Jehovah's Witnesses

MISCELLANEOUS 1 — *Quiz 66*

1 Which scientist used kites to conduct electrical experiments?

2 What are the famous last words of Julius Caesar?

3 In medicine, which is the most widespread parasitic infection?

4 What is the name given to subsoil that is permanently frozen?

5 Who played Jason Colby in 'The Colby's'?

6 Who wrote the musical 'Can-Can'?

7 The action of John Le Carré's book 'A Small Town in Germany' takes place in which small town?

8 In which TV series did Patrick McGoohan play No. 6?

9 Which actor's real name was Emanuel Goldenberg?

10 What is the longest river in France?

11 Which birds fly in groups called skeins?

12 What is the more common name of diluted acetic acid?

13 Who wrote 'Rob Roy'?

14 Which inventor had a research laboratory at Menlo Park?

15 In which year did the Dunkirk evacuation take place?

Answers 1 Benjamin Franklin **2** Et tu Brute **3** Malaria **4** Permafrost **5** Charlton Heston **6** Cole Porter **7** Bonn **8** The Prisoner **9** Edward G. Robinson **10** Loire **11** Geese **12** Vinegar **13** Sir Walter Scott **14** Edison **15** 1940

1   In which country is the Atacama Desert?

2   What did Richard J. Gattling invent in 1862?

3   What flower did singer Billie Holiday always wear in the right side of her hair?

4   The character of The Mad Hatter in 'Alice in Wonderland' is said to be patterned after which British Prime Minister?

5   Which city is served by Haneda airport?

6   At which sport would you use a penholder grip?

7   What did the Lateran Treaty of 1929 establish??

8   Who was the 5 ½ inch high boy in stories by the Brothers Grimm?

9   What is Mr Spock's home planet in 'Star Trek'?

10   In the Bible, whose brother was Aaron?

11   In the 1960s Anette Funicello starred in a series of beach movies with which actor/singer?

12   Who is Snoopy's sister in the comic strip 'Peanuts'?

13   Who was the youngest daughter of Tsar Nicolas II of Russia?

14   Who were the first aviators to fly across the Atlantic non-stop?

15   Who was the father of Alexander the Great?

Answers 1 Chile 2 The machine gun 3 Gardenia 4 Gladstone 5 Tokyo 6 Table tennis 7 The Vatican City as an independent state 8 Tom Thumb 9 Vulcan 10 Moses 11 Frankie Avalon 12 Belle 13 Anastasia 14 Alcock and Brown 15 Philip of Macedonia

MISCELLANEOUS 1   *Quiz 68*

1   Which city is served by Schipol airport?

2   What is the disease pertussis more commonly known as?

3   On which vessel did Jason and the Argonauts sail in search of the Golden Fleece?

4   Who wrote 'Northanger Abbey'?

5   Which actor husband of Elizabeth Taylor took his stage name from his school drama teacher?

6   Which two English Classic horse races are restricted to fillies only?

7   Jimmy Porter was the central character in John Osborne's 'Look Back in Anger'. Which other term was used to describe this character?

8   Which TV series had 'Who loves ya, baby' as its catchphrase?

9   What are the names of the twins in the Bee Gees pop group?

10 Which French novelist was romantically involved with composer Frederic Chopin?

11 Who lost to Billie Jean King in the Battle of the Sexes tennis match in 1973?

12 In which city is the Doge's Palace?

13 Which music hall star was known as The Prime Minister of Mirth?

14 Who was the first Roman Catholic president of the United States?

15 Which astronaut hit the first golf ball on the moon?

Answers 1 Amsterdam 2 Whooping cough 3 Argo 4 Jane Austen 5 Richard Burton 6 1000 Guineas and Oaks 7 Angry Young Man 8 Kojak 9 Maurice and Robin 10 George Sand 11 Bobby Riggs 12 Venice 13 George Robey 14 John F. Kennedy 15 Alan Shepard

1   How many letters are there in the Hawaiian alphabet?

2   In the TV series 'Dr. Who', what does the acronym TARDIS stand for?

3   In mythology, who is the Norse God of Thunder?

4   What does the S stand for in Harry S Truman?

5   'Vesti la guibba' is an aria from which opera?

6   In the first ever episode of Coronation Street, who lived at No.11 Coronation Street?

7   How many carats is pure gold?

8   Which actress was the first wife of Ronald Reagan?

9   Wands, Cups, Swords and Pentacles are suits in which deck of cards?

10   In mythology, which youth fell in love with his own reflection in a pool?

11   Which of the Seven Wonders of the Ancient World was built by King Nebuchadnezzar for his wife?

12   What is the name of the gamekeeper in 'Lady Chatterley's Lover'?

13   Who was the last prisoner to be held in the Tower of London?

14   What is a hand called in Bridge in which every card is a nine or under?

15   Which animal's home is called a sett?

Answers 1 12 **2** Time And Relative Dimensions In Space **3** Thor **4** Nothing (the S is merely an initial, note there is no dot after it) **5** I Pagliacci **6** Annie and Jack Walker (No.11 is the Rover's Return) **7** 24 **8** Jane Wyman **9** Tarot **10** Narcissus **11** The Hanging Gardens of Babylon **12** Mellors **13** Rudolf Hess **14** Yarborough **15** Badger

MISCELLANEOUS 1   *Quiz 70*

1   Of which country is Dacca the capital?

2   Which fictional character's landlady is Mrs Hudson?

3   The character Fallon appeared in 'Dynasty' and which other TV series?

4   Who wrote 'An Elegy Written in a Country Churchyard'?

5   The Inferno is the longest race in which sport?

6   The asteroid belt lies between which two planets?

7   In which part of the human body is the Organ of Corti?

8   In which opera does Lieut. Pinkerton appear?

9   Who, in his lifetime, sold only one painting, 'Red Vinyard'?

10 What kind of creature is a snapper?

11 When Mike Tyson was jailed for rape, what was the name of his victim?

12 What, between Italy and Sicily, is Charybdis?

13 Who plays juror No.8 in the movie '12 Angry Men'?

14 What is the official language of Haiti?

15 What in America was the original name for a cinema?

Answers 1 Bangladesh 2 Sherlock Holmes 3 The Colbys 4 Gray 5 Skiing (a slalom) 6 Mars and Jupiter 7 Ear 8 Madame Butterfly 9 Van Gogh 10 Fish 11 Desiree Washington 12 A whirlpool 13 Henry Fonda 14 French 15 Nickelodeon

1   What nationality was explorer Ferdinand Magellan?

2   To which sea in the North Atlantic do eels migrate each year to breed?

3   Who, in the Bible was the first person to be born?

4   As one of his labours, what had Hercules to do with the Cretan bull?

5   What name is given to the first day of Lent?

6   What is the name of the stew or soup thickened with okra?

7   Which was the first US city to host the modern Olympic Games?

8   Who sculpted 'Behold the Man'?

9   Of the nine muses, who is the muse of dance?

10 Who, in the title of a Shakespeare play are Valentine and Proteus?

11 Who wrote the Western classic 'Riders of the Purpole Sage'?

12 What did the St. Louis Rams win in 2000?

13 Native to Australia, what is a goanna a type of?

14 Who is the patron saint of book-keepers, accountants and tax collectors?

15 How many lines are there in a sonnet?

Answers 1 Portuguese **2** Sargasso Sea **3** Cain **4** Capture it **5** Pentecost **6** Gumbo **7** St.Louis **8** Epstein **9** Terpsichore **10** Two Gentlemen of Verona **11** Zane **12** The Superbowl **13** Lizard **14** Matthew **15** 14

MISCELLANEOUS 1   *Quiz 72*

1   The Dominican Republic declared itself independent from which country in 1821?
2   In which year did the first convict ships arrive in Port Jackson, Australia?
3   Which actress played the poison dwarf in 'Dallas'?
4   Who wrote the play 'A Streetcar Named Desire'?
5   What palace was given to Henry VIII by Cardinal Wolsey?
6   What computer language was invented by James Backus?
7   Which US president introduced a doctrine under which it was held that the American continents were not to open to future colonisation by any European power?
8   What is the world's oldest republic?
9   Ludwig Von Kochel catalogued the works of which composer?
10 In 1908 aged 3, what did Pu Yi become the last of?
11 What Ford vehicle letter in 1927 denoted the car that succeeded the model T?
12 Which woman's tennis player became, aged 16, the youngest player to win the US Open?
13 Which British newspaper is the oldest Sunday newspaper in the world?
14 What is the text of an opera called?
15 Kampala stands on the shores of which lake?

Answers 1 Spain 2 1788 3 Charlene Tilton 4 Tennessee Williams 5 Hampton Court 6 Fortran 7 James Monroe (The Monroe Doctrine) 8 San Marino 9 Mozart 10 China's last emperor 11 Model A 12 Tracy Austin 13 Observer 14 Libretto 15 Victoria

80

MISCELLANEOUS 1 *Quiz 73*

1   Boris Karloff received fourth billing at the end of which horror movie which premiered in 1931?

2   Which is New York's largest borough?

3   By what nickname was gardener Lancelot Brown better known?

4   In what type of building was Maria Marten famously murdered in 1927?

5   In 1976, which band were branded 'rotten punks' by the US press, making them a symbol for punk rock?

6   Alice Keppel was the mistress of which English king?

7   What was ended by the 21st Amendment of the US Constitution?

8   The last episode of which cult TV series was completed by the BBC in 1974?

9   In which movie starring Matt Damon and Robin Williams does a therapist try to figure out a destructively angered Boston youth?

10 Who wrote the 'Jungle Book'?

11 Who travelled to Africa to search for David Livingstone?

12 In which TV series did Wayne Rogers play Trapper John?

13 In which decade was Nelson Mandela jailed in South Africa?

14 Of where is a Sard a native?

15 Who became the first US unelected vice-president when he succeeded Spiro Agnew in 1973?

Answers 1 Frankenstein **2** Queens **3** Capability **4** A red barn **5** The Sex Pistols **6** Edward VII **7** Prohibition **8** Monty Python's Flying Circus **9** Good Will Hunting **10** Rudyard Kipling **11** Henry Morton Stanley **12** M.A.S.H **13** The 60s **14** Sardinia **15** Gerald Ford

MISCELLANEOUS 1

Quiz 74

1 From which country did Iceland finally win total independence in June 1944?

2 Which poet lived with his sister at Dove Cottage, Grasmere, in the English Lake district?

3 A covey is the group name for what type of bird?

4 What sport is played by the Carolina Panthers?

5 What is another name for the Russian Wolfhound?

6 What, in 1926, did 'Variety' Magazine describe as a new development in radio?

7 Which rock group disbanded four months after the death of its founder and guiding spirit Jerry Garcia?

8 What type of creature is a blind snake?

9 The Mozambique Channel separates which island from mainland Africa?

10 In which US state is Anchorage?

11 In Roman times, by what name was Lucius Domitius Ahenobarbus better known?

12 Who, in 1988, became the first woman elected to govern a Muslim nation?

13 Who was Fred Astaire's dancing partner in his first film, 'Dancing Lady'?

14 Who defeated Muhammed Ali in his 61st and last fight?

15 Where in Australia was the first convict settlement established?

Answers 1 Denmark 2 Wordsworth 3 Partridge 4 American Football 5 Borzoi 6 Television 7 The Grateful Dead 8 Lizard 9 Madagascar 10 Alaska 11 Nero 12 Benazir Bhutto 13 Joan Crawford 14 Trevor Berbick 15 Botany Bay

1   At the age of 22 Beethoven noted in his diary that he had enough money for his first music lesson with which fellow composer?

2   In which Italian city was the Mona Lisa recovered two years after it had been stolen from the Louvre in Paris?

3   What type of creature is a keeshund?

4   Which town in central Spain is famous for its swords and knives?

5   What are close encounters of the second kind?

6   Is nyctaphobia the fear of darkness, dirt or poverty?

7   Tommy Bolin, who died of a heroin overdose in 1976, was lead guitarist with which rock group?

8   The language Afrikaans derives from which European language?

9   What are double loops, radial loops, arches, whorles and ulna loops?

10 What do the French call Shrove Tuesday?

11 What colour are Venetian gondolas painted?

12 Thought to be the first of its kind, what was the German, 'Avisa Relation oder Zeitug', which appeared in 1609?

13 Titan, Mimas, Rhea and Dione are just five of the 20 known moons of which planet?

14 Magyar is the official language of which country?

15 A cygnet is the young of which animal?

Answers 1 Joseph Haydn **2** Florence **3** A Dutch barge dog **4** Toledo **5** Physical evidence of UFOs **6** Darkness **7** Deep Purple **8** Dutch **9** Fingerprints **10** Mardi Gras **11** Black **12** The first regular newspaper **13** Venus **14** Hungary **15** Swan

MULTIPLE CHOICE

MULTIPLE CHOICE

Quiz 1

1   The Sea Swallow is an alternative name for which bird?
    a   seagull
    b   penguin.
    c   tern
    d   cormorant

2   Who, on being executed said: "This is a sharp medicine, but it will cure all diseases"?
    a   Marie Antoinette
    b   Sir Walter Raleigh
    c   Mary Queen of Scots
    d   Charles I

3   What religion was founded by Bodhidhama?
    a   Zen Buddhism
    b   Islam
    c   Hinduism
    d   Sikhism

4   Of what is Tribology the study?
    a   lubrication and friction
    b   hormones
    c   animal behaviour
    d   tissues of organisms

5   In what sport would you see a Western Roll?
    a   ten pin bowling
    b   wrestling
    c   high jump
    d   judo

6   Who, when he was murdered whilst playing poker, held two aces and two eights, a hand which from then on was known as Dead Man's Hand?
    a   Wyatt Earp
    b   Jesse James
    c   Billy the Kid
    d   Wild Bill Hickok

7   Murganah is the slave girl in which story?
    a   The Count of Monte Christo
    b   The Canterbury Tales
    c   Ali Baba and the 40 Thieves
    d   Don Quixote

8   How was Herbert Khaury better known in the world of entertainment?
    a   Iggy Pop
    b   Tiny Tim
    c   Vanilla Ice
    d   Adam Ant

9   Who is the Greek goddess of Spring?
    a   Dionysus
    b   Ninhusay
    c   Pan
    d   Persephone

10 Diet is the Parliament of which country?
    a   Poland
    b   Japan
    c   Thailand
    d   Norway

Answers 1 c, 2 b, 3 a, 4 a, 5 c, 6 d, 7 c, 8 b, 9 d, 10 b.

MULTIPLE CHOICE *Quiz 2*

1 Lillie Langtry was the mistress of which British king?
   a Edward VII
   b Charles II
   c George V
   d Henry VIII

2 What was the real first name of Coco Chanel?
   a Maria
   b Leslie
   c Gabrielle
   d Amelia

3 By what is the last bugle call of the day otherwise known?
   a last post
   b reveille
   c sun set
   d lights out

4 In the USA, the nation's gold is stored at Fort Knox. Where is the nation's silver supply stored?
   a Chase Manhatten Bank vaults
   b West Point
   c Princeton University
   d The Pentagon Vaults

5 What is Gerald R. Ford's middle name?
   a Raymond
   b Robert
   c Ricardo
   d Rudolph

6 The Aztecs were natives of which country?
   a Mexico
   b Bolivia
   c Colombia
   d Peru

7 In the classic song 'Chattanooga Choo Choo', what is the nickname of the woman the singer is to meet at his hometown station?
   a Cutie Pie
   b Funny Face
   c Truly Truly Fair
   d Chi Chi

8 What was invented by O.A. North in 1869?
   a the toilet roll holder
   b moth balls
   c the toothpaste tube
   d the coat hanger

9 King Zog was the ruler of which country?
   a Albania
   b Bulgaria
   c Nicaragua
   d Romania

10 What does the dish marrons glace consist of?
   a rice with saffron
   b cracked wheat with lemon and mint
   c candied chestnuts
   d stuffed fruit pancake

Answers 1 a, 2 c, 3 a, 4 b, 5 d, 6 a, 7 b, 8 d, 9 a, 10 c.

1   What instrument was played by jazz great Count Basie?
 a   trombone
 b   piano
 c   clarinet
 d   tenor sax

2   What did my true love give to me on the 11th day of Christmas?
 a   ladies dancing
 b   maids-a-milking
 c   lords-a-leaping
 d   drummers drumming

3   Which capital city was once called Edo?
 a   Copenhagen
 b   Rangoon
 c   Tokyo
 d   Edinburgh

4   A chattering is the collective group name for which bird?
 a   chaffinch
 b   crow
 c   crane
 d   chough

5   What was the original name of movie mogul Sam Goldwyn?
 a   Goldrush
 b   Goldstein
 c   Goldfish
 d   Goldberg

6   What is the fifth book of the Pentateuch?
 a   Numbers
 b   Deuteronomy
 c   Exodus
 d   Genesis

7   Which comedian, who attacked American culture, was born Alfred Schneider in 1926, and died of a drug overdose in 1966?
 a   Alan King
 b   Alan Sherman
 c   Lennie Bruce
 d   Al Murrey

8   Dancer was the Secret Service code name for which First Lady?
 a   Barbara Bush
 b   Rosalyn Carter
 c   Nancy Reagan
 d   Hillary Clinton

9   What is the world's northernmost desert?
 a   Gobi
 b   Mojave
 c   Kalahari
 d   Nubian

10   What is a female donkey called?
 a   Annie
 b   Jenny
 c   Sally
 d   Jill

Answers 1 b, 2 a, 3 c, 4 d, 5 c, 6 b, 7 c, 8 b, 9 a, 10 b.

Quiz 4

1 In American football, which city has a team called the Oilers?
a Cleveland
b Houston
c Buffalo
d Indianapolis

2 Apart from Bill Clinton, who is the only other American president to have been impeached?
a John Quincy Adams
b James Buchanan
c Andrew Johnson
d Richard Nixon

3 Who wrote the song 'Alexander's Ragtime Band'?
a Cole Porter
b Irving Berlin
c George Gershwin
d Jerome Kern

4 Kim Campbell was the first female Prime Minister of which country?
a Canada
b New Zealand
c Australia
d The Republic of Ireland

5 In the Chinese calendar, the year 2002 is the year of which animal?
a snake
b tiger
c horse
d dragon

6 What nationality was the explorer Christopher Colombus?
a Italian
b English
c Portuguese
d Spanish

7 Which part of a flower contains pollen?
a stamen
b sepal
c anther
d pistil

8 Karroo is a plateau area in which country?
a Turkey
b Saudi Arabia
c Belgium
d South Africa

9 In the favourite song of Long John Silver in the novel 'Treasure Island', how many men on a Dead Man's Chest?
a 20
b 15
c 10
d 14

10 What is the meaning of the French phrase *bon mot*?
a witty saying
b good luck
c already done
d all together

Answers 1 b, 2 c, 3 b, 4 a, 5 c, 6 a, 7 c, 8 d, 9 b, 10 a.

MULTIPLE CHOICE   *Quiz 5*

1   Who wrote the 'Moonlight Sonata'?
    a   Schubert
    b   Beethoven
    c   Chopin
    d   Mozart

2   In mythology, two of the three Graces were
    Aglaia and Thalia, who was the third?
    a   Tisiphone
    b   Diomedes
    c   Euphrosyne
    d   Daphne

3   Milwaukee lies on which of North
    America's great lakes?
    a   Erie
    b   Ontario
    c   Superior
    d   Michigan

4   Ariel and Miranda are moons of which
    planet?
    a   Saturn
    b   Uranus
    c   Jupiter
    d   Neptune

5   Leon Bismark were the real first names of
    which jazz great?
    a   Dizzy Gillespie
    b   Jelly Roll Morton
    c   Bix Biederbecke
    d   Woody Herman

6   *Proboscidea* is the scientific name of which
    creature?
    a   anteater
    b   crocodile
    c   rhinoceros
    d   elephant

7   What does a calorimeter measure?
    a   energy
    b   altitude
    c   heat
    d   latitude

8   What was the name of the dog in the story
    'Three Men in a Boat'?
    a   Montmorency
    b   Scamper
    c   Peritas
    d   Boatswain

9   Of what is bryology the study?
    a   tree rings
    b   mosses
    c   bird's eggs
    d   fungi

10 In which movie, made in 1956, does Elvis
    Presley play Clint Reno?
    a   Jailhouse Rock
    b   King Creole
    c   Loving You
    d   Love Me Tender

Answers 1 b, 2 c, 3 d, 4 b, 5 c, 6 d, 7 c, 8 a, 9 b, 10 d.

MULTIPLE CHOICE

Quiz 6

1 The Java Trench, the greatest ocean depth, is part of which ocean?
   a   Pacific
   b   Atlantic
   c   Arctic
   d   Indian

2 What is the meaning of the Latin phrase *ex-cathedra*?
   a   with meaning
   b   from the chair
   c   from cause to effect
   d   by God's grace

3 Which English king died in a fall from his horse, called Sorrel?
   a   Richard III
   b   William III
   c   Richard I
   d   Henry II

4 What was the nationality of Sigmund Freud?
   a   Austrian
   b   English
   c   Swiss
   d   German

5 How old was the character Jack Crabb who was played in the 1970 movie 'Little Big Man' by Dustin Hoffman?
   a   91
   b   101
   c   111
   d   121

6 Which boxer is on the cover of the Beatles 'Sgt Pepper's Lonely Hearts Club Band' album?
   a   Henry Cooper
   b   Sonny Liston
   c   Joe Frazier
   d   Muhammed Ali

7 Which drink is made of corn flavoured with Juniper Berries?
   a   rum
   b   brandy
   c   slivovitz
   d   gin

8 What is the approximate capacity of a 10-gallon hat?
   a   6 pints
   b   7 pints
   c   8 pints
   d   10 pints

9 Which country, other than China, India and the USA, has the world's highest population?
   a   Pakistan
   b   Malaysia
   c   Indonesia
   d   Germany

10 How many years marriage is celebrated by a tin anniversary?
   a   5
   b   8
   c   10
   d   15

Answers 1 d, 2 b, 3 b, 4 a, 5 d, 6 b, 7 d, 8 a, 9 c, 10 c.

MULTIPLE CHOICE — Quiz 7

1 What is the nickname of blues singer McKinley Morgenfield?
   a Howlin' Wolf
   b Memphis Slim
   c Bo Diddley
   d Muddy Waters

2 In the dish devils on horseback, what type of fruit is stuffed and wrapped in bacon?
   a prune
   b peach
   c avocado
   d pear

3 Patagonia is an area on which continent?
   a Africa
   b Asia
   c South America
   d Europe

4 Cedric Errol is the title character of which book?
   a The Invisible Man
   b Little Lord Fauntleroy
   c The History Man
   d Lucky Jim

5 What is the name of 411 Elm Street in Dallas from where Lee Harvey Oswald is alleged to have shot President Kennedy on November 22, 1963?
   a Kruger's Variety Theater
   b Texas School Book Depository
   c Grassy Knoll House
   d The Dallas Academy of Modern Dance

6 Love Apple is the original name of which fruit?
   a fig
   b pineapple
   c tomato
   d pomegranate

7 Who was the first tennis player to achieve the Grand Slam of holding the Wimbledon, US, Australian and French titles simultaneously?
   a Rod Laver
   b Fred Perry
   c Don Budge
   d Bill Tilden

8 What was the first name of Spain's General Franco?
   a Juan
   b Francisco
   c Frederico
   d Pedro

9 The Camp David Agreement of 1978 was a Peace Treaty between which two nations?
   a India-Pakistan
   b Iran-Iraq
   c USA-Russia
   d Egypt-Israel

10 How many eyes does a bee have?
   a 2
   b 3
   c 4
   d 5

Answers 1 d, 2 a, 3 c, 4 b, 5 b, 6 c, 7 c, 8 b, 9 d, 10 d.

MULTIPLE CHOICE

Quiz 8

1   Algophobia is a fear of what?
   a   Arithmetic
   b   Pain
   c   Pleasure
   d   Seaweed

2   The popular children's characters the 'Mr. Men' were created by Roger Hargreaves. Which was the first one he created in 1971?
   a   Mr Greedy
   b   Mr Happy
   c   Mr Nosey
   d   Mr Tickle

3   Who was the first artist to top the US movie and music charts in the same week?
   a   Cher
   b   Jennifer Lopez
   c   Madonna
   d   Barbra Streisand

4   Which song has been a hit for Nat 'King' Cole, Donny Osmond and Rick Astley?
   a   Mona Lisa
   b   Together Forever
   c   Too Young
   d   When I Fall In Love

5   And which song has been a hit for the Ronettes, Dave Edmunds and the Ramones?
   a   Baby I Love You
   b   Be My Baby
   c   Don't Come Close
   d   Girls Talk

6   Formed in 1982, from which country does the Cirque du Soleil originate?
   a   Brazil
   b   Canada
   c   France
   d   Spain

7   Founded in 1741 by Moravian missionaries, the steel producing city of Bethlehem is in which state of the USA?
   a   Michigan
   b   New York
   c   Pennsylvania
   d   Wisconsin

8   Which driver won his third Monte Carlo Rally in a row in 2001?
   a   Richard Burns
   b   Tommi Makinen
   c   Colin McCrae
   d   Carlos Sainz

9   The first time the Miss World contest was held outside the UK was in 1989 Where was it held that year?
   a   Bangkok
   b   Hong Kong
   c   Las Vegas
   d   Sun City

10 In January 2001, Wanda Allen became the first woman to be executed in which US state since 1903?
   a   Colorado
   b   Kansas
   c   Oklahoma
   d   Utah

Answers 1 b, 2 d, 3 b, 4 d, 5 a, 6 b, 7 c, 8 b, 9 b, 10 c.

1 Where did Ken Warby set a world water speed record of 317.6 mph in 1978?
  a Blowering Dam Reservoir, Australia
  b Lake Eyre, Australia
  c Revier Canal, Michigan, USA
  d Lake Washington, USA

2 Which city was the home town of Sylvester Stallone's movie character Rocky Balboa?
  a Chicago
  b Detroit
  c New York
  d Philadelphia

3 Which of the following would a limnologist study?
  a Limbs of the body
  b Illuminations
  c Lakes
  d Snails

4 Written by Mary Renault, in which period are the historical novels 'The Last Of The Wine' and 'The King Must Die' set?
  a Medieval England
  b Ancient Greece
  c France during the Revolution
  d Czarist Russia

5 What is a quant?
  a A drinking cup
  b A poem consisting of four lines
  c A pole for propelling a punt
  d An Australian tree

6 Rockingham Castle and Rockingham Forest are in which English county?
  a Cambridgeshire
  b Leicestershire
  c Lincolnshire
  d Northamptonshire

7 The great West Indian cricketer Sir Garfield Sobers played for which Australian state side between 1961 and 1964?
  a Queensland
  b South Australia
  c Victoria
  d Western Australia

8 From which language is the word ketchup derived?
  a Chinese
  b Greek
  c Hindi
  d Turkish

9 When the world's longest running play 'The Mousetrap' began it's run in 1952, who was a member of the cast for the first eighteen months?
  a Richard Attenborough
  b Richard Burton
  c John Gielgud
  d John Mills

10 How many James Bond movies were made during the 1970s?
  a 3
  b 4
  c 5
  d 6

Answers 1 a, 2 d, 3 c, 4 b, 5 c, 6 d, 7 b, 8 a, 9 a, 10 c.

MULTIPLE CHOICE — *Quiz 10*

1 Which town is the home of Scottish football club Raith Rovers?
   a Coatbridge
   b Dumfries
   c Kirkcaldy
   d Paisley

2 A worldwide top-selling album released in 2000, the 'Beatles 1' album contains all their UK and US No.1 hit singles. How many tracks has it?
   a 23
   b 25
   c 27
   d 29

3 In which month of the year are the saints days of St..Luke and St. Francis of Assisi?
   a September
   b October
   c November
   d December

4 Bette Graham invented and patented the correction fluid known as Liquid Paper. She was also the mother of which member of the Monkees pop group?
   a Mickey Dolenz
   b Davy Jones
   c Mike Nesmith
   d Peter Tork

5 By what name is Australia's men's hockey team known?
   a Emus
   b Kangaroos
   c Kookaburras
   d Wallabies

6 At the 2000 Olympics, what did the tri-athletes fear most about having to swim in Sydney Harbour ?
   a Jellyfish
   b Pollution
   c Sharks
   d Speedboats

7 Prior to the start of the 2000 Olympics, who carried the Olympic torch through the streets of Sydney as bearer No.147?
   a Prince Albert of Monaco
   b Chelsea Clinton
   c Bill Gates
   d Greg Norman

8 In which year were both Charlie Chaplin and Adolf Hitler born?
   a 1888
   b 1889
   c 1890
   d 1898

9 Of which film actress did Marlene Dietrich once say: "Every time she sins she builds a church. That's why there are so many Catholic churches in Hollywood"?
   a Gloria Grahame
   b Celeste Holm
   c Rosalind Russell
   d Loretta Young

10 The identity of the subject of Frans Hals famous portrait painting 'The Laughing Cavalier' is not known. The only thing known is his age, which is inscribed on the canvas. How old was he?
   a 26   b 36
   c 46   d 56

Answers 1 c, 2 c, 3 b, 4 c, 5 c, 6 a, 7 a, 8 b, 9 d, 10 a.

MULTIPLE CHOICE

Quiz 11

1   Which king of England succeeded his
    father John to the throne in 1216?
    a   Edward I
    b   Henry III
    c   Richard II
    d   William IV

2   Which driver won his first Formula One
    Grand Prix race in 123 starts when he won
    the German Grand Prix in 2000?
    a   Rubens Barrichello
    b   Andrea De Cesaris
    c   Heinz-Harold Frentzen
    d   Nicola Larini

3   Batman is a town in the centre of the oil-
    producing region of which country?
    a   Iraq
    b   Iran
    c   Saudi Arabia
    d   Turkey

4   What type of creature is a Scottish Fold?
    a   Cat
    b   Chicken
    c   Rabbit
    d   Sheep

5   The Plaka is the oldest quarter of which
    city?
    a   Athens
    b   Prague
    c   Rome
    d   Vienna

6   What is an axolotl?
    a   A nerve in the brain
    b   A multi-axled vehicle
    c   A type of mortice lock
    d   A species of salamander

7   The Panama Canal was officially opened
    by which US president?
    a   Calvin Coolidge
    b   Herbert Hoover
    c   Theodore Roosevelt
    d   Woodrow Wilson

8   In which opera did Maria Callas make her
    last appearance at Covent Garden?
    a   'Carmen'
    b   'La Boheme'
    c   'Madame Butterfly'
    d   'Tosca'

9   After Adam, Eve, Cain and Abel who is
    the next person mentioned in the Bible?
    a   Enoch
    b   Jubal
    c   Lamech
    d   Zillah

10 What is a kudzu?
    a   Antelope
    b   Bird
    c   Jewish settlement
    d   Climbing plant

Answers 1 b, **2** a, **3** d, **4** a, **5** a, **6** d, **7** d, **8** d, **9** a, **10** a.

MULTIPLE CHOICE *Quiz 12*

1 Outlawed from 1603 to 1774, which Scottish clan was known as the 'Faceless Clan'?
  a Campbells
  b MacGregors
  c MacLeods
  d MacDonalds

2 From which country does tennis player Andres Gomez, winner of the 1990 French Championships, come?
  a Ecuador
  b Peru
  c Portugal
  d Spain

3 Pelé once said that he was born for soccer just as which composer was born for music?
  a Beethoven
  b Brahms
  c Liszt
  d Mozart

4 Who was king of France from 1643 to 1715?
  a Louis XIII
  b Louis XIV
  c Louis XV
  d Louis XVI

5 How did Pierre Curie, the physicist and chemist and husband of Marie, die?
  a Drowned when the Titanic sank
  b Knocked down by a cart in a Paris street
  c From radiation poisoning
  d By committing suicide

6 Which one of the following James Bond novels was published first?
  a 'Dr. No'
  b 'From Russia With Love'
  c 'Goldfinger'
  d 'Thunderball'

7 Who was born in Urbino, Italy on 6 April 1483 and died on 6 April 1520?
  a Donatello
  b Michelangelo
  c Raphael
  d Leonardo Da Vinci

8 In March 1974, which country became the first Arab country to have women police officers?
  a Algeria
  b Jordan
  c Kuwait
  d Tunisia

9 What's the first name of Dolby, the American who developed the famous system which reduces background hiss on recordings?
  a Charles
  b Donald
  c Ray
  d Thomas

10 During a concert in the Portuguese capital Lisbon, which singing superstar said to the audience: 'I love you Spain'?
  a Celine Dion
  b Gloria Estefan
  c Whitney Houston
  d Madonna

Answers 1 b, 2 a, 3 a, 4 b, 5 b, 6 b, 7 c, 8 d, 9 c, 10 c.

1 What was the name of Lord Baden-Powell's sister with whom he formed the Girl Guides?
   a Adelaide
   b Agnes
   c Alexandra
   d Alice

2 In which African country is the village of Lassa, where Lassa fever was first identified?
   a Angola
   b Mozambique
   c Nigeria
   d Somalia

3 In which country was the comedy film actor Leslie Nielsen born?
   a Australia
   b Canada
   c Wales
   d USA

4 Tennis. Tony Wilding in 1913 was the last man from which country to win the men's singles at Wimbledon?
   a Canada
   b New Zealand
   c South Africa
   d UK

5 Jack Kelly, the father of Princess Grace of Monaco, won an Olympic gold medal in which sport in 1920?
   a Athletics
   b Boxing
   c Fencing
   d Rowing

6 In which city did Hugh Heffner open his first Playboy Club on 29 February 1960?
   a Chicago
   b Detroit
   c Las Vegas
   d Los Angeles

7 Who was the first Antiguan to play test cricket for the West Indies?
   a Gordon Greenidge
   b Alvin Kallicharran
   c Viv Richards
   d Andy Roberts

8 According to the Bible, Genesis chapter 7 verse 6, how old was Noah when the flood of the waters was upon the earth?
   a 600 years old
   b 666 years old
   c 900 years old
   d 969 years old

9 In which city was the famous operatic tenor Enrico Caruso born?
   a Florence
   b Milan
   c Naples
   d Rome

10 In 1912, Albert Berry made the first parachute drop from an aeroplane whilst flying over which city?
   a San Francisco
   b Santa Fe
   c Seattle
   d St. Louis

Answers 1 b, 2 c, 3 b, 4 b, 5 d, 6 a, 7 d, 8 a, 9 c, 10 d.

Quiz 14

1   Mary Tudor was proclaimed queen of England at Framlingham Castle. In which county is Framlingham?
a   Dorset
b   Norfolk
c   Suffolk
d   Warwickshire

2   In 1959, what was elected to the city council of Sao Paulo, Brazil in protest of the price of meat and beans?
a   Elephant
b   Giraffe
c   Hippopotamus
d   Rhinoceros

3   What is the fear of going to bed?
a   Clinophobia
b   Coitophobia
c   Hypnophobia
d   Nyctophobia

4   How many books are there in the New Testament of the Bible?
a   17
b   27
c   37
d   47

5   Which is the most northerly of these US cities?
a   Boston
b   Chicago
c   Philadelphia
d   Seattle

6   Which actress provided the voice of Jane in the 1999 Disney animated film 'Tarzan'?
a   Cate Blanchett
b   Minnie Driver
c   Liz Hurley
d   Gwyneth Paltrow

7   What is a jota?
a   Bird
b   Notepad
c   Punctuation mark
d   Spanish dance

8   In 1990, which heavy metal band figured in a US court case about the suicides of two of their fans?
a   Black Sabbath
b   Iron Maiden
c   Judas Priest
d   Saxon

9   What is the setting for Michael Frayn's play 'Noises Off'?
a   Monastery
b   Newspaper Office
c   Prison
d   Theatre

10   What nationality was the first woman to reach the summit of Mount Everest?
a   British
b   Chinese
c   Japanese
d   New Zealander

Answers 1 c, 2 d, 3 a, 4 b, 5 d, 6 b, 7 d, 8 c, 9 d, 10 c.

MULTIPLE CHOICE

Quiz 15

1 Which was the first of London's Underground lines to be built?
a Central
b Circle
c District
d Metropolitan

2 Where was the artist Pablo Picasso born?
a Barcelona
b Malaga
c Marbella
d Seville

3 In which state was US president Dwight D Eisenhower born?
a Alabama
b California
c Georgia
d Texas

4 With what type of painting do you associate the artist Thomas Girtin?
a Abstract
b Landscapes
c Portraits
d Still-life

5 The American slang word for boss, 'honcho', often used in the phrase head honcho, is derived from which language?
a Chinese
b Japanese
c Portuguese
d Spanish

6 Which was the last country to stage both the Summer and Winter Olympics in the same year?
a Germany
b Italy
c Japan
d USA

7 In which year were the first of the Dead Sea Scrolls discovered?
a 1946
b 1947
c 1948
d 1949

8 Which of the following is the furthest west?
a Barbados
b Haiti
c Jamaica
d Puerto Rico

9 Which of the Louis' ruled France from 1610-1643?
a Louis XIII
b Louis XIV
c Louis XV
d Louis XVI

10 Mireya Moscoso became the first woman president of which country?
a Costa Rica
b El Salvador
c Guatemala
d Panama

Answers 1 d, 2 b, 3 d, 4 b, 5 b, 6 a, 7 b, 8 c, 9 a, 10 d.

1   Who was the first British monarch to be born at Buckingham Palace?
    a   Anne
    b   George IV
    c   Victoria
    d   William IV

2   Where was movie star Keanu Reeves born?
    a   Barcelona
    b   Beirut
    c   Berlin
    d   Bombay

3   Where was TV chat show host Jerry Springer born?
    a   Las Vegas
    b   Liverpool
    c   London
    d   Louisville

4   Gymnastics. Which country was the first to win the men's team event at the Olympics three times in succession?
    a   Italy
    b   Japan
    c   USA
    d   USSR

5   Which one of the following Italian composers was born first?
    a   Puccini
    b   Rossini
    c   Verdi
    d   Vivaldi

6   Who was voted foreign statesman of the 20th century by listeners of the Moscow Echo radio station?
    a   Winston Churchill
    b   Charles de Gaulle
    c   Franklin D Roosevelt
    d   Margaret Thatcher

7   What was silent film star 'Buster' Keaton's first name?
    a   Joseph
    b   Michael
    c   Stanley
    d   Walter

8   The winner of the 1999 Miss Universe beauty contest was the first ever entrant from which African country?
    a   Botswana
    b   Lesotho
    c   Namibia
    d   Swaziland

9   In which US state would you find the Garden of the Gods, an area of remarkable formations of eroded red sandstone rocks resembling animals, gargoyles and church spires?
    a   Arizona
    b   Colorado
    c   New Mexico
    d   Utah

10 In 1860, which was the first US state to withdraw from the Union to form the Confederacy?
    a   North Carolina
    b   South Carolina
    c   Virginia
    d   West Virginia

Answers 1 d. 2 b. 3 c. 4 a. 5 d. 6 a. 7 a. 8 a. 9 b. 10 b.

1   Of the following English monarchs, which one reigned the longest?
   a   Edward III
   b   Henry III
   c   Richard III
   d   William III

2   Who was the first boxer to regain the world heavyweight title?
   a   Muhammad Ali
   b   Joe Frazier
   c   Floyd Patterson
   d   Mike Tyson

3   Who composed the 'Academic Festival Overture'?
   a   Bach
   b   Beethoven
   c   Bizet
   d   Brahms

4   In 1959 Alaska and Hawaii became the 49th and 50th states of the USA. On 14 February 1912, which had become the 48th?
   a   Arizona
   b   Montana
   c   New Mexico
   d   Utah

5   In which year were women allowed to compete in athletics events at the Olympic Games for the first time?
   a   1908
   b   1928
   c   1948
   d   1968

6   What first name is shared by the poet Byron, actor and director Orson Welles and singer Van Morrison?
   a   George
   b   John
   c   Robert
   d   William

7   Which one of the following Oscar winners is the daughter of parents who have both won Oscars?
   a   Jane Fonda
   b   Anjelica Huston
   c   Liza Minnelli
   d   Vanessa Redgrave

8   Swimming. In which year were events using the butterfly stroke first contested at the Olympics?
   a   1896
   b   1936
   c   1956
   d   1976

9   The Spar group of shops originated in which country in 1932?
   a   Belgium
   b   Denmark
   c   Netherlands
   d   Sweden

10   In area, which is the smallest of the following countries?
   a   Austria
   b   Belgium
   c   Denmark
   d   Switzerland

Answers 1 b, 2 c, 3 d, 4 a, 5 b, 6 a, 7 c, 8 c, 9 c, 10 b.

Quiz 18

1   Before Tony Blair, only one other man during the 20th century became British Prime Minister without having any previous ministerial experience. Who?
a   Herbert Asquith
b   Winston Churchill
c   Ramsey MacDonald
d   John Major

2   Football. Who won the 1999 Women's World Cup after a penalty shoot-out?
a   China
b   Germany
c   Norway
d   USA

3   If someone is described as winsome, what are they?
a   Aggressive
b   Charming
c   Greedy
d   Ill

4   Pope John Paul I was elected Pope in August 1978 but died how many days later?
a   13
b   23
c   33
d   43

5   In 1999, which Hollywood star escaped injury when the helicopter he was piloting crashed on landing during a training flight near Los Angeles?
a   Tom Cruise
b   Michael Douglas
c   Harrison Ford
d   Keanu Reeves

6   Native to Central and South America, what is a manakin?
a   Bird
b   Cat
c   Lizard
d   Snake

7   How many Oscar nominations did the film Gladiator receive?
a   10
b   11
c   12
d   13

8   Uri Geller renewed his marriage vows on 7 March 2001. In which city had Geller married his wife Hanna ten years previously?
a   Budapest
b   Jerusalem
c   New York
d   Vienna

9   Rugby Union. Who was the first player to score 1,000 points in international rugby?
a   Serge Blanco
b   Grant Fox
c   Neil Jenkins
d   Michael Lynagh

10   Songwriter John Phillips, who died in 2001, was a member of which vocal group?
a   Beach Boys
b   Four Seasons
c   Four Tops
d   Mamas and the Papas

Answers 1 c, 2 d, 3 b, 4 c, 5 c, 6 a, 7 c, 8 a, 9 c, 10 d.

103

MULTIPLE CHOICE

Quiz 19

1   In which year did Queen Victoria celebrate her Golden Jubilee?
    a   1867
    b   1877
    c   1887
    d   1897

2   The obsolete unit of distance known as a league was equal to how many miles?
    a   3
    b   5
    c   10
    d   100

3   In which country did the Giro system of transferring money originate in 1883?
    a   Austria
    b   France
    c   Italy
    d   Switzerland

4   What nationality was the mural painter Diego Rivera?
    a   Brazilian
    b   Cuban
    c   Mexican
    d   Spanish

5   Which US president once said: "Whenever I can I always watch the Detroit Tigers on radio"?
    a   Jimmy Carter
    b   Gerald Ford
    c   Richard Nixon
    d   Ronald Reagan

6   The composers Mendelssohn and Brahms were both born in which city?
    a   Berlin
    b   Bonn
    c   Hamburg
    d   Munich

7   In which year did Charles Darwin return on HMS Beagle after a five year voyage and the battle of the Alamo took place?
    a   1826
    b   1836
    c   1846
    d   1856

8   Football. What 'feat' did Argentina's Martin Palermo achieve in a match against Colombia in 1999?
    a   He was sent off without having touched the ball
    b   He missed three penalties
    c   He scored an own goal with his very first touch of the ball
    d   He scored three own goals

9   Which strait separates Greenland and Iceland?
    a   Bering Strait
    b   Davis Strait
    c   Denmark Strait
    d   Hudson Strait

10 In which year did Earl Tupper found the Tupperware Company?
    a   1938
    b   1948
    c   1958
    d   1968

Answers 1 c, 2 a, 3 a, 4 c, 5 b, 6 c, 7 b, 8 b, 9 c, 10 a.

1 Which Scottish castle is the ancestral home of the Dukes of Argyll?
   a Inveraray
   b Scone
   c Stirling
   d Urquhart

2 For her role in which one of the following films did Meryl Streep win an Oscar?
   a 'The French Lieutenant's Woman'
   b 'Ironweed'
   c 'Out Of Africa'
   d 'Sophie's Choice'

3 Contested between amateur golfers of the USA and Britain and Ireland, in which year was the Walker Cup first competed for?
   a 1922
   b 1932
   c 1952
   d 1962

4 What is a pergola?
   a Framework for climbing plants
   b Pathway of crazy paving
   c Ornamental pond
   d Summerhouse

5 Arthur was the real first name of which one of the Marx Brothers?
   a Chico
   b Groucho
   c Harpo
   d Zeppo

6 Which Hollywood star caused a stir in 1951 when she unofficially adopted a boy on a trip to London?
   a Jayne Mansfield
   b Marilyn Monroe
   c Debbie Reynolds
   d Jane Russell

7 Ruby Stevens was the real name of which Hollywood actress?
   a Joan Crawford
   b Bette Davis
   c Joan Fontaine
   d Barbara Stanwyck

8 In which US state is the city of Kalamazoo?
   a Maine
   b Massachusetts
   c Michigan
   d Minnesota

9 Which fruit is obtained from the tree, *Prunus persica*?
   a Apricot
   b Cherry
   c Peach
   d Plum

10 In ancient Roman and Biblical times, what was a publican?
   a Gladiator
   b Innkeeper
   c Judge
   d Tax collector

Answers 1 a, 2 d, 3 a, 4 a, 5 c, 6 d, 7 d, 8 c, 9 c, 10 d.

MULTIPLE CHOICE

Quiz 21

1   Of the following, who was the oldest when he first became British Prime Minister?
a   James Callaghan
b   William Gladstone
c   Edward Heath
d   David Lloyd George

2   In sport, what did 36 year-old Margaret MacGregor achieve in Seattle in 1999?
a   she achieved a perfect score in ten-pin bowling
b   she beat a greyhound in a race
c   she achieved a nine dart finish
d   she beat a man in a boxing match

3   Which rival Hollywood actress was Bette Davis referring to when she said: "She has slept with every star at MGM except Lassie"?
a   Joan Crawford
b   Katherine Hepburn
c   Rosalind Russell
d   Jane Wyman

4   What are the names of the lizards plotting the frogs' downfall in Budweiser TV ads?
a   Curly and Spike
b   Frank and Louie
c   Johnny and Vinnie
d   Tom and Jerry

5   What was Vladimir Putin talking about when he said: "It is not just a sport you know. It's a philosophy. It's respect for your elders and your opponent. It's not for weaklings"?
a   Basketball
b   Chess
c   Judo
d   Orienteering

6   What is a granadilla?
a   A type of armadillo
b   A type of dance
c   A fruit cocktail
d   A type of climbing plant

7   In which year was actor Tom Cruise born?
a   1958
b   1960
c   1962
d   1964

8   In 1827, which botanist first put forward the theory that the continuous random movement of minute particles in a fluid is caused by collisions between the particles and the molecules of the fluid?
a   Robert Black
b   Robert Brown
c   Robert Green
d   Robert Grey

9   Basse-Terre and Grande-Terre are the two large islands of which French overseas department?
a   French Polynesia
b   Guadeloupe
c   Marquesas Islands
d   New Caledonia

10 Fort-de-France is the capital of which French overseas department?
a   French Guiana
b   Martinique
c   Mayotte
d   Reunion

Answers 1 a, 2 d, 3 a, 4 b, 5 c, 6 d, 7 c, 8 c, 9 b, 10 b.

Quiz 22

1 Of the following poets who was born first?
   a Byron
   b Keats
   c Shelley
   d Tennyson

2 In September 1999, in which country was Rachel Goldwyn jailed for singing a protest song?
   a China
   b Myanmar
   c Pakistan
   d Thailand

3 Football. How many countries entered for the 2002 World Cup?
   a 168
   b 186
   c 189
   d 198

4 What letter was used by writer Sir Arthur Quiller-Couch as his pseudonym?
   a C
   b Q
   c X
   d Z

5 In which city are the headquarters of Greyhound Links Inc., the famous providers of inter-city bus networks throughout the USA?
   a Chicago
   b Dallas
   c New Orleans
   d Seattle

6 Becks beer is brewed in which German city?
   a Berlin
   b Bremen
   c Cologne
   d Munich

7 In which country was the film actor Edward G. Robinson born?
   a Britain
   b Hungary
   c Romania
   d USA

8 Where was the musical conductor Leopold Stokowski born?
   a London
   b New York
   c Paris
   d Warsaw

9 Who wrote Bobby Vee's hit 'Rubber Ball' and Ricky Nelson's 'Hello Mary Lou'?
   a Neil Diamond
   b Billy Joel
   c Gene Pitney
   d P J. Proby

10 To which group of musical instruments does the marimba belong?
   a Brass
   b Percussion
   c Strings
   d Woodwind

Answers 1 a. 2 b. 3 d. 4 b. 5 d. 6 b. 7 c. 8 a. 9 c. 10 b.

MULTIPLE CHOICE   *Quiz 23*

1   The rationing of which commodity ended in Britain on 26 May 1950?
   a   Bread
   b   Chocolate
   c   Clothes
   d   Petrol

2   Golf. Who won the Open championship at Muirfield in 1959, at Carnoustie in 1968 and Royal Lytham in 1974?
   a   Jack Nicklaus
   b   Arnold Palmer
   c   Gary Player
   d   Peter Thomson

3   In which year was the composer Tchaikovsky born?
   a   1812
   b   1840
   c   1870
   d   1893

4   Which musical is based on the Borodin opera 'Prince Igor'?
   a   Carousel
   b   Kismet
   c   Kiss Me Kate
   d   West Side Story

5   Philomel is a poetic name for which bird?
   a   Albatross
   b   Eagle
   c   Lark
   d   Nightingale

6   Which of the following Russian spacecrafts' name means 'east'?
   a   Salyut
   b   Soyuz
   c   Sputnik
   d   Vostok

7   How many years elapsed between the end of the American War of Independence and the start of the American Civil War?
   a   68
   b   78
   c   88
   d   98

8   A hog is a pig, usually a castrated male A hogget is a young what?
   a   Deer
   b   Goat
   c   Pig
   d   Sheep

9   In which year did the Austro-Prussian or Seven Weeks' War take place?
   a   1756
   b   1763
   c   1862
   d   1866

10   Which king of France was known as Louis the Fat?
   a   Louis I
   b   Louis II
   c   Louis VI
   d   Louis VIII

Answers 1 d, **2** c, **3** b, **4** b, **5** d, **6** d, **7** b, **8** d, **9** d, **10** c.

MULTIPLE CHOICE

Quiz 24

1 The famous London store Harrods describes itself as Harrods of where...?
   a Kensington
   b Knightsbridge
   c Mayfair
   d Piccadilly

2 Athletics. The first official world record for the 3000 metres steeplechase was set in 1954. What nationality was the man who set that first record?
   a American
   b Belgian
   c Hungarian
   d Kenyan

3 In which century were rockets first used in warfare?
   a 11th
   b 13th
   c 15th
   d 20th

4 The Bible. According to Acts chapter 19 verse 35, where did the town clerk stop a riot?
   a Antioch
   b Corinth
   c Ephesus
   d Tarsus

5 What does a pteridologist study?
   a Ferns
   b Food poisoning
   c Molluscs
   d Pterodactyls

6 The columns of the Parthenon are what type?
   a Corinthian
   b Doric
   c Ionic
   d Tuscan

7 Which French writer died in a car accident in 1960?
   a Honore de Balzac
   b Simone de Beauvoir
   c Albert Camus
   d Jean-Paul Sartre

8 Which former Formula One world motor racing champion died of a heart attack whilst competing in the Bathhurst 1000 Endurance race in Australia in October 1992?
   a Jack Brabham
   b Phil Hill
   c Denny Hulme
   d James Hunt

9 In which century was Joan of Arc canonized?
   a 15th
   b 16th
   c 19th
   d 20th

10 Which one of the following refers to the rump or hindquarters of a horse?
   a Croup
   b Gaskin
   c Poll
   d Stifle

Answers 1 b, 2 c, 3 c, 4 c, 5 a, 6 b, 7 c, 8 c, 9 d, 10 a.

1   Who, in 1947, founded the Royal Philharmonic Orchestra?
a   John Barbiroli
b   Thomas Beecham
c   Malcolm Sargent
d   Henry Wood

2   Cricket. The first ever test match played in India took place in which city?
a   Bombay
b   Calcutta
c   Delhi
d   Madras

3   In which year was that first test match played in India?
a   1930
b   1931
c   1932
d   1933

4   Astronomer and scientist Galileo died in the same year that scientist and mathematician Isaac Newton was born. Which year?
a   1622
b   1642
c   1672
d   1692

5   Reckoned to be one of the great novels of world literature, who wrote 'Dead Souls'?
a   Sholom Aleichem
b   Isaac Babel
c   Nikolai Gogol
d   Ivan Turgenev

6   How did Italian dictator Benito Mussolini die?
a   In an air crash
b   Executed by the Allies after the Nuremberg trials
c   In prison of old age
d   Shot by Italian partisans

7   According to the title of an Edna O'Brien novel, which 'is a wicked month'?
a   March
b   April
c   May
d   August

8   In what field was Leonide Massine a well-known name during the 20th century?
a   Dancing
b   Gymnastics
c   Painting
d   Writing

9   Giovanni Battista Montini became which 20th century Pope?
a   John XXIII
b   John Paul I
c   Paul VI
d   Pius XII

10   Henry Fielding wrote the novels 'Tom Jones' and 'Joseph Andrews'. Who has directed move versions of both?
a   Federico Fellini
b   Tony Richardson
c   John Schlesinger
d   Franco Zeffirelli

Answers 1 b, 2 a, 3 d, 4 b, 5 c, 6 d, 7 d, 8 a, 9 c, 10 b.

1   British actor Oliver Reed died on which island?
   a   Crete
   b   Cyprus
   c   Malta
   d   Sicily

2   What nationality was Charles Jewtraw, the first ever gold medal-winner at the Winter Olympics ?
   a   American
   b   Australian
   c   British
   d   Canadian

3   What was the name of Jack Benny's manservant in his long-running TV series?
   a   Chester
   b   Chichester
   c   Rochester
   d   Winchester

4   Who wrote the novel 'Germinal'?
   a   Flaubert
   b   Camus
   c   Zola
   d   Voltaire

5   What are muniments?
   a   Architectural columns
   b   Military weapons
   c   Paintings
   d   Title deeds

6   What nationality was the painter Ren`é Magritte?
   a   Belgian
   b   Dutch
   c   French
   d   Swiss

7   Who composed the oratorio 'Israel In Egypt'?
   a   Beethoven
   b   Handel
   c   Mozart
   d   Verdi

8   Which American composed the piano sonata 'The Concord Sonata'?
   a   Burl Ives
   b   Charles Ives
   c   Frederick Ives
   d   George Ives

9   Where did Anne Frank die?
   a   Auschwitz
   b   Belsen
   c   Buchenwald
   d   Treblinka

10   Uxoricide is the crime of killing one's what?
   a   Father
   b   Husband
   c   Mother
   d   Wife

MULTIPLE CHOICE   Quiz 27

1   Immortalised in nursery rhyme, the Grand Old Duke of York was the son of which king?
    a George I
    b George II
    c George III
    d George IV

2   Football. Who were runners-up in the World Cup in 1982 and 1986?
    a Argentina
    b Italy
    c Netherlands
    d West Germany

3   Who composed 'The Abduction from the Seraglio'?
    a Beethoven
    b Haydn
    c Mozart
    d Schubert

4   What female name, in Greek, means 'a bee'?
    a Margaret
    b Melinda
    c Melissa
    d Miranda

5   Who was the original choice of producer Hal Wallis to play Rick in the 1942 movie 'Casablanca'?
    a Clark Gable
    b Alan Ladd
    c George Raft
    d Ronald Reagan

6   In January 1992, Annelise Coberger became the first skier from which country to win a World Cup race?
    a Australia
    b Netherlands
    c New Zealand
    d South Africa

7   What was the most popular name given to boys born in Cologne in 1991?
    a Clint
    b Hans
    c Jurgen
    d Kevin

8   In 1992, Michael Foale became Britain's first astronaut when he was a member of the crew of which US space shuttle craft?
    a Atlantis
    b Challenger
    c Columbia
    d Discovery

9   What was the name of the writer of children's books, E. Nesbit?
    a Edith
    b Edna
    c Eleanor
    d Elizabeth

10 Broadcast to 70 countries worldwide, which band opened the 'Concert For Life', a tribute to Freddie Mercury and a fundraiser for Aids awareness in April 1992?
    a Def Leppard
    b Extreme
    c Guns N' Roses
    d Metallica

Answers 1 c, 2 d, 3 c, 4 c, 5 d, 6 c, 7 d, 8 a, 9 a, 10 d.

1   In which year did Florence Nightingale die?
    a   1880
    b   1890
    c   1900
    d   1910

2   Golf. In 1992, who became the first woman to win the US and British Open titles in the same year?
    a   Beth Daniel
    b   Laura Davies
    c   Alison Nicholas
    d   Patty Sheehan

3   Which French composer wrote the humorous orchestral piece 'Divertissement'?
    a   Jacques Ibert
    b   Maurice Ravel
    c   Erik Satie
    d   Ambroise Thomas

4   Which French dramatist wrote 'Andromaque'?
    a   Pierre Corneille
    b   Moliere
    c   Jean Racine
    d   Edmond Rostand

5   What is the currency of Haiti?
    a   Dollar
    b   Gourde
    c   Peso
    d   Quetzal

6   How many competitors took part in the first Winter Olympic Games held in 1924?
    a   294
    b   311
    c   495
    d   625

7   In which century was work begun on the construction of the Leaning Tower of Pisa?
    a   12th
    b   13th
    c   14th
    d   15th

8   Five of the first twenty US presidents had which first name?
    a   Andrew
    b   George
    c   James
    d   John

9   In December 1991, which became the first country within the European Community to recognise Croatia and Slovenia as independent states?
    a   Belgium
    b   France
    c   Germany
    d   Italy

10 Which is the most northerly of these South American cities?
    a   Bogota
    b   Caracas
    c   Georgetown
    d   Lima

Answers 1 d, 2 d, 3 a, 4 c, 5 b, 6 a, 7 a, 8 c, 9 c, 10 b.

1 Founded in 1832, which is England's third oldest university?
   a Birmingham
   b Durham
   c Manchester
   d Newcastle

2 Yachting. What was the name of the American boat when they lost the America's Cup for the first time in 1983?
   a Freedom
   b Intrepid
   c Liberty
   d Stars And Stripes

3 Which US state is home to Hoosiers?
   a Idaho
   b Illinois
   c Indiana
   d Iowa

4 How old was Alexander the Great when he died?
   a 32
   b 52
   c 72
   d 92

5 Who was Johnny Carson's first ever guest on his 'Tonight' show on 2 October 1962?
   a George Burns
   b Bing Crosby
   c Bob Hope
   d Groucho Marx

6 And who was Carson's last ever guest on 21 May 1992?
   a Cher
   b Bette Midler
   c Dolly Parton
   d Barbra Streisand

7 In 1992, which former Formula One world motor racing champion was badly injured whilst practising for his first ever Indianapolis 500?
   a Alan Jones
   b Nelson Piquet
   c Alain Prost
   d Keke Rosberg

8 What is actor Michael Keaton's real surname?
   a Caine
   b Douglas
   c Landon
   d Smith

9 The Albert Canal runs from Antwerp to which other Belgian city?
   a Brussels
   b Charleroi
   c Ghent
   d Liege

10 Mentioned in the Bible, Antioch was a city in ancient Syria. It's present day name is Antakya. In which country is Antakya?
   a Iran
   b Iraq
   c Syria
   d Turkey

Answers 1 b, 2 c, 3 c, 4 a, 5 d, 6 b, 7 b, 8 b, 9 d, 10 d.

1 Which British engineer was born in the Derbyshire village of Wormhill, near Buxton in 1716?
a James Brindley
b George Stephenson
c Thomas Telford
d Richard Trevithick

2 Boxing. At what weight was Joe Brown the undisputed world champion between 1956 and 1962?
a Bantamweight
b Featherweight
c Lightweight
d Middleweight

3 What, in 1940, was the destination of the first of the Bob Hope and Bing Crosby series of 'Road' films?
a Bali
b Morocco
c Singapore
d Zanzibar

4 In which country was actress Victoria Principal born?
a Canada
b India
c Japan
d New Zealand

5 Name the first cricketer to be given a knighthood whilst still actively playing first class cricket?
a Don Bradman
b Colin Cowdrey
c Richard Hadlee
d Garfield Sobers

6 Which former linebacker with the Seattle Seahawks American Football team starred in the 1991 action movie 'Stone Cold'?
a Steve Austin
b Brian Bosworth
c Walter Payton
d John Riggins

7 With which group do you associate singer David Clayton Thomas?
a Bachman-Turner Overdrive
b Blood Sweat And Tears
c Creedence Clearwater Revival
d Earth Wind And Fire

8 Which actor played Captain Christopher Pike, commander of the Enterprise, in the pilot episode of the TV series 'Star Trek'?
a Jeffrey Hunter
b Jack Lord
c Tom Selleck
d Robert Wagner

9 On which holiday island would you find Arrecife airport?
a Fuerteventura
b Gran Canaria
c Lanzarote
d Tenerife

10 Which capital city was badly damaged by an earthquake in 1923?
a Algiers
b Belgrade
c Mexico City
d Tokyo

Answers 1 a, **2** c, **3** c, **4** c, **5** b, **6** b, **7** b, **8** a, **9** c, **10** d.

MULTIPLE CHOICE   *Quiz 31*

1   Before moving to America and making
    their fortune, James and William Horlicks
    first made their famous drink in the small
    town of Ruardean. In which English
    county is Ruardean?
    a   Devon
    b   Gloucestershire
    c   Somerset
    d   Wiltshire

2   Who played the title role in the 1968 film
    Inspector Clouseau?
    a   Alan Alda
    b   Alan Arkin
    c   Peter Sellers
    d   George Segal

3   Baseball. In 1992, who became the first
    Canadian team to win the World Series?
    a   Calgary Flames
    b   Edmonton Oilers
    c   Montreal Expos
    d   Toronto Blue Jays

4   Who said: "It can never be too big – be it
    salary, diamonds or breasts"?
    a   Brigitte Nielsen
    b   Dolly Parton
    c   Joan Rivers
    d   Raquel Welch

5   Apart from being the name of a country,
    Luxembourg is also the name of a province
    in which country?
    a   Belgium
    b   France
    c   Germany
    d   Netherlands

6   In June 1965, who became the first
    American astronaut to do a 'space walk'?
    a   Eugene Cernan
    b   Richard Gordon
    c   Ed White
    d   John Young

7   Ted Van Der Parre was the first man from
    which country to win the title of the
    World's Strongest Man?
    a   Canada
    b   Denmark
    c   Netherlands
    d   South Africa

8   By what name is *Solanum tuberosum*
    commonly known?
    a   Carrot
    b   Pea
    c   Potato
    d   Turnip

9   In which US state was Dolly Parton born?
    a   Alabama
    b   Kentucky
    c   Tennessee
    d   Texas

10 Which actress won Oscars in 1932 and
    1970?
    a   Lillian Gish
    b   Helen Hayes
    c   Katharine Hepburn
    d   Jessica Tandy

Answers 1 b, 2 b, 3 d, 4 a, 5 a, 6 c, 7 c, 8 c, 9 c, 10 b.

1   On 13 June 1999, which British athlete followed in the footsteps of Linford Christie to become the second European to run the 100 metres in less than 10 seconds?
    a   Darren Campbell
    b   Dwain Chambers
    c   Jason Gardener
    d   Ian Mackie

2   What was Ross Perot's share of the total vote in the 1992 US presidential election?
    a   9%
    b   14%
    c   19%
    d   24%

3   In which country was the artist Marc Chagall born?
    a   France
    b   Romania
    c   Russia
    d   Switzerland

4   Which part of the body is affected by Vincent's disease?
    a   Feet
    b   Heart
    c   Lungs
    d   Mouth

5   Alfred Hitchcock was famous for appearing in cameo roles in his films. In the 1951 film 'Strangers On A Train' he is seen getting on a train carrying what?
    a   Briefcase
    b   Double Bass
    c   Suitcase
    d   Tuba

6   And what type of hat was Hitchcock wearing during his appearance in 'Psycho'?
    a   Beaver fur
    b   Fedora
    c   Fez
    d   Stetson

7   Charlotte Bronte's novel 'Villette' is set in which European city, a city in which she had worked as an English teacher?
    a   Amsterdam
    b   Brussels
    c   Copenhagen
    d   Paris

8   The Egyptian goddess Hathor, the goddess of fertility and love, was usually portrayed as which creature?
    a   Cat
    b   Cow
    c   Dog
    d   Lioness

9   In the TV series 'Star Trek', what was Dr McCoy's first name?
    a   George
    b   James
    c   Leonard
    d   William

10 What is a carambola?
    a   Horse-drawn carriage
    b   Latin-American dance
    c   Tropical fruit
    d   Musical instrument

Answers 1 b, 2 c, 3 c, 4 d, 5 b, 6 d, 7 b, 8 b, 9 c, 10 c.

1 In 1978, Prince Michael of Kent married Marie-Christine von Reibnitz in which city?
   a Berlin
   b Munich
   c Salzburg
   d Vienna

2 What was the nickname of the German swimmer Michael Gross?
   a Albatross
   b Dolphin
   c Penguin
   d Shark

3 In which US state are the Adirondack Mountains?
   a New Hampshire
   b New Jersey
   c New Mexico
   d New York

4 The world's largest pyramid, the largest monument ever constructed, is to be found in which country?
   a Egypt
   b Mexico
   c Peru
   d Thailand

5 In which constellation is the open star cluster known as Pleiades to be found?
   a Aquarius
   b Gemini
   c Libra
   d Taurus

6 Leonard Slye was the real name of which movie cowboy?
   a Gene Autry
   b Tom Mix
   c Tex Ritter
   d Roy Rogers

7 In the TV western series 'Bonanza', the Cartwright's Ponderosa ranch was situated in which US state?
   a Arizona
   b Nevada
   c New Mexico
   d Utah

8 Similarly, in which US state was the High Chaparral in the TV series of that name, located?
   a Arizona
   b Nevada
   c New Mexico
   d Utah

9 Which actor appeared in the 1939 movie 'Dark Victory' and the 1947 movie 'Dark Passage'?
   a Humphrey Bogart
   b James Cagney
   c George Raft
   d Edward G. Robinson

10 The Bio-Bio is a river in which country?
    a Australia
    b Chile
    c South Africa
    d Thailand

Answers 1 d, 2 a, 3 d, 4 b, 5 d, 6 d, 7 b, 8 a, 9 a, 10 b.

MULTIPLE CHOICE

1 What was the name of Hugh Grant's character in the film 'Four Weddings And A Funeral'?
   a Charles
   b David
   c Matthew
   d Tom

2 Which is the only one of the following religious movements to be founded in the 20th century?
   a Seventh Day Adventists
   b Jehovah's Witnesses
   c Mormons
   d Church of the Nazarene

3 What women's fashion item was introduced by Frenchman Roger Vivier?
   a Strapless bra
   b Culottes
   c French knickers
   d Stiletto heeled shoe

4 Golf. Which country won the 1998 Dunhill Cup at St. Andrews with the same three players that won the trophy in 1997?
   a Australia
   b South Africa
   c Spain
   d USA

5 What aviation 'first' was achieved by Mrs. T. W. Evans of Miami on 28 October 1929?
   a First woman to parachute from a plane
   b First woman to fly across America solo
   c First woman to give birth on a planed
   d First female flight attendant

6 'All the world's a stage, and all the men and women merely players' is a line from which Shakespeare play?
   a As You Like It
   b Hamlet
   c The Taming Of The Shrew
   d Twelfth Night

7 Shirley MacLaine won an Oscar for her performance in which one of the following films?
   a The Apartment
   b Irma La Douce
   c Terms Of Endearment
   d The Turning Point

8 During the French Revolution, what were the tricoteuses?
   a An elite force of the king's men
   b The women knitting by the guillotine
   c The combined flags of the revolutionary forces
   d The executioners who operated the guillotine

9 Inti, Viracocha and Apu Ilapu were all gods of which ancient civilisation?
   a Aztec
   b Byzantine
   c Egyptian
   d Incas

10 Harbin is a city in which country?
   a China
   b Iran
   c Saudi Arabia
   d Thailand

Answers 1 a. 2 d. 3 d. 4 b. 5 c. 6 a. 7 c. 8 b. 9 d. 10 a.

119

MULTIPLE CHOICE

Quiz 35

1   Sir Christopher Wren was a professor at Oxford University from 1661 to 1673 in what subject?
a   Architecture
b   Astronomy
c   Geography
d   Physics

2   Which Shakespeare play opens with the words: 'In sooth, I know not why I am so sad: It wearies me; you say it wearies you' ?
a   Hamlet
b   King Lear
c   The Merchant of Venice
d   Romeo and Juliet

3   In which field is the Prix Goncourt awarded in France?
a   Art
b   Films
c   Literature
d   Music

4   In January 1986, in which French city did the launching ceremony for the Channel Tunnel take place?
a   Lille
b   Nantes
c   Paris
d   Rouen

5   In which country was Sonia, the widow of former Indian Prime Minister Rajiv Gandhi, born?
a   Britain
b   France
c   Italy
d   USA

6   Which US city was described by Dorothy Parker as '72 suburbs in search of a city' and by Raymond Chandler as 'having all the personality of a paper cup'?
a   Chicago
b   Los Angeles
c   New York
d   San Francisco

7   What is a rampion?
a   Insect
b   Plant
c   Star
d   Tool

8   Bryce Canyon National Park and Zion National Park are scenic attractions in which US state?
a   Colorado
b   Nevada
c   New Mexico
d   Utah

9   The cover of which of his albums shows Billy Joel leaning against a wall holding a trumpet?
a   Glass Houses
b   52nd Street
c   The Nylon Curtain
d   The Stranger

10 Lotte Lenya, at one time married to Kurt Weill, played Rosa Klebb in which James Bond movie?
a   Dr. No
b   From Russia With Love
c   Goldfinger
d   Thunderball

Answers 1 b, 2 c, 3 c, 4 a, 5 c, 6 b, 7 b, 8 d, 9 b, 10 b.

Quiz 36

1   The first book published by Penguin was entitled 'Ariel'. It was a biography of which poet?
    a   Byron
    b   Keats
    c   Shelley
    d   Wordsworth

2   In which Shakespeare play does a dog called Crab appear?
    a   The Comedy of Errors
    b   The Merchant of Venice
    c   The Merry Wives of Windsor
    d   The Two Gentlemen of Verona

3   How many books about the land of Oz did L. Frank Baum write?
    a   1
    b   14
    c   27
    d   60

4   And what did the L in L. Frank Baum stand for?
    a   Leighton
    b   Leon
    c   Lloyd
    d   Lyman

5   Which publishing company was founded by Virginia and Leonard Woolf?
    a   Arcturus
    b   Hogarth Press
    c   Pan
    d   Penguin

6   Marshall Royal was what?
    a   British soldier
    b   Canadian sculptor
    c   New Zealand Prime Minister
    d   US jazz musician

7   Which city was the setting for the children's book 'Emil And The Detectives' written by Erich Kaestner?
    a   Amsterdam
    b   Berlin
    c   Brussels
    d   Vienna

8   In which city was James Earl Ray, the man convicted of killing Martin Luther King, apprehended?
    a   London
    b   Los Angeles
    c   New York
    d   Paris

9   After performing at a gig in Memphis in 1976, who was apprehended by a security guard after climbing over the wall at Elvis Presley's Graceland mansion?
    a   Peter Frampton
    b   Billy Joel
    c   Bruce Springsteen
    d   Steve Tyler

10 Nicely-Nicely Johnson is a character in which musical?
    a   Carousel
    b   Guys And Dolls
    c   The Music Man
    d   West Side Story

Answers 1 c, 2 d, 3 b, 4 d, 5 b, 6 d, 7 b, 8 a, 9 c, 10 b.

MULTIPLE CHOICE   *Quiz 37*

1   Writers Enid Blyton and Agatha Christie both had which second name?
    a   Margaret
    b   Marjorie
    c   Martha
    d   Mary

2   In which Shakespeare play does the pedantic scholar Holofernes appear?
    a   Love's Labour's Lost
    b   The Merry Wives of Windsor
    c   Much Ado About Nothing
    d   The Taming of the Shrew

3   'The Art of the Fugue' was the last (unfinished) work of which composer?
    a   Bach
    b   Beethoven
    c   Mozart
    d   Schubert

4   Who played frontier scout Flint McCullough in the TV western series 'Wagon Train'?
    a   Ward Bond
    b   Robert Fuller
    c   Robert Horton
    d   Doug McClure

5   When table tennis was first introduced into the Olympic Games in 1988, two countries shared the four gold medals. China was one, who was the other?
    a   Japan
    b   South Korea
    c   Sweden
    d   Yugoslavia

6   The Craters of the Moon National Monument is in which US state?
    a   Alaska
    b   Hawaii
    c   Idaho
    d   Utah

7   Which two members of U2 performed the theme of the 1996 movie 'Mission Impossible'?
    a   Bono and The Edge
    b   Bono and Larry Mullen
    c   The Edge and Adam Clayton
    d   Larry Mullen and Adam Clayton

8   In chapter 5 of which book of the New Testament will you find the following words: 'But the fruit of the Spirit is love, joy, peace, long suffering, gentleness, goodness, faith, meekness, temperance against such there is no law'?
    a   Colossians
    b   Ephesians
    c   Galatians
    d   Philippians

9   What is the name of Giovanni's servant in Mozart's opera 'Don Giovanni'?
    a   Bartolo
    b   Cherubino
    c   Leporello
    d   Masetto

10 And what is the proper name of the character Mimi in Puccini's 'La Boheme'?
    a   Barbarina
    b   Lucia
    c   Marcellina
    d   Susanna

Answers 1 d, 2 a, 3 a, 4 c, 5 b, 6 c, 7 d, 8 c, 9 c, 10 b.

1   The Rt..Hon. Sir Archibald Philip Primrose was the British Prime Minister from March 1894 to June 1895. By what title was he known?
   a   Viscount Palmerston
   b   Earl of Rosebery
   c   Marquess of Salisbury
   d   Duke of Wellington

2   Boxing. Who, in 1954, was the first Argentinian to win a world title?
   a   Juan Manuel Fangio
   b   Mario Kempes
   c   Pascual Perez
   d   Hugo Porta

3   What kind of creature is a cuckoo wrasse?
   a   Bird
   b   Butterfly
   c   Fish
   d   Snake

4   Which song writing duo's songs feature in the show 'Smokey Joe's Cafe'?
   a   Bacharach and David
   b   Goffin and King
   c   Leiber and Stoller
   d   Rodgers and Hart

5   What is a shebeen?
   a   A cudgel
   b   An elf
   c   A ghost
   d   An illegal drinking place

6   Which country is the setting for Puccini's opera 'Turandot'?
   a   China
   b   Egypt
   c   Italy
   d   Japan

7   Which one of the following is the title of a Tchaikovsky opera?
   a   The Queen of Clubs
   b   The Queen of Diamonds
   c   The Queen of Hearts
   d   The Queen of Spades

8   Which continent is the setting for the Graham Greene novel 'The Heart Of The Matter'?
   a   Africa
   b   North America
   c   South America
   d   Asia

9   In which country did a financial scandal known as the 'Stavisky affair' prompt serious rioting in 1934?
   a   France
   b   Poland
   c   Russia
   d   USA

10   Who, on the TV comedy show 'Rowan and Martin's Laugh-In' said the catchphrase: "Very interesting, but stupid" in a German accent?
   a   Henry Gibson
   b   Arte Johnson
   c   Dick Martin
   d   Dan Rowan

Answers 1 b, 2 c, 3 c, 4 c, 5 d, 6 a, 7 d, 8 a, 9 a, 10 b.

MULTIPLE CHOICE

Quiz 39

1　At which prison was the infamous Dr Crippen hanged on 23 November 1910?
a　Newgate
b　Pentonville
c　Wandsworth
d　Wormwood Scrubs

2　Which Canadian achieved a hat-trick of men's world figure skating titles between 1989 and 1991?
a　Kurt Browning
b　Donald Jackson
c　Donald McPherson
d　Brian Orser

3　From which island did the character Sophia Petrillo in the US TV comedy show 'The Golden Girls', originate?
a　Cuba
b　Crete
c　Sardinia
d　Sicily

4　What's the name of the birdcatcher in Mozart's 'The Magic Flute'?
a　Monostatos
b　Papageno
c　Sarastro
d　Tamilo

5　The Wallis and Futuna islands are an overseas territory of which country?
a　Denmark
b　France
c　Portugal
d　USA

6　What did the Romans call Armorica?
a　Aragon
b　Brittany
c　Castile
d　Lorraine

7　Ceuta is a Spanish enclave within which country?
a　Algeria
b　Mexico
c　Morocco
d　Portugal

8　Which was Charles Dickens' last completed novel?
a　Great Expectations
b　Little Dorrit
c　Our Mutual Friend
d　A Tale Of Two Cities

9　What, in ancient Rome was hecatomb?
a　A place used for public debate
b　A large burial chamber
c　A series of incantations
d　A great public sacrifice

10　And what is a moko?
a　A traditional Maori tattoo
b　A type of monkey
c　A Tibetan monk
d　A traditional character in Japanese theatre

Answers 1 b, 2 a, 3 d, 4 b, 5 b, 6 b, 7 c, 8 c, 9 d, 10 a.

1   Which British politician auditioned for the part in the film 'National Velvet' which was given to Elizabeth Taylor?
    a   Betty Boothroyd
    b   Barbara Castle
    c   Margaret Thatcher
    d   Shirley Williams

2   Golf. In 1994, who became the first player to win the US PGA title with a four round score of under 270?
    a   Ernie Els
    b   Greg Norman
    c   Jose-Maria Olazabal
    d   Nick Price

3   Who was described by Rudolf Nureyev as the world's greatest dancer?
    a   Fred Astaire
    b   Gene Kelly
    c   Vaslav Nijinsky
    d   Wayne Sleep

4   Which Oscar-winning actress was on the board of Pepsi-Cola?
    a   Joan Crawford
    b   Bette Davis
    c   Olivia de Havilland
    d   Katharine Hepburn

5   What is Microsoft founder Bill Gates' middle name?
    a   Harvey
    b   Henry
    c   Howard
    d   Hugh

6   What is a coulis?
    a   A cucumber salad
    b   A crushed ice drink
    c   A fresh fruit sauce
    d   A dish made of cauliflower

7   Ballet dancer Carlos Acosta comes from which country?
    a   Argentina
    b   Chile
    c   Cuba
    d   Mexico

8   What is a gastrocnemius?
    a   An expert on food
    b   A muscle in the leg
    c   A mollusc
    d   An intestinal bacteria

9   What is a ratite?
    a   A flightless bird
    b   A type of crystal
    c   A musical instrument
    d   A type of palm tree

10 Wacke is a form of what?
    a   Tribal dance
    b   Children's game
    c   Linen material
    d   Rock

Answers 1 d, **2** d, **3** a, **4** a, **5** b, **6** c, **7** c, **8** b, **9** a, **10** d.

1 In which city was the school that originally inspired Ronald Searle to create St. Trinians?
   a Belfast
   b Cardiff
   c Edinburgh
   d London

2 Which country won the first ever Olympic baseball competition in 1992?
   a Cuba
   b Japan
   c Taiwan
   d USA

3 What type of creature is a gelada?
   a Antelope
   b Bird
   c Monkey
   d Snake

4 Which French revolutionary became minister of justice in 1792 but he himself was guillotined in 1794?
   a Eduard Danton
   b Georges Danton
   c Raymond Danton
   d Philippe Danton

5 In which movie did Humphrey Bogart say: "When you're slapped, you'll take it and like it"?
   a The African Queen
   b The Big Sleep
   c Casablanca
   d The Maltese Falcon

6 In ancient Greece, what was a kithara?
   a A type of stringed instrument
   b A type of clothing
   c A type of sword
   d A type of cat

7 In which country were a group known as the Dekabrists involved in a revolt in December 1825?
   a China
   b France
   c India
   d Russia

8 Who was known as 'Chief of the Beautiful River'?
   a Cochise
   b Hiawatha
   c Tecumseh
   d Uncas

9 Who composed the 'Abraham Lincoln Symphony'?
   a Jet Harris
   b Phil Harris
   c Rolf Harris
   d Roy Harris

10 The Flaminian Way was an ancient Roman road that ran from Rome to a town now known as what?
   a Bari
   b Brindisi
   c Perugia
   d Rimini

Quiz 42

1   With which country do you associate the Iron Age culture known as Nok?
    a   Australia
    b   Canada
    c   Nigeria
    d   Norway

2   Spica is the brightest star in which constellation?
    a   Gemini
    b   Leo
    c   Pisces
    d   Virgo

3   Which American city is known as "the cradle of the Confederacy'?
    a   Montgomery, Alabama
    b   Richmond, Virginia
    c   Atlanta, Georgia
    d   Columbus, South Carolina

4   Which Shakespeare character says: "O, what a rogue and peasant slave am I"?
    a   Falstaff
    b   Hamlet
    c   Othello
    d   Shylock

5   What is the literal meaning of Beelzebub?
    a   Lord of the flies
    b   Lord of the isles
    c   Lord of the rings
    d   Lord of the planets

6   Who recorded 'Shop Around', Motown's first million seller?
    a   Marvelettes
    b   Miracles
    c   Mary Wells
    d   Stevie Wonder

7   What is niello?
    a   A type of cherry
    b   A type of black compound
    c   A type of Italian dance
    d   A type of Italian marble

8   In falconry, what name is given to the leather strap fastened to the leg of a hawk to which a leash may be attached?
    a   Bess
    b   Jess
    c   Ness
    d   Tess

9   Albert Fall 'achieved' what first?
    a   First US vice-president
    b   First person to go over Niagara Falls in a barrel and survive
    c   First person to be imprisoned whilst holding a US cabinet post
    d   First person to walk across the USA

10   What type of creature is a langur?
    a   Anteater
    b   Bird
    c   Cat
    d   Monkey

Answers 1 c, 2 d, 3 a, 4 b, 5 a, 6 b, 7 b, 8 b, 9 c, 10 d.

MULTIPLE CHOICE

Quiz 43

1   Which was Thomas Hardy's last novel?
 a   Far From The Madding Crowd
 b   Jude The Obscure
 c   The Mayor Of Casterbridge
 d   Tess Of The D'Urbervilles

2   What is a polymath?
 a   A lie-detector
 b   A multi-molecular structure
 c   A person with wide-ranging knowledge
 d   A sum with more than one answer

3   A turning point in the American War of Independence was the surrender of British troops on 17 October 1777. Where did that surrender take place?
 a   Concord
 b   Lexington
 c   Saratoga
 d   Valley Forge

4   Which native American plains-dwelling tribe, of Algonquin stock, were known to other tribes as 'dog-eaters'?
 a   Arapaho
 b   Cheyenne
 c   Pawnee
 d   Shoshoni

5   Born in France of English parents, with what do you associate Alfred Sisley?
 a   Films
 b   Literature
 c   Music
 d   Painting

6   Which Asian capital city is located on the Chao Phraya river?
 a   Bangkok
 b   Jakarta
 c   Phnom Penh
 d   Pyongyang

7   Which Japanese bridge was the first major suspension bridge to use a single cable?
 a   Ajigawa
 b   Kanmon
 c   Konohana
 d   Minato

8   Where is the Garagum Canal?
 a   Afghanistan
 b   Kazakstan
 c   Turkmenistan
 d   Uzbekistan

9   What's the name of the cartoon strip created by American Chic Young and which by the 1960s was syndicated in more than 1500 newspapers throughout the world?
 a   Blondie
 b   Garfield
 c   Jane
 d   Peanuts

10 Alfredo Stroessner was president of which country from 1954 to 1989?
 a   Bolivia
 b   Chile
 c   Colombia
 d   Paraguay

Answers 1 b, **2** c, **3** c, **4** a, **5** d, **6** a, **7** c, **8** c, **9** a, **10** d.

Quiz 44

1   In which year did suffragette Emily Davison throw herself under the king's horse?
    a   1911
    b   1912
    c   1913
    d   1914

2   Avianea is the national airline of which country?
    a   Sri Lanka
    b   Indonesia
    c   Colombia
    d   Jordon

3   What relation was Napoleon III to Napoleon I?
    a   nephew
    b   brother
    c   grandson
    d   son

4   What Indian term means a man who washes clothes?
    a   syce
    b   doolie
    c   mahout
    d   dhobi-wallah

5   What is the name given to a sculptor's workbench?
    a   banker
    b   lawyer
    c   teacher
    d   doctor

6   What was the nickname of singer Billie Holiday?
    a   Lady Blue
    b   Lady Madonna
    c   Lady Day
    d   Lady in Red

7   Which hotel was the venue for the first Academy Awards presentation on May 16, 1929?
    a   Washington Hotel
    b   Lincoln Hotel
    c   Jackson Hotel
    d   Roosevelt Hotel

8   Whose law states that at constant pressure the volume of a gas varies directly with its absolute temperature?
    a   Edward's Law
    b   Charles' Law
    c   Andrew's Law
    d   Philip's Law

9   What, in Spain, is a bodega?
    a   inn
    b   police station
    c   bakery
    d   wine store

10 What nationality was dancer Isadora Duncan?
    a   French
    b   American
    c   Brazilian
    d   British

Answers 1 c, 2 c, 3 a, 4 d, 5 a, 6 c, 7 d, 8 b, 9 d, 10 b.

MULTIPLE CHOICE

Quiz 45

1 Where was the location of the 1960 Olympic Games?
   a Melbourne
   b Rome
   c Helsinki
   d Tokyo

2 In which sport would a competitor perform a choctow?
   a ice-skating
   b dressage
   c diving
   d judo

3 Shalwar is what type of clothing?
   a short-sleeved Indian blouse or bodice
   b Indian man's high-collared coat
   c baggy trousers as worn in Pakistan
   d bright toga worn in Ghana

4 What creature is able to jump over 100 times its own length?
   a flea
   b aphid
   c kangaroo
   d crane fly

5 How many pips are there on a set of 28 dominoes?
   a 152
   b 168
   c 184
   d 206

6 What, in 1849, did Walter Hunt invent?
   a the safety pin
   b soles for shoes
   c the elastic band
   d the paintbrush

7 'On My Way To a Star' was the theme song of which singer in his vintage TV show?
   a Andy Williams
   b Bing Crosby
   c Dean Martin
   d Perry Como

8 Which Indian chief led the Indians in 1876 at the Battle of the Little Big Horn?
   a Crazy Horse
   b Geronimo
   c Running Bear
   d Sitting Bull

9 The farandole is a national dance of which country?
   a Spain
   b France
   c Portugal
   d Italy

10 On a flower, what is another name for the petals?
    a pistil
    b anther
    c corolla
    d sepals

Answers 1 b, 2 a, 3 c, 4 a, 5 b, 6 a, 7 d, 8 a, 9 b, 10 c.

MULTIPLE CHOICE *Quiz 46*

1 Which of the following was the one time fight manager of Muhammed Ali?
   a Antonio Aberdeen
   b Angelo Dundee
   c Enrico Sterling
   d Mario Edinburgh

2 What kind of imaginary creature is Jodie in the novel/movie 'The Amityville Horror'?
   a rabbit
   b dog
   c pig
   d snake

3 What type of fabric is shantung?
   a jute
   b silk
   c wool
   d cotton

4 What in Japan is a Samisen?
   a three-stringed musical instrument
   b portable charcoal grill
   c gateway of a Shinto temple
   d sliding screen made of paper

5 What was the name of the racing car driven by Dick Dastardly in the TV cartoon series 'The Wacky Races'?
   a Road Runner
   b Storm Chaser
   c Mean Machine
   d Side Winder

6 What gas is used as a refrigerant and in fizzy drinks and aerosols?
   a carbon dioxide
   b ethylene
   c cyanogen
   d nitrous oxide

7 The movies 'The Music Man', 'My Fair Lady' and 'Porgy and Bess' were all set in which year?
   a 1892
   b 1902
   c 1912
   d 1922

8 Wilt Chamberlain was the first person to be paid $100,000 a season in which sport?
   a American football
   b basketball
   c hockey
   d baseball

9 A convocation is the group name for which type of bird?
   a crow
   b quail
   c eagle
   d hummingbird

10 What type of food is zuppa inglese?
   a Neapolitan ice-cream
   b frozen pudding with preserved fruit
   c meringue with cream and fresh fruit
   d Italian trifle

MULTIPLE CHOICE

Quiz 47

1 Which explorer discovered Newfoundland?
   a Jacques Cartier
   b Eric the Red
   c Louis Hennepin
   d John Cabot

2 What was Walt Disney's middle name?
   a Elijah
   b Elliot
   c Elias
   d Elvis

3 Which creatures feed on Mulberry leaves?
   a silkworm
   b locust
   c koala bear
   d Hercules moth

4 Which is the only European country without an army?
   a Monaco
   b Andorra
   c Vatican City
   d Liechtenstien

5 Which king of England was called 'The Merry Monarch'?
   a Henry VIII
   b George III
   c Charles II
   d Edward VII

6 The song 'Getting To Know You' comes from which musical?
   a South Pacific
   b The King and I
   c Flower Drum Song
   d Porgy and Bess

7 Which US President was rumoured to have carried on a 28 year affair with a black slave Sally Hemings?
   a Thomas Jefferson
   b John Adams
   c Abraham Lincoln
   d James Knox Polk

8 Why was the American poet and author Edgar Allan Poe thrown out of West Point in 1831?
   a for writing erotic literature
   b for cheating at poker
   c he showed up for inspection stark naked
   d he appeared in the officers mess dressed in drag

9 For what would a crewel needle be used?
   a embroidery
   b stitching fabric together
   c by a doctor for injecting a patient
   d leatherwork

10 In the vintage TV show 'The Munsters', what type of creature was Grandpa's pet Igor?
   a one-eyed polecat
   b vulture
   c bat
   d snake

Answers 1 d. 2 c. 3 a. 4 d. 5 c. 6 b. 7 a. 8 c. 9 a. 10 c.

1   Which one of the following is not a
    Cambridge University college?
    a   Clare
    b   Emmanuel
    c   Mary
    d   Selwyn

2   Which one of the following actresses has not
    appeared in a film with her mother?
    a   Laura Dern
    b   Mia Farrow
    c   Jane Fonda
    d   Melanie Griffith

3   Which one of the following is not one of
    Aesop's fables?
    a   Androcles and the Lion
    b   The Fox and the Grapes
    c   The Tortoise and the Hare
    d   The Wolf in Sheep's Clothing

4   Which one of the following was not born in
    Russia?
    a   The composer Irving Berlin
    b   The composer George Gershwin
    c   Singer and entertainer Al Jolson
    d   Actor George Sanders

5   Who is the only one of the following who
    did not die suffering from tuberculosis?
    a   Jane Austen
    b   Emily Bronte
    c   John Keats
    d   D.H. Lawrence

6   Which one of the following capital cities is
    not a seaport?
    a   Ankara
    b   Colombo
    c   Helsinki
    d   Phnom Penh

7   Which one of the following cities does not
    stand on the river Danube?
    a   Belgrade
    b   Budapest
    c   Prague
    d   Vienna

8   Which one of the following songs does not
    feature in 'The Sound Of Music'?
    a   Do-Re-Mi
    b   Feed The Birds
    c   I Have Confidence In Me
    d   Sixteen Going On Seventeen

9   Which one of the following is not a
    chemical element?
    a   Americium
    b   Californium
    c   Einsteinium
    d   Euphonium

10 Which one of the following is not a parent
    of twins?
    a   Mel Gibson
    b   Jerry Hall
    c   Donald Sutherland
    d   Margaret Thatcher

Answers 1 c, 2 c, 3 a, 4 b, 5 a, 6 a, 7 c, 8 b, 9 d, 10 b.

MULTIPLE CHOICE — Odd-one-out 2

1 Of the following England cricketers, who is the only one actually born in England?
   a Andrew Caddick
   b Graeme Hick
   c Nasser Hussain
   d Mark Ramprakash

2 Which one of the following birds is not a member of the falcon family?
   a Eagle
   b Hobby
   c Kestrel
   d Merlin

3 Which one of the following works of Beethoven is a piano concerto and not a piano sonata?
   a 'Appassionata'
   b 'Emperor'
   c 'Moonlight'
   d 'Pathetique'

4 Which one of the following cities does not stand on the river Rhine?
   a Basle
   b Bonn
   c Cologne
   d Geneva

5 Which one of the following is not a study of living creatures?
   a Herpetology
   b Ichthyology
   c Ornithology
   d Seismology

6 Soccer. Which one of the following Frenchmen did not play in the 1998 World Cup final against Brazil?
   a Anelka
   b Desailly
   c Leboeuf
   d Petit

7 Which one of the following was not a Knight of the Round Table?
   a Galahad
   b Gawain
   c Ivanhoe
   d Lancelot

8 Which one of the following was not discovered by Sir Humphry Davy?
   a Calcium
   b Helium
   c Potassium
   d Sodium

9 Which one of the following figures has more than four sides?
   a Parallelogram
   b Pentagon
   c Rhombus
   d Trapezium

10 Which one of the following English kings never married?
    a Edward II
    b Henry II
    c Richard II
    d William II

Answers 1 d, 2 a, 3 b, 4 d, 5 d, 6 a, 7 c, 8 b, 9 b, 10 d.

1 Which one of the following does not flow into the North Sea?
   a Humber
   b Mersey
   c Tyne
   d Wear

2 Which one of the following is not the size of a wine bottle?
   a Balthazar
   b Jeroboam
   c Melchior
   d Methuselah

3 Which one of the following is not a form of quartz?
   a Amethyst
   b Cairngorm
   c Jasper
   d Turquoise

4 Which one of the following films is not based on an Elmore Leonard novel?
   a 'Get Shorty'
   b 'Jackie Brown'
   c 'Out Of Sight'
   d 'Pulp Fiction'

5 Which one of the following jazz musicians was a saxophonist and not a trumpeter?
   a Louis Armstrong
   b John Coltrane
   c Miles Davis
   d Dizzy Gillespie

6 Which is the only one of the following that lies within the Tropics?
   a Alice Springs
   b Cairo
   c Karachi
   d Mexico City

7 Which one of the following plays was not written by Peter Shaffer?
   a 'Amadeus'
   b 'Equus'
   c 'The Royal Hunt Of The Sun'
   d 'Sleuth'

8 Which one of the following films was not set during World War Two?
   a 'The Bridge At Remagen'
   b 'The Bridge On The River Kwai'
   c 'The Bridges At Toko-Ri'
   d 'A Bridge Too Far'

9 Which one of the following is not both the name of a country and a river?
   a Hungary
   b Jordan
   c Paraguay
   d Zaire

10 Which one of the following is not a lobe of the brain?
   a Frontal
   b Occipital
   c Spatial
   d Temporal

MULTIPLE CHOICE

Odd-one-out 4

1   Which one of the following was not the subject of a play written by Shakespeare?
a   Henry IV
b   Henry V
c   Henry VI
d   Henry VII

2   Which one of the following is not a former French colony?
a   Nepal
b   Republic of Niger
c   Tunisia
d   Vietnam

3   Which one of the following cities has never been Japan's capital?
a   Kyoto
b   Nara
c   Tokyo
d   Yokohama

4   Which one of the following is not a satellite of Jupiter?
a   Callisto
b   Europa
c   Ganymede
d   Hyperion

5   Which one of the following is not a star constellation?
a   Andromeda
b   Medusa
c   Pegasus
d   Perseus

6   In Shakespeare's play 'Macbeth', which one of the following characters is not killed?
a   Banquo
b   Duncan
c   Macbeth
d   Macduff

7   Which one of the following is not named after a Frenchman?
a   Croissant
b   Guillotine
c   Leotard
d   Silhouette

8   Which one of the following mythological creatures does not have wings?
a   Centaur
b   Griffin
c   Harpy
d   Pegasus

9   Which one of the following is not a kind of antelope?
a   Capybara
b   Dik-Dik
c   Impala
d   Nilgai

10   Which one of the following women has not been married to Dudley Moore?
a   Bo Derek
b   Suzy Kendall
c   Brogan Lane
d   Tuesday Weld

Answers 1 d, 2 a, 3 d, 4 d, 5 b, 6 d, 7 a, 8 a, 9 a, 10 a.

MULTIPLE CHOICE   *Odd-one-out 5*

1   Which one of the following did not become British Prime Minister?
    a   Clement Attlee
    b   James Callaghan
    c   Hugh Gaitskell
    d   Harold Wilson

2   Which one of the following days of the week is not named after an ancient God?
    a   Monday
    b   Tuesday
    c   Wednesday
    d   Thursday

3   Which one of the following is not one of Canada's prairie provinces?
    a   Alberta
    b   Manitoba
    c   Ontario
    d   Saskatchewan

4   Which one of the following is not a rabbit in Watership Down?
    a   Bigwig
    b   Fiver
    c   Harvey
    d   Hazel

5   Of the following, three are ancient Roman coins and one is an ancient Greek coin. Which is the Greek coin?
    a   Narius
    b   Obolus
    c   Sesterce
    d   Solidus

6   Which one of the following was not a Roman emperor?
    a   Augustus
    b   Claudius
    c   Romulus
    d   Tiberius

7   Which one of the following is not a prime number?
    a   7
    b   9
    c   11
    d   13

8   Which one of the following art galleries is not located in it's country's capital city?
    a   Louvre
    b   Prado
    c   Tate
    d   Uffizi

9   Which one of the following was not an impressionist painter?
    a   Matisse
    b   Monet
    c   Pissarro
    d   Renoir

10 Which one of the following is not a ship built by Brunel?
    a   Great Britain
    b   Great Eastern
    c   Great Western
    d   Great Yarmouth

Answers 1 c, 2 a, 3 c, 4 c, 5 b, 6 c, 7 b, 8 c, 9 a, 10 d.

MULTIPLE CHOICE

Odd-one-out 6

1   Name the only one of the following not to be beheaded?
a   Anne Boleyn
b   Catherine of Aragon
c   Lady Jane Grey
d   Mary, Queen of Scots

2   Of the following films, in which one did Julie Andrews not appear?
a   'Funny Girl'
b   'Mary Poppins'
c   'Thoroughly Modern Millie'
d   'Victor/Victoria'

3   Which one of the following films was not directed by Robert Redford?
a   'A River Runs Through It'
b   'Ordinary People'
c   'Quiz Show'
d   'The Sting'

4   Which one of the following operas was not written by Verdi?
a   'Aida'
b   'Nabucco'
c   'Rigoletto'
d   'Tosca'

5   Which one of the following films was not directed by Alan Parker?
a   'The Commitments'
b   'Evita'
c   'Fame'
d   'Saturday Night Fever'

6   Which one of the following ballets was not written by Tchaikovsky?
a   'Giselle'
b   'The Nut Cracker'
c   'The Sleeping Beauty'
d   'Swan Lake'

7   Which one of the following has not sung the theme song for a James Bond movie?
a   Shirley Bassey
b   Bing Crosby
c   Tom Jones
d   Nancy Sinatra

8   Which one of the following is not the son of a film actor?
a   Ed Begley Jnr.
b   Lon Chaney Jnr.
c   Harry Connick Jnr.
d   Douglas Fairbanks Jnr.

9   Which one of the following films has won the Oscar for Best Picture?
a   'E.T.'
b   'Jaws'
c   'Rocky'
d   'Star Wars'

10 Which one of the following musicals was not written by Rodgers and Hammerstein?
a   'My Fair Lady'
b   'Oklahoma'
c   'South Pacific'
d   'The Sound Of Music'

Answers 1 b, 2 a, 3 d, 4 d, 5 d, 6 a, 7 b, 8 c, 9 c, 10 a.

MULTIPLE CHOICE

Odd-one-out 7

1 Which one of the following kings of England did not belong to the house of Tudor?
a Edward V
b Edward VI
c Henry VII
d Henry VIII

2 Which of the following Shakespeare plays did Laurence Olivier not direct a movie version of?
a 'Hamlet'
b 'Henry V'
c 'Macbeth'
d 'Richard III'

3 Which one of the following films was not directed by Warren Beatty?
a 'Bonnie And Clyde'
b 'Dick Tracy'
c 'Heaven Can Wait'
d 'Reds'

4 Which one of the following animals is a rodent?
a Badger
b Beaver
c Stoat
d Weasel

5 Which one of the following does not fall within the scope of physics?
a Boyle's Law
b Gresham's Law
c Lenz's Law
d Ohm's Law

6 Which one of the following played the trumpet not the piano?
a Count Basie
b Duke Ellington
c Earl Hines
d King Oliver

7 Which one of the following is not a volcano?
a Paricutin
b Mount Pelee
c Roraima
d Vesuvius

8 Which one of the following was a psychologist, not a philosopher?
a Alfred Adler
b Georg Hegel
c Friedrich Nietzsche
d Ludwig Wittgenstein

9 Which one of the following films did not feature Marilyn Monroe in?
a 'Gentlemen Prefer Blondes'
b 'Meet Me In St. Louis'
c 'The Misfits'
d 'The Prince And The Showgirl'

10 There have been three versions of the film 'A Star Is Born' (one made in 1937, one in 1954 and one in 1976). Of the following actresses, which one did not appear in any of them?
a Judy Garland
b Janet Gaynor
c Jane Powell
d Barbra Streisand

Answers 1 a, **2** c, **3** a, **4** b, **5** b, **6** d, **7** c, **8** a, **9** b, **10** c.

MISCELLANEOUS

MISCELLANEOUS 2 — Quiz 1

1 Which is the shortest modern European alphabet with only twenty-one letters?

2 What is the motto of the Special Air Service (SAS) division of the British Army?

3 Which American anti-slave campaigner was hanged in 1869 after an abortive raid on the federal arsenal in Virginia?

4 What nationality was the composer Borodin?

5 Who was the senator who became Elizabeth Taylor's seventh husband in 1976?

6 Who was the American journalist who was held hostage in Lebanon for 2454 days, finally being freed in 1991?

7 In 1917 Finland declared its independence from which country?

8 In 1961, who released their first record 'Surfin'' which made it to No.75 on the US charts?

9 What innovation in golf was patented in 1899 by George F. Bryant?

10 Onyx is an appropriate gift for which wedding anniversary – 5th 7th or 9th?

11 What is meant by the Latin phrase *a tergo*?

12 What was the former method of execution in Spain by means of strangling or breaking the neck with an iron collar?

13 Which rock group was disbanded two months after the death of its drummer John Bonham?

14 What was ended by the 13th Amendment to the US Constitution?

15 What was the Tin Donkey, which in 1915 was the first of its kind?

Answers 1 Italian 2 Who Dares Wins 3 John Brown 4 Russian 5 John Warner 6 Terry Anderson 7 Russia 8 The Beach Boys 9 A wooden tee 10 Seventh 11 From behind 12 Garrotte 13 Led Zeppelin 14 Slavery 15 An all metal plane

Quiz 2

1 Which country had a police force called the Tonton Macoutes?

2 What would you find in a formicary?

3 Which Greek millionairess died in 1989 in Argentina?

4 What was the profession of the Frenchman Auguste Escoffier?

5 In basketball, the Rockets are a Major League team of which city?

6 Who was the first British sovereign to make regular use of Buckingham Palace when in residence in London?

7 Of where is Sofia the capital?

8 What is meant by the musical term *andante*?

9 Which saint's day falls on 17 March?

10 In a bullfight, what is the mounted man with a lance called?

11 Which city has a soccer team called Ajax?

12 What Latin phrase, meaning bounteous mother, is used of Universities and schools?

13 Which Dutch explorer discovered New Zealand?

14 Who became the first black world heavyweight boxing champion in 1918?

15 Which keyboard instrument was patented in 1848 by Alexandre Debain in Paris?

Answers 1 Haiti 2 Ants 3 Christina Onassis 4 A chef 5 Houston 6 Queen Victoria 7 Bulgaria 8 At a moderate tempo 9 St.Patrick 10 A picador 11 Amsterdam 12 Alma mater 13 Abel Tasman 14 Jack Johnson 15 The harmonium

MISCELLANEOUS 2

Quiz 3

1   Who duetted with Celine Dion on the 1997 hit 'Tell Him'?

2   What nationality was the philosopher Immanuel Kant?

3   On which island was the painter El Greco born?

4   What is the meaning of the phrase *cri de coeur*?

5   In which US city did the movie 'Gone With the Wind' have its premiere?

6   Who were the one-eyed giants of Greek mythology?

7   What did Canada add to its national flag in 1964?

8   Who succeeded Oliver Cromwell as Lord Protector of England?

9   Which city is served by Zaventum airport?

10 What famous event took place off Griffin's Wharf in Massachusetts in 1773?

11 At eight minutes plus, which single in 1971 became one of the longest ever songs to ever hit the pop charts?

12 At what age must a cardinal retire?

13 Who wrote '2001, A Space Odyssey'?

14 What two colours make up the Greek flag?

15 What market town in England was named Corinium in Roman times, when it was the second largest town in Britain?

Answers 1 Barbra Streisand 2 German 3 Crete 4 Cry from the heart 5 Atlanta 6 Cyclops 7 A maple leaf 8 His son, Richard Cromwell 9 Brussels 10 The Boston Tea Party 11 Don McLean's American Pie 12 80 13 Arthur C. Clarke 14 Blue and white 15 Cirencester

1   What are the names of the two ancient Cretan scripts, one of which was deciphered in 1952 and one of which is still undeciphered?

2   What first was achieved by the Dutch vessel 'Curacao' in April 1827?

3   Which pope excommunicated King Henry VIII of England?

4   What was the name of the aircraft in which the Wright Brothers made their first successful flight in a powered aircraft?

5   In which country did tarot cards originate?

6   What in Britain are Derby, Dunlop, Leicester and Orkney types of?

7   Which ventriloquist had a dummy called Archie Andrews?

8   What is the name of the lace shawl worn over the head and shoulders by Spanish women?

9   Which hereditary warrior class of Japan boasted that they never drew their sword without using it and never gave their word without keeping it?

10   What continent has, for its size, the most coastline?

11   Who, in the 18th-century wrote 'The Beggar's Opera'?

12   Which Spanish woman tennis player won the 1994 French and US Open Championships?

13   What is the name given to crude iron obtained from blast furnaces after the ore has been treated?

14   What is the largest seabird?

15   ...and what is the largest land bird capable of flight?

Answers 1 Linear A and Linear B (deciphered)   **2** The first steamer to cross the Atlantic   **3** Pope Paul III   **4** The Wright Flyer   **5** Italy   **6** Cheeses   **7** Peter Brough   **8** Mantilla   **9** Samurai   **10** Europe   **11** John Gay   **12** Aranxa Sanchez Vicario   **13** Pig iron   **14** Albatross

MISCELLANEOUS 2

Quiz 5

1 What type of paper did Albert L. Jones patent in 1871?

2 Who wrote and recorded 'Blue Suede Shoes' in 1955?

3 What are anthracite, bituminous and lignite types of?

4 Who, in 1958, issued a recorded Christmas message from an orbiting space satellite: "To all mankind, America's wish for Peace on Earth and Good Will to Men Everywhere"?

5 Ron Wood is a long-standing member of which rock group?

6 Who played James Bond in 'Tomorrow Never Dies'?

7 Which is the only planet that is not named after a god of classical mythology?

8 Which rock group was formed in 1967 by Ian Anderson and Glenn Cornick?

9 What colours are the vertical stripes of the Italian flag?

10 What is another name for the card game 'chemin de fer'?

11 Who starred as Fast Eddie Felson in 'The Hustler'?

12 What is the capital of Lebanon?

13 What nationality was the composer Haydn?

14 In what sport might you perform an eskimo roll?

15 What colour is a female blackbird?

Answers 1 Corrugated paper 2 Carl Perkins 3 Coal 4 President Eisenhower 5 The Rolling Stones 6 Pierce Brosnan 7 Earth 8 Jethro Tull 9 Green, white, red 10 Baccarat 11 Paul Newman 12 Beirut 13 Austrian 14 Canoeing 15 Brown

MISCELLANEOUS 2

Quiz 6

1   What is the largest artery in the human body?

2   Which major sea is so shallow that it has no tides?

3   What island in the Indian ocean was described by Mark Twain as the prototype of heaven?

4   Who, in the reign of Charles I became Britain's first poet laureate?

5   What from earth is eclipsed when the moon moves between the earth and the sun?

6   In the United Kingdom, at what age must a magistrate retire?

7   In 1971, a TV movie 'The Homecoming: A Christmas Story', introduced which family to TV audiences?

8   In mythology the wife of Odin gave her name to which day of the week?

9   Who was the king of Epirus who after having spent nearly all of his life in battle was killed by a heavy tile dropped by an old woman in a street fight?

10 Invented during the reign of Henry VIII what was the Scavenger's Daughter?

11 What method of cleaning was accidentally discovered in 1849 when a tailor M. Jolly-Bellin upset a lamp containing oil and turpentine on his clothes?

12 Who is the Roman goddess of Dawn?

13 Where in France is a twenty-four hour race for motor cars held annually?

14 In 1973, who published an exposé of the Soviet prison system 'Gulag Archipelago', which led to his expulsion from the Soviet Union?

15 What coloured square is the centre of the Blue Peter flag?

Answers 1 Aorta **2** The Mediterranean **3** Mauritius **4** Ben Jonson **5** The Sun **6** 70 **7** The Waltons **8** Friday (Freya) **9** Pyrrhus **10** An instrument of torture **11** Dry-cleaning **12** Aurora **13** Le Mans **14** Alexander Solzhenitsyn **15** White

MISCELLANEOUS 2

Quiz 7

1   Which Beach Boy drowned aged 39 in 1983?

2   Who was the communications officer in the original TV series 'Star Trek' played by Michelle Nichols?

3   In which US state did the Wounded Knee massacre of Sioux Indians take place in 1890?

4   The name of which city in South America means Vale of Paradise?

5   Which singer appeared on a Jamaican postage stamp in 1982?

6   What is the meaning of the French term *haute couture*?

7   In Roald Dahl's 'Charlie and the Chocolate Factory', who is the factory owner?

8   The groat is an obsolete silver coin of which country?

9   Which English cathedral has a crooked spire?

10 In which ocean is Easter Island?

11 In 'Alice in Wonderland', what did the croquet players use instead of mallets?

12 …and what did they use instead of balls?

13 Who were the opposing countries in the Battle of Bunker Hill?

14 What classical tune was used as the theme tune for 'The Lone Ranger'?

15 The Granth is the holy book of which religion?

Answers 1 Dennis Wilson 2 Lt. Cmdr. Uhura 3 South Dakota 4 Valparaiso 5 Bob Marley 6 High fashion 7 Willy Wonka 8 England 9 Chesterfield 10 Pacific 11 Flamingoes 12 Hedgehogs 13 USA and Britain 14 The William Tell Overture 15 Sikhism

1   In which city is the only royal palace in the United States?

2   Who did Rajiv Gandhi succeed as Prime Minister of India?

3   What type of creature is a grampus?

4   Who composed the 'Ride of the Valkyries'?

5   When Johnny Cash entertained the inmates of San Quentin prison, a future country singer was in the audience serving time for burglary. Can you name him?

6   Who wrote 'The Catcher in the Rye'?

7   Who, in the Bible, performed the Dance of the Seven Veils?

8   Who is the eldest son of Tony Blair?

9   In which country is the House of Bernadotte the ruling dynasty?

10 Who was the British commander defeated by George Washington at the Battle of Princeton?

11 At the age of 84, who was the oldest ever British Prime Minister?

12 …and at 24, who was the youngest?

13 To what in 1847 did the Californian town of Yerba Buena change its name?

14 Who wrote the 'Lord of the Rings'?

15 What, in 1959, became America's 49th state?

Answers 1 Honolulu 2 His mother, Indira 3 A killer whale 4 Wagner 5 Merle Haggard 6 J.D.Salinger 7 Salome 8 Euan 9 Sweden 10 Cornwallis 11 Gladstone 12 William Pitt the Younger 13 San Francisco 14 J.R.R.Tolkien 15 Alaska

MISCELLANEOUS 2   Quiz 9

1   Who was the first female singer to be inducted into America's Rock and Roll Hall of Fame?

2   Boadicea was queen of which tribe of people?

3   What musical was based on a Christopher Isherwood novel, 'Goodbye to Berlin'?

4   The ancient city of Carthage is now in which country?

5   How many dice are used in the game of Backgammon?

6   In which US state is the Keek telescope, which in 1995 located the most distant galaxy up to then discovered, some 15 billion light years away?

7   What in Russia is Izvestia?

8   Dolomite is an ore of which metal?

9   In which city was the TV series 'Ironside' set?

10 Who is the patron saint of fishermen?

11 In the Hans Christian Anderson fairy story what does the Ugly Duckling turn into?

12 Which is the world's windiest continent?

13 The former headquarters of the French Foreign Legion, Sadi Ben Abbas, is in which country?

14 Who wrote 'Private Lives' for his long-time friend Gertrude Lawrence?

15 In the book 'Treasure Island', what is the name of the ship?

Answers 1 Aretha Franklin 2 Iceni 3 Cabaret 4 Tunisia 5 2 6 Hawaii 7 A newspaper 8 Magnesium 9 San Francisco 10 St. Peter 11 A swan 12 Antarctica 13 Algeria 14 Noel Coward 15 Hispaniola

MISCELLANEOUS 2 *Quiz 10*

1 In which part of the body are the deltoid muscles?

2 What is the name of Dick Turpin's horse?

3 From which country in South America does the monkey puzzle tree originate?

4 Which English artist first illustrated Lewis Carroll's 'Alice's Adventures in Wonderland?

5 Who wrote the 1997 bestseller 'A Thin Red Line'?

6 Orsino, Olivia, Viola, Malvolio and Festa are characters in which Shakespeare play?

7 E is the international car registration letter for which country?

8 Who is the minstrel in Robin Hood's band of merry men?

9 What is measured by an anemometer?

10 Vienna stands on which river?

11 In Morse Code, what letter is represented by - - ?

12 What do American's call what the British refer to as maize?

13 Who wrote 'The Day of the Triffids'?

14 Whose marooning for four years on an uninhabited island in the South Pacific following a quarrel, inspired Daniel Defoe to write the story 'Robinson Crusoe'?

15 What in South America is a llano?

Answers 1 Shoulder 2 Black Bess 3 Chile 4 John Tenniel 5 Tami Hoag 6 Twelfth Night 7 Spain 8 Alan A Dale 9 Wind speed 10 Danube 11 O 12 Corn 13 John Wyndham 14 Alexander Selkirk 15 A grassy plain

MISCELLANEOUS 2

Quiz 11

1   On which river in North America are the Horseshoe Falls?

2   What picture did Thomas Gainsborough paint in 1774 to prove to Sir Joshua Reynolds that blue could be used for the mass of a picture?

3   The Notre Dame cathedral in France is an example of what type of architecture?

4   What type of camel has two humps?

5   What contribution in 1900 did Mr Dwight F. Davis of St. Louis, Missouri make to the world of sport?

6   Which year in 18th-century Britain was only 354 days long due to the change-over to the Gregorian calendar?

7   Who is the King of Spain?

8   Sam Phillips, the music producer whose career was intertwined with that of Elvis Presley, founded which record label?

9   Who was the fourth wife of Henry VIII?

10 At what sport is Nancy Lopez a famous name?

11 In which middle east country is Mount Hermon?

12 The name of what, in Australia, is derived from an Aborigine word for 'I don't understand'?

13 In the MG motor car, what do the letters MG stand for?

14 Who, in 1924, wrote 'Rhapsody in Blue'?

15 The name of which Roman god means 'shining father' in Latin?

Answers 1 Niagara 2 Blue Boy 3 Gothic 4 Bactrian 5 He presented the Davis Cup for tennis 6 1752 7 Juan Carlos 8 Sun 9 Anne of Cleves 10 Golf 11 Syria 12 Kangaroo 13 Morris Garages 14 George Gershwin 15 Jupiter

Quiz 12

1   'Everything I Do (I Do It For You)' sung by Bryan Adams is the theme song from which movie?

2   Addis Ababa is the capital of which country?

3   What is the theme of the Ernest Hemingway novel 'Death in the Afternoon'?

4   The cymric is a longhaired version of what type of cat?

5   What is the most common Spanish surname?

6   Who, in the 1984 Los Angeles Olympics, won four gold medals and duplicated Jesse Owens' feat in the 1936 Olympics?

7   Whom did Martha Dandridge Curtis (or as she was at the time of her marriage, Martha Curtis, a widow) marry in 1759?

8   Who in Greek and Roman mythology is the god of wine?

9   Quinine is obtained from the bark of which tree?

10 Of which actor did Howard Hughes remark that his ears made him look like a taxi cab with both doors open?

11 Who in 1876 was shot in the back by Jack McCall while holding a 'Dead Man's Hand' at poker?

12 What is the name of the forest in Shakespeare's 'As You Like It'?

13 Althing is the parliament of which country?

14 Which American state is known as the Old Dominion and is thought to have been named from the nickname of an English queen?

15 Who attempted to assassinate Ronald Reagan in 1981?

Answers 1 Robin Hood, Prince of Thieves 2 Ethiopia 3 Bullfighting 4 Manx 5 Garcia 6 Carl Lewis 7 George Washington 8 Bacchus 9 Cinchona 10 Clark Gable 11 Wild Bill Hickok 12 Forest of Arden 13 Iceland 14 Virginia (Elizabeth I, The Virgin Queen) 15 John W. Hinckley

1   The Koran is the Holy Book of which religion?

2   What type of weapon is a poniard?

3   What is uniquely strange about the book 'Gadsby', written by Ernest Vincent Wright?

4   The marimba is a type of which instrument?

5   What is the common name of Beethoven's 'Symphony No.3 in E flat'?

6   What did the Romans call the goddess Aphrodite?

7   Who was the lover of the French philosopher Peter Abelard?

8   Which day of the week was named after the mythological son of Woden?

9   Which Lord opened the tomb of Tutankhamen in November 1922?

10 Which saying is derived from the name of a Cambridge horse hirer who always gave his customers the horse nearest to the stable door?

11 In which European mountain range is the Ordesa National Park?

12 The Peninsular War of 1808 to 1814 was fought on which peninsular?

13 David Ben Gurion was the first Prime Minister of which country?

14 What is chiromancy an alternative name for?

15 Whom did Pocahontas marry in 1614?

Answers 1 Islam 2 Dagger 3 It does not contain the letter E 4 Xylophone 5 Eroica 6 Venus 7 Heloise 8 Thursday 9 Carnarvon 10 Hobson's Choice 11 Pyrenees 12 Iberian 13 Israel 14 Palmistry 15 John Rolfe

MISCELLANEOUS 2

1 Apart from French, German and Romansch, what is the fourth official language of Switzerland?

2 Where in Europe are the only wild apes to be found?

3 Which country is the world's largest producer of coffee?

4 In which city was the world's first underground train service opened in 1863?

5 Who wrote 'The Thin Man'?

6 Sir John A. MacDonald was the first Prime Minister of which country?

7 How did Sue Rosenkawitz achieve fame in Cape Town on 11 January 1974?

8 In a novel by Victor Hugo, who kills the villain Archdeacon Frollo?

9 In which country is the River Spey?

10 Who wrote 'On the Beach' and 'A Town Like Alice'?

11 Who, in 1922, was the first athlete to swim 100 metres in under 1 minute?

12 'Ol' Man River' comes from which musical?

13 Who created the detective Hercule Poirot?

14 The Brabanconne is the national anthem of which country?

15 How many pairs of ribs are there in the human body?

Answers 1 Italian 2 Gibraltar 3 Brazil 4 London 5 Dashiell Hammet 6 Canada 7 She gave birth to the first surviving sextuplets 8 Quasimodo 9 Scotland 10 Nevil Shute 11 Johnny Weismuller 12 Showboat 13 Agatha Christie 14 Belgium 15 12

MISCELLANEOUS 2

Quiz 15

1 Becky Sharpe is a character in which novel?

2 Which English monarch was crowned in 1559?

3 What was unique about the crew of the yacht America 3 when they won an America's Cup race in 1995?

4 Who wrote the opera 'Tosca'?

5 Which novel was ceremoniously burnt by a thousand Muslims in 1989?

6 Who in mythology rode a horse called Xanthus?

7 What type of headgear was first worn in the late 18th-century by John Etherington of London?

8 Which Beatle was married to Barbara Bach?

9 How many acres are there in a square mile?

10 Which cartoon character was introduced in 1929 by E.C. Segar in his Thimble Theater comic strip?

11 Malev is the airline of which Eastern European country?

12 What was the name of the Allied offensive in the 1991 Gulf War?

13 What did Colonel Thomas Blood famously steal in 1675?

14 Which US state has the most numbers of population?

15 Albert De Salvo is notoriously better known by what nickname?

Answers 1 Vanity Fair 2 Elizabeth I 3 They were all female 4 Puccini 5 The Satanic Verses 6 Achilles 7 The top hat 8 Ringo Starr 9 640 10 Popeye the Sailor Man 11 Hungary 12 Desert Storm 13 The Crown Jewels 14 California 15 The Boston Strangler

1   Which fruit is a cross between an orange and a tangerine?

2   SO2 is the chemical formula for which chemical?

3   Bluebottle is the alternative name for what insect?

4   Who went to sea in a beautiful pea green boat?

5   Who, in 2000 was the official Labour Party candidate for the Lord Mayor of London?

6   Which character in Othello says: "I will play the swan, And die in music"?

7   Who wrote 'The Lady in the Lake'?

8   Who had a 1968 hit with 'I Close My Eyes and Count to Ten'?

9   Which Russian leader once said: "If one cannot catch the bird of paradise, better take a wet hen"?

10   What birds are sometimes referred to as Mother Carey's chickens?

11   After the 2000 Sydney Olympics, how many Gold Medals had been won, in total, by British rower Steve Redgrave?

12   Who, in 1704, wrote the satire 'The Battle of the Books'?

13   What, in the 13th-century was otherwise known as 'The Great Charter'?

14   In what part of the human body is the fibula?

15   Which artist had his so-called blue, pink and brown periods?

Answers 1 Clementine 2 Sulphur Dioxide 3 Blowfly 4 The Owl and the Pussycat 5 Frank Dobson 6 Emilia 7 Raymond Chandler 8 Dusty Springfield 9 Khrushchev 10 Stormy Petrels 11 Five 12 Jonathan Swift 13 Magna Carta 14 The leg (calf) 15 Picasso

1   Which football pools winner said: "I'm going to spend, spend, spend"?

2   What was the nickname of the American outlaw Robert LeRoy Parker?

3   Which actor played Bobby Ewing in 'Dallas'?

4   Which ancient riddle poses the question: 'What walks on four legs in the morning, two legs in the afternoon and three legs in the evening'?

5   ...and what is the answer to the riddle?

6   ...and who famously solved the riddle?

7   Of which saints day is it said that if it rains, it will rain for a further 40 days and 40 nights?

8   Which three countries comprise Scandinavia?

9   What relative was George IV to William IV?

10 What sport is the subject of David Story's book 'This Sporting Life'?

11 Rotorua is a health resort in which country?

12 RCH is the International car index mark for which country?

13 What name is often given to the third molar teeth, which are the last teeth to appear in a human being?

14 How many races are there in the Motor Racing Formula One Grand Prix season?

15 To what was Tennyson referring when he wrote, 'Into the valley of death rode the six-hundred'?

Answers 1 Vivien Nicholson 2 Butch Cassidy 3 Patrick Duffy 4 The Riddle of the Sphinx 5 Man 6 Oedipus 7 St.Swithin's Day 8 Denmark, Norway, Sweden 9 Brother 10 Rugby League 11 New Zealand 12 Chile 13 Wisdom teeth 14 16 15 The Charge of the Light Brigade

1   Which Shakespeare character said: "I am pigeon-livered and lack gall to make oppression better"?

2   In 2000 a ten-mile bridge opened in Europe linking Malmo with which capital city?

3   Which writer created Lord Peter Wimsey?

4   Which member of the Royal Family set up a company called Ardent in 1993?

5   Of what is Pharmacology the study?

6   Jill Craigie was the wife of which former leader of the British Labour Party?

7   Hamadryad is an alternative name for what type of snake?

8   Jean Valjean is the hero of which Victor Hugo novel?

9   Where would you expect to find a northing?

10   Molise is a region of which country?

11   First proposed by Ronald Reagan, for what is SDI an acronym?

12   Which sport consists of two Major Leagues in the USA, the National League (NL) and the American League (AL)?

13   To what position was Michael Martin elected in 2000?

14   What kind of fish is a sockeye?

15   Which branch of biology deals with the study of animals?

MISCELLANEOUS 2   *Quiz 19*

1   Which city was the first capital of the Kingdom of Italy until 1865?

2   King Zog was the last ruler of which country?

3   What did Winston Churchill refer to as a riddle wrapped in a mystery inside an enigma?

4   Who wrote the musical 'A Little Night Music'?

5   What is measured by an ammeter?

6   How was Jeanne D' Arc better known in history?

7   What is a rhinoceros horn made out of?

8   In America the Hudson river runs through which great city?

9   Which marine crustacean has a front pair of legs modified as pincers, one for crushing and one for cutting?

10 In which ocean are the Midway Islands?

11 Astronauts Young and Crippen made their first flight in which type of space vehicle on 12 April, 1981?

12 On the Beaufort scale, a speed of 12-18 kph (8-12 mph) is described as what type of breeze?

13 Developed in England from war-horses, what is the largest breed of horse?

14 Which Shakespeare character says: 'Yet I do fear thy nature; It is too full o' the milk of human kindness'?

15 Native to Europe, what is a medlar?

Answers 1 Turin **2** Albania **3** The Soviet Union **4** Stephen Sondheim **5** Electric current **6** Joan of Arc **7** Hair **8** New York **9** Lobster **10** Pacific **11** Space Shuttle **12** Gentle **13** Shire **14** Lady Macbeth **15** A small tree

1 According to the title of a Shakespeare play, what city is Timon from?

2 What in the human body are affected by Paget's disease?

3 What sport provides the background to the novels of Dick Francis?

4 In 1912, which British hero's last words were: "I am just going outside and I may be some time"?

5 Who played Queen Elizabeth I in 'Shakespeare in Love'?

6 What is meant by the musical term *arco*?

7 The flag of Sweden consists of a gold cross on what coloured background?

8 Felicitas Julia is the ancient name for which European capital city?

9 Which small constellation in the night sky features on the national flags of Australia and New Zealand?

10 In which English county is Fountains Abbey?

11 Which creature is called herisson in heraldry?

12 Whose 'Symphony No.40 in C' is known as 'Jupiter'?

13 What in the human body are classified by types known as True, False and Floating?

14 Whose was the briefest US Presidency?

15 At which sport would you be competing if you were stealing bases?

Answers 1 Athens 2 Bones 3 Horse racing 4 Captain Lawrence Oates 5 Judi Dench 6 With the bow 7 Blue 8 Lisbon 9 The Southern Cross 10 Yorkshire 11 Hedgehog 12 Mozart 13 Ribs 14 William Henry Harrison 15 Baseball

1   Is Shanghai north or south of Beijing?

2   What plant is the original source of the heart drug *digitalis*?

3   What, in Buddhism, is the sum of a person's actions in previous existences?

4   The nightingale is a member of which bird family?

5   What is the name for a word or phrase that reads the same both forwards and backwards, such as 'level', or 'Dennis and Edna sinned'?

6   What, because of its yellow colour, is pyrite sometimes known as?

7   What state of Australia was formerly known as Van Dieman's Land?

8   Which two layers of the earth's atmosphere are separated by the tropopause?

9   In which Scottish city is Sauchiehall Street?

10   In the Bible, for looking back at which two cities was Lot's wife turned into a pillar of salt?

11   Which actor was both one of 'The Dirty Dozen' and 'The Magnificent Seven'?

12   Telesto is the thirteenth natural satellite of which planet?

13   What is the name given to rowing when there is just one rower with two oars?

14   Which tree is also called a Rowan tree?

15   What is the name of the white-faced character created by the French mime-artist Marcel Marceau?

Answers 1 South **2** Foxglove **3** Karma **4** Thrush **5** Palindrome **6** Fool's Gold **7** Tasmania **8** Stratosphere and Troposphere **9** Glasgow **10** Sodom and Gomorah **11** Charles Bronson **12** Saturn **13** Sculling **14** Mountain Ash **15** Bip

1   A native of South Africa, what type of creature is a marabou?

2   What was the name of George Washington's very first railway locomotion?

3   What element was discovered in the Sun's atmosphere in 1869 by Sir Joseph Norman Lockyer?

4   Winnipeg is the capital of which Canadian province?

5   Hassan II became monarch of which African country in 1981?

6   Who, in 1865, founded the Salvation Army?

7   Which novel by Joseph Heller is set on a Mediterranean island of Pianosa?

8   A leveret is the young of which creature?

9   In the name of the singer B. B. King, what does the B. B. stand for?

10   Why did King John only seal the Magna Carta and not sign it?

11   What type of drink is Manzanilla?

12   In motor racing, what is signalled by a yellow flag?

13   Who wrote 'The Invisible Man'?

14   In which city is the TV series 'Friends' set?

15   What breed of dog, a member of the greyhound family, is also known as Arabian hound, or gazelle hound?

Answers 1 A type of stork 2 The Blucher 3 Helium 4 Manitoba 5 Morocco 6 William Booth 7 Catch 22 8 Hare 9 Blues Boy 10 He could not write 11 Sherry 12 Danger, no overtaking 13 H.G.Wells 14 New York 15 Saluki

Quiz 23

1   What is the capital of Romania?

2   'Summertime' is a song from which George Gershwin musical?

3   In which round in the 2000 Wimbledon tennis championships did Venus Williams defeat her sister Serena?

4   In what language does footballer David Beckham have his wife's name tattooed on his forearm?

5   What is said to be the 11th Commandment?

6   According to the song, sung by Gene Autry in 'Ride, Tenderfoot, Ride', in how many more months and days will I be out of the calaboose?

7   The film 'Sleepy Hollow', took its name from the novel 'The Legend of Sleepy Hollow', by which writer?

8   What creature was once called a camelopard because it resembled a cross between a camel and a leopard?

9   Edgar Degas specialised in paintings of which of the arts?

10 Who said about taking a course in speed reading: "I read War and Peace in ten minutes; its about Russia"?

11 What is referred to, and by whom, in a 1816 novel by Mary Wollstonecroft Shelley as, 'he is my Adam'?

12 What kind of creature is a meerkat?

13 Which character in 'The Arabian Nights' was the son of Mustafa the Tailor?

14 Which cartoon rooster of Warner Brother's cartoons said: "I say, I say howdy, son"?

15 Which boxer was portrayed by Paul Newman in the 1956 movie, 'Somebody Up There Likes Me'?

Answers 1 Bucharest 2 Porgy and Bess 3 Semi-final 4 Hindi 5 Thou shall not be found out 6 Eleven more months and ten more days 7 Washington Irving 8 Giraffe 9 Ballet 10 Woody Allen 11 Dr. Frankenstein referring to his monster 12 Mongoose 13 Aladdin 14 Foghorn J. Leghorn 15 Rocky Graziano

MISCELLANEOUS 2 *Quiz 24*

1 Who was Cock Robin's sweetheart in 'Who Killed Cock Robin'?

2 ...and who did kill Cock Robin?

3 ...and with what weapon?

4 In which decade of the 19th-century did Queen Victoria become Queen of England?

5 Who wrote the oft-quoted line: "A rose is a rose is a rose is a rose"?

6 Which American Civil War general led his famous march to the sea?

7 Which country always leads the Olympic procession at the opening ceremony?

8 Which romantic character created by novelist Gabriel Telleg is the main character of the opera 'Don Giovanni'?

9 The Latin name for which bird is *Pica Pica*?

10 At which US nuclear reactor did a nuclear accident occur in 1979?

11 How was the 2nd emperor of Rome, Claudius Nero Caesar better known?

12 What painter was portrayed in the 1956 movie 'Lust for Life' by Kirk Douglas?

13 Cape Verde is the most westerly point of which continent?

14 The wine marsala comes from which region of Italy?

15 The statue Christ of the Andes stands on the border between Argentina and which other country?

Answers 1 Miss Jenny Wren 2 The Sparrow 3 Bow and arrow 4 30s (1837) 5 Gertrude Stein 6 Sherman 7 Greece 8 Don Juan 9 Magpie 10 Three Mile Island 11 Tiberius 12 Van Gogh 13 Africa 14 Sicily 15 Chile

MISCELLANEOUS 2 — Quiz 25

1 Which American newspaper once carried the famously incorrect headline: "Dewey Defeats Truman"?

2 A stamp with the inscription Parsanes would be from which middle-east country?

3 The Nuggets (basketball) and Broncos (football) are major league teams of which US city?

4 The name of which bird would be used for a hole in one at a par four in golf?

5 Ga is the symbol for which element?

6 Who became Chancellor of Germany in 1982?

7 What type of dog is a Maltese?

8 In the Greek alphabet, what is the name for the letter O?

9 What, in the 16th-17th-century, was a pavana?

10 A nephron is the functional unit of which organ in the human body?

11 In which movie does Clint Eastwood play a disc jockey harassed by a disturbed fan?

12 Who is the patron saint of the impossible?

13 Which one of the James Brother's Wild West outlaw gang died peacefully at the age of 72, never having been convicted of a crime?

14 The final words of which American gangster and racketeer were: "The bullet hasn't been made that can kill me"?

15 The measurements of which Muppet Show character are 27-20-32?

Answers 1 Chicago Tribune 2 Iran 3 Denver 4 Albatross 5 Gallium 6 Helmut Kohl 7 Spaniel 8 Omicron 9 A dance 10 Kidney 11 Play Misty for Me 12 St. Jude 13 Frank 14 Legs Diamond 15 Miss Piggy

Quiz 26

1   Is the tree named in Latin, as *Fagus Sylvatica* ash, beech or elm?

2   Which ex-politician took part in his own play, 'The Accused', on the West End stage in 2000?

3   In which country in 2000 did the Mayon volcano erupt?

4   In the traditional rhyme, where would you ride to see a fine lady with rings on her fingers and bells on her toes?

5   In cookery, florentine means served with which vegetable?

6   Whom did Timothy Laurence marry in 1989?

7   In the book by Washington Irving, for how many years did Rip Van Winkle sleep?

8   Earl Hammer Jr. was the creator and narrator of which TV series?

9   What was the nickname of Meadow Lemon who was the famed clown member of the Harlem Globetrotters basketball team?

10 In which country in 1913 was actress Vivien Leigh born?

11 The second line of Verlaine's ode to which season is: 'pierce my heart with dull languor'?

12 What were the surnames of Shakespeare's Romeo and Juliet?

13 The Yucatan Channel lies between Cuba and which country on the American continent?

14 Which address in London is famous for being the fictional home of Sherlock Holmes?

15 Richard III was killed at which battle which ended the War of the Roses?

Answers 1 Beech 2 Jeffrey Archer 3 The Philippines 4 Banbury Cross 5 Spinach 6 Princess Anne 7 20 8 The Waltons 9 Meadowlark 10 India 11 Autumn 12 Montague and Capulet 13 Mexico 14 221B Baker Street 15 Bosworth Field

167

1 What nickname, meaning 'of great soul', was given to Indian leader Ghandi?

2 What does the K stand for in Jerome K. Jerome?

3 Which numbered train engine is mentioned in the song, 'On the Atchison, Topeka and the Santa Fe'?

4 Apart from Ford and Bush (twice), can you name the other two US presidents whose names only consisted of four letters?

5 Who was the grand daughter of William Randolph Hearst kidnapped by the SLA in 1974?

6 What type of clock was invented by Levi Hutchins in 1787?

7 In Shakespeare's 'Merchant of Venice', who would not have given a ring for a wilderness of monkeys?

8 What is the more common name of the flowering plant *helianthus*?

9 In which sport might you assume the egg position?

10 What was the name of the first space station?

11 Which of Jesus Christ's twelve apostles committed suicide?

12 Who created the fairy tale character Red Riding Hood?

13 Which Hungarian-born composer was the father-in-law of Richard Wagner?

14 Who is the wayward woman in Somerset Maugham's novel 'Rain', who is stranded on the Pacific Island of Pago Pago?

15 What was the name of the 'golden lion' which appeared in several 'Tarzan' books?

Answers 1 Mahatma 2 Klapka 3 Engine 49 4 Polk and Taft 5 Patty Hearst 6 The alarm clock 7 Shylock 8 Sunflower 9 Skiing 10 Skylab 11 Judas Iscariot 12 The Brothers Grimm 13 Franz Liszt 14 Sadie Thompson 15 Jad-Bal-Ja

1   The 10th President of the USA was the first to get married in office. Can you name him?

2   Ultra was the British code name for which German cipher machine?

3   Who, in a book by E. Nesbit, are Peter, Phyllis and Roberta?

4   What was the pseudonym of the French writer and philosopher Francois Marie Arouet?

5   In the very first message over the telephone, who said: "Mr Watson, come here, I need you"?

6   What aquatic creature killed John Wayne in the 1943 movie 'Reap the Wild Wind'?

7   How was Arthur Wellesley, who lived from 1769-1852 better known?

8   What is the capital of Jamaica?

9   What is the name of Tony Blair's only daughter?

10 What did Liam Gallagher and ex-wife Patsy Kensit name their son, in tribute to a pop music icon?

11 What in area is the largest country in Africa?

12 Which is the world's largest bay?

13 'Where's the Rest of Me' is the autobiography of which US president?

14 How many pounds are there in a hundredweight?

15 Which movie shares with 'Ben Hur' the distinction of winning 11 Oscars?

Answers 1 John Tyler 2 Enigma 3 The Railway Children 4 Voltaire 5 Alexander Graham Bell (Thomas Watson was his assistant) 6 An octopus 7 The Duke of Wellington 8 Kingston 9 Kathryn 10 Lennon 11 Sudan 12 Hudson 13 Ronald Reagan 14 112 15 Titanic

MISCELLANEOUS 2 — Quiz 29

1   What is the name of the Reverend in the game of Cluedo?

2   In which country is Disappointment Lake?

3   The song 'Any Dream Will Do' is from which Andrew Lloyd-Webber/Tim Rice musical?

4   What are the colours of the three vertical stripes on the flag of France?

5   Which Shakespeare play opens with the lines: 'Now is the winter of our discontent made glorious summer'?

6   Jill and Hob are the female and male of which creature?

7   At 77 who became America's oldest astronaut?

8   What first was achieved by Sally Ride in 1983?

9   What is the name of the aromatic gum resin obtained from trees of the genus *Boswellia*?

10   Who was the chief rabbit in the book 'Watership Down'?

11   What is the name of the Japanese dish of vinegared rice with raw fish?

12   In what type of building did the St.Valentine's Day massacre take place?

13   Who wrote 'Northanger Abbey'?

14   Cinnabar is the main ore of which metal?

15   What is the official name of New York's Sixth Avenue?

Answers 1 Green 2 Australia 3 Joseph and His Amazing Technicolour Dreamcoat 4 Blue, white, red 5 Richard III 6 Ferret 7 John Glenn 8 First US woman in space 9 Frankincense 10 Hazel 11 Sushi 12 A garage 13 Jane Austen 14 Mercury 15 Avenue of the Americas

MISCELLANEOUS 2
Quiz 30

1   Why is Easter Island so named?

2   In the Bible, which king was the son of David and Bathsheba?

3   Who was the Persian who wrote the classic poem 'The Rubaiyat'?

4   The colony of Pennsylvania was founded by which Quaker in 1681?

5   Which Venetian explorer in the 14th-century travelled to China where he became a diplomat for Kublai Khan?

6   What is another name for the meerkat?

7   Which part of the human body is studied by a phrenologist?

8   First sold in 1878, what became the registered trademark for petroleum jelly?

9   What sport takes place annually at the Henley Regatta?

10 Which English king fought at the Battle of Agincourt?

11 Besides his prolific output of music, how many children did J.S. Bach find time to father; was it 5, 10, 15 or 20?

12 'The Descent of Man' was the subsequent volume to which influential book by Charles Darwin?

13 In 1888, who was the first person to market a camera simple enough for an amateur to operate?

14 Which rock 'n' roll icon's first hit was 'Tutti Frutti' in 1955?

15 What is crystallomancy another name for?

Answers 1 It was discovered on Easter Sunday **2** Solomon **3** Omar Khayyam **4** William Penn **5** Marco Polo **6** The Suricate **7** Skull **8** Vaseline **9** Rowing **10** Henry V **11** 20 **12** The Origin of Species **13** George Eastman **14** Little Richard **15** Crystal gazing

MISCELLANEOUS 2 — Quiz 31

1 Which actor played the lead in 'The Asphalt Jungle'?

2 In 'The Arabian Nights', where were the Forty Thieves hiding when Ali Baba's female slave Morgiana poured hot oil on them?

3 Who was Dictator-president of Uganda from 1971-79?

4 What was discovered by aviator James Angel while he was flying over Venezuela in 1935?

5 What is the nickname of Jack Dawkins in Charles Dicken's 'Oliver Twist'?

6 A Baldwin is a famous make of which musical instrument?

7 Which famous novel was written in 1924 by Percival Christopher Wren, an ex-member of the French Foreign Legion?

8 Which dish, consisting of chicken, peas and carrots in a white sauce was created by Thomas Jefferson, 3rd US President?

9 Who was the father of Luke Skywalker in the 'Star Wars' film?

10 On which date in Britain does the Summer solstice occur?

11 Where do arboreal animals live?

12 What is the traditional meaning of the surname Mercer?

13 A doe is the female of which creatures?

14 What is meant by the phrase *hic et ubique*?

15 Which mythological animal had the body and head of a woman and the feet and wings of a vulture?

Answers 1 Sterling Hayden 2 In large jars 3 Idi Amin 4 The Angel Falls (the world's highest waterfall) 5 The Artful Dodger 6 Piano 7 Beau Geste 8 Chicken-a-la-King 9 Darth Vader 10 June 21 11 In trees 12 Textile dealer 13 Rabbit and deer 14 Here and everywhere 15 Harpy

1   What is the literal meaning of the word 'Kremlin'?

2   Where in the US would you find the inscription: "Give me you tired, your poor; your huddled masses; yearning to breathe free"?

3   What in 17th-century India did the Emperor Shah Jahan build for his wife Mumtaz?

4   Traditionally what does a cooper manufacture?

5   What is meant by the musical term *allargando*: agitatedly, becoming faster or becoming slower?

6   In what type of auction is the price progressively lowered until a buyer accepts?

7   The stars Caster and Pollux are in which constellation in the night sky?

8   What A is also known as an idiot board?

9   What does a cutler make, sell or repair?

10 For how many years in Genesis 5:27 was Methuselah said to have lived?

11 What is the fruit of the plant *citrus aurantum*?

12 The Pentathlon consists of running, riding, fencing, swimming and which other sport?

13 What Cistercian order of monks are noted for their austerity and vow of silence?

14 The Yak is a native of which region of the world?

15 What is the name given to pedestrian light-controlled crossing?

Answers 1 Citadel **2** On the Statue of Liberty **3** Taj Mahal **4** Barrels **5** Becoming slower **6** Dutch **7** Gemini **8** Autocue **9** Knives **10** 969 years **11** Orange **12** Pistol shooting **13** Trappist **14** Tibet **15** Pelican crossing

MISCELLANEOUS 2 — Quiz 33

1   In which London borough are the Houses of Parliament situated?

2   What did George Eliot describe as: 'snowy, flowy, blowy, showery, flowery, bowery, hoppy, croppy, droppy, breezy, sneezy and freezy'?

3   What in the human body is the more common name for the trachea?

4   Which creature sold a ring to the Owl and the Pussycat for a shilling?

5   The resorts of Tremezzo and Menaggio are on the shores of which Italian lake?

6   Which of the tropics lies immediately to the north of Cuba; Cancer or Capricorn?

7   Found in the Premier Diamond mine in Transvaal in 1905, what is the name of the largest diamond ever found?

8   Whose law states that work expands so as to fill the time available for its completion?

9   In Britain it is a chemist's shop, what is it in the USA?

10 What in aviation is meant by the abbreviation, STOL?

11 What is the more common name of Dvorak's 'Symphony No. 9'?

12 Who created the character Noddy?

13 How many years marriage are celebrated by a pearl anniversary?

14 Which British army was victorious at the Battle of El Alamein?

15 Which Indian statesman had the nickname Pandit?

Answers 1 Westminster 2 The months of the year 3 Windpipe 4 Pig 5 Como 6 Cancer 7 Cullinan 8 Parkinson's Law 9 A drug store 10 Short Take Off and Landing 11 New World 12 Enid Blyton 13 Thirty 14 Eighth 15 Nehru

1   The women of which religion wear a yashmak in public?

2   What is the provincial capital of Nova Scotia?

3   In legend, who rode a sea-horse called a hippocampus?

4   Into what state do Just Souls go, which are barred from heaven through not being baptised?

5   Who was the first king of Rome?

6   In which month of the year does the American Superbowl final take place?

7   To Westerners, what is Hatha the most common form of?

8   What female Christian name means 'wished for child'?

9   Who is supposed to have said: "Eureka! (I have it)"?

10 Which people are organised politically into the modern Inkatha movement?

11 What eight-letter word beginning with 'A' are the words 'post' and 'stop'?

12 In the Christian calendar, what name is given to the twelfth day after Christmas?

13 What measure is equal to 4 inches of a horse's height?

14 What is hypegiaphobia the fear of?

15 Which North American river was a major transportation route during the Klondike gold rush?

Answers 1 Muslim **2** Halifax **3** Neptune **4** Limbo **5** Romulus **6** January **7** Yoga **8** Mary **9** Archimedes **10** Zulus **11** Anagrams **12** Epiphany **13** Hand **14** Responsibility **15** Yukon

MISCELLANEOUS 2   *Quiz 35*

1 What is meant by the prefix 'geo'?
2 Which female Christian name is the Cornish form of Guinevere?
3 What type of ape lives on the Rock of Gibraltar?
4 What game was invented by Anthony Pratt of Birmingham, England in 1943?
5 What do Americans call a dinner jacket?
6 Which group of stars in the night sky represents a hunter with belt and sword?
7 What R is the North American caribou a type of?
8 Which country was formerly called Northern Rhodesia?
9 What is the sweet liqueur made of raw egg yolks and brandy?
10 What is the homophone for sail?
11 Who was the founder of the religious sect 'The Plymouth Brethren'?
12 What E is the technique of which Rembrandt was the greatest master?
13 What is the pseudonym of the British detective story writer Phyllis Dorothy White?
14 Which fruit is also called Chinese gooseberry?
15 Of what is triskaidekaphobia the fear?

1 What is the name of the river sacred to Hindus?

2 The name of what place in Scotland lends its name to a dish of small whole haddock, hot smoked to a brown colour?

3 What is the US term for the game of noughts and crosses?

4 The eggs of which fish are used to produce caviar?

5 Who was the founder of the British police force from whom the term 'bobby' is obtained?

6 What was the name of the many-headed monster in Greek legend, killed by Heracles, which grew two more heads whenever one was cut off?

7 A mandrill is a type of what creature?

8 What is the largest city in Switzerland?

9 Which Wagner opera is based on the legend of a 13th-century poet's seduction by Venus?

10 In Morse Code, which letter is represented by . - (dot/dash)?

11 What is the name of the muscular tissue in the eye that surrounds the pupil and is situated immediately in front of the lens?

12 Which mythological creature had the head and wings of an eagle, the body of a lion and a serpent's tail?

13 In the Old Testament, which two cities of Palestine were known as the cities of the plain?

14 Which Athenian philosopher was condemned to die by drinking hemlock?

15 In which part of the human body are the olfactory glands?

Answers 1 Ganges 2 Arbroath Smokie 3 Tick-tack-toe 4 Sturgeon 5 Sir Robert Peel 6 Hydra 7 Monkey 8 Zurich 9 Tannhauser 10 A 11 Iris 12 Griffon 13 Sodom and Gomorrah 14 Socrates 15 Nose

MISCELLANEOUS 2   Quiz 37

1   In a game of table tennis (ping pong), the winner is of a game is the first to reach what total by 2 clear points?

2   What is the name given the aquatic larva of frogs and toads?

3   In which country is the seaport of Trieste?

4   Who were the priestesses of the goddess Vesta who tended the eternal fire at her shrine in Rome?

5   Into which continent is the Waddell Sea a large inlet of the South Atlantic ocean?

6   In which city in America is the Guggenheim museum?

7   Whose over-flattering portrait of Anne of Cleves resulted in Henry VIII agreeing to marry her before he had even met her?

8   Which musical instrument is played by both exhaling and inhaling?

9   Porcine is the adjective for which animal?

10   What would be cultivated in an arboretum?

11   Arcadia was an idyllic rural region of which country?

12   Who recorded the 1972 album 'Ziggy Stardust'?

13   In boxing, what weight comes between flyweight and featherweight?

14   Which are the highest type of clouds, stratocumulus or cirrus?

15   The name of which rebellion in China in 1900 was so called because the rebels belonging to a secret society were named the Fists of Righteous Harmony?

Answers 1 21 2 Tadpole 3 Italy 4 The Vestal Virgins 5 Antarctica 6 New York 7 Holbein 8 Harmonica (or mouth organ) 9 Pig 10 Trees 11 Greece 12 David Bowie 13 Bantamweight 14 Cirrus 15 Boxer Rebellion

1   Which American president had the first names Stephen Grover?

2   In the 14th-century, the nickname of which Prince of Wales referred to the colour of armour he was said to have worn at the Battle of Crecy?

3   The Quetzal is the unit of currency of which Central American country?

4   What is a Hunter's band a type of?

5   Whose picture in England in World War I appeared on recruiting posters with the slogan 'Your Country Needs You'?

6   Which European capital city stands on the River Pedieas?

7   What is the name given to the ninth month of the Muslim year?

8   Who wrote 'The Prime of Miss Jean Brodie'?

9   What is the common name of the small carnivorous mammal, *Mustele erminea*?

10 Which former British Prime Minister was created the 1st Earl of Stockton?

11 Which Russian became the youngest ever world chess champion at the age of 22 in 1985?

12 Which is the only US state that shares a border with just one other state?

13 Kicking Horse Pass is a pass through which range of mountains?

14 A colotatura is a type of which singing voice?

15 In the First World War, a doughboy was an infantryman of which country?

Answers 1 Cleveland **2** Edward, the Black Prince **3** Guatemala **4** Knot **5** Lord Kitchener **6** Nicosia (Cyprus) **7** Ramadan **8** Muriel Spark **9** Stoat **10** Harold MacMillan **11** Gary Kasparov **12** Maine **13** The Rockies **14** Soprano **15** USA

1   Which ancient measure of length was based on the length of the arm from fingertip to elbow?

2   Which American tree-dwelling marsupial reputedly deters predators by pretending to be dead?

3   Which Italian actor was the star of Fellini's 'La Dolce Vita' (1961) and Antonioni's 'La Notte' (1961)?

4   Which ship carried the Pilgrim Fathers to America?

5   Which city in Saudi Arabia is the birthplace of Mohammed?

6   What was the name of the official bodyguard of Roman emperors created by Augustus in 27BC?

7   What was designed by Thomas Sheraton?

8   Where, in London, is there a track for riding horses called Rotten Row?

9   Of what is dendrochronology a method of dating?

10 After World War I, Transylvania became part of which country?

11 What is the name given to travellers in a group or convoy, especially through a desert?

12 In which country is Tangiers?

13 The names of which couple in an 18th-century English ballad can now refer to any devoted elderly married couple?

14 What in the bible is the Decalogue?

15 A pibroch is a set of martial or funeral musical variations played on which instrument?

Answers 1 Cubit 2 Possum (or opossum) 3 Marcello Mastroianni 4 The Mayflower 5 Mecca 6 Praetorian Guard 7 Furniture 8 Hyde Park 9 Trees 10 Romania 11 Caravan 12 Morocco 13 Derby and Joan 14 The Ten Commandments 15 Bagpipes

Quiz 40

1 Ipswich is the administrative centre of which English county?

2 Who is the narrator in most of Conan Doyle's 'Sherlock Holmes' short stories and novels?

3 What is the US name for what in Britain is known as the game of draughts?

4 Fyns is the second largest island of which country?

5 What type of creature is a harvestman?

6 Which Austrian composer wrote 'The Creation' in 1798?

7 Which breed of dog for herding sheep and cattle, and developed in Australia, was named after a champion sheepdog of the 1870s?

8 Formed by Kenneth MacAlpine in the 9th-century, the kingdom of Alba was the foundation of which modern country?

9 In the New Testament, the Apostles were mainly written by which saint?

10 What was the first capital of the USA from 1789 to 1790?

11 What C is a gas used in welding and as a chemical weapon and rocket propellant?

12 What is meant by the Latin phrase *in vitro*?

13 Which metal, similar to iron and noted for its deep-blue colour is used as an alloy in the manufacture of cutting steels and magnets?

14 In which decade did Walt Disney open his Disneyland amusement park in California?

15 In Africa, what type of animal is a dik-dik?

Answers 1 Suffolk **2** Dr Watson **3** Checkers **4** Denmark **5** Spider **6** Haydn **7** Kelpie **8** Scotland **9** St.Paul **10** New York **11** Cyanogen **12** In an artificial environment **13** Cobalt **14** 1950s (1955) **15** Antelope

MISCELLANEOUS 2 — Quiz 41

1   Which country was originally called Staten Land when it was discovered in the 17th-century?

2   Which one of the 12 Apostles of the New Testament is symbolised by loaves in medieval art because of his participation in the miracle of loaves and fishes?

3   How, in the 16/17th-century was the Scottish outlaw Robert McGregor better known?

4   What is the US term for a gramophone?

5   Who, in Greek mythology, was the messenger and herald of the gods?

6   In British royalty, who is the youngest daughter of King George VI?

7   In Australia, the state of New South Wales borders on which ocean?

8   Which European capital city was formerly called Kristiana?

9   What was the name of the son of the novelist A.A. Milne who was the inspiration for his books?

10   No is a form of theatre in which country?

11   What form of calcium sulphate is used for casts for broken limbs?

12   The Cutty Sark is a famous ship now moored at Greenwich in London. In the 18th-century this ship was used to bring which product from China?

13   Which planet is furthest from earth, Mars or Venus?

14   In which country is the African port of Mogadishu?

15   Which woman, the subject of a book of the Old Testament, became Queen of the Persian King Ahasuerus and used her influence to frustrate a plot to massacre Persian Jews?

Answers 1 New Zealand 2 St. Philip 3 Rob Roy 4 Phonograph 5 Hermes 6 Princess Margaret 7 Pacific 8 Oslo 9 Christopher Robin 10 Japan 11 Plaster of Paris 12 Tea 13 Mars 14 Somalia 15 Esther

182

1 Which is the largest national park in the USA?
2 Which actress, in the film 'All About Eve', said: "Fasten your seatbelts, its going to be a bumpy night"?
3 Goulash is a traditional stew in which country?
4 Beth, waw, mem and shim are all letters in which alphabet?
5 What did Thomas Moule publish in the 19th-century?
6 In which prison was Rudolf Hess imprisoned up to his death in 1987?
7 Who was the British admiral after whom the inn in the novel 'Treasure Island' was named?
8 Who, in Roman mythology, was the wife of Jupiter?
9 In Greek mythology, who opened the box releasing all the evils into the world?
10 Which member of the cat family found on the American continent is otherwise known as puma, mountain lion, catamount and panther?
11 Which is the world's largest snake?
12 What sport, apart from skiing takes place on a piste?
13 Who is the patron saint of carpenters?
14 What does a twitcher watch out for?
15 Of what are Pitmanscript, Gregg and Teeline types of?

Answers 1 Yellowstone 2 Bette Davis 3 Hungary 4 Hebrew 5 Maps 6 Spandau 7 Benbow 8 Juno 9 Pandora 10 Cougar 11 Anaconda 12 Fencing 13 St. Joseph 14 Birds 15 Shorthand

1   Which sports stadium in New York is affectionately known as the house that Babe Ruth built?

2   Of what is pedology the study?

3   Copra is the dried kernel of which fruit?

4   What L is the eyepiece or magnifying glass as used by a jeweller?

5   Who wrote 'Lucia d'Lammermoor'?

6   What are you doing if you are in a state of erubescence?

7   Discovered by Gallileo in 1610, Europa is the second natural satellite of which planet?

8   What D does a nyctophobiac fear?

9   In which classic book are there a race of brutish ape-like people called Yahoos?

10   What R is the active form of vitamin A found in margarines, oily fish and dairy fats?

11   Orly airport is to the south of which city?

12   What is a 'quizzing glass' an archaic term for?

13   Which element has the atomic No. 40 and the symbol Zr?

14   Who was the giant watchman in Greek mythology with 100 eyes?

15   Mossad is the secret service of which country?

Answers 1 The Yankee Stadium 2 Soil 3 Coconut 4 Loupe 5 Donizetti 6 Blushing 7 Jupiter 8 Dark 9 Gulliver's Travels 10 Retinol 11 Paris 12 Monocle 13 Zirconium 14 Argos 15 Israel

1 In which mythological country did C.S. Lewis set his novel, 'The Lion, The Witch and the Wardrobe'?

2 Whom, in AD62 did Poppaea marry?

3 Which male Christian name, beginning with O, is the Italian form of Roland?

4 What is the name of the tower of volcanic rock in Wyoming used as a setting for the movie 'Close Encounters of the Third Kind'?

5 What surname is shared by US artist James Abbott McNeil and British artist Rex?

6 What would be studied by a vulcanologist?

7 Which British TV comedy was set in a fictional prison called Slade?

8 Which US general was nicknamed Black Jack, and gave his name to a nuclear missile?

9 Which strong, brown type of wrapping paper's name is taken from the German word for strength?

10 What shape is cordate?

11 What do xylophagous insects eat?

12 What is an Eskimo's nukluk a type of?

13 Found especially in a river, what is an eyot?

14 What do Americans call what the British refer to as an estate agent?

15 What was the name of King David's father in the Bible?

MISCELLANEOUS 2   *Quiz 45*

1 In which film did Julie Andrews play Gertrude Lawrence?

2 What is a Morris column used for?

3 What is the common name for the condition myopia?

4 Peter Noone was the leader of which pop group who were at the height of their popularity in the 1960s?

5 'The Rainbow' was the prequel to which D.H. Lawrence novel?

6 In which great bay are the Nicobar Islands?

7 A skulk is the collective noun for which creature?

8 In 1986, Greg Le Mond was the first non-European to win which annual sporting event?

9 Bartlett, comice and conference are types of what fruit?

10 Which US male singer had a hit with 'Piece of the Action' in 1985?

11 The Elgin Marbles, now in the British Museum, were originally taken from which building?

12 In which film did Yul Brynner play King Mong Kat?

13 What did my true love give to me on the 8th day of Christmas?

14 What in the human body are controlled by the lumbrical muscles?

15 In Shakespeare's 'A Midsummer Night's Dream', who is the Queen of the Fairies?

Answers 1 Star 2 Advertisements 3 Short-sightedness 4 Herman's Hermits 5 Women in Love 6 Bay of Bengal 7 Fox 8 Tour de France 9 Pear 10 Meat Loaf 11 The Parthenon in Greece 12 The King and I 13 8 maids-a-milking 14 Finger movement 15 Titania

Quiz 46

1 Through what on their body do fish breathe?

2 Which patron saint of the British Isles does not have his cross on the Union Jack?

3 Which French novelist wrote 'Madame Bovary'?

4 How many players are there in a women's lacrosse team?

5 Which instrument derives its name from the fact that it can be played soft or loud according to the pressure on the keys?

6 What is the third colour of the rainbow?

7 What day in the Church calendar is the first day of Lent and a day of special public sorrow for sin?

8 On the Fahrenheit scale, what temperature is boiling point?

9 The tapir is a native of what continent?

10 What country would you first reach if you travelled south-east from Sicily?

11 Who in Greek legend is the youth who fell in love with his own reflected image?

12 On a Plimsoll line, what is meant by the abbreviation WNA?

13 Who wrote 'Ode to a Grecian Urn'?

14 What is the name of the hard resin, used in varnishing, which is produced on the bark of trees by insects?

15 In the 19th-century, Paul Kruger was president of which country?

Answers 1 Gills **2** St. David **3** Gustave Flaubert **4** 12 **5** Pianoforte **6** Yellow **7** Ash Wednesday **8** 212 **9** South America **10** Tunisia **11** Narcissus **12** Winter North Atlantic **13** Keats **14** Shellac **15** South Africa

MISCELLANEOUS 2 — Quiz 47

1 What is the name of the British territory on the Iberian Peninsula?

2 Which sweet, syrupy, organic liquid is the basis of all fats and oils, and is also used in the manufacture of explosives?

3 The letters RF on a stamp would indicate it is from which country?

4 In which country does the River Rhine rise?

5 On which part of the body do grasshoppers have their ears?

6 Which of the Seven Wonders of the Ancient World was at Alexandria?

7 In which ocean does Iceland lie?

8 Which future US president was born in a small log cabin in Kentucky in 1809?

9 What is the meaning of the musical term cantabile?

10 San Juan is the capital of which island in the West Indies?

11 In which Eastern European country would you find the town of Ploesti and the port of Constantsa?

12 Which snake is used by Indian snake charmers to sway to music of their pipes?

13 Which profession gets its name from the Latin word for lead?

14 Which Christian denomination was started in 1799 by John and Charles Wesley?

15 Which of the disciples of Jesus was the brother of Andrew, and a fisherman?

Answers 1 Gibraltar **2** Glycerine **3** France **4** Switzerland **5** Hind legs **6** The lighthouse **7** Atlantic **8** Lincoln **9** In a singing style **10** Puerto Rico **11** Rumania **12** Cobra **13** Plumbing **14** Methodist **15** Simon Peter

MISCELLANEOUS 2 *Quiz 48*

1   What nationality was composer Franz Schubert?

2   Snake-necked and Hawk's Bill are kinds of what creature?

3   Which imaginary island was created by Sir Thomas More in 1516?

4   What city on the shores of the Mediterranean Sea was originally a Greek colony called Massilia?

5   What is the name of the flat circular disc of vulcanised rubber used in the game of ice-hockey?

6   What, in Japan, are Hokkaido, Shikoko and Kyushu?

7   What part of Robert Jenkin's anatomy caused a war between England and Spain in 1751?

8   How, in Russia, in the 19th and early 20th-century was Vladimir Ilyich Ulyanov better known?

9   What was the pen name of Mrs Bland, a children's writer, several of her books being about the Bastable family?

10 What is the nearest relative of the cassowary?

11 Quicklime is an alkaline powder obtained by strongly heating which other material?

12 What type of creature is a blue beveren?

13 Which French king, who reigned from 1643-1715, professed to hold his power from God and is supposed to have said: "*L'etat c'est moi*" (I am the State)?

14 The story of the Pied Piper took place in which German town?

15 What is the name of the three-headed dog that in classical mythology guards the entrance to Hades?

Answers 1 Austrian 2 Turtle 3 Utopia 4 Marseilles 5 Puck 6 Islands 7 His ear 8 Lenin 9 E. Nesbit 10 Ostrich 11 Chalk 12 Rabbit 13 Louis XIV 14 Hamelin 15 Cerberus

MISCELLANEOUS 2 — Quiz 49

1 What is the name given to a writ, issued to the official in charge of a detained person, to bring him before a court to investigate the lawfulness of the detention?

2 Who in the Bible was the son of Isaac and the brother of Esau?

3 Who is the mighty hunter of Greek mythology recognised by his girdle, sword and club?

4 The name of what piece of music means, literally, an opening?

5 Sir Walter Scott's novel 'Kenilworth' is set during the reign of which British monarch?

6 The country of Peru is on the shores of which ocean?

7 If a person is defranchised, what has he lost his right to do?

8 Who was the first man to transmit speech by electricity?

9 How many hoops are there in a croquet game?

10 The Duckbilled Platypus is a native of which country?

11 What is the popular name for the most north-easterly part of Great Britain?

12 Who painted the Adoration of the Magi?

13 Which letter in Morse code is represented by – – (dash dash)?

14 The port of Agadir is in which country?

15 What colour is sulphur?

Answers 1 Habeas Corpus 2 Jacob 3 Orion 4 Overture 5 Elizabeth I 6 Pacific 7 The Right to vote 8 Alexander Graham Bell 9 6 10 Australia 11 John o'Groats 12 Leonardo Da Vinci 13 M 14 Morocco 15 Yellow

1   Coal and longtailed are types of which bird family?

2   William IV was the uncle of which monarch?

3   What chemical substance is formed by the interaction of an acid and a base?

4   In the Christian church, Maundy Thursday commemorates which event?

5   Who, in mythology, was the father of Romulus, the founder of Rome?

6   What is the modern name of the rocky fortress which the Moors named Gabel-al-Tarik (the Rock of Tarik)?

7   Which alloy of tin and lead was originally used for making plates and mugs?

8   In a Plimsoll line, what is meant by the abbreviation TF?

9   Which of the Bronte sisters wrote 'The Tenant of Wildfell Hall'?

10 The ounce is another name for what type of leopard?

11 What nationality was the composer Chopin?

12 In the game of darts, what is the value of the outer bull?

13 In a famous carol, which town is known as Royal David's City?

14 In which part of the human body is the cochlea?

15 With which three countries does Luxembourg share borders?

Answers 1 Tit **2** Victoria **3** Salt **4** The institution of Holy Communion at the Last Supper **5** Mars **6** Gibraltar **7** Pewter **8** Tropical Freshwater **9** Anne **10** Snow leopard **11** Polish **12** 25 **13** Bethlehem **14** Ear **15** Belgium, France, Germany

MISCELLANEOUS 2 — Quiz 51

1   Who was the famous monster of Greek legend, part woman, part beast, who dwelt near Thebes?

2   What nationality was Jonathan Swift, who wrote 'Gulliver's Travels'?

3   What is the name of the milky fluid obtained from trees which is used to produce rubber?

4   The molecule of what substance contains two hydrogen atoms and one oxygen atom?

5   Of what is entymology the study?

6   Of where is Amman the capital?

7   The republics if Estonia, Latvia and Lithuania border the shores of which sea?

8   How many innings are there for each team in a game of baseball?

9   Which is the only mammal with the power of active flight?

10 In which English county is Lizard Point?

11 What is the name given to the clusters of flowers born by trees such as hazel, birch and oak?

12 In chess, which piece can move diagonally in a straight line but keeping to the colour of the square on which it starts?

13 What point of the compass comes midway between WbW and WbN?

14 Who was the commander-in-chief of the Greeks in the Trojan War who was murdered by his wife Clytemnestra?

15 Which lower level of clouds are commonly called 'rain clouds'?

Answers 1 Sphinx **2** English (he was born and educated in Dublin, but both his parents were English, making him English also) **3** Latex **4** Water **5** Insects **6** Jordan **7** Baltic **8** 9 **9** Bat **10** Cornwall **11** Catkins **12** Bishop **13** WNW **14** Agamemnon **15** Nimbus

1   Cider is the fermented juice of which fruit?

2   What ancient Roman silver coin was called a penny in the New Testament, its first letter being used as a symbol for a pre-decimal British penny?

3   Pomelo or Shaddock are alternative names for which type of fruit?

4   In Classical mythology, how are Aglia, Thalia and Euphrosyne better known?

5   Storthing is the parliament of which European country?

6   Which American university is in Newhaven, Connecticut?

7   Grevy's and Chapman's are two species of which animal, native to Africa?

8   Sanskrit was an old literary language of which country?

9   Which carnivorous American animal, related to the bear, lives in trees, moves about at night and has a long black and white ringed tail?

10   What is a quassia a type of?

11   Which month is named after the Latin goddess of growth and increase?

12   Which iron ore, an oxide of iron, is named in Greek after its blood-red colour?

13   Which star in the constellation Little Bear is, when visible, an indication of practically true north?

14   What name, meaning fiftieth (day), is given to the Sunday prior to the beginning of Lent?

15   What food fish is the young of herrings and sprat?

Answers 1 Apples 2 Denarius 3 Grapefruit 4 The Three Graces 5 Norway 6 Yale 7 Zebra 8 India 9 Racoon 10 Tree 11 May (Maia) 12 Haematite 13 Polaris (Pole Star) 14 Quinquagesima 15 Whitebait

1   Which 61 mile long canal links the Baltic and North Seas?

2   How many pieces does each player have in the game of backgammon?

3   Which metric unit of weight was originally the weight of a cubic centimetre of distilled water at freezing point?

4   The Menai Bridge links Wales with which island?

5   The Angel Falls are on which Venezuelan river?

6   The wildebeest is known by which other name, once immortalised in a song by Michael Flanders and Donald Swan?

7   What is the name given to the equinox which occurs around 21st June?

8   Of what are Mechlin, Valenciennes and Honiton types?

9   What nautical measurement is the speed of one sea-mile per hour?

10   What is the name of a stoat in its white winter coat?

11   The Incas were the hereditary rulers of which South American country?

12   Which bird of the stork family, common in Central Africa, was a sacred bird to the Ancient Egyptians?

13   Which Greek epic poem describes the siege of Troy?

14   What instrument is used in land surveying for measuring vertical and horizontal angles?

15   In the early part of the 20th-century, the Olympic was the sister ship of which White Star liner?

Quiz 54

1   What was the name of the Scandinavian God of Poetry?

2   The mocking bird is a member of which family of birds?

3   In which country is Mount Logan?

4   In London, The Monument, a 202 feet high Doric column near the north end of London Bridge, was erected to commemorate which event?

5   Which American anthem is sung to the tune of the British National anthem, 'God Save the Queen'?

6   What name is given to the period of four years between each Olympic Games?

7   The Sea Elephant is the largest of what type of creature?

8   Who were the wandering poets and minstrels of Southern France who flourished in the 11-13th centuries?

9   What name is given to violent circular storms in the China Seas?

10 Which branch of mathematics deals with the relation of angles and sides of triangles to one another?

11 Carbuncle is a less valuable type of which gemstone?

12 What is another more common name for a Gazelle Hound, which is believed to be one of the breeds Noah collected into the Ark?

13 Which great palace, built in the 16/17th-centuries at Paris, has now disappeared except for wings connected to the Louvre?

14 Which green poisonous deposit forms on copper with the action of acids?

15 What planet is also known as Evening Star or Morning Star?

MISCELLANEOUS 2   Quiz 55

1   What hot, parching wind blows from the Sahara in a northerly direction over the Mediterranean and Southern Europe?

2   Which metallic element has the property of catching fire if dropped in hot water?

3   Which is the largest member of the dog family?

4   What form of defence in a criminal prosecution is a Latin word meaning elsewhere?

5   Apart from America, which is the only other country in the world to which alligators are native?

6   What to a Native American Indian is a calumet?

7   The Ancient Greek town of Delphi, famous for the Temple of Apollo, was on the south slope of which mountain?

8   What is the famous series of stories written in the 14th-century by the Italian Boccaccio?

9   What is the name of the square cap worn by Roman Catholic and some Anglican clerics?

10 Which month of the year obtains its name from the Latin verb for 'to open'?

11 Which artery carries blood from the right ventricle to the lungs?

12 Which is the highest register of male voice, which enables the singer to reach notes higher than with his natural voice?

13 The peregrine is a type of which bird?

14 What on a ship is a jib?

15 What title was formerly given to the Emperors of Germany and Austria?

Answers 1 Sirocco 2 Sodium 3 The Wolf 4 Alibi 5 China 6 A pipe of peace 7 Mount Parnassus 8 Decameron 9 Biretta 10 April 11 The pulmonary artery 12 Falsetto 13 Falcon 14 A sail 15 Kaiser

1   Who became president of Poland in 1990?

2   Who invented the internal combustion engine?

3   Ronald Reagan shares his middle name with the last name of which 20th-century British Prime Minister?

4   Salt Lake City is the capital of which US state?

5   Which movie star who died in 1995 was known as the 'sweater girl'?

6   In India, what is a durzi?

7   Who won best actor Oscar in 1985 for his role in 'Kiss of the Spider Woman'?

8   Who, in 1814, wrote the poem 'The Star Spangled Banner'?

9   What was developed in 1989 by Tim Berners-Lee, a British computer specialist?

10   What bird is a merganser a type of?

11   If pentad is a group of five, how many is ennead a group of?

12   In the Bible, who was the father of Cain, Abel and Seth?

13   Which former Wimbledon tennis champion was born in Weisbaden, Germany on 16 February, 1959?

14   What were the first names of the two brothers Grimm, famous for their fairy tales?

15   What is the birthstone for April?

Answers 1 Lech Walesa 2 Rudolf Deisel 3 Wilson 4 Utah 5 Lana Turner 6 A tailor 7 William Hurt 8 Francis Scott Key 9 The World Wide Web 10 Duck 11 Nine 12 Adam 13 John McEnroe 14 Jacob and Wilhelm 15 Diamond

1   The name of which month of the year means (in Latin) the month of purification?

2   Who played Charlie Allnut, the boat owner, in the movie 'The African Queen'?

3   What was the name of the Illinois Central express on which Casey Jones lost his life in 1900?

4   On what, in America, would you find the inscription: 'Proclaim Liberty throughout all the land unto all their inhabitants thereof'?

5   ...and from which book of the Bible is the quotation obtained?

6   How, in the world of entertainment, were LaVerne, Patti and Maxine better known in the 1940s and 1950s?

7   Who won best actress Oscar in 1990 for her role in 'Misery'?

8   Which country and western singer was known as the Silver Fox and was an originator of the countrypolitan sound?

9   To what does the adjective volucrine refer?

10 Lockjaw is another name for which medical condition?

11 What is the common name for the African bird *struthio camelus*?

12 Who created Captain Horatio Hornblower?

13 What are timbels, tabors and tablas types of?

14 What is the name of the whole note O?

15 In which year in the 1980s did the Tiannanmen Square massacre take place in China?

Answers 1 February **2** Humphrey Bogart **3** Cannonball **4** The Liberty Bell **5** Leviticus (25:10) **6** The Andrews Sisters **7** Kathy Bates **8** Charlie Rich **9** Birds **10** Tetanus **11** Ostrich **12** C.S. Forester **13** Drum **14** Semibreve **15** 1989

1   What were James Cagney's famous last words in the movie 'White Heat'?

2   In Britain it is a nappy, what is it called in America?

3   Olerosa is a sweet-medium type of which drink?

4   What is trichology the study of?

5   Nyasaland is the former name of which African republic?

6   What was the name of the Greenpeace vessel sunk by French agents in Auckland harbour in July 1985?

7   What is the meaning of the Africaan word boer?

8   What U is the twentieth letter of the Greek alphabet?

9   Zen is a mystical form of what religion?

10 Who wrote 'Uncle Vanya'?

11 What D is a small writing desk with side drawers?

12 Who is the Hindu god of love?

13 What type of bomb is an enhanced radiation weapon?

14 Joan Plowright is the widow of which British actor?

15 In which country would you find San José, Fray Bentos and Salto?

Answers 1 Look Ma! Top of the World 2 Diaper 3 Sherry 4 Hair 5 Malawi 6 Rainbow Warrior 7 Farmer 8 Upsilon 9 Buddhism 10 Chekhov 11 Davenport 12 Kama 13 Neutron 14 Lord (Laurence) Olivier 15 Uruguay

1   What are salmon called during the first two years of their life?

2   What is the philosophy of morals and moral choices?

3   Which American president had a sign on his desk: 'The buck stops here'?

4   Quantas is the national airline of which country?

5   Where in 1945 did a conference take place between Churchill, Stalin and Roosevelt?

6   Which famous furnishings company was founded by Sir Terence Conran?

7   Flying Fish Cove is the capital of which Australian island?

8   What does a wainwright build or repair?

9   If Orient is East, what is West?

10   What is the name of the theory that energy transferences occur in bursts of limited quantity?

11   What G is the name of sixteen popes, the last being in 1946?

12   What is meant by the prefix *tetra-*?

13   In the James Bond stories, of which criminal organisation is Ernst Stavro Blofeld the head?

14   In horse racing, at which French racecourse is the Prix de L'Arc de Triomphe held annually?

15   Who made journey's of exploration in the vessel Endeavour?

Answers 1 Parr 2 Ethics 3 Truman 4 Australia 5 Yalta 6 Habitat 7 Christmas Island 8 Wagons 9 Occident 10 Quantum 11 Gregory 12 Four 13 Spectre 14 Longchamps 15 Captain Cook

MISCELLANEOUS 2

1   In America it is a transom, what is it called in Britain?

2   What is the name of the hourglass-shaped toy that is thrown and caught on a cord between the hands?

3   What male Christian name means 'bringer of treasure'?

4   What C is an 18th-century Italian writer of erotic memoirs?

5   The Black Pearl was the nickname of which Portuguese soccer player?

6   What is topiary?

7   What is meant by the musical term *grazioso*?

8   Who was the youngest daughter of the prophet Mohammed?

9   Who wrote the opera 'The Tales of Hoffman'?

10 What A is another name for the egg plant?

11 Who is the former KGB chief who was USSR leader from 1982-1984?

12 What creature lives in a dray?

13 For what is spondulix a slang term?

14 Who was the wicked hypnotist of George du Maurier's novel 'Trilby'?

15 What R is a match of three in bridge or whist?

MISCELLANEOUS 2   *Quiz 61*

1 What type of book is a Baedeker?

2 What A is the national airline of Russia, code name SU?

3 What large vehicular word means in Sanskrit 'protector of the world'?

4 What male Christian name means 'dark water'?

5 Which American writer created the character Pudd'nhead Wilson in his 1894 detective story?

6 What would be kept in a quiver?

7 Which British aviator married Amy Johnson in 1932?

8 What is the capital of Morocco?

9 What would you find in a book called a missal?

10 What are trefoil, ogee, lancet and parabolic types of?

11 What G is another name for the eucalyptus tree?

12 What shape is described as cuneal or sphenoid?

13 Standing on the Arabian Sea, what is the principal seaport of Pakistan?

14 What code name was used by the US for the project from 1942 which developed the atomic bomb?

15 What ology is concerned with the study of unidentified flying objects?

MISCELLANEOUS 2 *Quiz 62*

1 What girl's name in Greek originally meant 'bright shining one'?

2 In language, what word means the use of words starting with the same letter or sound, for example big black box?

3 What V is a finely calibrated scale named after a 17th-century French mathematician?

4 What type of creature is a Portuguese man-of-war?

5 For what is vespertillian an adjective?

6 What was the name of the 19th-century US engineer who designed the giant fairground wheel that now bears his name?

7 What is the name of Sherlock Holmes' faithful housekeeper?

8 If recto is odd-numbered pages of a book, what are the left-handed even-numbered pages called?

9 What is the main ingredient of the dish angels-on-horseback?

10 What, especially in the Southern US states, is 'Moonshine'?

11 Who in past times would wear a coxcombe and motley and carry a bauble?

12 John, Lionel and Ethel were part of which famous acting family of the first half of the 20th-century?

13 What shape is described as ensform, gladiate or xiphoid?

14 Which tree produces edible fruit called persimmons?

15 Who was the beggar in Jesus' parable of the rich man and the poor man?

---

15 Lazarus

8 Verso 9 Oysters 10 Whiskey 11 A jester 12 Barrymore 13 Sword 14 Ebony

Answers 1 Helen 2 Alliteration 3 Vernier 4 Jellyfish 5 Bats 6 Ferris 7 Mrs Hudson

MISCELLANEOUS 2   *Quiz 63*

1   What D is a fine delicate China made at Meissen in Germany since 1710?

2   What was the former name of the country now known as Myanmar?

3   What J would you be likely to see using Indian Clubs?

4   Sophy was the title of the king of which middle east country in ancient times?

5   Who, in medieval stories, is the lover of Cressida?

6   What was invented in 1839 by a West Point cadet Abner Doubleday?

7   Which American President said: "Liberty, when it begins to take root, is a plant of rapid growth"?

8   What is the better-known name of Israel Beer Josephat (1816-99), the British founder of the first news agency?

9   What S are cantle, skirt, flap and pommel all parts of?

10   Which cave is celebrated in Mendelssohn's 'Hebrides Overture'?

11   Which palace is the official residence of the French president?

12   Whose law states that 'work expands so as to fill the time available for its completion'?

13   In Greek mythology, who used a shield called the aegis?

14   What was the name of the character played by Leslie Howard in 'Gone With the Wind'?

15   Which nocturnal beetle is also known as glow-worm or lightning bug?

1 Which science-fiction wrote the 'Foundation Trilogy'?

2 What would you find in a vespiary?

3 What bird of pray is also known as fish hawk or fish eagle?

4 What is musophobia the fear of?

5 What U is a church or religious movement known as 'the Moonies'?

6 In which country is the Imola motor racing circuit?

7 What L is an adjective pertaining to the left side of a vessel?

8 A species of which bird is called pipits?

9 Of which precious stone did John Ruskin write: 'The chemistry of it is more like a medieval doctors prescription than the making of a respectable mineral'?

10 Of where is Libreville the capital?

11 What F is a person who shoes horses?

12 Which resort island in Brooklyn, New York, was named from the Dutch word for rabbit?

13 What was the name of the Roman practise of killing every tenth man in a cowardly or mutinous military unit?

14 What is the more common name for the human disease *varicella*?

15 What was the married name of the 19th-century writer on cookery, Isabella Mary Mayson?

Answers 1 Isaac Asimov 2 Wasps 3 Osprey 4 Mice 5 Unification 6 Italy 7 Larboard 8 Wagtail 9 Amethyst 10 Gabon 11 Farrier 12 Coney 13 Decimation 14 Chicken pox 15 Mrs Beeton

MISCELLANEOUS 2 — Quiz 65

1 Who is the Australian feminist and author of 'The Female Eunuch'?

2 What predominantly Irish Christian name means 'small dark one'?

3 What creature is a cayman a type of?

4 Who, in Greek mythology, was turned into the laurel which became Apollo's sacred tree?

5 What was the former name of Ho-Chi Minh City?

6 What P are the type of people connected by the names Jeremiah and Cassandra?

7 What L would be kept in a chest or wooden trunk called a kist?

8 Mustapha Kemal, elected President of Turkey in August 1925, was better known by what name?

9 Whom did George Bush defeat to become US President in 1988?

10 Which modern city was known as Byzantium from 660 BC-AD 330?

11 A whooper is a type of which bird?

12 What V means that a dish is served with white grapes?

13 What C is Fuller's Earth?

14 In the human body, what are lumber, sacral, median, ulnar, digital, maxilliary and tibial types of?

15 What adjective pertains to the 'Muse of Dancing'?

Answers 1 Germaine Greer 2 Keiron 3 Crocodile 4 Daphne 5 Saigon 6 Pessimists 7 Linen 8 Ataturk 9 Michael Dukakis 10 Istanbul 11 Swan 12 Veronique 13 Clay 14 Nerves 15 Terpsichorean

1 Who, in Greek mythology, were the semi-divine female beings who by their songs lured men to destruction?

2 Which Florentine adventurer gave his name to America?

3 How many prongs does a tuning fork have?

4 What is another word for a lariat?

5 Native to the Himalayas, what is a deodar?

6 How many degrees longitude represents one hour in time?

7 Who devised the term 'horse power' when he discovered that a strong horse could raise a weight of 150 pounds 4 feet in 1 second?

8 Who created the fictional barrister Horace Rumpole?

9 In Arthurian legend, who was the evil sorceress who plotted the overthrow of her brother King Arthur?

10 Which Shakespeare play opens with the words: 'If music be the food of love, play on'?

11 In which TV series did Farrah Fawcett-Majors play Jill Munroe?

12 On what part of a shoe would you find the aglets?

13 Which size of champagne bottle comes between Salmanazar and Nebuchadnezzar?

14 How many players are there in a hurling team?

15 Who is the author of the poem 'Gunga Din'?

Answers 1 Sirens 2 Amerigo Vespucci 3 2 4 Lasso 5 A tree 6 15 7 James Watt 8 John Mortimer 9 Morgan Le Fay 10 Twelfth Night 11 Charlie's Angels 12 They are the plastic ends at the end of the laces 13 Balthazar 14 15 Rudyard Kipling

MISCELLANEOUS 2   *Quiz 67*

1 In which famous TV series did Antonio Fargas play Huggy Bear Brown?

2 What type of clock was invented in 1656 by Christian Huygens?

3 Peter Hurd painted the official portrait of which American President, who remarked when it was unveiled in January 1967, that it was the ugliest thing he ever saw?

4 What kind of creature was Benito Mussolini's pet, Italia Bella, which travelled around with him?

5 What was the first American-bred and trained horse to win the Grand National Steeplechase in England?

6 Which architect designed New York's Guggenheim Museum?

7 Who, in 1988, won best actress Oscar for her role in 'The Accused'?

8 Mohammed Ali Jinnah helped to found which country in 1947?

9 Which Hungarian inventor produced the first ball-point pen in 1938?

10 On its return to earth in June 1971, inside which Soviet spacecraft were the three cosmonauts found dead in their seats?

11 In which country was the Archbishop of Canterbury's envoy, Terry Waite taken hostage in 1987?

12 Is downstage a theatrical term for the part of the stage nearest, or furthest away from the audience?

13 What motel chain was founded by an American hotelier, Kemmons Wilson in 1952 in Memphis, Tennessee?

14 What is the name of the valve containing an anode, a cathode and a control grid, that was invented in 1906 by L. De Forest?

15 The Spaniard Andres Segovia was a virtuoso on which instrument?

Answers 1 Starsky and Hutch 2 The Pendulum Clock 3 Lyndon Johnson 4 A lion 5 Jay Trump 6 Frank Lloyd Wright 7 Jodie Foster 8 Pakistan 9 Laszlo Biro 10 Soyuz II 11 Lebanon 12 Nearest 13 Holiday Inn 14 Triode 15 Guitar

1   Who was the mayor of New York from 1933-1945 who gave his name to one of that cities airports?

2   What is the name given to the post which supports the handrail at either end of a flight of stairs?

3   Who succeeded Hirohito as Emperor of Japan?

4   Who was the US industrialist who developed the current scoring system for contract bridge?

5   According to Longfellow, which Indian was married to Minnehaha?

6   What A is a liquorice-flavoured spice used in cooking?

7   What name is given to a sentence which contains every letter of the alphabet, for example, the quick brown fox jumps over the lazy dog?

8   With which animal is a cynomaniac obsessed?

9   What is the name of the rope with weights attached which is used by horsemen for catching cattle by snaring their legs?

10   A joanna is a slang term for which musical instrument?

11   An urubu is a Central American type of what bird?

12   What Z was a German optician whose factory at Jena became noted for producing lenses and microscopes?

13   At which Ugandan town in 1976 did a dramatic rescue of Israelies take place, whose plane had been hijacked by terrorists?

14   What M is a doubling-up system in gambling, especially at roulette?

15   To what do piscary laws refer?

Answers 1 La Guardia 2 Newel 3 Akihito 4 Vanderbilt 5 Hiawatha 6 Aniseed 7 Pangram 8 Dogs 9 Bolas 10 Piano 11 Vulture 12 Zeiss 13 Entebbe 14 Martingale 15 Fishing

1 In the Japanese martial art of Kendo, what are shiani?

2 Of what is polemology the study?

3 What is meant by the suffix - 'ling'?

4 Who is the eponymous heroine of a 1913 Eleanor Porter novel, whose name has become synonymous with excessive optimism?

5 Who was the Italian renaissance painter whose works include 'La Donna Valeta' and 'The Marriage of the Virgin'?

6 When did Mao Tse-Tung die?

7 What is Job's tears – a type of grass or a type of wine?

8 What are anise, burnet and hyssop types of?

9 What K is a variety of cabbage with curly leaves?

10 What have upright centre pins called gnomens?

11 For what, in the reign of Charles II did Francis Stewart model?

12 What port is at the Atlantic end of the Panama Canal?

13 What O is a figure of speech such as cruel to be kind?

14 What river is crossed in Florence by the Ponte Vecchio?

15 Who was Rafael Sabatini's famous pirate captain?

Answers 1 The Bamboo swords 2 Wars 3 Young 4 Pollyanna 5 Raphael 6 1976 7 Grass 8 Herbs 9 Kale 10 Sundials 11 Britannia 12 Colon 13 Oxymoron 14 The Arno 15 Captain Blood

1   Hapsburg was the name of the former royal family of which European country?

2   Which fruit is a cross between a grapefruit and a tangerine?

3   The card game cooncan is similar to which other popular game?

4   What is burnt to produce an ash called kelp?

5   Which American president said: "The ballot is stronger than the bullet"?

6   What Y is a language which is a compound of Hebrew and German?

7   What name is given to the ridge between the shoulder-blades of a horse?

8   Who said that the upward thrust exerted on a body immersed in fluid equals the weight of fluid dispersed?

9   What M is a synthetic dye produced in 1859 and named after a battle?

10 Which Carthaginian soldier was defeated by Scipio at Zama in 202BC?

11 What D is a minstrel song which became the battle hymn of the confederacy during the American Civil War?

12 What is the name of the leather loop worn around a scout's neckerchief?

13 How often does a Mohammedan pray each day?

14 Semperflorens is a variety of what plant?

15 How many players are there in a volleyball team?

Answers 1 Austria 2 Ugli 3 Rummy 4 Seaweed 5 Lincoln 6 Yiddish 7 Withers 8 Archimedes 9 Magenta 10 Hannibal 11 Dixie 12 Woggle 13 Five times 14 Begonia 15 6

MISCELLANEOUS 2

Quiz 71

1   In ancient Rome, what name was given to the 15th day of March, May, July and October, and the 13th of other months?

2   In which city was Martin Luther King assassinated in 1968?

3   Dale Evans who died in February 2001 was the widow of which famous screen cowboy?

4   Who, in 1988, wrote 'A Brief History of Time'?

5   What is pulled by a coolie?

6   Who sculpted 'The Burghers of Calais'?

7   What is the name of the stadium in which cycle races take place?

8   What is the currency unit of The Netherlands?

9   What type of flowering garden plant originated from Mexico and includes the varieties ball and collerette?

10 In which US state will you find Wichita and Topeka?

11 What is the name of the twelve-a-side stick and ball game played in the Scottish Highlands?

12 The Rowan is an alternative name for which tree?

13 Memphis was the ancient capital of which country?

14 Which order of mammals includes kangaroos and wallabies?

15 What land bird has the largest wing span?

Answers 1 Ides 2 Memphis 3 Roy Rogers 4 Stephen Hawking 5 A rickshaw 6 Rodin 7 Velodrome 8 Guilder 9 Dahlia 10 Kansas 11 Shinty 12 Mountain Ash 13 Egypt 14 Marsupials 15 Condor

1 Who was the Roman goddess of flowers?

2 What is the root-like stem of the tropical plant, Zingibar officinale?

3 What fictitious, but appropriately named, brand of piano was owned by Fred and Wilma Flintstone in the TV series 'The Flintstones'?

4 How in the world of rock 'n' roll music is Richard Penniman better known?

5 How big, in square feet, is a regulation boxing ring?

6 Which 1973 Woody Allen movie was set in the year 2173?

7 In which year in the 20th-century did America celebrate its Bicentennial?

8 In the TV series 'Fantasy Island', which character's first words in each episode were: "La Plane, la plane"?

9 Which composer was portrayed by Richard Chamberlain in the 1970 movie 'The Music Lovers'?

10 Panama hats are made in which South American country?

11 What famous announcement was made by concert hosts to signify to fans that an Elvis Presley concert was over?

12 Which is the only film in which John Wayne died of natural causes?

13 What was the Academy Award winning song in the 1970 Disney movie 'Pinocchio'?

14 What is the positive masculine and light principle of Chinese philosophy and religion?

15 What is the common name of *Allium cepa*, a biennial plant of the lily family native to South West Asia?

ENTERTAINMENT

General Entertainment

GENERAL ENTERTAINMENT

Quiz 1

1 Who recorded the 1985 Album of the Year 'Graceland'?

2 Who starred as Jim Rockford in 'The Rockford Files'?

3 Who wrote 'Eine Kleine Nachtmusik'?

4 In which movie did Vivien Leigh play Blanche Du Bois?

5 In a vintage TV series which family lived at 5/8 Crestview Drive, Beverley Hills?

6 Who played Captain Spalding in 'Animal Crackers' and Rufus T. Firely in 'Duck Soup'?

7 Which 1996 movie about the Salem witchcraft trials starred Daniel Day-Lewis and Winona Ryder?

8 Who played Steven Taylor in 'Doctor Who'?

9 In which 1977 movie did Diane Keaton first play opposite Woody Allen?

10 Who played New York book editor Martin Tupper in the 90s TV comedy series 'Dream On'?

11 Which 70s pop star, the son of an East End docker, was born David Cook in July 1947?

12 Who wrote The Byrds hit 'Mr Tambourine Man'?

13 What was the name of Ian Dury's backing group?

14 Who duetted with David Bowie on the Christmas hit single 'Peace On Earth'?

15 Which character, the subject of several movies and TV series was originally created by Bob Kane and published in DC Comics?

Answers 1 Paul Simon 2 James Garner 3 Mozart 4 A Streetcar Named Desire 5 The Clampitts 6 Groucho Marx 7 The Crucible 8 Peter Purves 9 Annie Hall 10 Brian Benben 11 David Essex 12 Bob Dylan 13 Blockheads 14 Bing Crosby 15 Batman

ENTERTAINMENT

Quiz 2

1 For which role did Tom Hanks win best actor Oscar in 1994?

2 Which rock band had an album called 'Zenyatta Mondatta'?

3 Which film company has Lady Liberty at the start of each of its films?

4 Which actress was dubbed the Platinum Blond?

5 What was the title of Steven Spielberg's movie version of the Peter Pan story?

6 Whose first big hit was '(They Long To Be) Close To You'?

7 In whose 1964 spoof recording 'The Twelve Gifts of Christmas' does he list 'an automatic vegetable slicer that works when you see it on television, but not when you get it home'?

8 The 1961 song 'The Lion Sleeps Tonight' by the Tokens was recorded by several artists including The Weavers and Carl Denver under which alternative title?

9 Who in 1996 won a recording contract by singing a hymn 'Jesus Loves Me' at her audition?

10 The Rev. Susan Brown officiated at whose Scottish wedding on December 22, 2000?

11 The 'Attan' is a national dance of which country?

12 Which French artist was portrayed on screen by Jose Ferrer in the 1952 movie 'Moulin Rouge'?

13 What nationality was the composer Chopin?

14 What instrument was played by jazz great Earl 'Fatha' Hines?

15 In 1859, the French Opera House, the first great opera house in America, was built in which city – New York, Chicago or New Orleans?

GENERAL ENTERTAINMENT   Quiz 3

1   'Looks like we're in for nasty weather' is a line from which 1969 hit record by Credence Clearwater Revival?

2   Which German composer wrote the oratorios of 'Elijah' and 'St.Paul'?

3   Who played Captain Von Trappe in 'The Sound of Music'?

4   Which singers backing group is The Vagabonds?

5   What was the only No.1 hit record for Jerry Lee Lewis?

6   What is the name of the butler in 'The Addams Family'?

7   In the TV series 'Knotts Landing', a spin off from 'Dallas' what was the surname of Abby and Gary?

8   Who was the youngest of the five Marx brothers, Gummo, Chico or Zeppo?

9   Who wrote 'The Sabre Dance'?

10 Who plays Mitch Buchanan in 'Baywatch'?

11 Which composer died in New York City in 1989 aged 101?

12 Regis Philbin is the host of the American version of which successful world wide quiz show?

13 Jodie Foster played FBI agent Clarice Starling in which movie?

14 What nationality is Nicole Kidman?

15 In which film did Frank Sinatra sing 'High Hopes'?

Answers 1 Bad Moon Rising **2** Mendelssohn **3** Christopher Plummer **4** Jimmy James **5** Great Balls of Fire **6** Lurch **7** Ewings **8** Zeppo **9** Khachaturian **10** David Hasselhoff **11** Irving Berlin **12** Who Wants To Be a Millionaire? **13** Silence of the Lambs **14** Australian **15** A Hole In the Head

GENERAL ENTERTAINMENT — *Quiz 4*

1 In America, for what type of film and TV genre is an Annie awarded?

2 In which 1999 movie does Denzel Washington play a bedridden forensics expert leading the hunt for a serial killer?

3 What was the name of Celine Dion's hit from the movie 'Titanic'?

4 "We never close" was the motto of which London theatre?

5 What was the name of Gene Hackman's character in 'The French Connection'?

6 Who in 1986 was 'Addicted to Love'?

7 Who wrote the book and lyrics for the musical 'My Fair Lady'?

8 When asked by Oprah Winfrey on her TV show: "How does music come to you?" Who replied: "It is really a gift from God",

9 What nationality was composer Bela Bartok?

10 Which TV series is set in General Memorial Hospital?

11 Who duetted with Diana Ross on 'Endless Love'?

12 For which movie did George Burns win an Oscar for best actor in a supporting role in 1975?

13 Which actor, who played an Irish con artist in 'Waking Ned' was killed in a car crash in Scotland in November 1999?

14 What was the stage name of John Lydon of The Sex Pistols?

15 How is rapper Sean Combs better known in the world of entertainment?

Answers 1 Animation 2 The Bone Collector 3 My Heart Will Go On 4 The Windmill 5 Popeye Doyle 6 Robert Palmer 7 Alan Jay Lerner 8 Stevie Wonder 9 Hungarian 10 ER 11 Lionel Ritchie 12 The Sunshine Boys 13 Ian Bannen 14 Johnnie Rotten 15 Puff Daddy

GENERAL ENTERTAINMENT
Quiz 5

1   In how many movies did Harrison Ford play Indiana Jones?

2   What type of film was made in the Almeria desert of Spain during the 1960s?

3   Who sang the United Kingdom's winning entry 'Save Your Kisses for Me' in the 1976 Eurovision Song Contest?

4   'Ode To Joy' is from which composer's ninth symphony?

5   What is the name given to the traditional French clown with whitened face and conical hat popular in seaside shows?

6   What nationality are singers Bryan Adams and Anne Murrey?

7   Jim Morrison was vocalist with which rock group?

8   What was the name of the missionary played by Ingrid Bergman in 'The Inn of the Sixth Happiness'?

9   'Barbarella' and 'Night Games' are two of the films of which French director?

10 With which of the arts would you associate Egon Madsen?

11 Born 1942 in England, which TV and film actor performed in the musicals 'Hello Dolly' and 'Phantom of the Opera'?

12 In which city is La Scala opera house?

13 Sting was the former lead singer with which group?

14 Who directed the horror slasher flicks 'Scream' and 'Nightmare on Elm Street'?

15 The movie 'Forbidden Planet' was based on which Shakespeare play?

Answers 1 Three **2** Spaghetti Western **3** Brotherhood of Man **4** Beethoven **5** Pierrot **6** Canadian **7** The Doors **8** Gladys Aylward **9** Roger Vadim **10** Ballet **11** Michael Crawford **12** Milan **13** The Police **14** Wes Craven **15** The Tempest

This quiz is all about television programmes.

1 In the TV series 'The Waltons', what were the first names of Grandpa and Grandma Walton?

2 Name the actor who appeared in the TV series' 'Bonanza', 'Little House On The Prairie' and 'Highway To Heaven'.

3 In 1997, actor Dave Thompson was sacked from his role of which Teletubby?

4 What's the name of the high school featured in the TV series 'Happy Days'?

5 Who played the title role in the 1990s detective series 'Father Rowling Investigates'?

6 In the cult sci-fi series 'Sapphire And Steel', Joanna Lumley played Sapphire. Which actor played Steel?

7 Name the male soldier who dressed in women's clothing in the series M.A.S.H.

8 Never seen, only heard, what was the name of the wealthy estate owner in the series 'Magnum PI' who's voice was provided by Orson Welles?

9 Name the actor who played Spock in 'Star Trek'.

10 In the American TV police drama series 'CHIPS'. What does CHIPS stand for?

11 'Daktari' was a 1960s TV series. Daktari being a Swahili word which means what in English?

12 Name the actress who played Rock Hudson's wife in 'McMillan And Wife'.

13 Detective Bobby Simone and Lieutenant Arthur Fancy are characters in which series?

14 Which actress played Laurie Partridge in 'The Partridge Family' and Grace Van Owen in 'LA Law'?

15 Who played the title role in the detective series 'Remington Steele'?

GENERAL ENTERTAINMENT   *Quiz 7*

1   Anna Leonowens is the English governess in which musical?

2   In which movie does Meryl Streep play Sarah Woodruff in the title role?

3   Born 1899, who starred, produced, co-directed and scored the wartime movie, 'In Which We Serve'?

4   In which movie does Robert Carlyle play Gary 'Gaz' Schofield?

5   What musical instrument is connected with the Frenchman Paul Tortelier?

6   Which French singer was known as The Little Sparrow?

7   Rock musician Keith Emerson is associated with which rock group?

8   What nationality is pop star Ricky Martin?

9   Which actor was paralyzed in a 1995 accident during a horse-jumping competition?

10 With which of the arts do you associate the name Victoria de las Angeles?

11 Who is the blind Italian tenor who sang at the 2000 Sydney Olympic games?

12 Which English actor was married to Elizabeth Taylor from 1952-57?

13 What is the name of the imaginary 6-foot-tall rabbit in a comedy by Mary Chase?

14 Which singer was portrayed by Diana Ross in the movie 'Lady Sings the Blues'?

15 What in 1948 was the first British movie to win best film Oscar?

Answers 1 The King and I 2 The French Lieutenant's Woman 3 Noel Coward 4 The Full Monty 5 Cello 6 Edith Piaf 7 Emerson, Lake and Palmer 8 Puerto Rican 9 Christopher Reeve 10 Opera 11 Andrea Bocelli 12 Michael Wilding 13 Harvey 14 Billie Holiday 15 Hamlet

GENERAL ENTERTAINMENT   *Quiz 8*

1   Rhythm-and-blues musician Ronald Bell is associated with which group?
2   Who recorded the album, 'Don't Shoot Me, I'm Only the Piano Player'?
3   Which legendary country and western singer died in 1953 aged 30 as a consequence of alcohol and drug abuse?
4   The 1991 play 'Through the Grapevine' was the story of which musical legend?
5   Who had a 1964 hit with 'Little Children'?
6   Born in 1888, who is the French entertainer whose trademark was a straw hat and bow-tie?
7   Which jazz great was known as the 'King of Swing'?
8   Which entertainer was born Francis Gumm in 1922?
9   Which silent film star was dubbed 'America's Sweetheart'?
10 Who wrote the play 'Rosencrantz and Guildenstern are Dead'?
11 Which German actress starred in the film 'Blue Angel'?
12 Who wrote the opera 'Carmen'?
13 Who wrote the music for 'Gone With the Wind'?
14 From which Gilbert and Sullivan opera is the song 'When I was a lad'?
15 Who was the lyric-writing brother of George Gershwin?

Answers 1 Kool and the Gang 2 Elton John 3 Hank Williams 4 Marvin Gaye 5 Billy J. Kramer and the Dakotas 6 Maurice Chevalier 7 Benny Goodman 8 Judy Garland 9 Mary Pickford 10 Tom Stoppard 11 Marlene Dietrich 12 Bizet 13 Max Steiner 14 HMS Pinafore 15 Ira Gershwin

GENERAL ENTERTAINMENT   *Quiz 9*

1   Which English theatrical manager, born in 1844, was associated with the production of operas by Gilbert and Sullivan?

2   Who wrote the opera 'La Boheme'?

3   Which group had a hit in 1973 with 'You Won't Find Another Fool Like Me'?

4   Michael Nesmith is associated with which pop group founded in the 1960s?

5   Who played Victor Frankenstein in the 1994 movie 'Mary Shelley's Frankenstein'?

6   Which actor played Norm in 'Cheers'?

7   Whose vocal partner is Daryl Hall?

8   Who sang Ireland's winning entry 'All Kinds of Everything' in the 1970 Eurovision Song Contest?

9   Which country music star broke into the pop charts during the 1980s with 'To All the Girls I've Loved Before'?

10 Who was on the 'Banks of the Ohio' in 1971 and 'Hopelessly Devoted to You' in 1978?

11 Who wrote the musical 'Pal Joey' with Richard Rodgers?

12 'Uptight' was the first hit for which artist?

13 Robert Redford and Paul Newman play two conmen in which movie?

14 Who wrote the Everly Brothers record 'Claudette' for his wife Claudette Frady?

15 Frank Loesser wrote which musical in 1950 which had characters created by Damon Runyon?

Quiz 10

1   Who played the Acid Queen in Ken Russell's film version of the rock-opera 'Tommy'?
2   With which opera singer did Freddy Mercury re-record Barcelona in 1992?
3   In 1999 which 91-year old American comedian joked: "I think it was 1951, I signed a lifetime contract with NBC, it expired 20 years ago'?
4   Which country singer has appeared in the movies '9 to 5' and 'Straight Talk'?
5   In which movie did Shirley Temple sing 'On the Good Ship Lollipop'?
6   Who won Oscars for her roles in 'Woman in Love' and 'A Touch of Class'?
7   In which movie does Pat O'Brian play a priest Father Connoly and James Cagney play a gangster Rocky Sullivan?
8   What instrument is played by Billy Preston?
9   Whose backing group were the Jordanaires?
10 In the Cary Grant/Katherine Hepburn film 'Bringing Up Baby', what was the baby?
11 Which actress has a life jacket named after her?
12 Who is the husband of Melanie Griffith who directed her in the 1999 movie 'Crazy in Alabama'?
13 Whose first No. 1 hit was 'Rivers of Babylon'?
14 Which of the Spice Girls was nicknamed Sporty Spice?
15 Johnny Nash had a hit with 'Tears on My Pillow', but who had a hit later with the same title but a different tune?

GENERAL ENTERTAINMENT   Quiz 11

1 In America, which long-running radio show traces its roots to a local radio show called 'WSM Barn Dance' which broadcast live country music beginning in 1925?

2 Who wrote the song 'They Didn't Believe Me'?

3 Produced by Rodgers and Hammerstein in 1943, which musical had ballets, choreographed by Agnes de Mille, that were an integral part of the plot?

4 Which TV series features the characters Hannibal Hayes and Jed 'Kid' Curry?

5 Which classic cartoon was created by Matt Groening?

6 Who played the girl in 'The Exorcist'?

7 The movie 'Jaws' was based on a novel by which author?

8 Whose 1973 Record of the Year was 'Killing Me Softly With His Song'?

9 Who wrote the 'Brandenburg Concertos'?

10 'Down Hearted Blues' was in 1923 the first recording by which artist known as the Empress of the Blues?

11 Which TV series stars, among others, Jennifer Aniston and Courtney Cox?

12 In which Hitchcock movie does Cary Grant get attacked by a crop-dusting aeroplane?

13 Johnny Cash recorded in Folson and which other prison?

14 What instrument was played on stage by country great Roy Acuff?

15 Who had a hit in 1963 with 'Good Golly Miss Molly'?

Answers 1 Grand Ole Opry **2** Jerome Kern **3** Oklahoma **4** Alias Smith and Jones **5** The Simpsons **6** Linda Blair **7** Peter Benchley **8** Roberta Flack **9** Bach **10** Bessie Smith **11** Friends **12** North by Northwest **13** San Quentin **14** Fiddle **15** Jerry Lee Lewis

1 Which American pianist and composer wrote 'Raindrops Keep Falling On My Head'?

2 What relation is Lorna Luft to Liza Minelli?

3 Which film actress was born Lucy Johnson and was once married to Frank Sinatra?

4 For which film did Gary Cooper win best actor Oscar in 1952?

5 What instrument was played by jazz great Bix Beiderbecke?

6 What was the name of the ranch in the TV series 'The Virginian'?

7 Which actor plays Freddy Krueger in the 'Nightmare on Elm Street' series?

8 Which American film actress was known in the 1920s as the 'It Girl'?

9 Who sang the theme song for the Bond film 'For Your Eyes Only'?

10 In which musical did Bjorn Ulvaeus of Abba collaborate with Tim Rice?

11 James Arness played Marshall Matt Dillon of Dodge City in which vintage TV series?

12 Larry Parks is famous for miming the voice of which entertainer in two movies in the 1940s?

13 "Guess Who?" were the first words spoken by which character in his debut cartoon Knock Knock?

14 'Ready To Take a Chance Again' was sung by which singer/songwriter as the theme of the 1978 movie 'Foul Play'?

15 Prior to marrying rock guitarist Eric Clapton, Patti Boyd had been married to which one of the Beatles?

GENERAL ENTERTAINMENT   *Quiz 13*

1   What was the name of the character played by Robert Vaughn in the cult series 'The Man From U.N.C.L.E'?

2   What did U.N.C.L.E. stand for?

3   In which Swiss resort is the Golden Rose festival and awards ceremony held annually?

4   Which female singer played a paranoid schizophrenic in the 1994 made-for-TV movie 'Out Of Darkness'?

5   Which US actor played the leading character Norman Grant in the 1980s sci-fi mini-series 'Space'?

6   What instrument does Zoot play in the Muppet Show?

7   The US version of the British comedy series 'Till Death Us Do Part' was called 'All In The Family'. What was the name of the US equivalent of Alf Garnett in that series?

8   Which real-life sisters starred in a 1991 made-for-TV movie re-make of the classic 'Whatever Happened To Baby Jane'?

9   Name the actor who played the title roles in the series 'Perry Mason' and 'Ironside'.

10 Two actresses played the role of Miss Ellie in 'Dallas'. One was Barbara Bel Geddes, who was the other?

11 In which comedy series was actress Elizabeth Montgomery constantly twitching her nose?

12 What was the title of the series in which Jan-Michael Vincent played hi-tec helicopter pilot Stringfellow Hawke?

13 Name the actress who played Tara King in 'The Avengers'.

14 Which actor played Mike Gambit in 'The New Avengers'?

15 What was the name of the character played by Joanna Lumley in 'The New Avengers'?

Answers 1 Napoleon Solo 2 United Network Command For Law Enforcement 3 Montreux 4 Diana Ross 5 James Garner 6 Saxophone 7 Archie Bunker 8 Vanessa and Lynn Redgrave 9 Raymond Burr 10 Donna Reed 11 Bewitched 12 Airwolf 13 Linda Thorson 14 Gareth Hunt 15 Purdey

1 The Ken Russell film 'The Music Lovers' was about the life of which composer?
2 What is the connection between actress Mary Pickford and the mother of Elvis Presley?
3 Who was born at 415 Monroe Street, Hoboken, New Jersey on December 12, 1915?
4 The 1974 movie 'The Odessa File' was based on a 1972 novel of the same name by which author?
5 In a famous TV series of the 1960s who was Dr. Richard Kimble otherwise known as?
6 Mary Travers became famous as a member of which pop trio in the 1960s?
7 The movie 'Watership Down' featured the song 'Bright Eyes' by which artist?
8 Which TV show starring Valerie Harper in the title role was a spin-off from 'The Mary Tyler Moore Show'?
9 'Moonlight Serenade' was the theme tune of which American big band?
10 Who composed the opera 'Rigoletto'?
11 What is the better known name of Arthur Stanley Jefferson?
12 Which famous Parisian variety theatre, famous for its elaborate revues, was opened in 1869?
13 What nationality was composer Frederick Delius?
14 Who played the killer in the film 'Rear Window'?
15 What type of entertainment does the satellite TV channel Paramount specialise in?

Answers 1 Tchaikovsky 2 They were both born with the same birth name - Gladys Smith 3 Frank Sinatra 4 Frederick Forsyth 5 The Fugitive 6 Peter, Paul and Mary 7 Art Garfunkel 8 Rhoda 9 Glenn Miller 10 Verdi 11 Stan Laurel 12 The Folies-Bergere 13 British 14 Raymond Burr 15 Comedy

1 In which movie does Ewan McGregor play Nick Leeson?

2 'Love, exciting and new.....come aboard, we're expecting you', were lines crooned by Jack Jones at the beginning of each episode of which TV series?

3 'Death in Venice' was the last opera of which composer?

4 Dave Evans (The Edge) is a member of which rock band?

5 'Gundam Wing' is an animation TV series which originated in which country?

6 Annette Bening played opposite which actor in the movie 'American Beauty'?

7 Which Irish rock musician received a honorary knighthood in 1986?

8 Which film actress was born Maria Magdaline von Losch?

9 Who had a hit in 1970 with 'Everything is Beautiful'?

10 For which movie did Anna Paquin win an Oscar for best Actress in a Supporting Role in 1993?

11 What instrument is played by jazz great Dave Brubeck?

12 Released in 1982, which album by Michael Jackson sold more that 20 million copies to become the biggest-selling album in history?

13 Monica Geller is a character in which TV sitcom?

14 In which movie does Meg Ryan simulate an orgasm in a crowded restaurant?

15 What character was played by Cary Grant in 'The Philadelphia Story' and by Bing Crosby in the remake 'High Society'?

Answers 1 Rogue Trader **2** The Love Boat **3** Benjamin Britten **4** U2 **5** Japan **6** Kevin Spacey **7** Bob Geldof **8** Marlene Dietrich **9** Ray Stevens **10** The Piano **11** Piano **12** Thriller **13** Friends **14** When Harry Met Sally **15** Dexter Haven

1   Clint Eastwood played Rowdy Yates in which classic TV western series?

2   Robert De Niro played Travis Bickle in which movie?

3   In which 1999 movie does Meryl Streep play Roberta Guaspari who started a violin program for poor children in East Harlem in New York?

4   Which 1979 movie starring Bette Midler was supposedly based on the life of Janis Joplin?

5   Who composed 'The Planets Suite'?

6   In 'The Wizard of Oz', the lion wants courage, what does the scarecrow want?

7   Casse-Noisette is the French name for which Tchaikovsky ballet?

8   'A Policeman's Lot is not a Happy One' is from which Gilbert and Sullivan opera?

9   The name of which type of rock music was obtained from a William Burroughs novel?

10 In the movie 'Saving Private Ryan', who plays Private Ryan?

11 'Jeux Sans Frontiers' is the International name for which team game show?

12 Which group were 'Sultans of Swing' in 1979 and 'On Every Street' in 1992?

13 Which French jazz violinist was one of the members of the Hot Club de France?

14 What is Barney and Betty's surname in The Flintstones?

15 Who played Tulse McCauley in the 1960 movie 'Flaming Star'?

1 The film 'The Coal miner's Daughter' tells the life story of which country singer?

2 In which European city is the Abbey Theatre?

3 The zapateado is a national dance of which country?

4 Who played the Fat Man in 'The Maltese Falcon'?

5 What was the real first name of jazz great Dizzy Gillespie?

6 Who was the New York City detective played in movies and the TV series by Richard Roundtree?

7 Who composed 'The Entertainers' used in the 1973 movie 'The Sting'?

8 Which remark by John Lennon so upset a Radio Station in Texas that they ceremoniously burnt all the Beatles records in protest?

9 Helen Kane, whose theme song was 'I Wanna Be Loved By You', was known in America by what nickname?

10 Which actor made his last movie appearance in the 1964 film 'The Killers'?

11 ...and on whose story was 'The Killers' based?

12 Which English king was portrayed by Peter O'Toole in the movies 'Becket' and 'The Lion in Winter'?

13 Who wrote 'Cavalleria Rusticana'?

14 ...and what in English does 'Die Fledermaus' mean?

15 Who plays Rachel Green in 'Friends'?

Answers 1 Loretta Lynn 2 Dublin 3 Spain 4 Sidney Greenstreet 5 John 6 Shaft 7 Scott Joplin 8 "We're more popular than Jesus now" 9 The Boop-A-Doop Girl 10 Ronald Reagan 11 Ernest Hemingway 12 Henry II 13 Mascagni 14 The Bat 15 Jennifer Aniston

1 The name of which rock and roll band of the late 1970s and early 1980s stood for Knights in the Service of Satan?

2 What was the name of the family pet lion in the TV series 'The Addams Family'?

3 In which 1962 Gene Chandler hit is the word 'Duke' sung 132 times?

4 A pop superstar in his own right, who was the only artist to have toured with Elvis Presley, the Beatles and The Eagles?

5 Who played Queen Charlotte opposite Nigel Hawthorne's King George III in the movie 'The Madness of King George'?

6 For which newspaper does Clark Kent (Superman) work?

7 At which film festival is the Golden Palm awarded for the best film?

8 Who was born at 1112 North Jay Street, Tacoma, Washington on May 2, 1904?

9 Who played Mork of Ork in the TV series 'Mork and Mindy'?

10 Whose son was record producer Terry Melcher who had previously owned the house where Sharon Tate was killed by the Charles Manson clan?

11 Who played Lt Felix Unger in the TV series 'The Odd Couple'?

12 'You're Still the One' was a hit for which pop star?

13 Which was the first musical to have its sound track released on a record album?

14 Who made her film debut in 1941 in the Argentinian movie 'Only the Valiant'?

15 'On the Banks of the Wabash' is the official song of which US state?

Answers 1 Kiss **2** Kit Kat **3** Duke of Earl **4** Roy Orbison **5** Helen Mirren **6** Daily Planet **7** Cannes **8** Bing Crosby **9** Robin Williams **10** Doris Day **11** Tony Randall **12** Shania Twain **13** Oklahoma **14** Eva Duarte (Eva Peron) **15** Indiana

Quiz 19

This quiz is all about the television programme 'Frasier.'

1 Which city is the setting for 'Frasier'?

2 What is the name of the cafe frequented by Frasier and his brother Niles?

3 What type of programme is presented by Gill Chesterton at the Radio Station?

4 What is the first name of Frasier's father?

5 ...and which actor plays Frasier's father?

6 Which actress plays Daphne Moon?

7 What is the name of the cute dog which belongs to Frasier's father?

8 What is the nickname of the sports presenter at the Radio Station?

9 Who plays Niles Crane, Frasier's brother?

10 What is the number of Frasier's apartment?

11 Daphne is a native of which English city?

12 Which actress plays man-mad Roz, Frasier's producer at the Radio station?

13 Which English actress and entertainer made a cameo appearance in Frasier as Daphne's mother?

14 In the theme song, sung by Kelsey Grammar (Frasier) at the end of each episode, what type of food does Frasier say he doesn't know what to do with?

15 Who was the divorce attorney whom Daphne ditched at the altar in favour of Niles?

Answers 1 Seattle 2 Café Nervosa 3 Cooking 4 Marty 5 John Mahon 6 Jane Leeves 7 Eddie 8 Bulldog 9 David Hyde Pierce 10 1901 11 Manchester 12 Peri Gilpin 13 Millicent Martin 14 Squashed salad and scrambled eggs 15 Donny

GENERAL ENTERTAINMENT   *Quiz 20*

1   Samantha and Darren Stephens were the main characters in which 60s/70s TV series?

2   Which pop group had their only No.1 hit with 'Chanson D'amour'?

3   What part was played by Charlton Heston in 'The Ten Commandments'?

4   Who wrote 'Air on a G-String'?

5   What is the name of the barber in Rossini's opera 'The Barber of Seville'?

6   In which TV series did Barbara Feldon play Agent 99?

7   In which movie do Fred Astaire and Judy Garland perform 'A Couple of Swells'?

8   Who wrote the music for 'An American in Paris'?

9   Which opera was composed by Verdi to commemorate the opening of the Suez Canal?

10 Whom did Priscilla Beaulieu marry on 1 May 1967?

11 Which hymn, when recorded by the Royal Scots Dragoon Guards in 1972, became the first million-selling record featuring bagpipes?

12 Who played Hans Christian Anderson in the 1952 movie of the same name?

13 Which 5ft 4ins tall comic strip character has a wife named Flo?

14 The original version of which TV series consisted of 78 episodes filmed from September 5 1966 to April 4 1969?

15 The Faces and Barracudas were opposing gangs in which 70s film musical?

Answers 1 Bewitched **2** Manhattan Transfer **3** Moses **4** J.S. Bach **5** Figaro **6** Get Smart **7** Easter Parade **8** George Gershwin **9** Aida **10** Elvis Presley **11** Amazing Grace **12** Danny Kaye **13** Andy Capp **14** Star Trek **15** Saturday Night Fever

GENERAL ENTERTAINMENT
Quiz 21

1   With whom did David Bowie duet on the No. 1 hit 'Dancing in the Street'?

2   How is the female politician who was appointed US Ambassador to Ghana in 1974 best remembered in the world of entertainment?

3   Who was the American vaudeville star known as the 'Last of the Red Hot Mamas'?

4   Which American jazz musician wrote 'Mood Indigo'?

5   Which entertainer once said: "I was born at the age of twelve on an MGM lot"?

6   In which 1971 movie is Dennis Weaver terrorised and chased in his car by a large tank truck?

7   What is unusual about the character ODO in 'Star Trek – Deep Space Nine'?

8   The Meanies are the villains in which Beatles movie?

9   Who plays the nurse who tends Ralph Fiennes in 'The English Patient'?

10 The film 'Kiss Me Kate' is based on which Shakespeare play?

11 Who played Demi Moore's husband in the movie 'Indecent Proposal'?

12 Which male film star played a female in all his films?

13 Of the Marx brothers, whose real name was Julius?

14 In 'Hergé's Adventures of Tin Tin', what is the name of Tin Tin's dog?

15 Which pop singer has the middle names Damita Jo?

Answers 1 Mick Jagger 2 Shirley Temple 3 Sophie Tucker 4 Duke Ellington 5 Judy Garland 6 Duel 7 He is a shape-shifter 8 Yellow Submarine 9 Juliette Binoche 10 The Taming of the Shrew 11 Woody Harrelson 12 Lassie 13 Groucho 14 Snowy 15 Janet Jackson

GENERAL ENTERTAINMENT   *Quiz 22*

1   What is the name of the villain in 'Star Wars'?

2   Who are Katherine, Rocky, Adam, Tanya and Tommy better known as?

3   Which Italian actress starred in 'A Countess From Hong Kong' and 'The Millionairess'?

4   In which European city is the opera 'La Boheme' set?

5   Who wrote the music for 'Starlight Express'?

6   Who started to broadcast his weekly 'Letter From America' in 1946?

7   In 'Batman and Robin', what is Robin's real name?

8   How many movements are there usually in a concerto?

9   In which movie does Montgomery Clift play a priest who is told of a murder in confessional?

10 Who wrote the song 'White Christmas'?

11 Who recorded 'Pearl's a Singer' in 1977 and 'Gasoline Alley' in 1983?

12 Keith Richard is famous as the rhythm guitarist with which rock group?

13 What is the meaning of Kemo Sabi, which Tonto calls the Lone Ranger?

14 Who was the British member of the Monkees?

15 Who played the Ringo Kid in John Ford's classic movie 'Stagecoach'?

Answers 1 Darth Vader 2 The Power Rangers 3 Sophia Loren 4 Paris 5 Andrew Lloyd Weber 6 Alistair Cooke 7 Dick Grayson 8 3 9 I Confess 10 Irving Berlin 11 Elkie Brooks 12 Rolling Stones 13 Trusty Scout 14 Davy Jones 15 John Wayne

GENERAL ENTERTAINMENT · Quiz 23

1   Anni-Frid Lyngstad was a member of which pop group?

2   What was John Lennon's first solo hit record?

3   In which film musical did Lee Marvin sing 'Wanderin' Star'?

4   In the movie 'The Agony and the Ecstasy', which painter is played by Charlton Heston?

5   Which fictional character has been portrayed in the movies more than any other?

6   Who wrote the Joe Cocker hit 'With a Little Help From My Friends'?

7   What did my truelove give to me on the 10th day of Christmas?

8   Which Stephen Sondheim musical was based on an Ingmar Bergman film 'Smiles of a Summer Night'?

9   In which film musical does Maurice Chevalier sing 'Thank Heaven For Little Girls'?

10   'Ain't Misbehavin' was the theme song of which piano playing jazz great?

11   Who played Charlene Robinson in the Australian soap 'Neighbours'?

12   Which famous TV series cigar-smoker partook of 'Garcia y Vega Elegantes' brand of cigars?

13   Which cartoon was the first to be given a X-certificate?

14   What instrument was played by jazz great Artie Shaw?

15   Lieut. Pinkerton is a character in which Puccini opera?

Answers 1 Abba 2 Give Peace a Chance 3 Paint Your Wagon 4 Michaelangelo 5 Sherlock Holmes 6 Lennon and McCartney 7 10 pipers piping 8 A Little Night Music 9 Gigi 10 Fats Waller 11 Kylie Minogue 12 Lt.Colombo 13 Fritz the Cat 14 Clarinet 15 Madame Butterfly

GENERAL ENTERTAINMENT — *Quiz 24*

1 In 1995 Neil Young collaborated with which pop group on the album 'Mirror Ball'?

2 Who wrote the internationally acclaimed thriller 'The Mask of Demetrios'

3 Which instrument is pitched an octave above a flute?

4 Who were John Belushi and Dan Ackroyd otherwise known as?

5 Pete Best was one of the original members of which rock group?

6 Who was responsible for the distinctive laugh of cartoon character Woody Woodpecker?

7 Who played Andy Hardy in a series of films in the 1940s?

8 The Attractions are the backing group for which pop star?

9 In which vintage TV series did Brodrick Crawford play Dan Matthews?

10 …and what was his famous catchphrase in the series?

11 Who was the first person to cross Niagara Falls on a tightrope?

12 Julie Andrews played which character whose address was 17 Cherry Tree Lane?

13 Who played Sue Ellen in 'Dallas'?

14 'All the President's Men' was an exposure of which US 1970s scandal?

15 'He's So Fine' by the Chiffons was likened to which song by George Harrison?

Answers 1 Pearl Jam 2 Eric Ambler 3 Piccolo 4 Blues Brothers 5 The Beatles 6 Mel Blanc 7 Mickey Rooney 8 Elvis Costello 9 Highway Patrol 10 Ten Four 11 Blondin 12 Mary Poppins 13 Linda Gray 14 Watergate 15 My Sweet Lord

GENERAL ENTERTAINMENT   *Quiz 25*

1 In which TV series did James Garner live in a trailer?

2 Probably the most frequently sung song in the UK and USA, which song was composed in 1892 under the original title of 'Good Morning To You'?

3 The Harlettes female vocal trio were the backing group for which female singer?

4 Which TV series is set in Bedrock?

5 The actress Susan Blackline played the first victim in which 1975 blockbuster movie?

6 Who played Napoleon Solo in the TV series 'The Man From U.N.C.L.E'?

7 What was the nickname of Jimmy Doyle, played by Gene Hackman in 'The French Connection'?

8 Who in a 1942 Disney feature length cartoon movie became the Great Prince of the Forest?

9 Who wrote the words for 'Auld Lang Syne'?

10 Which one of the Marx Brothers was Arthur?

11 How in the world of pop music is Marvin Lee Aday better known?

12 Which cartoon series is set in Jellystone Park?

13 In which 90s movie does a London bookshop owner fall for an American film star?

14 What is the nationality of the pop group 'A-ha'?

15 Whose catchphrase is 'Hello, Possums'?

Answers 1 The Rockford Files 2 Happy Birthday to You 3 Bette Midler 4 The Flintstones 5 Jaws 6 Robert Vaughn 7 Popeye 8 Bambi 9 Robert Burns 10 Harpo 11 Meat Loaf 12 Yogi Bear 13 Notting Hill 14 Norwegian 15 Dame Edna Everage

GENERAL ENTERTAINMENT

Quiz 26

1 Bernard Jewry, aka Shane Fenton, is best known by what stage name?

2 Which 50s vocalist, who died in 2000 as a result of a riding accident, had a string of hit records including 'She Wears Red Feathers' in 1953?

3 In the song 'Tie a Yellow Ribbon Round the Old Oak Tree', how many long years had the singer spent in prison?

4 How is Debbie Harry best known in the world of entertainment?

5 Which cartoon character has a 30 inch chest which increases to 60 inch when expanded?

6 In which prison is Steve McQueen held in solitary confinement in the movie 'Papillon'?

7 Who played Mrs Robinson in the 1967 movie 'The Graduate'?

8 Complete the title of the pop group, Cliff Bennett and the... ...

9 Who composed the ballet 'A Midsummer Night's Dream'?

10 What did my true love give to me on the 4th day of Christmas?

11 The writing of which traditional English song is improbably attributed to King Henry VIII?

12 In 1962, which recording by the Tornados became the first British instrumental to top the US charts?

13 Which English actress was the daughter of a Dutch Baroness?

14 The song 'Windmills of Your Mind' is from the soundtrack of which movie?

15 In a 1943 movie a future US Senator played the father of a future US President. Can you name the two actors?

Answers 1 Alvin Stardust 2 Guy Mitchell 3 3 4 Blondie 5 Popeye 6 Devil's Island 7 Anne Bancroft 8 Rebel Rousers 9 Mendelssohn 10 4 Calling birds 11 Greensleeves 12 Telstar 13 Audrey Hepburn 14 The Thomas Crown Affair 15 George Murphy and Ronald Reagan

GENERAL ENTERTAINMENT

Quiz 27

1   Which semi-classical instrumental group included John Williams and Herbie Flowers?

2   'This Night Can Last Forever' from Billy Joel's 1983 album 'An Innocent Man' is based on a melody by which classical composer?

3   Whose hit single 'Crazy' entered the UK charts in 1990, twenty-seven years after her death?

4   Name the pop group whose four members included Eric Clapton and whose chart successes included 'I Feel Free'?

5   Can you complete the title of the song 'Maria…' which was a 1969 chart hit for Gene Pitney?

6   What was the stage name of Stuart Goddard who had a hit record in the 1980s with 'Goody Two Shoes'?

7   Paul Anka wrote which song, which was the English version of 'Comme D'Habitude'?

8   Which Tchaikovsky work is usually accompanied by a scored cannon, mortar effects and bells?

9   The subtitle of which Delibe's ballet is 'The Girl with the Enamel Eyes'?

10 Who had a chart hit with 'YMCA' in 1983?

11 Which 1941 film featured 'The Warsaw Concerto'?

12 In which Puccini opera does The Polka Inn feature?

13 Which is the smallest note, a crotchet or quaver?

14 In Holst's 'The Planets', which planet is the bringer of Jollity?

15 Whose book 'Father of the Blues' was published in the year of his death in 1958?

Answers 1 Sky **2** Beethoven **3** Patsy Cline **4** Cream **5** Elena **6** Adam Ant **7** My Way **8** 1812 Overture **9** Coppelia **10** Village People **11** Dangerous Moonlight **12** The Girl of the Golden West **13** Crotchet **14** Jupiter **15** W.C. Handy

ENTERTAINMENT

This quiz is all about television programmes.

1 Which city was the setting for 'Cagney and Lacey'?

2 Better known for her role in another TV series, who played Chris Cagney in the pilot film of Cagney and Lacey?

3 Who played Hannibal Smith in 'The A Team'?

4 Who played the title role in the award winning comedy series 'Murphy Brown'?

5 In the Australian soap 'Neighbours', what is the surname of the family consisting of Karl, Susan and their children Mal, Libby and Billy?

6 In Coronation Street, what was Emily's surname before she became a Bishop?

7 Who played the wheelchair-bound character in the 1998 made-for-TV remake of Hitchcock's movie 'Rear Window'?

8 Who was Bo and Luke's female cousin in 'The Dukes Of Hazzard'?

9 Name the American actor who played Dempsey in the police drama series 'Dempsey And Makepeace'.

10 What single letter was the title of a sci-fi series which featured a character called Mike Donovan battling against an invasion of reptile-like aliens on earth?

11 Which former Miami Vice star went on to become Nash Bridges?

12 Set in Philadelphia, what was the title of the light-hearted drama series about upwardly mobile friends that included characters named Michael, Elliot, Hope, Nancy, Gary, Melissa and Ellyn?

13 Which comedy series was set in the fictional town of Cicely, Alaska?

14 Which drama series featured an ex-cop turned radio presenter named Jack Killian?

15 Name the British sitcom featuring Joe McGann, Diana Weston and Honor Blackman that was based on the US sitcom 'Who's The Boss'.

Answers 1 New York 2 Loretta Swit (Hotlips in M.A.S.H) 3 George Peppard 4 Candice Bergen 5 Kennedy 6 Nugent 7 Christopher Reeve 8 Daisy 9 Michael Brandon 10 V 11 Don Johnson 12 Thirtysomething 13 Northern Exposure 14 Midnight Caller 15 The Upper Hand

GENERAL ENTERTAINMENT — *Quiz 29*

1 Complete the title of this song 'In the Year...', which was the one hit wonder of Zager and Evans in 1969.

2 In a Mozart opera, whose servant is Leporello?

3 With whom did Elton John record his first UK No.1 hit 'Don't Go Breaking My Heart'?

4 For which Audrey Hepburn movie did Henry Mancini write 'Moon River'?

5 In which film does Donald O'Conner perform the classic number 'Make 'Em Laugh'?

6 'Send in the Clowns' comes from which musical?

7 George Takic played which role in the original series of 'Star Trek'?

8 The Coconuts were the backing group for which artist?

9 What in the TV series 'The Dukes of Hazzard', was General Lee?

10 Which pop star named himself after a German composer?

11 In which film does Olivia Newton-John sing 'Hopelessly Devoted To You'?

12 Which Shakespeare play is called in theatrical circles The Scottish Play, because it is unlucky to mention its name?

13 What is the name of Walt Disney's flying elephant?

14 What instrument was played classically by Vladimir Horowitz?

15 Which musical was based on the George Bernard Shaw play 'Pygmalion'?

Answers 1 2525 2 Don Giovanni 3 Kiki Dee 4 Breakfast at Tiffany's 5 Singing in the Rain 6 A Little Night Music 7 Mr Sulu 8 Kid Creole 9 The Car 10 Engelbert Humperdinck 11 Grease 12 Macbeth 13 Dumbo 14 Piano 15 My Fair Lady

Quiz 30

1 Who played Cathy Gale in 'The Avengers'?

2 How is Harry Wayne Casey, who recorded with the Sunshine Band, more commonly referred to?

3 Which hit record for the New Seekers was originally heard as a Coca-Cola television jingle?

4 'I Got Stung One Night' was the last of which type of record by Elvis Presley issued in October 1958?

5 The Osmond Brothers made their television debut on which singer's show in December 1962?

6 Marc Almond was lead singer with which rock group?

7 Which role did David Essex play on stage in the musical 'Evita'?

8 Which group had a No.1 with 'Needles and Pins'?

9 In which 1995 blockbuster movie does Kevin Costner play 'The Mariner' and Dennis Hopper play 'The Deacon'?

10 In the world of country music who is The Man in Black?

11 What nationality is singer Bjork?

12 In which TV series are the first names of the two main characters Fox and Dana?

13 Amati and Guarneri are famous makes of which musical instrument?

14 Which country is the setting for Bizet's opera 'The Pearl Fishers'?

15 Which rock group were previously called New Yardbirds?

Answers 1 Honor Blackman 2 KC 3 I'd Like To Teach the World to Sing 4 78 rpm 5 The Andy Williams Show 6 Soft Cell 7 Che Guevara 8 The Searchers 9 Waterworld 10 Johnny Cash 11 Icelandic 12 The X-Files 13 Violin 14 Ceylon (Sri Lanka) 15 Led Zeppelin

GENERAL ENTERTAINMENT　　　*Quiz 31*

1　What was the name of Bob Marley's backing group?

2　Lionel Hampton introduced which instrument into jazz?

3　What type of instrument in Ireland is a bodhran?

4　In which Spanish dance does the man represent a matador and the woman represent the cloak?

5　In the movie 'The Bodyguard', who plays the singer requiring protection?

6　Dame Myra Hess was a celebrated classical performer on which instrument?

7　Who in 1938 wrote the music for the ballet 'Billy the Kid'?

8　The song 'Nobody Does It Better' featured in which James Bond film?

9　The aria 'Nessun Dorma' is from which Puccini opera?

10　The Composer Franz Liszt was a virtuoso performer on which instrument?

11　In which Gilbert and Sullivan opera does the Lord Chancellor marry a fairy?

12　What is the popular name for Schubert's 'Quintet in A for piano and strings'?

13　In the Popeye cartoon series who is Popeye's hamburger loving friend who has an IQ of 326?

14　Which US female vocal/instrumental group had a hit with 'Walk Like An Egyptian'?

15　Which actor was the first male to appear as a centrefold in Cosmopolitan magazine?

Answers 1 The Wailers 2 Vibraphone (xylophone) 3 A drum 4 Pasa Doble 5 Whitney Houston 6 Piano 7 Aaron Copland 8 The Spy Who Loved Me 9 Turandot 10 Piano 11 Iolanthe 12 The Trout Quintet 13 J. Wellington Wimpy 14 The Bangles 15 Burt Reynolds

GENERAL ENTERTAINMENT   *Quiz 32*

1   In which musical is the dawning of the Age of Aquarius celebrated?

2   Who asked 'How Do You Do It?' in 1963?

3   What in America are referred to as Mother Goose Songs?

4   Which opera features the 'Tavern of Lillas Pastia'?

5   Can you name a David Essex hit which has the title of a play by Shakespeare?

6   …and can you name a Shakespeare titled hit for Adam Faith?

7   What instrument was played by jazz great Erroll Garner?

8   Who, in the 1960s were Bobby Hatfield and Billy Medley?

9   What instrumentalist had a hit with 'Annie's Song' in 1978?

10 Who directed the movie 'Halloween'?

11 In which movie does Gary Cooper play an about-to-retire sherriff Will Kane?

12 Which opera singer sang at the wedding of Prince Charles and Lady Diana?

13 In which TV series is the main character DCI Jane Tennison?

14 'Stand By Your Man' was a hit for which country artist in 1975?

15 Who played Casey Jean (CJ) Parker in Baywatch?

Answers 1 Hair **2** Gerry and the Pacemakers **3** Nursery Rhymes **4** Carmen **5** A Winter's Tale **6** As You Like It **7** Piano **8** The Righteous Brothers **9** James Galway **10** John Carpenter **11** High Noon **12** Kiri Te Kanawa **13** Prime Suspect **14** Tammy Wynette **15** Pamela Anderson

GENERAL ENTERTAINMENT

Quiz 33

1   Which Johnny Mathis No.1 hit of 1976 was also known as 'Soleado'?

2   Which Andrew Lloyd Webber musical is performed on roller skates?

3   ...and who collaborated with Lloyd Webber on this musical?

4   Which is longer, a minim or a crotchet?

5   Who composed 'The Dream of Gerontius'?

6   Pete Townshend is associated with which rock group?

7   What historical character was played by Mel Gibson in the movie 'Braveheart'?

8   George Michael and Andrew Ridgeley formed which pop duo?

9   What were the names of the opposing gangs in the movie 'Quadrophenia'?

10 Lindsey Buckingham is a member of which rock group?

11 Adelaide Hall was a singer of what type of music?

12 'Who's Sorry Now' was the first hit record, in 1958, for which artist?

13 Which of Paul McCartney's songs was originally entitled 'Scrambled Eggs'?

14 Which famous composer served as a special constable in Hampstead in World War I?

15 Who wrote the ballet 'The Firebird'?

Answers 1 When a Child is Born **2** Starlight Express **3** Richard Stilgoe **4** Minim (two crotchets) **5** Edward Elgar **6** The Who **7** William Wallace **8** Wham **9** Mods and Rockers **10** Fleetwood Mac **11** Jazz **12** Connie Francis **13** Yesterday **14** Edward Elgar **15** Igor Stravinsky

This quiz is all about television programmes.

1   What's the first name of Richard Chamberlain's Dr Kildare?

2   The first name of Makepeace in the police drama series 'Dempsey And Makepeace'?

3   The first name of Cannon the private eye played by William Conrad?

4   The first name of Smart the secret agent in the 1960s comedy series 'Get Smart'?

5   Played by Bob Crane, the first name of Hogan in 'Hogan's Heroes'?

6   The first name of McMillan in the series 'McMillan And Wife'?

7   What's the first name of the cartoon character Mr Magoo?

8   Played by Barry Newman, the first name of the lawyer Petrocelli?

9   Played by Richard Roundtree in the 1970s detective series, what is the first name of Shaft?

10   The surname of Lucille Ball's character in the comedy series 'Here's Lucy'?

11   The maiden name of Valerie Harper's character in the comedy series 'Rhoda'?

12   The surname of Roseanne Barr/Arnold's character in 'Roseanne'?

13   The first name of Gene Barry's character in the detective series 'Burke's Law'?

14   Played by Raymond Burr, what is the first name of the wheelchair-bound cop Ironside?

15   The surname of father and son lawyers played by E.G.Marshall and Robert Reed in the 1960s drama series 'The Defenders'?

Quiz 35

1   Who wrote the music for the Astaire/Rodgers film 'Top Hat'?
2   In the Hitchcock film 'The Trouble With Harry', what was the trouble with Harry?
3   In a classic Orson Welles movie, who lives in Xanadu?
4   In which movie does Elvis Presley sing 'Wooden Heart'?
5   Who directed and starred in 'Reservoir Dogs'?
6   The US soap 'The Bold and the Beautiful' is set in which city?
7   'Why Do Fools Fall In Love' was a No. 1 hit for which artist in 1956?
8   In which movie did Liz Hurley play Vanessa Kensington?
9   Which animal goes water skiing in the movie 'Honky Tonk Freeway'?
10 In which year were Academy awards first presented?
11 What was the real first name of Duke Ellington?
12 Which artist made the famous recording of 'Fever'?
13 Which 1973 Clint Eastwood movie was set in the Western town of Lago?
14 Who sang the theme song for the TV series 'Rawhide'?
15 Which flamboyant entertainer had a swimming pool in the shape of a piano?

Answers 1 Irving Berlin 2 He was dead 3 Citizen Kane 4 G.I. Blues 5 Quentin Tarantino
6 Los Angeles 7 Frankie Lymon and the Teenagers 8 Austin Powers: International Man of
Mystery 9 An elephant 10 1928 11 Edmund 12 Peggy Lee 13 High Plains Drifter
14 Frankie Laine 15 Liberace

ENTERTAINMENT

Quiz 36

1 The sisters Nicole and Nathalie Appleton are associated with which pop group?

2 Joel Grey won an Oscar for Best Actor in a Supporting Role in 1972 for his performance in which musical?

3 Which boxer was portrayed in the 1980 movie 'Raging Bull' by Robert De Niro?

4 Lara's Theme is the theme from which 1965 movie?

5 ...and with lyrics, what is the song entitled?

6 What is the name of the saloon owned and run by Frenchy (Marlene Dietrich) in the 1939 movie 'Destry Rides Again'?

7 Natalie Wood portrayed which striptease artist in the film 'Gypsy'?

8 What was the middle name of John Lennon before he changed it to Ono?

9 In which film musical does Ethel Merman play the U.S. Ambassador to the country of Lichtenburg?

10 Phil Lynott is connected with which rock group?

11 What is the English translation of the aria 'Vesti la gubba' from the opera 'Pagliacci'?

12 ...and what is the English translation of 'Pagliacci'?

13 ...and who wrote the opera 'Pagliacci'?

14 Which instrument did bandleader Tommy Dorsey play?

15 After writing his last opera 'William Tell', the composer Rossini devoted the rest of his life to which hobby?

Answers 1 All Saints 2 Cabaret 3 Jake La Motta 4 Doctor Zhivago 5 Somewhere My Love 6 Last Chance Saloon 7 Gypsy Rose Lee 8 Winston 9 Call Me Madame 10 Thin Lizzy 11 On With the Motley 12 The Clowns 13 Leoncavallo 14 Trombone 15 Cooking

GENERAL ENTERTAINMENT

Quiz 37

1 Who, in 1969, sang about 'A Boy Named Sue'?

2 Who composed 'The Entry of the Queen of Sheba', which is often played as a bride walks down the aisle?

3 The song 'I'm Always Chasing Rainbows' is based on which composer's 'Fantasie-Impromptu in C sharp minor'?

4 Who composed the music for several Steven Spielberg films, including 'Jaws?

5 'I Love Paris' is from which Cole Porter musical?

6 A trumpet was the only instrument found in whose tomb in 1922?

7 Majel Barrett played head nurse Lt. Christine Chapel in which cult TV series?

8 What was the name of Enoch Light's orchestra?

9 Which cult actor died in a car crash on 20 September 1955?

10 Which is the only fictional place visited in the Hope/Crosby Road films?

11 Which brothers wrote the music for the film 'Saturday Night Fever'?

12 Bernie Taupin has co-written many hits with which superstar?

13 Which US male vocal group were 'At the Hop' in 1958?

14 In which 1998 movie does Annette Bening play a book illustrator who uses her psychic powers to discover where a child murderer is to strike next?

15 Who plays DI Jack Frost in 'A Touch of Frost'?

Answers 1 Johnny Cash 2 Handel 3 Chopin 4 John Williams 5 Can-Can 6 Tutankhamun 7 Star Trek 8 The Light Brigade 9 James Dean 10 Utopia 11 The Gibb Brothers 12 Elton John 13 Danny and the Juniors 14 In Dreams 15 David Jason

1 Who played Jack Lemmon's accident-prone assistant in 'The Great Race'?

2 Which TV series featured the characters Charles and Caroline Ingalls?

3 Tchaikovsky wrote three ballets, 'Swan Lake', 'The Nutcracker' and which other?

4 What song from their 1937 film 'Way Out West' was a surprise hit for Laurel and Hardy in 1975?

5 The sub-title of which Gilbert and Sullivan opera is 'The Lass Who Loved a Sailor'?

6 The Theme from the 'Bridge on the River Kwai' incorporated which march written by Kenneth J. Alford in 1914?

7 What was the nickname of Major Margaret Houlihan in M.A.S.H?

8 What is the nickname of muppet Simon Smith in the TV series 'The Muppet Show'?

9 Whose Broadway revues from 1907 to 1931 were designed to 'Glorify the American Girl'?

10 Count Almaviva and Rossina are lovers in which Rossini opera?

11 Whose secretary was Della Street?

12 The mazurka is the national dance of which country?

13 Which dancer with the Kirov Ballet defected to the West in 1974?

14 Which of the Spice Girls was Emma Bunton?

15 Who played Obi-Wan Kenobi in 'Star Wars'?

Answers 1 Peter Falk 2 Little House on the Prairie 3 The Sleeping Beauty 4 The Trail of the Lonesome Pine 5 HMS Pinafore 6 Colonel Bogey 7 Hot lips 8 Scooter 9 Florenz Ziegfeld 10 The Barber of Seville 11 Perry Mason 12 Poland 13 Mikhail Baryshnikov 14 Baby Spice 15 Alec Guinness

1 What was the nickname of jazz great Thomas Wright Waller?

2 What type of entertainment was provided by Peter Brough and Ray Allen?

3 What was the nickname of the straightfaced American comedian Joseph Francis Keaton?

4 In the partnership of Gilbert and Sullivan, who wrote the music?

5 In the film 'The Jazz Singer', who declared: "You ain't heard nothin' yet folks"?

6 What actor was dubbed The King of Hollywood?

7 Elliot Ness was the hero of which TV series?

8 What is the US equivalent of the British Music Hall?

9 Which actress appeared in the Road films with Hope and Crosby?

10 In theatrical terms what is Kensington Gore?

11 Who said: "All I need to make a comedy is a park, a policeman and a pretty girl"?

12 In Alfred Hitchcock's 1951 film 'Strangers on a Train', one of the strangers was played by Farley Granger, who played the other?

13 What in the 19th-century was Astles' and Spangler's?

14 What type of music was popularised by Scott Joplin?

15 Which showman said: "There's a sucker born every minute"?

Answers 1 Fats 2 Ventriloquism 3 Buster 4 Sullivan 5 Al Jolson 6 Clark Gable 7 The Untouchables 8 Vaudeville 9 Dorothy Lamour 10 Imitation blood 11 Charlie Chaplin 12 Robert Walker 13 A circus 14 Ragtime 15 P.T. Barnum

1   Who composed the musicals 'On the Town' and 'West Side Story'?

2   Which Mexican town is associated with Herb Alpert?

3   Who, in 1936, composed 'Peter and the Wolf'?

4   Fred Astaire starred in vaudeville as a double-act with his sister. What was her name?

5   What is the name of Elvis Presley's home, now a museum in Memphis?

6   In Shakespeare's 'A Midsummer Night's Dream', who is King of the Fairies?

7   Who played the part of Robert Jordan in the film version of Hemingway's 'For Whom The Bell Tolls'?

8   Which character was played by Stanley Holloway in 'My Fair Lady'?

9   Which vocal/instrumental group were 'Glad All Over' in 1963?

10 What was the nickname of blues artist Peter Chatman?

11 Which music by Ravel does Bo Derek make love to Dudley Moore in the 1979 movie '10'?

12 What is the best-known work of the British composer Sir Hubert Parry?

13 Who played the gangster Rico in the film 'Little Caesar'?

14 Who founded the silent film company Keystone in 1912?

15 Which 1950s TV series starred Jack Webb?

Answers 1 Leonard Bernstein 2 Tijuana 3 Prokofiev 4 Adele 5 Graceland 6 Oberon 7 Gary Cooper 8 Alfred Doolittle 9 Dave Clark Five 10 Memphis Slim 11 Bolero 12 Jerusalem 13 Edward G.Robinson 14 Mack Sennett 15 Dragnet

GENERAL ENTERTAINMENT   *Quiz 41*

1   Kenny Jones replaced Keith Moon as the drummer in which rock group?

2   Which theatre in London first staged the operas of Gilbert and Sullivan?

3   Who wrote and played the theme music on the harmonica for the 1953 film 'Genevieve'?

4   Developed in the 1950s by Leo Fender, what type of instrument was a Stratocaster?

5   Whose rock album, 'The Division Bell' included a track 'Keep Talking', featuring Stephen Hawking?

6   Which of the Beatles made a charity record 'Nobody's Child' for his wife's Romanian Angel appeal?

7   Who, with Annie Lennox, formed the Eurythmics?

8   Which Richard Strauss opera features 'The Dance of the Seven Veils'?

9   Who, in 1967, sang about Simon Smith and his Amazing Dancing Bear?

10 What nationality was soprano Jenny Lind?

11 Who wrote the lyrics of 'South Pacific'?

12 Who was nicknamed The Master?

13 Who had a 1973 No.1 hit with 'Merry Xmas Everybody'?

14 Which instrument is called Faggott in Germany?

15 Who played Wanda Gerschwitz in the movie 'A Fish Called Wanda'?

Answers 1 The Who **2** Savoy **3** Larry Adler **4** Guitar **5** Pink Floyd **6** George Harrison **7** Dave Stewart **8** Salome **9** Alan Price **10** Swedish **11** Oscar Hammerstein II **12** Noel Coward **13** Slade **14** Bassoon **15** Jamie Lee Curtis

GENERAL ENTERTAINMENT   *Quiz 42*

1 Which of the Beatles albums sold most copies in the UK?

2 In which movie did Humphrey Bogart say: "Here's looking at you kid"?

3 Who in the 1970s was dubbed the 'Queen of Disco'?

4 Matt Monroe sang the theme song for which Bond movie?

5 In 'Kojak', by what name did Theo Kojak refer to his brother George?

6 What instrument does Sharon play in the Corrs?

7 Who directed 'Blazing Saddles'?

8 In the 1930s and 1940s Nigel Bruce played Dr. Watson. Who played Sherlock Holmes?

9 The name Brian Ferry is associated with which rock group?

10 Who played the drums with the Dave Clark Five?

11 Duran Duran took their name from which Jane Fonda movie?

12 Who in a Peter, Paul and Mary song lived in a land called Honalee?

13 Which film star is also an International bridge player?

14 In which film did Rex Harrison talk to the animals?

15 Which No. 1 record by Chuck Berry was banned by the BBC?

Answers 1 Sergeant Pepper's Lonely Hearts Club Band 2 Casablanca 3 Donna Summer 4 From Russia With Love 5 Stavros 6 Violin 7 Mel Brooks 8 Basil Rathbone 9 Roxy Music 10 Dave Clark 11 Barbarella 12 Puff the Magic Dragon 13 Omar Sharif 14 Dr Dolittle 15 My Ding A Ling

GENERAL ENTERTAINMENT

Quiz 43

1   Which musical set in the slums of New York City is based on Shakespeare's 'Romeo and Juliet'?

2   In the TV series 'Roots', who was the son of Kizzy and Tom Kea?

3   What was the name of Olive Oyl's boyfriend for 10 years before she met Popeye?

4   George Frederick Handel became a naturalized subject of which country?

5   In the song 'The Naughty Lady of Shady Lane', how old was the naughty lady?

6   Which rock & roll legend was born at 1911 6th street, Lubbock, Texas on September 7th 1936?

7   Who played Sonny Hooper in the 1978 movie 'Hooper'?

8   What instrument is played by classical artist Julian Bream?

9   The characters Pamina and Papageno appear in which Mozart opera?

10 At which venue in July 1985 did the US Live Aid concert take place?

11 Which two actors who share the same surname have played Dr. Who?

12 The movie 'Apocalypse Now' is based on the book 'Heart of Darkness' by which author?

13 Which actor played opposite Myrna Loy in a series of 'Thin Man' movies?

14 In the 1951 movie 'Quo Vadis', which Roman emperor was played by Peter Ustinov?

15 The Quarrymen was the original name of which pop group?

Answers 1 West Side Story **2** Chicken George **3** Ham Gravy **4** Britain **5** 9 days **6** Buddy Holly **7** Burt Reynolds **8** Guitar **9** The Magic Flute **10** JFK Stadium, Philadelphia **11** Tom and Colin Baker **12** Joseph Conrad **13** William Powell **14** Nero **15** The Beatles

1   Abbreviated to TW3, what was the name of the first British satire TV show which originated in the 1960s?

2   'If I Said You Have A Beautiful Body Would You Hold It Against Me?', was a 1979 hit for which US vocal duo?

3   Who is the blind jazz pianist who settled in America from England in the 1940s, and wrote 'Lullaby of Birdland'?

4   Who wrote 'The Carnival of the Animals'?

5   'Take Me Home Country Road' was a 1973 hit for which artist?

6   Henry Mancini was a pianist and arranger with which big band in the 1940s?

7   What instrument was played by Dennis Brain?

8   Which song by Jimmy Durante was played on the soundtrack of 'Sleepless in Seattle'?

9   What nationality was composer Edward Grieg?

10 Which pop singer, born Steven Georgiou in London in 1947, retired from music in the 1970s and devoted himself to religious studies, having converted to Islam?

11 In the TV series 'Thunderbirds', what is the name of Lady Penelope's chauffeur?

12 What nationality is Buffy Saint-Marie?

13 Brian and Michael's 1978 hit 'Matchstick Men and Matchstick Cats and Dogs' was a tribute to which painter?

14 Which jazz great had a big band called 'The Herd'?

15 Which of the Spice Girls was Geri Halliwell?

GENERAL ENTERTAINMENT   *Quiz 45*

1   In the remake of which movie does Jessica Lange recreate the role made famous by Fay Wray?

2   In which century did Maurice Ravel write 'Bolero'?

3   Who wrote the opera 'Fair Maid of Perth'?

4   Which pop group obtained its name from the London postal code for Walthamstow?

5   In which movie did Greta Garbo first speak on screen?

6   Who composed the five 'Pomp and Circumstance' marches?

7   Ravi Shankar is a virtuoso on which instrument?

8   Whose Unfinished symphony was his 'No. 8 in B minor'?

9   Which conductor founded the London Symphony Orchestra?

10 Who directed the film 'Lawrence of Arabia'?

11 Who played Big Chris Sting in the movie 'Lock, Stock and Two Smoking Barrels'?

12 Which British rock group took its name from a Beano-comic character?

13 Which Jerry Herman musical was based on the Thornton Wilder play 'The Matchmaker'?

14 The names of Neil Tennant and Chris Lowe are associated with which pop group?

15 Which actor was the most decorated US soldier in World War II?

Answers 1 King Kong **2** 20th **3** Bizet **4** East 17 **5** Grand Hotel **6** Elgar **7** Sitar **8** Schubert **9** Sir Thomas Beecham **10** David Lean **11** Vinnie Jones **12** Thin Lizzy **13** Hello Dolly **14** Pet Shop Boys **15** Audie Murphy

1   Which American comedian/actor had a hit in 1985 with the song 'You Look Marvellous'?

2   Which US city is referred to in song as 'you toddlin' town'?

3   Name the duo who created the cartoon characters Tom and Jerry, Huckleberry Hound, The Flintstones and Scooby Doo?

4   Who starred as Wild Bill Hickok in the 1996 movie 'Wild Bill'?

5   Name the US actor with the Greek sounding name who appeared in the film 'West Side Story', '633 Squadron' and 'Kings Of The Sun'.

6   In the TV series, what make and model of car did Starsky and Hutch drive around in?

7   Rocky and Bullwinkle are cartoon characters. Rocky is a squirrel, what type of creature is Bullwinkle?

8   In which US state were singers Buddy Holly, Janis Joplin and Willie Nelson all born?

9   He collaborated with several lyricists and composed the music for the songs 'I've Got The World On A String', 'Over The Rainbow' and 'Get Happy', Name him?

10 In the song 'Waiting For The Robert E. Lee', what is the Robert E. Lee?

11 Brad Pitt married which actress in July 2000?

12 Which New Zealand-born actor often performs in a rock band known as 30 Odd Foot Of Grunts?

13 According to the words of Noel Coward's song 'Mad Dogs And Englishmen', where do they 'strike a gong, and fire off a midday gun'?

14 In which country was film director Pedro Almodovar born?

15 The musical piece 'Finlandia' was written by which composer?

Answers 1 Billy Crystal 2 Chicago 3 Hanna and Barbera 4 Jeff Bridges 5 George Chakiris 6 Ford Torino 7 Moose 8 Texas 9 Harold Arlen 10 A paddle steamer 11 Jennifer Aniston 12 Russell Crowe 13 Hong Kong 14 Spain 15 Sibelius

GENERAL ENTERTAINMENT   *Quiz 47*

1   Gavin Taylor was the first character to die in which British TV soap?

2   In August 1971 former Beatle George Harrison organised a concert in Madison Square Garden, New York to aid the victims of famine and war in which country?

3   'Get Me To The Church On Time', 'Wouldn't It Be Lovely' and 'With A Little Bit Of Luck' are all songs from which musical?

4   'To Hell And Back' is the title of the autobiography of which rock star?

5   Elyot and Amanda are the two leading characters in which Noel Coward play?

6   Velma, Daphne, Freddy and Shaggy are companions of which cartoon character?

7   Who starred as Lucas McCain in the 1960s TV western series 'The Rifleman'?

8   Which word, Italian for air, is used in opera to describe a solo song with instrumental accompaniment?

9   In which American TV drama series was the main character assisted by a character named Sam Fujiyama?

10 'Neither Shaken Nor Stirred' is the title of a biography of which actor?

11 And which actor compiled an almanac of information entitled 'Not Many People Know That'?

12 Which actor, star of the film 'Matrix', appeared with his rock band at the 1999 Glastonbury festival?

13 With which form of entertainment do you particularly associate Darcey Bussell?

14 Which US city was the setting for the TV series 'Starsky And Hutch'?

15 With which British entertainer do you associate the phrase 'Turned out nice again'?

Answers 1 Brookside 2 Bangaladesh 3 My Fair Lady 4 Meatloaf 5 Private Lives 6 Scooby Doo 7 Chuck Connors 8 Aria 9 Quincy 10 Sean Connery 11 Michael Caine 12 Keanu Reeves 13 Ballet 14 Los Angeles 15 George Formby

GENERAL ENTERTAINMENT   *Quiz 48*

1 Which British actress won a Tony award in 1999 for her performance in the play 'Amy's View'?

2 In which country was the famous escapologist Harry Houdini born?

3 Who, in 1982, became the first person to have three musicals running in New York and three running in London at the same time?

4 What's the name of the muskrat who was Deputy Dawg's sidekick?

5 Who played 'Dex' Dexter in 'Dynasty'?

6 Who was the original leading male dancer in 'Riverdance' and then went on to produce a show entitled 'Lord Of The Dance'?

7 Famous for her legs, which Hollywood star of the 1940s and 1950s once said: "There are two reasons why I'm in the movies – and I'm standing on both of them"?

8 The musical 'Mamma Mia' features the songs of which group?

9 'A Doll's House', 'Ghosts' and 'Hedda Gabler' are all plays written by which Norwegian dramatist?

10 In what style of jazz or blues piano playing does the left hand establish a driving repetitive rhythm, while the right provides a variety of syncopation?

11 With which musical instrument do you associate Charlie Christian and Django Reinhardt?

12 The song 'Seventy Six Trombones' comes from which musical?

13 Which Hollywood tough-guy actor was involved in the first ever 'palimony' case in 1979?

14 Maria Callas, Marc Bolan, Bing Crosby and Elvis Presley all died in which year?

15 Which American-born rock star was buried in Paris in July 1971?

Answers 1 Judi Dench 2 Hungary 3 Andrew Lloyd Webber 4 Muskie 5 Michael Nader 6 Michael Flatley 7 Betty Grable 8 Abba 9 Henrik Ibsen 10 Boogie-Woogie 11 Guitar 12 The Music Man 13 Lee Marvin 14 1977 15 Jim Morrison

1   Which duo wrote the musical 'Gigi'?

2   With which instrument do you associate the Austrian musician Fritz Kreisler?

3   An Italian film director, he made the films 'Shoeshine', 'Bicycle Thieves', 'A Place For Lovers' and 'Indiscretion Of An American Wife'. As an actor he appeared in the TV series 'The Four Just Men' with Jack Hawkins, Dan Dailey and Richard Conte. Name him.

4   Founded in Moscow in 1780, what is the name of Russia's principal ballet company?

5   'Parsley, sage, rosemary and thyme' is the second line of which song?

6   Which musical, set in Czarist Russia, is the story of Tevye the dairyman?

7   Which 19th century German composer wrote a set of 18 waltzes for singers and piano entitled 'Liebeslieder Waltzer'?

8   Name the Welsh composer and songwriter who wrote the song 'We'll Gather Lilacs'?

9   What was the first name of the famous Italian tenor, Caruso, who died in 1921?

10 Name the French vocal group, popular in the 1960s, who sang 18th century music, especially that of Bach, in a swing/jazz style?

11 How many musicians are there in a quintet?

12 The song 'The Folks Who Live On The Hill' was written by whom?

13 What is the deep-toned Aboriginal wind instrument popularised by Rolf Harris called?

14 'Don't know why there's no sun up in the sky' are the first words of which popular song?

15 What nationality was the bass-baritone singer Peter Dawson?

Answers 1 Lerner and Loewe **2** Violin **3** Vittorio De Sica **4** Bolshoi **5** Scarborough Fair **6** Fiddler On The Roof **7** Brahms **8** Ivor Novello **9** Enrico **10** Swingle Singers **11** 5 **12** Jerome Kern **13** Didgeridoo **14** Stormy Weather **15** Australian

1   Which British actress was known as the 'Jersey Lily'?

2   In which musical would you hear the songs 'Climb Every Mountain' and 'Sixteen Going On Seventeen'?

3   According to the popular song 'birds do it, bees do it – even educated fleas do it' – do what?

4   Henry, Jane, Peter and Bridget - what is the surname of this family of actors?

5   In which country was playwright Tom Stoppard born?

6   Born Anthony Robert MacMillan in Scotland, which rather portly actor took the surname of a legendary jazz saxophonist?

7   Which Rodgers and Hammerstein musical features the song 'People Will Say We're In Love'?

8   According to the song, in which US city is the 'house of the rising sun'?

9   'Wakey wakey' was the catchphrase of which British bandleader?

10 Who is Popeye's great rival for Olive Oyl's affections?

11 With which musical instrument do you associate Dame Myra Hess?

12 Which star of stage and screen was known as the 'Brazilian Bombshell'?

13 What was the name of the spoof group created by Neil Innes that was a thinly disguised parody of the Beatles?

14 According to the old song, how long is the Camptown racetrack?

15 And according to the title of the song, with which US state do you associate the yellow rose?

Answers 1 Lillie Langtry 2 The Sound Of Music 3 Fall in love 4 Fonda 5 Czechoslovakia 6 Robbie Coltrane 7 Oklahoma 8 New Orleans 9 Billy Cotton 10 Bluto 11 Piano 12 Carmen Miranda 13 The Rutles 14 5 miles 15 Texas

Quiz 51

1   Complete the title of the following Prokofiev opera – 'The Love For Three ....'?

2   Pete Seeger, Lee Hays, Ronnie Gilbert and Fred Helleman founded which American folk group in the late 1940s. They helped to popularize songs such as 'Goodnight Irene' and 'Kisses Sweeter Than Wine'?

3   Which musical instrument did comedian Jack Benny play, and base his stand-up comedy routine around?

4   The Lindy Hop was a dance inspired by an achievement of which man in 1927?

5   Who wrote the musical 'Annie Get Your Gun'?

6   In London, which concert hall is the traditional home of the Promenade concerts?

7   She was born Cherilyn Sarkasian La Piere. By what name is she better known?

8   What does the acronym RADA stand for?

9   With which female ventriloquist do you associate the puppet Lambchop?

10 Name the Scottish music-hall entertainer who wrote the songs 'Roamin' In The Gloamin' ' and 'Keep Right On To The End Of The Road'?

11 In which musical is the song 'Big Spender' featured?

12 In which Caribbean dance do people pass under a bar or pole whilst leaning backwards?

13 From which opera does the aria 'One Fine Day' come?

14 'My little chickadee' is a phrase associated with which US comedian and actor?

15 Lys Assia won the very first Eurovision Song Contest in 1956 representing which country?

Answers 1 Oranges **2** The Weavers **3** Violin **4** Charles Lindbergh **5** Irving Berlin **6** Royal Albert Hall **7** Cher **8** Royal Academy of Dramatic Art **9** Shari Lewis **10** Harry Lauder **11** Sweet Charity **12** Limbo **13** Madame Butterfly **14** W. C. Fields **15** Switzerland

1   Who wrote the songs 'Beautiful Dreamer' and 'Jeannie With The Light Brown Hair'?

2   Name the British contralto who died of cancer at the height of her career in 1953.

3   With whom did Lorenz Hart write the musicals 'The Boys From Syracuse' and 'Pal Joey'?

4   In which country was jazz pianist Oscar Peterson born?

5   In 1998, which tenor organised a charity concert in his home town of Modena, during which he sang with the Spice Girls?

6   Also in 1998, who became the first actress to win an Emmy and an Oscar in the same year?

7   How many musicians are there in a sextet?

8   According to the song 'Home, where grass is greener, where honey bees hum melodies and orange trees scent the breeze' is where?

9   The song 'So Deep Is The Night' is an arrangement of music written by which classical composer?

10   Which of Sigmund Romberg's operettas features the 'Riff Song'?

11   Name the Austrian-born British tenor who wrote and sang 'My Heart And I'?

12   With which female singer did Billy Eckstine record the song 'Passing Strangers'?

13   In which city was composer Frederick Delius born?

14   Which pianist's real name is Philippe Pages?

15   What is the English title of the Welsh folk song 'Ar Hyd y Nos'?

Answers 1 Stephen Foster 2 Kathleen Ferrier 3 Richard Rodgers 4 Canada 5 Luciano Pavarotti 6 Helen Hunt 7 6 8 Pasadena 9 Chopin 10 The Desert Song 11 Richard Tauber 12 Sarah Vaughan 13 Bradford 14 Richard Clayderman 15 All Through The Night

Quiz 53

1   Near blind from birth, he was jazz music's first supreme keyboard virtuoso. Born in Toledo, Ohio in 1909/10 he died in 1956. Name him.

2   What nationality was the composer Christian Sinding?

3   What is the English title of Mozart's opera 'Die Zauberflote'?

4   Which bandleader was dubbed 'King of the Hi-De-Ho' for his scat-type vocals?

5   What was the nickname of jazz saxophonist Julian Adderley?

6   Then known as Force, the group Europe represented which country at the 1982 Eurovision Song Contest?

7   Which virtuoso jazz drummer started out in a vaudeville act as 'Baby Trapps the Drum Wonder'?

8   The first UK album chart appeared in November 1958. The first album to top that chart stayed in the charts for 70 weeks. It was the soundtrack from which Rodgers and Hammerstein movie?

9   What nationality was the 20th century composer John Henry Antill?

10 Which rock star was married for a short time to Erin Everly, daughter of Don Everly of the Everly Brothers?

11 At the 1998 Golden Raspberry Awards, who won the award for worst actress for her performance in the film 'GI Jane'?

12 'Goodness Had Nothing To Do With It' was the title of which Hollywood sex symbol's autobiography?

13 Born Alfredo Arnold Cocozza in 1921, which American tenor died from a heart attack at the age of 38 following drug and alcohol problems?

14 Who composed the opera 'Fierrabras'?

15 In the musical 'My Fair Lady', what did Eliza admit that she 'could have done all night and still have begged for more'?

Answers 1 Art Tatum **2** Norwegian **3** The Magic Flute **4** Cab Calloway **5** Cannonball **6** Sweden **7** Buddy Rich **8** South Pacific **9** Australian **10** Axl Rose **11** Demi Moore **12** Mae West **13** Mario Lanza **14** Schubert **15** Danced

1   Based on a Victor Hugo novel, and popular throughout the world, which stage musical was the subject of a 10th anniversary gala concert at the Royal Albert Hall in October 1995?

2   Which of Henry VIII's wives was the subject of an opera by the 19th century Italian composer Donizetti?

3   Which pop legend celebrated his birthday with a lavish party at the Hammersmith Palais in 1997?

4   Of the famous musical pair, Gilbert and Sullivan, which one died of a heart attack in 1911 after saving a young woman from drowning?

5   Which German-born conductor, pianist and composer was the conductor of the London Symphony Orchestra from 1969 to 1979?

6   Born in 1932, name the French-born composer noted for his film scores, including the Oscar-winning Summer Of '42?

7   Which Lloyd Webber musical features the song 'Any Dream Will Do'?

8   According to the old song, Burlington Bertie rises at what time?

9   Which film star is known as the 'Muscles from Brussels'?

10   According to the popular song, what did 'my very good friend the milkman' suggest?

11   Which musical was almost called 'My Lady Liza'?

12   What was the title of the unsuccessful sequel to the musical 'No, No, Nanette'?

13   If Edward Ellington was 'Duke' and William Basie was 'Count', what was Joe Oliver?

14   Which opera singer was the first to sell a million records?

15   Which pianist was known as the 'Rhinestone Rubenstein'?

Answers 1 Les Misérables 2 Anne Boleyn 3 Elton John 4 Gilbert 5 Andre Previn 6 Michel Legrand 7 Joseph And The Amazing Technicolour Dreamcoat 8 Ten Thirty 9 Jean-Claude Van Damme 10 That You Should Marry Me 11 My Fair Lady 12 Yes, Yes, Yvette 13 King 14 Enrico Caruso 15 Liberace

Quiz 55

1   According to his song, how old was Al Jolson's 'Sonny Boy'?

2   In which Lloyd Webber musical do Pearl, Dinah, Rusty, Greaseball, Electra and Poppa appear?

3   'Tony's' are the US theatre equivalent of the movies Oscars. Which Lloyd Webber musical won seven Tony awards in 1995?

4   What physical disability did the pianist Paul Wittgenstein have?

5   Who is said to have invented 'scat' singing when he forgot the words of 'Heebie Jeebies' during a 1926 recording?

6   Billy, Deek, Hoppy and Charlie were the members of which American singing group who were originally railway porters and celebrated their 50th year in show business in 1980?

7   Which of Handel's works did Mark Gottlieb perform submerged in a swimming pool in Washington DC in 1975?

8   Which English university awarded the composer Haydn a doctorate?

9   The classic jazz tunes 'Round Midnight' and 'Straight No Chaser' were written by which American jazz pianist and composer?

10 Hagerup was the middle name of which Norwegian composer?

11 Which character in the Australian TV soap 'Neighbours' has been played by actresses Kylie Flinker, Sacha Close and Melissa Bell?

12 Which famous oratorio was first performed in Dublin in April 1742?

13 Which Australian operatic soprano established her reputation at Covent Garden in 1959 with her performance in the title role of Donizetti's Lucia di Lammermoor?

14 'In olden days a glimpse of stocking was looked on as something shocking' is a line from which popular song?

15 And which song from 'The Sound Of Music' refers to 'warm woollen mittens'?

Answers 1 3 **2** Starlight Express **3** Sunset Boulevard **4** He only had one arm **5** Louis Armstrong **6** The Ink Spots **7** The Water Music **8** Oxford **9** Thelonious Monk **10** Edvard Grieg **11** Lucy Robinson **12** The Messiah **13** Joan Sutherland **14** Anything Goes **15** My Favourite Things

GENERAL ENTERTAINMENT

Quiz 56

This quiz is all about American television programmes.

1 What was the name of the 'talking' horse in the title role of a 1960s comedy series?

2 A scatty receptionist called Agnes Dipesto and a clerk named Herbert Viola who longed to be a detective were characters in which comedy drama series?

3 Which actress played the title role in the 1970s series 'Wonder Woman'?

4 In the detective series 'Columbo', what breed was the detective's dog Fang?

5 The characters Captain Dobey and Huggy Bear appeared in which police series?

6 In which TV detective series did a dog call Freeway appear?

7 Ex-president Gerald Ford, his wife Betty and former Secretary of State Henry Kissinger all appeared in an episode of which series?

8 Name the actor who played 'Hawkeye' Pierce in M.A.S.H and Dr. Gabriel Lawrence in 'ER'.

9 Shirley Jones, Susan Dey and David Cassidy were all members of which family?

10 Who stars as Vallery Irons in the series 'VIP'?

11 Pianist, songwriter and actor Hoagy Carmichael played a ranch hand named Jonesy in which 1960s western series?

12 Name the actor who played the title role in the 1960s series 'Batman'.

13 Which Hollywood star appeared as Jason Colby in 'The Colbys'?

14 Who worked for the funeral home of Gateman, Goodbury & Graves?

15 Name the actor who played the title role in the 1970's series 'Banacek'.

1 Which Baywatch actress was born Tara Leigh Patrick in Cincinnati in 1972 and married controversial basketball star Denis Rodman in November 1998?

2 He was born in Peru, Indiana in 1891 and died in 1964. Name this famous American composer and lyricist.

3 Nicholas Hammond who played Friedrich, the eldest of the Von Trapp boys in the 1965 movie 'The Sound Of Music', went on to play which super-hero in a 1970s American TV series?

4 Played by Jonathan Frakes, who is Jean-Luc Picard's Number One in 'Star Trek: The Next Generation'?

5 Which cartoon character said: "Heavens to Murgatroyd" and "Exit stage left"?

6 Which dance became popular in 1989 when accompanied by a record made by the group Kaoma?

7 According to the title of a Samuel Beckett play, what are Vladimir and Estragon doing?

8 'Mr. Snow' is the title of the song that features in which Rodgers and Hammerstein musical?

9 What title is shared by a 1996 hit for the group Ash and a James Bond movie?

10 With which cartoon character do you associate the phrase 'Drat and double drat'?

11 Founded in 1975 by Clive Davis, the name of which record label is derived from the Greek word meaning 'the best'? The label's first hit record was Barry Manilow's 'Mandy'.

12 In which musical does the song 'They Call The Wind Maria' feature?

13 Actress Angelina Jolie is the daughter of which actor?

14 'The Million Dollar Mermaid' is the title of who's autobiography?

15 Who starred opposite Virginia McKenna in 'The King And I' at the London Palladium in 1979?

Answers 1 Carmen Electra **2** Cole Porter **3** Spiderman **4** William Riker **5** Snagglepuss **6** Lambada **7** Waiting For Godot **8** Carousel **9** Goldfinger **10** Dick Dastardly **11** Arista **12** Paint Your Wagon **13** Jon Voight **14** Esther Williams **15** Yul Brynner

ENTERTAINMENT

1 On 16 December 2000 the world's longest running play – it opened in London in November 1952 - was performed for the 20,000th time. Name it.

2 Who was once one of Benny Hill's Angels in the UK before finding fame in the US by playing the character of Daphne Moon in the TV sitcom 'Frasier'?

3 Patty, Maxene and Laverne were the first names of which singing sisters?

4 The song 'As Long As He Needs Me' features in which musical?

5 Whose play 'The Importance Of Being Earnest' was first performed in 1895?

6 What name is given to the solo dance, traditionally performed by sailors, which is named after the instrument it was originally danced to?

7 Name the 52 year-old guitarist who was nominated in ten categories at the 2000 Grammy awards, winning in eight of them.

8 Which French actress returned to the stage in November 1915 after having her right leg amputated the previous February?

9 With which musical instrument do you associate Vanessa Mae?

10 Which Gilbert and Sullivan operetta is set in Venice?

11 Which female pop star wrote the 1999 best-selling book 'If Only'?

12 What is the name of the magical island featured in the musical 'South Pacific'?

13 Name the actor/singer, often compared with Sinatra, who appeared in the films 'Memphis Belle', 'Little Man Tate', 'Hope Floats' and 'Copycat'.

14 According to the title of his popular song, what did Ivor Novello want to keep burning?

15 Which of Handel's musical works contains the famous 'Hallelujah Chorus'?

Answers 1 The Mousetrap 2 Jane Leeves 3 Andrews Sisters 4 Oliver 5 Oscar Wilde
6 Hornpipe 7 Carlos Santana 8 Sarah Bernhardt 9 Violin 10 The Gondoliers 11 Geri
Halliwell 12 Bali Ha'i 13 Harry Connick Jnr. 14 The home fires 15 The Messiah

275

1. In which TV sci-fi series is a character called John Crichton catapulted across time and space into a raging battle in a parallel universe?

2. The All Saints song 'Pure Shores' is featured on the soundtrack of which Leonardo DiCaprio movie?

3. Which stage musical written by Willy Russell and first seen in 1983 is about twins separated at birth?

4. Which actor was born Bernard Schwartz in New York in 1925?

5. Which British actress is the star of the 2001 blockbuster movies 'Pearl Harbour'?

6. According to the traditional English song, which fair did 'old uncle Tom Cobbleigh and all' go to?

7. Which female entertainer had a hit in 1955 with the song 'Under The Bridges Of Paris', appeared as Catwoman in the 1960s TV series Batman and in 1989 featured with Bronski Beat on the song 'Cha Cha Heels'?

8. What's the name of the summer camp referred to in Allan Sherman's comedy record 'Hello Muddah Hello Faddah'?

9. The actress Talia Shire is the sister of which film director?

10. Which actress was born in Japan, raised in Norway and appeared in several films directed by the Swede, Ingmar Bergman?

11. Which English comedian was known as 'The Cheeky Chappie'?

12. Which popular World War One music hall song contains the lyrics: 'What's the use of worrying' and 'Smile, smile, smile'?

13. Which composer wrote the musical piece 'Rhapsody In Blue'?

14. Name the country estate in Sussex which is famous for it's summer season of operas.

15. Celine Dion sang the winning song in the 1988 Eurovision Song contest representing which country?

Answers 1 Farscape 2 The Beach 3 Blood Brothers 4 Tony Curtis 5 Sarah Michelle Gellar 6 Widdicombe Fair 7 Eartha Kitt 8 Camp Granada 9 Francis Ford Coppola 10 Liv Ullmann 11 Max Miller 12 Pack Up Your Troubles In Your Old Kit Bag 13 George Gershwin 14 Glyndebourne 15 Switzerland

1 Who starred as the vigilante in the 'Death Wish' films?

2 Who starred in 'Last Tango in Paris' and 'The Passenger'?

3 Who starred as Daisy Miller in the 1974 film version of Henry Miller's novel of the same name?

4 In films, who played both Mike Hammer and Martin Luther?

5 Which actor took Sean Penn under his wing?

6 Which British comedian was the Punch and Judy Man?

7 In the 1950 film 'Born Yesterday', which actress won an Oscar for her role as Broderick Crawford's mistress?

8 What was the name of the character played by Malcolm McDowell in 'A Clockwork Orange'?

9 Who was the star of 'Seven' and 'Johnny Suede'?

10 Where in France are the films 'Jean de Florette' and 'Manon des Sources' set?

11 What was the title of the film by Alan Parker that told the prison memoirs of Billy Hayes?

12 Name the follow-up to Mary Poppins.

13 Which film mogul was renowned for illiteracies such as: "I'll tell you in two words – Im possible"?

14 Who was the star of 'Blue Collar' and later 'Homicide: Life On The Street'?

15 Which comedian starred in 'The Fatal Glass of Beer'?

Answers 1 Charles Bronson 2 Maria Schneider 3 Cybill Shepherd 4 Stacy Keach 5 Robert Duvall 6 Tony Hancock 7 Judy Holliday 8 Alex De Large 9 Brad Pitt 10 Provence 11 Midnight Express 12 Bedknobs and Broomsticks 13 Sam Goldwyn 14 Yaphet Kotto 15 WC Fields

Cinema

CINEMA   *Quiz 1*

1   Which comedy duo achieved top billing for the first time in the 1941 film 'Buck Privates'?

2   Who won best actress Academy Award in 1979 for playing the title role in 'Norma Rae'?

3   Who is the mother of actress Carrie Fisher?

4   In which 1952 musical did Jean Hagen play silent film beauty Lina Lamont?

5   Who played dancer Gaby Gerard opposite Fred Astaire in the 1953 musical 'The Band Wagon'?

6   In the 1992 movie 'Hoffa', who played Teamster boss Jimmy Hoffa in the title role?

7   Can you name the director of the 1987 film 'Wall Street'? His father was a broker to whom the film was dedicated.

8   Who played Madison the Mermaid in the 1984 comedy 'Splash'?

9   In which movie do Meg Ryan and Tom Hanks first star together?

10 In which 1988 comedy do Alec Baldwin and Geena Davis play a couple drowned in a car accident who return to their house as ghosts?

11 Who played Edward Scissorhands in the 1990 movie of the same name?

12 In the 1953 movie 'House of Wax', the character Paul Cavanagh was played by Charles Buchinsky. In later movies, what did this actor change his name to?

13 In the 1954 musical 'Brigadoon', who played Gene Kelly's fellow American with whom he stumbles across the town of 'Brigadoon' while hunting in the Scottish Highlands?

14 Which leading man in MGM comedies of the late 1940s and early 1950s was the brother-in-law of President John F. Kennedy?

15 Who, in 1962, played the title role in 'Lawrence of Arabia'?

Answers 1 Bud Abbot and Lou Costello 2 Sally Field 3 Debbie Reynolds 4 Singin' in the Rain 5 Cyd Charisse 6 Jack Nicholson 7 Oliver Stone 8 Daryl Hannah 9 Joe Versus the Volcano (1990) 10 Beetlejuice 11 Johnny Depp 12 Charles Bronson 13 Van Johnson 14 Peter Lawford 15 Peter O' Toole

CINEMA

Quiz 2

1   Who played the manipulative junkie, Renton, in the 1995 film 'Trainspotting'?

2   Name the 1969 film in which Rossano Brazzi, Noel Coward, Benny Hill and Michael Caine all featured.

3   Which actor provides the voice of Rocky the Rooster in 'Chicken Run'?

4   Name the British-born male actor who appeared in 'The Love Bug', 'Mary Poppins' and 'Bedknobs And Broomsticks'.

5   Which actor played Major Eric Fincham in 'Von Ryan's Express' and Father Collins in 'Ryan's Daughter'?

6   Which country is the setting for the 1971 film 'Walkabout' starring Jenny Agutter?

7   What was the first name of Dustin Hoffman's character in 'Rain Man'?

8   Name the actress who appeared in such films as films 'Dangerous', 'Jezebel' and 'Whatever Happened To Baby Jane?'.

9   Which actor provides the voice of the mouse Stuart Little in the movie of that name?

10 Who was Meryl Streep's male co-star in the 1981 movie 'The French Lieutenant's Woman'?

11 Name the actor who appeared in 'The Full Monty' and played Fred Flintstone in 'The Flintstones In Viva Rock Vegas'.

12 Which Hollywood tough-guy, known for his gangster roles in films like 'Scarface', was also a very good dancer, appearing in films such as 'Rumba' and 'Bolero' with Carole Lombard?

13 Who played the title role in the two Crocodile Dundee films?

14 Who played the flustered priest Father Gerald in 'Four Weddings And A Funeral'?

15 Who sang the theme song of the James Bond movie 'Moonraker'?

CINEMA

Quiz 3

1 Which group recorded the theme song of the Bond movie 'The World Is Not Enough'?

2 Which film company pioneered the wide-screen format known as Cinemascope with their 1953 movie 'The Robe'?

3 What's the surname of Dorothy, the central character in 'The Wizard Of Oz'?

4 Robin Williams played a manic US armed forces radio DJ in which 1987 film?

5 Which actor did Demi Moore harass in 'Disclosure'?

6 Who played the title role in the 1970 movie 'Patton'?

7 Which month of the year features in the title of a 1989 film starring Kevin Kline, Susan Sarandon, Elizabeth Mastrantonio and Harvey Keitel?

8 Starring Tom Cruise and Nicole Kidman, what is the title of the last movie made by director Stanley Kubrick?

9 Which film director, famous for his westerns, was born Sean Aloysius O'Fearna?

10 The 1984 film 'Ghostbusters' was set in which US city?

11 In which 1946 film did Henry Fonda play Wyatt Earp and Victor Mature play Doc Holiday?

12 Who played the villain, Alec Trevelyan, in the James Bond movie 'Goldeneye'?

13 One of 32 possible candidates to represent the USA at archery at the 2000 Olympics, which movie star had an archery range installed on the set of the movie 'Stuart Little' to enable her to practice?

14 In the 1999 version of 'The Thomas Crown Affair', who reprised the 1968 roles of Steve McQueen and Faye Dunaway?

15 What is the name of the character played by Bruce Willis in the 'Die Hard' series of films?

Answers 1 Garbage 2 20th Century-Fox 3 Gale 4 Good Morning Vietnam 5 Michael Douglas 6 George C. Scott 7 January (The January Man) 8 Eyes Wide Shut 9 John Ford 10 New York 11 My Darling Clementine 12 Sean Bean 13 Geena Davis 14 Pierce Brosnan and Rene Russo 15 John McClane

CINEMA   *Quiz 4*

These questions are all connected to one another

1   Which actor, who was born Gwyllyn Samuel Newton in 1916, first made his name in the 1946 movie 'Gilda' opposite Rita Hayworth?

2   ...and in which 1957 musical did Rita Hayworth star alongside Kim Novak and Frank Sinatra?

3   ...and in which 1948 Hitchcock thriller did Kim Novak star opposite James Stewart?

4   ...and in that film which actress, who played Miss Ellie in Dallas, played James Stewart's former fiancee Midge Wood?

5   ...and in which Hitchcock film does James Stewart play opposite Grace Kelly as a wheelchair-bound man who witnesses a murder from his apartment?

6   ...and for her supporting role in which 1953 movie set in Africa and starring Ava Gardner and Clark Gable, did Grace Kelly receive an Oscar nomination?

7   ...and who did Clark Gable star opposite in his last film role 'The Misfits'?

8   ...and which actor, who also starred in 'The Misfits' played Robert E. Lee Prewitt in 'From Here to Eternity'?

9   ...and in 'From Here to Eternity' who plays the female lead who has a famous roll in the sand with Burt Lancaster?

10 ...and in which oddly named 1980 western does Burt Lancaster star alongside Amanda Plummer and Diana Lane in the title roles?

11 ...and in which 1992 film does Amanda Plummer appear with Emilio Estevez who plays a car race driver who dies in 1991 and finds his body snatched into year 2009?

12 ...and in which 1988 movie, also starring Keifer Sutherland, does Emilio Estevez play Billie the Kid?

13 ...and in the 1993 film 'The Three Musketeers', who is the brother of Emilio Estevez who plays the musketeer Aramis?

14 ...and in the 1948 version of 'The Three Musketeers', which song and dance man played D'Artagnan opposite Lana Turner?

15 ...and for which 1957 movie, later to become a TV series, did Lana Turner receive an Academy Award nomination?

Answers 1 Glenn Ford 2 Pal Joey 3 Vertigo 4 Barbara Bel Geddes 5 Rear Window 6 Mogambo 7 Marilyn Monroe 8 Montgomery Clift 9 Deborah Kerr 10 Cattle Annie and Little Britches 11 Freejack 12 Young Guns 13 Charlie Sheen 14 Gene Kelly 15 Peyton Place

CINEMA

Quiz 5

1   Elmo Lincoln, Gordon Scott, Christopher Lambert and Miles O'Keeffe have all played which movie hero?

2   Which actor played San Francisco cop Nick Curran in 'Basic Instinct'?

3   By appearing in 'Double Trouble' and 'A Hard Day's Night', this British actor is the only actor to have appeared in movies with both Elvis Presley and The Beatles. He also appeared in the first three 'Carry On' films. Name him.

4   Who played horror film director James Whale in the movie 'Gods And Monsters'?

5   Which British-born actor co-starred opposite Ingrid Bergman in 'Indiscreet'?

6   Which 1999 Disney film was described in publicity handouts as 'An epic of miniature proportions'?

7   Which character has been played in films by Clark Gable, Marlon Brando and Mel Gibson?

8   Who won an Oscar for Best Actor for his performance in 'Life Is Beautiful'?

9   Who plays the title role in 'Patch Adams'?

10 In which film does Michael Keaton appear as a dead father who comes back to life as a snowman?

11 According to the title of their movie, who did Cher, Maggie Smith and Judi Dench have tea with?

12 'Shakespeare In Love' received 13 Oscar nominations. How many did it win?

13 Who sang 'Now You Has Jazz' with Bing Crosby in 'High Society'?

14 Robert Donat, Kenneth More and Robert Powell have all starred in movie versions of which John Buchan novel?

15 Who directed the films 'Spartacus', 'Full Metal Jacket' and '2001: A Space Odyssey'?

Answers 1 Tarzan 2 Michael Douglas 3 Norman Rossington 4 Ian McKellen 5 Cary Grant 6 A Bug's Life 7 Fletcher Christian 8 Roberto Benigni 9 Robin Williams 10 Jack Frost 11 Mussolini 12 7 13 Louis Armstrong 14 The Thirty Nine Steps 15 Stanley Kubrick

Quiz 6

This quiz is all about romantic and "tear-jerker" films.

1   In Gone With The Wind, which actress played Melanie Wilkes who married Ashley, the man who Scarlett O'Hara wanted?

2   And what's the name of Scarlett and Rhett Butler's daughter who dies in a riding accident?

3   The 1932 movie 'A Farewell To Arms' was set during which war?

4   Who played the title role of the female plumber in the 1946 movie 'Cluny Brown'?

5   Who played the title role in the 1954 movie 'Sabrina' that also featured Humphrey Bogart and William Holden?

6   In which 1981 film do Jeremy Irons and Meryl Streep say farewell?

7   In which 1942 film does Bette Davis say to Paul Henreid: "Oh Jerry, don't let's ask for the moon. We have the stars"?

8   And in which 1950 film as Margo Channing does Bette Davis say: "Fasten your seat belts it's going to be a bumpy night"?

9   Name the co-stars who become romantically linked in the 1984 movie 'Romancing The Stone'.

10 Complete the title of the following Steve McQueen and Natalie Wood movie: 'Love With The...'?

11 In which movie did Frank Sinatra sing 'Lady Is A Tramp' and Kim Novak 'My Funny Valentine'?

12 Which actress is Burt Reynolds love interest in 'Smokey And The Bandit'?

13 Name the actor and actress who tie the knot in the 1955 movie 'Guys And Dolls'.

14 What is the first name of Ryan O'Neal's character in 'Love Story'?

15 Who plays Count Almasy in 'The English Patient'?

Answers 1 Olivia de Havilland 2 Bonnie Blue 3 World War One 4 Jennifer Jones 5 Audrey Hepburn 6 The French Lieutenant's Woman 7 Now, Voyager 8 All About Eve 9 Michael Douglas and Kathleen Turner 10 Proper Stranger 11 Pal Joey 12 Sally Field 13 Marlon Brando and Jean Simmons 14 Oliver 15 Ralph Fiennes

1 In 'To Sir With Love' (1967), who plays the West Indian teacher who reforms a bunch of tough East End teenagers?

2 In the National Lampoon series of movies Chevy Chase plays the husband. Who plays his wife?

3 Which actress made her feature debut in 1982 as the soap opera actress who shares a dressing room with 'Tootsie'?

4 Who plays the TV weatherman trapped in a replay of the same 24 hours in the 1993 movie 'Groundhog Day'?

5 Who played Tarzan in the 1984 movie 'Greystoke: Legend of Tarzan, Lord of the Apes'?

6 In the 1951 classic comedy 'The Lavender Hill Mob', what do the gang mould the stolen gold bullion into?

7 Which actress starred opposite Cary Grant in the 1963 movie 'Charade'?

8 Who played Alex Grenville, opposite Peter Finch in the 1971 drama 'Sunday Bloody Sunday'?

9 Which part was played by Gary Oldman in the 1991 movie 'JFK'?

10 Which former vaudevillian played Osgood E. Fielding III who fell in love with Jack Lemmon's Daphne in the 1969 comedy 'Some Like It Hot'?

11 ....and what were Osgood's final words in the movie upon discovering that Daphne was really a man?

12 Who played the Twins in the 1988 movie of the same name?

13 Born Hugh J. Krampe in 1925, this actor played in many movies, mostly in supporting roles, but went on to achieve his greatest success playing Sheriff Wyatt Earp on TV. Can you name him?

14 In his last film 'The Shootist', John Wayne plays the title role and James Stewart plays the doctor. Who plays the widow?

15 Who starred opposite Mickey Rooney in the 1939 musical 'Babes in Arms'?

Answers 1 Sidney Poitier 2 Beverly D'Angelo 3 Geena Davis 4 Bill Murray 5 Chistopher Lambert 6 Miniature Eiffel Towers 7 Audrey Hepburn 8 Glenda Jackson 9 Lee Harvey Oswald 10 Joe E. Brown 11 Well, nobody's perfect 12 Arnold Schwarzenegger and Danny De Vito 13 Hugh O'Brian 14 Lauren Bacall 15 Judy Garland

CINEMA   *Quiz 8*

1 The career of which actress took off after her scantily-clad appearance in the 1966 movie 'One Million Years BC'?

2 Which French actress starred in the 1965 Roman Polanski film 'Repulsion' and the 1983 Tony Scott movie 'The Hunger'?

3 Name the actor who played the father of Indiana Jones in 'Indiana Jones And The Last Crusade'.

4 Who was Meryl Streep's male co-star in 'The Bridges Of Madison County'?

5 Name Marilyn Monroe's female co-star in 'Gentlemen Prefer Blondes'.

6 Which 1998 computer-generated animated film featured the voices of several Hollywood stars including Woody Allen, Gene Hackman and Sharon Stone?

7 Which rock star appeared in the films 'Ned Kelly', 'Performance' and 'Freejack'?

8 In which of the 'Star Wars' series of films did the furry little creatures known as Ewoks appear?

9 Which company produced 'Seven Brides For Seven Brothers' and 'Singing In The Rain'?

10 Who played the Soviet submarine commander in 'The Hunt For Red October'?

11 Which series of films features the partnership of Murtaugh and Riggs?

12 Who directed the films 'A Hard Day's Night', 'Robin and Marian', several films featuring the 'Three Musketeers' and 'Superman II' and 'Superman III'?

13 Which American wild west character has been portrayed in movies by Robert Taylor, Audie Murphy, Paul Newman, Kris Kristofferson and Emilio Estevez?

14 Which three letters are the title of a 1988 thriller starring Dennis Quaid and Meg Ryan?

15 In the film industry they are known as 'group jeopardy movies'. What other popular name is given to these type of films?

Answers 1 Raquel Welch 2 Catherine Deneuve 3 Sean Connery 4 Clint Eastwood 5 Jane Russell 6 Antz 7 Mick Jagger 8 Return Of The Jedi 9 M-G-M 10 Sean Connery 11 Lethal Weapon 12 Richard (or Dick) Lester 13 Billy the Kid 14 D.O.A 15 Disaster movies

CINEMA   *Quiz 9*

1   Name the British actor who played the villain in the following films: 'Die Hard', 'Quigley Down Under' and 'Robin Hood: Prince Of Thieves'.

2   Which English photographer and designer won academy awards for his costume and set designs for 'My Fair Lady'?

3   Who won an Oscar for Best Actor for his performance in the 1944 movie 'Going My Way'?

4   Which film company uses the symbol of a snow covered mountain top at the start of their productions?

5   The 1992 film 'Hear My Song' was loosely based on part of the life of which Irish tenor?

6   For his performance in which film, released in 1979, did Dustin Hoffman win his first Oscar?

7   Michael Sinnott was the real name of which silent film producer and director who was known as the 'king of comedy'?

8   Who played Rosemary in the 1968 movie 'Rosemary's Baby'?

9   In The Wizard Of Oz, what's the name of the little people Dorothy meets when first entering the land of Oz?

10 What is the name of the wacky pet detective played in films by Jim Carrey?

11 Who played Fanny Brice in 'Funny Girl' and 'Funny Lady'?

12 What breed of dog is the star of the Beethoven films?

13 'Oliver's Story' was the sequel to which film?

14 Who was the female star of the first two of the Halloween series of films?

15 Released in 1967, Tiger Tanaka and Kissy Suzuki are characters in which James Bond movie?

Answers 1 Alan Rickman 2 Cecil Beaton 3 Bing Crosby 4 Paramount 5 Josef Locke 6 Kramer vs Kramer 7 Mack Sennett 8 Mia Farrow 9 Munchkins 10 Ace Ventura 11 Barbra Streisand 12 St. Bernard 13 Love Story 14 Jamie Lee Curtis 15 You Only Live Twice

CINEMA

Quiz 10

1 Born Harleen Carpenter in 1911, can you name the actress who starred as Gwen Allen opposite James Cagney in the 1931 movie 'The Public Enemy'?

2 Which actor/singer played a heroic swordsman in 'The Princess Bride' (1987) in which he uttered the lines: "I am Inigo Monoya. You killed my father. Prepare to die"?

3 In the silent film comedy 'The General' starring Buster Keaton, in what many consider his masterpiece, who or what is The General?

4 In which 1973 spoof horror does Vincent Price murder his victims by recreating famous scenes from Shakespeare plays?

5 In which movie does Diana Rigg marry James Bond, played by George Lazenby?

6 Which actor was born Maurice Joseph Micklewhite at Bermondsey, England in 1933?

7 In which 1986 film does Bob Hoskins play a petty crook, just out of prison, who is given the job of chauffeuring a call girl on her nightly rounds?

8 Which former 'Cheers' star was given his first leading role in 'White Men Can't Jump' in 1992?

9 Who wrote the comedy 'Barefoot in the Park', which was made into a film starring Robert Redford and Jane Fonda in 1967?

10 Who played the ill-fated mother of the anti-Christ opposite Gregory Peck in 'The Omen' in 1976?

11 ...and how many sequels to the original 'Omen' movie were made?

12 Which actress played Dudley Moore's love interest in the 1981 comedy 'Arthur'?

13 In the 1939 movie 'Wuthering Heights', who played Heathcliff to Merle Oberon's Cathy?

14 In 1956 who played Phileas Fogg in 'Around the World in 80 Days'?

15 In which 1962 movie do Bette Davis and Joan Crawford play sisters Jane and Blanche Hudson?

Answers 1 Jean Harlow 2 Mandy Patinkin 3 A train 4 Theatre of Blood 5 On Her Majesty's Secret Service 6 Michael Caine 7 Mona Lisa 8 Woody Harrelson 9 Neil Simon 10 Lee Remick 11 Three 12 Liza Minnelli 13 Laurence Olivier 14 David Niven 15 Whatever Happened to Baby Jane?

1 Which sport is featured in 'Bull Durham', 'Field Of Dreams' and 'A League Of Their Own'?

2 Which actor, best known for his tough-guy roles, directed the 1983 John Travolta movie 'Staying Alive'?

3 Which 1952 classic western was based on a story called 'The Tin Star' and featured a memorable Tex Ritter song?

4 Which country was the setting for the Oscar winning film 'The Piano'?

5 Name the debonair British-born actor who appeared in 'The Dawn Patrol', 'The Charge Of The Light Brigade', 'Around The World In Eighty Days' and 'Separate Tables'.

6 Name the 1984 Paul McCartney film that featured the song 'No More Lonely Nights'.

7 Widely viewed as a documentary of their break-up, which 1970 Beatles film won an Oscar for best original song score?

8 Played by Burt Kwouk, what was the name of Inspector Clouseau's valet in the Pink Panther films?

9 Name the British film company who specialised in horror films in the 1950s and 1960s with films such as 'The Quatermass Experiment' and 'The Curse of Frankenstein'.

10 Which Oscar-winning actor was born Krishna Banji in Yorkshire in 1943?

11 Considered to be the first movie masterpieces, who directed the silent films 'The Birth Of A Nation' and 'Intolerance'?

12 The battle of Rorke's Drift was the subject of which 1964 film?

13 Who produced and starred in the 1975 film 'Shampoo'?

14 Who played the title role in the 1972 movie 'Young Winston'?

15 Who directed the 1960 classic thriller 'Psycho'?

Answers 1 Baseball 2 Sylvester Stallone 3 High Noon 4 New Zealand 5 David Niven 6 Give My Regards To Broad Street 7 Let It Be 8 Cato 9 Hammer 10 Ben Kingsley 11 D. W. Griffith 12 Zulu 13 Warren Beatty 14 Simon Ward 15 Alfred Hitchcock

CINEMA

Quiz 12

This quiz is all about quotations.

1. "A man's got to know his limitations" is the last line of which Clint Eastwood movie?

2. Which western movie ends with the words: "Thank God for that. For a moment there I thought we were in trouble"?

3. "You played it for her, you can play it for me. Play it!" is a famous line from which film?

4. In which film did Mae West say: "It's not the men in your life that counts, it's the life in your men"?

5. Although it has been said in a different context by people in other movies, with which actor is the phrase "I'll be back" most associated?

6. Which actress said the line: "Would you be shocked if I changed into something more comfortable" in the 1930 film Hell's Angels?

7. And which actress in another 1930 film said: "Gif me a visky, ginger ale on the side and don't be stingy, baby"?

8. In which 1976 movie does Robert De Niro say: "You talkin' to me? You talkin' to me? You talkin' to me? Then who the hell else are you talkin' to? You talkin' to me"?

9. "Ray, it's looking at me Ray" is a quote from which 1984 movie?

10. In which film did Groucho Marx say: "Either he's dead or my watch has stopped"?

11. Which actor, preparing for his 1990 role as Hamlet said: "I'm playing Shakespeare – and I may not win"?

12. In which film did Humphrey Bogart say: "I don't know why the Germans would want this God-forsaken place"?

13. Who said in 'Witness For The Prosecution': "If you were a woman, Miss Plimsoll, I would strike you"?

14. In which 1960 film did Laurence Olivier say: "Let me know where you're working tomorrow night. I'll come and see you"?

15. What is the name of the Clint Eastwood character with whom you associate the phrase: "Go ahead, make my day"?

Answers 1 Magnum Force 2 Butch Cassidy And The Sundance Kid 3 Casablanca 4 I'm No Angel 5 Arnold Schwarzenegger 6 Jean Harlow 7 Greta Garbo 8 Taxi Driver 9 Ghostbusters 10 A Day At The Races 11 Mel Gibson 12 The African Queen 13 Charles Laughton 14 The Entertainer 15 Harry Callahan

CINEMA

Quiz 13

1 Name the actress who co-starred with Richard Gere in 'An Officer And A Gentleman'.

2 Who played Barney Rubble to John Goodman's Fred Flintstone in the 1994 movie 'The Flintstones'?

3 Buddy Ebsen had to drop which role in a famous 1939 film because he was allergic to metallic paint?

4 In the Rambo films, what was Rambo's christian name?

5 Gladys Knight sang the theme song of which James Bond movie?

6 The 1966 film 'Blow Up' was reputedly based on which photographer?

7 Which 1944 film starring Elizabeth Taylor and Mickey Rooney, included footage of the 'Grand National' that were actually shot on a Pasadena golf course?

8 Starring Rita Hayworth and Kim Novak, in which 1957 film did Frank Sinatra sing 'The Lady Is A Tramp'?

9 Who played Mr. Freeze in the 1997 movie 'Batman And Robin'?

10 Name the actor who co-starred with Doris Day in 'Move Over Darling'.

11 Which actress, who became deaf in infancy as a result of *roseola infantum*, won an Oscar for her performance in 'Children Of A Lesser God'?

12 Which of the Superman series of films was sub-titled 'The Quest For Peace'?

13 Which country is the setting for the 1983 film 'Local Hero' featuring Burt Lancaster?

14 Which 1998 Disney animated film was based on a Chinese folk story?

15 Which former British music hall comedian starred in the 1930s comedy films 'Oh, Mr. Porter' and 'Ask A Policeman'?

Answers 1 Debra Winger **2** Rick Moranis **3** The Tin Man (in the Wizard of Oz) **4** John **5** Licence To Kill **6** David Bailey **7** National Velvet **8** Pal Joey **9** Arnold Schwarzenegger **10** James Garner **11** Marlee Matlin **12** Superman IV **13** Scotland **14** Mulan **15** Will Hay

CINEMA | *Quiz 14*

1 Who played Beverley Hills plastic surgeon Ernest Menville in the 1992 comedy 'Death Becomes Her'?

2 In which 1979 movie did Meryl Streep win her first Oscar (for supporting actress)?

3 Who played Damien In the Omen film, 'The Final Conflict' (1981)?

4 Who co-wrote the screenplay of 'Jurassic Park' from his own novel on which the film was based?

5 Who played ex-CIA agent Jack Ryan in the 1992 movie 'Patriot Games'?

6 ...and who played Jack Ryan in the 1990 thriller 'The Hunt for Red October'?

7 In which movie did Sean Connery first play James Bond?

8 Who played Princess Leia Organa in the movie 'Star Wars'?

9 Which actor was born in 1909 at Hobart, Tasmania and was the son of a distinguished American marine biologist?

10 Who won the 1939 Best Actor Oscar for his role as Charles Chipping in 'Goodbye, Mr. Chips'?

11 In which classic 1950 movie does James Stewart play a whimsical inebriate Elwood P. Dowd?

12 In which 1958 movie does Burl Ives play Big Daddy Pollitt?

13 Who played the title role in the 1964 film 'Becket'?

14 Which 1980 Stanley Kubrick film stars Jack Nicholson as a caretaker of an isolated resort hotel and Shelley Duvall as his panic stricken wife?

15 Which actor was Oscar-nominated for the 1997 film 'The Apostle'?

Answers 1 Bruce Willis 2 Kramer vs Kramer 3 Sam Neill 4 Michael Crichton 5 Harrison Ford 6 Alec Baldwin 7 Dr No 8 Carrie Fisher 9 Errol Flynn 10 Robert Donat 11 Harvey 12 Cat On a Hot Tin Roof 13 Richard Burton 14 The Shining 15 Robert Duvall

CINEMA

Quiz 15

1   Which English monarch was played by Quentin Crisp in the 1993 movie adaptation of Virginia Woolf's novel 'Orlando'?

2   The 1990 film 'Havana' was the seventh movie made together by director Sydney Pollack and which actor?

3   Which 'spaghetti' western had the Italian title 'Il Buono, Il Brutto, Il Cattivo'?

4   Which actor was born Thomas C. Mapother IV in 1962, using his middle name as his screen surname?

5   'Eight legs, two fangs and an attitude' was an advertising slogan used for which 1990 movie starring Jeff Daniels?

6   Name the actor who played the title role in Sam Peckinpah's 1965 western 'Major Dundee'.

7   Born Susan Tomaling, which American actress uses the surname of her ex-husband, actor Chris?

8   In the 1984 movie 'All Of Me', Steve Martin inherits the soul of a character played by which actress?

9   Which actor, a cousin of Ian Fleming, played the villain Scaramanga in the 1974 James Bond movie 'The Man With The Golden Gun'?

10 Lauren Bacall, Ingrid Bergman, Sean Connery and Vanessa Redgrave were all train passengers in which 1974 movie?

11 Mia Farrow, Barbara Hershey and Dianne West appeared in which 1986 Woody Allen film?

12 Which 1960s pop group starred in a 'psychedelic trip of a movie' entitled 'Head'?

13 Which real-life married couple played the title roles in the 1990 film 'Mr. & Mrs. Bridge'?

14 Who played Maid Marian in the 1983 film 'The Adventures of Robin Hood'?

15 Also starring Patrick Bergin and Sean Bean, in which 1992 film did Harrison Ford take over the role of Jack Ryan?

Answers 1 Elizabeth I 2 Robert Redford 3 The Good, The Bad And The Ugly 4 Tom Cruise 5 Arachnophobia 6 Charlton Heston 7 Susan Sarandon 8 Lily Tomlin 9 Christopher Lee 10 Murder On The Orient Express 11 Hannah And Her Sisters 12 The Monkees 13 Paul Newman and Joanne Woodward 14 Olivia de Havilland 15 Patriot Games

1   In which 1978 Sam Peckinpah movie does Kris Kristofferson play a character known as 'Rubber Duck'?

2   Which 1981 movie starring Sean Connery is something akin to 'High Noon in outer space'?

3   Sigourney Weaver and Melanie Griffith were office rivals in which 1988 movie?

4   In the 1989 film 'The Tall Guy', Jeff Goldblum plays a comedian's straight man. Who plays the comedian?

5   Who co-wrote and starred in the 1991 film 'American Friends'? He played an Oxford don based on his real life great-grandfather.

6   Who played the private eye in the 1973 film 'Shamus'?

7   Which actor played the gunman English Bob in Clint Eastwood's western 'Unforgiven'?

8   Who played the title role in the 1985 biblical epic 'King David'?

9   Which 1993 Michael Douglas movie has 'kid with missile launcher' amongst the cast credits?

10 Complete the title of the following film starring Clint Eastwood and Jeff Bridges – 'Thunderbolt And…'?

11 According to the title of a 1988 film starring Gene Hackman and Willem Dafoe, which US state was 'burning'?

12 The name of the diner featured in the 1990 film starring Susan Sarandon and James Spader is also the title of the film, what is it?

13 As an actor, who appeared as a child in the 1962 musical 'The Music Man' and later in John Wayne's 'The Shootist? He has also directed several films, among them 'Backdraft', 'Parenthood' and 'Apollo 13'. Name him.

14 Who co-starred with Burt Lancaster as a couple of ageing ex-cons in the 1986 movie 'Tough Guys'?

15 Based on an Edgar Allan Poe story, which film starring Vincent Price was about blood-letting in 16th century Spain?

Answers 1 Convoy 2 Outland 3 Working Girl 4 Rowan Atkinson 5 Michael Palin 6 Burt Reynolds 7 Richard Harris 8 Richard Gere 9 Falling Down 10 Lightfoot 11 Mississippi 12 White Palace 13 Ron Howard 14 Kirk Douglas 15 Pit And The Pendulum

CINEMA   Quiz 17

1   According to the title of a 1974 Martin Scorcese film, who 'doesn't live here anymore'?

2   Which singer provided the singing voice of Prince Karl in the 1954 film 'The Student Prince'? He was also scheduled to play the part but was dropped because he was vastly overweight.

3   And which actor played Prince Karl in that movie?

4   Name the male singer who appeared in the musicals 'Annie Get Your Gun', 'Show Boat' and 'Kiss Me Kate'.

5   Which female singer appeared in the musicals 'Tea For Two', 'On Moonlight Bay' and 'I'll See You In My Dreams'?

6   Name the actress who played the civilian astrophysicist in the 1986 film 'Top Gun'.

7   Who played the title role in the 1995 movie 'Rob Roy'?

8   Who co-starred with Gene Wilder in 'Silver Streak', 'Stir Crazy' and 'See No Evil, Hear No Evil'?

9   Who directed ''Do The Right Thing', 'Malcolm X', 'School Daze' and 'She's Gotta Have It'?

10 Name the 1948 film in which Humphrey Bogart plays Fred C. Dobbs, a gold prospector in Mexico.

11 What is the name of Indie's boy companion in 'Indiana Jones And The Temple of Doom'?

12 Who played the title role in the 1997 film 'Wilde'?

13 Name the actress who appeared in the 1966 film 'Georgy Girl' and the 1988 murder mystery movie 'D.O.A.'?

14 In the 1967 film 'Doctor Dolittle', what type of creature was Pushme-Pullyou, an animal with two heads facing opposite ways?

15 Which Swedish-born actress appeared in the movies 'The Cincinnati Kid, Carnal Knowledge', 'Tommy' and 'Grumpy Old Men'?

Answers 1 Alice **2** Mario Lanza **3** Edmund Purdom **4** Howard Keel **5** Doris Day **6** Kelly McGillis **7** Liam Neeson **8** Richard Pryor **9** Spike Lee **10** The Treasure Of The Sierra Madre **11** Short Round **12** Stephen Fry **13** Charlotte Rampling **14** Llama **15** Ann-Margret

1 Which actress, who won best actress Academy Award in 1958 for 'I Want To Live!' was born Edythe Marrener in 1918?

2 Who played Rose Sayer opposite Humphrey Bogart in 'The African Queen'?

3 Which composer was played by Edward G. Robinson in the 1970 film 'Song of Norway'?

4 In which 1958 film did Dirk Bogarde play Sydney Carton?

5 In 1978, Donald Pleasance starred with Jamie Lee Curtis in the first of which series of films?

6 ...and who is the mother of Jamie Lee Curtis?

7 In 'A Few Good Men' (1992) who plays Navy attorney Lt. Daniel Kaffe?

8 Which actor did Meg Ryan marry in 1991?

9 In which 1986 film does Kathleen Turner travel back in time to re-live her romance with her future husband?

10 Which famous bandleader was featured with his orchestra in the 1941 film 'Sun Valley Serenade'?

11 Who played Charlie Chaplin in the 1992 biography 'Chaplin'?

12 Which 1992 movie, starring Sir Anthony Hopkins and Emma Thompson, is an adaptation of an E. M. Forster novel?

13 Which songwriting team wrote the musical 'Camelot'?

14 Which comedy team spent 'A Day at the Races' in 1937?

15 Who, in 1967, was 'Cool Hand Luke'?

Quiz 19

1 What sport was the subject of the 1986 Gene Hackman/Dennis Hopper movie 'Hoosiers'?

2 In which 1958 film, based on an Ernest Hemingway novel does Spencer Tracy appear throughout the entire film?

3 What contribution did Dimitri Tiomkin make to the film 'High Noon'?

4 Who played the title role in the 1973 movie 'Serpico'?

5 Who starred as Louise in the 1991 movie 'Thelma and Louise'?

6 …and what do Thelma and Louise deliberately do when surrounded by cops at the end of the film?

7 In which 1989 film does Tom Cruise play real-life paralyzed Vietnam war veteran Ron Kovik?

8 In 'The Magnificent Seven' (1960), Yul Brynner, Steve McQueen, Horst Buchholz, Charles Bronson, Brad Dexter and James Coburn are six of the seven. Who is the seventh?

9 Who directed the 1956 religious epic 'The Ten Commandments'?

10 …and who directed the original silent version of 'The Ten Commandments' in 1923?

11 Ruby Keeler, who starred in some of the classic musicals of the 1930s, was married to which showbiz legend?

12 Which actress/dancer frequently stole the show with her tap dancing routines in several musicals, including 'On the Town', and was born Lucille Ann Collier in 1919?

13 Who starred as Lisa Bouvier opposite Gene Kelly in 'An American in Paris'?

14 In which 1990 film does Jeremy Irons play the aristocratic Claus von Bulow, accused of attempting to murder his wife played by Glenn Close?

15 Which singer appears in the 1993 movie 'Body of Evidence'?

Answers 1 Basketball 2 The Old Man And The Sea 3 He wrote the music 4 Al Pacino 5 Susan Sarandon 6 Drive over the top of the Grand Canyon 7 Born On the Fourth of July 8 Robert Vaughan 9 Cecil B. De Mille 10 Also Cecil B. De Mille 11 Al Jolson 12 Ann Miller 13 Leslie Caron 14 Reversal of Fortune 15 Madonna

CINEMA

Quiz 20

This quiz is all about Disney animated feature films.

1   In the 1992 film 'Aladdin', the vizier Jafar had a parrot who's name was that of which Shakespearean character?

2   And what was the name of the Sultan's daughter in 'Aladdin'?

3   Which film released in 1989 was based on a story by Hans Christian Andersen?

4   Which American singer/songwriter provided the voice for Dodger in the 1988 movie 'Oliver & Company'?

5   Which was the last animated movie to be personally supervised by Walt Disney?

6   In the 1940 movie 'Pinocchio', what kind of creature was J. Worthington Foulfellow?

7   What was the name of the fat cat in 'Cinderella'?

8   Who duetted with Peabo Bryson on the Oscar-winning song 'Beauty And The Beast' from the film of the same name?

9   Which 1940 film was updated for 2000?

10 Released worldwide in 2001, which film features the characters Kusco, Pacha, Yzma and Kronk?

11 Which 1941 film is set to a circus background?

12 In 'The Lion King', what is the name of Simba's father?

13 What is the title of the 1981 film which features Tod and Copper, two childhood animal friends forced to become enemies?

14 Written by Alan Menken and Tim Rice, 'A Whole New World' was the theme song for which film?

15 Complete the title of this 1990 film – 'The Rescuers Down ......'?

CINEMA

Quiz 21

1 Who appeared in the starring role in the movie 'Body Heat' opposite Kathleen Turner?

2 Which 'Star Trek' regular directed the 1987 comedy '3 Men and a Baby'?

3 In which 1993 horror does Warwick Davis make his debut as a sinister pint-sized Irish fairy?

4 In which movie does Woody Allen play Alvy Singer?

5 In which 1979 movie are the crew members of the spaceship Nostromo mercilessly killed off one by one?

6 In the 1983 movie 'Silkwood', who plays Oklahoma factory worker Karen Silkwood?

7 In 'Gone With the Wind' what did Scarlett O'Hara say to Rhett Butler, which prompted the response of: "Frankly, my dear, I don't give a damn"?

8 Who played Quasimodo in 1939 and Henry VIII in 1933?

9 Which movie icon made her last appearance in 'Sextette' in 1978, which was a movie based on her own play?

10 ...and which of the Beatles also starred in that film?

11 Who played Col. Nicholson in the 1957 epic 'The Bridge on the River Kwai'?

12 Which 1964 film was based on Harold Robbins novel about a millionaire plane manufacturer, and was the last film in which Alan Ladd appeared?

13 Which 1979 drama starring Anthony Franciosa and Carroll Baker was from a novel and screenplay by Jackie Collins?

14 Which Jerome Kern musical has been adapted to the screen three times; in 1929, 1936 and 1957?

15 Which 1953 Cole Porter musical starring Howard Keel and Kathryn Grayson was originally made in 3-D?

Answers 1 William Hurt 2 Leonard Nimoy 3 Leprechaun 4 Annie Hall 5 Alien 6 Meryl Streep 7 "Rhett, Rhett, if you go, where shall I go, what shall I do?" 8 Charles Laughton 9 Mae West 10 Ringo Starr 11 Alec Guinness 12 The Carpetbaggers 13 The World is Full of Married Men 14 Showboat 15 Kiss Me Kate

CINEMA   *Quiz 22*

1   Which writer was played by Christopher Plummer in the film 'The Man Who Would Be King'?

2   In the 1954 movie 'The Naked Jungle', what caused the jungle to be naked?

3   In which 1938 movie did Bette Davis win her second Oscar playing a tempestuous Southern belle opposite Henry Fonda?

4   In which 1992 film do Tom Cruise and Nicole Kidman sail for America and seek their destiny in the 1893 Oklahoma gold rush?

5   Who played opposite Marlon Brando in the erotic drama 'Last Tango in Paris'?

6   Who plays brothel proprietor Mona Strangley in 'The Best Little Whorehouse in Texas'?

7   Which film director married Jane Fonda in 1965?

8   Which actress slaps Lee Marvin repeatedly in the 1967 cult movie 'Point Blank'?

9   Which rock star was 'The Man Who Fell to Earth' in 1976?

10 In 'The Exorcist', who plays the normal 12-year-old whose body is possessed by the Devil?

11 Who played the title role in the 1992 movie 'Malcolm X'?

12 Who played rock 'n' roll icon Tina Turner in the 1993 movie 'What's Love Got to Do With It?'?

13 Who, in 1982, was 'Conan the Barbarian'?

14 In the movie 'Star Wars', which character reassures Luke Skywalker: "The force will be with you – always"?

15 Who played Sherlock Holmes in the 1959 film 'The Hound of the Baskervilles'?

Quiz 23

1 'Happy Talk' and 'Some Enchanted Evening' are songs from which 1958 musical?

2 In which 1952 film does James Stewart play Buttons, a circus clown?

3 In which of the Crosby/Hope Road films do Joan Collins and Peter Sellers make cameo appearances?

4 Which 1964 Stanley Kubrick film starring Peter Sellers had the alternative title, 'How I Learned to Stop Worrying and Love the Bomb'?

5 Which Swedish actress and former model was at one time married to Peter Sellers?

6 In which town in England was Michael Caine's 1971 cult movie 'Get Carter' filmed?

7 In the 1985 movie 'Fletch', who plays investigative reporter I. M. Fletcher in the title role?

8 In which 1969 anti-war musical did Sir Richard Attenborough make his directing debut?

9 In the 1978 'Superman' movie, which cinema icon plays Superman's father Jor-El?

10 In which 1972 movie does a crewman say to the Captain (Leslie Neilson): "I never saw anything like it – an enormous wall of water coming towards us"?

11 Who played Captain Philip Francis Queeg in 'The Caine Mutiny'?

12 Who directed the 1984 film 'Paris, Texas'?

13 In which 1953 musical does Howard Keel star as Wild Bill Hickock opposite Doris Day?

14 Frank Langella is best known for playing the title role in which 1979 horror movie?

15 Madonna was tempestuously married to which actor, whose movies include, 'Taps' (1981) and 'Bad Boys' (1983)?

All the following films were nominated for the Oscar for Best Picture but did not win.

1   Based on a novel, it was about sex in a little American town. Made in 1957, Lana Turner, Arthur Kennedy, Russ Tamblyn and Hope Lange all appeared in it.

2   Again based on a best-selling novel, which 1959 film was set in the north of England and told of a young man's search for success, and starred Laurence Harvey and Simone Signoret.

3   Based on a James Hilton novel, which 1942 filmed starred Ronald Colman as Charles Rainier, a prosperous man who loses his memory as a result of shellshock in the First World War.

4   Henry Fonda, Jane Darwell and John Carradine feature in this 1940 film about the Joad family and their migration from the Dust Bowl to California during the depression.

5   Directed by Rob Reiner and also starring Tom Cruise and Demi Moore, Jack Nicholson was nominated for the Oscar for Best Supporting Actor for his performance as a US marine commander in this 1992 movie about the trial of two marines charged with murder.

6   A Merchant-Ivory film, it won Emma Thompson the Oscar for Best Actress and Vanessa Redgrave was nominated for Best Supporting Actress. The film also featured Anthony Hopkins and was based on an E. M. Forster novel.

7   Barbra Streisand produced, directed and starred in this 1991 film which featured Nick Nolte as a man in a midlife crisis.

8   Also featuring Annette Bening, Harvey Keitel and Ben Kingsley, Warren Beatty co-produced and acted in this 1991 gangster movie.

9   Another gangster film, this Martin Scorcese film looked at New York Mafia life and featured Robert De Niro, Joe Pesci and Ray Liotta.

10 This film was based on the true story of a young American's disappearance in Chile and starred Jack Lemmon and Sissy Spacek.

11 Yet another gangster movie, this one features Burt Lancaster as a small time ageing mafia hood and Susan Sarandon as an ambitious young woman.

12 Directed by Alan Parker, and featuring Brad Davis, this film is a sordid story about a young American busted for smuggling hash in Turkey and his subsequent harsh imprisonment and later escape.

Answers 1 Peyton Place 2 Room At The Top 3 Random Harvest 4 The Grapes Of Wrath 5 A Few Good Men 6 Howards End 7 The Prince Of Tides 8 Bugsy 9 Goodfellas 10 Missing 11 Atlantic City 12 Midnight Express

CINEMA

Quiz 25

1 Name the English actress who appeared in the films 'Four Weddings And A Funeral', 'The English Patient' and 'The Horse Whisperer'.

2 What species of shark was the one featured in the original 'Jaws' movie?

3 Who played Anne Boleyn in the film 'Anne of the Thousand Days'?

4 Who sang the theme song for the Bond movie 'Thunderball'?

5 The hero of 28 western novels written by Clarence E. Mulford, he was portrayed in over 60 feature films by William Boyd. Name this fictional cowboy hero.

6 The song 'Some Day My Prince Will Come' featured in which Disney full-length animated film?

7 What is the title of Richard Attenborough's movie about a 1930s Canadian frontiersman and pioneering eco-warrior starring Pierce Brosnan?

8 Which actress played Natalie Cook in the 2000 movie 'Charlie's Angels'?

9 In which 1991 movie thriller does one of the main characters say: "I do wish we could chat longer, but I'm having an old friend for dinner"?

10 Julie Walters appears in which film about a boy in a mining community in the north-east of England who becomes a ballet dancer?

11 'Jesus Christ: Lust For Glory' was one of several titles originally considered for which comedy film?

12 'We are Siamese, if you please' is sung by a pair of snooty cats in which Disney animated film?

13 Who plays the title role in the 2000 film 'Shaft', a re-working of the 1970s classic starring Richard Roundtree?

14 In the film 'Zulu', the Zulu chief Cetewayo was played by which real life Zulu Chief?

15 Who directed the movies 'MASH', 'The Long Goodbye', 'Nashville' and 'Pret-A-Porter'?

Answers 1 Kristin Scott Thomas **2** Great White **3** Genevieve Bujold **4** Tom Jones **5** Hopalong Cassidy **6** Snow White And The Seven Dwarfs **7** Grey Owl **8** Cameron Diaz **9** The Silence Of The Lambs **10** Billy Elliot **11** Monty Python's Life Of Brian **12** The Lady And The Tramp **13** Samuel L. Jackson **14** Chief Buthelezi **15** Robert Altman

CINEMA   *Quiz 26*

1 Robbie Coltrane and Whoopi Goldberg have both appeared in films where their characters disguised themselves as what?

2 Released in 1976, 'Family Plot', was the last movie made by which famous director?

3 Who wrote the screenplays for 'Four Weddings And A Funeral' and 'Notting Hill'?

4 Based on Marvel comic characters, name the film released in 2000 starring Patrick Stewart?

5 What type of British aircraft were featured in the 1964 film '633 Squadron'?

6 Name the actor who played the title role in the Disney movie 'Inspector Gadget'.

7 Which member of the Monty Python team appeared as Q's assistant in the James Bond movie 'The World Is Not Enough'?

8 Which actor played Daryl Van Horn in the 1987 film 'The Witches Of Eastwick'?

9 Name the director of 'Beetlejuice', 'Edward Scissorhands', 'Ed Wood' and 'Mars Attacks!'.

10 Name the actress famous for romping naked in the 1933 film 'Ectasy'.

11 Who plays a robot in 'Bicentennial Man'?

12 Which actor played double roles as the US president and his look-alike in the 1994 film 'Dave'?

13 Name the British actress who was nominated, but did not win, an Oscar for her performance in 'Tumbleweeds'.

14 In which James Bond movie does the character Oddjob appear?

15 Who provides the voice of Woody in the 'Toy Story' films?

Answers 1 Nuns 2 Alfred Hitchcock 3 Richard Curtis 4 X-Men 5 Mosquito 6 Matthew Broderick 7 John Cleese 8 Jack Nicholson 9 Tim Burton 10 Hedy Lamarr 11 Robin Williams 12 Kevin Kline 13 Janet McTeer 14 Goldfinger 15 Tom Hanks

CINEMA

Quiz 27

1   Which actress appeared in the films 'Sliding Doors', 'Shakespeare In Love' and 'The Talented Mr. Ripley'?

2   Following his death, Warner Brothers re-released which 1971 Stanley Kubrick movie that Kubrick himself had asked to be taken out of circulation some 20 years previously?

3   Who played Dorothy in the 1939 film 'The Wizard Of Oz'?

4   Famously played in films by Peter Sellers, what's the first name of the bungling Inspector Clouseau?

5   Name the actress who appeared in the 1980's movies 'Sea Of Love' and 'The Big Easy'.

6   In the film version of Evita starring Madonna, who plays Che Guevara?

7   Which actress plays the title role in the 'Erin Brockovich'?

8   Which actress appeared in the John Wayne movie 'Stagecoach' and won an Oscar for her performance as Edward G. Robinson's moll in 'Key Largo'?

9   In the 'Toy Story' films, what is the name of Woody and Buzz Lightyear's owner?

10 In which 1991 film does actor Alan Rickman say the line: "I'll cut his heart out with a rusty spoon"?

11 Which film studio made the 1972 Oscar-winning movie 'The Godfather'?

12 Which actor played Mr. White in 'Reservoir Dogs'?

13 Celia Johnson meets Trevor Howard at a railway station in which 1945 film?

14 Which British actor made his last screen appearance in the Ridley Scott epic 'Gladiator'?

15 Starring Fred Astaire, Petula Clark and Tommy Steele, which 1968 film featured the songs 'Old Devil Moon' and 'How Are Things In Glocca Morra'?

15 Finian's Rainbow

Prince Of Thieves 11 Paramount 12 Harvey Keitel 13 Brief Encounter 14 Oliver Reed

Barkin 6 Antonio Banderas 7 Julia Roberts 8 Claire Trevor 9 Andy 10 Robin Hood:

Answers 1 Gwyneth Paltrow 2 A Clockwork Orange 3 Judy Garland 4 Jacques 5 Ellen

CINEMA   *Quiz 28*

1 Who was the director of 'Lawrence of Arabia?

2 Which writer of 'Four Weddings and A Funeral' received an MBE in 1995?

3 Which Italian actor, star of 'Three Coins in the Fountain' died at the end of 1994?

4 Who was the Prince of Wales in 'The Madness of King George'?

5 Who starred in 'The Hunger', 'Labyrinth' and 'Merry Christmas Mr Lawrence'?

6 Who starred opposite Charlie Sheen in 'Terminal Velocity'?

7 Who played the title role in the 1987 movie 'Nadine'?

8 Which film starring Esther Williams featured the song 'Baby It's Cold Outside'?

9 Who was the muse in the 1999 film of the same name?

10 In the 1968 film 'Villa Rides', who played Pancho Villa?

11 The Sorcerer' was the subtitle of which 1994 film?

12 Who played the young William Shakespeare in 'Shakespeare in Love'?

13 In which film did Richard Dreyfus star as a child psychiatrist?

14 Who portrayed Mrs March in the 1994 movie 'Little Women'?

15 Who portrayed Edward Scissorhands?

Answers 1 David Lean 2 Richard Curtis 3 Rossano Brazzi 4 Rupert Everett 5 David Bowie 6 Nastassia Kinski 7 Kim Basinger 8 Neptune's Daughter 9 Sharon Stone 10 Yul Brynner 11 Highlander 12 Joseph Fiennes 13 Silent Fall 14 Susan Sarandon 15 Johnny Depp

MUSIC

MUSIC

Pop music 1

1 Which rock guitarist was born Saul Hudson in Stoke-on-Trent, England in 1965 where he spent the first eleven years of his life before moving to the USA?

2 Name the Nigerian-born singer who sold over 6 million copies of her debut album 'Diamond Life'.

3 T Rex had four UK No. 1 hits between March 1971 and June 1972. 'Hot Love' was the first, what was the last?

4 'Rock The Casbah', 'London Calling' and 'Should I Stay Or Should I Go' are all songs recorded by which punk-rock band?

5 Name the female singer who appeared with Westlife on their recording of 'Against All Odds'?

6 Who appeared as Madonna's chauffeur in the video for her song 'Music'?

7 Whigfield sang about which night of the week?

8 Which British 'boy band' had a hit in 1998 with the song 'More Than A Woman'?

9 And which American group had a hit with 'More Than A Woman' in 1978?

10 What instrument is Vanessa Mae famous for playing?

11 Acclaimed by critics as one of the best albums of 1999, 'On How Life Is' was recorded by which singer who has been compared with Nina Simone and Billie Holiday?

12 'Disco 2000' was a hit in 1995 for which group?

13 An incident at the 1973 Oscar's ceremony inspired Ray Stevens to write and record which 1974 chart topping song on both sides of the Atlantic?

14 In 1953, who became the first vocal group to top the UK charts with 'Broken Wings'?

15 In 2000, who released her version of the Don McLean song 'American Pie'?

Answers 1 Slash **2** Sade **3** Metal Guru **4** The Clash **5** Mariah Carey **6** Ali G **7** Saturday **8** 911 **9** Tavares **10** Violin **11** Macy Gray **12** Pulp **13** The Streak **14** The Stargazers **15** Madonna

MUSIC

Pop groups 1

Complete the name of the following groups:

1   Bobby 'Boris' Pickett and the ....?
2   Joan Jett and the ....?
3   Lisa Loeb and ....?
4   Gary Puckett and the ....?
5   Emile Ford and the ....?
6   Desmond Dekker and the ....?
7   Huey Lewis and the ....?
8   Kool and the ....?
9   Gladys Knight and the ....?
10 Bob Seger and the ....?
11 KC and the ....?
12 Somethin' Smith and the ....?
13 Boyd Bennett and his....................?
14 Gene Vincent and the ....?
15 Little Anthony and the ....?

Answers 1 Crypt Kickers **2** Blackhearts **3** Nine Stories **4** Union Gap **5** Checkmates **6** Aces **7** News **8** Gang **9** Pips **10** Silver Bullet Band **11** Sunshine Band **12** Redheads **13** Rockets **14** Blue Caps **15** Imperials

311

MUSIC

Pop music 2

1   According to the title of a Four Seasons hit song 'Big Girls Don't …' what?

2   'Steptacular' was a 1999 UK chart-topping album for which British group?

3   Which singer topped the UK singles charts with 'Dreams' in 1993 and 'Rise' in 2000?

4   What sport is the central theme of the video for Robbie Williams' song 'She's The One'?

5   Name the American singer of the 1960s hits 'Runaway', 'Swiss Maid' and 'Little Town Flirt' who died from a self-inflicted gunshot wound on 8 February 1990.

6   What were the first names of the pop duo The Carpenters?

7   According to the title of Benny Hill's hit, who was the 'fastest milkman in the west'?

8   'Shang-A-Lang', 'Bye Bye Baby' and 'Give A Little Love' were all hits in the 1970s for which British group?

9   Name the female singer who appeared with the Pet Shop Boys on the 1987 hit 'What Have I Done To Deserve This?'

10 The Platters, Teddy Pendergrass, Yazoo and Portishead have all had hits with completely different songs that had the same two word title. What title?

11 'Help Me Rhonda', 'Barbara Ann' and 'Lady Lynda' were all hits for which group?

12 A barber, a banker, a fireman and a nurse all feature in the lyrics of which Beatles' song?

13 The group the Cardigans who's hits include 'Lovefool' and 'My Favourite Game', originate from which country?

14 Complete the name of this American group – Hootie and the…?

15 'Mama Told Me Not To Come' was a hit in 1970 for which American group?

Answers 1 Cry **2** Step **3** Gabrielle **4** Ice Skating **5** Del Shannon **6** Richard and Karen **7** Ernie **8** Bay City Rollers **9** Dusty Springfield **10** Only You **11** Beach Boys **12** Penny Lane **13** Sweden **14** Blowfish **15** Three Dog Night

MUSIC — Musical instruments

1. What term, consisting of two hyphenated rhyming words, is sometimes applied to two mechanical cranked instruments, the barrel organ and barrel piano?

2. What instrument is Ravi Shankar famous for popularising?

3. The name of what instrument, developed in Hawaii in the late 19th-century has an Hawaiian name meaning flea?

4. The single-headed Middle-eastern darabuka and the double-headed Japanese tsuzumi are types of which musical instrument?

5. What instrument was played by jazz great Jelly Roll Morton?

6. Closely related to the bugle and flugelhorn, which trumpet-like instrument now has its most prominent place in marching, military and brass bands?

7. The name of which percussion instrument is derived from two Greek words meaning wood and sound?

8. Which Hungarian composer included a triangle solo in his first piano concerto (1849) called the 'Triangle concerto'?

9. Andres Segovia was a virtuoso performer of which musical instrument?

10. The B-flat soprano is the most common size of which woodwind instrument?

11. Vivaldi, who composed 'The Four Seasons', was a virtuoso on which musical instrument?

12. The Spanish-born Pablo Casals was the most prominent 20th-century performer of which musical instrument?

13. Which free-reed musical instrument, in which wind is supplied to the reeds by bellows, was invented in Berlin in 1822?

14. In the Marx Brothers movies, what instrument was played by Chico?

15. The kinnor of the ancient Hebrews, the instrument of King David, was a type of which stringed musical instrument?

Answers 1 Hurdy-Gurdy 2 Sitar 3 Ukulele 4 Drum 5 Piano 6 Cornet 7 Xylophone 8 Franz Liszt 9 Guitar 10 Clarinet 11 Violin 12 Cello 13 Accordion 14 Piano 15 Lyre

1 'Resurrection Symphony' and the 'Symphony Of A Thousand' are works by which Austrian-born composer?

2 Who was known as the 'Waltz King', composing many famous waltzes such as 'The Blue Danube'? Was it Johann Strauss the Elder or Johann Strauss the Younger?

3 What was the first name of Strauss, the German composer who died in 1949. One of his best known works being the opera 'Der Rosenkavalier'?

4 Who composed the famous 'Pomp and Circumstance' march?

5 Who wrote the 'Marriage of Figaro'?

6 Which 19th century Russian composer wrote the opera 'Boris Godunov'?

7 Name the 20th century German composer who's best known work is the oratorio 'Carmina Burana'.

8 The choral works 'Psalmus Hungaricus' and 'Te Deum' are major works of which Hungarian composer?

9 Which 20th century French composer wrote the ballet 'Les Biches' and the opera 'Les Mamelles de Tiresias'?

10 Which German composed the 'Rhenish Symphony' in the mid-19th century?

11 And which 19th century German composer wrote the opera 'Camacho's Wedding'?

12 BWV numbers are used to identify the works of which composer?

13 Which Puccini opera was completed after his death by Franco Alfano?

14 Name the Italian who composed the symphonic poem 'Fountains Of Rome'. The leading Italian composer of his time, he died in 1936.

15 Three major composers were born in 1685. Bach, Handel and which Italian who was also a noted harpsichordist and organist?

Answers 1 Gustav Mahler 2 Johann Strauss the Younger 3 Richard 4 Edward Elgar 5 Mozart 6 Modest Mussorgsky 7 Carl Orff 8 Zoltan Kodaly 9 Francis Poulenc 10 Robert Schumann 11 Felix Mendelssohn 12 Johann Sebastian Bach 13 Turandot 14 Ottorino Respighi 15 Domenico Scarlatti

MUSIC   *Pop albums 1*

Who recorded the following albums:-

1   Revolver / Rubber Soul / Abbey Road?
2   Nevermind / In Utero / Incesticide?
3   Pet Sounds / Smiley Smile / Sunflower?
4   Automatic For The People / Out Of Time / New Adventures In Hi-Fi?
5   The Dark Side Of The Moon / Wish You Were Here / The Wall?
6   The Rise And Fall Of Ziggy Stardust And The Spiders From Mars / Hunky Dory / Aladdin Sane?
7   Electric Ladyland / Are You Experienced / Axis:Bold As Love?
8   Blonde On Blonde / Blood On The Tracks / Highway 61 Revisited?
9   The Joshua Tree / Achtung Baby / The Unforgettable Fire?
10 Rumours / Mirage / Behind The Mask?
11 The Queen Is Dead / Meat Is Murder / Strangeways Here We Come?
12 Exile On Main Street / Let It Bleed / Beggars Banquet?
13 What's Going On / Here, My Dear / Let's Get It On?
14 (What's The Story) Morning Glory / Definitely Maybe / Be Here Now?
15 Forever Changes / Out Here / Reel To Reel?

Answers 1 The Beatles 2 Nirvana 3 Beach Boys 4 R.E.M 5 Pink Floyd 6 David Bowie 7 Jimi Hendrix Experience 8 Bob Dylan 9 U2 10 Fleetwood Mac 11 The Smiths 12 Rolling Stones 13 Marvin Gaye 14 Oasis 15 Love

MUSIC — Music of the World

1 Name the 20th century Spanish composer, blind from the age of three, who was the first contemporary composer to combine the sound of the guitar with that of an orchestra, his work 'Concierto de Aranjuez' being a typical example.

2 Which 20th century Brazilian composer and conductor wrote a series of suites entitled 'Bachianas Brasileiras' in which he treats Brazilian-style melodies in the manner of Bach?

3 What nationality was the composer Carl August Nielsen who died in 1931?

4 In which country was composer Arnold Schoenberg born?

5 By what name is Haydn's 'Symphony No.104 in D' known?

6 'Harold In Italy' is a symphony written by which 19th century French composer?

7 Which British composer wrote the children's opera, 'Noyes Fludde', a musical rendition of a 14th century miracle play?

8 Who composed the opera 'Tristan And Isolde'?

9 Which composer died in Vienna on 5 December 1791 at the age of 35?

10 According to Rossini, which German composer had 'beautiful moments but awful quarter hours'?

11 Popular in the 1970s and 1980s, the instrumental group Tangerine Dream came from which country?

12 For which musical instrument was Liszt's 'Liebestraume' written?

13 'La Brabanconne' is the title of the national anthem of which European country?

14 What nationality was the composer Erik Satie?

15 And what was the nationality of pianist and composer Isaac Albeniz?

Answers 1 Joaquin Rodrigo **2** Heitor Villa-Lobos **3** Danish **4** Austria **5** London Symphony **6** Hector Berlioz **7** Benjamin Britten **8** Richard Wagner **9** Mozart **10** Richard Wagner **11** Germany **12** Piano **13** Belgium **14** French **15** Spanish

MUSIC — Pop music 3

1   Name the former member of the Beatles who died in Germany in 1962 following a brain haemorrhage.

2   Guitarist Paul 'Bonehead' Arthur and bass player Paul 'Guigsy' McGuigan both quit which rock band in 1999?

3   Who wrote the Manfred Mann hits 'Just Like A Woman', 'The Mighty Quinn' and 'If You Gotta Go, Go Now'?

4   Which singer, once married to Elizabeth Taylor, topped the UK charts in 1953 with the songs 'Outside Of Heaven' and 'I'm Walking Behind You'?

5   On 3 July 1999, fans from around the world gathered in Cheltenham, his home town, to commemorate the 30th anniversary of the death of which former member of the Rolling Stones?

6   Who topped the UK singles charts for seven weeks in 1998 with 'Believe'?

7   Which group released albums entitled 'Modern Life Is Rubbish' and 'The Great Escape'?

8   Nancy and Frank Sinatra topped the UK charts in 1967 with which song?

9   Which instrument did George Harrison play on the Beatles recordings of 'Norwegian Wood' and 'Within You Without You'?

10 In 1999, 'Music To Watch The Girls By' gave which American singer his first UK top ten hit since 1973?

11 Which song was a hit for Doris Day in 1954, for Kathy Kirby in 1963 and for Daniel O'Donnell in 1995?

12 Berry Gordy Jnr. founded which recording company in Detroit in 1959?

13 Who's recording of 'We Have All The Time In The World' became a hit in 1994, 23 years after his death?

14 What nationality are the group Ace Of Base?

15 'Rock Lobster', 'Love Shack', 'Roam' and 'Good Stuff' were all hits for which group?

Answers 1 Stuart Sutcliffe 2 Oasis 3 Bob Dylan 4 Eddie Fisher 5 Brian Jones 6 Cher 7 Blur 8 Something Stupid 9 Sitar 10 Andy Williams 11 Secret Love 12 Tamla Motown 13 Louis Armstrong 14 Swedish 15 B-52's

MUSIC

Song lyrics

Identify the popular (not pop) songs from which the following lyrics come:

1 'I get no kick from champagne, mere alcohol doesn't thrill me at all'?

2 'One day they may tell you, you will not go far, that night you open and there you are. Next day on your dressing room they hang a star!'?

3 'Father's name was Hezikiah, mother's name was Anna Maria, Yanks, through and through! Red, white and blue'?

4 'I'm as corny as Kansas in August, I'm as normal as blueberry pie......, High as a flag on the fourth of July'?

5 'In olden days, a glimpse of stocking was looked upon as something shocking'?

6 'I get too hungry for dinner at eight, I like the theatre but never come late'?

7 'All the rams that chase the ewe sheep, are determined there'll be new sheep and the ewe sheep aren't even keeping score'?

8 'In the Philippines, there are lovely screens to protect you from the glare; In the Malay states they have hats like plates which the Britishers won't wear'?

9 'You like potato and I like po-tah-to, you like tomato and I like to-mah-to'?

10 'Holding hands at midnight beneath a starry sky'?

11 'I'm wild again, beguiled again, a simpering, whimpering child again'?

12 'Like the beat, beat, beat of the tom-tom; When the jungle shadows fall, like the tick, tick, tock of the stately clock, as it stands against the wall'?

13 'There's no love song finer, but how strange the change from major to minor'?

14 'Let me be by myself in the evenin' breeze, and listen to the murmur of the cottonwood trees, send me off forever but I ask you please'?

15 'I've tried so not to give in, I've said to myself this affair never will go so well, but why should I try to resist'?

Answers 1 I Get A Kick Out Of You 2 There's No Business Like Show Business 3 Yankee Doodle Dandy 4 I'm In Love With A Wonderful Guy 5 Anything Goes 6 The Lady Is A Tramp 7 June Is Bustin' Out All Over 8 Mad Dogs And Englishmen 9 Let's Call The Whole Thing Off 10 Nice Work If You Can Get It 11 Bewitched, Bothered And Bewildered 12 Night And Day 13 Every Time We Say Goodbye 14 Don't Fence Me In 15 I've Got You Under My Skin

MUSIC

Pop groups 2

Complete the names of the following groups:

1   Dion and the ....?
2   Maurice Williams and the ....?
3   Little Caesar and the ....?
4   Joey Dee and the ....?
5   Booker T and the ....?
6   Billy J. Kramer and the ....?
7   Jr. Walker and the ....?
8   Wayne Fontana and the ....?
9   Sam The Sham and the ....?
10 Paul Revere and the ....?
11 Gary Lewis and the ....?
12 Tommy James and the ....?
13 ? (Question Mark) and the ....?
14 Archie Bell and the ....?
15 Commander Cody and His.....................?

Answers 1 Belmonts 2 Zodiacs 3 Romans 4 Starlighters 5 M.G's 6 Dakotas 7 All Stars 8 Mindbenders 9 Pharaohs 10 Raiders 11 Playboys 12 Shondells 13 Mysterians 14 Drells 15 Lost Planet Airmen

319

Classical music 2

1 'O Fortuna' is the opening chorus of which oratorio?

2 Which French composer wrote the orchestral piece 'Pavane'?

3 And which French composer wrote piano pieces known as 'Trois Gymnopedies'?

4 'Adagio for Strings' is the best known work of which 20th century US composer?

5 Which Italian composer wrote the one-act opera 'Gianni Schicchi'?

6 'The Shepherd's Hymn' features in which Beethoven symphony?

7 Who composed the symphonic poem 'Also sprach Zarathustra'?

8 Which German composer's 'Symphony No. 4' is known as the 'Italian Symphony'?

9 In 1899, which English composer wrote the piece 'Chanson de Matin' (Song of the Morning)?

10 Which composer's 'cantata No. 208' is known as 'Sheep May Safely Graze'?

11 What name is given to Beethoven's 'piano concerto No.5'. Is it Emperor, Kreutzer or Trout?

12 What nationality was the composer Alexandre Luigini?

13 The music for the ballet 'Gayaneh' was written by which 20th century Armenian-born composer?

14 The opera 'Thais' was written by which French composer?

15 Often attributed to Purcell, which English composer actually wrote 'Trumpet Voluntary'?

Answers 1 Carmina Burana 2 Gabriel Faure 3 Erik Satie 4 Samuel Barber 5 Puccini 6 Pastoral or 6th 7 Richard Strauss 8 Felix Mendelssohn 9 Edward Elgar 10 Johann Sebastian Bach 11 Emperor 12 French 13 Aram Ilich Khachaturian 14 Jules Massenet 15 Jeremiah Clarke

MUSIC	Pop groups 3

Complete the names of the following groups:

1   Harold Melvin and the ....?
2   Disco Tex and the ....?
3   Jimmy James and the ....?
4   Rick Dees and his ....?
5   Jonathan Richman and the ....?
6   Ian Dury and the ....?
7   Tom Petty and the ....?
8   Bob Marley and the ....?
9   Kid Creole and the ....?
10   Bruce Hornsby and the ....?
11   Edie Brickell and the ....?
12   Hootie and the ....?
13   Simon Dupree and the ....?
14   Smokey Robinson and the ....?
15   Graham Parker and the ....?

Answers 1 Blue Notes 2 Sex-O-Lettes 3 Vagabonds 4 Cast of Idiots 5 Modern Lovers 6 Blockheads 7 Heartbreakers 8 Wailers 9 Coconuts 10 Range 11 New Bohemians 12 Blowfish 13 Big Sound 14 Miracles 15 Rumour

Pop music 4

1 Which former member of the Beatles released the solo albums 'All Things Must Pass', 'Living In The Material World' and 'Cloud Nine'?

2 Which guitarist/singer was a member of the Yardbirds, Bluesbreakers, Cream and Blind Faith?

3 Under the alias Apollo C. Vermouth, which of the Beatles produced the Bonzo Dog Doo-Dah Band's hit 'I'm The Urban Spaceman'?

4 Dave Guard, Bob Shane and Nick Reynolds formed which folk trio in San Francisco in 1957. They had a big hit in the UK with the song 'Tom Dooley'?

5 Name the singer who had a hit in 1962 with 'Dream Baby' and a hit in 1963 with 'In Dreams'?

6 Who wrote the song 'Roll Over Beethoven'?

7 What is the surname of Billy Joe in Bobbie Gentry's hit song 'Ode To Billy Joe'?

8 And in that song, what was the name of the bridge that Billy Joe jumped off?

9 The Monkees sang about the 'last train to .... ' where?

10 Name the Brazilian-born singer who had a hit with the song 'Feelings' in 1975?

11 'In the town where I was born' is the first line of which Beatles' song?

12 Which guitarist was born Brian Rankin in Newcastle-upon-Tyne on 28 October 1941?

13 Which song has been a hit for Harold Melvin and the Bluenotes, Thelma Houston and the Communards?

14 Who wrote the Monkees hit 'A Little Bit Me A Little Bit You'?

15 Which T Rex song was given the title 'Bang A Gong' in the US to avoid confusion with another song?

Answers 1 George Harrison 2 Eric Clapton 3 Paul McCartney 4 Kingston Trio 5 Roy Orbison 6 Chuck Berry 7 MacAllister 8 Tallahachie Bridge 9 Clarksville 10 Morris Albert 11 Yellow Submarine 12 Hank Marvin 13 Don't Leave Me This Way 14 Neil Diamond 15 Get It On

MUSIC

Pop albums 2

Who recorded the following albums:-

1   Sign 'O' The Times / Lovesexy / Graffiti Bridge?
2   Kind Of Blue / Bitches Brew / Amandla?
3   Physical Graffiti / In Through The Out Door / Houses Of The Holy?
4   Blue / Court And Spark / Hejira?
5   Mellow Gold / Odelay / Midnight Vultures?
6   Hounds Of Love / The Sensual World / The Red Shoes?
7   Trout Mask Replica / Doc At The Radar Station / Clear Spot?
8   Born To Run / Tunnel Of Love / The River?
9   Experience / The Fat Of The Land / Music For The Jilted Generation?
10 Songs In The Key Of Life / Music Of My Mind / Talking Book?
11 Transformer / Rock 'N' Roll Animal / New York?
12 Astral Weeks / St. Dominic's Preview / Poetic Champions Compose?
13 Mellon Collie And The Infinite Sadness / Siamese Dream / Pisces Iscariot?
14 Woodface / Together Alone / Temple Of Low Men?
15 After The Goldrush / Harvest / Weld?

MUSIC — Pop music 5

1   Not released as a single in the US, which Fleetwood Mac recording reached No. 9 in the UK charts in February 1983?

2   'Telegraph Road' is a track on which Dire Straits album?

3   Which UK group had hits with their versions of 'Tears Of A Clown' in 1979 and 'Can't Get Used To Losing You' in 1983?

4   Which group fronted by Ian McCulloch had 11 top 40 hits between 1981 and 1988?

5   Which Prince song, featured in the movie 'Purple Rain', gave him his first US No.1 and was the top selling single of 1984?

6   Marvin Gaye won his first Grammy award in 1983. It was for Best Male Vocal Performance of which song?

7   Who's debut album 'Licensed To Ill' was the first rap album to top the US charts?

8   Name the female singer who provided the vocals on the Crusaders hit 'Street Life'.

9   In 1985, which British female singer became the first ever to achieve top ten hits in the US pop, R&B, country, dance and adult contemporary charts?

10 Which female singer topped the US and UK album charts in 1980 with the album 'Guilty'?

11 Which member of Police recorded under the name of Klark Kent?

12 'I Am What I Am' was which female singer's only UK top twenty hit during the 1980s?

13 Which Bananarama song was a US No.1 hit in 1986?

14 Soft Cell's hit 'Tainted Love' was written by Ed Cobb. Cobb had been a member of which group who had a big hit in both the US and UK in 1958 with 'Big Man'?

15 Which Def Leppard album spent 96 weeks in the US Top 40 and was the first heavy metal album to sell a million copies in CD format?

Answers 1 Oh Diane 2 Love Over Gold 3 The Beat 4 Echo and the Bunnymen 5 When Doves Cry 6 (Sexual) Healing 7 Beastie Boys 8 Randy Crawford 9 Sheena Easton 10 Barbra Streisand 11 Stewart Copeland 12 Gloria Gaynor 13 Venus 14 The Four Preps 15 Hysteria

MUSIC — Classical music 3

1   Which Russian composer wrote the satiric opera 'The Nose'?

2   Which Bavarian-born 18th century composer wrote the opera 'Orfeo ed Eurydice'?

3   Noted for his religious music, which Russian composed the piece known as 'The Creed'?

4   What nationality was the composer Charles Gounod?

5   The son of a doctor from Sierra Leone and a British mother, which composer is best known for the trilogy for solo voices, chorus and orchestra 'Song of Hiawatha'?

6   In which century did the Italian composer Vincenzo Bellini live?

7   Who wrote the 'Wine, Women and Song' waltz?

8   What nationality was the pianist, composer and conductor Carl Reinecke?

9   Whose 'Waltz No. 3 in F' is known as the 'Cats Waltz'?

10 Written in the 20th century, Erwartung and Pierrot Lunaire are works of which composer?

11 His interest in gypsy music laid the foundations for which composer's 'Hungarian Rhapsodies'?

12 Which opera features the 'March of the Toreadors'?

13 Fiordiligi, Dorabella, Guglielmo, Ferrando and Don Alfonso are all characters in which of Mozart's operas?

14 And in which Gilbert and Sullivan opera do the characters Captain Corcoran, Dick Deadeye and Little Buttercup appear?

15 Which Russian-born composer wrote the music for the ballet 'Pulcinella'?

Answers 1 Dmitri Shostakovich 2 Christoph Gluck 3 Aleksandr Grechaninov 4 French 5 Samuel Coleridge-Taylor 6 19th 7 Johann Strauss the Younger 8 German 9 Frédéric Chopin 10 Arnold Schoenberg 11 Franz Liszt 12 Carmen 13 Cosi Fan Tutte 14 HMS Pinafore 15 Igor Stravinsky

MUSIC   *Pop albums 3*

Who recorded the following albums:-

1   Bat Out Of Hell / Welcome To The Neighbourhood / Bad Attitude?

2   Legend / Exodus / Natty Dread?

3   Ten / Vs / Vitalogy?

4   A Night At The Opera / Made In Heaven / News Of The World?

5   Brothers In Arms / Making Movies / On Every Street?

6   Bringing It All Back Home / Infidels / Slow Train Coming?

7   Older / Faith / Listen Without Prejudice?

8   Younger Than Yesterday / Fifth Dimension / Ballad Of Easy Rider?

9   Know Your Enemy / Everything Must Go / This Is My Truth Tell Me Yours?

10 The Pretender / Running On Empty / Late For The Sky?

11 Touch / Revenge / We Too Are One?

12 Their Satanic Majesties Request / Goat's Head Soup / Steel Wheels?

13 Arrival / Voulez-Vous / Super Trouper?

14 Nylon Curtain / Piano Man / River Of Dreams?

15 Don't Shoot Me I'm Only The Piano Player / Breaking Hearts / Reg Strikes Back?

Answers 1 Meatloaf **2** Bob Marley and the Wailers **3** Pearl Jam **4** Queen **5** Dire Straits **6** Bob Dylan **7** George Michael **8** The Byrds **9** Manic Street Preachers **10** Jackson Browne **11** Eurythmics **12** Rolling Stones **13** Abba **14** Billy Joel **15** Elton John

326

1 One of Tamla Motown's most successful acts, which group had hits with 'My Girl', 'Get Ready', 'Ball Of Confusion', 'Just My Imagination' and 'Papa Was A Rollin' Stone'?

2 Marshall Bruce Mathers III is the real name of which rap star?

3 Name the US group who had a hit in the UK in both 1977 and 1990 with the song 'Black Betty'?

4 What four letter word beginning with H is used to describe the part of a pop song which you easily remember, usually the chorus?

5 Name the Hollywood movie star who appeared with Wendy Fraser on the 1988 hit 'She's Like The Wind'?

6 Complete the title of the following song which was a hit for both Marc Cohn and Cher – 'Walking In ......'?

7 Which song recorded by Herman's Hermits was a million seller in the USA but was never released as a single in the UK because they thought the arrangement was too corny for the British market?

8 By what name did Richard Penniman become known as a rock 'n' roller?

9 Lenny Bruce, Leonard Bernstein and Leonid Brezhnev are mentioned in which R.E.M. song?

10 Under what name is William Broad better known as a pop star?

11 Which female singer once worked as a French and Spanish interpreter at Miami airport?

12 From which country do Martha and The Muffins originate?

13 In 1986, who sang: 'We don't have to take our clothes off to have a good time'?

14 In 1989, who became the first female teenager to top the US singles and album charts simultaneously?

15 What does the kd in kd Lang stand for?

Answers 1 The Temptations 2 Eminem 3 Ram Jam 4 Hook 5 Patrick Swayze 6 Memphis 7 Mrs. Brown You've Got A Lovely Daughter 8 Little Richard 9 It's The End Of The World As We Know It 10 Billy Idol 11 Gloria Estefan 12 Canada 13 Jermaine Stewart 14 Debbie Gibson 15 Kathy Dawn

MUSIC — Disney Music

1   In 'The Little Mermaid' which character sings 'Under The Sea'?

2   Which former teen idol provides the singing voice for Captain Li Shang in 'Mulan'?

3   Which Disney movie featured a number called the 'Chimney-Sweep Ballet'?

4   Nominated for an Oscar, the song 'The Age Of Not Believing' featured in which 1971 Disney movie?

5   Which famous animation movie featured the Oscar-nominated song 'Love Is A Song'?

6   Which 1941 film featured another Oscar-nominated song 'Baby Mine'?

7   In the 1992 movie 'Aladdin', which character sings the song 'Prince Ali'?

8   Apart from the end title duet, the theme song for 'Beauty And The Beast' is sung by which character whose voice is provided by Angela Lansbury?

9   Hayley Mills achieved minor chart success with which song featured in the 1961 movie 'The Parent Trap'?

10 Which 1940 film featured music by Bach, Tchaikovsky, Beethoven, Stravinsky and others?

11 Which movie featured the song 'Hakuna M-a-t-a-t-a'?

12 Featured in 'Lady And The Tramp' which female vocalist sang 'He's A Tramp'?

13 And which singing 'superstar' sings the theme for 'The Emperor's New Groove'?

14 Which 1946 film featured 'Zip-a-dee Doo-Dah'?

15 Which 1997 film features the songs 'Zero To Hero' and 'A Star Is Born'?

Answers 1 Sebastian 2 Donny Osmond 3 Mary Poppins 4 Bedknobs And Broomsticks 5 Bambi 6 Dumbo 7 The Genie 8 Mrs. Potts 9 Let's Get Together 10 Fantasia 11 The Lion King 12 Peggy Lee 13 Tom Jones 14 Song Of The South 15 Hercules

1 When his recording of 'Hold On To The Nights' topped the US charts in 1988, who became the first male singer to notch four US top 3 hits from a debut album?

2 Their first million-selling single was 'Dream On' in 1976 and their first UK top twenty hit was 'Love In An Elevator' in 1989. Name this American rock group?

3 What title is shared by Don McLean's 1970 debut album and Carole King's 1971 chart-topping album?

4 Which Hollywood actress sang on the Was (Not Was) hit 'Shake Your Head'?

5 Name the only US top ten hit the Kinks had during the 1970s.

6 Name the title of Bruce Springsteen's first double album, released in 1980.

7 Who did the Beach Boys team up with on the 1987 hit 'Wipeout'?

8 And with which British rock band did the Beach Boys record 'Fun Fun Fun' in 1996?

9 Which singing group were originally called the Four Aims before changing their name in 1956?

10 In 1987, which Michael Jackson album became the first album to enter both the US and UK album charts at number one?

11 Which Australian group started their career in 1977 as The Farriss Brothers, with three brothers named Farriss in their line-up?

12 The burning down of Montreux Casino in 1971 was immortalised by which Deep Purple song?

13 Name the drummer of the Eagles who had solo success with songs such as 'Dirty Laundry', 'The Boys Of Summer' and 'The End Of The Innocence'.

14 "I want you, I need you, but there ain't no way I'm ever gonna love you, now don't be sad" are lyrics from which Meat Loaf song?

15 Not released as a single in the UK, which Beatles song topped the US charts in June 1970?

Answers 1 Richard Marx 2 Aerosmith 3 Tapestry 4 Kim Basinger 5 Lola 6 The River 7 The Fat Boys 8 Status Quo 9 Four Tops 10 Bad 11 INXS 12 Smoke On The Water 13 Don Henley 14 Two Out Of Three Ain't Bad 15 The Long And Winding Road

MUSIC *ABBA*

1 Before joining Abba, Benny Andersson was the piano player for which other popular Swedish group?

2 Who was Benny married to – Agnetha or Frida?

3 And under what name did Benny and Bjorn sing as a duo – The Hip Cats, The Hootenanny Singers or West Bay?

4 Who was known as the groups 'fifth member', he was their manager and co-wrote some of their earlier hits?

5 Which US singer/songwriter provided the English lyrics for their song 'Ring Ring'?

6 With which song did they win the Eurovision Song Contest?

7 And in which year?

8 And where did they win it – Basle, Brighton or Brussels?

9 And which country came second – Italy, Norway or the UK?

10 Which member of the group was born in Norway?

11 Which song gave them their first US No.1 hit single?

12 Which song features the following lyrics: 'I'm nothing special, in fact I'm a bit of a bore/If I tell you a joke, you've probably heard it before'?

13 Which hit song is subtitled ('A Man After Midnight')?

14 The title of which hit show featuring their songs is taken from the title of one of them?

15 'If you change your mind, I'm the first in line' are lyrics from which song?

Answers 1 The Hep Stars 2 Frida 3 The Hootenanny Singers 4 Stig Anderson 5 Neil Sedaka 6 Waterloo 7 1974 8 Brighton 9 Italy 10 Frida 11 Dancing Queen 12 Thank You For The Music 13 Gimme Gimme Gimme 14 Mamma Mia 15 Take A Chance On Me

MUSIC — Song lyrics 2

1 'I believe that children are our future, teach them well and let them lead the way' are lyrics from which Whitney Houston hit song, also recorded by George Benson?

2 Which song contains the line: 'Beelzebub has a devil put aside for me'?

3 'You talk like Marlene Dietrich' are the opening words of which 1969 UK chart-topping song?

4 Which Everly Brothers song contains the following lyrics: 'The movie wasn't so hot, it didn't have much of a plot, we fell asleep, our goose is cooked, our reputation is shot'?

5 From which Elvis Presley hit song do the following lyrics come: 'When no-one else can understand me, when everything I do is wrong, you give me hope and consolation, you give me strength to carry on'?

6 The lyrics 'She looked good, she looked fine and I nearly lost my mind' come from which 1964 chart-topper on both sides of the Atlantic?

7 From which Eric Clapton song do the following lyrics come: 'I feel wonderful because I see the love light in your eyes. And the wonder of it all is that you just don't realise how much I love you'?

8 'Okay, so you're Brad Pitt' are lyrics from which Shania Twain song?

9 Which Robert Palmer song contains the following lyrics: 'You see the signs but you can't read, you're running at a different speed, your heart beats at double time, another kiss and you'll be mine – one-track mind you can't be saved'?

10 'You check out Guitar George he knows all the chords, mind he's strictly rhythm he doesn't want to make it cry or sing, and an old guitar is all he can afford when he gets up under the lights to play his thing' are words from which Dire Straits song?

11 From which song do the following lyrics come: 'But February made me shiver, with every paper I'd deliver, bad news on the doorstep, I couldn't take one more step, I can't remember if I cried, when I read about his widowed bride'?

12 'Watching every motion in my foolish lover's game, on this endless ocean finally lovers know no shame, turning and returning to some secret place inside, watching in slow motion as you turn around and say' are lyrics from which song?

Answers 1 Greatest Love Of All 2 Bohemian Rhapsody 3 Where Do You Go To My Lovely 4 Wake Up Little Susie 5 The Wonder Of You 6 Do Wah Diddy Diddy 7 Wonderful Tonight 8 That Don't Impress Me Much 9 Addicted To Love 10 Sultans Of Swing 11 American Pie 12 Take My Breath Away

MUSIC   *Pop music 8*

1   Their most famous song is 'Born To Be Wild'. Which rock band took their name from the title of a novel written by Hermann Hesse?

2   Not related, what surname is shared by Andy, John and Roger, all one-time members of Duran Duran?

3   Eddie Van Halen played lead guitar on which 1983 Michael Jackson hit single?

4   'Appetite For Destruction' was the title of which rock band's debut album?

5   Which Simon and Garfunkel song did Bob Dylan include on his 1970 album 'Self Portrait'?

6   In 1978, Elton John released his first album without Bernie Taupin lyrics. Name it.

7   Which member of Queen wrote 'Radio Ga Ga'?

8   In 1986, Bruce Springsteen reputedly refused an offer of $12 million from Chrysler to use which one of his songs in a series of commercials?

9   Which Beatles song was recorded in June 1967, the final session being shown 'live' on worldwide television as part of the first ever global TV link-up?

10 Who wrote the Tina Turner song 'Private Dancer'?

11 In 1991, Natalie Cole revived one of her father's most memorable songs. Which song?

12 Which song was a hit for Elvis Presley and Fine Young Cannibals?

13 Name the song, written by Eric Clapton as a tribute to his son Conor, which was a hit on both sides of the Atlantic in 1992.

14 Which aptly titled song was released by David Bowie in July 1969 to coincide with the Apollo moon landing?

15 Who played piano on the Hollies 1969 recording of 'He Ain't Heavy, He's My Brother'?

Answers 1 Steppenwolf 2 Taylor 3 Beat It 4 Guns N' Roses 5 The Boxer 6 A Single Man 7 Roger Taylor 8 Born In The USA 9 All You Need Is Love 10 Mark Knopfler 11 Unforgettable 12 Suspicious Minds 13 Tears In Heaven 14 Space Oddity 15 Elton John

MUSIC

Pop music 9

1   Which group had hits in the 1990s with 'Everything About You' and 'Cats In The Cradle'?

2   In 1972, 'Mother And Child Reunion' was the first solo hit in the UK for which American singer?

3   Which group released an album entitled 'Mwng' which is Welsh for 'mane' and is sung entirely in Welsh?

4   Name the group who topped the UK charts in 1996 with the singles 'Breathe' and 'Firestarter'?

5   Born in Dumbarton, Scotland, which singer/songwriter was the frontman of 'Talking Heads'?

6   Popular in the 1960s and 1970s, the name of which group is often abbreviated to CSN & Y?

7   What make of car can be seen half-submerged in a swimming pool on the cover of the Oasis album 'Be Here Now'?

8   Which singer is known as the 'groover from Vancouver'?

9   'Dream Lover', 'Mack The Knife', 'Lazy River' and 'If I Were A Carpenter' were all hits for which singer?

10 A collection of classic rock 'n' roll tracks, who recorded the album 'Run Devil Run'?

11 Who released an album entitled 'Willennium'?

12 Whitney Houston first topped the UK singles charts in 1985 with which song?

13 Which pop star was born Georgios Panayiotou in 1963?

14 Which female singer was found dead at the Landmark Hotel, Hollywood on 4 October 1970?

15 Six Isle of Man postage stamps were issued on 12 October 1999 in honour of which pop group?

14 Janis Joplin   15 Bee Gees

10 Paul McCartney   11 Will Smith   12 Saving All My Love For You   13 George Michael

Byrne   6 Crosby, Stills, Nash and Young   7 Rolls-Royce   8 Bryan Adams   9 Bobby Darin

Answers 1 Ugly Kid Joe   2 Paul Simon   3 Super Furry Animals   4 The Prodigy   5 David

MISCELLANEOUS

MISCELLANEOUS 3

Quiz 1

1   Annapurna is a mountain in which mountain range?

2   The Russian composer Sergei Prokofiev died on 5 March 1953. This news was overshadowed by the death of which other famous Russian on the very same day?

3   American actor David Soul has been involved with the charitable organisation WSPA. What does WSPA stand for?

4   What kind of foodstuff is Monterey Jack?

5   Which US cavalry regiment did Custer lead to disaster at the Little Bighorn?

6   And in which US state would you find Custer County and a city named Custer?

7   Where was Olivia Newton-John born – Cambridge or Oxford?

8   Which British monarch served a 60 year apprenticeship as Prince of Wales before becoming king?

9   Whose presidential campaign slogan was: 'All The Way With LBJ'?

10 Which historic house on the Isle of Wight saw a 30% increase in visitors following the release of the film 'Mrs. Brown'?

11 Who famously sang 'Happy Birthday' to President Kennedy in 1962?

12 In November 1998 which former movie sex symbol turned animal lover flew to Scotland to assist in the successful efforts to save a collie named Woofie from being put down?

13 In which country was King Juan Carlos of Spain born?

14 Which famous Russian writer died at a railway station in 1910?

15 The name of which lizard is derived from the Greek for 'on the ground' and 'lion'?

Answers 1 Himalayas 2 Joseph Stalin 3 World Society For The Protection Of Animals 4 Cheese 5 7th 6 South Dakota 7 Cambridge 8 Edward VII 9 Lyndon B. Johnson 10 Osborne House 11 Marilyn Monroe 12 Brigitte Bardot 13 Italy 14 Leo Tolstoy 15 Chameleon

Quiz 2

1   AOL are an internet service provider. What does AOL stand for?

2   Derived from the Latin for 'Greek hay', what F is a herb of the pea family whose aromatic seeds are used as spice?

3   Which Baltic state is bordered by Estonia, Russia, Belarus and Lithuania?

4   Which part of London is famous for a power station and a dog's home?

5   In 1902, who succeeded his uncle, Lord Salisbury, as British Prime Minister?

6   What name is shared by a market town in Nottinghamshire UK and the largest city in New Jersey, USA?

7   What does the fc stand for in the designer fashion label fcuk?

8   The coronation of which king of England took place in Gloucester Cathedral in 1216?

9   The name of which North African city literally means 'white house'?

10 What does the W in George W. Bush stand for?

11 In which country was Samuel Cunard, founder of the famous shipping line, born?

12 Which deceased former emperor of Ethiopia is regarded by members of the Rastafarian religion as the Messiah?

13 Shades of which colour can be described as cobalt and prussian?

14 Emperor Ming the Merciless was the arch enemy of which sci-fi hero?

15 The famous stone circle, Stonehenge, is in which English county?

MISCELLANEOUS 3

Quiz 3

1   In 1819, from which country did the USA obtain the land now known as Florida?

2   Who died after being shot whilst watching a performance of the play, 'Our American Cousin', in 1865?

3   DKNY is a well known designer fashion label. What does DKNY stand for?

4   In which country is Lake Winnipeg?

5   According to the Bible, how many loaves did Jesus use to feed the five thousand?

6   Who, on his death in 1883, was remembered on his gravestone as 'Queen Victoria's Beloved Friend' ?

7   Following the Second World War, in which year did clothes rationing end in Britain?

8   How many of Henry VIII's children succeeded him on the throne of England?

9   Sacked by the English in 1388 it was ceded to Cromwell in 1658 and in 1662 was sold back to the French by Charles II. Name this port in northern France.

10 Name the legendary Greek hero who led the Argonauts to find the Golden Fleece.

11 What are the first names of Elvis Presley's daughter?

12 The Romans called it Sabrina and it's Welsh name is Hafren. Name this British river.

13 Which herb is also known as 'boneset' or 'knitbone' because of it's supposed healing qualities?

14 In which year did Edward VIII abdicate?

15 A Salopian is a native of which English county?

15 Shropshire

Answers 1 Spain 2 Abraham Lincoln 3 Donna Karan New York 4 Canada 5 5 6 John Brown 7 1949 8 3 9 Dunkirk 10 Jason 11 Lisa Marie 12 Severn 13 Comfrey 14 1936

338

1   Which range of hills are sometimes referred to as 'the backbone of England'?

2   Who was the mother of King James I of England?

3   Which Soviet physicist and dissident was awarded the Nobel Peace Prize in 1975?

4   Mount Elbert is the highest peak in which North American mountain range?

5   Which of the Channel Islands is only 3 square miles in area, St. Anne being it's chief town?

6   If Arthur C. Clarke's Space Odyssey is 2001, what is his Final Odyssey?

7   Known to the French as persil, which herb with curled aromatic leaves is used in cooking?

8   In the world of computing and the world wide web, what does ISP stand for?

9   In which city was John Lennon shot dead in December 1980?

10 Which place in Georgia, USA, the birthplace of Kim Basinger and where the members of the group REM spent their formative years, is also the name of a European capital city?

11 In 1979, Greenland gained it's independence from which country?

12 Which English stately home, seat of the Dukes of Devonshire, is sometimes referred to as the 'Palace in the Peaks'?

13 Who designed Madonna's famous conical-busted basque?

14 Which American singer, famous for his relaxed style, died on 12 May 2001, just days short of his 89th birthday?

15 The singers Neil Young, Joni Mitchell and Alanis Morissette were all born in which country?

Answers 1 The Pennines 2 Mary, Queen of Scots 3 Andrei Sakharov 4 The Rockies 5 Alderney 6 3001 7 Parsley 8 Internet Service Provider 9 New York 10 Athens 11 Denmark 12 Chatsworth House 13 Jean-Paul Gaultier 14 Perry Como 15 Canada

MISCELLANEOUS 3   Quiz 5

1   Which of Henry VIII's wives was the mother of Edward VI?

2   Name the British nurse executed by the Germans in 1915 for helping allied soldiers escape from German-occupied Belgium.

3   Who founded the Order Of The Missionaries Of Charity in Calcutta in 1948?

4   In which German city is the famous Oktoberfest beer festival held?

5   The forces of which country invaded Abyssinia in October 1935?

6   Which couple were shot dead at a police road-block in Louisiana on 23 May 1934?

7   In which year did Edward the Confessor, Harold and William I all occupy the throne of England?

8   What is the official language of Paraguay?

9   The name of which Australian island, off the north coast of Queensland, the chief town being Port Kennedy, is also the name of a day of the week?

10 In a game of chess, which is the only piece which cannot move backwards?

11 According to sailor's folklore, what is the name of the ghost ship that is supposed to haunt the seas around the Cape of Good Hope? The story became popular in the 19th century and inspired an opera by Wagner.

12 From which language is the word helicopter derived?

13 Created by Augustus in 27 BC, what name was given to the official bodyguard of Roman emperors?

14 In which year of the 1950s did sugar rationing end in Britain?

15 Ornithology is the study of what?

Answers 1 Jane Seymour **2** Edith Cavell **3** Mother Teresa **4** Munich **5** Italy **6** Bonnie and Clyde **7** 1066 **8** Spanish **9** Thursday Island **10** Pawn **11** The Flying Dutchman **12** Greek **13** Praetorian Guard **14** 1953 **15** Birds

1   Bulgaria, Georgia, Romania, Turkey and the Ukraine all have shorelines on which inland sea?

2   Which of Henry VIII's wives was beheaded for adultery in 1536?

3   In heraldry, what word is the term used to describe a creature in a sleeping position?

4   In October 1942, over 300 lives where lost when the British cruiser Curacao sank after colliding with which ocean liner?

5   Dark Muscovado and Light Muscovado are both types of what?

6   In the 16th century, the prophecies of which man were collected together in the work entitled 'Centuries'?

7   Which Australian city was known as Palmerston between 1869 and 1911?

8   Which independent African kingdom is bordered to the north, west and south by South Africa and to the east by Mozambique? Mbabane is the administrative capital and Lobamba the royal capital.

9   Name the American financier, who in 2001 became the world's first paying space tourist.

10 Derived from the Swedish for commissioner, what name is given to an official who investigates citizens' complaints against the government or it's servants?

11 In which battle of 1743 did George II become the last British monarch to command his troops in battle?

12 Who, during the Vietnam War, was known as 'Hanoi Jane'?

13 The flag of which European country consists of a black double-headed eagle on a red background?

14 Which country won the 2001 Eurovision Song Contest?

15 What nationality was the explorer Vasco da Gama?

Answers 1 Black Sea 2 Anne Boleyn 3 Dormant 4 Queen Mary 5 Sugar 6 Nostradamus 7 Darwin 8 Swaziland 9 Dennis Tito 10 Ombudsman 11 Dettingen 12 Jane Fonda 13 Albania 14 Estonia 15 Portuguese

1   Aerophobia is a fear of flying, agoraphobia is a fear of open spaces, what is acrophobia a fear of?

2   In computing, how is a modulator-demodulator more commonly known?

3   Wystan Hugh were the forenames of which 20th century British poet?

4   In 1968, the Oscars ceremony was postponed for two days after whose assassination?

5   Founded in Washington D.C., which monthly magazine provides the armchair traveller with vivid articles and pictures on geography, archaeology, anthropology and exploration?

6   Which former world heavyweight boxing champion died in an air crash on 31 August 1969, just hours short of his 46th birthday?

7   It's Afrikaans name is Kaapstad. By what name do we know this city?

8   Now a museum, which house, the former home of the Duke of Wellington, used to be known as No. 1 London?

9   Which animal appears on the flag of the Falkland Islands?

10 On 31 March 1854, Japan and which other country signed the Treaty of Kanagawa?

11 The site of one of Africa's largest cellulose and paper-pulp factories and situated on the Como river, Kango is a town in which country?

12 Uluru is the aborigine name for which Australian landmark?

13 Who was Britain's Prime Minister when HM Queen Elizabeth II was born?

14 What is the French word for key and also the name of a symbol used in music notation?

15 What is the name of the ancient temple on the Acropolis in Athens that was dedicated to the goddess Athena?

Answers 1 Heights 2 Modem 3 W. H. Auden 4 Martin Luther King 5 National Geographic Magazine 6 Rocky Marciano 7 Cape Town 8 Apsley House 9 A Sheep 10 USA 11 Gabon 12 Ayers Rock 13 Stanley Baldwin 14 Clef 15 Parthenon

MISCELLANEOUS 3 *Quiz 8*

1   On which of New Zealand's islands is the capital Wellington situated?

2   Which British monarch died in 1901?

3   During which year of the Second World War did the Duke of Kent, the youngest brother of King George VI, die in a flying boat accident?

4   Zulfikar Ali Bhutto and his daughter, Benazir, have both been Prime Ministers of which country?

5   What name is given to the region within the Arctic Circle that stretches across northern Norway, Sweden, Finland and into the Kola peninsula of Russia?

6   The aid agency Oxfam was founded in which city?

7   In which decade of the 20th century was Halley's Comet last seen?

8   Which 'King of the Wild Frontier' was born in Greene County, Tennessee on 17 August 1786?

9   What nationality was Geiger who gave his name to the geiger counter?

10 Locating ocean-going vessels, flight navigation and in-car maps depend on a service provided by a network of satellites known as GPS. What does GPS stand for?

11 Known locally as Vlissingen, by what name is this Dutch seaport known in English?

12 What is the plural of talisman?

13 Which sign of the zodiac comes after Leo and before Libra?

14 On which bank of the river Nile do the famous pyramids of Giza stand – east or west?

15 In heraldry, what colour is gules?

Answers 1 North 2 Queen Victoria 3 1942 4 Pakistan 5 Lapland 6 Oxford 7 1980s 8 Davy Crockett 9 German 10 Global Positioning System 11 Flushing 12 Talismans 13 Virgo 14 West 15 Red

MISCELLANEOUS 3 — Quiz 9

1 In which decade of the 20th century was the famous Sydney Harbour Bridge officially opened?

2 In architectural terms, what is a postern?

3 Said to have lived in a tub, who founded the philosophical sect known as the Cynics?

4 Name the Australian golfer who won the US PGA championship in 1979 and the US Open in 1981.

5 What was the surname of Julius and Ethel, the married couple found guilty of spying and executed at Sing Sing prison in 1953?

6 Who was the shrewish wife of the philosopher Socrates, fabled for her bad temper?

7 What is the common name of the wasp *Vespa crabro*?

8 In which US state is the College of William and Mary, the country's second oldest institution of higher education after HArvard?

9 What name is given to the migration of Mohammed from Mecca to Medina in 622 AD?

10 In the 1970s TV series Harry O starring David Janssen, what did the O stand for?

11 Also according to legend, which forest was the home of Robin Hood?

12 If Batman is Bruce Wayne and Robin is Dick Grayson, who is Batwoman?

13 Algeria and Tunisia both gained independence from which country?

14 Who was four years late in collecting his Nobel Prize for Literature which was originally awarded in November 1970?

15 By what popular name was the Boeing B-17 bomber known?

Answers 1 1930s 2 A back or side door or gate 3 Diogenes 4 David Graham 5 Rosenberg 6 Xanthippe 7 Hornet 8 Virginia 9 Hegira or Hejira 10 Orwell 11 Sherwood Forest 12 Kathy Kane 13 France 14 Aleksandr Solzhenitsyn 15 Flying Fortress

Quiz 10

1   British Prime Miinister Tony Blair was born in which city?

2   In physics, what N is the central core of the atom?

3   Which one of Henry VIII's wives was Spanish-born?

4   Which star constellation is known as the 'water bearer'?

5   By what name were the series of military expeditions organised in western Christendom to recover the Holy Places of Palestine from Muslim occupation between 1095 and 1291, known?

6   Name the Prime Minister of Australia from 1968 until 1971 who fostered Australia's involvement in the Vietnam War.

7   What is the Spanish word for black?

8   What are inhabitants of the island of Lesbos called?

9   In March of which year of the 1960s did John Lennon marry Yoko Ono and Paul McCartney marry Linda Eastman?

10 In which decade of the 20th century did Nestlé first market Nescafé, the world's first instant coffee?

11 Which 20th century American poet, born of the 'beat' movement, published 'Howl and other poems' in 1956 and 'Kaddish and other poems' in 1961?

12 What are a cat's *vibrissae* more commonly known as?

13 Vendredi is French for which day of the week?

14 Which seabird is also known as bottlenose or sea parrot?

15 What is the main ingredient of the Swiss food dish Rosti?

Answers 1 Edinburgh **2** Nucleus **3** Catherine of Aragon **4** Aquarius **5** The Crusades **6** John Gorton **7** Negro **8** Lesbosians **9** 1969 **10** 1930s **11** Allen Ginsberg **12** It's whiskers **13** Friday **14** Puffin **15** Potatoes

1　Which common Irish surname means 'descendant of the sea warrior'?

2　Triton and Nereid are satellites of which planet?

3　Which famous park was officially opened in New York in 1876?

4　In a symphony orchestra, which is the only stringed instrument that is not played with a bow?

5　The Tupamaros were an active guerrilla group during the 1960s and 1970s in which South American country?

6　Name the Norwegian playwright who wrote 'Ghosts', 'An Enemy Of The People' and 'The Master Builder'.

7　Which US president ordered the dropping of the first atomic bomb?

8　The 'Bouncing Czech' and 'Captain Bob' were nicknames given to whom?

9　Name the hilly area on the border between Syria and Israel which was the location of several biter Arab-Israeli confrontations during the 1950s, 1960s and 1970s.

10　What is the middle colour of the spectrum?

11　On which island would you find the Arecibo radio telescope?

12　Which is closest to Britain – the North Pole or the South Pole?

13　'Bring me my bow of burning gold! Bring me my arrows of desire! Bring me my spear! O clouds unfold! Bring me my chariot of fire!' are words from which hymn?

14　Gascony was a former duchy of which country?

15　With which African country do you associate the political groups FRELIMO and RENAMO?

Answers 1 Murphy 2 Neptune 3 Central Park 4 Harp 5 Uruguay 6 Henrik Ibsen 7 Harry S. Truman 8 Robert Maxwell 9 Golan Heights 10 Green 11 Puerto Rico 12 North Pole 13 Jerusalem 14 France 15 Mozambique

Quiz 12

1   In the Bible, according to the sermon on the mount, who shall 'inherit the earth'?

2   What type of creature is a stonechat?

3   Name the newspaper heiress kidnapped by the Simbionese Liberation Army in 1974.

4   What was the popular name for the East German secret police who were disbanded shortly after the Berlin Wall came down in 1989?

5   Which one of the 'Seven Deadly Sins' begins with G?

6   What is the name of Brunel's iron steamship that was brought back to Bristol from the Falkland Islands in 1970?

7   Which Swedish retailer was founded in the 1940s by Ingvar Kamprad?

8   What nationality was the chemist Johan Gadolin?

9   Name the British soldier who died leading his men in the capture of Quebec in 1759.

10 Which English potter opened a factory which he named Etruria in 1769?

11 In which year of the 1960s did Valentina Tereshkova become the first woman in space?

12 Which burger chain took it's name from a character featured in 'Popeye' cartoons?

13 In which book of the Old Testament is the story of Noah's Ark told?

14 Which British airline took it's name from the initials of the ship broking firm which launched it in 1953?

15 Bing Crosby died in 1977 whilst playing golf in which country?

MISCELLANEOUS 3 — Quiz 13

1 Which of the Bronte sisters married Arthur Bell Nicholls in 1854 and died during pregnancy the following year?

2 What is the official language of San Marino?

3 In which Canadian province is the country's capital Ottawa situated?

4 The atmosphere of Venus primarily consists of which gas?

5 What nationality was the Nobel prize winning nuclear physicist Niels Bohr?

6 The psychic performer Uri Geller was born in which country?

7 What does the acronym MORI, as in MORI poll, stand for?

8 CO is the chemical formula for what?

9 What nationality is Peter Abrahams, author of the novels 'Mine Boy' and 'The View From Coyoba'?

10 In religious art, who are symbolised together as a group by an angel, a winged lion, a winged ox and an eagle?

11 In which year of the 1950s did Edmund Hillary and Sherpa Tenzing become the first climbers to reach the summit of Mount Everest?

12 What surname is derived from a person who made or sold arrows in medieval times?

13 Caracas is the capital of which South American country?

14 Which world leader was given the nickname 'The Beard' by the United States Intelligence Service?

15 Which austere religious sect, having strict standards of behaviour and shunning many secular trades and professions, was founded in 1830 by J. N. Darby?

Answers 1 Charlotte 2 Italian 3 Ontario 4 Carbon dioxide 5 Danish 6 Israel 7 Market and Opinion Research International 8 Carbon Monoxide 9 South African 10 The four evangelists 11 1953 12 Fletcher 13 Venezuela 14 Fidel Castro 15 Plymouth Brethren

Quiz 14

1   In 1993, Lotus Cars were sold by their parent company General Motors to which classic sports car manufacturer?

2   Cr is the chemical symbol for what?

3   'Each little flower that opens, Each little bird that sings, He made their glowing colours, He made their tiny wings' are words from which hymn?

4   Which dance is particularly associated with singer Chubby Checker?

5   What do birds do when they nidificate?

6   Fuerteventura, Lanzarote and Tenerife are all part of which island group?

7   In which city was Terry Waite taken hostage in 1987?

8   Which Jewish religious movement was founded by Ba'al Shem Tov?

9   How many times does the word 'Ha' appear in the title of Roddy Doyle's novel about Paddy Clarke?

10 What middle name is shared by Bill Clinton and William Hague?

11 To a male Australian, what are his strides?

12 What name is given to the four days in the Christian calendar devoted to prayer and fasting? The main day is 25 April and the other three days are the three days before Ascension Day.

13 What is the name of the news agency founded by Israel Josephat which uses his adopted name?

14 What A is a bird belonging to the genus *Prunella* and is also known as shufflewing?

15 Calabria, Umbria, Lombardy and Tuscany are all regions in which country?

Answers 1 Bugatti 2 Chromium 3 All Things Bright And Beautiful 4 The Twist 5 Make or build a nest 6 Canary Islands 7 Beirut 8 Hasidism 9 3 10 Jefferson 11 Trousers 12 Rogation days 13 Reuters 14 Accentor 15 Italy

1 Alaskan malamute and schnauzer are both types of what?

2 How many astronauts were aboard each Gemini space flight made during the 1960s?

3 Which German region would you visit to witness the Oberammergau passion play?

4 What word can mean a type of punctuation mark and is also part of the large intestine?

5 How many sides does a nonagon have?

6 In 1918 the German army used a long-range gun to shell Paris from 70 miles away. By what nickname, after the daughter of the manufacturer, was it known?

7 What name is given to the white knee length pleated skirt worn as traditional dress by men in Greece and Albania?

8 In which Italian city was the explorer Marco Polo born?

9 What does the acronym AWOL stand for?

10 Andy Warhol became known for his colourful reproductions of everyday objects, such as which brand of canned soup tins?

11 According to the Old Testament (Exodus 24), on which mountain did Moses receive the tablets of the law?

12 Which breed of dog took it's name from the man who developed it, a night watchman and dogpound guard in Germany?

13 Which British landmark was bought by American oil tycoon Robert McCullough in 1968?

14 A kibbutz is a Jewish settlement. What is the plural of kibbutz?

15 From which country does the dance known as a 'tarantella' originate?

Answers 1 Dog 2 2 3 Bavaria 4 Colon 5 9 6 Big Bertha 7 Fustanella 8 Venice 9 Absent without leave 10 Campbell's 11 Mount Sinai 12 Doberman 13 London Bridge 14 Kibbutzim 15 Italy

Quiz 16

1   Who was president of Chile from 1973 until 1990?

2   What was Bing Crosby's real first name? Was it Tom, Dick or Harry?

3   In November 1965, Rhodesia announced its UDI. What did UDI stand for?

4   Described as the 'greatest mind and paramount icon of our age' who did Time magazine name as their 'Person of the 20th Century'?

5   Name the castle on the Isle of Wight where Charles I was imprisoned.

6   The name of which type of pasta is derived from the Italian for 'little cords'?

7   'The Girl With Enamel Eyes' is the alternative title of which two act ballet first performed in Paris in 1870?

8   What type of creature is an addax?

9   Who was Lord Mayor of Cologne from 1917 to 1933?

10 Name the American saxophonist and singer who fronted the All-Stars who died aged 53 in 1995.

11 Who in 1843 on the day before his 73rd birthday, was appointed Poet Laureate?

12 *Ocimum basilicum* is the botanical name for which herb?

13 Which former tennis player, he won the Australian Open in 1977 and was a regular around New York's nightlife, was found dead on September 1994?

14 Which household appliance was patented by Percy Spencer, an American working for Raytheon, in the 1940's?

15 Name the Italian city which stages horse races through the main square during the annual Palio festival.

Answers 1 General Pinochet 2 Harry 3 Unilateral Declaration of Independence 4 Albert Einstein 5 Carisbrooke 6 Spaghetti 7 Coppelia 8 Antelope 9 Konrad Adenauer 10 Junior Walker 11 William Wordsworth 12 Basil 13 Vitas Gerulaitis 14 Microwave Oven 15 Siena

Quiz 17

1 On which island was Napoleon Bonaparte born in 1769?

2 Which famous German automatic pistol was named after the man who first developed it in 1902?

3 The battles of Edgehill and Naseby were fought during which war?

4 Which popular female author, sometimes referred to as BTB, once worked for the Yorkshire Post newspaper?

5 What is the surname of Robert, the American engineer who in the mid-1960s invented the synthesizer?

6 In planning the marketing of a new product a company may use a SWOT analysis. What does the acronym SWOT stand for?

7 By what nickname was the convicted criminal Robert Stroud known?

8 From which country does the bread called ciabatta originate?

9 On 22 March 2000, Bill Clinton said: 'I've wanted to come here all my life' when visiting which world-famous building?

10 In 1803, from which country did the USA buy some 800,000 square miles of land between the Mississippi river and the Rocky Mountains in a deal known as the 'Louisiana Purchase'?

11 Named after it's American owner, which major department store was opened in London's Oxford Street in 1909?

12 According to the title of his popular song, what did Ivor Novello want to keep burning?

13 In which city would you find Goulandris Natural History Museum and the Acropolis Museum?

14 In 330 AD which Roman emperor re-named the ancient city of Byzantium after himself?

15 Which 15th century French patriot was known as the 'Maid of Orleans'?

1   In New Zealand, what does the saying 'up the boohai' mean?

2   If ursine means 'bear-like' or relating to bears, what creature does hircine refer to?

3   What was the name of the private militia of the Duvalier family during their regime in Haiti from the mid-1950s until the late 1980s?

4   What sort of creature is a whydah or whidah?

5   Which of the Bronte sisters wrote 'Wuthering Heights'?

6   What do the initials of the meat substitute TVP stand for?

7   An estimated 12,000 people were killed when which Moroccan port was devastated by an earthquake on 29 February 1960?

8   What name, from French, is given to eyeglasses held in place by means of a clip over the bridge of the nose?

9   And what French term describes cooking food, particularly meat, encased in pastry?

10 The name of which order of mammal is derived from the Latin word for 'purse'?

11 Who was Muhammad Ali's opponent in the fight known as the 'Thriller In Manila'?

12 What is the basic material used in origami?

13 What nationality was the famous philosopher Confucius?

14 Which war was sparked off by the assassination of Archduke Franz Ferdinand in Sarajevo?

15 Charles Lindbergh made the first solo, non-stop flight across which ocean in 1927?

Answers 1 Completely lost **2** Goat **3** Tonton Macoutes **4** Bird **5** Emily **6** Textured Vegetable Protein **7** Agadir **8** Pince-Nez **9** En croute **10** Marsupial **11** Joe Frazier **12** Paper **13** Chinese **14** World War One **15** Atlantic

MISCELLANEOUS 3   Quiz 19

1   After being besieged for 118 days by the Boers, which South African town was relieved by the British general Sir Redvers Buller on 28 February 1900?

2   Which alpine rail tunnel, then the longest rail tunnel in the world, was opened in 1906?

3   Which Biblical character was thrown into a lion's den?

4   The Periodic Table is a list of chemical elements. What is No. 1 in that list?

5   Orville was one of the pioneering aviators the Wright brothers. What was the name of the other?

6   Which month of the year takes it's name from the Roman festival of purification?

7   According to the fairy tale, who had to leave the ball before midnight?

8   In which Italian city is the gondola a popular form of transport?

9   In tennis, what score comes after deuce?

10 Which royal house ruled England throughout the 16th century?

11 Derived from the Latin for 'licking', what word describes a syrupy medicinal preparation taken to relieve coughs and sore throats?

12 Which famous English landscape painter was born in East Bergholt, Suffolk in 1776?

13 A large European grouse, it's name is derived from the Gaelic for 'horse of the woods'. Name it.

14 Which high-kicking dance, performed by a female chorus, originated in the music halls of 19th century Paris?

15 In architecture, fenestration is the arrangement of what in a building?

Answers 1 Ladysmith 2 Simplon Tunnel 3 Daniel 4 Hydrogen 5 Wilbur 6 February 7 Cinderella 8 Venice 9 Advantage 10 Tudor 11 Linctus 12 John Constable 13 Capercaillie 14 Cancan 15 Windows

Quiz 20

1   What cord connects a fetus with the placenta?

2   A former title used by Japanese emperors, it literally means 'honourable palace gate'. What is it?

3   In 1979, the Ayatollah Khomeini returned to Iran after 14 years exile in which European country?

4   In heraldry, which creature is termed an 'urchin'?

5   And in heraldry, which creature is usually depicted as a small lizard surrounded by flames, signifying faith and constancy?

6   The dark-reddish brown pigment obtained from the inky secretion of cuttlefish and used as a dye and an ink since Roman times is called what?

7   Situated on the Seyhan river, Adana is a city in which country.

8   Who was the sixth and last wife of Henry VIII?

9   According to the Bible, what was Job's outstanding quality?

10 With regard to Mexican food, what name is given to a kind of thin pancake made from corn meal which takes it's name from the Spanish for 'a little round cake' ?

11 Which saint, one of the apostles, his feast day is 28 October, is traditionally represented holding a saw because according to tradition he was martyred by being cut in half with a saw?

12 The composer Mozart was born in which Austrian city in 1756?

13 The jet pack used by astronauts for untethered space walks is known as a MMU. What does MMU stand for?

14 Name the man who was president of the Philippines between 1965 and 1986.

15 In terms of modern science, particularly with regard to food products, what do the initials GM stand for?

Answers 1 Umbilical cord 2 Mikado 3 France 4 Hedgehog 5 Salamander 6 Sepia 7 Turkey 8 Catherine Parr 9 Patience 10 Tortilla 11 St Simon 12 Salzburg 13 Manned Manoeuvring Unit 14 Ferdinand Marcos 15 Genetically Modified

MISCELLANEOUS 3

Quiz 21

1 Pb is the chemical symbol for what?

2 In February 2001, a US space probe landed on which asteroid?

3 What was the name of the submarine which sank during sea trials in Liverpool Bay in June 1939 with the loss of 99 lives?

4 Which European country restored it's monarchy in 1975?

5 Which cartoon character won his first Oscar for the 1958 cartoon feature 'Knighty Knight, Bugs'?

6 According to the Bible, whom did Jesus raise from the dead?

7 Which device was used to behead people during the French Revolution?

8 Actress Kate Hudson is the daughter of which actress?

9 Seven kings of which country have been named Haakon?

10 A misogynist is a man who hates what?

11 The word 'entrepreneur' comes from which language?

12 In December 1999, Richard Branson sold 49% of Virgin Atlantic to which other airline?

13 Elf is German for what number?

14 From the French for 'knee breeches', what name is given to women's knee-length trousers, cut with very full legs to resemble a skirt?

15 Whilst suffering acute depression, the artist Vincent Van Gogh cut off part of an ear. Was it his left or right ear?

Answers 1 Lead 2 433 Eros 3 Thetis 4 Spain 5 Bugs Bunny 6 Lazarus 7 Guillotine 8 Goldie Hawn 9 Norway 10 Women 11 French 12 Singapore Airlines 13 11 14 Culottes 15 Left

Quiz 22

1   What is the name of the Russian who gave his name to the famous AK47 assault rifle?

2   Which two primary colours are mixed to make purple?

3   Established as an independent kingdom in 1946, which country in the Middle East has a seven-pointed white star on it's national flag representing the first seven verses of the Koran?

4   Who was the most famous conspirator in a plot led by Robert Catesby?

5   Which English word for a type of dwelling is derived from the Gujarati word meaning 'of Bengal' ?

6   What is a pashmina?

7   In what did Cleopatra supposedly bathe to remain beautiful?

8   What is the name of the sedative drug which caused deformities in babies born in the late 1950s and early 1960s?

9   Which popular female country and western singer was killed in a plane crash in March 1963?

10 What type of creature is a fulmar?

11 Name the American-born cartoonist of the Monty Python comedy team.

12 What was the nationality of Rachmaninov, the composer, pianist and conductor who lived from 1873 to 1943?

13 Whose tomb was discovered by Howard Carter and Lord Carnarvon in 1922?

14 If you were suffering from an attack of 'horripilation', what would you have?

15 Who was born the son of a customs official in Braunau, upper Austria in 1889?

Answers 1 Kalashnikov **2** Red and Blue **3** Jordan **4** Guy Fawkes **5** Bungalow **6** A type of shawl **7** Ass's milk **8** Thalidomide **9** Patsy Cline **10** Bird **11** Terry Gilliam **12** Russian **13** Tutankhamen **14** Goose flesh **15** Adolf Hitler

MISCELLANEOUS 3 — *Quiz 23*

1 In January 2001, oil spilt from the stricken tanker 'Jessica' posed a threat to the unique wildlife on which group of islands?

2 Name the 17th century Italian sculptor and architect responsible for the building of several fountains in Rome including the famous fountain of the four river gods in the Piazza Navona.

3 Tarabulus is the Arabic name for two cities. One is the capital of an African country, the other a port in Lebanon. By what name do we know these cities?

4 An ornamental shrub, also known as the butterfly bush, takes it's name from the British botanist who discovered it. What is it?

5 In which American city in 1999 were demonstrators involved in violent protests during meetings of the World Trade Organisation?

6 US space shuttles are officially referred to by the initials STS. What does STS stand for?

7 Mohammed Idris Al Senussi reigned from 1951 until 1969. He was the first, and to date, the only king of which North African country?

8 Gordie Howe and Wayne Gretsky are famous names in which sport?

9 Who was the President of Tanzania largely instrumental in the ousting of Idi Amin from Uganda?

10 What was the name of the Greenpeace ship sunk in Auckland harbour in 1985?

11 Writer P. L. Travers created the character Mary Poppins. What do the initials P .L. stand for?

12 A hexagon is a polygon with how many sides?

13 Name the former Cameroon World Cup star who was named Africa's Footballer of the 20th Century by African Soccer magazine.

14 Phobos and Deimos are satellites of which planet?

15 In which country did the dance, the gavotte, originate?

Answers 1 Galapagos **2** Gian Lorenzo Bernini **3** Tripoli **4** Buddleia (after A. Buddle) **5** Seattle **6** Space Transportation System **7** Libya **8** Ice hockey **9** Julius Nyerere **10** Rainbow Warrior **11** Pamela Lyndon **12** 6 **13** Roger Milla **14** Mars **15** France

Quiz 24

1   DA is an abbreviation for which legal official in the US?

2   What name did father and son, Malcolm and Donald Campbell, give to their vehicles in which they both set world land and water speed records?

3   On which Greek island was Prince Philip, the Duke of Edinburgh born?

4   On 17 November 1913, the steamship 'Louise' became the first ship to pass through which canal?

5   Name the Belgian-born guitarist who was one of Europe's first jazz virtuosos.

6   'Bolero' is one of the most popular works of which French composer?

7   In which American city was John F. Kennedy assassinated in 1963?

8   Who is the patron saint of Spain?

9   Which member of the Marx Brothers was famous for his cigar and funny walk?

10 Cartoon film animator Walter Lantz died aged 93 in 1994. What character was his most famous creation?

11 Which country ruled the African country of Zaire prior to it's independence?

12 In which month of the year is St. Patrick's Day celebrated?

13 The holy town of Lourdes is situated in the foothills of which mountain range?

14 How did American financier John Jacob Astor IV die in 1912?

15 In Roman numerals, what number is represented by L?

Answers 1 District Attorney **2** Bluebird **3** Corfu **4** Panama Canal **5** Django Reinhardt **6** Maurice Ravel **7** Dallas **8** St. James **9** Groucho **10** Woody Woodpecker **11** Belgium **12** March **13** Pyrenees **14** He was a passenger on the Titanic **15** 50

MISCELLANEOUS 3   *Quiz 25*

1   Name the American-born clarinettist and soprano saxophone player who achieved worldwide recognition after a tour of Europe in 1919. After the Second Word War he lived in Paris, where he died in 1959.

2   The Brow, Mumbles, Pruneface and Flattop were all opponents of which fictional detective?

3   During which war did the My Lai massacre take place?

4   What is the name of the notorious fracture in the earth's crust which runs through California?

5   If first, second and third are ordinal – what are one, two and three?

6   According to the stories surrounding Robin Hood, which one of his followers was the son of a miller?

7   Tennis. Three Americans lost to Bjorn Borg in Wimbledon men's singles finals. They were John McEnroe, Jimmy Connors and which other?

8   Who was president of the USA from 1981 to 1989?

9   The name of which dinosaur is derived from the Greek words for 'thunder' and 'lizard'?

10 What type of animal is affected by a disease known as 'strangles'?

11 Which Indian state was hit by a cyclone in 1999 that was dubbed the 'storm of the century'?

12 In the 1950s, which Japanese company marketed the first transistor radio?

13 Name the island in New York harbour which served as an entry centre for immigrants to the USA between 1892 and 1943.

14 In which country was the feminist and author Germaine Greer born?

15 Cochon is the French word for which creature?

Answers 1 Sidney Bechet 2 Dick Tracy 3 Vietnam War 4 San Andreas Fault 5 Cardinal 6 Much 7 Roscoe Tanner 8 Ronald Reagan 9 Brontosaurus 10 Horse 11 Orissa 12 Sony 13 Ellis Island 14 Australia 15 Pig

1   Commodore William Warwick who died in 1999, was the first captain of which ocean liner?

2   Name the last of Hitler's fleet of so-called 'unsinkable battleships' that was sunk by Lancaster bombers in the Norwegian fjords on 12 November 1944.

3   Regulus, Denebola and Algeiba are the brightest stars in which constellation?

4   What was constructed between 1806 and 1836 to celebrate the victories of Napoleon?

5   What is the French word for cheese?

6   Which ageing 'playboy' married Kimberley Conrad in 1989?

7   Name the 20th century Italian-born American composer who wrote the operas 'Amelia Goes To The Ball' and 'Amahl And The Night Visitors'.

8   Aristotle and Plato were ancient Greek philosophers. Which one was born first?

9   What was American gangster 'Lucky' Luciano's first name?

10 What is the surname of Andre and Edouard, the French brothers who invented the removable tyre in 1891?

11 Famagusta is a port on which Mediterranean island?

12 Formed in London in 1884, which society was named after the ancient Roman general Fabius Maximus?

13 In which country was the poet Fleur Adcock born?

14 By what name was the Colt 45 revolver popularly known?

15 Name any year during which Pius XII was Pope.

Answers 1 QE2 **2** Tirpitz **3** Leo **4** Arc de Triomphe **5** Fromage **6** Hugh Hefner **7** Gian-Carlo Menotti **8** Plato **9** Charles **10** Michelin **11** Cyprus **12** Fabian Society **13** New Zealand **14** The peacemaker **15** Any year between 1939 and 1958 inclusive

MISCELLANEOUS 3   *Quiz 27*

1   Which notorious London prison was demolished in 1902 and replaced by the Central Criminal Court (Old Bailey)?

2   In which country was movie star Mel Gibson born?

3   Which English adventurer, once a favourite of Elizabeth I, was beheaded during the reign of James I on 29 October 1618?

4   In the 'Arabian Night' stories, what were the magic words used by Ali Baba to gain entrance to the cave of the 40 thieves?

5   What type of ancient creature was found preserved in the frozen wastes of Siberia in 1999?

6   Antibes is a tourist resort in which European country?

7   What type of lettuce is named after the Greek island from which it originates?

8   Which serious disease affecting trees was first described in the Netherlands in 1919?

9   The original ' carpetbaggers' were people trying to profit from the disruption following which war?

10 According to the Bible, who led the Israelite forces at the battle of Jericho?

11 What seven letter word is the opposite of convex?

12 What is a female fox called?

13 With which composer is the German town of Bayreuth associated?

14 What type of bird is a greylag?

15 Name the ancient Greek warrior who was killed by a poisoned arrow shot into his heel.

Answers 1 Newgate 2 USA 3 Walter Raleigh 4 Open sesame 5 Mammoth 6 France 7 Cos 8 Dutch Elm disease 9 American Civil War 10 Joshua 11 Concave 12 Vixen 13 Richard Wagner 14 Goose 15 Achilles

MISCELLANEOUS 3   Quiz 28

1   Who was on the British throne between 1760 and 1820?

2   What nationality was the prince who lived from 1394 until 1460 and known as Henry the Navigator?

3   Regarded as one of the foremost composers of the first half of the 20th century, who wrote the opera 'Duke Bluebeard's Castle' and the ballet 'The Miraculous Mandarin'?

4   To which animals does the adjective 'feline' refer?

5   Which sign of the zodiac is known as the Scales?

6   From which war does the term 'fifth column' meaning a group of hostile infiltrators, originate?

7   Which of the seven deadly sins begins with the letter C?

8   What colour is traditionally associated with envy or jealousy?

9   In which city was Martin Luther King assassinated?

10 What type of creature is a bleak?

11 The name of the capital of the Tamil Nadu region of India is associated with curries. What is it?

12 Genghis Khan and his grandson Kublai Khan were leaders of which race of Asiatic people?

13 In the Bible, who was the father of Cain and Abel?

14 The marabou stork is native to which continent?

15 16th century Spaniards believed there was a region of South America made entirely of gold. What name did they give it?

14 Africa 15 El Dorado

Answers 1 George III 2 Portuguese 3 Bela Bartok 4 Cats 5 Libra 6 Spanish Civil War 7 Covetousness 8 Green 9 Memphis 10 A fish 11 Madras 12 Mongols 13 Adam

363

1   Fought in September 1854, the battle of Alma took place during which war?

2   What nationality is the operatic soprano Montserrat Caballe?

3   All the kings of the house of Hanover who ruled Britain were named George except for one. What was his name?

4   Which film star's death at the age of 31 in August 1926 reportedly led to worldwide hysteria and several suicides?

5   In September 1967, which European country switched from driving on the left of the road to driving on the right?

6   From which city did Napoleon make his famous retreat in 1812?

7   From which country does Capodimonte porcelain come?

8   What is John Montagu, an 18th century compulsive gambler, said to have invented because he refused to leave his gaming table for lunch?

9   Donnerstag is German for which day of the week?

10   What is the common name given to drugs such as propranolol, oxprenolol and metoprolol that are used to reduce high blood pressure, treat angina and control abnormal heart rhythms?

11   Which prison was demolished after the death of it's last inmate Rudolf Hess?

12   In 1908, the American car firms Buick and Oldsmobile merged to form which company?

13   In which town was the National Library of Wales founded in 1911?

14   Which wide-brimmed hat takes it's name from the Spanish word for 'shade'?

15   What type of citrus fruit is a shamouti?

Answers 1 Crimean War 2 Spanish 3 William (IV) 4 Rudolph Valentino 5 Sweden 6 Moscow 7 Italy 8 The sandwich (he was the 4th Earl of Sandwich) 9 Thursday 10 Beta-blockers 11 Spandau 12 General Motors 13 Aberystwyth 14 Sombrero 15 Orange

1   Originating in Latin America, what name is given to the dance consisting of three steps and a kick to each bar performed by a number of people in single file?

2   Which navigational instrument, invented by John Hadley in 1730, has an horizon glass and an index mirror?

3   During World War Two, Operation Barbarossa was the code name for the German invasion of which country?

4   In 1903, Jack Root became the first ever world champion at which boxing weight?

5   What was the artist Picasso's first name?

6   Which Christian period of fasting and penance begins on Ash Wednesday?

7   Ar is the chemical symbol for which gas?

8   What is the name given to the 11th century embroidered linen strip which depicts the Norman conquest of England?

9   What do you do when you nictate?

10 Which east coast US city has areas known as Chelsea, Dorchester and Winchester?

11 If you ordered pamplemousse as part of your breakfast in a French hotel, what would you get?

12 Parturition is the act or process of what?

13 To which type of animal does the adjective 'ovine' refer?

14 Which US President issued the Emancipation Proclamation?

15 Name the Chinese leader who was ousted by the Communists in 1949. He fled to Formosa, now Taiwan, where he established the Republic of China.

Answers 1 Conga 2 Sextant 3 Russia 4 Light-heavyweight 5 Pablo 6 Lent 7 Argon 8 Bayeux Tapestry 9 Blink 10 Boston 11 Grapefruit 12 Giving birth 13 Sheep 14 Abraham Lincoln 15 Chiang Kai-shek

MISCELLANEOUS 3 — Quiz 31

1   Shogi is a Japanese form of which board game?

2   Which American rider won the 500cc world motor cycling championship in 1984, 1986, 1988 and 1989?

3   Which European capital city contains a medieval inner city called the Altstadt and has a skyline dominated by St. Stephen's Cathedral?

4   What nationality was the playwright Henrik Ibsen?

5   Which famous furniture designer was born in Otley, West Yorkshire in 1718?

6   DCL are the Roman numerals for what number?

7   What is the name of the substance released by body tissues in allergic reactions such as hay fever?

8   Of which country was Sukarno the first president?

9   In which city did Anne Frank write her famous diary while hiding from the Nazis?

10 What sort of creature is a hake?

11 On which Spanish 'costa' is Torremolinos?

12 Which Roman emperor was assassinated in the Senate House on the Ides of March?

13 Who came to power on 1 January 1959 when he overthrew the government led by Fulgencio Batista?

14 According to Alexander Pope 'a little learning' is what?

15 In show jumping, what name is given to a competition that tests a horse's ability to jump large fences?

Answers 1 Chess **2** Eddie Lawson **3** Vienna **4** Norwegian **5** Thomas Chippendale **6** 650 **7** Histamine **8** Indonesia **9** Amsterdam **10** Fish **11** Costa Del Sol **12** Julius Caesar **13** Fidel Castro **14** A dangerous thing **15** Puissance

1   What was the name of the IBM computer that beat reigning world chess champion Gary Kasparov in a six game series in New York in 1997?

2   'The Lord is my shepherd; I shall not want' is the first line of which psalm?

3   What name is the Russian equivalent of John?

4   Carlos Menem, Leopoldo Galtieri and Juan Peron have all been president of which country?

5   In 1976, Israeli troops stormed a hi-jacked plane in a dramatic rescue at which Ugandan airport?

6   Which French term meaning odds and ends, is used in English for miscellaneous small objects, ornaments, trinkets etc.?

7   Name the loose fitting garment consisting of a piece of cloth draped around the body and worn by the citizens of ancient Rome.

8   What kind of school for young children literally means 'children's garden' in German?

9   Three days of rioting, known as the 'July Revolution' took place in which city in 1830?

10 When a conductor faces a symphony orchestra are the cellos to his or her left or right?

11 In February 1996, Joan Collins won a New York court case against which book publishers?

12 How is 19 written in Roman numerals?

13 What type of creatures are the eastern diamondback and fer-de-lance?

14 Which London nightclub was opened in Berkeley Square in 1963 by Mark Birley and named after his sister?

15 One of the apostles, he was a tax collector until he became a follower of Jesus. He is the patron saint of accountants, bankers and custom officers and his feast day is 21 September. Name him.

Answers 1 Deep Blue 2 23rd 3 Ivan 4 Argentina 5 Entebbe 6 Bric-a-brac 7 Toga 8 Kindergarten 9 Paris 10 Right 11 Random House 12 XIX 13 Snakes 14 Annabel's 15 St. Matthew

1 Who was the first president of the USA?

2 Which fruit is obtained from the tree *Prunus persica*?

3 Is Fiji north or south of the equator?

4 Winston Churchill and Charlie Chaplin had the same middle name, what name?

5 In 1951, who founded the Free Presbyterian Church of Ulster?

6 The name of which type of horse is derived from the Spanish for 'dove like'?

7 The triathlon is a sport involving running, swimming and which other discipline?

8 'Schnozzle' was the nickname of which American entertainer?

9 In 1990, Dr. Carmen Lawrence became the first woman premier of any Australian state. Which state?

10 Popular in the 1920s, which very short mannish hairstyle worn by women was named after an English public school?

11 In which month of the year is the Christian feast of the Annunciation of the Virgin Mary, also known as Lady Day, celebrated?

12 In which cathedral was Thomas a Becket murdered in 1170?

13 In which German town did optical equipment manufacturer Carl Zeiss open his first workshop in 1846?

14 Having a high gluten content, which variety of wheat is the most commonly used in making pasta?

15 Which German boxer became world heavyweight champion in 1930?

Answers 1 George Washington 2 Peach 3 South 4 Spencer 5 Ian Paisley 6 Palomino 7 Cycling 8 Jimmy Durante 9 Western Australia 10 Eton crop 11 March 12 Canterbury 13 Jena 14 Durum 15 Max Schmeling

1 What type of animal is a Lipizzaner?

2 On which continent did the Boer Wars take place?

3 Whom did Jacqueline Kennedy, widow of John F. Kennedy, marry in 1968?

4 Which 20th century Italian writer and chemist wrote a volume of memoirs and autobiographical reflections entitled 'The Periodic Table' consisting of 21 sections, each named after a chemical element?

5 Name the Scottish missionary and explorer of Africa who in 1857 published the book entitled 'Missionary Travels'.

6 Used with reference to the explosive power of a nuclear weapon, what word is used to describe the equivalent explosive force of one million tons of TNT?

7 From which country do the drinks ouzo and retsina originate?

8 Name the English poet who died in Rome at the age of 26 in 1821.

9 In which country was the infamous William Bligh imprisoned by mutinous soldiers during the so-called 'Rum Rebellion' of 1808?

10 What is a bouzouki?

11 Beluga, sevruga and osetrova are the three main types of what?

12 The name of which tropical fruit is derived from it's resemblance to the cone of a conifer?

13 Which tennis player stormed off court after losing to Steffi Graf in the final of the 1999 French Open?

14 Bardolatry is a word meaning an excessive admiration of which famous person?

15 Who wrote the popular children's book 'Heidi'?

Answers 1 Horse **2** Africa **3** Aristotle Onassis **4** Primo Levi **5** David Livingstone **6** Megaton **7** Greece **8** John Keats **9** Australia **10** Musical instrument **11** Caviare **12** Pineapple **13** Martina Hingis **14** William Shakespeare **15** Johanna Spyri

1   In religious doctrine, especially Roman Catholic, what name is given to the place or state in which souls are believed to undergo a limited amount of suffering to make amends for their sins?

2   Found in Africa, what type of creature is a waterbuck?

3   Renal is an adjective which relates to which part of the body?

4   Who is the patron saint of Wales?

5   Apiphobia is a fear of what?

6   In July 1985 Britain lifted restrictions on imports from which South American country?

7   King Charles, Cavalier King Charles and English Springer are all types of which breed of dog?

8   Which Asian capital city was known as Batavia until 1949?

9   Which edible nut of the American hickory tree is similar to a walnut?

10 Alderbaran is the brightest star in which constellation?

11 Fidelity, Bravery, Integrity is the motto of which American organisation?

12 What was the name of the cloned sheep which attracted much media attention in 1997?

13 Which pistol that fires a coloured flare for signalling purposes was named after a US naval ordnance officer?

14 Where would you normally find cerumen?

15 What is the more common name for the medical condition nyctalopia?

Answers 1 Purgatory 2 Antelope 3 Kidneys 4 St. David 5 Bees 6 Argentina 7 Spaniel 8 Jakarta 9 Pecan 10 Taurus 11 FBI 12 Dolly 13 Very pistol 14 In your ear, it's earwax 15 Night blindness

1 Which legendary chief of the Onondaga tribe of native Americans was the subject of a famous poem by Henry Longfellow?

2 Which famous sportsman was presented with a gold medal during the 1996 Olympics to replace the one he threw away in the 1960s?

3 What sort of movies are sometimes referred to as 'horse operas'?

4 Which word for the act of killing someone painlessly, especially to relieve suffering, is derived from the Greek for 'easy death'?

5 Carmine is a vivid shade of which colour?

6 Name the island where Gulliver discovered a race of little people in the novel 'Gulliver's Travels'.

7 In May 1999 who succeeded Benjamin Netanyahu as Israel's Prime Minister?

8 Under Genoese control from the 14th century, which Mediterranean island was sold to France in 1768?

9 The face of which British soldier and politician appeared on one of the most famous of all recruiting posters with the slogan 'Your country needs you'?

10 On what date in July do the French celebrate Bastille Day?

11 What type of buildings did Don Quixote mistake for evil giants?

12 Is Hong Kong north or south of the equator?

13 In which decade of the 20th century was insulin first used to treat diabetes?

14 Jomo Kenyatta was Prime Minister and president of which African country?

15 According to tradition, Mount Nebo in Jordan contains the tomb of which Biblical leader?

Answers 1 Hiawatha 2 Muhammad Ali 3 Westerns 4 Euthanasia 5 Red 6 Lilliput 7 Ehud Barak 8 Corsica 9 Lord Kitchener 10 14th 11 Windmills 12 North 13 1920s 14 Kenya 15 Moses

1   Originating in the USA, what word means a payment awarded to a non-married partner after the break-up of a long term relationship?

2   Can you name the following Asian politician? He was one of the most influential communist leaders of the 20th century; he was President of his country from 1954 until his death in 1969; he worked as a gardener, a street sweeper, a waiter and an oven stoker during a stay in France between 1917 and 1923.

3   Which famous Englishman was born on 23 April 1564 and died on 23 April 1616?

4   Who is the Patron Saint of Catania and bell-founders and according to legend had her breasts cut off?

5   Built in the 1880s, the Home Insurance building is acknowledged as the world's first skyscraper. In which American city was it built?

6   What type of creature is a drill?

7   Former US President Jimmy Carter's full name is James E. Carter. What does the E stand for?

8   A penny-farthing was an early form of what type of vehicle?

9   Which German physician was the founder of homeopathy?

10 The archer is the symbol of which sign of the zodiac?

11 Name the American playwright who wrote 'Barefoot In The Park' and 'The Odd Couple'.

12 In geometry, what name is given to a quarter of the circumference of a circle?

13 What nationality was the composer Franz Schubert?

14 Kelp and laverbread are types of what?

15 Where would a troglodyte live?

Answers 1 Palimony 2 Ho Chi-Minh 3 William Shakespeare 4 St Agatha 5 Chicago 6 Monkey 7 Earl 8 Bicycle 9 Samuel Hahnemann 10 Sagittarius 11 Neil Simon 12 Quadrant 13 Austrian 14 Seaweed 15 In a cave

MISCELLANEOUS 3 *Quiz 38*

1   Which 20th century US president founded the Peace Corps, an organisation of volunteers providing Third World countries with skilled manpower, especially teachers and agriculturalists?

2   In music, what note has the time value of half a semibreve?

3   Name the German arms manufacturing company who developed the World War One artillery piece known as Big Bertha.

4   The Folketing is the parliament of which country?

5   What nationality was Charles Darrow, inventor of the game Monopoly?

6   Who made his first fortune with Pergamon Press, which originally published scientific research journals?

7   Karl Marx and writer George Eliot were both buried in which London cemetery?

8   The story of Noah's Ark is told in which book of the Old Testament?

9   With which librettist did composer Arthur Sullivan collaborate on fourteen popular comic operas?

10 Which European golfer won the US Masters in 1994 and 1999?

11 The word for which form of physical exercise is derived from the Greek words for air and life?

12 In which country did Robert Clive help to establish British rule during the 18th century?

13 Dimanche is French for which day of the week?

14 Which sign of the zodiac is represented by a lion?

15 The Thinker and The Kiss are two famous works of which sculptor?

Answers 1 John F. Kennedy 2 Minim 3 Krupp 4 Denmark 5 American 6 Robert Maxwell 7 Highgate Cemetery 8 Genesis 9 W. S. Gilbert 10 Jose Maria Olazabal 11 Aerobics 12 India 13 Sunday 14 Leo 15 Rodin

MISCELLANEOUS 3   *Quiz 39*

1 Because he was entrusted with the 'keys of the Kingdom of Heaven', two crossed keys are the symbol of which apostle?

2 At the age of forty, which legendary American boxer, a multi-world champion, had his first fight in Britain when he fought Nate Miller on 10 April 1999?

3 What nationality was the 17th century painter Jan Vermeer?

4 Which war was described by 'Time' magazine in 1983 as 'a fight between two bald men over a comb'?

5 What name is given to the pouch worn hanging from a belt in front of the kilt in Scottish highland dress?

6 Found in North America, what sort of creature is a chuckwalla?

7 Name the park to the west of Paris which contains Longchamp racecourse.

8 In 1996, which European airline brightened up it's image by putting stickers of Tintin and other cartoon characters on the fuselages of it's aircraft?

9 Name the anchorage where the German navy scuttled itself in 1919.

10 Which queen of England was known as the 'Virgin Queen'?

11 By what acronym is radio detecting and ranging more commonly known?

12 Which herb, native to the Mediterranean region, is sometimes called vegetable oyster or oyster plant?

13 Who wrote, in 1988, 'A Brief History of Time'?

14 Which US president was known as 'Honest Abe' ?

15 If you are suffering from aphonia, you have lost your what?

Answers 1 St. Peter **2** Thomas 'Hit Man' Hearns **3** Dutch **4** The Falklands War **5** Sporran **6** Lizard **7** Bois Du Boulogne **8** Sabena **9** Scapa Flow **10** Elizabeth I **11** RADAR **12** Salsify **13** Stephen Hawking **14** Abraham Lincoln **15** Voice

MISCELLANEOUS 3 *Quiz 40*

1   Mazzini and Garibaldi did much to unite which country?

2   Dom Mintoff was a leading politician on which Mediterranean island?

3   An osier is what species of tree?

4   What kind of plant is a saguaro?

5   What is the product of a male zebra and a female horse called?

6   In which year of the 1950s did Roger Bannister become the first man to run a sub-four minute mile?

7   Which famous British actor was married to Vivien Leigh and Joan Plowright?

8   Born in 1811, Chang and Eng were the world's first officially recorded what?

9   To depilate, means to remove what?

10 Apart from a pawn, which is the only other piece that can make the opening move in a game of chess?

11 What kind of creature is the cartoon character Speedy Gonzales?

12 An elver is a young what?

13 What word was coined by Jim Henson to describe his creations which were a blend of marionettes and puppets?

14 By what name is the insect *Mantis religiosa* more commonly known?

15 What does the O and J stand for in O. J. Simpson?

Answers 1 Italy 2 Malta 3 Willow 4 Cactus 5 Zorse 6 1954 7 Laurence Olivier 8 Siamese twins 9 Hair 10 Knight 11 Mouse 12 Eel 13 Muppets 14 Praying Mantis 15 Orenthal James

1 What surname is shared by the 9th and 23rd presidents of the USA?

2 Which Italian artist and architect is supposed to have drawn a perfect circle as an example of his work in order to secure a Papal commission?

3 What is the more common name of trichloromethane?

4 Name the American poet who made broadcasts in Italy supporting the Fascists during the Second World War.

5 Which American journalist and author wrote the monumental history, 'The Rise And Fall Of The Third Reich'?

6 Which soft, fine net material, used for making veils and dresses, takes it's name from the town in the Correze department of France where it was first made?

7 In London, which street runs between Oxford Circus and Piccadilly Circus?

8 Which one of the seven deadly sins was portrayed in medieval art as a rider thrown from his horse?

9 French Prime Minister from 1942 to 1944, he was executed in 1945 after being found guilty of conspiracy against the state and collaborating with the Germans. Can you name him?

10 In December 2000 he signed a lucrative 10 year contract: in which sport is Alex Rodriguez a big name?

11 What are the Palatine, Aventine, Capitoline, Quirinal, Viminal, Esquiline and Caelian?

12 Name the place in northern Italy where in 1976 a leak from the chemical works contaminated the surrounding area, killing animals and causing people to suffer from skin disorders and other ailments.

13 What nationality was Ernst Mach, the physicist after whom Mach numbers were named?

14 In which country was former Israeli Prime Minister David Ben Gurion born?

15 'The Ambassadors' is considered to be the masterpiece of which American novelist?

Answers 1 Harrison 2 Giotto 3 Chloroform 4 Ezra Pound 5 William Shirer 6 Tulle 7 Regent Street 8 Pride 9 Pierre Laval 10 Baseball 11 The seven hills of Rome 12 Seveso 13 Austrian 14 Poland 15 Henry James

1   What name links a sports team in Sheffield, England with one in Pittsburgh, USA?

2   Name the Italian ocean liner which sank off the coast of Massachusetts after colliding with another vessel on 26 July 1956.

3   Which 19th century US president married Martha Wayles Skelton?

4   What does the B in Cecil B. De Mille stand for?

5   Who is the patron saint of Portugal?

6   Can you name the South African author of the novels 'Elephant Song' and 'A Time To Die'?

7   Which 19th century American philosopher, poet and essayist wrote: 'Nothing great was ever achieved without enthusiasm'?

8   What name was given to the religious revival in the American colonies during the 18th century that was inspired by the preaching of George Whitefield and Jonathan Edwards?

9   In the 1930s, the American company Bally were forerunners in the development of which games machine?

10   Which bird did Wordsworth describe as 'a blithe newcomer'?

11   What is the name of the well preserved Inca city discovered in 1911 that is named after the mountain that rises above it?

12   In 1962, who became the first American to orbit the earth?

13   The plays 'The Shadow Of A Gunman', 'Juno And The Paycock' and 'Red Roses For Me' were written by which Irish dramatist?

14   First performed in Paris in 1841, which ballet in two acts by Adolphe Adam concerns the ghosts of young girls who die of grief before their wedding day after being deserted by their lovers?

15   What name was given to the government of Germany from 1919 to 1933, named after the town in which the constitution was formulated?

Answers 1 Steelers 2 Andrea Doria 3 Thomas Jefferson 4 Blount 5 St. Anthony of Padua 6 Wilbur Smith 7 Ralph Waldo Emerson 8 The Great Awakening 9 Pinball 10 Cuckoo 11 Machu Picchu 12 John Glenn 13 Sean O'Casey 14 Giselle 15 Weimar Republic

MISCELLANEOUS 3 — Quiz 43

1   On 6 December 1917, several munition ships exploded in the harbour of which Canadian port, killing over 1500 and making 20,000 people homeless?

2   Which Anglo-Saxon missionary and saint is known as the 'apostle of Germany'?

3   Name the German architect who was director of the Bauhaus school of design from 1919 to 1928.

4   The Small-endians and the Big-endians appeared in the adventures of which literary character?

5   Which sport did British comedian Norman Pace liken to 'playing golf from a helicopter'?

6   What name is given to the three wars fought between Rome and Carthage?

7   Which city in Cilicia was the birthplace of St. Paul?

8   Name the Egyptian astronomer and geographer who lived in the second century AD and who produced his *Geographa Hyphegesis*, an extensive guide to geography.

9   What name is given to the diode valve which is the source of microwaves in a microwave oven?

10 Sent into orbit by the Russians, what was the name of the Samoyed who was the first dog in space?

11 Who was the Democrat candidate beaten by George Bush in the 1988 US presidential election?

12 Name the mongoose in Kipling's 'Jungle Book'.

13 Which Frenchman wrote: 'If God did not exist it would be necessary to invent him'?

14 Adrastea is a satellite of which planet?

15 Turkish-born Canadian portrait photographer Yousef Karsh, famous for his wartime studies of Churchill and other national leaders, signed himself as 'Karsh of ......' which city?

Answers 1 Halifax 2 St. Boniface 3 Walter Gropius 4 Lemuel Gulliver 5 Polo 6 Punic Wars 7 Tarsus 8 Ptolemy 9 Magnetron 10 Laika 11 Michael Dukakis 12 Rikki Tikki Tavi 13 Voltaire 14 Jupiter 15 Ottawa

1   The Imperial Hotel in Tokyo and the Guggenheim Museum in New York are two of the best known public buildings designed by which American architect?

2   What was the name of the 16th century Flemish geographer, best known for his cylindrical map projection that was named after him?

3   In 1995, who at his third attempt was finally elected president of France?

4   Who was the president of the Confederate States during the American civil war?

5   After her husband had been assassinated in 1983, who became president of the Philippines in 1986?

6   Which religious movement was founded by John Thomas in New York in 1848?

7   Supposedly started by Mrs. O'Leary's cow kicking over an oil lamp, fire almost completely destroyed which US city in 1871?

8   Which former American hero turned traitor conspired unsuccessfully to surrender the vital West Point position to the British in 1780 during the American War of Independence?

9   An American man of letters, he wrote stories such as 'The Legend Of Sleepy Hollow'. He reached the height of his career when he was appointed US ambassador to Spain in 1842. Can you name him?

10 Which city is the home of the Italian soccer team Sampdoria?

11 And which city in northern Spain is the home of Real Sociedad?

12 Imprisoned with Hitler, who is said to have taken down 'Mein Kampf' from Hitler's dictation?

13 In J. M. Barrie's 'Peter Pan', what is the surname of the children Wendy, Michael and John?

14 And according to Peter Pan, what happens every time a child says: "I don't believe in fairies"?

15 Which international organisation was founded in England in 1929 to promote sound horsemanship among people under the age of twenty one?

Answers 1 Frank Lloyd Wright 2 Gerardus Mercator 3 Jacques Chirac 4 Jefferson Davis 5 Corazon Aquino 6 Christadelphians 7 Chicago 8 Benedict Arnold 9 Washington Irving 10 Genoa 11 San Sebastian 12 Rudolf Hess 13 Darling 14 A fairy drops down dead 15 The Pony Club

MISCELLANEOUS 3 — Quiz 45

1   Who is the US politician after whom the Prohibition Act of 1919 was named?

2   What's the name of the austere sect, an offshoot of the Quakers that was formed in the 18th century by Ann Lee?

3   Who were the American brother and sister pairing who won the mixed doubles at Wimbledon in 1980?

4   Which British soldier died leading his men in the capture of Quebec in 1759?

5   Which publication, originally reprinting condensations of other articles from other magazines, first appeared in the US in 1922?

6   What was the name of German terrorist Andreas Baader's female partner?

7   And what was the name of the urban guerrilla organisation they headed?

8   Which 19th century Russian dramatist wrote the historical drama 'Boris Godunov'?

9   Which artist was appointed court painter to Charles IV of Spain in 1786?

10 Which German bacteriologist discovered Salvarsan, a compound used in the treatment of syphilis, before the introduction of antibiotics?

11 Which ancient Roman satirist wrote the '16 Satires'?

12 Name the American who was commander-in-chief of UN forces in the Korean War until relieved of his command in April 1951.

13 Who was US president when the armistice ending the Korean War was signed on 27 July 1953?

14 In March 1988, Mike Tyson had his first fight outside the USA when he defended his world heavyweight title against Tony Tubbs. In which city did that fight take place?

15 President of the United Nations General Assembly 1952/3, he was awarded the Nobel peace prize in 1957 and was Prime Minister of Canada from 1963 to 1968. Can you name him?

Answers 1 Andrew Volstead 2 Shakers 3 John and Tracy Austin 4 General James Wolfe 5 Reader's Digest 6 Ulrike Meinhof 7 The Red Army Faction 8 Alexander Pushkin 9 Goya 10 Paul Ehrlich 11 Juvenal 12 Douglas MacArthur 13 Dwight D. Eisenhower 14 Tokyo 15 Lester Pearson

1   Plato's 'Phaedo' is an eloquent account of who's death?

2   Can you name the founder president of the African National Council in 1971 who headed the government in Zimbabwe for a short time before the 1980 election swept Robert Mugabe into power?

3   By what name was the Swiss-born French architect Charles Edouard Jeanneret better known?

4   Golf. Who partnered Davis Love III when the USA won the World Cup in 1992, 1993 and 1994?

5   Who was the governor-general of Batavia who commissioned Abel Tasman to explore the South Pacific?

6   King Camp Gillette patented the safety razor in 1895; who in 1931 patented and marketed the first electric razor?

7   What nationality was explorer Christopher Columbus?

8   By what name is the fungal infection *tinea pedis* more commonly known?

9   In which country was Arnold Schwarzenegger born?

10   Thomas Munzer and John of Leiden were prominent leaders of which 16th century sect that taught the doctrine of pacifism?

11   Ganesh, one of the principle Hindu deities, is portrayed by having the head of which beast on a human body?

12   Which religious person was originally known as Giovanni Bernadone?

13   Which Italian statesman, writer and political philosopher wrote 'The Prince'?

14   Which 18th century German philosopher who coined the term 'categorical imperative'?

15   Which scientific instrument was invented by Dutchman Hans Jansen and his son Zacharias in the late 16th century?

Answers 1 Socrates 2 Bishop Abel Muzorewa 3 Le Corbusier 4 Fred Couples 5 Antony Van Dieman 6 Colonel Jacob Schick 7 Italian 8 Athlete's foot 9 Austria 10 Anabaptists 11 Elephant 12 St. Francis of Assisi 13 Niccolo Machiavelli 14 Immanuel Kant 15 Microscope

MISCELLANEOUS 3 — Quiz 47

1 Which Spanish missionary was known as the 'Apostle of the Indies'?

2 Which thermoplastic material was invented by the American Hyatt brothers in 1870?

3 Enver Hoxha was leader of which country from 1946 to 1985?

4 Whichof the Canary Islands is known for its 'Mountains of Fire'?

5 Which novelist was a deputy inspector in the New York customs office in the middle to late 19th century?

6 What does the F. W. stand for in the name of international retailer F. W. Woolworth?

7 Golf. Name the American who won the 1989 Open at Royal Troon.

8 Nelson Rockefeller was governor of which US state during the 1950s and 1960s?

9 Which saint, the mother of Constantine the Great, reputedly visited Jerusalem in 326 AD and founded the basilicas on the Mount of Olives and at Bethlehem?

10 By what more familiar term is the habit, bruxism (often done whilst asleep) more commonly known?

11 In September 1995, which German sportsman was made a special envoy for education and sports by UNESCO?

12 Which Himalayan kingdom is known locally as Druk-Yul which means 'Realm of the Dragon'?

13 Name the actress who was married to Steve McQueen from 1973 to 1978.

14 According to a Cole Porter song who 'regrets she's unable to lunch today'?

15 The first jet aircraft to be constructed with engines at the rear of the fuselage rather than on the wings was French. What was it's name?

Answers 1 St. Francis Xavier 2 Celluloid 3 Albania 4 Lanzarote 5 Herman Melville 6 Frank Winfield 7 Mark Calcavecchia 8 New York 9 St. Helena 10 Grinding your teeth 11 Michael Schumacher 12 Bhutan 13 Ali McGraw 14 Miss Otis 15 Caravelle

1   With which Greek island do you associate the poet Sappho?

2   What is the English translation of the title of the children's book of verse, 'Struwwelpeter'?

3   According to Jonathan Swift, 'Promises and pie-crusts are made to be ..... ' what?

4   The USA had four presidents during the 1920s – Woodrow Wilson, Calvin Coolidge, Herbert Hoover and which other?

5   Which walled town in central Spain, noted for it's gothic cathedral, was the birthplace of St. Teresa?

6   In 1964, which French writer was awarded, but declined to accept the Nobel Prize for literature?

7   Named after the physician who identified it, by what other name is adrenal insufficiency known as?

8   In 1943, American playwright Eugene O'Neill became the father-in-law of a man who was only six months his junior and a lot more famous worldwide. Who was that man?

9   According to folklore, which bird can predict bad weather and if seen near a ship will bring a storm?

10 Opened in 1966, the world's first successful tidal power station was built on which French river?

11 Lauren Bacall was married (at different times) to Humphrey Bogart and which other actor?

12 By what other name is a medical operation known as a 'suction curettage' more commonly known?

13 Name the Spanish composer and pianist who died when the ship 'Sussex' was torpedoed in 1916.

14 What nationality is former UN secretary-general, Javier Perez de Cuellar?

15 Known as Berlin until 1916, the city of Kitchener is in which country?

Answers 1 Lesbos 2 Shock-headed Peter 3 Broken 4 Warren Harding 5 Avila 6 Jean-Paul Sartre 7 Addison's Disease 8 Charlie Chaplin 9 Albatross 10 Rance 11 Jason Robards 12 Abortion 13 Enrique Granados 14 Peruvian 15 Canada

MISCELLANEOUS 3 — Quiz 49

1 Which US state is nicknamed the 'Diamond State'?

2 Name the actress to whom Tom Cruise was married before Nicole Kidman.

3 Adherence of which religion believes that Ahura Mazda, the good god, is in conflict with Ahriman, the evil god?

4 In 1981, the government of which country resigned after revelations of strong links with the Freemason's Lodge known as P2?

5 Which item of clothing, popularised by Greta Garbo in the 1930s, was once again a popular fashion item following Faye Dunaway's role in the movie 'Bonnie And Clyde'?

6 Which viral disease takes it's name from the Nigerian village where it was first reported in 1969?

7 16 October 1995 saw the largest gathering of black people in Washington since Martin Luther King made his famous 'I have a dream' speech in 1963. What name was given to that gathering?

8 A constituent of baking powder, which colourless crystalline acid found in many fruits is used as an additive in soft drinks and confectionery?

9 In 1884, which American-born inventor produced the first automatic machine gun?

10 By what name is the edible seafish *Hippoglossus hippoglossus* commonly known?

11 In 1933 which American aviator made the first solo flight around the world?

12 Spacewalks are referred to as EVAs. What does EVA stand for?

13 In astronomical terms, what does the abbreviation QSO stand for?

14 Which insect was the symbol of Napoleon III of France?

15 In medicine, aetiology or etiology is the study of what?

Answers 1 Delaware 2 Mimi Rogers 3 Zoroastrianism 4 Italy 5 Beret 6 Lassa fever 7 Million men march 8 Tartaric acid 9 Hiram S. Maxim 10 Halibut 11 Wiley Post 12 Extra-vehicular activity 13 Quasi-stellar object 14 Bee 15 Cause of a disease or a condition

1   Which Scottish glen is known as the 'glen of weeping'?

2   Supreme Greasepaint, the first make-up specially designed for the movie industry, was developed by which famous name in the world of cosmetics?

3   Actresses Ursula Andress and Linda Evans were both married to which actor and director?

4   Which religion's most sacred books contain the teachings of Mahavira?

5   In 1981, President Reagan announced the dismissal of 12,000 striking members of the PATCO trade union. What was their occupation?

6   In which opera by Meyerbeer is Vasco da Gama shipwrecked and falls in love with an African slave girl?

7   Name the American author who wrote the trilogy of novels – 'Rabbit Run', 'Rabbit Redux' and 'Rabbit Is Rich'.

8   That 'Rabbit' trilogy spans 30 years in the life of a salesman. What type of salesman?

9   Jean, Jacques, Daniel and Nicolas were the forenames of which family of Swiss mathematicians?

10   Which player ended 28 months in the tennis wilderness by winning the women's singles at the 1996 Australian Open championship?

11   The music for the ballet 'Appalachian Spring' was written by which 20th century American composer?

12   Legendary pool player Rudolph Wolderone died the day before his 83rd birthday in January 1996. By what name was he better known?

13   Before making a fortune from the manufacture of firearms, which American inventor is best remembered for his invention of the cotton gin, a machine that separates cotton fibre from the seeds?

14   Which reclusive American actor published his autobiography 'Songs My Mother Taught Me' in 1994?

15   What title was borne by Abu Bakr who succeeded Mohammed in 632. The title was given to the rulers of Baghdad and then the sultans of the Ottoman Empire until it was abolished in 1924?

Answers 1 Glencoe 2 Max Factor 3 John Derek 4 Jainism 5 Air traffic controllers 6 L'Africaine 7 John Updike 8 A car salesman 9 Bernoulli 10 Monica Seles 11 Aaron Copland 12 Minnesota Fats 13 Eli Whitney 14 Marlon Brando 15 Caliph

MISCELLANEOUS 3

Quiz 51

1   What is the standard monetary unit of Japan?

2   In which European country did armed soldiers burst into the parliament building and take some 350 MPs hostage during an attempted right-wing coup in 1981?

3   Close up pictures of Halley's Comet were sent back to earth by which European space probe in 1986?

4   What's the surname of 'Big Bill' who in 1920 became the first American to win the men's singles at Wimbledon?

5   Grenadine is a syrup made from the juice of which fruit?

6   The Statue of Liberty was given to the USA by which nation in 1884?

7   Which Greek shipping tycoon died aged 86 in March 1996?

8   Which motor car manufacturer was founded by Giovanni Agnelli in Turin in 1899?

9   Created by American writer Rex Stout, who was the phenomenally fat private eye who was assisted by a character called Archie Godwin?

10 In July 1992, which of Puccini's operas was broadcast live on worldwide TV, being performed at the exact times and in the locations specified in the opera?

11 The 'Kenny method', named after Australian nurse Elizabeth Kenny, was used as a treatment for which medical condition?

12 Some of the earliest war photographs were taken at the battle of Antietam. During which war was this battle fought?

13 Which medical condition, the name is no longer in technical use, was known in medieval times as the 'king's evil'?

14 Name the French poet whose collective work entitled 'Les Fleurs Du Mal' contained several erotic poems which led to him being convicted of obscenity and he died in poverty in 1867.

15 What object is draped over the branch of a tree in Salvador Dali's painting 'The Persistence Of Memory'?

MISCELLANEOUS 3   *Quiz 52*

1   Name the American astronaut, who in 1984 became the first man to make an 'untethered' spacewalk.

2   Which inlet of the Firth of Clyde was the site of a US Polaris nuclear submarine base from 1961 until 1992?

3   The son of a celebrated archaeologist, he was the conductor of the Berlin Philharmonic orchestra from 1922 until his death in 1954. Can you name him?

4   What type of Australian eucalyptus tree is mentioned in the song 'Waltzing Matilda'?

5   Who, in May 1996, was made an honorary citizen of Warsaw?

6   The Kuiper Crater is on which planet?

7   Walker Smith was the real name of which famous world welter and middleweight boxing champion of the 1940s and 1950s?

8   And which world heavyweight boxing champion, he won the title at the age of 37, was born Arnold Cream?

9   Situated on both banks of the Karun river, Ahvaz is a city in which country?

10 Name the feminist, a constant companion of Jean-Paul Sartre, who wrote 'The Second Sex'.

11 Often seen in the 17th and 18th centuries, what was a peruke?

12 In the Jewish religion, what name is given to the scrolls which contain the text of the Pentateuch?

13 What nationality was the first pilot to be saved by an ejector seat?

14 Born in Scotland, who was Canada's first Prime Minister?

15 In the story of 'Peter Pan', Peter has to return to the Darling's house because on his first visit he left without what?

MISCELLANEOUS 3 — *Quiz 53*

1 Which amphibian was the symbol of Francis I of France?

2 Born in Paris, he settled in America and in 1919 founded the New Symphony Orchestra. His works often used unconventional percussion instruments. Name this composer.

3 In which city in the north of England would you find the Royal Armouries Museum?

4 Jerry Rawlings twice led successful coups (in 1979 and 1981) to overthrow the government of which African country?

5 Which French author, born the son of a doctor in Rouen in 1821, claimed as a schoolboy to be 'disgusted with life' and said of his most famous heroine Madame Bovary 'c'est moi'?

6 The IFAW is an organisation that cares for animals. What does IFAW stand for?

7 In nautical terms, what is a grapnel?

8 What name is given to carving with an incised or sunken design, the opposite of cameo?

9 What is the name of the ship used by Amundsen for his successful expedition to the South Pole in 1911?

10 Known as 'the voice of New England', which American poet won the Pulitzer prize in 1924, 1931 and 1937?

11 Canonized in 1925, which 19th century French nun was known as the 'Little Flower of Jesus'?

12 In which country would you find the famous Ipanema beach?

13 Bonnie and Clyde were infamous bank robbers. What were their surnames?

14 Who was the Roman governor of Judaea who condemned Christ to death?

15 Which breed of dog originating from Flanders that was used as a guard dog on barges, has a stocky tailless body with short legs and a fox-like head with erect ears?

Answers 1 Salamander 2 Edgar Varese 3 Leeds 4 Ghana 5 Gustave Flaubert 6 International Fund for Animal Welfare 7 An anchor 8 Intaglio 9 Fram 10 Robert Lee Frost 11 St. Theresa 12 Brazil 13 Parker and Barrow 14 Pontius Pilate 15 Schipperke

1. An American, in 1932 he isolated heavy water. He won the Nobel prize for chemistry in 1934 and was director of the atomic bomb project from 1940 to 1945. Name him.

2. Name the religious order founded by St. Bruno in 1084, the name being derived from the location of it's first community La Grande Chartreuse.

3. In October 1996, which Oscar-winning duo were lost for 48 hours in the back of a New York taxi?

4. With which profession is Harley Street in London associated?

5. Of which ballet company was Rudolf Nureyev a member when he defected to the west in 1961?

6. Who's work on dreams was published in 1900 under the title 'The Interpretation Of Dreams'?

7. *Amoebiasis* is a parasitic infection of which specific part of the body?

8. Name the French writer and dramatist who gained international success with his play 'Cyrano de Bergerac'.

9. When he was a crew member of Gemini 3 in 1965, who became the first man to go into space twice?

10. Immortalised in song and nursery rhyme, who was acquitted of murdering her father and stepmother with an axe?

11. The SS were the elite Nazi military corps. In German, what did SS stand for?

12. What name was given to the terrorist group responsible for the assassination of Franz Ferdinand in Sarajevo in 1914?

13. What name is given to the cocktail made up of gin, cointreau and lemon juice that first made it's mark in London in 1919 but was perfected by Harry"s Bar in Paris?

14. Name the New York newspaper first published on 10 April 1841.

15. Associated with Frank Sinatra, who wrote the song 'My Kind Of Town'?

Answers 1 Harold Clayton Urey 2 Carthusians 3 Wallace and Gromit 4 Medical profession 5 Kirov 6 Sigmund Freud 7 Intestines 8 Edmond Rostand 9 Virgil 'Gus' Grissom 10 Lizzie Borden 11 Schutzstaffel 12 The Black Hand 13 White Lady 14 New York Tribune 15 Jimmy Van Heusen

1. Famous for his falsetto warble and his version of 'Tiptoe Through The Tulips', who died at the age of 64 in 1996?

2. What's the title of the novel written by Rumer Godden about nuns, passion and the Himalayas?

3. Adolf Hitler was sent to prison in 1923 for attempting to overthrow the Bavarian government in which city?

4. What was Hitler's original family name?

5. Opened in 1906, which famous hotel was the first important steel-framed building to be built in London?

6. What is your pollex?

7. Levodopa is a drug now commonly used in the treatment of which degenerative disease?

8. What is the meaning of the word rugose?

9. Which Norwegian artist painted the picture entitled 'The Scream'?

10. Who was the famous pupil of Anne M. Sullivan?

11. Which American company were the first to manufacture nylon?

12. In 1997, who won a Grammy award in the Best Spoken Word or Non-Musical Category for her recorded version of the best selling book about child rearing, 'It Takes A Village'?

13. Name the town in the Tuscany region of Italy famous for it's white marble as used by Michelangelo.

14. What kind of creature is an affenpinscher?

15. Which Hollywood actor published two volumes of autobiography during the 1970s entitled 'The Moon's A Balloon' and 'Bring On The Empty Horses'?

Answers 1 Tiny Tim 2 The Black Narcissus 3 Munich 4 Schicklgruber 5 The Ritz 6 Thumb 7 Parkinson's disease 8 Wrinkled 9 Edvard Munch 10 Helen Keller 11 Du Pont 12 Hillary Clinton 13 Carrara 14 A dog 15 David Niven

1   Said never to have lost a battle, which Federal general was ordered by Grant to make the Shenandoah valley 'a barren waste' during the American Civil War?

2   In 1517, Martin Luther nailed his 95 theses to a church door in which German town?

3   In 1841, who was the first vice-president of the USA to become president on the death of a president?

4   And to date, who is the only US president who's second term of office did not immediately follow his first?

5   In 1898, which French novelist wrote an open letter entitled 'J'accuse' which attacked the French government over their persecution of the army officer Alfred Dreyfus?

6   Which British woman, a novelist and TV writer, was responsible for the Egg Marketing Board slogan 'Go to work on an egg'?

7   Reckoned to be the oldest trophy in international sport, it was badly damaged by a Maori protestor in New Zealand in March 1997. Which trophy?

8   What is the proper first name of golfer Tiger Woods?

9   Atomic number 67, which metallic element's name is derived from the Latin name for Stockholm?

10 And which metallic element, atomic number 24, is alloyed with iron and nickel in the manufacture of stainless steel?

11 Name the Russian-born actor and director who is said to be the founder of 'method acting'.

12 First published in the USA in 1923, which international news and general interest magazine became famous for it's 'Man of the Year' issue?

13 Usually formed by the top of a volcano that has subsided, what geographical term describes a crater flanked by steep cliffs?

14 Specifically, to what geographical feature does the adjective riparian refer?

15 First known as Bible Students, which religious movement was started by Charles Taze Russell in the early 1870s?

Answers 1 Philip Henry Sheridan 2 Wittenburg 3 John Tyler 4 Grover Cleveland 5 Emile Zola 6 Fay Weldon 7 The America's Cup 8 Eldrick 9 Holmium 10 Chromium 11 Konstantin Stanislavsky 12 Time 13 Caldera 14 River bank 15 Jehovah's Witnesses

MISCELLANEOUS 3 — Quiz 57

1   Previously relatively unknown, which American golfer won the 1997 Open at Troon?

2   From which country does the Uzi machine gun originate?

3   In which country was Semtex explosive developed?

4   Name the 18th century French philosopher who wrote: "Man is born free and everywhere he is in chains".

5   Which Anton Chekhov play tells of the destruction of a family estate for the construction of a new housing development?

6   In 1869, which American patented automatic air brakes for railway carriages?

7   What nickname, referring to it's colour, was given to the British army standard issue flintlock musket of the 18th century that was still in use at the battle of Waterloo in 1815?

8   The Mangla Dam is in which Asian country?

9   What is the broad sash tied in a large flat bow at the back and worn as part of Japanese national costume called?

10 One of the code names of the five beachheads used for the D-Day landings was named after which US state?

11 And which one of the five beachheads had the same name as the largest city in Nebraska?

12 Elton John donated sponsorship money for his 1993 world tour to his Aids foundation. Which cosmetics company sponsored that tour?

13 Name the US Secretary of State who resigned in protest over President Carter's desperate plan to rescue US embassy staff held hostage in Iran.

14 The name of which metallic element, isolated by Humphry Davy, is derived from an ancient Greek city in Thessaly near where it was first found?

15 Comprising over 90% of the population, which is the largest ethnic group in China?

Answers 1 Justin Leonard 2 Israel 3 Czechoslovakia 4 Jean Jacques Rousseau 5 The Cherry Orchard 6 George Westinghouse 7 Brown Bess 8 Pakistan 9 Obi 10 Utah 11 Omaha 12 Revlon 13 Cyrus Vance 14 Magnesium 15 Han

1 What is the loincloth worn by Indian men which consists of a wide length of cotton wrapped around the waist with the end rolled up and tucked between the legs called?

2 Tennis. In 1973, which American pairing were the first ever winners of the world's doubles championship?

3 What is the common name for ethanoic acid?

4 And what is the common name for methanoic acid?

5 What name was given to the literary movement in the USA in the 1950s of which William Burroughs and Jack Kerouac were prominent writers?

6 About 70% of Venezuela's total oil production is obtained in and around which lake?

7 What nationality is author Gabriel Garcia Marquez?

8 Of which constellation is Hamal the brightest star?

9 What name is given to the dogma of the Roman Catholic church which states that the Virgin Mary was conceived free from original sin?

10 American astronomer Carl Sagan popularised the study of space through his TV programme of the early 1980s. What was the programme called?

11 Which island is sometimes referred to as 'the teardrop of India'?

12 Which American poet wrote 'The Defence Of Fort McHenry', the words of which were adopted for the American national anthem 'The Star-Spangled Banner'?

13 The Alice mentioned in the Joseph McCarthy and Harry Tierney song 'Alice-blue Gown' was the daughter of which US president?

14 What name is given to the large group of plants that are formed by the mutually beneficial association between fungi and algae?

15 Name the South African Prime Minister who survived an attempt on his life in 1960 but was assassinated in 1966.

Answers 1 Dhoti **2** Stan Smith and Bob Lutz **3** Acetic acid **4** Formic acid **5** The Beat Movement **6** Lake Maracaibo **7** Colombian **8** Aries **9** The Immaculate Conception **10** Cosmos **11** Sri Lanka **12** Francis Scott Key **13** Theodore Roosevelt **14** Lichens **15** Hendrik Verwoerd

MISCELLANEOUS 3 — Quiz 59

1. In April 1996, which European country's general election saw a victory for the Olive Tree Alliance, producing the country's first truly left of centre government since World War Two?

2. Speedway. Which country were the first ever winners of the world team championship in 1960?

3. Name the tanker which ran aground in Prince William Sound, Alaska in 1989 causing a massive oil spillage.

4. 'The Seven Books On The Structure Of The Human Body' containing some of the first accurate descriptions of human anatomy was the major work of which 16th century Flemish anatomist?

5. What is the title of Australia's national anthem?

6. Which 20th century US president is the only one in history to have three different vice-presidents during his time in the White House?

7. What did the E stand for in the name of American confederate general Robert E. Lee?

8. Which religious sect was founded in 1954 by American philosopher and science fiction writer Lafayette Ronald Hubbard?

9. Which famous soldier was Britain's Prime Minister between 1828 and 1830?

10. On 8 December 1997, Jenny Shipley was sworn in as which country's first woman Prime Minister?

11. Sometimes referred to as the Eastern Highlands, which range of Australian mountains extend some 2,300 miles from Cape York Peninsula in the north down to Victoria in the south?

12. Spoken on the gallows in 1880, who's alleged last words were: "Such is life"?

13. If you travelled due south from Trinidad, which South American country would be your next landfall?

14. And if you travelled due west from Madagascar, which African country would be your next landfall?

15. Which branch of physics is the study of heat and it's relationship with other forms of energy?

Answers 1 Italy 2 Sweden 3 Exxon Valdez 4 Andreas Vesalius 5 Advance Australia Fair 6 Franklin D. Roosevelt 7 Edward 8 Church of Scientology 9 The Duke of Wellington 10 New Zealand 11 Great Dividing Range 12 Ned Kelly 13 Venezuela 14 Mozambique 15 Thermodynamics

1. The Akosombo Dam provides which African country with hydro-electric power?

2. Which US president was nicknamed 'Baby Dumpling' by his family, 'Hotshot' at school and 'Toadthrush' by Private Eye magazine?

3. Which Dutch tennis player lost in the finals of the women's singles, women's doubles and mixed doubles at Wimbledon in 1977?

4. Name the social reformer who in 1916 founded the first American birth control clinic, for which she was imprisoned.

5. Which US mountain range extends north-east to south-west from the Mohawk river to Alabama, separating the Mississippi-Missouri lowlands from the Atlantic coastal plain?

6. John the Perfect and John the Unfortunate were kings of which country?

7. Name the writer whose first novel 'Valley Of The Dolls' was a best-seller.

8. Give either of the names of the two Doberman guard dogs featured in the TV series 'Magnum P. I'.

9. In ancient times, which Greek mountain was held sacred to Apollo and the Muses?

10. Which award-winning author was once an advertising copywriter and counts amongst his work the slogan used in ads for fresh cream cakes 'Naughty – but Nice'?

11. Stella McCartney, daughter of Paul, was appointed head designer of which French fashion house in 1997?

12. Also in 1997, which Italian woman said: "Everything you see I owe to spaghetti"?

13. The original cathedral church of Venice was built in the 9th century to house the relics of which saint?

14. What was the surname of the singer known as Mama Cass?

15. Mount Chimborazo is the highest point of which South American country?

Answers 1 Ghana 2 Jimmy Carter 3 Betty Stove 4 Margaret Sanger 5 Appalachian Mountains 6 Portugal 7 Jacqueline Susann 8 Zeus or Apollo 9 Mount Parnassus 10 Salman Rushdie 11 Chloe 12 Sophia Loren 13 St. Mark 14 Elliot 15 Ecuador

MISCELLANEOUS 3

Quiz 61

1 Which idea of James Van Alen's was first used in a 'Grand Slam' tennis tournament in 1970?

2 Of which singer was it once said: "If she burnt her bra, it would take three days for the fire to go out"?

3 Which major American city and port is sometimes referred to as Crescent City because of it's location on a bend in the Mississippi river?

4 If you added the faces of a tetrahedron, a dodecahedron and an icosahedron together, how many faces would you have in total?

5 Which affluent literary character seduces Daisy Buchanan, a former lover who is married to a neighbour?

6 Situated in the Bavarian Alps, near the Austrian border, what is the highest mountain in Germany?

7 Which 20th century American humorous writer is remembered for his outrageous lines such as: "A bit of talcum is walcum" and "Candy is dandy but liquor is quicker"?

8 What does the D.W. stand for in the name of silent film director D. W. Griffith?

9 Name the manager of Elvis Presley who died aged 87 in 1997.

10 Which spice is obtained from the dried outer covering of the nutmeg?

11 Of the two infamous 19th century bodysnatchers – Burke and Hare – which one escaped death by hanging by turning king's evidence?

12 Which female name grew in popularity after Grace Kelly played a character with the name in the 1956 film 'High Society'?

13 A 19th century French poet, he abandoned writing at the age of 20 to become an explorer and gun-runner during which time his ex-lover Verlaine published his work without his permission claiming he was dead. Name the poet.

14 Which metallic element, symbol Os, is used in the making of pen nibs and light-bulb filaments and like platinum is a useful catalyst?

15 What are formed during the process known as orogenesis?

Answers 1 Tie-Break 2 Dolly Parton 3 New Orleans 4 36 (4 + 12 + 20) 5 Jay Gatsby 6 Zugspitze 7 Ogden Nash 8 David Wark 9 'Colonel' Tom Parker 10 Mace 11 Hare 12 Tracy 13 Arthur Rimbaud 14 Osmium 15 Mountains

1 American Football. Which team lost three Superbowls in four years, 1974, 1975 and 1977 after having lost previously in 1970?

2 The coronations of most of the French kings took place in which city in the Marne department in north eastern France?

3 Which American writer of short stories was born William Sydney Porter in 1862? He started writing whilst in prison for embezzlement where he adopted which pseudonym.

4 Kitzbuhel is a ski resort in which country?

5 And in which country is the ski resort of Val Gardena?

6 Which American compiled a book of 'Familiar Quotations' in 1855?

7 Van Gogh cut off part of his own left ear during a quarrel with which other artist?

8 Which French composer was influenced in his early years by friendships with a number of impressionist painters and by the Javanese gamelan music he heard at the 1889 Paris Exposition?

9 To which breed of dog was Longfellow referring when he wrote: 'A traveller, by the faithful hound, half-buried in the snow was found'?

10 Of which French writer did philosopher A.J. Ayer say: "I much prefer his plays to his philosophy. Existentialism works much better in the theatre than in theory"?

11 Who had an occasional role as Guinan, the female bartender in the Ten Forward lounge in the TV series 'Star Trek: The Next Generation'?

12 What is the name of Princess Anne's daughter?

13 What were composer G. F. Handel's first names?

14 And what were the famous composer J. S. Bach's first names?

15 Who, shortly before her 57th birthday on 26 November 1996 said: "I may be nearly 57 but I'm still wild. I don't want to go on stage all dressed up and just stand before the microphone"?

MISCELLANEOUS 3 — Quiz 63

1 What type of creature created panic among players and spectators at the Lipton Tennis Championships in Florida on 21 March 1997 causing a match between Venus Williams and Ginger Helgeson to be held up for 18 minutes until the creature was trapped and caught?

2 In which year of the 1980s was the wreck of the Titanic discovered?

3 French chemist Joseph Niepce took the first what in 1826?

4 Which 19th century American writer offered the advice: "Beware of all enterprises that require new clothes"?

5 In which novel does Tolstoy describe a Russian wolf hunt using borzois?

6 The opera 'The Snow Maiden' was written in the early 1880s by which Russian composer?

7 The town of Golden, Colorado is the home of which brand of beer?

8 Which beer is made in Wisconsin and is said to be 'the beer that made Milwaukee famous'?

9 Name the actor who won the Oscar for Best Supporting Actor for his role in the 1971 film 'The Last Picture Show'. Earlier in his career he appeared in several westerns, most notably 'She Wore A Yellow Ribbon' and 'Wagon Master'.

10 Which film star is a cousin of two former New Zealand cricket captains?

11 The 1968 film 'The Planet Of The Apes' was based on the novel 'Monkey Planet' written by which French author who died in 1994?

12 In which South American capital city would you find Palermo Park and the famous Teatro Colon opera house?

13 According to the traditional Irish song, who 'wheeled her wheelbarrow through streets broad and narrow'?

14 In which German city was the composer Johannes Brahms born?

15 Which rock band, best remembered for their song 'Born To Be Wild', took their name from a 1920s novel by German-born writer Hermann Hesse?

Answers 1 A rat 2 1985 3 Photograph 4 Henry David Thoreau 5 War And Peace 6 Nikolai Rimsky-Korsakov 7 Coors 8 Schlitz 9 Ben Johnson 10 Russell Crowe 11 Pierre Boulle 12 Buenos Aires 13 Sweet Molly Malone 14 Hamburg 15 Steppenwolf

MISCELLANEOUS 3 *Quiz 64*

1   Name the American dramatist who wrote the play 'The Little Foxes', later adapted into a movie starring Bette Davis.

2   Which Australian cricketer, considered to be the greatest ever batsman, died in February 2001 aged 92?

3   Whose first sight of the interior of the White House prompted her to say: "It looks like it's been furnished by discount stores. There is no trace of the past"?

4   Irish president Eamon De Valera presented US president John F. Kennedy with a dog called Shannon. What breed of dog was it?

5   In which 1961 Disney comedy film was a substance called 'flubber' invented?

6   Mozart's 'Symphony No. 38 in D Major' was named after which European city to commemorate it's first performance during his visit there in 1787?

7   Executed at the Nuremberg trials, which German politician had been ambassador to the UK from 1936 to 1938 and then German foreign minister until 1945?

8   In which country did McDonalds open their first beef-free restaurant on 13 October 1996?

9   Name the small island off the coast of Nova Scotia, the scene of many shipwrecks, which is known as 'the graveyard of the Atlantic'.

10 In which year did the evacuation of allied troops from the beaches of Dunkirk take place?

11 Nearly a third of the total population of Illinois live in which US city?

12 Which dancer and actress, at one time engaged to Frank Sinatra, appeared with Sinatra in the movie 'Can-Can' and with Elvis Presley in the film 'G.I. Blues'?

13 Which computer peripheral was first conceived and designed by American Douglas Engelbart?

14 Which British writer was born in Bombay in 1865, some of his best novels and short stories being set in India?

15 John Diefenbaker was Prime Minister of which country from 1957 to 1963?

Answers 1 Lillian Hellman **2** Donald Bradman **3** Jacqueline Kennedy **4** Cocker Spaniel **5** The Absent Minded Professor **6** Prague **7** Joachim von Ribbentrop **8** India **9** Sable Island **10** 1940 **11** Chicago **12** Juliet Prowse **13** Mouse **14** Rudyard Kipling **15** Canada

1 Which American novelist wrote: "If you pick up a starving dog and make him prosperous, he will not bite you. This is the principal difference between a dog and man"?

2 The composer Richard Strauss was born in which German city in 1864?

3 Cooperstown, New York is acclaimed as the birthplace of which sport, it being the location for the sport's National Hall Of Fame?

4 In 1996, which actress said she was 'dead chuffed' to receive an Emmy for her role in 'Prime Suspect'?

5 The Coromandel Coast is the name given to part of the south-east coast of which Asian country?

6 Who inherited the Australian Consolidated Press group from his father Frank?

7 The Vedas are the sacred scriptures of which religion?

8 In which country are the mountain ranges known as the Inland and Seaward Kaikouras?

9 There are two Colorado rivers in the USA. The most famous runs through the Grand Canyon, the other flows through which state capital city?

10 Who is the French director of the 1973 Oscar winning best foreign film 'Day For Night', who appeared in the 1977 movie 'Close Encounters Of The Third Kind'?

11 In Norse mythology, what is the name given to the fates – Urth, Verthandi and Skuld – the three females who shaped the life of man?

12 The Dutch artist Vincent Van Gogh died in which country?

13 The Mount Rushmore National Memorial is a gigantic sculpture of the heads of four US presidents. They are Washington, Jefferson, Lincoln and which other?

14 Which actor played the title role in the 1960s TV medical drama series 'Ben Casey'?

15 Who was Britain's Prime Minister at the outbreak of World War One?

1 Famous for it's knitted goods, which sparsely inhabited island is situated in the North Sea between the Orkney and Shetland Islands?

2 Name the American general who owned a white Bull Terrier named Willie who accompanied the troops during the Second World War.

3 Zaccaria, Ismaela and Fenena are all characters in which Verdi opera?

4 With which sport do you associate the Italians Luca Cadalora, Loris Capirossi and Max Biaggi?

5 Jan Smuts was Prime Minister of which country from 1919 to 1924 and again from 1939 to 1948?

6 Who wrote the stories about Brer Rabbit and his friends which were narrated by Uncle Remus?

7 In 1996, which 80 year-old Hollywood actor became a father for the twelfth time when his former secretary Kathy Benvin gave birth to a boy named Ryan?

8 Kairouan is an ancient holy Islamic city in which African country?

9 Which two European countries are connected by the Pass of Roncesvalles?

10 What does the R stand for in the name of former US president Gerald R. Ford?

11 Born in the West Indies in 1830, which French impressionist painter participated in all eight of the impressionist exhibitions between 1874 and 1886 and was noted for his encouragement of younger painters such as Cézanne and Gauguin?

12 Who played Steve Keller in the TV series 'The Streets Of San Francisco' before becoming a Hollywood star?

13 Cape Trafalgar, where the famous naval battle of 1805 took place, is off the coast of which country?

14 In Herman Melville's novel 'Moby Dick', what is the name of Captain Ahab's ship?

15 What's the name of the ginger tom in T.S. Eliot's 'Old Possum's Book Of Practical Cats' known as the 'Napoleon of Crime'?

---

1   Name the Bavarian-born composer who wrote the opera 'Orfeo'.

2   Which British soldier and inventor designed the first tank to have caterpillar tracks which enabled it to crush barbed wire and climb over trenches?

3   What's the surname of Leon and Michael, brothers who both won boxing gold medals at the 1976 Olympics and who both went on to become world champions in the professional ranks?

4   Edwin Landseer's painting 'Dignity And Impudence' features a large dog and a small dog sharing a kennel. What breed is the large dog?

5   Which actress played Mindy opposite Robin Williams' Mork in the TV series 'Mork And Mindy'?

6   What was the nickname of American gangster George Kelly?

7   Name the American statesman and scientist who used the pseudonym Richard Saunders for articles he contributed to 'Poor Richard's Almanac', a publication he himself started?

8   Who is missing from this list of Czar Nicholas II's children – Alexis, Olga, Tatania, Maria and…?

9   In which West African country was president Samuel Doe captured by rebel forces and put to death in September 1990?

10 Which is the most easterly of the Canary Islands?

11 What type of birds caused the postponement of a US space shuttle launch in June 1995?

12 Which city situated in the foothills of the Himalayas was the summer capital of India from 1865 to 1939?

13 Which acid, used as an antiseptic, in food preparation and dyestuffs is the active constituent of aspirin?

14 Braidism, after James Braid who introduced it into medicine, is another name for what?

15 Which US president is the subject of Walt Whitman's poem 'When Lilacs Last In The Courtyard Bloom'd'?

Answers 1 C. W. Gluck **2** Ernest Swinton **3** Spinks **4** Bloodhound **5** Pam Dawber **6** Machine-Gun **7** Benjamin Franklin **8** Anastasia **9** Liberia **10** Lanzarote **11** Woodpeckers **12** Simla **13** Salicylic **14** Hypnosis **15** Abraham Lincoln

1   In which Puccini opera do the characters Edmondo, Des Grieux and Geronte di Ravoir appear?

2   Tennis player Andre Agassi's father Emmanuel emigrated to the US from which country?

3   Published in 1898, which George Bernard Shaw play was not performed until 1902, mainly because of it's controversial treatment of the subject of prostitution?

4   Which famous American general travelled with a pack of 40 coursing dogs and was racing the dogs the day before he left on a fateful expedition in 1876?

5   Name the Italian-born painter famous for his portraits of Queen Elizabeth II and John F. Kennedy.

6   Which is the most northerly of Japan's four main islands?

7   Epidemic or classical typhus (not to be confused with typhoid fever) is spread from person to person by what?

8   Bob Hope and Bing Crosby appeared in seven 'Road' films. Singapore, Zanzibar, Morocco, Rio, Bali and Hong Kong were the destinations in six of them, what was the title of the fourth in the series, released in 1946?

9   In which year of the 1950s was the 'Treaty of Rome' signed which led to the establishment of the EEC?

10 Name the character played by Doug McClure in the TV western series 'The Virginian'.

11 Undulant fever is another name for which infectious disease that affects farm animals?

12 Australians refer to which of their states as the 'cabbage patch'?

13 In Jack London's novel 'The Call Of The Wild', what's the name of the dog who became leader of the sled team and then ran away to join a wolf pack?

14 In which country was the sculptor and woodcarver Grinling Gibbons born?

15 Which long, narrow bay, an inlet of the Atlantic Ocean between Nova Scotia and New Brunswick, is famous for it's high tides from which electricity is generated?

Answers 1 Manon Lescaut 2 Iran 3 Mrs. Warren's Profession 4 George Armstrong Custer 5 Pietro Annigoni 6 Hokkaido 7 Lice 8 Road To Utopia 9 1957 10 Trampas 11 Brucellosis 12 Victoria 13 Buck 14 The Netherlands 15 Bay of Fundy

1   'Vision Of A Knight' and 'The Marriage Of The Virgin' are works by which Italian Renaissance painter?

2   What was the name of the deadly virus which struck in Zaire in 1995?

3   In 1931, Zeppo Marx of the Marx Brothers and his wife acquired two dogs in England. The dogs, official names Asra of Ghazni and Westmill Omar, became the foundation dogs of which breed in America?

4   In which year was Olaf Palme, the Swedish premier, shot?

5   'Manon' is the title of an opera written by which French composer?

6   What, in medical terms, is the name given to a fracture in which the broken bone pierces the skin?

7   What name is given to a fracture of a bone of a child in which the bone is partly bent and splinters only on the convex side of the bend?

8   The name Soweto, the township outside Johannesburg, is derived from which three words?

9   In 1988, he managed the George Bush presidential campaign and after winning the election Bush made him secretary of state. Name him.

10 Highly acclaimed Japanese film director Akira Kurosawa's 1985 film 'Ran' is a samurai version of which Shakespeare play?

11 And Kurosowa's film 'The Throne Of Blood' was his adaptation of which Shakespeare play?

12 Which Hungarian-born American architect designed the UNESCO building in Paris, completed in 1958?

13 The five highest waterfalls in Europe are all to be found in which country?

14 Name the 19th century Italian composer who wrote the opera 'La Gioconda'.

15 Peter Wolf was lead singer of the rock group the J. Geils Band for 16 years. He was married for a short time to which Hollywood actress?

Answers 1 Raphael 2 Ebola 3 Afghan Hound 4 1986 5 Jules Massenet 6 Compound fracture 7 Greenstick fracture 8 South Western Township 9 James Baker 10 King Lear 11 Macbeth 12 Marcel Lajos Breuer 13 Norway 14 Amilcare Ponchielli 15 Faye Dunaway

MISCELLANEOUS 3

1 Athletics. In 1994, which Irishman became the first man over the age of 40 to run a sub-4 minute mile? A great favourite on the indoor circuit in the US, in 1983 he had set the world indoor record for the mile which was not broken until the late 1990s.

2 Name the lake in Ethiopia that is the source of the Blue Nile.

3 The court musician to the Duke of Mantua, which Italian composer of around 50 operas lived from 1671 to 1750 and was an influence on J. S. Bach?

4 'The Prince And The Pauper' and 'A Connecticut Yankee In King Arthur's Court' are novels written by which American author?

5 An unsuccessful assassination attempt was made on the life of which African leader in Addis Ababa on 26 June 1995?

6 Name the female American writer who went to live in Paris in 1903 and became the patron of avant garde artists such as Picasso and Braque.

7 Prince Aly Khan was the third husband of which Hollywood film actress?

8 In which novel does Emile Zola depict life in a French mining community?

9 The Johann Wyss novel 'Swiss Family Robinson' was first published in which language?

10 On which Mediterranean island could you visit the walled city of Medina, take a cruise to the spectacular Blue Grotto or laze on the beach at Mellieha Bay?

11 And on which Aegean island could you visit the Valley of the Butterflies, see the Acropolis at Lindos or stay in the lively resort of Ixia?

12 Name the American champion of women's rights and dress reform who lived from 1818 to 1894 and gave her name to an item of clothing.

13 Which 4th century Roman christian and martyr is the patron saint of virgins? Her emblem is a lamb and her feast day is 21 January.

14 Following judicial approval in January 1995, which animals were re-introduced into the USA's Yellowstone National Park after an absence of 60 years?

15 The orchestral rhapsody 'Espana' is the best known work of which 19th century French composer?

Answers 1 Eamonn Coghlan 2 Lake T'ana 3 Tomaso Albinoni 4 Mark Twain 5 President Mubarak of Egypt 6 Gertrude Stein 7 Rita Hayworth 8 Germinal 9 German 10 Malta 11 Rhodes 12 Amelia Bloomer 13 St. Agnes 14 Wolves 15 Emmanuel Chabrier

MISCELLANEOUS 3 — Quiz 71

1 According to Christian tradition, which saint was the mother of the Virgin Mary, whose feast day is 26 July?

2 Of the 11 founder members of OPEC, which was the only South American country?

3 In August 1995, which of the Leeward Islands had to be evacuated due to the threat of a volcanic eruption?

4 Name the English baroque architect, trained by Wren, who collaborated with Vanbrugh on the building of Castle Howard and Blenheim Palace.

5 The sea, or shipping forecast areas of North Utsire and South Utsire are off the coast of which country?

6 In space technology, what is 'comsat' short for?

7 Which novel by Dostoyevsky tells of a father murdered by one of his sons?

8 How many events are there in an heptathlon?

9 Which Hollywood actress and her fiancé Tom Green were saved by the barking of their dog Flossie when fire destroyed their home in February 2001?

10 Held every twelve years and lasting several weeks, what is the name of the religious festival that attracts millions of Hindus to the river Ganges?

11 Which US city has an area known as Foggy Bottom, a nickname sometimes given to the city itself?

12 What name is given to rain that has absorbed sulphur dioxide and oxides of nitrogen from the atmosphere?

13 Jodie Foster played Clarice Starling in the movie 'The Silence Of The Lambs' but which actress played the role in the sequel, 'Hannibal'?

14 On what date is Armistice Day celebrated?

15 In the Bible, the Gospel according to whom is the first book of the New Testament?

MISCELLANEOUS 3 *Quiz 72*

1. Which 17th century English Cavalier poet wrote one of his best known poems 'To Althea, From Prison' while he was in prison?

2. After his initial meeting with British Prime Minister Tony Blair in February 2001, US president George W. Bush was asked by reporters what they had in common. Bush replied by saying they both used which product?

3. What activity links the following films – 'Blood And Sand', 'The Kid From Spain' and 'The Sun Also Rises'?

4. Of the comedy duo Abbott and Costello, who died first?

5. Which city on the river Vienne is the centre of the French porcelain industry?

6. What is the main ingredient of a soubise sauce which provides it's distinctive flavour?

7. What is the meaning of the prefix 'kara' in Japanese words such as karate and karaoke?

8. How many dancers feature in a 'pas de deux'?

9. Is Provence in the north or south of France?

10. What are the playing periods in a game of Polo called?

11. In the 'Jungle Book', what type of creature was Baloo?

12. What breed of dog was Nana, the dog featured in 'Peter Pan'?

13. Name the beef dish which gets it's name from a Russian count.

14. Who, in a 1977 film said: "Hey, don't knock masturbation. It's sex with someone I love"?

15. Tennis. After her career seemed to be in ruins, who marked her comeback by winning her first 'Grand Slam' tournament, the 2001 Australian Open championship?

Answers 1 Richard Lovelace **2** Colgate toothpaste **3** Bullfighting **4** Lou Costello **5** Limoges **6** Onion **7** Empty **8** 2 **9** South **10** Chukkas **11** Bear **12** Newfoundland **13** Beef Stroganoff **14** Woody Allen **15** Jennifer Capriati

MISCELLANEOUS 3 — Quiz 73

1   On 28 February 2001, which US city suffered it's worst earthquake in more than half a century?

2   Name the physician and naturalist whose collection of books, manuscripts, pictures etc, formed the nucleus of the British Museum.

3   Which member of the Rolling Stones broke both his legs in a car accident in November 1990?

4   Who became emperor of Japan after the death of Hirohito in 1989?

5   The volcano Cotopaxi is situated in which South American country?

6   Who was vice-president to Lyndon Johnson between 1964 and 1969 but was beaten to the US presidency by Richard Nixon?

7   In the Bible, Noah released two different species of bird to find out if there was any dry land. One was a dove, what was the other?

8   Russian president Boris Yeltsin announced his surprise resignation on 31 December of which year?

9   Which city was the capital of Hungary from 1526 until 1784? Situated on the river Danube it is now the capital of Slovakia.

10 Who played a character called Pedro Jiminez in the film 'The Dirty Dozen' and had a hit with the song 'If I Had A Hammer'?

11 Which seaport and resort in south-east Spain was called Lucentum by the Romans and Al-Akant by the Moors?

12 Traditionally, which herb is used in the making of a pesto sauce?

13 Which former US president once said: "It's true hard work never killed anybody but I figure why take the chance"?

14 In 1872, the Holtermann nugget, the largest gold-bearing nugget ever found, was mined in which country?

15 In the 1970s TV western series 'Alias Smith And Jones', was Hannibal Heyes known as Smith or Jones?

Answers 1 Seattle 2 Hans Sloane 3 Ronnie Wood 4 Akihito 5 Ecuador 6 Hubert Humphrey 7 Raven 8 1999 9 Bratislava 10 Trini Lopez 11 Alicante 12 Basil 13 Ronald Reagan 14 Australia 15 Smith

1   Is Patagonia part of North or South America?

2   According to the book of Kings in the Old Testament, Elisha cured the Syrian captain Naaman of which disease?

3   Who was on the English throne when the Black Death swept across Europe in the 14th century?

4   What are the slender tactile spines or bristles that hang from the jaws of certain fishes, such as carp, called?

5   Who lived to the greatest age – John Lennon or Elvis Presley?

6   During the time of the Vietnam War, who was known as 'Hanoi Jane'?

7   The famous cycle race, the Tour de France, traditionally ends in which city?

8   Which one of the famous comedy duo, Laurel and Hardy, died first?

9   The aviation pioneers, the Wright brothers were born four years apart but which one died thirty-six years before the other – Orville or Wilbur?

10 Which South American country runs some 2,700 miles north to south but is never more than 250 miles wide, east to west?

11 Sloppy Joe's Bar in Key West, Florida has become famous for it's association with which writer?

12 Which boxer once said: "I've seen George Foreman shadow box, and the shadow won"?

13 The support groups Alcoholics Anonymous and Gamblers Anonymous were both initially started in which country?

14 Carlton Barrett and Peter Tosh in 1987 and Junior Braithwaite in 1999 were all shot dead in Jamaica. At one time or another, all three were members of which musical group?

15 What relation is King Juan Carlos of Spain to the country's previous monarch Alfonso XIII?

Answers 1 South 2 Leprosy 3 Edward III 4 Barbels 5 Elvis Presley 6 Jane Fonda 7 Paris 8 Oliver Hardy 9 Wilbur 10 Chile 11 Ernest Hemingway 12 Muhammad Ali 13 USA 14 The Wailers 15 Grandson

CATEGORIES

Art & Literature

ART & LITERATURE — Art 1

1 'Las Meninas' is the masterpiece of which Spanish painter (1599-1660) who Manet referred to as The Painter of Painters?

2 Whose painting of a 'Bowl of Fruit, Bottle and Violin' was done in 1914 during the artist's Synthetic Cubist period?

3 Which French Post Impressionist painted poster designs connected with the Moulin Rouge?

4 Whose four paintings of sunflowers dating from August and September 1888 were intended to decorate the Yellow House in Arles?

5 Anthony van Dyck is best remembered for his representations of which British king?

6 Who painted 'The Virgin of the Rocks' around 1503-06?

7 Which Spanish artist painted a famous portrait of The Duke of Wellington in 1812?

8 Peter Paul were the first names of which artist born in Flanders in 1577?

9 'The Umbrellas' is a famous painting by which French Impressionist?

10 Whose most famous painting is 'The Rake's Progress'?

11 Which French painter born in 1834 is famous as a painter of ballet scenes?

12 'The Self Portrait aged Sixty-Three' is of which Dutch artist painted during the final year of his life in 1669?

13 What nationality was the 15/16th century Renaissance painter Raphael?

14 Which French painter who was faced with increasing poverty after retiring from stockbroking in 1891, left Paris to work in Tahiti where many of his most famous paintings were produced?

15 Who painted the Sistine chapel of the Vatican in Rome?

Answers 1 Velazquez 2 Picasso 3 Toulouse-Lautrec 4 Van Gogh 5 Charles I 6 Leonardo Da Vinci 7 Goya 8 Rubens 9 Renoir 10 William Hogarth 11 Degas 12 Rembrandt 13 Italian 14 Gauguin 15 Michelangelo

ART & LITERATURE   *20ᵗʰ Century Literature 1*

1 Who wrote the futuristic novel 'The Running Man' under the pseudonym Richard Bachman?

2 Name the American novelist who wrote 'As I Lay Dying', 'Intruder In The Dust', 'Absalom, Absalom!' and 'The Sound And The Fury'?

3 'The Stranger', 'The Plague' and 'The Fall' are all English titles of which 1957 Nobel prize for-literature-winning French novelist?

4 Which writer created the detective Charlie Chan?

5 Said to have started the vogue for tough realism in gangster stories, what was the pen name of Rene Raymond?

6 Which John Steinbeck novel is based on the biblical story of Cain and Abel?

7 Which writer, born in Iran and brought up in Rhodesia, wrote 'The Grass Is Singing', 'The Golden Notebook' and 'The Fifth Child'?

8 Name the American novelist and short story writer who wrote 'The Age Of Innocence' and 'The Buccaneers'?

9 Name the Austrian-born American novelist who made her name when 'Grand Hotel' was published in 1930?

10 Which American novelist wrote 'Tobacco Road' and 'God's Little Acre'?

11 Name the American writer of macabre fantasy and science fiction who published 'The Case Of Charles Dexter Ward' and 'At The Mountains Of Madness' in the 1920s and 1930s?

12 The Finnish writer Tove Jansson created a family of creatures which include Snufkin, Fillyjonk and the Snork Maiden. What did she call these creatures?

13 Born in Newark, New Jersey in 1933, which author wrote the novels 'The Anatomy Lesson', 'Portnoy's Complaint' and 'Goodbye Columbus'?

14 Born in Sydney, Australia in 1935 his novels include 'Schindler's Ark', 'The Chant Of Jimmie Blacksmith' and 'The Playmaker'. Name him.

15 Name the American novelist who published the novels 'Martin Arrowsmith' and 'Elmer Gantry' during the 1920s?

Answers 1 Stephen King 2 William Faulkner 3 Albert Camus 4 Earl Biggers 5 James Hadley Chase 6 East Of Eden 7 Doris Lessing 8 Edith Wharton 9 Vicki Baum 10 Erskine Caldwell 11 H. P. Lovecraft 12 Moomins 13 Philip Roth 14 Thomas Keneally 15 Sinclair Lewis

ART & LITERATURE — *What the Dickens! 1*

1 Wackford Squeers is the schoolmaster in which Dickens' novel?

2 Published in 1837, which was Dickens' first novel?

3 Which novel by Dickens was said to be strongly autobiographical?

4 In the preface to which book does Dickens write: 'I have endeavoured in this ghostly little book to raise the ghost of an idea'?

5 Who wrote the musical 'Oliver', which was based on Dickens' novel 'Oliver Twist'?

6 Which novel by Dickens was set during the Gordon riots?

7 Charles Dickens was born near which port on the South coast of England?

8 What pen name was used by Dickens, which he used in the work 'Sketches by…'?

9 What is the first name of the son in the novel 'Domby and Son'?

10 'It was the best of times, it was the worst of times' are the opening words of which Dickens' novel?

11 For what was Charles Dickens' father imprisoned when Charles was aged 12?

12 What was the pseudonym of H.K. Browne who illustrated most of Charles Dickens' work?

13 What is the name of the convict in 'Great Expectations'?

14 In which church is Charles Dickens buried?

15 Which Dickens' character has been played in the movies by George C Scott (1982), Alec Guinness (1948) and Lon Chaney (1922)?

Answers 1 Nicholas Nickleby 2 The Pickwick Papers 3 David Copperfield 4 A Christmas Carol 5 Lionel Bart 6 Barnaby Rudge 7 Portsmouth 8 Boz 9 Paul 10 A Tale of Two Cities 11 Debt 12 Phiz 13 Magwitch 14 Westminster Abbey 15 Fagin

ART & LITERATURE   *Art 2*

1. Who painted 'The Madonna and Child with Saint John the Baptist and Saint Nicholas of Bari' (The Ansidei Madonna) in 1505?

2. Which Venetian painter, whose works include 'Venus and Adonis' (1554) was court painter to the Holy Roman Emperor Charles V?

3. Which leading French impressionist painter is famous for several scenes of his beloved garden at Giverny?

4. Can you name the English portrait painter whose subjects include his portrait (1783-5) of Mrs Siddons, the daughter of the actor Roger Kemble?

5. Which Italian religious painter killed an opponent in a duel in 1606? His works include 'Salome receives the Head of St. John the Baptist'.

6. Who, in 1812, painted 'The Hay Wain'?

7. Who was the English portrait painter (1878-1961) whose subjects include Dylan Thomas (1938) and Tallulah Bankhead (1933), which is now in the National Portrait Gallery in Washington D.C.?

8. Henri Matisse was the leader of which short-lived movement in French painting (1905-10) whose name literally meant the wild beasts?

9. Which French painter (1883-1955) was the son of painter Suzanne Valadon, who was his only art teacher?

10. Which English painter and specialist in the drawings of birds, was also a noted humorist and master of the limerick?

11. Which American painter and leading figure in the artistic avant-garde of Paris in the 1920s was a noted photographer?

12. Which American painter's works include 'Harmony in Grey and Green', 'Miss Cicily Alexander', and 'The Artist's Mother'?

13. The British artist George Stubbs is famous for his paintings of which animal?

14. Who, in 1924, painted 'The Laughing Cavalier'?

15. Which Spanish surrealist's 1955 work, 'The Sacrament of the Last Supper' is in the National Gallery of Art in Washington D.C.?

Answers 1 Raphael 2 Titian 3 Monet 4 Gainsborough 5 Caravaggio 6 Constable 7 Augustus John 8 Fauvism 9 Maurice Utrillo 10 Edward Lear 11 Man Ray 12 James Whistler 13 Horses 14 Frans Hals 15 Salvador Dali

1   Name the American author who wrote the novels 'V', 'The Crying Of Lot 49', 'Gravity's Rainbow', 'Vineland' and 'Mason & Dixon'?

2   What was the name of the very fast horse given to Gandalf by King Theoden in Tolkein's 'The Lord Of The Rings'?

3   Who wrote the love poem 'A Red, Red Rose' which starts with the lines – 'O my love is like a red, red rose; That's newly sprung in June'?

4   The detectives Cordelia Gray and Adam Dalgleish were created by which female thriller writer?

5   Name the Canadian novelist who's first book was the phenomenally successful 'Anne Of Green Gables'?

6   'Indecent Obsession', 'The Ladies Of Missalonghi', 'The Thorn Birds' and 'Morgan's Run' are all novels written by which Australian author?

7   Who's greatest work was 'Faust', a poetic drama of the aspirations of man?

8   What is the first name of Smiley, the spy created by writer John Le Carré?

9   Who wrote the Booker Prize winning novel 'The English Patient' which was adapted into a successful film?

10 What was the surname of the character William, created by writer Richmal Crompton?

11 Which former tennis player, has co-written with Liz Nickles, several thrillers featuring a former tennis champion turned sleuth named Jordan Myles?

12 Name the American writer of children's stories who wrote the Katy series of books, including 'What Katy Did'?

13 Expelled by the Soviet Writer's Union, which writer had to take the unprecedented step of refusing the Nobel prize for Literature in 1958?

14 Name Don Quixote's squire?

15 Name the Spanish novelist who achieved fame with his vivid portrayal of World War One, 'The Four Horsemen Of The Apocalypse'?

14 Sancho Panza 15 Vicente Ibanez
Ondaatje 10 Brown 11 Martina Navratilova 12 Susan Coolidge 13 Boris Pasternak
Montgomery 6 Colleen McCullough 7 Johann Wolfgang Von Goethe 8 George 9 Michael
Answers 1 Thomas Pynchon 2 Shadowfax 3 Robert Burns 4 P. D. James 5 Lucy Maud

ART & LITERATURE — *What the Dickens! 2*

1 During which decade of the 19th-century did Dickens die?

2 …and which novel did he leave unfinished at his death?

3 In 'A Christmas Carol', who was the clerk to Ebeneezer Scrooge?

4 The 'Ivy Green' is a poem from which work by Dickens?

5 The court case of Jarndyce v Jarndyce features in which Dickens' novel?

6 Betsy Trotwood is the aunt of which character?

7 Dickens fathered how many children, 5, 8 or 10?

8 In which novel do Mr and Mrs Fezziwig appear?

9 In 'A Tale of Two Cities', what are the two cities?

10 What was the profession of Ellen Ternan, with whom Dickens had a relationship which led to his separation from his wife in 1858?

11 In which book does Augustus Snodgrass appear?

12 Which Dickens' character isolates herself in her cobweb-festooned mansion in the novel 'Great Expectations'?

13 Gradgrind is the central character of which novel?

14 In the 1935 movie version of 'David Copperfield' which screen comedian played Mr Micawber?

15 The title character of which Dickens' novel was born at Marshalsea Prison, which was the same prison in which Dickens' father was incarcerated?

Answers 1 1870s (1870) 2 The Mystery of Edwin Drood 3 Bob Cratchit 4 Pickwick Papers 5 Bleak House 6 David Copperfield 7 10 8 A Christmas Carol 9 London and Paris 10 Actress 11 Pickwick Papers 12 Miss Havisham 13 Hard Times 14 W.C.Fields 15 Little Dorrit

ART & LITERATURE   *20ᵗʰ Century Literature 2*

1   Born in Trinidad of Indian descent, which novelist wrote the novels 'A House For Mr. Biswas', 'In A Free State' and 'A Bend In The River'?

2   What's the title of the book published in 1979 by Kit Williams which contained a riddle that for two years involved millions of readers around the world in the search for a golden hare?

3   Who wrote the poem 'Annus Mirabilis' which opens with the lines – 'Sexual intercourse began in nineteen sixty three (which was rather late for me) – between the end of the Chatterley ban and the Beatles' first LP'?

4   Born in London of Australian parents, who in 1973, became the first Australian to win the Nobel prize for Literature?

5   How is Dolores Haze better known in an eponymous novel first published in Paris in 1955?

6   What is the name of the heroine of Truman Capote's novel 'Breakfast At Tiffany's'?

7   Born in Prague, who wrote the novels 'The Trial and 'The Castle', both published after his death in 1924?

8   In which novel by Australian author Patrick White does Oliver Halliday, the wannabe 'nature poet' appear?

9   Who has written a series of best-selling novels featuring the heroine Emma Harte?

10 Published in 1958, 'Exodus' is the best known book of which American author?

11 Published in 1926, 'The Sun Also Rises' helped to establish the reputation of which American novelist?

12 James Farrell's Studs Lonigan trilogy of novels tells of life on the south side of which US city?

13 Name the American writer who died at the age of 44 in 1940 with his novel 'The Last Tycoon' left unfinished?

14 Holden Caulfield is the main character of which American novel that was rather controversial when first published in 1951?

15 'From Feathers To Iron', 'An Italian Visit' and 'The Magnetic Mountain' are all collections of poems written by whom?

Answers 1 V. S. Naipaul 2 Masquerade 3 Philip Larkin 4 Patrick White 5 Lolita 6 Holly Golightly 7 Franz Kafka 8 Happy Valley 9 Barbara Taylor Bradford 10 Leon Uris 11 Ernest Hemingway 12 Chicago 13 F. Scott Fitzgerald 14 The Catcher In The Rye 15 Cecil Day Lewis

ART & LITERATURE — *Works of Shakespeare 1*

1 Polonius and his children Laertes and Ophelia are characters in which play?

2 Shylock is the leading male character in which play?

3 'Once more unto the breach, dear friends, once more'; 'Or close the wall up with our English dead' are quotations from which play?

4 Which war forms the background for 'Troilus and Cressida'?

5 What is the 'sack' of which Sir John Falstaff is so fond of in 'Henry IV'?

6 The King of Britain, the King of France, the Duke of Burgundy, the Duke of Cornwall and the Duke of Albany are all characters in which play?

7 Oberon, Titania and Puck are all characters in which play?

8 From which play does the following quotation come: 'The quality of mercy is not strained, it droppeth as the gentle rain from heaven'?

9 In 'Twefth Night', who is the uncle of Olivia?

10 Vincentio, Duke of Vienna is the central character of which play?

11 What name is shared by one of the main characters in 'Two Gentlemen Of Verona' and minor characters in 'Titus Andronicus' and 'Twelfth Night'?

12 And what name is shared by a leading character in 'The Merchant Of Venice' and lesser characters in 'The Tempest', 'Twelfth Night', 'Much Ado About Nothing' and 'Two Gentlemen Of Verona'?

13 Othello is set in Venice and on which Mediterranean island?

14 What is the name of Hamlet's mother?

15 Which physically obese and comical character appears in both 'Henry IV' and 'The Merry Wives Of Windsor'?

Answers 1 Hamlet 2 The Merchant Of Venice 3 Henry V 4 Trojan War 5 Wine 6 King Lear 7 A Midsummer Night's Dream 8 The Merchant Of Venice 9 Sir Toby Belch 10 Measure For Measure 11 Valentine 12 Antonio 13 Cyprus 14 Gertrude 15 Falstaff

ART & LITERATURE — What the Dickens! 3

1 Which nurse was drunk with an umbrella in 'Martin Chuzzlewit'?

2 'God bless us, every one' is the last line of which novel?

3 Which Dickens' character said: "annual income 20 pounds, annual expenditure 19 pounds. Result? Happiness. Annual income, 20 pounds; annual expenditure, 21 pounds. Result? Misery"?

4 What is the name of the school where Nicolas Nickleby teaches?

5 In which novel does Little Emily appear?

6 ...and Little Nell is the central character of which novel?

7 The final words of which great Dickens' hero are: "It is a far, far better thing I do, than I have ever done; it is a far, far better rest that I go to than I have ever known"?

8 In 'Great Expectations', what is the full name of the main character Pip?

9 In 'A Christmas Carol', which ghost is described as a spirit of a kind, generous and hearty nature?

10 Who is the wooden-legged villain in the novel 'Our Mutual Friend'?

11 In which novel does a Christmas Party take place at Dingly Dell?

12 Which British stage and screen entertainer, who was once married to Joan Collins played the Artful Dodger in the 1948 film version of 'Oliver Twist'?

13 In which novel does the villainous Uriah Heep appear?

14 In 'Bleak House', how does the character Krook earn his living?

15 Who was the lame son of Bob Cratchit in 'A Christmas Carol'?

Answers 1 Mrs Sarah Gamp 2 A Christmas Carol 3 Mr Micawber 4 Dotheboys Hall 5 David Copperfield 6 The Old Curiosity Shop 7 Sydney Carton 8 Philip Pirrip 9 Ghost of Christmas Present 10 Silas Wegg 11 Pickwick Papers 12 Anthony Newley 13 David Copperfield 14 He is a rag and bone man 15 Tiny Tim

ART & LITERATURE

Art 3

1 Which celebrated painter of landscapes of America's Wild West was born in Bolton, England in 1837?

2 Name the 20th century Australian painter who made his name with a series of 'Ned Kelly' paintings?

3 Which surrealist artist once described his paintings as 'hand-painted dream photographs'?

4 The 17th century French landscape painter Claude Gelee is better known by the name he adopted from the province where he was born. What was the name?

5 Which French impressionist painter produced a series of works of subjects under different aspects of light including 'Haystacks' and the almost abstract 'Waterlilies'?

6 The Venetian painter Jacopo Robusti, a son of a silk dyer adopted a name meaning 'little dyer'. What is that name by which he is more familiarly known?

7 Which artist was forced to flee Rome in 1606 after he had killed a man after a tennis match?

8 Which Spanish artist, he died in 1828, produced a series of sardonic etchings entitled 'The Disasters Of War' condemning the Napoleonic invasion of Spain?

9 Which Venetian artist painted many portraits of Holy Roman Emperor Charles V during the 16th century?

10 'Le Moulin de la Galette' is one of the best known works of which Limoges born artist?

11 Born in Aix-en-Provence, which artist's works include 'The Suicide's' House and 'The Card Players'?

12 In which country was Willem de Kooning, one of America's leading avant-garde painters, born?

13 Spanish Guitar Player and Olympia are major works of which 19th century French artist?

14 Which 19th century English artist painted 'The Light Of The World' and 'The Finding Of Christ In The Temple'?

15 By what name is renaissance painter Guido di Pietro better known?

Answers 1 Thomas Moran 2 Sidney Nolan 3 Salvador Dali 4 Claude Lorraine 5 Claude Monet 6 Tintoretto 7 Caravaggio 8 Goya 9 Titian 10 Pierre Auguste Renoir 11 Paul Cezanne 12 The Netherlands 13 Edouard Manet 14 Holman Hunt 15 Fra Angelico

ART & LITERATURE *20ᵗʰ Century Literature 3*

1 Which Australian-born novelist wrote 'The Devil's Advocate', 'The Shoes Of The Fisherman', 'The Tower Of Babel' and 'The Clowns Of God'?

2 Adapted into films 'The Postman Always Rings Twice' and 'Double Indemnity' are novels written by which American author?

3 In the 1930s, which writer published the monumental US trilogy comprising of '42nd Parallel', '1919' and 'The Big Money'?

4 Name the Dutch detective created by Nicholas Freeling?

5 Which British author published the cynical novels 'Chrome Yellow' and 'Point Counter Point' in the 1920s?

6 Who wrote the Cold War thriller 'The Hunt For Red October'?

7 Name the Italian author whose first two novels were entitled 'The Name Of The Rose' and 'Foucault's Pendulum'?

8 'Words Without Music', 'The Last Of England' and 'The Cost Of Seriousness' are all collections of which Australian poet?

9 What's the title of Roald Dahl's sequel to 'Charlie And The Chocolate Factory'?

10 Who wrote the novel 'The Witches Of Eastwick' on which the popular film starring Jack Nicholson was based?

11 'The Fifth Element', 'Carpe Jugulum' and 'The Dark Side Of The Sun' were all written by which sci-fi novelist?

12 Published in 1952, who wrote the novel 'The Old Man And The Sea', a classic tale of fisherman versus marlin?

13 Complete the title of John Gray's best-selling book 'Men Are From Mars, Women Are From …'?

14 Which US diplomat, a former secretary of state and Nobel peace prize winner, published the books 'The White House Years' in 1979 and 'Years Of Upheaveal' in 1982?

15 Which famous fictional lawyer first appeared in the novel 'The Case Of The Velvet Claws' published in 1933?

Answers 1 Morris West 2 James M. Cain 3 John Dos Passos 4 Piet van der Valk 5 Aldous Huxley 6 Tom Clancy 7 Umberto Eco 8 Peter Porter 9 Charlie And The Great Glass Elevator 10 John Updike 11 Terry Pratchett 12 Ernest Hemingway 13 Venus 14 Henry Kissinger 15 Perry Mason

Art & Literature *20th Century Artistic Works*

1 Which Nigerian-born novelist wrote 'Anthills Of The Savannah'?

2 Born in Rome in 1880, he went to Paris at the age of 20 where he wrote his famous 'Chanson du mal-aime' or 'Song of the Poorly Loved'. Name this poet?

3 With which field of the arts do you associate Yasujiro Ozu?

4 'Rekviem' (or Requiem) is one of the major works of which Russian poet recognized at her death in 1966 as the greatest woman Russian poet?

5 Published in 1966, 'Death of a Naturalist' was the first poetry collection of which Irish poet who won the Nobel Prize for Literature in 1995?

6 Published in 1940, which Ernest Hemingway novel was about the Spanish Civil War?

7 Name the US novelist whose first and finest novel was the semi-autobiographical 'Go Tell It On The Mountain'?

8 Published in 1965, 'Ariel' is a collection of the later poems of which American female who died in 1963?

9 'Autumn Rhythm' is the title of a mural-size canvas of which US painter?

10 A National Book award-winner, 'Herzog' published in 1964 was written by which Canadian-born American writer?

11 The 1956 movie 'The Seventh Seal' is considered to be a masterpiece of which film-maker?

12 Really the story of his own life, which French novelist produced the 13-volume 'A la Recherche du Temps Perdu'?

13 Published in 1946 'North and South' was the first book of poetry published by which Pulitzer prize-winning US female poet?

14 What was the nationality of the essayist, poet and short-story writer Jorge Luis Borges whose works have become classics of 20th century world literature?

15 With what do you associate Andre Kertesz?

Answers 1 Chinua Achebe 2 Guillaime Apollinaire 3 Films 4 Anna Akhmatova 5 Seamus Heaney 6 For Whom The Bell Tolls 7 James Baldwin 8 Sylvia Plath 9 Jackson Pollock 10 Saul Bellow 11 Ingmar Bergman 12 Marcel Proust 13 Elizabeth Bishop 14 Argentinian 15 Photography

ART & LITERATURE

The Bible

1   Which book of the Old Testament recounts the wanderings of the Israelites in the wilderness?

2   The first miracle performed by Jesus took place at a wedding feast in which town?

3   To which land did Cain go after killing Abel?

4   His name means 'son of good luck', who was the youngest son of Jacob?

5   According to the book of Genesis, with what type of wood did Noah build the Ark?

6   And what sign did God give to Noah as a promise that the earth would not be flooded again?

7   Which man did God test by asking him to sacrifice his only son, later allowing him to sacrifice a ram instead?

8   According to the Book of Revelations, who were the two attendant powers of Satan?

9   In the Old Testament, who was the father of David?

10 In the New Testament, who's gospel starts with the words: 'In the beginning was the Word, and the Word was with God, and the Word was God'?

11 According to chapter 9 of the book of Proverbs, how many pillars has wisdoms' house?

12 How many psalms are there in the book of Psalms?

13 Which book of the Old Testament tells of the burning fiery furnace and the writing on the wall?

14 According to the book of Judges, with what did Samson slay one thousand men?

15 Which book of the Old Testament tells the story of a blameless man who loses his money, his health and his family, everything except his belief in God?

Answers 1 Numbers 2 Cana 3 Land of Nod 4 Benjamin 5 Gopher wood 6 A Rainbow 7 Abraham 8 Gog and Magog 9 Jesse 10 St. John 11 7 12 150 13 Daniel 14 The jawbone of an ass 15 Job

CATEGORIES

What the Dickens! 4

1   In the 1958 film version of 'A Tale of Two Cities', who plays Sydney Carton?

2   Which central Dickens' character marries Madeline Bray?

3   In 'Oliver Twist', who is the Beadle who is horrified when Oliver asks for more?

4   John Harmon is a character in which Dickens' novel?

5   The solicitor Jaggers appears in which novel?

6   Dora Spenlow and Agnes Wickfield were the wives of which eponymous Dickens' character?

7   In 'Great Expectations', who is the blacksmith and brother-in-law of Pip with whom he works as an apprentice?

8   What is the first name of the title character 'Little Dorrit'?

9   In which novel does the character Bucket appear?

10   Kit Nupples is the friend of which of Dickens' central characters?

11   In the 1920s, British censors objected to the release of a silent film version of which Dickens' novel because they felt it might encourage hooliganism in England?

12   Sam Weller is a servant in which Dickens' novel?

13   Who does Sydney Carton sacrifice his life for in 'A Tale of Two Cities'?

14   What is the name of the dwarf in 'The Old Curiosity Shop'?

15   In 'Great Expectations', who is the love of Pip's life?

Answers 1 Dirk Bogarde 2 Nicolas Nickleby 3 Mr Bumble 4 Our Mutual Friend 5 Great Expectations 6 David Copperfield 7 Joe Gargery 8 Amy 9 Hard Times 10 Little Nell 11 Oliver Twist 12 Pickwick Papers 13 Charles Darnley 14 Quilp 15 Estella

Who wrote the following novels:

1   The Magnificent Ambersons / The Gentleman From Indiana / Monsieur Beaucaire?
2   The Postman Always Rings Twice / The Magician's Wife / Rainbow's End?
3   The Sheltering Sky / The Spider's House / Up Above The World?
4   Under The Net / The Flight From The Enchanter / Jackson's Dilemma?
5   Wide Sargasso Sea / Postures / Voyage In The Dark?
6   The Magus / Mantissa / Maggott?
7   Ironweed / The Ink Truck / Very Old Bones?
8   Tobacco Road / God's Little Acre / In Search Of Bisco?
9   Blindness / Living / Loving?
10   Sophie's Choice / Lie Down In Darkness / The Confessions of Nat Turner?
11   Ragtime / Welcome To Hard Times / Billy Bathgate?
12   The Death Of The Heart / The Last September / The House In Paris?
13   Angle Of Repose / The Big Rock Candy Mountain / Remembering Laughter?
14   A High Wind In Jamaica / Gertrude's Child / In Hazard?
15   The Wapshot Chronicles / The Wapshot Scandal / Oh What A Paradise It Seems?

Answers 1 Booth Tarkington 2 James M. Cain 3 Paul Bowles 4 Iris Murdoch 5 Jean Rhys 6 John Fowles 7 William Kennedy 8 Erskine Caldwell 9 Henry Green 10 William Styron 11 E.L.Doctorow 12 Elizabeth Bowen 13 Wallace Stegner 14 Richard Hughes 15 John Cheever

ART & LITERATURE   *Works of Shakespeare 2*

1   Which play has scenes set in a wood near Athens?

2   Which play opens with the exclamation 'Boatswain!'?

3   Complete the title of the following poem – 'The Rape Of ....'?

4   The prologue to which play begins 'Two households, both alike in dignity'?

5   Ferdinand, king of Navarre, Dull a stupid constable and Costard a clown, are all characters in which play?

6   In 'Twelfth Night', who is the steward to Olivia?

7   Which character, shortly before he kills himself, says to Gratiano: 'Be not afraid, though you do see me weapon'd; Here is my journey's end, here is my butt'?

8   In Hamlet, who is described as being 'a fellow of infinite jest, of most excellent fancy'?

9   Nathaniel, Joseph, Nicholas, Philip and Walter are all servants of which character in 'The Taming Of The Shrew'?

10   Which forest is the setting for 'As You Like It'?

11   In a scene of which play do the characters Princess Katherine and her lady-in-waiting Alice converse in French?

12   Which character is described as 'a poor, infirm, weak and despised old man'?

13   Which is the only one of Shakespeare's plays in which the action all takes place in one day and in one place?

14   The greater part of 'Romeo And Juliet' takes part in Verona, but part of Act 5 is set in which other Italian city?

15   'Tush! never tell me; I take it much unkindly' are the opening words of which play?

Answers 1 A Midsummer Night's Dream 2 The Tempest 3 Lucrece 4 Romeo And Juliet 5 Love's Labour's Lost 6 Malvolio 7 Othello 8 Yorick 9 Petruchio 10 Forest of Arden 11 Henry V 12 King Lear 13 The Tempest 14 Mantua 15 Othello

ART & LITERATURE   *The Bible 2*

1   What name is given to the 21 books of the New Testament that were written as letters?

2   In which book of the Old Testament would you find the following words: 'for a living dog is better than a dead lion'?

3   According to the Old Testament, who was awoken by a ship-master and told to call upon his God?

4   Which book of the Old Testament comes between Leviticus and Deuteronomy?

5   What is the content of St. Luke, chapter 11 verses 2 to 4?

6   Verse 15 of chapter 7 of whose gospel refers to 'wolves in sheep's clothing'?

7   According to chapter 9 of the Gospel of St. John, what miracle did Jesus perform at the pool of Siloam?

8   Which is the last book of the Old Testament.

9   According to Exodus, chapter 8, what was the first of the plagues inflicted on the Egyptians?

10 In the Old Testament, who single-handedly killed a lion and a bear that had attacked his father's sheep, before going on to his more famous conquest?

11 Which is the shortest book of the Old Testament, comprising of just one chapter?

12 According to the Gospel of St. Matthew, chapter 6 verse 24, you cannot serve God and … what?

13 Who was the sister of Aaron and Moses?

14 Isaac was the son of Abraham. Who was his mother?

15 Name the woman mentioned in chapters 4 and 5 of the book of Judges who was a judge and a military leader?

Answers 1 Epistles 2 Ecclesiastes 3 Jonah 4 Numbers 5 The Lord's Prayer 6 Matthew 7 He cured a blind man 8 Malachi 9 The rivers were turned into blood 10 David 11 Obadiah 12 Mammon 13 Miriam 14 Sarah 15 Deborah

CATEGORIES

ART & LITERATURE *20ᵗʰ Century Literature 4*

1   Name the Bulgarian-born writer, who in 1981 became the first British citizen since Winston Churchill to win the Nobel Prize for Literature?

2   Which best-selling book by Jung Chang tells the story of 20th century China through the lives of three different women – grandmother, mother and daughter?

3   What is the first name of the Roald Dahl character who lives with his cruel aunts after his parents are eaten by a rhinoceros?

4   Later adapted into a successful film, who wrote the novel 'One Flew Over The Cuckoo's Nest'?

5   In which famous novel would you find the opinion – 'If you want a picture of the future, imagine a boot stamping on a human face – for ever'?

6   Which biochemist turned science fiction writer who died in 1992, wrote a series of novels known as the 'Foundation' novels and the so-called 'Robot' novels?

7   Which female authors first novel 'Pearls' sold over 1.5 million copies and was translated into every European language?

8   What is the title of Shirley Conran's first novel which was a best-seller and later adapted into a TV drama series?

9   In 1940, which American writer published the novel 'Lassie Come Home' which was adapted into a popular film?

10   In Hugh Lofting's story of Dr. Dolittle, what is the name of the doctor's parrot?

11   'Bitter Medicine' and 'Killing Orders' are two of the crime novels concerning a female private investigator in the Loop district of Chicago. Name the author?

12   'The Black Marble', 'The Choirboys' and 'The Secrets Of Harry Bright' are crime novels centred around members of the Los Angeles Police Department. Can you name their author?

13   Who made his name with the best-selling novel 'How Green Was My Valley' which was adapted into a film?

14   Which French writer and resistance fighter wrote the novels 'La Condition Humaine' and 'L'Espoir'?

15   Frederick Forsyth took part of a quotation from Shakespeare's Julius Caesar for the title of which of his novels?

Answers 1 Elias Canetti 2 Wild Swans 3 James 4 Ken Kesey 5 Nineteen Eighty Four 6 Isaac Asimov 7 Celia Brayfield 8 Lace 9 Eric Knight 10 Polynesia 11 Sara Paretsky 12 Joseph Wambaugh 13 Richard Llewellyn 14 Andre Malraux 15 The Dogs Of War

ART & LITERATURE   Art 4

1   Name the Romanian sculptor whose early works include one of a young girl kneeling called 'The Prayer'?

2   Where would you find the Pio-Clementino Museum and the Chiaramonti Sculpture Gallery?

3   In 1768, who became the first president of the Royal Academy?

4   Which American-born artist was also famous as a wit and the author of 'The Gentle Art Of Making Enemies'?

5   The large painting entitled 'Raft Of The Medusa' is the considered masterpiece of which French artist?

6   And the 'Avenue, Middelharns' is considered to be the masterpiece of which Dutch landscape painter?

7   For which monarch did Benvenuto Cellini make his famous gold saltcellar in 1540?

8   Regarded as one of the greatest exponents of classicism, what nationality was the 17th century painter Nicolas Poussin?

9   Which 16th century Venetian artist painted the portraits known as 'Young Man With Cap And Gloves' and 'Man With A Glove'?

10 'Hermes Carrying The Infant Dionysus' and 'Aphrodite Of Cnidos' are two of the most famous works of which ancient Greek sculptor?

11 Name the Russian czar who first commissioned Fabergé to make his famous imperial Easter eggs in 1884?

12 Best remembered for his work 'The Statue of Liberty', which French sculptor carved the massive Lion of Belfort that towers over the French city of Belfort?

13 In which country was the 20th century sculptor Ossip Zadkine born?

14 Born in Italy in 1856, which US portrait painter achieved considerable success with his elegant portraits of celebrities such as Robert Louis Stevenson, Madame X and John D. Rockefeller?

15 Famous for her scenes of circus, gypsy and ballet life, which painter became a member of the Royal Academy in 1936?

Answers 1 Constantin Brancusi 2 The Vatican 3 Joshua Reynolds 4 James McNeill Whistler 5 Theodore Gericault 6 Meindhert Hobbema 7 Francis I of France 8 French 9 Titian 10 Praxiteles 11 Alexander III 12 Frederic-Auguste Bartholdi 13 Russia 14 John Singer Sargent 15 Dame Laura Knight

ART & LITERATURE   *20ᵗʰ Century Literature 5*

1 Who wrote the novels 'The Pied Piper', 'No Highway' and 'Round The Bend'?

2 Who won the 1962 Pulitzer Prize for non-fiction for his book 'The Making of the President', 1960?

3 Which American-born author wrote the lusty comic novel 'The Ginger Man'. His other works include 'The Onion Eaters' and 'A Fairy Tale Of New York'?

4 What is the title of Louis Golding's best known novel, the story of a street in a provincial city where Jews live on one side and Gentiles on the other?

5 Which Russian revolutionary leader wrote 'The Prelude To Bolshevism' and 'The Road To Tragedy'?

6 Which Shanghai-born author wrote the novels 'Empire Of The Sun' and 'Crash'?

7 Which country was the setting for James Clavell's 1986 novel 'Whirlwind' – Iran, Japan or Kenya?

8 'Cry This Peacock', 'Where Shall We Go To This Summer' and 'Clear Light Of Day' are all novels of which female Indian author?

9 Under what name does American Ursula Kroeber write science fiction and fantasy stories?

10 Which two US science fiction writers collaborated to write 'The Space Merchants'?

11 'Speak, Memory' is the title of the autobiography of which Russian-born American novelist who died in 1977?

12 Which US novelist and story writer wrote 'Ten North Frederick', 'Butterfield 8' and 'From The Terrace', all of which were adapted into films?

13 Which US novelist, he died in 1997, wrote 'Hawaii' and 'Centennial'?

14 'The Moor's Last Sigh' and 'The Ground Beneath Her Feet' were written by which Anglo-Indian writer?

15 Name the US born novelist and travel writer who had his first commercial success in 1975 with 'The Great Railway Bazaar' describing his four month train journey through Asia. His novels include 'Jungle Lovers' and 'The Mosquito Coast'?

Answers 1 Nevil Shute 2 Theodore White 3 J.P.Donleavy 4 Magnolia Street 5 Alexander Feodorovitch Kerensky 6 J.G. Ballard 7 Iran 8 Anita Desai 9 Ursula K. Le Guin 10 Frederik Pohl and C.M. Kornbluth 11 Vladimir Nabokov 12 John O'Hara 13 James A. Michener 14 Salman Rushdie 15 Paul Theroux

ART & LITERATURE *Works of Shakespeare 3*

1 Cicero, Calpurnia and Claudius are characters in which play?

2 From which play do the following lines come: 'All that glisters is not gold, often have you heard that told'?

3 In which play does a foolish knight named Sir Andrew Aguecheek appear?

4 In which lesser known play does a character named Pandar and his wife keep a bordello?

5 Another lesser known play, it is set in Athens and the surrounding woods, name it?

6 Proculeius, Thyreus and Gallus are minor characters in which play?

7 In which play do the characters Elbow a comic constable and Froth a foolish gentleman appear?

8 Bernardo and Francisco are two sentries who set the scene in the opening of which play?

9 Leontes, king of Sicilia is a leading character in which play?

10 Launcelot Gobbo is a comic servant of which Shakespearean character?

11 In 'Twelfth Night', which character is tricked into wearing 'yellow stockings, cross gartered' believing that his mistress Olivia would fall in love with him wearing them?

12 In 'The Merry Wives Of Windsor', who hides in a laundry basket?

13 In Act III Scene III of which play is there a stage direction Exit, pursued by a bear?

14 Which play opens with the line: 'Hence! home, you idle creatures, get you home'?

15 What name is used by Viola when disguised as a man in 'Twelfth Night'?

Answers 1 Julius Caesar 2 The Merchant Of Venice 3 Twelfth Night 4 Pericles 5 Timon Of Athens 6 Antony And Cleopatra 7 Measure For Measure 8 Hamlet 9 The Winter's Tale 10 Shylock 11 Malvolio 12 Falstaff 13 The Winter's Tale 14 Julius Caesar 15 Cesario

1   With which art movement do you associate Arp, Duchamp and Schwitters?

2   Correggio's famous work 'The Assumption of the Virgin' can be seen on the cupola of the cathedral of which Italian city?

3   Which Japanese master artist and printmaker was responsible for 'The Breaking Wave off Kanagawa' and 'Thirty-Six Views of Mount Fuji'?

4   'Susannah and the Elders' and 'Flight into Egypt' are works of which late Renaissance painter of the Venetian school?

5   Name the American illustrator, noted for his illustrations of buxom girls and particularly for his World War One recruiting poster of a pointing Uncle Sam?

6   In which Italian city is Da Vinci's famous fresco painting 'The Last Supper' to be found?

7   'The Marriage at Cana' and 'The Adoration of the Kings' are works of which major painter of the 16th century Venetian school?

8   In which European city is the Kunsthistorisches museum which houses collections of fine art?

9   What nationality was the artist Jan Vermeer?

10   Which English painter was famous for his scenes of the industrial north with their matchstick figures?

11   The name of which 15th century Florentine painter loosely translates as 'Big Tom' or 'Clumsy Tom'?

12   And which Florentine artist's name literally translates as 'Little barrel'?

13   Which painter is best remembered for his portraits of the leading figures of the American Revolution and as the founder of the first major museum in the US?

14   What name was given to the group of German artists founded in Germany in 1905 that included Ernst Kirchner, Erich Heckel and Fritz Bleyl?

15   And which art movement was founded in Munich in 1911 and whose founding members were Franz Marc and Wassily Kandinsky?

Answers 1 Dada 2 Parma 3 Hokusai 4 Jacopo Bassano 5 James Montgomery Flagg 6 Milan 7 Paolo Veronese 8 Vienna 9 Dutch 10 L.S. Lowry 11 Masaccio 12 Botticelli 13 Charles Willson Peale 14 Die Brucke (or The Bridge) 15 Der Blaue Reiter (or The Blue Rider)

Geography

GEOGRAPHY   *Quiz 1*

1   In which country are the Kaitaur Falls on the Potaro River, the second highest falls in the world?

2   Ross Island, which contains the 1000-metre high active volcano Mount Erebus, is in which continent?

3   The Franklin River is in which Australian state?

4   In which city could you dine in the CN tower revolving restaurant and enjoy views over Lake Ontario?

5   What is the former name of Harare, the capital of Zimbabwe?

6   Which US state has borders with Iowa and Colorado?

7   What island, slightly larger than Washington DC, lies 18 miles off the coast of Venezuela in the Southern Caribbean?

8   Jakarta, the capital, is on which Indonesian island?

9   In which ocean is Tristan de Cunha?

10 In which Australian state is Adelaide?

11 Bahrain lies in which stretch of water?

12 Andorra lies in which mountain range?

13 Providence is the capital of which US state?

14 Where in the British isles is Lady Isabella, the world's largest water wheel?

15 In which Italian city can you cross over the River Arno on the Ponte Vecchio?

Answers 1 Guyana 2 Antarctica 3 Tasmania 4 Toronto 5 Salisbury 6 Nebraska 7 Aruba 8 Java 9 South Atlantic 10 South Australia 11 The Persian Gulf 12 The Pyrenees 13 Rhode Island 14 The Isle of Man 15 Florence

GEOGRAPHY

Quiz 2

1 Of where is Sophia the capital?
2 The Quachita river is in which country?
3 In which US state is Stone Mountain Park which contains the worlds largest bas-relief sculpture?
4 Which republic lies partly in Europe and partly in Asia?
5 Which lake, also called Bodensee, lies partly in Germany and partly in Switzerland?
6 Sugar Loaf mountain overlooks which city?
7 Mount Washington is the highest peak in which US state?
8 Which is the largest island of Japan?
9 What is the world's largest sea?
10 Which two countries are separated by the Kattegat?
11 The Vistula is the longest river in which East European country?
12 In which ocean is Western Samoa?
13 The Rio Grande forms the borders between which two countries?
14 The Valley is the capital of which of the Leeward Islands?
15 Which stretch of water separates the Isle of Wight from mainland Britain?

Answers 1 Bulgaria 2 USA 3 Georgia 4 Turkey 5 Constance 6 Rio de Janeiro 7 New Hampshire 8 Honshu 9 Coral Sea 10 Denmark and Sweden 11 Poland 12 South Pacific 13 USA and Mexico 14 Anguilla 15 The Solent

GEOGRAPHY   Quiz 3

1   In which African country do the natives speak English and spend shillings?

2   The River Danube rises in which country?

3   Which US state has borders with Kansas, Illinois and Arkansas?

4   The Levant is a general name given to the eastern shores of which sea?

5   Where in Britain would you find Aubrey holes, bluestone horseshoe and avenue ditch?

6   Which tourist attraction is to be found in Tuscany on the River Arno?

7   Which US state has the sugar maple as its state tree and is the leading US producer of maple syrup?

8   The address of which country's Prime Minister is at 24 Sussex Drive?

9   In which Central American republic would you be if you were travelling between the towns of San Miguel and San Vicente?

10 The Moselle River forms part of the border between Germany and which other country?

11 In which US state is Fresno?

12 Which country is nicknamed 'The Cockpit of Europe' because of the number of battles throughout history fought on its soil?

13 What is the capital of Libya?

14 In which US state is Milwaukee?

15 Which province and ancient kingdom in the Republic of Ireland consists of the countries of Galway, Leitrim, Mayo. Roscommon and Sligo?

Answers 1 Tanzania 2 Germany 3 Missouri 4 Mediterranean 5 Stonehenge 6 The Leaning Tower of Pisa 7 Vermont 8 Canada 9 El Salvador 10 Luxembourg 11 California 12 Belgium 13 Tripoli 14 Wisconsin 15 Connaught

440

CATEGORIES

1   What is the highest mountain in Great Britain south of the Scottish border?

2   In which country is the port of St. Malo?

3   In which of North America's great lakes would you find the islands of Bass, Kelly's and Pellee?

4   On which river in Germany des the porcelain producing town of Meissen stand ·

5   What islet is connected to the French mainland by a causeway and is crowned by a Benedictine monastery?

6   'Rosecliffe'. the Mansion on Bellevue Avenue, used as the home of Jay Gatsby in the 1974 movie 'The Great Gatsby' is in which US state?

7   Sevastapol in the Crimea is on the shores of which sea?

8   In which country would you be if you were trudging across the Simpson Desert?

9   Which city in Arizona was originally called Stjukshon, an Indian word meaning 'village of the dark spring at the foot of the mountains'?

10   What is the second largest city of Portugal famous for the export of its port wines?

11   Which island in the Ionian sea has the Greek name Kerkira?

12   Where was the explorer David Livingston when he said: 'Scenes so lovely must have been gazed on by angels in their flight'?

13   The island of Gozo is four miles North of which larger island?

14   In which suburb of the city is Lisbon airport situated?

15   Mount Rainier is the highest peak of which US state?

Answers 1 Snowdon 2 France 3 Erie 4 River Elbe 5 Mont St.Michel 6 Rhode Island (Newport) 7 Black 8 Australia 9 Tucson 10 Oporto 11 Corfu 12 Victoria Falls 13 Malta 14 Potela 15 California

GEOGRAPHY

Quiz 5

This quiz is all about islands.

1 Which island is one of the New England states?
2 Prince Edward Island is a Maritime province of which country?
3 The capital Wellington stands on which of New Zealand's islands?
4 Which European capital city is divided by canals into about 90 islands joined by about 400 bridges?
5 In which ocean are Queen Charlotte Islands?
6 The Aran Islands are at the mouth of which bay in the Republic of Ireland?
7 What is another name for the Islas Malvinas?
8 Which rocky islet in the Atlantic Ocean was part of a French penal colony from 1852-1946?
9 Which island in the South Pacific ocean became home to the mutineers of HMS Bounty in 1790?
10 What was Bedloe's Island renamed by a US act of Congress in 1956?
11 Hamilton is the capital of which island in the North Atlantic ocean?
12 In which sea is the Dodecanese island group?
13 Which islands belonging to Denmark lie midway between the Shetland Islands and Iceland?
14 Which island borough of New York was known as the borough of Richmond until 1975?
15 Which is the second largest island of Japan?

Answers 1 Rhode Island 2 Canada 3 North Island 4 Amsterdam 5 Pacific 6 Galway Bay 7 Falkland Islands 8 Devil's Island 9 Pitcairn Island 10 Liberty Island 11 Bermuda 12 Aegean 13 Faero Island 14 Staten Island 15 Hokkaido

CATEGORIES

Quiz 6

1 Which US city was originally a settlement called Franklinton and is the seat of Franklin County on the Scioto River?

2 Which country is separated from Ethiopia by the RedSea?

3 What is the main port of Italy?

4 Where would you be is you were taking holidays on National Founding Day, Respect for the Aged Day and Labour Thanksgiving Day?

5 In which European city are the 17th-century Charlottenborg Palace and the Christiansborg Palace?

6 In which US state did the 'Gunfight at the OK Corral' take place?

7 Where would you be if people were speaking Spanish and spending sucre?

8 Mount Logan is the highest peak in which country?

9 What is the name of the extinct volcano in Edinburgh?

10 Which is Europe's highest capital city?

11 What are the three principle rivers of France?

12 Which country in South America was originally inhabited by the Guarani Indians?

13 On which Mediterranean island is Palermo?

14 In which state is Harvard University?

15 Name the two cities in England that have a population exceeding 1 million.

Answers 1 Colombus 2 Yemen 3 Genoa 4 Japan 5 Copenhagen 6 Arizona 7 Ecuador 8 Canada 9 Arthur's Seat 10 Madrid 11 Seine, Loire, Rhone 12 Paraguay 13 Sicily 14 New Jersey 15 London and Birmingham

GEOGRAPHY   *Quiz 7*

1   Which US territory is the largest of the Mariana Islands?

2   Where would you be if you saw vehicles with the International Vehicle registration sign RP?

3   Which three countries apart from the former Yugoslavia, share borders with Greece?

4   Situated in the Caribbean Sea, what is the collective name for the islands of Curacao, Aruba, Bonaire, St. Marten, St. Eustatius and Saba?

5   In terms of population, which is the largest US state?

6   What is the third largest port in France?

7   Which is the chief of the seven hills of Rome?

8   Between Iraq and Turkey, the River Euphrates flows through which country?

9   Lesotho is a kingdom completely land-locked within which other country?

10 What in the Netherlands is polder?

11 In which ocean are the Seychelles?

12 The Palk Strait separates which two countries?

13 What is the name of the large area of rolling moorland in Germany between the rivers Weser and Elba?

14 To which group of Greek islands do Cos, Rhodes and Patmos belong?

15 Which US city is located on the Maumee River at Lake Erie?

CATEGORIES

GEOGRAPHY   *Quiz 8*

1   Lisbon stands at the mouth of which river?

2   What is the longest river in France?

3   In which Australian state is Darwin?

4   Apart from Rome, how many cities in Italy have a population over 1 million?

5   What in America is the Palmetto state?

6   In which ocean is Madagascar?

7   In which US city is Sears Tower?

8   Which country is bounded by Suriname to the East, Venezuela to the West and Brazil to the South?

9   On his Kon-tiki expedition, Thor Heyerdahl sailed to Tuamoto Island from which South American country?

10 In which country is the Hague?

11 Brisbane is the capital of which Australian state?

12 In the US, which city is at the junction where the Allegheny and Monongahela rivers join the form the Ohio River?

13 By what other name is the Funchal Islands known?

14 Which is the furthest distance from London – Paris or Dublin?

15 San Juan is the capital of which US overseas territory?

1   Which US territory and Atoll was discovered by the captain of HMS Cornwallis in 1807 and includes Sand Island and Hikina Island?

2   What colour are the four stars on the flag of New Zealand?

3   Which is the largest of the Greek islands in the eastern Mediterranean Sea?

4   The island of Mauritius has been ruled by which three European countries?

5   After the Caspian Sea, which is the world's largest lake?

6   What is Germany's largest port?

7   What is the largest active volcano in Europe?

8   Wyendotte Cave in Crawford County, which contains Monumental Mountain, is in which US state?

9   In which ocean are the Marshall Islands?

10 Vinson Massif is the highest elevation on which continent?

11 What in Alaska is Katmai?

12 Dakar is the capital of which African country?

13 The Wadden Islands are in the north of which country?

14 The US state of Georgia is on the coast of which ocean?

15 What term, in geography refers to one of two extremities of the axis around which the earth rotates?

Answers 1 Johnson Atoll **2** Red **3** Crete **4** France, Britain, Portugal **5** Lake Superior **6** Hamburg **7** Mount Etna **8** Indiana **9** Pacific **10** Antarctica **11** A volcano **12** Senegal **13** The Netherlands **14** Atlantic **15** Pole

GEOGRAPHY   *Quiz 10*

This quiz is all about countries.

1. Which country has a shoreline on the Red Sea and land borders with several countries including Egypt, Ethiopia, Kenya, Uganda, Chad and Libya?

2. Which European country is divided into 26 cantons, six of which are designated 'semi-cantons' but function as full cantons?

3. The name of which Central American country literally means 'rich coast' ?

4. A sabra is a native of which country?

5. Which South American country has land borders with ten other countries?

6. In which country's name does the letter U appear three times in the first five letters?

7. In which present day country is the old land known as Sheba now situated?

8. Which European country is also the first name of Kim Basinger and Alec Baldwin's daughter?

9. Name the only country through which both the equator and Tropic of Capricorn pass?

10. Which African country has both western and eastern borders with Mozambique?

11. Iran's most easterly point borders which country?

12. In 1856 which country became the first to use a secret ballot for government elections?

13. The elements Erbium, Yttrium, Ytterbium and Terbium are all named after the town of Ytterby where they were discovered. In which country is Ytterby?

14. St. George's is the capital of which island country, one of the Windward Islands?

15. In which South American country are Spanish and Guarani spoken?

Answers 1 Sudan 2 Switzerland 3 Costa Rica 4 Israel 5 Brazil 6 Uruguay 7 The Yemen 8 Ireland 9 Brazil 10 Malawi 11 Pakistan 12 Australia 13 Sweden 14 Grenada 15 Paraguay

GEOGRAPHY   Quiz 11

1   In which town in Kent would you find the promenade 'The Pantiles'?

2   The Shatt-al-Arab river is formed by the union of whch two rivers?

3   Riga is the capital of which European city?

4   Which six countries border the Black Sea?

5   On which River does Berlin stand?

6   Mount Marcy is the highest peak of which North American mountain range?

7   What did the country of Upper Volta become in 1984?

8   The commercial cetre of which Illinois city is called 'The Loop'?

9   Which of these two rivers is the longest - the River Forth or the River Tees?

10 In which US State is the coastal resort of Hollywood?

11 The Vestmann Islands are situated off which European country?

12 In which African country is the town of Debra Markos?

13 In which European country is the cathedral town of Teruel?

14 In which country would you find the ruins of Tell el Amerna?

15 Tegucigalpa, the capital of Honduras, stands on which river?

Answers 1 Royal Tunbridge Wells 2 Tigris and Euphrates 3 Latvia 4 Bulgaria, Georgia, Romania, Russia, Turkey and Ukraine 5 River Spree 6 Adirondack mountains 7 Burkina Faso 8 Chicago 9 Forth 10 Florida 11 Iceland 12 Ethiopia 13 Spain 14 Egypt 15 Choluteca River

CATEGORIES

1   What is the regional capital of Bavaria in Germany?

2   Milwaukee stands on which of North America's Great Lakes?

3   Which, by area, is the largest country in South America?

4   Which two countries make up the island of Hispaniola?

5   Apart from Flemish and German, what is the other official language of Belgium?

6   Which explorer was first to cross the Antarctic?

7   What is the most southerly point of Britain?

8   The ancient country of Babylonia is now part of which modern country?

9   Ischia is an island of which European country?

10 Fyn is the second largest island of which country?

11 Ben Nevis is in which range of mountains?

12 Which African country has borders with Zaire, Zambia and Namibia?

13 Which country is separated from Saudi Arabia by the Persian Gulf?

14 In which city in Portugal is a bridge designed by the French engineer Gustav Eiffel?

15 Castles in Spain are so numerous that they have given their name to which region
    and former kingdom in Central Spain at the foot of the Cantabrian mountains?

Answers 1 Munich 2 Michigan 3 Brazil 4 Dominican Republic and Haiti 5 Walloon
6 Vivian Fuchs 7 Lizard Point, Cornwall 8 Iraq 9 Italy 10 Denmark 11 Grampians
12 Angola 13 Iran 14 Oporto 15 Castil or Castilla

GEOGRAPHY   *Quiz 13*

1   On which of North America's Great Lakes does Cleveland stand?
2   Which bridge in Venice links the Doge's Palace with the state prison?
3   Name the three cities in Germany that have a population over 1 million?
4   The refinery at Mina al Fahal is the main oil-terminal of which middle eastern monarchy?
5   Which republic within the commonwealth lies at the southern tip of the Malaysian peninsula?
6   What is the most southerly province of Portugal?
7   In which mountain range is Spain's highest point at Mulhacen?
8   Hadrian's Wall ran from Bowness on the Solway Firth to Wallsend near the mouth of which river?
9   The Khyber Pass links which two countries?
10 Kosovo lies within which area of the former Yugoslavia?
11 The Battle of the Nile in 1798 took place in which bay in northern Egypt?
12 Zululand is a region of South Africa situated in which province?
13 The Maritime Alps run along the border between which two countries?
14 In which country is Arnhem?
15 Can you name the six US states that comprise New England?

Connecticut, Maine, New Hampshire, Vermont, Massachusetts
10 Serbia 11 Abukir 12 Natal 13 France and Italy 14 The Netherlands 15 Rhode Island,
5 Singapore 6 The Algarve 7 Sierra Nevada 8 Tyne 9 Afghanistan and Pakistan
Answers 1 Erie 2 The Bridge of Sighs 3 Berlin, Hamburg and Munich 4 Oman

GEOGRAPHY   *Quiz 14*

1   The Northern part of which country is called Oesling?

2   The name of which US state is derived from two French words meaning Green and Mountain?

3   Marston Moor, the scene of a battle during the English Civil War, is near to which English city?

4   Napier is a city in which country?

5   Where in Europe is the world's largest port?

6   What is the capital of Guernsey?

7   What is the Hook of Holland?

8   The Guadaloupe Mountains are a branch of which mountain range?

9   Jervis Bay is an inlet on the eastern coast of which Australian state?

10 In which ocean is the Bismarck Archipelago?

11 New Caledonia is a dependent state of which country?

12 The River Douro forms part of the border between which two countries?

13 Port Moresby is the capital of which country?

14 Which territory in the Northern part of the Indian sub-continent is claimed by both India and Pakistan and has been partitioned since 1947?

15 What is the name of the inlet of the North Sea within the Netherlands which is separated by a dam built in 1932?

Answers 1 Luxembourg 2 Vermont 3 York 4 New Zealand 5 Rotterdam 6 St. Peter Port 7 A port in the southeast Netherlands 8 The Rocky Mountains 9 New South Wales 10 Pacific 11 France 12 Spain and Portugal 13 Papua New Guinea 14 Kashmir 15 Zuider Zee

This quiz is all about mountains.

1 What is the third highest mountain in Africa, after Mount Kilimanjaro and Mount Kenya?

2 Which mountain range in Africa has the same name as a town in South Wales?

3 The Wrangell mountains are in which US state?

4 What is the name of the highest peak in Austria?

5 At some 2,277 feet, Mount Botrange is the highest point of which European country?

6 What is the highest peak in the Ecuadorian Andes?

7 Mount Toubkal is the highest point of which African mountain range?

8 The peak of Rysy, at an elevation of 8,199 feet is the highest point of which European country?

9 What is the highest peak in British Columbia?

10 Ben Lomond is a mountain mass in which Australian state?

11 Musala is the highest point of which country - Bulgaria, Greece or Romania?

12 What is the world's third highest mountain after Everest and K2?

13 Baldy Mountain is the highest peak in which Canadian province?

14 Mount La Marmora is the highest point of which Mediterranean island?

15 In which Asian country are the Palkonda Hills?

Answers 1 Margherita Peak 2 Aberdare 3 Alaska 4 Grossglockner 5 Belgium 6 Chimborazo 7 Atlas Mountains 8 Poland 9 Mount Fairweather 10 Tasmania 11 Bulgaria 12 Kanchenjunga 13 Manitoba 14 Sardinia 15 India

CATEGORIES

GEOGRAPHY   *Quiz 16*

1   What is the highest mountain in Greece?
2   Which port in Belgium is a world centre for the cutting of diamonds?
3   Which country, which forms part of Lapland, contains the greatest number of Lapps?
4   The name of which South American capital city means Good Winds?
5   The Galapagos Islands are a territory of which country?
6   Four US states meet at one point, two of them are Arizona and New Mexico, which are the other two?
7   Which river flows through Glasgow?
8   Which country lies opposite Spain across the Straits of Gibraltar?
9   Which volcano is on the Lipari Islands, off Sicily?
10 What is the name of the famous pleasure garden in Copenhagen?
11 The Grenadines are part of which larger group of islands in the eastern Caribbean Sea?
12 Abadan is a city of which middle-eastern country?
13 What, in the Quebec Province of Canada, is or are Trois-Rivières (Three Rivers)?
14 In which country is Algoa Bay a large inlet of the Indian Ocean?
15 The Malabar Coast is a long narrow coastal plain of which country?

Answers 1 Mount Olympus 2 Antwerp 3 Norway 4 Buenos Aires 5 Ecuador 6 Colorado and Utah 7 Clyde 8 Morocco 9 Stromboli 10 Tivoli 11 Windward Islands 12 Iran 13 A city 14 South Africa 15 India

1 Which sea in Northern Europe is bounded by several countries including Sweden, Finland, Poland and Germany?

2 In which country do the White and Blue Niles converge?

3 In which sea are the Ryukyu Islands?

4 A road tunnel runs from Pelerins in France to Entreves in Italy under which mountain?

5 What do the French refer to Iles Normandes?

6 Which city is served by Aldergrove airport?

7 The Andaman Islands lie East of India in which great bay?

8 The Barents Sea is part of which ocean?

9 The canalization of which river has given Rhine shipping direct access to Luxembourg?

10 In which country is the Great Slave Lake?

11 Which two countries are either side of the mouth of the River Plate?

12 What is the highest mountain in the British Isles?

13 The River Rhone flows into which sea?

14 The ancient country of Moab, east of the Dead Sea is now part of which modern country?

15 Which volcano is sometimes called Puebla Volcano after the state in Mexico where it is located?

Answers 1 The Baltic Sea **2** Sudan **3** China Sea **4** Mont Blanc **5** The Channel Islands
6 Belfast **7** The Bay of Bengal **8** Arctic **9** Moselle **10** Canada **11** Argentina and Uruguay
12 Ben Nevis **13** Mediterranean **14** Jordan **15** Popocatepetl

This quiz is all about the USA.

1   Montpelier is the capital of which New England state?

2   Name the only state in which I is the only vowel in it's name?

3   Bordering on Virginia and Maryland, which bay is the largest inlet on the USA's Atlantic coast?

4   The names of two states end in the letter D. One is Maryland, what is the other?

5   Name the city in Ohio, the birthplace of aviator Orville Wright, where Bosnian peace talks were held in 1995?

6   New Haven, New Britain and New London are all cities in which state?

7   The collapse of which bridge in 1940, only four months after it's completion, led to modification in the design of suspension bridges?

8   The US military academy of West Point is in which state?

9   The site of the battle of Gettysburg is to be found in which US state?

10   A regular landing site for returning space shuttles, Edwards air force base is in which state?

11   Which Californian beach resorts name is given to a type of surfboard known technically as a long board?

12   Which city is sometimes referred to as the 'Athens of the New World' and also often dubbed as the 'Hub of the Universe'?

13   Which present day state capital was the first capital of the Confederate states during the American civil war?

14   In area, Alaska, Texas and California are the three largest states, which is the fourth largest?

15   In which state would you find the volcanic area known as the Valley of Ten Thousand Smokes?

1   What are the vast treeless plains of central Argentina called?

2   What is Bedloe's Island now called in the USA?

3   What is the capital of Trinidad and Tobago?

4   What is called The Eternal City?

5   The isle of Elba belongs to which country?

6   What in the Rocky Mountains is a Chinook?

7   Which is the second largest of the Dodecanese islands which is thought to be the birthplace of the physician Hippocrates?

8   In which country is the health and vacation resort of Yalta?

9   Which natural pass in the US, near the point where the states of Kentucky, Tennessee and Virginia meet, was made famous in song by Lonnie Donegan?

10 Andalucia is an autonomous region of which country?

11 What is another name for the Left Bank in Paris located near to the River Seine?

12 Which US city is famous for its Grand Ole Opry radio broadcasts?

13 Which mountain range forms the north boundary of the Sahara Desert?

14 What line of latitude is the International Date Line?

15 In which US state is the Badlands National Park?

CATEGORIES

1   Kathmandu is the capital of which country?

2   Which is the largest island in Canada and the fifth largest in the world?

3   The aurora borealis are the northern lights, what name is given to the southern lights?

4   What is the longest river solely in England?

5   The Great Barrier Reef is off the coast of which Australian state?

6   In which river is Ile St. Louis?

7   The Rio Grande flows into which body of water which is an arm of the Atlantic Ocean?

8   In which US state would you find the Cajun people?

9   The ancient kingdom of Northumbria included all of England north of which river?

10   On which island is the city of Spanish Town?

11   Which country, consisting of nine atolls in the Pacific Ocean was formerly called Ellice Islands?

12   Which is the southernmost of the New England states of the US?

13   Which lake in Southern Manitoba in Canada is a remnant of a prehistoric lake called Lake Agassiz?

14   On which continent is Marie Byrd Land?

15   Which large gulf is an arm of the Arafura Sea in Northern Australia?

Answers 1 Nepal 2 Baffin Island 3 Aurora Australis 4 Thames 5 Queensland 6 Seine 7 Gulf of Mexico 8 Louisiana 9 Humber 10 Jamaica 11 Tuvalu 12 Connecticut 13 Lake Winnipeg 14 Antarctica 15 Gulf of Carpentaria

GEOGRAPHY   *Quiz 21*

1   Saxony was a former state of which country?

2   Which mountain in South Dakota contains the carved heads of four American presidents?

3   What cave on the Island of Staffa, off the coast of Argyllshire, is named after a half-mythical Scottish hero?

4   The Jara mountain range straddles the border between France and which other country?

5   The Ebro is the longest river of which country?

6   The French island of Saint-Pierre et Miquelon is off the coast of which country?

7   Baile Atha Cliath is the gaelic name for which city?

8   What is the name of the road, originally built by Napoleon, between Nice and Genoa, which is cut into the precipitous cliffs overhanging the Mediterranean?

9   Which Canadian city is the capital of Nova Scotia?

10 What is the main port of France?

11 John F. Kennedy airport and La Guardia airport are situated on which island?

12 What is the name of the strait which separates San Francisco Bay from the Pacific Ocean?

13 What is the capital of Sicily?

14 Tobermory is the chief town of which Scottish island?

15 What is the name of the salt lake situated between Israel and Jordan?

Answers 1 Germany 2 Rushmore 3 Fingal's Cave 4 Switzerland 5 Spain 6 Canada 7 Dublin 8 The Corniche 9 Halifax 10 Marseilles 11 Long Island 12 Golden Gate 13 Palermo 14 Mull 15 Dead Sea

GEOGRAPHY — Quiz 22

1   What is the longest river in India?

2   Basse Terre is one of two islands and also the capital of which island group?

3   At 12.00 hours GMT what time is it in Lisbon?

4   In which country is the promontory known as the Giant's Causeway?

5   Conakry is the capital of which West African republic?

6   What is the largest railway port in Europe?

7   The rivers Ruhr, Main. Moselle and Necker are tributaries of which river?

8   Which lake is the lowest point in Australia?

9   What is the name of the North wind which blows down from the mountains in Italy and Spain?

10 Euboea, Limnos and Kos are three of which group of islands?

11 Which country in Europe is just over half the size of Scotland, has a coastline 4500 miles long and nowhere higher than 570 feet?

12 Which town in Northern Italy is famous for violins made there by the Stradivari family?

13 The port of Ghent is in which country?

14 Which wooded valley in Central Scotland features in the poem 'Lady of the Lake' and the novel 'Rob Roy'?

15 Which US state is known as the Heart of Dixie?

Answers 1 Ganges 2 Guadeloupe 3 12.00 4 Northern Ireland 5 Guinea 6 Antwerp 7 Rhine 8 Eyre 9 Tramontana 10 Aegean Islands 11 Denmark 12 Cremona 13 Belgium 14 The Trossachs 15 Alabama

GEOGRAPHY   Quiz 23

1   Monte Corno is the highest peak in which Italian range of mountains?

2   Which island was previously known as Formosa?

3   Mount Ossa is the highest peak of which Australian state?

4   Which two Spanish cities have a population in excess of 1 million?

5   Which sea bounds The Netherlands to the north and west?

6   The Straits of Hormuz is the entrance to which body of water?

7   What in Hawaii is Mauna Loa?

8   What memorial to Hans Andersen is in Copenhagan harbour?

9   How is the Collegiate Church of St. Peter in London better known?

10 In England, the Clifton Suspension Bridge spans which river?

11 The Caribbean Sea is an arm of which ocean?

12 What, in Rome, is the more familiar name for the Flavian Amphitheatre?

13 What, in Egypt, are Chehren and Mycerimus?

14 Which region of Spain is known as the land of Don Quixote and Sancho Panza?

15 In which Italian city is the Cathedral of St. Mark?

Quiz 24

This quiz is all about rivers.

1 Name the river in Guyana, some 215 miles in length, which enters the Atlantic Ocean at Georgetown?

2 Which river, a major battleground during the American Civil War, joins the Potomac at Harpers Ferry?

3 The Russian city of St. Petersburg stands on the delta of which river?

4 In which country does a river called the Thames flow through the town of Thames and into the Firth of Thames?

5 On which river does the Italian city of Verona stand?

6 And which river flows through the Italian city of Milan?

7 In geology, what is the term used to describe sands and gravels carried by rivers and deposited along the course of the river?

8 Which river rises in the Welsh mountains, flows south through places like Builth Wells, Hereford and Monmouth before joining the Severn near Chepstow?

9 In which African country do both the Limpopo and Zambezi rivers reach the sea?

10 The French city of Lyon stands at the confluence of the Rhone and which other river?

11 The German city of Hamburg stands at the confluence of the Alster and which other river?

12 Which river of Central Europe rises in the Beskids range of the Carpathian mountains and over 1,000 kilometres later enters the Baltic Sea near Gdansk?

13 Which North American river, it has the same name as a US state, forms the state boundary between Vermont and New Hampshire and drains into the Long Island Sound at New Haven?

14 Which French river flows into the English Channel just south of Le Havre?

15 On which river does Prague stand?

Answers 1 Demerara 2 Shenandoah 3 Neva 4 New Zealand 5 Adige 6 Olona 7 Alluvium or Alluvial 8 Wye 9 Mozambique 10 Saone 11 Elbe 12 Vistula 13 Connecticut 14 Seine 15 Vltava

GEOGRAPHY   Quiz 25

1   The remains of the Biblical towns of Sodom and Gomorrah are said to lie under which sea?

2   The Kiel Canal links which two seas?

3   Which is the largest lake in Canada?

4   Table Bay overlooks which city in South Africa?

5   The Gobi Desert extends over which two countries?

6   What in Scotland is known as the granite city?

7   Heligoland, an island in the North Sea, belongs to which country?

8   When moving West across the International Date Line, is a day lost or gained?

9   In which Scottish firth is the isle of Arran?

10 Which island in Southeast Massachusetts is separated from Cape Cod by Vineyard Sound?

11 What is the lowest region of the atmosphere?

12 What is the capital of Croatia?

13 Which is the largest of New Zealand's islands. North or South?

14 Cape Horn is the southern extremity of which South American archipelago?

15 The chrysanthemum is the national symbol for which country?

Answers 1 The Dead Sea **2** Baltic and North Sea **3** The Great Bear Lake **4** Cape Town **5** China and Mongolia **6** Aberdeen **7** Germany **8** Gained **9** Firth of Clyde **10** Martha's Vineyard **11** Troposphere **12** Zagreb **13** South **14** Tierra del Fuego **15** Japan

GEOGRAPHY

Quiz 26

1 In which US state is Amarillo?

2 Which country is now officially called Myanmar?

3 Cape Catastrophe is in which Australian state?

4 Auld Reekie is the nickname for which Scottish city?

5 Ashanti is a region of which African country?

6 Which country lies to the north of Belize and Guatemala?

7 Lutecia was the Roman name for which European city?

8 The Strait of Bonifacio separates Corsica from which other island?

9 The site of the Biblical city of Troy is in which modern country?

10 Which European capital city is on the island of Zealand?

11 In Spain, what is the regional capital of Catalonia?

12 What is spanned by the Rialto Bridge?

13 What is the name of the self-governing community belonging to Denmark lying between Scotland and Ireland?

14 On what river does Rome stand?

15 Jaffa is a part of which city in Israel which now incorporates its name?

Answers 1 Texas 2 Burma 3 South Australia 4 Edinburgh 5 Ghana 6 Mexico 7 Paris 8 Sardinia 9 Turkey 10 Copenhagen 11 Barcelona 12 The Grand Canal in Venice 13 The Faeroe Islands 14 Tiber 15 Tel Aviv-Jaffa

1   In which county in Northern Ireland are the Mourne Mountains?
2   What in Scotland is the meaning of the prefix 'Inver'?
3   The river Rhine flows through which country before entering the North sea?
4   What in France are Petit St. Bernard and Tourmalet?
5   Which Greek island lies close to the coast of Albania?
6   Bangui stands on which river, which is an anagram of its name?
7   Which Most Serene Republic lies within Italy?
8   Which US state has the lowest population?
9   Which county is nicknamed the Garden of England?
10 Aquineum was the Roman name for which Eastern European capital city?
11 In which US state is Daytona Beach?
12 Washington is on the same degree of latitude as which European capital city?
13 Attica is a region of which country?
14 Which African country was formerly called French Sudan?
15 Delos is the smallest of which group of islands in the Aegean Sea?

Answers 1 Co. Down 2 River Mouth 3 The Netherlands 4 Mountain Passes 5 Corfu 6 Ubangi 7 San Marino 8 Alaska 9 Kent 10 Budapest 11 Florida 12 Lisbon 13 Greece 14 Mali 15 Cyclades

In which city are the following buildings to be found?

1   The Blue Mosque and the Mosque of Suleyman?
2   The Jin Mao Building?
3   The Cathedral of St. Basil and the Rossiya Hotel?
4   The John Hancock Centre?
5   The Strozzi Palace and Santa Maria del Fiori cathedral?
6   The Potala Palace, a major pilgrimage site for Buddhists?
7   The Seagram Building?
8   The Rijksmuseum?
9   The Australia Square Tower?
10 The Guggenheim Museum?
11 The Liebighaus Museum of sculpture and the Goethe Museum and Library?
12 The cathedral of St. Vitus and the Bedrich Smetana Museum?
13 The Schonbrunn Palace, Albertina Museum and Burgtheater?
14 The Petronas Towers?
15 The T & C Tower?

Answers 1 Istanbul 2 Shanghai 3 Moscow 4 Chicago 5 Florence 6 Lhasa 7 New York 8 Amsterdam 9 Sydney 10 New York 11 Frankfurt 12 Prague 13 Vienna 14 Kuala Lumpur 15 Kao-hsiung in Taiwan

1   The Golfe de Gascogne is the South of which bay?

2   What is the name of the vast sand bank in the central North sea to the north of Norfolk?

3   The Isle of Sheppey lies at the mouth of which river?

4   The name of which large city in Japan is an anagram of the capital of Japan?

5   Which national monument in Wyoming was featured in the movie Close Encounters of the Third Kind?

6   Which region of Canada near the Alaskan border became famous when gold was discovered there in 1896?

7   Which is the Republic of Ireland's longest river?

8   Used mainly in the US states on the Gulf of Mexico, what is the meaning of the word Bayou?

9   In which European country is the 81 mile long Albert Canal?

10   Which city in England has a Bridge of Sighs?

11   Lake Garda is the largest lake in which country?

12   In which mountain range is the Matterhorn?

13   The Trent unites with which other river to form the Humber river?

14   What is the name of the spa in France which, from 1940-44 was the seat of the French government?

15   What is the largest lake in Great Britain?

Answers 1 The Bay of Biscay 2 Dogger Bank 3 Thames 4 Kyoto 5 Devil's Tower 6 Klondyke 7 Shannon 8 A sluggish creek flowing through swampy terrain 9 Belgium 10 Cambridge 11 Italy 12 Alps 13 Ouse 14 Vichy 15 Loch Lomond

CATEGORIES

1 Which ancient city, now occupied by the towns of Al-Karnak and Luxor was for many centuries the capital of Ancient Egypt?

2 Manama is the capital of which country?

3 Which English city was once known as Aquae Sullis because of its hot natural springs?

4 In Africa, the Namibia desert merges with which other desert to the south?

5 What are the names of the two large islands off the west coast of Italy?

6 In which island group would you find the port of Scapa Flow?

7 From which of the Marshall Islands were the population relocated on the island of Rongerik in 1946 due to US nuclear testing?

8 Which country has the word Hellas on its postage stamps?

9 What structure stands at the centre of the Etoile at the top of the Champs Elysees in Paris?

10 The Gulf of Suez is an arm of which sea?

11 The Moluccas Islands in Eastern Indonesia are known by what other name?

12 In which city is the annual Running of the Bulls?

13 The name of which European capital city means Merchant's Harbour?

14 In which country are Angel Falls, the world's highest waterfalls, situated?

15 In which country is the extinct volcano Aconcagua?

Answers 1 Thebes 2 Bahrain 3 Bath 4 Kalahari 5 Sardinia and Corsica 6 The Orkneys 7 Bikini 8 Greece 9 Arc de Triomphe 10 The Red Sea 11 The Spice Islands 12 Pamplona 13 Copenhagen 14 Venezuela 15 Argentina

467

GEOGRAPHY — *Quiz 31*

1 What river is known to Germans as Donau?

2 What is the name of the wind that blows towards Italy from the South?

3 The Gulf of Venice is the northern part of which sea?

4 Which is the second largest province in Canada?

5 What are the citizens of Cannes called?

6 If you travel East from Cheyenne in Wyoming which is the next state you would enter?

7 St. George's Channel lies between which two countries?

8 The river Niagara flows from Lake Erie to which other of North America's Great Lakes?

9 What is the name of the whirlpool in the Lofoten Islands off Norway?

10 What is the largest region of Italy?

11 What is the largest island of the Outer Hebrides?

12 Which country has its North-West coast on the Ligurian Sea?

13 What in the British Isles are Drumlins?

14 Prior to reunification, what was the capital of West Germany?

15 Porcupine Bank is to the west of which country?

Answers 1 The Danube 2 Sirocco 3 The Adriatic 4 Ontario 5 Cannois 6 Nebraska 7 Wales and The Republic of Ireland 8 Ontario 9 Maelstrom 10 Sicily 11 Lewis 12 Italy 13 Rocky outcrops left behind by glaciation 14 Bonn 15 The Republic of Ireland

1 Which ancient city near Naples was rediscovered in 1748?

2 What is Scotland's longest river?

3 The name of which ocean is derived from one of the Titans of Greek mythology?

4 The Red Sea is an arm of which ocean?

5 Which sea is connected with the Aegean Sea by the Bosporus?

6 In which African country is Tsavo national park?

7 Ninety Mile Beach is in which Australian state?

8 In which country is the Gower Peninsula?

9 How many republics comprise the former USSR?

10 Sherpas are natives of which country?

11 Vindabona was the Roman name for which city?

12 Where in Colorado would you find the Old Faithful geyser?

13 Lake Tiberias is an alternative name for which sea?

14 St. Mary's, St. Agnes and St. Martins are part of which island group?

15 In which modern country was the Mausoleum at Helicarnassus, one of the Seven Wonders of the Ancient World?

Answers 1 Pompeii 2 Tay 3 Atlantic Ocean 4 Indian 5 Black Sea 6 Kenya 7 Victoria 8 Wales 9 15 10 Nepal 11 Venice 12 Yellowstone Park 13 Sea of Galilee 14 Scilly-Isles 15 Turkey

GEOGRAPHY   *Quiz 33*

This quiz is all about rivers.

1   Which river in Argentina has the same name as a river in the USA?

2   The longest river in the Northern Territory of Australia shares its name with which Australian state?

3   Austria's second largest city, Graz, stands on which river?

4   Which river flows through Cambrai and Valenciennes in France and Oudenaarde and Ghent in Belgium?

5   Name the river in Belize whose name is also that of the title of a John Wayne western?

6   What name is shared by a major tributary of the Amazon and an island in the Atlantic?

7   Some 2,700 miles in length, and flowing from the hills of Tibet, through China, Myanmar, Laos, Cambodia and Vietnam, which is the longest river in south-east Asia?

8   What name is shared by a British river and a river in northwestern Ontario, Canada?

9   There is a Magdalena river in Mexico and which South American country?

10 The line of which river, it rises in the hills near Saint-Quentin and flows westwards to the English Channel, was of great strategic importance during World War One?

11 The Berbice is a river in which South American country?

12 The name of which Greek river traditionally means 'river of woe'. In ancient times it was thought to go to Hades because it flowed through dark gorges and went underground in several places?

13 Buller, Clutha, Mataura and Wanganui are all rivers in which country?

14 What name is shared by a river in southwestern England and northern Tasmania?

15 In which country would you find the Tone and Yodo rivers?

Answers 1 Colorado **2** Victoria **3** Mur **4** Scheldt **5** Hondo **6** Madeira **7** Mekong **8** Severn **9** Colombia **10** Somme **11** Guyana **12** Acheron **13** New Zealand **14** Tamar **15** Japan

GEOGRAPHY   *Quiz 34*

1   Which small island lies off the coast of Tuscany, Italy?

2   Lake Maggiore is partly in Italy and partly in which other country?

3   The Aram Islands are in which Irish bay?

4   On which river does Balmoral Castle stand?

5   Sao Miguel is the largest of which group of islands in the mid-Atlantic?

6   Lake Kariba, created by the Kariba Dam, is an expansion of which African river?

7   In which US state is Gettysburg?

8   The Great Gray owl is the provincial bird of which Canadian province?

9   Saint Thomas, Saint John and Saint Croix are the three islands of which US Island group in the Lesser Antilles?

10   In which Indian city is the Golden Temple?

11   Where in England is the Royal Observatory?

12   In which country is the Nubian desert?

13   What in Australia is a billabong?

14   On which Hawaiian island is Honolulu?

15   In which country is Mount Herman?

Answers 1 Elba 2 Switzerland 3 Galway Bay 4 Dee 5 Azores 6 Zambezi 7 Pennsylvania 8 Manitoba 9 US Virgin Islands 10 Amritsar 11 Cambridge 12 Sudan 13 A waterhole 14 Oahu 15 Syria

Quiz 35

1   On which river does Londonderry stand?

2   The name of which republic of the former Yugoslavia means black mountain?

3   The north-west corner of which country is called Thrace?

4   In which country is Lough Neagh?

5   In which years in the 20th-century did San Francisco suffer major earthquakes?

6   In which desert is the world's driest place?

7   In which African country is the Serengeti National Park?

8   The Empire State building is in which borough of New York?

9   In which US state is Omaha?

10 Which is the world's saltiest sea?

11 …and which is the least salty?

12 With an area of just 2 square miles, which is the smallest of the Channel Islands?

13 Which strait separates the southern tip of South America from the island of Tierra del Fuego?

14 In which ocean is Micronesia?

15 Which is the largest city within the Arctic circle?

GEOGRAPHY
Quiz 36

1 Which is the world's northernmost capital city?
2 In which African country is Timbuktu?
3 Which country lies south of the Isle of Wight?
4 In which country is Marrakech?
5 Which river flows through Dublin?
6 Which is the largest landlocked country in Europe?
7 Luzon is an island of which country?
8 What was the former name of the Chinese capital Beijing?
9 Which country's national flag is completely green?
10 Which is the second largest of North America's Great Lakes?
11 The territory previously known as Prussia is now part of which modern country?
12 Hibernia was the Roman name for which country?
13 In which country are the Dolomite Alps?
14 The later name for which sea is 'Mare Germanicum'?
15 The highest point of which range of hills in England is Cleeve Cloud near Cheltenham?

Answers 1 Reykjavik, Iceland 2 Mali 3 France 4 Morocco 5 Liffy 6 Hungary 7 Philippines 8 Peking 9 Libya 10 Huron 11 Germany 12 Ireland 13 Italy 14 North Sea 15 Cotswolds

POT POURRI

Pot Pourri: General

Myths & Legends

1 In Hindu mythology, who is the goddess of death?

2 In medieval Jewish folklore what name was given to an image or automaton that could be brought to life by a charm. They were supposed to have been used as servants by rabbis?

3 In mythology, which famous Greek warrior was the son of Peleus, king of Thessaly and Thetis, a sea nymph?

4 In the Vedic phase of Hindu mythology, what A is the personification of the infinite. She supports the sky, sustains all existence and nourishes the earth?

5 Name the rock in the river Rhine noted for it's echo and association with a legend concerning a water nymph whose singing lured sailors to destruction?

6 In Norse mythology, what was the name of the mischief-making giant who had the ability to change his shape and sex. He was imprisoned in a cave for the murder of Balder?

7 The sorceress Circe turned the followers of Odysseus into what?

8 In Greek mythology, who was the brother of Electra who killed their mother and her lover?

9 In Norse mythology, what A is the race of warlike gods which include Odin, Thor and Tyr?

10 In Greek mythology, a personification of the soul, she lost her divine lover Cupid but was finally reunited with him in marriage in heaven. Name her?

11 Vulcan was the Roman god of fire. Who was the Greek god of fire, he was also the god of crafts?

12 According to Greek legend, which fire-breathing monster had a lion's head, a goat's body and a serpent's tail?

13 Who, in Greek mythology, was the god of wealth?

14 In Greek mythology, the Pleiades were the seven daughters of which Titan?

15 What was the name of the winged horse that sprang from the blood of Medusa when she was beheaded by Perseus?

Answers 1 Kali **2** Golem **3** Achilles **4** Aditi **5** Lorelei **6** Loki **7** Swine **8** Orestes **9** Aesir **10** Psyche **11** Hephaestus **12** Chimera **13** Plutus **14** Atlas **15** Pegasus

POT POURRI: GENERAL *The Name's the Same 1*

1 A city in Texas and the surname of Tracy, winner of the women's singles at the 1979 and 1981 US Open tennis championships?

2 A town in Kent, England and the surname of Evelyn, winner of the women's 100 metres at the 1984 Olympics?

3 The third largest city in Spain and the third largest city in Venezuela?

4 The surname of the 17th and 36th presidents of the USA?

5 An alpine flower and the title of a song featured in 'The Sound Of Music'?

6 A port in New Zealand and the surname of the man who invented logarithms?

7 A two-masted sailing vessel and the surname of a 17th century hangman?

8 The forename of dancer Baryshnikov and former Russian leader Gorbachev?

9 Which salad dressing, made from mayonnaise with ketchup, chopped gherkins etc, shares it's name with a group of islands?

10 A London railway station and one of the patron saints of children?

11 The surname of the 18th president of the USA and the surname of the Hollywood star whose real name was Archibald Leach?

12 A type of vegetable and the surname of a producer of James Bond movies?

13 The surname of post-war Wimbledon singles tennis champions Stan and Margaret?

14 The forename and surname of an American author of historical novels who lived from 1871 until 1947 and the forename and surname of a 20th century British Prime Minister?

15 A Biblical king and a group of islands in the Pacific Ocean?

Answers 1 Austin 2 Ashford 3 Valencia 4 Johnson 5 Edelweiss 6 Napier 7 Ketch 8 Mikhail 9 Thousand Island 10 St. Pancras 11 Grant 12 Broccoli 13 Smith 14 Winston Churchill 15 Solomon

POT POURRI: GENERAL   *Tools*

1   An auger bit is used to drill what type of material?

2   What machine tool shapes material by rapidly turning it against a stationary cutting device?

3   In the 6th-century AD the Spanish theologian St.Isidore of Seville made the first reference to which writing implement which was to be the principle writing tool for nearly 1300 years?

4   What part of a wheelbarrow is the fulcrum?

5   In the 1830s an American blacksmith John Deere was a pioneer in the development of which agricultural tool?

6   What C is a device used to determine small lengths, of which a vernier is one type?

7   Rip, chain and band are types of which tool?

8   What calibrated tool was the standard tool for engineers and scientists prior to the invention of the hand-held calculator?

9   What P is sometimes referred to as block and tackle?

10 What H is a tool or machine used to smooth ploughed land and sometimes cover seeds and fertilizers with earth?

11 For what purpose would a gardener use a dibber?

12 What J is a device used to raise an object too heavy to deal with by hand?

13 An electric version of which device was introduced in the 1930s by the American manufacturer Jacob Schick?

14 What type of craftsman would use a shearing hook, reed leggett and eaves hook?

15 Ball-pein, club, claw and bush are types of which tool?

Answers 1 Wood 2 Lathe 3 Quill pen 4 The wheel 5 The plough 6 Caliper 7 Saw 8 Slide rule 9 Pulley 10 Harrow 11 Making holes 12 Jack 13 Razor 14 Thatcher 15 Hammer

POT POURRI: GENERAL *Folk Lore & Fairy Tales*

1 In the 'Arabian Nights', who relates one of the tales to her husband Scharier each night to keep him from killing her?

2 Who wrote 'The Ugly Duckling' and 'The Emperor's New Clothes'?

3 Which children's character was introduced in 1667 by Frenchman Charles Perrault in Contes de ma mere l'Oie?

4 Which American president is said to have confessed as a child to chopping down a cherry tree?

5 What geographical feature is the mythological American lumberjack Paul Bunyan reputed to have dug?

6 Who created the Uncle Remus tales which featured the character Brer Rabbit?

7 Which character in 'Alice's Adventures in Wonderland' would often fade from sight until nothing but his grin remained?

8 By what nickname is John Chapman (1774-1847), who is reputed to have spread seeds from which grew orchards in America's Midwest, better known?

9 Who, in 1893, wrote 'The Tale of Peter Rabbit'?

10 The music for the Nursery Rhyme 'Twinkle Twinkle Little Star', written in the early 19th-century, comes from an adaptation by which composer of an early French tune?

11 What German word is preferred by scholars to designate the genre Fairy Tales?

12 Which Fairy story includes the line: 'fee-fi-fo-fum / I smell the blood of an Englishman'?

13 Which American author created Rip Van Winkle?

14 Who wrote the fairy tales 'Hansel and Gretel' and 'Snow White and the Seven Dwarfs'?

15 In which book by Kenneth Grahame do the characters Rat, Mole, Badger and toad appear?

POT POURRI: GENERAL — Legal Eagles

1 A codicil is a supplement or afterthought which is usually added to which document?

2 What phrase meaning in the chamber refers to proceedings that a judge hears with the public excluded from the court?

3 What S is a writ requiring a person to appear and give evidence in court?

4 Meaning he has sworn, what A is a sworn written statement?

5 Which Latin phrase means in the very act of committing a crime; red-handed?

6 What I is a written accusation, read out to the accused in court?

7 What Latin phrase, meaning 'you may have the body', is a writ requiring a person detained to be produced before a court and reasons given for his detention?

8 What D is a written statement made under oath and presented as evidence in court?

9 What phrase means premeditation, plan or conscious intent to commit a crime, especially of murder or violent crime leading to death?

10 What I is a court order to refrain from an act such as visiting a person or place?

11 What Latin phrase, meaning 'under a judge' means that something is under deliberation by the courts, and is not, therefore, open to public comment or discussion?

12 What T is a breach or violation of civil law, other than breach of contract?

13 What P is the establishing of the validity of a will?

14 What is signified by the Latin phrase *Men's rea*?

15 What L is negligence or unreasonable delay in pursuing a legal claim?

Answers 1 A will 2 In camera 3 Subpoena 4 Affidavit 5 *In flagrante delicto* 6 Indictment 7 *Habeas Corpus* 8 Deposition 9 Malice aforethought 10 Injunction 11 Sub judice 12 Tort 13 Probate 14 Criminal intent 15 Laches

POT POURRI: GENERAL — *Words & Phrases*

1 Which French phrase means 'according to the fashion'?

2 Which Latin phrase means 'not in control of oneís mind' or 'of unsound mind'?

3 Which phrase meaning a social blunder comes from the French for false step?

4 Which Latin phrase and the title of a film, means 'whither goest thou'?

5 Sometimes abbreviated on medical prescriptions as 'ung', *unguentum* is the Latin word for what?

6 Which Latin phrase meaning 'something for something' is a reciprocal exchange?

7 What word is the name given to the piece of crane-like equipment that suspends and lowers the lifeboats on a ship?

8 And what word is the name given to the built-in housing for a ship's compass?

9 What word is used to describe the art of decorating or carving shells or whales teeth as practised by sailors, especially in days gone by?

10 Used in meteorology, which word describes a change of wind direction in a clockwise direction?

11 And which word is used for a change of wind direction in an anti-clockwise direction?

12 What word is the term used to describe the curved upper surface of a liquid standing in a tube, produced by the surface tension?

13 What is the Japanese word which is given to a carved toggle, usually made of wood or ivory, that was originally used to tether a medicine box or purse worn dangling from the waist?

14 Which Latin phrase meaning 'the course of one's life' is commonly used in the business world in connection with job applications?

15 Which Latin phrase meaning 'without a day' is used in connection with disciplinary punishment, especially in a sporting context and in legal terms with reference to an adjournment, means no appointed date for resumption?

Answers 1 A La Mode 2 Non Compos Mentis 3 Faux Pas 4 Quo Vadis? 5 Ointment 6 Quid Pro Quo 7 Davit 8 Binnacle 9 Scrimshaw 10 Veering 11 Backing 12 Meniscus 13 Netsuke 14 Curriculum vitae 15 Sine die

POT POURRI: GENERAL *The Name's the Same 2*

1 The surname of a 20th century US president and a 20th century British Prime Minister?

2 The forename and surname of the American film actor who appears in the National Lampoon series of films and the name of a battle between the English family of Percy and the Scottish family of Douglas of which a ballad was written?

3 The fourth letter of the Greek alphabet and the word used to describe the flat alluvial area at the mouth of some rivers where the mainstream splits up into several tributaries?

4 The surname of the president of South Africa from 1883 to 1902 and a game reserve in north-east South Africa?

5 The river that flows through Philadelphia and a US state?

6 A Biblical town and the place in Pennsylvania where Nigel Mansell clinched victory in the 1993 Indy Car Championship?

7 The title of a song recorded by Nat 'King' Cole and Conway Twitty and a Da Vinci painting?

8 A type of Pacific salmon and a type of helicopter?

9 The name of a city in China and the word which meant to kidnap someone for enforced service at sea?

10 A man's forename and a grade of proficiency in martial arts such as judo and karate?

11 The forename and surname of a deceased Hollywood movie star and the forename and surname of the 1999 Turner Prize winner?

12 The title of a Barry Manilow song and a famous beach in Rio?

13 The name given to a type of West Indian ballad and the name of Jacques Cousteau's famous boat?

14 A man's forename and a city in Indiana which was the birthplace of Michael Jackson?

15 Another name for a macadamia nut and an Australian state?

Answers 1 Wilson 2 Chevy Chase 3 Delta 4 Kruger 5 Delaware 6 Nazareth 7 Mona Lisa 8 Chinook 9 Shanghai 10 Dan 11 Steve McQueen 12 Copacabana 13 Calypso 14 Gary 15 Queensland

POT POURRI: GENERAL   *Classical Mythology 1*

1 Who was the Greek warrior who killed himself at Troy because Achilles' armour was awarded to Odysseus?

2 Who was the daughter of Zeus and Leda who was described as the fairest woman in the world?

3 Who was the brother of Romulus, slain by him?

4 Triton, the demigod of the sea, was the son of which god of the sea?

5 Who opened the box containing all known ills?

6 …and afterwards what was the only thing left inside the box?

7 Who was the Roman god of woods and fields?

8 What geographical feature were inhabited by the nymphs Oreads?

9 Who was the Titan who held the world on his shoulders as a punishment for warring against Zeus?

10 Of what was Demeter the goddess?

11 Which nymph, after falling hopelessly in love with Narcissus faded away except for her voice?

12 What name for the abode of the dead is sometimes given to Pluto?

13 Who was the Gorgon beheaded by Perseus?

14 Which Greek warrior slew Hector at Troy?

15 Who was the Roman god of boundaries and landmarks?

Answers 1 Ajax **2** Helen **3** Remus **4** Poseidon **5** Pandora **6** Hope **7** Silvanus **8** Mountains **9** Atlas **10** Agriculture **11** Echo **12** Hades **13** Medusa **14** Achilles **15** Terminus

POT POURRI: GENERAL — *Dishes of the World*

1   In France, carbonade is a beef stew made with which type of drink?

2   What is the name of the pate made from goose or duck liver?

3   In Middle Eastern cooking, what is the name of thin lamb slices, flavoured with garlic and herbs, cut from a revolving spit?

4   In Spain, what P is a seasoned rice dish with chicken, shellfish and often vegetables?

5   What in Indian cooking is the name given to slightly leavened bread usually cooked in a clay oven?

6   What type of vegetable is an essential ingredient of moussaka?

7   What type of meat is used in coq au vin?

8   Dim Sum are small sweet or savoury snacks used in dishes from which country?

9   In France, what is the name given to a small piece of bread or toast with a savoury topping?

10 Parmentier means cooked or garnished with which vegetable?

11 What Indian term means cooked in a clay oven?

12 In Japan, what S is small snacks of raw fish and cold rice?

13 In Indonesia, what S is grilled marinated meat kebabs with peanut sauce?

14 In India, what K is cooked dry in curd with spices and vegetables?

15 In France, what J is a garnish of matchstick-thin strips of vegetables?

Answers 1 Beer 2 Pate de Foie Gras 3 Doner Kebab 4 Paella 5 Nan 6 Aubergine 7 Chicken 8 China 9 Canape 10 Potato 11 Tandoori 12 Sushi 13 Satay 14 Khorma 15 Julienne

POT POURRI: GENERAL — *Words & Phrases 2*

1 The phrase 'expletive deleted' widely used in the 1970s, entered popular use after the publication of transcripts relating to which scandal?

2 Tauromachy is the art or act of what?

3 In German-speaking countries, what name is given to the conductor or leader of an orchestra or choir?

4 What three-word phrase was coined by militant Black Panther leader Stokely Carmichael in 1966?

5 Meaning 'to the city and the world', what is the Latin phrase used for the name of special blessings given by the Pope?

6 What is the Latin name for the Lord's Prayer, taken from it's opening words in that language?

7 Which two word phrase was applied to soldiers who were regarded as expendable in times of war?

8 What word for a short, light piece of music also means something of little value and is also a game?

9 What musical composition is named after the Latin word for flight?

10 In art, what name is given to a halo of light over a holy figure. It is also the word for a type of cloud?

11 Which word derived from the Persian for 'spun' is a thin, crisp, lustrous plain-weave fabric of silk or rayon used for women's clothing?

12 Which term, taken from the French for 'to the point' means well acquainted with, fully informed or having a good or detailed knowledge of?

13 Taken from the French for 'accomplished fact', what term means something already done and beyond alteration?

14 What word is the name given to the Chinese puzzle in which a square, cut into a parallelogram, a square and five triangles, is formed into different figures?

15 Which word meaning blind and aggressive patriotism is derived from G.W. Hunt's music hall song 'We Don't Want To Fight'?

Answers 1 Watergate 2 Bullfighting 3 Kapellmeister 4 Black is beautiful 5 Urbi Et Orbi 6 Pater Noster 7 Cannon fodder 8 Bagatelle 9 Fugue 10 Nimbus 11 Taffeta 12 Au Fait 13 Fait Accompli 14 Tangram 15 Jingoism

POT POURRI: GENERAL — *Classical Mythology 2*

1 Who was the daughter of Cepheus who was chained to a cliff for a monster to devour, but was rescued by Perseus?

2 What horse was ridden by Bellerophon when he slew Chimera?

3 Who was the mortal loved by Zeus, who, in the form of a white bull, carried her off to Crete?

4 Which monsters had the heads of women and bodies of birds?

5 Leda was the mortal loved by Zeus in the form of what creature?

6 Who was the son of Aeson, who went to Colchis and brought back the Golden Fleece?

7 Dryads were nymphs who inhabited what areas of the countryside?

8 Who was the prophetess who was never believed, and who was slain with Agamemnon?

9 Which nymph, who was pursued by Apollo, was changed into a laurel tree?

10 Which female warriors in Asia Minor supported Troy against the Greeks?

11 Who was the beautiful boy who succeeded Hebe as cup-bearer to the gods?

12 Who was the goddess of victory?

13 Who was the monster, half man and half beast, who was kept in the labyrinth in Crete?

14 Who was the father of the Titans and the personification of heaven?

15 Who was the boatman who carried the souls of the dead to Hades across the Styx?

Answers 1 Andromeda 2 Pegasus 3 Europa 4 Harpies 5 A swan 6 Jason 7 Woods 8 Cassandra 9 Daphne 10 Amazons 11 Ganymede 12 Nike 13 Minotaur 14 Uranus 15 Charon

POT POURRI: GENERAL Myths & Legends 2

1 In Greek mythology, the wife of Heracles, who was the goddess of youth and cupbearer to the gods?

2 And how were Lachesis, Clotho and Atropos collectively known?

3 In Teutonic legend, what was the trade of Wayland or Weland?

4 In Germanic legend who owned a sword named 'Nothung'?

5 Who was the mother of Romulus and Remus?

6 And who was the mother of Castor and Pollux?

7 Who is the Greek goddess of the hearth and domestic life?

8 In Greek mythology, the monster Echidna was half woman, half what?

9 According to Greek legend, which king of Thebes fulfilled the prophecy that he would kill his father and marry his mother?

10 Hippolyte was the queen of which race of female warriors?

11 In Greek mythology, whom did Perseus save from a sea monster and marry?

12 According to legend, who was the last king of Troy?

13 Who was the Roman goddess of women and marriage, the equivalent of the Greek goddess Hera?

14 In Greek mythology, name the river across which the souls of the dead were ferried?

15 In Greek legend which Titan created man and endowed him with reason? He also stole fire from heaven to give to man.

Answers 1 Hebe 2 Fates or Three Fates 3 Smith or Blacksmith 4 Siegfried 5 Rhea Silvia 6 Leda 7 Hestia 8 Serpent or snake 9 Oedipus 10 Amazons 11 Andromeda 12 Priam 13 Juno 14 Styx 15 Prometheus

POT POURRI: GENERAL — *Flags of the World*

1 The flag of which country consists of three horizontal bands of blue, white and blue with an emblem known as the 'Sun of May' in the centre?

2 Which country's flag consists of blue and white horizontal stripes with the 'Sun of May' emblem in the top left hand corner?

3 The flag of which country bears the motto *Ordem e Progresso* which means order and progress in English?

4 Which country's flag is described as a red and blue ying-yang symbol surrounded by four black trigrams on a white background?

5 The flag of which US state features a buffalo with the state seal superimposed on the buffalo?

6 Which US state flag features a grizzly bear and a star?

7 The flag of Bolivia consists of three horizontal bands of red, yellow and which other colour?

8 Jamaica's flag consists of green, yellow and what other colour?

9 What colour is the large circle on the flag of Bangladesh?

10 What colour is the five pointed star on the flag of Morocco?

11 Which bird appears on the state flag of Western Australia?

12 What appears inside the white star in the centre of the flag of Northern Ireland?

13 The flag of the UK is known as the 'Union Jack'. Which US state incorporates a 'Union Jack' as part of it's flag?

14 Which three colours are common to the national flags of Chile, Luxembourg and Yugoslavia?

15 The national flag of which middle-eastern country has a seven-pointed white star that represents the first seven verses of the Koran?

Answers 1 Argentina 2 Uruguay 3 Brazil 4 South Korea 5 Wyoming 6 California 7 Green 8 Black 9 Red 10 Green 11 Black Swan 12 A red hand 13 Hawaii 14 Red, White and Blue 15 Jordan

POT POURRI: GENERAL *The Name's the Same 3*

1   A shade of green and the word for a man revered for his profound wisdom?

2   What M is a fine-quality coffee and a soft leather made from sheepskin?

3   A species of sandpiper and the word for an allotted or fixed period of work?

4   The forename and surname of the American pioneer and frontiersman who played a notable role in the settlement of Kentucky and Missouri around 1770 and the forename and surname of the British singer who had hits in the early 1970s with the songs 'Daddy Don't You Walk So Fast' and 'Beautiful Sunday'?

5   The first name of the 18th president of the USA and the title of a novel by James Joyce?

6   The surname of Clive, the former West Indian cricket captain and Harold, a daredevil comedian of silent movies?

7   The name of a German town which gave it's name to a type of man's hat and the title of a hit record for Procol Harum?

8   The name of a US daily newspaper and the title of a John Philip Sousa march?

9   The title of a poem by Rudyard Kipling and the title of a hit song for both Bread and Telly Savalas?

10 The forename of Runyan, writer of 'Guys And Dolls' and Hill, world motor racing champion?

11 The surname of the 16th president of the USA and a city in eastern-central England?

12 Cult actor James Dean's middle name and the surname of a 19th century English poet?

13 The surname of the 3rd US president and the real surname of comedian Stan Laurel?

14 The name of a wading bird similar to the avocet and one of a pair of long poles on which a person stands or walks?

15 The name of a bird of prey and an old US gold coin worth ten dollars?

Answers 1 Sage 2 Mocha 3 Stint 4 Daniel Boone 5 Ulysses 6 Lloyd 7 Homburg 8 Washington Post 9 If 10 Damon 11 Lincoln 12 Byron 13 Jefferson 14 Stilt 15 Eagle

POT POURRI: GENERAL — *It's a Dog's Life*

1 The name of which breed of dog means butterfly in French?

2 Which large dog is also known as the coach dog because it was used to precede or follow horse-drawn carriages?

3 Said to have originated in 17th-century Belgium, which breed of dog is named after a mythological animal which it is said to resemble?

4 Which dog, thought to have originated in Germany about the middle of the 16th-century is the result of interbreeding between the Irish Wolfhound and the Old-English Mastiff?

5 From which country does the Akita originate?

6 Which dog is trained in locating game to stand rigid with its nose in direction of the spot in which game is concealed?

7 What breed of domestic dog belonging to the hound family is also called the African barkless dog?

8 Which breed of hunting dog, for which records date from 3600BC, is known to have been used to hunt the gazelle and is, therefore, sometimes called the gazelle hound?

9 Which breed of terrier, formerly called the black-and-tan or rat terrier, now shares its name with an English city?

10 In which country did the Japanese Chin originate?

11 The name of which dog means badger dog in German?

12 Which bushy-haired dog having a small head with pointed snout and small upright ears is descended from the sledge dogs of Lapland, and is a forbear of the Pomeranian?

13 Which breed of dog, bred in China since the 17th century, has a name meaning lion dog, but because the hair grows in all directions over its face is also called the chrysanthemum-faced dog?

14 What breed of dog is named after a character in Sir Walter Scott's novel 'Guy Mannering'?

15 Which breed of dog is named from the inhabitants of Siberia, with whom the dog has always been closely associated?

Answers 1 Papillon 2 Dalmation 3 Brussels Griffon 4 Great Dane 5 Japan 6 Pointer 7 Basenji 8 Saluki 9 Manchester Terrier 10 China 11 Dachshund 12 Spitz 13 Shih Tzu 14 Dandie Dinmont terrier 15 Samoyed

POT POURRI: GENERAL — *Words & Phrases 3*

1 If ingress is the action of entering or going in, what is the word for the action of leaving or going out?

2 Which expression, meaning in a meaningless or complicated language, is derived from the name of an African tribal god Mama Dyumbo?

3 Which French phrase describes an alluring or seductive woman, especially one who causes men to love her to their own distress?

4 What does the Latin phrase *exempli gratia* mean in English?

5 What are you if you are referred to as 'sinistral'?

6 What word was army slang for a raw recruit and is now used in sport, especially golf and American football, to describe a first year professional?

7 What word describes an ancient Roman building used for administration and also applies to a church, such as St. Peter's in Rome?

8 What word meaning a person who suffers death rather than denounce their belief in a cause or religion, comes from the Latin for 'witness'?

9 What six-letter word beginning with G is the name Latin Americans give to a person from an English-speaking country?

10 What are the leaves of ferns and palm trees called?

11 What is the meaning of the phrase *in flagrante delicto*?

12 What word is an acknowledgement of a hit in fencing and also an acknowledgement of a witty reply?

13 Which seven letter word, meaning of little importance, is derived from the Latin word for the junction of three roads?

14 What nine letter word beginning with C is a rounded gemstone, especially a garnet cut without facets, and is also a skin eruption similar to a boil?

15 What five letter word beginning with B is the title given in certain countries to a woman of high rank, as in the case of the wife of the Aga Khan?

Answers 1 Egress 2 Mumbo Jumbo 3 Femme Fatale 4 For Example 5 Left-handed 6 Rookie 7 Basilica 8 Martyr 9 Gringo 10 Fronds 11 Caught in the act, redhanded etc. 12 Touché 13 Trivial 14 Carbuncle 15 Begum

POT POURRI: GENERAL   *Food & Drink 1*

1   What is the name of the spicy dish, originating from North Africa, that consists of steamed semolina served with a meat stew?

2   If you ordered calamares in a restaurant, what would you be eating?

3   In chinese cooking, what W is the name given to small savoury-filled dumplings served boiled in a broth?

4   What is the name of the Italian dessert made from coffee-soaked biscuits layered with a sweetened cream cheese?

5   What is the name of the Cajun dish, a type of paella containing shrimps, sausage, chicken and ham seasoned with chilli powder and cayenne?

6   Which rich, white sauce flavoured with herbs and seasonings takes itís name from the French Marquis who invented it?

7   Named after a town in north-east India, which high quality tea with a delicate 'grapey' taste is known as the 'champagne of teas'?

8   The name of which salad dish of shredded cabbage, mayonnaise, carrots and onions is derived from the Dutch for 'cabbage salad'?

9   Which Greek dip is made from yoghurt, cucumber, garlic and mint?

10 To what foodstuff does the adjective caseous apply?

11 In Indian cooking, what name is given to a small, fried, triangular spiced meat or vegetable pasty?

12 What name is given to the Mexican dish consisting of a tortilla filled with meat or cheese and served with a chilli sauce?

13 What name is given to Italian dumplings made from potato, semolina or flour and served with a cheese sauce?

14 Said to have been the personal drink of Bonnie Prince Charlie, the name of which Scottish liqueur is derived from the Gaelic for 'satisfying drink'?

15 Derived from French, what name is given to a small fireproof dish in which individual portions of food are cooked and served?

Answers 1 Couscous 2 Squid 3 Wun Tun or Won Ton 4 Tiramisu 5 Jambalaya 6 Bechamel 7 Darjeeling 8 Coleslaw 9 Tzatziki 10 Cheese 11 Samosa 12 Enchilada 13 Gnocchi 14 Drambuie 15 Cocotte

POT POURRI: GENERAL — *Green*

Either the question or answer refers to something green

1   What name was given to the forces commanded by Ethan Allen in the US between 1770 and 1775?

2   An acute, often fatal viral infection is sometimes called Marburg disease after the place in Germany where it was first described. By what other name is this disease known?

3   What is the common name of the cultivated variety of plum tree *Prunus italica*?

4   A tropical South American tree which produces extremely hard timber, it is also known as sweetwood or bebeeru. Name it.

5   A large European sandpiper, *Tringa nebularia*, is more commonly known as what?

6   Which traditional song begins with the words: 'Alas my love you do me wrong to cast me off discourteously'?

7   In which US state is the city of Greensboro, a major centre for the cotton and tobacco industries?

8   What type of bird is a green leek?

9   What is the name given to the parliament of Greenland?

10 The name of the team which won American Football's first ever Superbowl?

11 The first name of Green, the golfer who won the 1977 US Open?

12 Found in Australia, what type of plant is a greenhood?

13 The title of a hit for the Lemon Pipers on both sides of the Atlantic in 1968?

14 Which group released an album entitled 'Green' in 1988, it being their first on the Warner label?

15 Who was Gerard Depardieu's female co-star in the film 'Green Card'?

Answers 1 Green Mountain Boys 2 Green Monkey disease 3 Greengage 4 Greenheart 5 Greenshank 6 Greensleeves 7 North Carolina 8 Parrot 9 Landsting 10 Green Bay Packers 11 Hubert 12 Orchid 13 Green Tambourine 14 REM 15 Andie MacDowell

POT POURRI: GENERAL — *Myths & Legends 3*

1 In Greek and Roman mythology, what name is given to the river in the underworld, the water of which caused those who drank it to forget their former lives?

2 In Greek legend, who was the companion of Achilles killed by Hector whilst wearing the armour of Achilles?

3 In Greek mythology, who was goddess of the sea, the wife of Poseidon?

4 The ancient Egyptian goddess Hathor, the goddess of fertility and love was usually portrayed as which creature?

5 In Greek legend, who was the goddess of epic poetry and chief of the nine Muses?

6 In Germanic legend, who was the queen of Issland who had superhuman strength and vowed to marry only he who would prove himself stronger?

7 According to Greek mythology, which maiden lost a running race because she stopped to pick up three apples dropped by Hippomenes?

8 In the mythology of native Americans, what did they call their 'Great Spirit'?

9 In Greek mythology, who was the only mortal Gorgon?

10 Who was the ancient Egyptian god of the dead, renewal and rebirth?

11 According to Greek legend, Polyphemus was one of which race of giants?

12 Who was the Roman god of agriculture and the father of the gods?

13 In Greek legend, the minotaur was the offspring of a bull and the wife of king Minos. What was her name?

14 In Greek mythology, who was the goddess of the underworld and the daughter of Zeus and Demeter?

15 According to Roman mythology, Juno was the wife of which god?

Answers 1 Lethe 2 Patroclus 3 Amphitrite 4 Cow 5 Calliope 6 Brunhild 7 Atalanta 8 Manitou 9 Medusa 10 Osiris 11 Cyclops 12 Saturn 13 Pasiphae 14 Persephone 15 Jupiter

CATEGORIES

1   What creature is the emblem of St. Agnes, a Roman martyr and the patron saint of virgins?

2   According to legend, which saint offered a cloth to Jesus on his way to Calvary?

3   His Feast day is 3rd November, which son of the Duke of Guienne is the patron saint of hunting?

4   Who was the secretary of the Pope who was commissioned to carry out the first Latin translation of the Bible from the Hebrew?

5   Founder of the 'Poor Clares', Clare is known as St. Clare of … which Italian town?

6   And in 1958, the Pope designated Clare as the patron saint of which form of entertainment?

7   What is the emblem of St. Barbara – a bridge, a cannon, a sword or a tower?

8   Famous for his poetic epistles, which French-born prelate was the Bishop of Nola in Italy from 409 until 431AD?

9   What is the emblem of St. Sebastian, who lived in the 3rd century AD – an arrow, an athlete, a drum or a flower?

10   Which saint, whose name means 'honoured by God', was a disciple of Paul?

11   His Feast day is 5th June, who is known as the 'Apostle of Germany'?

12   Which Syrian monk and hermit is said to have lived for over 30 years on a small platform on the top of a tall pillar?

13   Who is the patron saint of cooks, housewives, dieticians and laundry workers?

14   Which French saint, a 4th century soldier who became Bishop of Tours and whose feast day is 11th November, reputedly gave his military cloak to a naked beggar and thus it became a symbol of charity?

15   His feast day is 14th July and his emblem is a cardinal's hat. Which Italian saint who lived in the 13th century was known as Doctor Seraphicus?

Answers 1 Lamb 2 Veronica 3 Hubert 4 Jerome 5 Assisi 6 Television 7 Tower 8 Paulinus 9 Arrow 10 Timothy 11 Boniface 12 Simeon Stylites 13 Martha 14 Martin 15 Bonaventure

Word Wise

1 What English word, meaning suave and affable, is derived from Old French, literally 'of good temper'?

2 In Roman times, what word meant a marketplace or public square, and place for public activity?

3 What would be the shape of a cupola roof?

4 What type of hut-like prefabricarted shelter of arched corrugated iron sheets is named after a 19/20th century British engineer?

5 What word related to the culture, language and peoples of Spain and other areas influenced by Spain?

6 What is the name given to a person born or living in the Orkneys?

7 What type of neckband derives its name from the French for Croatian after the Croatian mercenaries in France who wore such neckbands?

8 What, in Greek mythology, was a nereid?

9 What type of vegetable is a haricot?

10 What would a Maori be doing if he performed a 'haka'?

11 What, in a North African town, is the Kasbah?

12 What adjective means 'relating to the Moon'?

13 What clay-like material used in pottery means, in Italian, literally 'baked earth'?

14 In medieval France, what was a trouvier?

15 Philomel, in legend, refers to which bird and is named after Philomele, a princess in Greek legend who turned into such a bird?

Answers 1 Debonaire (De Bon Aire) **2** Forum **3** Dome shaped **4** Nissen hut **5** Hispanic **6** Orcadian **7** Cravat (cravate) **8** Sea nymph **9** A bean **10** A war dance **11** Market quarter **12** Lunar **13** Terracotta **14** A minstrel **15** Nightingale

CATEGORIES

1   A Texan resort and seaport, and a college at both Oxford and Cambridge universities?

2   A city in Minnesota, home of the famous Mayo clinic and the surname of a hero in a Charlotte Bronte novel?

3   The surname of Dorothy, American writer and radical social reformer and the surname of the American actress/singer whose real name is Kappelhoff?

4   Surname of George, a 1968 US presidential candidate and William, a Scottish hero?

5   The surname of two explorers – one an American with the first names Frederick Albert and the other British with the first name James?

6   The surname of the 23rd president of the USA and the surname of one of the Beatles?

7   The middle name of the creator of Tarzan and the surname of lyricist Tim?

8   Another name for Polaris or North Star and the surname of Reginald, the last Roman Catholic Archbishop of Canterbury?

9   The surname of the rock star whose real name is Vincent Furnier and the surname of the author of 'The Last Of The Mohicans'?

10 The name of the Italian biblical scholar and saint whose feast day is 30 September and the first name of the composer of the musical 'Show Boat'?

11 Surname of American poet Ezra, and the UK's unit of currency?

12 A measurement equal to 8 US quarts and the surname of the star of the movies 'To Kill A Mockingbird' and 'The Omen'?

13 A city in Florida and a character in Shakespeare's 'As You Like It'?

14 The surname of a famous British painter and the surname of the singer whose real name is Annie Mae Bullock?

15 The name of the French churchman who is the patron saint of publicans and inn-keepers and whose feast day is 11 November, and the surname of the star of the movies 'The Jerk' and 'Roxanne'?

Answers 1 Corpus Christi 2 Rochester 3 Day 4 Wallace 5 Cook 6 Harrison 7 Rice 8 Pole 9 Cooper 10 Jerome 11 Pound 12 Peck 13 Orlando 14 Turner 15 Martin

Pot Pourri: Who Said?

1 Who said: "Quitting smoking is easy, I've done it hundreds of times"?
   a Bette Davis
   b Mark Twain
   c Humphrey Bogart
   d Tallulah Bankhead

2 Who said: "The man who views the world at 50 the same as he did at 20 has wasted 30 years of his life"?
   a Albert Einstein
   b Aristotle
   c Sigmund Freud
   d Muhammed Ali

3 Who said: "The surest way to make a monkey out of a man is to quote him"?
   a Newt Gingrich
   b Will Rogers
   c Robert Benchley
   d George Bernard Shaw

4 Who said: "The person who knows how to laugh at himself will never cease to be amused"?
   a Andy Warhol
   b Al Capp
   c Shirley Maclaine
   d Nancy Astor

5 Who said: "I was married by a judge. I should have asked for a jury"?
   a Mickey Rooney
   b Groucho Marx
   c Arthur Miller
   d W.C. Fields

6 Who said: "I've been in more laps than a napkin"?
   a Zsa Zsa Gabor
   b Brigitte Bardot
   c Gypsy Rose Lee
   d Mae West

7 Who said: "If the aborigine drafted an IQ test, all of Western civilization would presumably flunk it"?
   a George Orwell
   b Mao Tse-tung
   c Joseph Stalin
   d Ghandi

8 Who said: "I have left orders to be awakened at any time in case of national emergency, even if I am in a cabinet meeting"?
   a Gerald Ford
   b Lyndon Baines Johnson
   c Ronald Reagan
   d Dan Quayle

9 Who said: "I never put on a pair of shoes until I've worn them at least five years"?
   a Liberace
   b Samuel Goldwyn
   c Imelda Marcos
   d Woody Allen

10 Who said: "I'm not a real movie star. I've still got the same wife I started out with twenty-eight years ago"?
   a Will Rogers
   b Bob Hope
   c Gregory Peck
   d John Wayne

Answers 1 b, **2** d, **3** c, **4** c, **5** b, **6** d, **7** d, **8** c, **9** b, **10** a.

POT POURRI: WHO SAID?   *Quiz 2*

1   Who said: "History will be kind to me for I intend to write it"?
   a   Voltaire
   b   Winston Churchill
   c   Benjamin Franklin
   d   Napoleon Bonaparte

2   Who said: "Sex alleviates tension. Love causes it"?
   a   James Thurber
   b   Oscar Wilde
   c   Elizabeth Taylor
   d   Woody Allen

3   Who said: "If you can't stand the heat, get out of the kitchen"?
   a   Herbert Hoover
   b   Dwight D. Eisenhower
   c   Harry S. Truman
   d   Franklin D. Roosevelt

4   Who said: "Politics is supposed to be the second oldest profession. I have come to realize that it bears a very close resemblance to the first" ?
   a   Henry Kissinger
   b   Ronald Reagan
   c   Richard Nixon
   d   Margaret Thatcher

5   Who said: "Start by doing what's necessary, then do what's possible, and suddenly you are doing the impossible"?
   a   St. Francis of Assisi
   b   Thomas Alva Edison
   c   Henry Ford
   d   Pope John Paul II

6   Who said: "The secret of staying young is to live honestly, eat slowly, and lie about your age"?
   a   Katherine Hepburn
   b   George Burns
   c   Lucille Ball
   d   Sophie Tucker

7   Who said: "Golf is a good walk spoiled"?
   a   Mark Twain
   b   Groucho Marx
   c   Robert Benchley
   d   Arnold Palmer

8   Who said: "New York now leads the world's great cities in the number of people around whom you shouldn't make a sudden move"?
   a   Bob Hope
   b   Danny De Vito
   c   David Letterman
   d   Ruby Wax

9   Who said: "The problem with people who have no vices is that generally you can be pretty sure they're going to have some pretty annoying virtues"?
   a   Sigmund Freud
   b   Elizabeth Taylor
   c   Mae West
   d   Lily Tomlin

10 Who said: "Arithmetic is being able to count up to twenty without taking off your shoes"?
   a   Snoopy
   b   Samuel Goldwyn
   c   Mickey Mouse
   d   Dan Quayle

Answers 1 b, 2 d, 3 c, 4 b, 5 a, 6 c, 7 a, 8 c, 9 b, 10 c.

POT POURRI: WHO SAID?   *Quiz 3*

1   Who said: "You can build a throne with bayonets, but you can`t sit on it for very long"?
    a   Mahatma Ghandi
    b   Henry Kissinger
    c   Boris Yeltsin
    d   Leo Tolstoy

2   Who said: "The length of a film should be directly related to the endurance of the human bladder"?
    a   Alfred Hitchcock
    b   Cecil B De Mille
    c   Walter Winchell
    d   Jack Warner

3   Who said: "Things should be made as simple as possible, but not any simpler"?
    a   Aristotle
    b   Albert Einstein
    c   Woodrow Wilson
    d   Bertrand Russell

4   Who said: "My problem lies in reconciling my gross habits with my nett income"?
    a   Ernest Hemingway
    b   Howard Hughes
    c   Errol Flynn
    d   John D. Rockefeller

5   Who said: "I'm going to stay in show business until I'm the last one left"?
    a   Bob Hope
    b   Jack Benny
    c   George Burns
    d   Milton Berle

6   Who said: "An intellectual snob is someone who can listen to the William Tell Overture and not think of The Lone Ranger"?
    a   David Letterman
    b   Jay Leno
    c   Johnny Carson
    d   Dan Rather

7   Who said: "Everything you can imagine is real"?
    a   Isaac Asimov
    b   Thomas Edison
    c   Madame Curie
    d   Pablo Picasso

8   Who said: "I could prove God statistically"?
    a   John Kenneth Galbraith
    b   Arthur C. Clarke
    c   George Gallup
    d   Walt Disney

9   Who said: "I feel sure that no girl would go to the altar if she knew all" ?
    a   Queen Victoria
    b   Elizabeth Taylor
    c   Princess Diana
    d   Bette Davis

10 Who said, "It is better to be looked over than overlooked" ?
    a   Rosalind Russell
    b   Mae West
    c   Katherine Hepburn
    d   Joan Rivers

Answers 1 c, **2** a, **3** b, **4** c, **5** c, **6** d, **7** d, **8** c, **9** a, **10** b.

CATEGORIES

1   Who said: "The New England Journal of
    Medicine reports that 9 out of 10 doctors
    agree that 1 out of 10 doctors is an idiot"?
    a   David Letterman
    b   Joan Rivers
    c   Jay Leno
    d   Dick Cavatt

2   Who said: "I don't know who my
    grandfather was, I am much more concerned
    to know what his grandson will be"?
    a   Robert E. Lee
    b   Sigmund Freud
    c   Charles De Gaulle
    d   Abraham Lincoln

3   Who said: "I married the first man I ever
    kissed. When I tell that to my children they
    just about throw up"?
    a   Barbara Bush
    b   Rosalynn Smith Carter
    c   Lady Bird Johnson
    d   Margaret Thatcher

4   Who said: "It's not the men in my life that
    count, it's the life in my men"?
    a   Zsa Zsa Gabor
    b   Mae West
    c   Rosanne Barr
    d   Gloria Swanson

5   Who said: "You can tell a lot about a fellows
    character by the way he eats jelly beans" ?
    a   Ronald Reagan
    b   Donald Trump
    c   Bill Clinton
    d   James Thurber

6   Who said: "Computers are useless They can
    only give you answers"?
    a   Bill Gates
    b   Charlie McCarthy
    c   Arthur Miller
    d   Pablo Picasso

7   Who said: "My husband said he wanted to
    have an affair with a redhead, so I dyed my
    hair" ?
    a   Joan Rivers
    b   Bette Midler
    c   Jane Fonda
    d   Shelley Winters

8   Who wrote: "He is winding the watch of his
    wit, by and by it will strike"?
    a   Charles Schulz
    b   William Shakespeare
    c   James Thurber
    d   George Bernard Shaw

9   Who said: "I've been on a calender, but
    never on time"?
    a   Coco Chanel
    b   Brigette Bardot
    c   Cher
    d   Marilyn Monroe

10 Who said: "It is a very sad thing that
    nowadays there is so little useless
    information"?
    a   Oscar Wilde
    b   Bertrand Russell
    c   Mick Jagger
    d   Voltaire

Answers 1 c, 2 d, 3 a, 4 b, 5 a, 6 d, 7 d, 8 b, 9 d, 10 a

POT POURRI: WHO SAID?

Quiz 5

1 Who said: "I believe we are on an irreversible trend toward more freedom and democracy – but that could change"?
   a Ronald Reagan
   b Samuel Goldwyn
   c Will Rogers
   d Dan Quayle

2 Who said: "Nancy Reagan fell down and broke her hair"?
   a Bill Cosby
   b Johnny Carson
   c Steve Martin
   d David Letterman

3 Who said: "If this is coffee, please bring me tea; but if this is tea, please bring me some coffee"?
   a Abraham Lincoln
   b Cary Grant
   c Gerald Ford
   d Noel Coward

4 Who said: "Whenever I'm caught between two evils, I take the one I've never tried"?
   a Bette Midler
   b Oscar Wilde
   c Mae West
   d Frank Sinatra

5 Who said: "I have opinions of my own…strong opinions…but I don't always agree with them"?
   a Bill Clinton
   b Al Capone
   c George Bush
   d Al Gore

6 Who said: "I believe in equality for everyone, except reporters and photographers"?
   a Ghandi
   b Lady Diana
   c Madonna
   d Frank Sinatra

7 Who said: "My husband and I didn't sign a pre-nuptual agreement. We signed a mutual suicide pact"?
   a Zsa Zsa Gabor
   b Rosanne Barr
   c Phyllis Diller
   d Elizabeth Taylor

8 Who said: "When I appear in public, people expect me to neigh, grind my teeth, paw the ground and swish my tail…none of which is easy"?
   a Joan Rivers
   b Sarah Ferguson
   c Katherine Hepburn
   d Princess Anne

9 Who said: "Money is better than poverty, if only for financial reasons" ?
   a Woody Allen
   b John Paul Getty
   c Bill Gates
   d Bob Hope

10 Who said: "I don`t think anyone should write their autobiography until after they`re dead"?
   a George Burns
   b Mark Twain
   c Samuel Goldwyn
   d Jack Benny

Answers 1 d. 2 b. 3 a. 4 c. 5 a. 6 c. 7 b. 8 d. 9 a. 10 c.

POT POURRI: WHO SAID?　　　*Quiz 6*

1　Who said: "I stopped believing in Santa Clause when my mother took me to see him in a department store, and he asked for my autograph"?
a　Judy Garland
b　Mickey Rooney
c　Elizabeth Taylor
d　Shirley Temple

2　Who said: "My one regret is that I am not somebody else"?
a　Will Rogers
b　Woody Allen
c　Bertrand Russell
d　Oscar Wilde

3　Who said: "Some weasel took the cork out of my lunch"?
a　Dean Martin
b　W.C. Fields
c　Ernest Hemingway
d　James Thurber

4　Who said: "There cannot be a crisis next weekMy schedule is already full"?
a　Henry Kissinger
b　Margaret Thatcher
c　Gerald Ford
d　Ronald Reagan

5　Who said: "The report of my death was an exaggeration"?
a　Alexandre Dumas
b　Pablo Picasso
c　Ralph Waldo Emerson
d　Mark Twain

6　Who said: "I don't know anything about music. In my business you don't have to"?
a　Madonna
b　Sid Vicious
c　Michael Jackson
d　Elvis Presley

7　Who said: "If you cannot convince them, confuse them"?
a　Voltaire
b　Richard Nixon
c　Harry S. Truman
d　Winston Churchill

8　Who said: "Never eat more than you can lift"?
a　Mohammed Ali
b　Oliver Hardy
c　Miss Piggy
d　Roscoe "Fatty" Arbuckle

9　Who said: "I'm tough, ambitious and I know exactly what I want"?
a　Madonna
b　Robert Kennedy
c　Indira Ghandi
d　Bill Clinton

10　Who said: "I'd marry again if I found a man who had fifteen million dollars, would sign over half to me, and guarantee that he'd be dead within a year" ?
a　Mae West
b　Bette Davis
c　Gipsy Rose Lee
d　Xaviera Holland

Answers 1 d, 2 b, 3 b, 4 a, 5 d, 6 d, 7 c, 8 c, 9 a, 10 b.

THE ULTIMATE GENERAL KNOWLEDGE QUIZ BOOK

POT POURRI: WHO SAID? *Quiz 7*

1 Who said: "Growing old is a case of mind over matter. If you don't mind, it doesn't matter"?
a George Burns
b Jack Benny
c Milton Berle
d Bob Hope

2 Who said: "Adults are obsolete children"?
a Goethe
b Lillian Helman
c Dr. Seuss
d Peter Pan

3 Who said: "I love California. I practically grew up in Phoenix"?
a Dan Quayle
b Linda Ronstadt
c Barry Goldwater
d Marilyn Vos Savant

4 Who said: "Gravitation can not be held responsible for people falling in love"?
a Isaac Newton
b Prince Charles
c Albert Einstein
d Elizabeth Taylor

5 What phrase, in 1947, was coined by columnist Herbert Bayard Swope ?
a The Bamboo Curtain
b Zero Option
c The Cold War
d The Iron Curtain

6 Who said: "Better a diamond with a flaw than a pebble without it"?
a Zsa Zsa Gabor
b Aristotle
c Confucius
d Liberace

7 Who said: "A desperate disease requires a desperate remedy"?
a Adolf Hitler
b Guy Fawkes
c George Patton
d Oliver Cromwell

8 Who said: 'I can live for two months on a good compliment"?
a Oscar Wilde
b Jack Benny
c George Bush
d Mark Twain

9 Who said: "Einstein was the creative philosophic mind of the century and I have been the creative literary mind of this century"?
a Ernest Hemingway
b Gertrude Stein
c Jackie Collins
d F. Scott Fitzgerald

10 Who said: "I appreciate your welcome. As the cow said to the Maine farmer, 'Thank you for a warm hand on a cold morning' "?
a James Thurber
b John F. Kennedy
c Henry Kissinger
d Ronald Reagan

Answers 1 b, 2 c, 3 a, 4 c, 5 c, 6 c, 7 b, 8 d, 9 b, 10 b.

508

POT POURRI: WHO SAID?   *Quiz 8*

1 Who said: "Life would be infinitely happier if we could only be born at the age of eighty and gradually approach eighteen"?
  a George Burns
  b Mark Twain
  c Ronald Reagan
  d Winston Churchill

2 Who said: "Give up spinach for Lent"?
  a Popeye
  b Ogden Nash
  c Olive Oyl
  d F. Scott Fitzgerald

3 Who said: "Making peace is harder than making war"?
  a Lyndon B. Johnson
  b Robert Kennedy
  c Adlai Stevenson
  d George Patton

4 Who said when it was suggested she was mad: "Of course, I know that. But tell me this: who on this planet is more mad than an Englishman? Hahahahaha!"?
  a Shirley MacLaine
  b Margaret Thatcher
  c Sarah Ferguson
  d Ruby Wax

5 Who said: "The public is always right"?
  a F. W. Woolworth
  b P. T. Barnum
  c H. G. Selfridge
  d C. B. DeMille

6 Who said: "Long live Quebec! Long live free Quebec!"?
  a Pierre Trudeau
  b Charles De Gaulle
  c John Diefenbaker
  d Georges Pompidou

7 What said: "Guess Who?"?
  a Groucho Marx
  b Jerry Lewis
  c David Letterman
  d Woody Woodpecker

8 Who said: "Common sense is the collection of prejudices acquired by the age 18"?
  a Woodrow Wilson
  b Woody Allan
  c Albert Einstein
  d P.G.Wodehouse

9 Who said: "We are ready for any unforseen event that may or may not occur"?
  a Gerald Ford
  b Mel Brooks
  c Ronald Reagan
  d Dan Quayle

10 Whose last words were: "It is very beautiful over there"?
  a Bing Crosby
  b Thomas Edison
  c Mark Twain
  d Rocky Graziano

Answers 1 b, 2 c, 3 c, 4 a, 5 d, 6 b, 7 d, 8 c, 9 d, 10 b.

POT POURRI: WHO SAID?

Quiz 9

1 Who said, in reply to a reporter`s sleeze allegations: "If I'd had as many affairs as you fellows claim, I'd be speaking to you from a jar in the Harvard Medical School."?
a Warren Beatty
b Frank Sinatra
c Bill Clinton
d Errol Flynn

2 Who said: "Good luck, Mr Gorsky"?
a Neil Armstrong
b John F. Kennedy
c Karin Carpenter
d Woody Allan

3 Who said: "The thing that impresses me most about America is the way parents obey their children"?
a Oscar Wilde
b Orsen Welles
c Robert Benchley
d Edward VIII, the Duke of Windsor

4 Who said, in a radio broadcast on October 1, 1939: "I cannot forecast to you the actions of Russia. It is a riddle wrapped in a mystery inside an enigma"?
a Joseph Stalin
b F. D. Roosevelt
c Winston Churchill
d Charles De Gaulle

5 Who said: "Middle age is when your age starts to show around your middle" ?
a George Burns
b Jack Nicklaus
c Ronald Reagan
d Bob Hope

6 Who said: "Husbands are like fires. They go out when unattended"?
a Zsa Zsa Gabor
b Judy Garland
c Joan Crawford
d Elizabeth Taylor

7 Who said:" I guess it was because we were so completely unlike in every way, but, like bacon and eggs, we seemed to be about perfect together – but not so good apart"?
a Oliver Hardy
b Dean Martin
c Richard Burton
d Lou Costello

8 Who said: "God does not play dice with the universe"?
a Stephen Hawking
b Havelock Ellis
c Albert Einstein
d Tycho Brahe

9 Which movie director when asked by an actress if her right or left profile was better, replied: "My dear, you're sitting on your best profile"?
a John Ford
b Alfred Hitchcock
c Busby Berkley
d Cecil B. De Mille

10 Which fictional detective character said: "She was the kind of blond that could make a bishop kick a hole through a stain-glass window" ?
a Frank Drebin
b Sam Spade
c Peter Gunn
d Philip Marlowe

Answers 1 b, 2 a, 3 d, 4 c, 5 d, 6 a, 7 b, 8 c, 9 b, 10 d.

POT POURRI: WHO SAID? — Quiz 10

1 Who said: " All I know is that I am not a Marxist"?
   a Lenin
   b Karl Marx
   c Stalin
   d Groucho Marx

2 Who said in the film 'All About Eve': "Fasten your seatbelts. It`s going to be a bumpy night" ?
   a Joan Crawford
   b Jane Russell
   c Bette Davies
   d Mae West

3 Who said:, "There is no man living who isn't capable of doing more than he thinks he can do" ?
   a Henry Ford
   b John Glenn
   c Martin Luther King
   d Benjamin Disraeli

4 Who said: "Contentment is natural wealth, luxury, artificial poverty"?
   a Aristotle
   b Einstein
   c Robert Burns
   d Socrates

5 Which American president said: "One man with courage makes a majority"?
   a Andrew Jackson
   b Jonn F. Kennedy
   c Abraham Lincoln
   d Harry Truman

6 Whose own epitaph was: "On the whole I`d rather be in Philadelphia"?
   a F. Scott Fitzgerald
   b Jack Benny
   c Robert Benchley
   d W.C. Fields

7 Who said: "Drama is life with the dull bits cut out"?
   a Clarke Gable
   b Alfred Hitchcock
   c Paul Hogan
   d Theodore Roosevelt

8 Who said: "A man who has committed a mistake and doesn't correct it is committing another mistake"?
   a Cherie Blair
   b Woody Allen
   c Confucius
   d Ogden Nash

9 Who said: "There is only one difference between a madman and me. I am not mad"?
   a Vincent van Gogh
   b Rasputin
   c Salvador Dali
   d Samuel Goldwyn

10 Who said: "We are not amused"?
   a Queen Victoria
   b Margaret Thatcher
   c Queen Elizabeth II
   d Anne Boleyn

Answers 1 b, 2 c, 3 a, 4 d, 5 a, 6 d, 7 b, 8 c, 9 c, 10 a.

People

PEOPLE — *Famous Names: Anagrams 1*

1   US jazz band leader and vibraphone player: PLANE MONOLITH (6,7)

2   Israeli Prime Minister (1977-83): ENHANCE IBM GEM (8,5)

3   Emperor of China (1279-94) who founded the Yuan dynasty: BLANK HAIKU(6,4)

4   Italian statesman (1469-1527) whose name is a synonym for cunning and duplicity: MANIC EVIL ALCOHOLIC (7,11)

5   The fourth secretary-general of the United Nations: WHITE MUDLARK(4,8)

6   Hungarian-born actor, real name Laszlo Lowenstein who made his debut in the classic 1933 film 'M': PORT REELER (5,5)

7   American pioneer and Indian fighter: BLEED A ONION (6,5)

8   First person to publish a set of rules for the card game of whist: HONED MELODY (6,5)

9   Author of the 1775 comedy 'The Rivals', in which the character Mrs. Malaprop appears: DRAIN HARSH CIDER (7,8)

10 French composer of 'Symphonie Fantastique' (1831) : COZIER BROTHEL (6,7)

11 Light-heavyweight world boxing champion who was nicknamed Old Moongoose: CHEERIO ROMA (6,5)

12 English conspirator (1628-1705) and principal informer in the so-called Popish plot: TOAST SUITE (5,5)

13 American film actress (1903-68) noted for her beauty, husky-voice and sophistication: HELL! HAUL DATABANK (8,8)

14 Actor who played Tom Thumb in the 1958 movie of the same name: SMARTLY SNUB (4,7)

15 Author of the play 'Fallen Angels' (1925) : ADORE CLOWN (4,6)

Answers 1 Lionel Hampton **2** Menachem Begin **3** Kublai Khan **4** Niccolo Machiavelli **5** Kurt Waldheim **6** Peter Lorre **7** Daniel Boone **8** Edmund Hoyle **9** Richard Sheridan **10** Hector Berlioz **11** Archie Moore **12** Titus Oates **13** Tallulah Bankhead **14** Russ Tamblyn **15** Noel Coward

PEOPLE

Nicknames 1

1 'Notre Dame de Sartre' was a nickname given to which French writer, essayist and constant companion of Jean-Paul Sartre?

2 Which British-born female Hollywood star was given the nickname of 'Hockey stick'?

3 Because of his ability to find his way out of difficult situations, which 20th century US president was known as 'Houdini in the White House'?

4 Which 20th century US president was known as the 'Houdini of American Politics' and 'Tricky Dicky'?

5 And which early US president was known as the 'Machiavelli of Massachusetts'?

6 What was the name of the hated wife of the camp commandant who was known as the 'Bitch of Buchenwald'?

7 Which operatic soprano was given the nickname 'Jessyenormous'?

8 Which 20th century German politician was known as 'der Alte' or 'The old man'?

9 Known for her ability to be heard in the next block, which American singer and entertainer was known as the 'Golden Foghorn'?

10 Referring to her evident weight problem, what nickname did the press give to heiress Christina Onassis?

11 What nickname was given to John Sirica, a judge who became known during the Watergate trial for pressing for severe punishment of the guilty parties?

12 Which former world record holder for the men's 110 metres hurdles was known as 'Skeets'?

13 Name the governor of New York unexpectedly beaten by Harry Truman in the 1948 US presidential election and given the nickname 'Man on the wedding cake'?

14 Which Irish flautist is known as the 'Man with the Golden Flute'?

15 Which French soldier was known as 'he bravest of the brave'?

Answers 1 Simone de Beauvoir 2 Julie Andrews 3 Franklin D. Roosevelt 4 Richard Nixon 5 John Adams 6 Ilse Koch 7 Jessye Norman 8 Konrad Adenauer 9 Ethel Merman 10 Thunderthighs 11 Maximum John 12 Renaldo Nehemiah 13 Thomas E. Dewey 14 James Galway 15 Marshal Michel Ney

PEOPLE — They changed their names 1

Under what names did the following persons become famous?

1 Francoise Sorya Dreyfus, a French actress, born 1932?

2 Anna Maria Louisa Italiano, actress born in New York 1931?

3 Francois Silly, French composer, vocalist and actor, born 1921?

4 Estelle Merle O'Brien Thompson, actress born 1911 died 1979?

5 Truman Streckfus Persons, American writer born 1924 died 1984?

6 Borge Rosenbaum, a Danish-born entertainer who died in 2000?

7 Jeffrey Hyman, punk singer born in Forest Hills 1952 died 2001?

8 Susan Abigail Tomalin, actress born in New York in 1946?

9 Ernest Evans, US singer associated with a popular 1960's dance?

10 Vito Rocco Farinola, singer born in Brooklyn 1928?

11 Sidney Leibowitz and Edith Gormezano, US husband and wife singing duo?

12 Patsy Ann McClenny, actress born in 1950 who appeared in the TV series 'Falcon Crest'?

13 Harris Glenn Milstead, noted for his comic transvestite roles?

14 Stefanie Zofia Federkiewicz, TV actress born in Hollywood in 1942?

15 Paul Hewson, rock star born in Dublin in 1960?

Answers 1 Anouk Aimee 2 Anne Bancroft 3 Gilbert Becaud 4 Merle Oberon 5 Truman Capote 6 Victor Borge 7 Joey Ramone 8 Susan Sarandon 9 Chubby Checker 10 Vic Damone 11 Steve Lawrence and Eydie Gorme 12 Morgan Fairchild 13 Divine 14 Stephanie Powers 15 Bono

PEOPLE — *Famous Names: Anagrams 2*

1 High-wire circus performer who fell to his death on March 22, 1978 at San Jose, Puerto Rico: RAKED ALL LAWN (4,8)

2 American movie director whose films include 'To Have and Have Not' (1944): HAD WORK WASH (6,5)

3 In U.S. history, a Gulf coast pirate who helped defend New Orleans against the British in the War of 1812: I FEEL FAT JAN (4,7)

4 She portrayed Paula McFadden in the 1977 movie 'The Goodbye Girl': SHAM OARSMAN (6,5)

5 Hollywood gossip columnist (1890-1966) born Elda Furry: HEED HARD POP (5,6)

6 Singer of the theme song for the 1974 movie 'Blazing Saddles': FEAR ALIEN INK (7,5)

7 Union officer in the American civil war who devised the game of baseball: BY ADORABLE NUDE (5,9)

8 Actor who portrayed Maxim de Winter in the 1940 movie 'Rebecca': OUR EVIL RELIANCE (8,7)

9 Inventor, in 1939, of the steam shovel: SLOW MILITIA (7,4)

10 The first entertainer to be invited to the Imperial Palace in Japan where, in 1973, she had an audience with the empress: ASS IN ROAD (5,4)

11 Pen-name of American journalist and novelist John Griffith: LACK DONJON (4,6)

12 Singer who wrote the book 'Twixt Twelve and Twenty' in 1958: OPEN BOAT (3,5)

13 Composer in 1922 of the 'Pastoral Symphony': VULGAR ANIMAL WHIPLASH (5,7,8)

14 American golfer who from 1950 to 1953 served in the United States Coastguard: PRONE MALLARD (6,6)

15 English author and feminist (1759-97) whose best-known work is 'A Vindication of the Rights of Woman' (1792): FATAL STORM CLOWNERY (4,14)

Answers 1 Karl Wallenda 2 Howard Hawks 3 Jean Laffite 4 Marsha Mason 5 Hedda Hopper 6 Frankie Laine 7 Abner Doubleday 8 Laurence Olivier 9 William Otis 10 Diana Ross 11 Jack London 12 Pat Boone 13 Ralph Vaughan Williams 14 Arnold Palmer 15 Mary Wollstonecraft

PEOPLE — Nicknames 2

1 A distinguished actor of the 1920s and 1930s who entered the film world in middle age, he earned the nickname 'First Gentleman of the Screen' from the number of films in which he was cast as a king, rajah or nobleman. Name him.

2 And which Canadian-born actress, she made many films in the 1920s and 1930s, was known as the 'First Lady of the Screen'?

3 Which 19th century US president was known as the 'Dude President'?

4 Which Italian composer was known as the 'Swan of Pesaro'?

5 Which 20th century US presidential candidate was known as 'Duke'?

6 'Grim Grom' and 'Mr. Nyet' were names given to which Russian foreign secretary?

7 What nickname was given to silent movie star, Francis X. Bushman?

8 Which operatic tenor was given the nickname 'The man with the Orchid-Lined Voice'?

9 What was the nickname of the the Chinese empress Zi Xi (or Tzu-hsi)?

10 Which prolific inventor was known as the 'Wizard of Menlo Park'?

11 Who is known as 'the Mother of the Blues'?

12 'The Divine Pagan' was a name given to which female Neoplatonist philosopher and mathematician?

13 Which 20th century French Prime Minister became known as the 'Tiger' for his attacks on other politicians?

14 A type of footwear, what nickname was given to the Dutch musical conductor Bernard Haitink?

15 Which king of the French was known as the 'Citizen king'?

Answers 1 George Arliss 2 Norma Shearer 3 Chester Arthur 4 Rossini 5 Michael Dukakis 6 Andrei Gromyko 7 The Handsomest Man in the World 8 Enrico Caruso 9 The Old Buddha 10 Thomas Edison 11 Ma Rainey 12 Hypatia 13 Georges Clemenceau 14 Clogs 15 Louis-Philippe

PEOPLE — *They changed their names 2*

Under what names did the following persons become famous?

1   Joan Alexandra Molinsky, US comedienne born in Brooklyn?

2   Joan de Havilland, actress born in 1917?

3   Harvey Lee Yearly, US actor?

4   Barbara Herzstein, actress born in Los Angeles?

5   Phyllis Driver, US actress and comedienne born in 1917?

6   Vladimir Palanuik, American tough-guy actor?

7   Robert Nankeville, British comedian and impressionist, born in 1959?

8   Francis Castelluccio, American singer born Newark, New Jersey in 1937?

9   Louis Gendre, French actor born in 1919?

10 Nastassja Nakszynski, actress born Berlin in the 1960s?

11 James Stewart, actor born London in 1913, died in 1993?

12 Derek Harris, actor, director and producer born Hollywood 1926 died 1998?

13 Tula Ellice Finklea, US dancer and actress born in 1921?

14 Harry Clifford Leek, US singer and actor?

15 Leo Jacoby, US actor born in 1911 died in 1976?

Answers 1 Joan Rivers 2 Joan Fontaine 3 Lee Majors 4 Barbara Hershey 5 Phyllis Diller 6 Jack Palance 7 Bobby Davro 8 Frankie Valli 9 Louis Jourdan 10 Nastassia Kinski 11 Stewart Granger 12 John Derek 13 Cyd Charisse 14 Howard Keel 15 Lee J. Cobb

Nicknames 3

1 The 'Yankee Clipper' was one of the nicknames given to which baseball player?

2 'Ten-cent Jimmy', 'Old Public Functionary' and the 'Bachelor President' were nicknames given to which US president?

3 Name the 8th president of the USA who was known as the 'little magician' to his friends and the 'sly fox' to his enemies. He was also known as the 'wizard of Kinderhook'.

4 Which Nazi minister of propaganda was known as the 'poison or poisoned dwarf'?

5 Known as 'Wild Bill', what did the initials of the American wild west hero J. B. Hickok stand for?

6 Which actor of both silent and talking films and a member of a famous acting family was known as 'The Great Profile'?

7 Which singing duo who co-starred in several films together between 1935 and 1942 were known as 'America's Sweethearts'?

8 'White Lightning' was the nickname of which Cuban athlete?

9 'Super-Mex' is a name given to which US golfer?

10 What is the nickname of Eric Esch, the IBA super-heavyweight boxer from Jasper, Alabama?

11 And which American boxer, he was world champion at three different weights simultaneously during the 1930s was known as 'Homicide Hank'?

12 Which Roman emperor was known as 'Restitutor Orbis' or 'Restorer of the World'?

13 And what was the nickname of the Roman general Quintus Fabius Maximus?

14 Which Gestapo chief was known as the 'Butcher of Lyons'?

15 And what nickname was given to Josef Mengele, the camp doctor at Auschwitz?

Answers 1 Joe DiMaggio 2 James Buchanan 3 Martin Van Buren 4 Josef Goebbels 5 James Butler 6 John Barrymore 7 Nelson Eddy and Jeanette MacDonald 8 Alberto Juantorena 9 Lee Trevino 10 Butterbean 11 Henry Armstrong 12 Aurelian 13 Cunctator or Delayer 14 Klaus Barbie 15 Angel of Death

PEOPLE — *Famous names: Anagrams 3*

1. Middleweight boxing champion of the world (1949-1951) nicknamed the 'Bronx Bull': JOKE AT MALTA (4,7)

2. Professional name of singer/songwriter Steveland Judkin Morris: WESTERN VIDEO (6,6)

3. The 12th president of the United States: CRAZY ROYAL HAT (7,6)

4. Actor who played Captain Bligh in the 1935 movie 'Mutiny on the Bounty': THE CARNAL GHOULS (7,8)

5. Author in 1961 of 'Night of the Iguana': NEW SMILE ESSENTIAL (9,8)

6. Actor who, in the 'Top Cat' cartoon series, was the voice of Officer Dibble: AN' KILL JENSEN (5,7)

7. Hollywood gossip columnist (1880-1972) who hosted the radio series 'Hollywood Hotel' and appeared in the 1937 movie of the same name: PULLS AN AEROSOL (7,7)

8. New Zealand-born short story writer whose works include 'The Garden Party' (1922): FEMININE TALKED RASH (9,9)

9. The birth name of sharp-shooting champion Annie Oakley: IS OBESE PHENOMENA (6,5,5)

10. Israeli Prime Minister who was portrayed by Peter Finch in the 1977 TV movie 'Raid on Entebbe': HAZY BRAIN KIT (7,5)

11. British physicist and chemist who discovered the laws of electrolysis: AMERICA HALF DAY (7,7)

12. Multimillionaire businessman who lost his life in the 1912 Titanic disaster: CHASE TROJAN JOB (4,5,5)

13. Actress who starred opposite James Cagney in the 1941 comedy 'The Bride Came C.O.D': VETTED BIAS (5,5)

14. The first president of Zambia (1964-91: NEAT NAKED HUNK (7,6)

15. Italian cardinal (1476-1507), the son of Pope Alexander VI, who gave up his church position to become a conqueror of cities and castles in Italy: AIR BASE CARGO (6,6)

Answers 1 Jake LaMotta 2 Stevie Wonder 3 Zachary Taylor 4 Charles Laughton 5 Tennessee Williams 6 Allen Jenkins 7 Louella Parsons 8 Katherine Mansfield 9 Phoebe Annie Moses 10 Yitzhak Rabin 11 Michael Faraday 12 John Jacob Aster 13 Bette Davis 14 Kenneth Kaunda 15 Caesar Borgia

PEOPLE — Identify the person

1   A French explorer, he claimed the area which he named Louisiana for France and was murdered by his mutinous followers in 1687?

2   The most celebrated of ancient Greek mathematicians, he was killed in 212 BC by a Roman soldier?

3   Religious hermit and one of the earliest monks, considered to be the founder of organized Christian monasticism, he was allegedly around 100 years old at the time of his death circa AD 350?

4   US diplomat who was awarded the Nobel Peace Prize in 1950?

5   Hungarian-born US newspaper editor and publisher after whom a well known literary prize is named?

6   Born in Cordoba in 1126, he was an influential Islamic religious philosopher who integrated Islamic traditions with ancient Greek thought?

7   US boxer who was Olympic light-heavyweight champion in 1976 and who was the world professional heavyweight champion for seven months in 1978?

8   Real name Margarita Cansino and born the daughter of a flamenco dancer in New York in 1918. A film star, she was called 'The Great American Love Goddess'?

9   A pioneer of the kindergarten education movement in the US, the best known work of this author is 'Rebecca Of Sunnybrook Farm'?

10 He was the man who developed nylon but took his own life before it went into commercial production?

11 Born in a slave hut in 1856, he became the most influential spokesman for black Americans between 1895 and 1915 and his autobiography was entitled 'Up From Slavery'?

12 Born in Massachusetts in 1820, she was the pioneer crusader for the women suffrage movement in the US?

13 Charlotte Mecklenburg-Strelitz was the wife of which British king, bearing him 15 children?

14 In 1892, who beat John L. Sullivan in the first world heavyweight title fight to use gloves and have three-minute rounds?

15 German whose optical theory led to great improvements in microscope design and in 1866 became optical director of the Zeiss optical works?

Answers 1 Rene-Robert La Salle 2 Archimedes 3 St. Anthony 4 Ralph Bunche 5 Joseph Pulitzer 6 Averroes 7 Leon Spink 8 Rita Hayworth 9 Kate Wiggin 10 Wallace Carothers 11 Booker T. Washington 12 Susan Anthony 13 George III 14 James J Corbett 15 Ernst Abbe

CATEGORIES

Nicknames 4

1   What was the nickname of the voluptuous Italian film actress Silvana Pampanini who appeared in light comedies in the 1950s?

2   Which movie matinee idol was given the nickname 'America's Boyfriend'. He was married to the 'World's Sweetheart' Mary Pickford?

3   Which 19th century US president was given the nickname 'American Caesar'?

4   And which 20th century US general also acquired the nickname 'American Caesar'?

5   Which British romantic novelist was given the nickname the 'Animated Meringue' by humorist Arthur Marshall?

6   Who was known as Beast 666 and earned the nickname 'The Wickedest Man in the World' for his practice of the black arts and his advocacy of drugs and satanic sexual rituals?

7   Name the commandant known as the 'Beast of Belsen'.

8   Big Green is the nickname of which college in Hanover, New Hampshire, one of the Ivy League colleges?

9   A major star of the silent movies, she appeared in 'Resurrection', who was known as the 'Biograph Girl'?

10 Which 20th century US president was known as 'The Boss', 'The Sphinx' and the 'New Deal Caesar'?

11 And which US rock star is known as 'The Boss'?

12 'Bubbles' is the nickname of which US soprano?

13 Who was nicknamed Brenda by the magazine 'Private Eye'?

14 Noted for his vitriolic reviews, US drama critic Alexander Woolcott was known as the 'Butcher of ...'?

15 Which 20th century British soldier was known as 'The Auk'?

Answers 1 Anatomic Bomb 2 Charles 'Buddy' Rogers 3 Ulysses S. Grant 4 Douglas MacArthur 5 Barbara Cartland 6 Aleister Crowley 7 Josef Kramer 8 Dartmouth College 9 Florence Lawrence 10 Franklin D. Roosevelt 11 Bruce Springsteen 12 Beverly Sills 13 Elizabeth II 14 Broadway 15 Claude Auchinleck

Science & Technology

SCIENCE & TECHNOLOGY

Quiz 1

1   What system of measurement is used for precious metals?

2   What instrument for detecting radioactivity is named after a 20th-century German physicist?

3   Brass is an alloy of which two minerals?

4   From what country does the Skoda motor car originate?

5   What in France is a TGV?

6   The US industrialist Leo Hendrick Baekeland, the inventor of Bakelite, was born in which country?

7   Which gas smells like rotten eggs?

8   Who made the first successful balloon flight in 1783, flying 9 km across Paris?

9   Which store in the UK, in 1898, was the first to have an escalator installed?

10 The pineal body, the parietal lobe and the frontal lobe are in which part of the human anatomy?

11 What, in our solar system, are Ceres, Palles, Juno and Vesta?

12 What is the SI unit of temperature?

13 How many chromosomes has a normal human body cell?

14 What does a cryometer measure?

15 Which plant, which has purplish-blue hood-shaped flowers, is also known as monk's-hood?

SCIENCE & TECHNOLOGY   *Quiz 2*

1   In which layer of the atmosphere does the ozone layer occur?
2   Which of the following did Benjamin Hall invent in 1900: the tractor, the safety pin or the zipper?
3   What was first constructed at Artois in France to obtain water from between layers of rock?
4   Which element has the symbol Au?
5   The Ripplecraft was the original name for which vehicle?
6   What is measured in Hertz?
7   Who was the English motor manufacturer who died a baron in 1941 and who pioneered the small motor car?
8   Which Scottish chemist founded the mineral oil industry of Scotland?
9   Which of the following were invented by a Greek Philo in 250BC: nails, springs or screws?
10 Which French educationalist perfected a system of reading for the blind?
11 What is the colour of the mineral beryl when it contains chromium?
12 Who, in 1929, propounded the Big Bang Theory?
13 What is the longest side of a right-angled triangle?
14 What colour does an alkali change litmus paper to?
15 What is the common name for calcium carbonate?

Answers 1 Stratosphere **2** The tractor **3** An artesian well **4** Gold **5** The hovercraft **6** Frequency **7** 1st Baron Austin **8** James Young **9** Springs **10** Louis Braille **11** Green **12** Edwin Hubble **13** Hypotenuse **14** Blue **15** Chalk

SCIENCE & TECHNOLOGY   *Quiz 3*

This quiz is all about astronomy.

1   What is the largest planet in our solar system?

2   Hyperion and Rhea are two of the moons of which planet?

3   Which spacecraft flew close to Jupiter in 1979, Saturn in 1981, Uranus in 1986 and Neptune in 1989?

4   Astronomers divide the whole sky into 88 areas. What are these areas called?

5   By what common name is the star Polaris referred to?

6   Which star in the constellation Centaurus, is also called by the Arabic name Rigil Kent, which means the foot of the Centaur?

7   Only visible from a latitude 35 degrees south, what is the common name of the constellation Crux?

8   What is the English name of the constellation Ursa Minor?

9   What is the brightest star in the constellation Lyra, and the fifth brightest star in the sky?

10 For what in astronomy does the abbreviation NCP stand for?

11 Which celestial body takes 29.5 days to complete a cycle of phases known as the synodic month?

12 Which term is applied to the planet Venus (or occasionally Mercury) when it appears in the eastern sky in the early morning before sunrise?

13 The Caloris Basin, a huge impact crater with a diameter a quarter of the planet, is the most significant single feature of which planet?

14 The asteroid belt lies between which two planets in our solar system?

15 Which comet follows an elongated elliptical orbit around the Sun, which takes 78 years to complete?

Answers 1 Jupiter 2 Saturn 3 Voyager 2 4 Constellations 5 Pole Star 6 Alpha Centauri 7 Southern Cross 8 The Little Bear 9 Vega 10 North Celestial Pole 11 The Moon 12 Morning Star 13 Mercury 14 Mars and Jupiter 15 Halley's Comet

528

1   What are goolet and ferula types of?

2   Which company's name is associated with the comet aircraft?

3   What in computer language do the initials ISDN stand for?

4   Which 3rd-century Greek mathematician wrote Elements of Geometry, which remained a standard text book until the 20th-century?

5   What medical apparatus was invented by a French doctor, Rene Theophile Hyacinthe Laennec, in 1816?

6   How many yards are there in a furlong?

7   What was first predicted around 600BC by a Greek scientist, Thales?

8   Which German physicist devised a temperature scale with a boiling point of 212 degrees?

9   What does a baroscope measure?

10   What is a dirigible a type of?

11   What did a Frenchman Joseph Marie Jacquard invent?

12   Which British leader of an Antarctic expedition died in 1912 whilst returning from the South Pole?

13   In what type of engine is fuel ignited by compression?

14   Who first succeeded in transmitting a radio signal across the Atlantic ocean?

15   What word means the bending of light when passing through a lens?

Answers 1 Boats 2 De Havilland 3 Integrated Services Digital Network 4 Euclid 5 The stethoscope 6 220 7 An eclipse of the sun 8 Fahrenheit 9 Atmospheric pressure 10 Airship 11 A type of loom 12 Robert Falcon Scott 13 Diesel 14 Marconi 15 Refraction

Quiz 5

This quiz is all about the human body.

1 What name is given to the first cervical vertebra, the one that supports the skull?

2 Veins on each side of the neck drain blood from the head and neck regions to the larger veins passing to the heart. What are they called?

3 What name is given to the fibrous protein that is found in the outer layer of the skin and is a major constituent of hair and nails?

4 What name is given to the fluid surrounding a fetus in the womb?

5 Where are the Billroth cords to be found?

6 And where in the body are the Kupffer cells?

7 Blepharitis is inflammation of which specific part of the body?

8 A lacrimal duct is the technical name for which part of your body?

9 Consisting of two parts, the medulla and cortex, what is the name of the glands situated above each kidney?

10 Acne is caused by an increase of secretion by which glands?

11 Coxa is the technical name for which part of the body?

12 Which part of the body is affected by keratitis?

13 What name is given to the membranous sac enclosing the heart?

14 Which part of the body is removed during a 'cholecystectomy'?

15 Gout is caused by a build up of which acid in, and around the joints?

Answers 1 Atlas 2 Jugular 3 Keratin 4 Amniotic fluid 5 Spleen 6 Liver 7 Eyelids 8 Tear duct 9 Adrenal glands 10 Sebaceous glands 11 Hipbone or hip joint 12 Eye (inflammation of the cornea) 13 Pericardium 14 Gall bladder 15 Uric acid

This quiz is all about birds.

1   *Passer domesticus* is the scientific name for which small, common non-migratory bird?

2   Which bird of the crow family, *corvus corax*, can sometimes be taught to talk?

3   The Secretary Bird is a native of which continent?

4   What is the common name given to about 24 species of birds of the genus *Vanellus*, many of which have sharp spurs at the base of the wing, which are native to every continent except North America and Antarctica?

5   The canary is a member of which bird family?

6   Also called 'man-'o-war bird', which ocean bird is noted for possessing a larger wingspan in proportion to its weight than any other bird?

7   Which common bird, also called mynas, were first introduced to the American continent in 1890, when 100 were brought to Central Park in New York City?

8   Regarded from ancient times as a symbol of courage and power, what is the common name of the *Aquila chrysaetos*?

9   The Umbrella Bird is native to which continent?

10 What is the common name collectively applied to numerous species of birds of the waterfowl family *Anatidae*?

11 What bird, which has not bred in Egypt for more than a century was, in ancient times, sacred to the Egyptians?

12 Rookeries are breeding grounds of which bird?

13 Which bird, similar to the heron, has evolved a number of dances, which include the nestling's excited bobbing on the return of its parents?

14 Which large bird with naked head and hooked bill feeds almost entirely on carrion, occasionally attacking wounded living animals?

15 Migrating flocks of which bird are reported in the Book of Exodus as having supplied food to the Israelites in the wilderness?

Answers 1 House sparrow 2 Raven 3 Africa 4 Lapwing 5 Finch 6 Frigate bird 7 Starling 8 Golden Eagle 9 South America 10 Duck 11 Ibis 12 Penguins 13 Crane 14 Vulture 15 Quail

SCIENCE & TECHNOLOGY   *Quiz 7*

1   Of what is petrology the study?

2   Who, in Glasgow in 1865, was the first British person to use antiseptic surgery?

3   What is an endoscope used to examine?

4   What is the more common name of sodium bicarbonate?

5   What, in the field of earth moving, do the initials JCB stand for?

6   What colour is topaz?

7   What element is used in flash guns?

8   Strontium produces what colour in fireworks?

9   What type of weapon is a Lee-Enfield?

10 Which scientist won the Nobel Prize for his discovery of photoelectric effect?

11 For what purpose would a doctor use a sphygmomanometer?

12 Which grows up from the ground, a stalactite or a stalagmite?

13 In radiation wavelength measurement, radio rays are the longest, what are the shortest?

14 If a cathode is a negative electrode, what is a positive electrode?

15 Galena is an ore of which metal?

Answers 1 Rock and minerals 2 Lord Lister 3 The inside of the body 4 Baking soda 5 J.C. Bamford 6 Yellow 7 Magnesium 8 Red 9 A rifle 10 Einstein 11 For measuring blood pressure 12 Stalagmite 13 Gamma rays 14 Anode 15 Lead

SCIENCE & TECHNOLOGY   *Quiz 8*

This quiz is all about astrology.

1   Which sign of the zodiac comes between Leo and Libra?

2   Which planet is said to influence the way we communicate?

3   Are you a fire, air, water or earth sign if you were born under Aquarius?

4   Which star sign is the first sign of the zodiac?

5   If you were born on New Years Day, which is your astrological sign?

6   What is the ruling planet of Scorpio?

7   Pisces and Scorpio are two of the water signs, name the third?

8   Which zodiac sign follows Aries?

9   Which animal is associated with Capricorn?

10 If your sign is Pisces you would of been born in either of which two months?

11 Which planet is most thought to bring good luck?

12 What three facts do astrologers need to compile a birth chart?

13 The name of which star sign, in Latin, means fishes?

14 Which planet is associated with the sign of Aries?

15 Which sign of the zodiac lies opposite to Cancer?

Answers 1 Virgo 2 Mercury 3 Air 4 Aries 5 Capricorn 6 Pluto 7 Cancer 8 Taurus 9 Goat 10 February or March 11 Jupiter 12 Date/place/time of birth 13 Pisces 14 Mars 15 Capricorn

533

SCIENCE & TECHNOLOGY

Quiz 9

1 Who was the German-born British physicist who worked on atomic bomb research in London during World War II and in 1950 was found guilty of spying for the Soviet Union?

2 What is the name of the letter Z in the Greek alphabet?

3 In 1945, H. L. Fizeau and J. Leon Foucault took the first photo of which of the following:, the sun, the moon or mars?

4 German silver is an alloy of copper and which other element?

5 What type of boat was built by the American, John Fitch, in 1786?

6 Types of what were invented by John Napier in 1614, Blaise Pascal in 1642, and in the 20th-century by William Burroughs and Dorr E. Felt?

7 Which English physicist discovered alpha, beta and gamma rays in 1899?

8 Named after a British scientist, what is the SI unit of energy equivalent to the amount of heat required to raise 1 gram of water through 1 degree centigrade?

9 How many litres are contained in a US gallon: 3.78 or 7.57?

10 In the metric system, what word/prefix stands for 1 million?

11 Invented by Dr. John Pemberton, what drink was originally described as 'esteemed brain tonic and intellectual beverage'?

12 What is the more common name of nitrous oxide?

13 Which Briton invented the power loom and the wool-combing machine?

14 In computer technology, what do the initials VGA stand for?

15 What year did Concorde first come into service?

Answers 1 Klaus Fuchs 2 Zeta 3 The sun 4 Nickel 5 Steamboat 6 Calculating machines 7 Ernest Rutherford 8 Joule 9 3.78 10 Mega 11 Coca-cola 12 Laughing gas 13 Edmund Cartwright 14 Video Graphics Array 15 1976

SCIENCE & TECHNOLOGY   *Quiz 10*

1 What colour is produced by adding together the primary colours of yellow and cyan?

2 Which psychologist differentiated people according to types, extroverted and introverted?

3 Which Scotsman invented hard road surfaces?

4 Sodium produces which colour in fireworks?

5 Which disease, carried by bark beetles, was first described in The Netherlands in 1919?

6 Prior to 1930, what was the world's highest building?

7 What did Sir Frank Whittle invent in 1930?

8 What was innovative about a pencil patented in 1858 by Hyman L. Lipman?

9 Which French philosopher and mathematician said: *Cogito ergo sum* ('I think, therefore I am')?

10 Which is the heaviest of the noble gases, neon, xenon or radon?

11 How is deoxyribonacleic acid better known?

12 What is measured in dynes: power, force or velocity?

13 On what area of the moon did Armstrong, Aldin and Collins make their landing on July 20, 1969?

14 What did the American physicist Benjamin Spock specialise in the care of?

15 Which Italian scientist had to face an inquisition and recant his views?

Answers 1 Green 2 Carl Jung 3 John McAdam 4 Yellow 5 Dutch Elm Disease 6 The Eiffel Tower 7 The jet engine 8 It had an attached eraser 9 Rene Descartes 10 Radon 11 DNA 12 Force 13 The Sea of Tranquility 14 Babies 15 Galileo

SCIENCE & TECHNOLOGY   *Quiz 11*

This quiz is all about astronomy.

1   Which is the nearest planet to the Sun?

2   Which comet crashed into the planet Jupiter in July 1994?

3   Which space station ended its life by crashing into the Pacific Ocean in March 2001?

4   What popular name is given to the event which occurred 15 billion years ago marking the beginning of our Universe?

5   76% of the Sun is comprised of which gas?

6   What is known as the Red Planet?

7   Ishtar Terra in the northern hemisphere and Aphrodite Terra in the equatorial region are the two main highland areas of which planet?

8   Which planet can experience a double-dawn because of the way it turns very slowly while following its elliptical orbit around the Sun?

9   Which brilliant constellation is also known as the Hunter?

10 Phobos and Delmos are the moons of which planet?

11 With an English name of Sea Monster, which is the largest constellation in the night sky by area?

12 Which famous Greek astronomer listed 49 constellations in the second century A.D.?

13 Which five planets are visible from earth at one time or another without the aid of a telescope?

14 In September 1990, a large white spot, an eruption of material from the lower atmosphere, developed on which planet?

15 Which planet was discovered on 18 February 1930 from the Lowell Observatory by Clyde Tombaugh?

Answers 1 Mercury 2 Shoemaker-Levy 3 Mir 4 Big Bang 5 Hydrogen 6 Mars 7 Venus 8 Mercury 9 Orion 10 Mars 11 Hydra 12 Ptolemy 13 Mercury, Venus, Mars, Jupiter, Saturn 14 Saturn 15 Pluto

SCIENCE & TECHNOLOGY

Quiz 12

This quiz is all about the living world.

1   Which cephalopod mollusc has a body which is supported by an internal calcareous leaf-shaped shell which gives buoyancy and when alarmed it emits an inky fluid?

2   Which member of the shark family has a long scythe-like extension of the upper tail lobe which it uses to thrash the water while circling it's prey, such as squid etc., forcing them into tighter groups before it attacks?

3   What is the name of the primitive bird found in South American swamps that cannot fly very well and has developed wings with claws on them to climb the dense undergrowth?

4   Name the tropical fish, of which there are over 6000 species, some of which guard their eggs by carrying them in their mouth?

5   Which carnivorous mammal is also called glutton?

6   Originating from the Perche district of France, what is a percheron?

7   Native to Corsica and Sardinia, but introduced to other parts of the world, what is a mouflon?

8   Often impaling it's small prey on thorny spikes, the butcherbird is more properly known by what name?

9   Which bird is the fastest of all living creatures, reaching speeds of over 200mph when stooping from great heights at an angle of 45 degrees?

10   Resembling large short-tailed mice, which small mammal is also known by the names mousehare – whistling hare, cony or rock rabbit?

11   What type of creature is a grayling?

12   What type of bird is a greylag?

13   From which country does the Angora goat originate?

14   What is the zoological term for the animal group which includes rabbits and hares?

15   What is the common name for the aquatic rodent *Castor fiber*?

14 Hagomorphs 15 Beaver

7 A sheep 8 Shrike 9 Peregrine falcon 10 Pika 11 Fish 12 Goose 13 Turkey

Answers 1 Cuttlefish 2 Thresher Shark 3 Hoatzin 4 Cichlid 5 Wolverine 6 A horse

SCIENCE & TECHNOLOGY — *Quiz 13*

1 What is the name of the theory that light and other forms of energy are given off as discrete packets?

2 What collective name is given to the group of gases which do not form compounds easily?

3 Which element is named from the Roman name for Paris?

4 Which element is used on luminous watch dials?

5 What is the poisonous gas emitted by car exhaust fumes?

6 Which is the largest planet in our solar system?

7 What term was first coined in 1965 by a computer scientist John McCarthy?

8 Which American inventor flew a kite in a thunderstorm to show that lightning bolts are huge electric sparks?

9 Which element has the symbol Na?

10 What measuring apparatus was invented in 1643 in Italy by Evangelista Torricelli?

11 Is the sun 73, 83 or 93 million miles away from the earth?

12 Which SI unit of pressure is named after a French physicist who discovered that the pressure of fluid is everywhere equal?

13 What apparatus for laboratory use was popularised by the German chemist whose name it now bears?

14 Discovered in 1840, but never built, the first computer would have covered an area the size of which of the following; a table tennis table, a tennis court or a soccer pitch?

15 ...and who in 1840 designed that first computer?

Answers 1 Quantum theory 2 Inert gases 3 Lutetium 4 Radium 5 Carbon Monoxide 6 Jupiter 7 Artificial intelligence 8 Benjamin Franklin 9 Sodium 10 The barometer 11 93 12 Pascal 13 Bunsen burner 14 Soccer pitch 15 Charles Babbage

This quiz is all about the living world.

1   What is the common name for the species of toad *Alytes obstetricans* which has an unusual breeding habit? As the eggs are laid, the male winds the two egg strings around his hind legs and keeps them there for about a month before hatching.

2   Which small rodent, which can be kept as a pet, is also known as a jird or sand rat?

3   Flies belong to which order of insect?

4   Native to North America, the road runner is a terrestrial species of which bird?

5   What type of creature is a quetzal?

6   Found in the forests of Central and South America, what type of creature is a basilisk?

7   What type of creature is a vervet?

8   Which large hook-billed seabird that breeds in Arctic and Antarctic regions is also known as Jaeger or Sea Hawk?

9   Which small timid ruminant mammal of south-east Asia is also known as the mouse deer?

10 What name is given to the unpaired fin on the back of a fish that maintains balance during locomotion?

11 What is the pupa of a moth or butterfly in a cocoon called?

12 *Felis rufa* is a North American wildcat that resembles a lynx. Sometimes referred to as the bay lynx, what is itís more common name?

13 Feeding off parasites on the backs of cattle and game animals, by what other name is the African bird the oxpecker commonly known?

14 What is the common name for the North American bear, *Ursus arctus horribilis*?

15 Unknown before 1901, which hoofed mammal is the closest living relative to the giraffe?

---

15 Okapi

Answers 1 Midwife Toad **2** Gerbil **3** Diptera **4** Cuckoo **5** Bird **6** Lizard **7** Monkey **8** Skua **9** Chevrotain **10** Dorsal **11** Chrysalis **12** Bobcat **13** Tick Bird **14** Grizzly bear

1   What is the name of the theory that the universe originated with a huge explosion?

2   What life-saving device was patented in 1872 by Thomas J. Martin?

3   What was the profession of Thomas Newcomen, who in 1712 constructed an early steam engine?

4   What is the name of a one-sided closed surface formulated by a German mathematician whose name it now bears?

5   What element has the symbol Sn?

6   In the metric system what word/prefix stands for 10?

7   What home and office comfort, used especially on hot sticky days, was invented by Willis Havilland Carrier?

8   The American microbiologist Albert Bruce Sabin discovered a vaccine for which disease?

9   Who invented the sliding-scale rule which bears his name and which can measure accurately to two decimal places?

10 What are Bq, Gy and Su units of?

11 What was invented in 1827 by John Walker, an English chemist, and sold for half a crown per box of fifty?

12 What is the name given to the halo of light around the sun and moon?

13 What are 1,148,576 bytes called?

14 What was invented in 1938 by a Hungarian called Lazlo Biro?

15 What is the heaviest of all the naturally occurring elements?

Answers 1 Big Bang theory 2 The fire extinguisher 3 Blacksmith 4 Klein bottle 5 Tin 6 Deca 7 Air conditioning 8 Polio 9 Pierre Vernier 10 Radiation 11 Matches 12 Corona 13 Gigabyte 14 The ballpoint pen 15 Uranium

SCIENCE & TECHNOLOGY   Quiz 16

This quiz is all about the human body.

1 Name the soft elongated gland, about 15cm long, and situated in the abdomen behind the stomach.

2 Usually due to an infection, what is inflammation of the urinary bladder called?

3 Opaque areas which develop on the lens of the eye causing vision to mist over are known as what?

4 What is the name of the important nerve that connects the brain with the throat, larynx, heart, lungs, stomach and gut?

5 Which part of the body is affected by nystagmus?

6 What is the name of the tubular passage extending from the mouth to the anus, through which food is passed and digested?

7 What is the name of the tubes through which eggs pass from the ovaries to the uterus?

8 Where in the human body is the ilium?

9 What name is given to the part of the small intestine between the jejenum and the caecum?

10 In which of the body's organs is the Bowman's capsule to be found?

11 What is the common name for the inflammatory condition of muscles and tendons in a particular part of the body known as epicondylitis?

12 Found in the ear, by what more common names are the malleus, incus and stapes bones known?

13 What is the collective name for the malleus, incus and stapes bones?

14 Erysipelas is an infectious disease of the skin characterised by fever and purplish lesions. By what other name is it known?

15 What name is given to a swelling of the thyroid gland, in some cases nearly doubling the size of the neck?

Answers 1 Pancreas 2 Cystitis 3 Cataracts 4 Vagus nerve 5 Eye 6 Alimentary canal 7 Fallopian tubes or oviducts 8 Hip or Pelvis 9 Ileum 10 Kidneys 11 Tennis elbow 12 Hammer, anvil and stirrup 13 The Ossicles 14 St. Anthony's Fire 15 Goitre

SCIENCE & TECHNOLOGY   *Quiz 17*

1   The ratio of the circumference of a circle to its diameter is denoted by which Greek letter?

2   What was developed shortly before World War II by a British team led by Sir Robert Watson-Watt?

3   What element, atomic number 74, has the symbol W?

4   What instrument, which demonstrates the rotation of the earth was invented by the French scientist Jean Bernard Foucault?

5   What are fitted to helicopters so they do not twist with the rotor blades?

6   What scale measures the hardness of minerals?

7   …and on this scale, which is the hardest mineral?

8   …and which is the softest?

9   What alloy contains 63% iron and 35% nickel?

10 What is the name of the layer of the earth's atmosphere which begins at about seven miles, or 37000 feet up?

11 In Roman numerals, what letter represents 1000?

12 What is measures in poundals; mass, force, volume or weight?

13 In which country was a type of margarine first produced in 1869?

14 Which German count was a leader in the field of the development of airships in the early 20th-century?

15 Which Greek physician was called the Father of Medicine?

Answers 1 Pi 2 Radar 3 Tungsten 4 Foucault's pendulum 5 Tail propellers 6 Mohs scale 7 Diamond 8 Talc 9 Invar 10 Stratosphere 11 M 12 Force 13 France 14 Zeppelin 15 Hippocrates

CATEGORIES

Quiz 18

1 The Hyundai motor car originated from which country?

2 What is the name given to an angle of more than 90 degrees?

3 Haematite is an ore of which metal?

4 What does not occur in an anechoic chamber?

5 What colour is formed by mixing blue, green and red lights?

6 What in the human body are triceps and biceps?

7 …and in which part of the body are they found?

8 Which planet has a total of 16 moons, including Europa, Gannymede, Leda and Thebe?

9 What, in computer terminology does ROM stand for?

10 What was invented by the Sumarians in Mesopotamia about 3500 BC to 3000 BC and is often referred to as the first great invention?

11 How many metres are there in a kilometre?

12 Which is the brightest planet seen from earth?

13 In computer terminology, what do the letters RAM stand for?

14 Which physicist discovered the Uncertainty Principle, or indeterminacy?

15 Who, in 1888 invented the pneumatic tyre?

Answers 1 South Korea 2 Obtuse 3 Iron 4 An echo 5 White 6 Muscles 7 Arm 8 Jupiter 9 Read-only Memory 10 The wheel 11 1000 12 Venus 13 Random Access Memory 14 Heisenberg 15 John B. Dunlop

Quiz 19

This quiz is all about astronomy.

1 The eccentric orbit of Pluto brings it temporarily closer to the Sun than which planet?

2 What is the common name of The Pleiades, a cluster of seven stars in the constellation Taurus?

3 Which star in the night sky is also known as The Demon Star, or Winking Demon, because it is really a binary system in which two stars regularly cross in front of each other as viewed from Earth?

4 Which constellation, the best known of all southern constellations, is the smallest constellation by area and contains a five-star cluster known as the Jewel Box?

5 The Dragon is the English name for which constellation in the Northern Hemisphere?

6 The seven stars in which constellation are known variously as the Plough, the Big Dipper and Charles's Wain?

7 The Hellas is a major impact basin of which planet, which is just over half the size of Earth, but has a year twice as long as ours?

8 Discovered in 1978, Charon is a satellite of which planet?

9 The first magnitude star Aldebaran, and the Crab Nebula, lie within the boundaries of which constellation?

10 Numbered 1566, with a diameter of 1.4 km, and discovered in 1949 by W. Baade, what is Icarus a type of?

11 Which planet is famous for its rings, which can be seen with a small telescope?

12 Which is the seventh major planet of the solar system in order from the Sun?

13 The orbit of which planet can take it closer to Earth than any other planet?

14 The first colour image of which planet was taken by Viking 1 when it landed in the Chryse Planitia region on 20 July 1976?

15 Titan is the largest moon of which planet?

Answers 1 Neptune 2 The Seven Sisters 3 Algol 4 Crux (The Southern Cross) 5 Draco 6 Ursa Major 7 Mars 8 Pluto 9 Taurus 10 Asteroid 11 Saturn 12 Uranus 13 Venus 14 Mars 15 Saturn

SCIENCE & TECHNOLOGY   *Quiz 20*

This quiz is all about plant life.

1   Native to northern Europe and Asia, what type of flower is a lady's slipper?

2   Traveller's Joy and Old Man's Beard are names given to which plant?

3   The ironbark is a species of which Australian tree?

4   Which flowering plant, native to North and Central America, is named after a gardener of Charles I?

5   To which genus of plants do carnations, pinks and sweet williams belong?

6   What is the common name for the root vegetable *Pastinaca sativa*?

7   Native to the eastern USA, what is the common name of the carnivorous plant *Dionaea muscipula*?

8   Is the periwinkle deciduous or evergreen?

9   What is the common name for the herb *Armoracia rusticana* whose fleshy, pungent roots are used to make a sauce, often used with roast beef?

10   Known for itís light grey bark, what is the common name of the tree *Betula pendula*?

11   What is the common name of the spring flower *Narcissus pseudonarcissus*?

12   By what more common name is the flower *Galanthus* known?

13   By what popular name is the plant *Kniphofia* or Torch Lily known?

14   *Helianthus annuus* provides bird-food from it's seed and also oil for culinary use. What is it's common name?

15   Which herb is also known as 'herb of grace'?

Answers 1 Orchid 2 Clematis 3 Eucalyptus 4 Tradescantia (after John Tradescant)
5 Dianthus 6 Parsnip 7 Venus Flytrap 8 Evergreen 9 Horseradish 10 Silver Birch
11 Daffodil 12 Snowdrop 13 Red Hot Poker 14 Sunflower 15 Ru

545

SCIENCE & TECHNOLOGY

Quiz 21

1   Who invented the electric lamp?

2   What type of creature was Ham, who survived a sub-orbital flight on 31 January 1961?

3   What type of camera was invented by Edwin Land in 1948?

4   What element has the symbol Pb?

5   Of what, introduced in 1982, was the Epson HX-20 the first of its kind?

6   Which planet has a great red spot as wide as the earth?

7   Who invented the Spinning Jenny?

8   How many sides has a nonagon?

9   What colour is formed by mixing green and red light?

10 Launched on January 31, 1958, what was the name of the first US satellite?

11 After hydrogen, what is the second most abundant element in the universe?

12 What is the name given to a quantum of electro-magnetic rotation such as light?

13 What is measured by a calorimeter – altitude, energy or heat?

14 What was the disability suffered by the road-building pioneer, John Metcalf?

15 The hour falls on which stroke of Big Ben – first or last?

Answers 1 Edison 2 Chimpanzee 3 Polaroid 4 Lead 5 Laptop computer 6 Jupiter 7 James Hargreaves 8 Nine 9 Yellow 10 Explorer 1 11 Helium 12 Photon 13 Heat 14 He was blind 15 First

SCIENCE & TECHNOLOGY — Quiz 22

1   What musical instrument was invented by Bartolommeo Christofori?

2   What kind of weapon is a Bofors?

3   What is known as the Red Planet?

4   What wind-powered device was first built in Persia around 500AD?

5   In the metric system, what word/prefix represents one-tenth?

6   Which German physicist laid down the principles of quantum theory?

7   In which science is Karl Fredrich Gauss one of the all-time greats?

8   How many dozen are there in a gross?

9   Which variety of quartz is violet to purple in colour and is the birthstone for February?

10 Of what was the Flemish geographer, Gerandus Mercator, an originator?

11 What is the name of the aircraft developed in 1969 in which two movable nozzles direct the engines thrust downwards for vertical take-off?

12 What type of vessel to explore ocean depths was invented in 1947 by Auguste Piccard?

13 Which astronomer discovered the planet Uranus?

14 Which part of a wheelbarrow is the fulcrum?

15 In broadcasting, what device is used to transform sound energy into electrical energy?

Answers 1 Piano 2 Anti-aircraft gun 3 Mars 4 Windmill 5 Deci 6 Max Planck 7 Mathematics 8 12 9 Amethyst 10 Maps 11 Hawker Siddeley Harrier 12 Bathycaphe 13 Herschell 14 The wheel 15 Microphone

SCIENCE & TECHNOLOGY

Quiz 23

This quiz is all about computer terms.

1   Which numbering system, used in the operation of computers, uses only two digits, 0 and 1?

2   What W is the name given to an unauthorised independent program that penetrates computers and replicates itself?

3   What does the acronym ROM stand for?

4   What term describes a permanent record of work done on a computer in the form of a paper printout?

5   What term is used for exploring the internet?

6   What does the acronym HTTP stand for?

7   What word, meaning the fifth element, is applied to Intel's fifth generation of sophisticated high-speed microprocessor?

8   What S is the name given to a computer that shares its resources and information with other computers on a network?

9   What unit consists of one billion bytes?

10   What printing device sprays tiny droplets of ink particles onto paper which are formed into characters by an electric field?

11   What C is a tiny wafer of silicon containing miniature electric circuits which can store millions of bits of information?

12   What rate is the speed of data transmission measured in bits per second?

13   What does the acronym RAM stand for?

14   What G is the cause of an unexpected malfunction?

15   What M describes software application technology that combines text and graphics with sound and animation?

Answers 1 Binary **2** Worm **3** Read-only memory **4** Hard copy **5** Surfing **6** Hypertext Transfer Protocol **7** Pentium **8** Server **9** Gigabyte **10** Jet **11** Chip **12** Baud Rate **13** Random access memory **14** Glitch **15** Multimedia

SCIENCE & TECHNOLOGY
Quiz 24

This quiz is all about birds.

1 What colour is the female blackbird?

2 The superstition about a bird which brings bad luck forms the theme of the 'Rime of The Ancient Marine'r by Samuel Taylor Coleridge. What is the name of the bird?

3 Which bird, nicknamed 'laughing jackass', is often heard on television and motion picture soundtracks to typify jungle sounds?

4 Which bird, also called mud hen or swamp hen, cannot take off from the land, but must run along the surface of the water to attain flight speed?

5 The trumpeter, which breeds in North America, is the largest type of which water bird?

6 Which large, long-legged bird sometimes builds nests on top of disused chimneys?

7 The name of which common American nocturnal bird, which spends its day resting on fallen leaves, describes its distinctive call?

8 Which bird has a large pouchlike flap suspended from its lower mandible which is used to capture and store fish?

9 Which bird exhibits elongated upper tail feathers and brilliant colours to attract females during courtship?

10 The peregrine is a type of which bird of prey?

11 What name was first given to a small European bird, *Erithacus rubecula*, of the thrush family, and was later applied by settlers in other parts of the world to birds of a similar appearance?

12 What is the common name for birds of the species *pica*?

13 The rhea of South America closely resembles which bird native to Africa?

14 Which nocturnal and flightless bird is only found in New Zealand and adjacent small islands?

15 Which large central and south American birds were greatly admired by pre-Colombian cultures and are found in their art and mythology?

Answers 1 Brown 2 Albatross 3 Kookaburra 4 Coot 5 Swan 6 Stork 7 Whippoorwill 8 Pelican 9 Peacock 10 Falcon 11 Robin 12 Magpie 13 Ostrich 14 Kiwi 15 Quetzal

SCIENCE & TECHNOLOGY   *Quiz 25*

1   How many degrees are there in a right angle?

2   Which is the nearest planet to the sun?

3   What heat treatment of milk to destroy germs was named after the French microbiologist who devised it?

4   Which solid provides the biggest volume for its surface area?

5   What is the only number that cannot be represented by a Roman numeral?

6   How many nautical miles are there in a league?

7   What is measured by an odometer – angles, speed or distance?

8   What element is used in a microchip?

9   What is the main constituent in the manufacture of glass?

10 Which element has the highest melting point?

11 How many teeth does an adult human have, assuming he has a full set?

12 Who invented dynamite?

13 In radio transmission, what does the abbreviation AM stand for?

14 What does an astrolobe measure the position of?

15 What, in mechanics, is the reaction force produced by the rotation of a shaft about its axis?

Answers 1 90 **2** Mercury **3** Pasteurization **4** Sphere **5** Zero **6** 3 **7** Distance **8** Silicon **9** Sand **10** Carbon **11** 32 **12** Alfred Nobel **13** Amplitude Modulation **14** Heavenly bodies **15** Torque

1　What device was invented in 1954 by C. H. Townes?

2　What colour is formed by adding together yellow, cyan and magenta?

3　In the metric system, what word/prefix stands for one-millionth?

4　One tablespoon is equal to how many teaspoons?

5　Hg is the chemical symbol for which element?

6　Which element is the best conductor of electricity?

7　What is the only gem which is of animal origin?

8　From which country does Indian ink originate?

9　Which star in the constellation Canis Major is also known as the Dog Star?

10　Of what is seismology the study?

11　Which French physicist gave his name to the SI unit of electric current?

12　Which famous motor car did Ferdinand Porsche design in 1937?

13　What colour is alabaster?

14　What measurement is equal to the imperial measure of 3.3 feet?

15　What alloy consists of a mixture of copper, tin and zinc?

Answers 1 Laser 2 Black 3 Micro 4 3 5 Mercury 6 Silver 7 Pearl 8 China 9 Sirius 10 Earthquakes 11 Ampere 12 Volkswagen Beetle 13 White 14 Metre 15 Gunmetal

This quiz is all about inventors and inventions.

1   Which machine, used in the textile industry was invented by James Hargreaves and was named after his daughter?

2   Whose most famous invention was the air-brake in 1869?

3   In which country was Alexander Graham Bell, the inventor of the telephone, born?

4   Which Frenchman invented the adding machine in 1642?

5   Who, in 1884, patented the first practical fountain pen containing its own ink reservoir?

6   The name of which inventor is now a synonym for the word raincoat?

7   Which artillery fragmentation shell is named after its inventor, an English artillery officer, and today broadly denotes any projectile fragments?

8   What C is a musical instrument invented by the British physicist Sir Charles Wheatstone?

9   Who was the English agriculturalist known for his 1701 invention of a machine drill that sowed seeds in rows?

10 Who, in 1793, invented the first cotton gin?

11 Who was the German physicist who invented the modern alcohol and mercury thermometers?

12 What type of camera was invented by Edwin Land in the 1940s?

13 What nationality was Adophe Sax, the inventor of the saxophone?

14 What was the name of the two French brothers who invented the first practical hot air balloon?

15 What is the best-known invention of Evangelista Torricelli?

Answers 1 Spinning Jenny 2 George Westinghouse 3 Scotland 4 Blaise Pascal 5 Lewis Waterman 6 Macintosh 7 Shrapnel 8 Concertina 9 Jethro Tull 10 Eli Whitney 11 Gabriel Fahrenheit 12 Polaroid 13 Belgian 14 Montgolfier 15 The barometer

CATEGORIES

Quiz 28

1 Which scale of wind velocity was named after a 19th-century English admiral?

2 Who built the first successful petrol-driven car?

3 What weapon was designed in 1866 by the British engineer Robert Whitehead?

4 What unit of weight equals 1000 kilograms?

5 What metallic element shares its name with a famous London theatre?

6 What is the acronym for 'sound navigation and ranging'?

7 Who first stated the laws of gravitation and light and also constructed the first reflection telescope?

8 What in the metric system is equivalent to a cubic decimeter and equals 1.76 English pints?

9 How many pounds are there in a kilogram?

10 What are Astra, Eutelsat, Intelsat and Telecom?

11 Who was the British engineer who invented the ACV (air cushion vehicle) in 1955?

12 Of what is metrology the study?

13 Who became Humphry Davy's assistant in 1813?

14 What is measured by a bolometer?

15 What is the name given to a quadrilateral which has all its sides equal, but no right-angels?

Answers 1 The Beaufort Scale 2 Karl Benz 3 Torpedo 4 Metric ton (tonne) 5 Palladium 6 Sonar 7 Isaac Newton 8 Litre 9 2.2 10 Satellites which transmit, or have transmitted, satellite television channels 11 Sir Christopher Cockerell 12 Measurement 13 Michael Faraday 14 Radiant energy 15 Rhombus

SCIENCE & TECHNOLOGY — Quiz 29

1   What was invented by the Scottish scientist Sir James Dewer?

2   Who first printed a book in English?

3   The name of which gas is derived from a Greek word meaning sun?

4   What R is an arc of light comprising the spectral colours?

5   What method of photocopying was developed in the 1930s by Chester F. Carlson?

6   In Troy weight how many ounces are there in a pound?

7   What word, from a Greek word meaning 'to hear', is a term used for the science of sound in general?

8   Who invented vulcanised rubber?

9   What measurement is a 360th part of a complete revolution?

10   Which instrument, that often appears to defy the laws of gravity, consists in its most common form of a wheel within another wheel?

11   What common substance is obtained from latex-producing tropical trees?

12   What in mathematics is the name given to a curve formed by the intersection of a cone?

13   Who invented the safety lamp formerly used by coal miners?

14   What element has the symbol K?

15   What does an oleometer measure the density of?

Answers 1 The thermos flask **2** William Caxton **3** Helium **4** Rainbow **5** Xerography **6** 12 **7** Acoustics **8** Charles Goodyear **9** Degree **10** Gyroscope **11** Rubber **12** Parabola **13** Sir Humphry Davy **14** Potassium **15** Oil

SCIENCE & TECHNOLOGY

Quiz 30

1   What J is the name given to a horizontal beam supporting a ceiling?

2   How many gills are there in a pint?

3   What L are stalagmites and stalactites formed from?

4   What type of mine clings to a ship's hull by magnetic means?

5   What gas is used in illuminated signs?

6   Who was the Gloucestershire physician who discovered vaccination?

7   What scheme did a French engineer, Thome de Germond, place before Napoleon III in 1856?

8   Which 13th-century English monk has been credited with the invention of gunpowder and the magnifying glass?

9   Which theory did Einstein publish first; special or general?

10 In the measurement of what material is 16 cu.ft equal to 1 cord foot?

11 How many degrees are there in a sign of the zodiac?

12 Until 1956, which unit of measurement was defined as 1/86,400 of a mean solar day?

13 What unit of work or energy is names from a Greek word meaning work?

14 What substance is softened by replacing calcium and magnesium ions with sodium and potassium?

15 Which dinosaur's name derived from the phrase 'earthquake lizard'?

SPORT

General Sport

1   Who, in 1975, was defeated by Muhammed Ali in the epic title fight 'Thrilla in Manila'?

2   Named in 1965 as the greatest professional golfer of all time, which golfing legend was nicknamed 'The Killer' and 'The Iceman'?

3   At which sport was Franz Klammer a world champion?

4   Which famous Belgian, nicknamed 'The Cannibal', won cycling's Tour de France five times in the 1960s and 1970s?

5   Which tennis player was not defeated at Wimbledon between losing to Arthur Ashe in 1975 and John McEnroe in 1981?

6   At which sport did Dick Button gain two Olympic victories, in 1948 and 1952?

7   Which US jockey, now confined to a wheelchair after a car accident, once said: "I reckon more horses are whipped out of the money than into it"?

8   Which former England soccer international goalkeeper of the 1940s became a journalist and was killed in the Manchester United Munich air disaster?

9   Which Olympic champion swimmer once said: "MGM put me in a G-string and asked me 'Can you climb that tree, can you lift that girl?' "?

10 Which baseball legend was the first black man to play in the major leagues, and led the Brooklyn Dodgers to six National league titles?

11 Which US body builder was five times winner of the Mr Universe competition and later became one of Hollywood's highest-paid film stars?

12 Which East German athlete of the 1980s and 1990s became the most successful long jumper in women's athletics history and has leapt 7 m or further more than 400 times?

13 Which British ski-jumper, known as 'The Eagle' became a legend in the 1980s because his performance at the Calgary Olympic games was so spectacularly bad?

14 The Oscar-winning movie 'Chariots of Fire' was the story of Eric Liddell and which other athlete?

15 Which Australian cricket legend who, if he had hit one more boundary in any one of his 80 test matches would have had an average of 100 runs, died in his nineties in 2001?

Answers 1 Joe Frazier 2 Ben Hogan 3 Skiing 4 Eddy Merckx 5 Bjorn Borg 6 Figure skating 7 Bill Shoemaker 8 Frank Swift 9 Johnny Weissmuller 10 Jackie Robinson 11 Arnold Schwarzenegger 12 Heike Drechsler 13 Eddie Edwards 14 Harold Abrahams 15 Sir Donald Bradman

GENERAL SPORT

Motor Sport

1 Who, in 1959, became the first Australian to win the Formula One world championship?

2 And who, in 1961, became the first American winner of Formula One's world championship?

3 Which South African won the Formula One world championship in 1979?

4 Name the French driver who won his first ever Formula One grand prix race, the 1995 Canadian Grand Prix, on his 31st birthday.

5 And which French driver recorded his first Formula One race victory when he won the 1996 Monaco Grand Prix?

6 Who was Formula One world champion in 1972 and 1974 and Indianapolis 500 winner in 1989 and 1993?

7 Who failed to qualify for the 1995 Indianapolis 500 after having won the race the previous year?

8 Which Formula One driver had his private plane confiscated by tax officials in 1996?

9 In 1965, who became the first British driver to win the Indianapolis 500?

10 Who, in 1991, became the first driver to win the first four races of a Formula One grand prix season?

11 Which driver won the 1982 Indianapolis 500 by the narrow margin of less than a second?

12 Name the Argentinian driver who won both Grand Prix races held in the US in 1978, one at Long Beach and one at Watkins Glen?

13 What make of car finished first, second and third at Le Mans in 2000 – Audi, Jaguar, Nissan or Porsche?

14 Which driver was the first to follow a Formula One world championship with an Indy Car championship?

15 Name the Indy Car champion of 1991 who tried his hand, none too successfully, at Formula One in 1993?

Answers 1 Jack Brabham 2 Phil Hill 3 Jody Scheckter 4 Jean Alesi 5 Olivier Panis 6 Emerson Fittipaldi 7 Al Unser Jnr. 8 Gerhard Berger 9 Jim Clark 10 Ayrton Senna 11 Gordon Johncock 12 Carlos Reutemann 13 Audi 14 Nigel Mansell 15 Michael Andretti

GENERAL SPORT *The Olympic Games*

1   What nationality was the athlete Paavo Nurmi, winner of nine gold medals?

2   Hillary Wolf, who appeared in the first two 'Home Alone' films as a sister of Macaulay Culkin, represented the USA at both the 1996 and 2000 Olympics in which sport?

3   Jaroslav Drobny won the Wimbledon men's singles title in 1954. In 1948 he was a member of the Czechoslovakian team that won an Olympic silver medal in which sport?

4   James Connolly became the first winner of a gold medal at the modern Olympics when he won which athletics field event in 1896?

5   Which US city staged the summer Olympics in 1932 and 1984?

6   Where in the US were the winter Olympics of 1932 and 1980 held?

7   Which city was due to stage the cancelled Games of 1916?

8   Tennis. The two girls who won the women's doubles for the USA at the 1992 Games, had the same surname. What name?

9   Which country are the reigning Olympic polo champions, winning the last time it was contested in 1936?

10 And which country won the rugby union tournament the last time it was contested, in 1924?

11 Between 1912 and 1956, with the exception of 1936, the winner of the individual modern pentathlon title came from which country?

12 With the exception of 1936, Canada won every Olympic ice hockey tournament between 1920 and 1952. Which country won in 1936?

13 Which team sport, invented in America in 1895 by William Morgan, became an Olympic sport in 1964?

14 In which year did British ice skater Robin Cousins win a gold medal?

15 Which female swimmer, representing East Germany, won six gold medals in 1988?

1 About which tennis player did Arthur Ashe remark: "Nasty drives you crazy but you have to love him"?

2 Who was the USSR gymnast who, aged 17, took the 1972 Munich Olympics by storm and whose routines set new standards in women's gymnastics?

3 Which West Indies cricketer, in 1994, in Antigua against England, broke the record for the highest test score with 375?

4 Which Argentinian soccer genius scored his famous 'Hand of God' goal against England in the 1986 World Cup finals in Mexico?

5 Which US athlete, who dominated the 400 m hurdles for more than a decade, took the oath at the 1984 Los Angeles Olympics?

6 What was the nickname of the US tennis player Richard Gonzales who was at the peak of his career in the 1950s?

7 Which boxer was portrayed by Paul Newman in the movie 'Somebody Up There Likes Me'?

8 At which Grand Prix circuit was Ayrton Senna killed in 1994?

9 Which British golfer won the British Open in 1969 and 11 months later the US Open by seven strokes?

10 Which Cuban runner won the men's 400m and 800m gold medals at the 1976 Montreal Olympics?

11 Who, in 1973, confronted a male tennis player directly in the 'Battle of the Sexes', defeating Bobby Riggs 6-4, 6-3, 6-3?

12 Which legendary Scottish-born soccer manager once said that 'football is more important than life or death'?

13 Which Welsh boxer, who from 1916-1923 was world flyweight champion, was known as 'the ghost with the hammer in his hands'?

14 Which US swimmer is, thanks to her movies, probably the most famous swimmer who never competed in the Olympics?

15 Which sport was dominated by Byron Nelson in the mid 1940s?

Answers 1 Ilie Nastase 2 Olga Korbut 3 Brian Lara 4 Diego Maradona 5 Ed Moses 6 Pancho 7 Rocky Graziano 8 Imola 9 Tony Jacklin 10 Alberto Juantorena 11 Billie Jean King 12 Bill Shankly 13 Jimmy Wilde 14 Esther Williams 15 Golf

GENERAL SPORT — *Olympic Games 2*

1   In 1984, Stephan van den Berg became the first Olympic boardsailing champion. Which country did he represent?

2   Robert Sullivan, husband of singer Bonnie Tyler, represented Great Britain at the 1972 Games in which sport?

3   Which Finnish athlete won the men's 5000 and 10,000 metres at both the 1972 and 1976 Games?

4   Which Russian athlete won the men's 100 and 200 metres at the 1972 Games?

5   Name the American who won both platform and springboard diving titles at the 1984 Olympics, a feat he repeated in 1988.

6   Known as the 'albatross', which German swimmer won the men's 200 metres freestyle and 100 metres butterfly in 1984 and the 200 metres butterfly in 1988?

7   Which Ethiopian athlete won the men's 5000 and 10,000 metres at the 1980 Games?

8   American Al Oerter won which athletics event at four consecutive Games between 1956 and 1968?

9   And at which event did Russian athlete Viktor Saneyev win three successive gold medals between 1968 and 1976?

10   Athletics. In 1908 Reginald Walker became the first non-American winner of the 100 metres title. Which country did he represent?

11   Whom did Lennox Lewis beat in the final of the 1988 super-heavyweight boxing competition?

12   Name the Cuban boxer who won the gold medal in the heavyweight division in 1972, 1976 and 1980.

13   In which female field event did British athletes win silver medals at every Games from 1936 to 1960?

14   What nationality was Rob De Castella who in 1992 became the first athlete to take part and finish in four Olympic marathon races?

15   Athletics. The winners of the men's 200 metres in both 1960 and 1980 came from which European country?

Answers 1 The Netherlands **2** Judo **3** Lasse Viren **4** Valeriy Borzov **5** Greg Louganis **6** Michael Gross **7** Miruts Yifter **8** Discus **9** Triple jump **10** South Africa **11** Riddick Bowe **12** Teofilo Stevenson **13** High Jump **14** Australian **15** Italy

GENERAL SPORT   *Soccer's World Cup 1*

1 Who scored two goals in Argentina's 3-1 win over Holland in the 1978 final?

2 Which Hungarian, he was to be the European Footballer of the Year in 1967, was the only player to score a hat-trick during the 1962 finals?

3 Pelé scored goals in the final stages of four successive World Cups – 1958, 1962, 1966 and 1970. Which West German player also scored in those final stages?

4 He played for the winning side in the 1958 and 1962 finals and managed the winners in 1970. Name him.

5 Who scored Italy's consolation goal in their 4-1 defeat by Brazil in the 1970 final?

6 In which country did the first World Cup finals take place in 1930?

7 Brazil's captain during the 1982 finals had the same name as which ancient Greek philosopher?

8 Which European country finished third in the 1974 and 1982 tournaments?

9 Why did Larry Gaetjens make the headlines in the 1950 tournament?

10 For which country did goalkeeper Antonio Carbajal play in the final stages in 1950, 1954, 1958, 1962 and 1966?

11 Which European country lost in the final in 1934 and 1962?

12 Against which Central American country did Hungary score 10 during the 1982 finals?

13 Which two teams, one European and one South American, were involved in a quarter-final match in 1954 known as the 'Battle of Berne'?

14 On their way to winning the competition in their own country in 1974, West Germany lost one match. Who beat them?

15 Name the captain of Argentina who was sent off in the quarter-final against England in 1966.

Answers 1 Mario Kempes 2 Florian Albert 3 Uwe Seeler 4 Mario Zagalo 5 Roberto Boninsegna 6 Uruguay 7 Socrates 8 Poland 9 He scored the goal when the USA surprisingly beat England 1-0 10 Mexico 11 Czechoslovakia 12 El Salvador 13 Hungary and Brazil 14 East Germany 15 Antonio Rattin

Boxing Quips

1   On being told his next opponent, Chuck Wepner, was another great white hope, who replied: "That's the only hope he's got"?

2   In 1979, which boxer who twice lost on points in the mid 1960s when challenging for the world title said: "I'm the best heavyweight in Canada and I'll still be the best when I'm dead seven years"?

3   Before fighting Billy Conn, which world heavyweight champion said: "He can run but he can't hide"?

4   Which contemporary of Jake LaMotta said: "Me and Jake LaMotta grew up in the same neighbourhood. You wanna know how popular Jake was? When we played hide and seek, nobody ever looked for LaMotta"?

5   And which famous world champion said: "Jake LaMotta and I fought six times. We almost got married"?

6   After Lennox Lewis lost his WBC title to Oliver McCall, who said: "Lennox Lewis has two chances of getting a rematch with McCall – no chance and slim. And slim has just left town"?

7   Which boxer once said: "My girlfriend boos when we make love because she knows it turns me on". Was it Hector Camacho, Julio Cesar Chavez or Roberto Duran?

8   Famous for his shaven head, which world middleweight champion once said: "With four sisters about the house, I could never get my hands on a comb"?

9   In 1990, which veteran heavyweight said: "I want to keep fighting because it is the only thing that keeps me out of hamburger joints. If I don't fight, I'll eat this planet"?

10 Which popular Welsh heavyweight once said: "I only have to read Joe Louis' name and my nose starts to bleed again"?

11 Which famous trainer once said: "Anyone who weighs over 200 pounds can punch – I don't care if it's a broad"?

12 With regard to his fight with Floyd Patterson in 1962 being switched, who said: "Don't matter where the fight is. My punches are just as hard in Chicago as New York"?

Answers 1 Muhammad Ali 2 George Chuvalo 3 Joe Louis 4 Rocky Graziano 5 Sugar Ray Robinson 6 Don King 7 Hector Camacho 8 Marvin Hagler 9 George Foreman 10 Tommy Farr 11 Angelo Dundee 12 Sonny Liston

Sporting Quotations

1   When talking about golf, which American entertainer said: "If you drink, don't drive. Don't even putt"?

2   What was Dick Allen referring to when he said: "If horses can't eat it, I won't play on it"?

3   Which legendary Australian swimmer once said: "I'm a woman first and a swimmer second. I attract trouble like worms attract birds"?

4   Who prompted the newspaper headline: "Moses finds the promised land" after breaking 8 minutes for the 3000 metres steeplechase?

5   And who said: "Being a decathlete is like having ten girlfriends. You have to love them all, and you can't afford losing one"?

6   Which former US president said: "Bob Hope says I have made golf a combat and contact sport. But I know I'm getting better at golf because I am hitting fewer spectators"?

7   A former partner, who said: "The best doubles pair in the world is John McEnroe and anyone else"?

8   What sport was Stan Fischler referring to here: "He who lives by the cheap shot dies by the crosscheck"?

9   Which woman, the first woman driver to take part in the Indianapolis 500, on being asked if female drivers were as strong as their male counterparts replied: "You drive the car, you don't carry it"?

10 And which member of the Unser family said on winning the Indianapolis 500: "It sure didn't make me the million dollars people said it would, but it sure made my ex-wife happy"?

11 Which New Zealand golfer, he won the Open in 1963, once said: "Being left-handed is a big advantage. No one knows enough about your swing to mess you up with advice"?

12 On suggestions that she might date 'Broadway' Joe Namath, which popular American singer of the 1950s and 1960s replied: "Who wants to go with a guy who has two bad knees and a quick release?"?

Answers 1 Dean Martin 2 Astroturf 3 Dawn Fraser 4 Moses Kiptanui 5 Daley Thompson 6 Gerald Ford 7 Peter Fleming 8 Ice Hockey 9 Janet Guthrie 10 Bobby Unser 11 Bob Charles 12 Connie Francis

Sporting Legends 3

1   Which basketball star featured in the movie 'Space Jam' with a host of cartoon characters including Bugs Bunny?

2   Which tennis player had, by the time she retired from singles play in 1994, won 167 singles titles including a record nine at Wimbledon?

3   Which USSR figure skater achieved success in the 1960s and 1970s with two partners, Alexai Ulanov and Alexander Zaitsev?

4   What nationality was 1979 World Motor Racing Champion Jody Schecter?

5   Which 14-year-old Romanian gymnast became an overnight sensation when she was awarded a perfect 10 for an asymmetric bars exercise in the Montreal Olympics

6   Which lady tennis player was known as 'Little Mo'?

7   At which sport in the 1960s did Peggy Fleming become a household name?

8   Who revolutionised high jumping when he used his flop technique to win an Olympic gold medal in Mexico in 1968?

9   What nationality was tennis player John Newcombe?

10 About which golfer did the great Bobby Jones remark: "He is playing an entirely different game - a game I'm not even familiar with."?

11 Which tennis player, famous for her two-handed backhand and baseline-dominated play was nicknamed 'The Ice Maiden'?

12 Who was the Argentinian racing driver (1911-1995) who won five world championships and was team leader of Mercedes-Benz, Alfa Romeo, Ferrari and Masarati?

13 Which Italian jockey rode his first winner Lizzy Hare, at Goodwood in 1987?

14 With which baseball team did Joe DiMaggio achieve icon status in the 1940s?

15 Which sport was dominated by the Italian, Giacomo Agostini in the 1960s and 1970s?

Answers 1 Michael Jordan 2 Martina Navratilova 3 Irina Rodnina 4 South African 5 Nadia Comaneci 6 Maureen Connolly 7 Figure Skating 8 Dick Fosbury 9 Australian 10 Jack Nicklaus 11 Chris Evert 12 Juan Manuel Fangio 13 Frankie Dettori 14 New York Yankees 15 Motor cycling

1 What nationality was Spyridon Louis, winner of the first modern Olympic marathon in 1896?

2 In which sport did Emmanuel Agassi, father of Andre, compete at the 1948 and 1952 Games?

3 Which country hosted the Summer Games of 1904, 1932, 1984 and 1996?

4 Which country hosted the Winter Games of 1924, 1968 and 1992?

5 A member of the US decathlon team at the 1912 Games, he was president of the International Olympic Committee from 1952 to 1972. Name him.

6 Name the rider from New Zealand who won the individual three-day event competition on his horse Charisma in both 1984 and 1988?

7 What was the name of the cartoon-style dog that was the mascot of the 1992 Games in Barcelona?

8 And what was the name of the bear who was the mascot for the 1980 Moscow Games?

9 An all-round sportsman, he carried the torch at the Melbourne Olympics in 1956 and went on to become a top snooker player. Name him.

10 Name the Briton who won gold medals in the three position, small bore rifle event in both 1984 and 1988.

11 First played in Germany around 1890, which team sport was introduced to the Games in 1936 as an 11-a-side outdoor game and did not appear again until 1972 when it was re-introduced as an indoor 7-a-side game?

12 Which country won the most medals, 29 in total, at the 1998 Winter Games?

13 Name the Dutch athlete, who in 1948 became the first woman to complete the 100 and 200 metres sprint double.

14 What nationality was athlete Percy Williams who won the 100 and 200 metres at the 1928 Games?

15 Which US athlete won the women's heptathlon at the 1988 and 1992 Games?

Answers 1 Greek **2** Boxing **3** USA **4** France **5** Avery Brundage **6** Mark Todd **7** Cobi **8** Mischa **9** Eddie Charlton **10** Malcolm Cooper **11** Handball **12** Germany **13** Fanny Blankers-Koen **14** Canadian **15** Jackie Joyner-Kersee

GENERAL SPORT — Sporting Legends 4

1 Which tennis player was described by Barbra Streisand as a Zen master, and at the height of his rebellious phase said: "Image is everything"?

2 What nationality was Abebe Bikila who won the marathon in the 1960 Rome Olympics?

3 Which American jockey, known as 'The Kentucky Kid' won three British leading jockey titles and , in 1985, won four out of five British classics?

4 The Frenchman Georges Carpentier was a famous name in which sport during the first quarter of the 20th-century?

5 In what year did Mats Wilander win three grand slam titles'?

6 In how many Tests did David Gower captain the England cricket team?

7 In the 1950s and 1960s Garrincha was a household name in which sport?

8 Which baseball player of the 1920s and 1930s was known as 'The Iron Horse' and was portrayed in the movie 'Pride of the Yankees' by Gary Cooper?

9 Who became the youngest player to win a US open tennis singles title when she defeated Chris Evert in 1979 at the age of 16 years nine months?

10 'One in a Million' (1937), was the first movie of which Norwegian-born 3-times Olympic gold medal ice-skating champion?

11 The meaning of the name of which Pakistan squash player is 'Conqueror of the World'?

12 In the 1968 Mexico Olympics, which 200m gold-medal winner raised a black-gloved clenched fisted 'black-power' salute on the medal ceremony podium?

13 The British Parliament adjourned to watch which competitors at the Winter Olympics in Sarajevo on 14 February 1984?

14 Who was the first boxer to regain the World Heavyweight boxing championship?

15 What nationality is 1960s football legend Eusebio?

Answers 1 André Agassi 2 Ethiopian 3 Steve Cauthen 4 Boxing 5 1988 6 32 7 Soccer 8 Lou Gehring 9 Tracy Austin 10 Sonja Henie 11 Jahangir Khan 12 Tommy Smith 13 Torvill and Dean's winning performance in the ice-dance to Ravel's 'Bolero' 14 Floyd Patterson 15 Portuguese

GENERAL SPORT   *Soccer's World Cup 2*

1 Who played in goal for Holland in the 1974 final and the 1978 final?

2 Which other South American country did Argentina beat 6-0 in the last match of the second stage of the 1978 competition, thus preventing Brazil from reaching the final?

3 In 1938, in France, which country became the first to win the World Cup outside their own country?

4 In the 1982 tournament, which African country drew with Italy, Peru and Poland?

5 Name the Frenchman who scored 13 goals during the 1958 finals.

6 And which West German player scored 10 goals during the 1970 finals?

7 Yugoslavia beat which African country 9-0 in the 1974 competition?

8 Who scored for West Germany in the 1974 final and the 1982 final?

9 Which European country reached the final stages for the first time in 1986?

10 Against which Asian country did Eusebio score four goals for Portugal in 1966?

11 Ramon Quiroga, known as 'El Loco', played in goal for which country in the 1978 and 1982 competitions?

12 Which was the first city to stage the final twice?

13 Who was the coach of the winning French team of 1998?

14 Which European country reached the final stages for the first time in 1994 but failed to score a goal in their three matches?

15 In 1994, which 17 year-old player from the Cameroon had the misfortune to become the youngest player to be sent off in the final stages of a World Cup?

Answers 1 Jan Jongbloed **2** Peru **3** Italy **4** Cameroon **5** Juste Fontaine **6** Gerd Muller **7** Zaire **8** Paul Breitner **9** Denmark **10** North Korea **11** Peru **12** Mexico City **13** Aime Jacquet **14** Greece **15** Rigobert Song

571

Sporting Greats

SPORTING GREATS

Quiz 1

All the answers begin with A.

1 Hank, a baseball player who made 755 home runs between 1954 and 1976?

2 The surname of Carmine and Giuseppe, the Italian brothers who dominated rowing's coxed pairs between 1981 and 1991?

3 Giacomo, the Italian motor cyclist who won 15 world titles?

4 Vasili, a Russian weight lifter who set 81 world records?

5 Greta, a swimmer who won the Olympic 100 metes freestyle for Denmark in 1948 and then went on to swim the English Channel six times and became a US citizen in 1958?

6 Nikolai, a Russian gymnast who won 13 medals at the Olympics between 1972 and 1980?

7 Jacques, the first cyclist to win the Tour de France five times?

8 Said, brilliant Moroccan middle distance runner of the 1980s?

9 Eddie, US jockey who won 4,779 races in a 30-year career that ended in 1961?

10 The name of the horse regarded by many as the greatest ever British steeplechaser, winning 3 consecutive Cheltenham Gold Cups 1964-6?

11 Alberto, the motor racing driver who won 9 consecutive Grand Prix between June 1952 and June 1953?

12 Arthur, tennis player who won the US Open in 1968 and Wimbledon in 1975?

13 Surname of soccer players Jose and Rodriguez, who were uncle and nephew? Jose played in Uruguay's World Cup winning team of 1930 and Rodriguez repeated the feat in 1950.

14 Paul, US weight lifter who was the first man to break the 500kg mark and was undefeated during his amateur career.

15 Surname of Fred, a famous New Zealand rugby coach and England cricketer?

Answers 1 Aaron 2 Abbagnale 3 Agostini 4 Alexeyev 5 Andersen 6 Andrianov 7 Anquetil 8 Aouita 9 Arcaro 10 Arkle 11 Ascari 12 Ashe 13 Andrade 14 Anderson 15 Allen

SPORTING GREATS

Quiz 2

All the answers begin with B.

1 Max, US heavyweight boxer who became world champion in 1934 and was known as 'Madcap Maxie' and the 'Playboy of the Ring'?

2 Roberto, Italian soccer player nicknamed 'The Divine Ponytail' because of his hairstyle?

3 Viktor, the Hungarian-born table tennis player who won 15 world titles at singles and doubles?

4 Iolande, Romanian high jumper who won 140 consecutive competitions between 1956 and 1967?

5 Bob, US long jumper who will always be remembered for his 'leap' at the 1968 Olympics?

6 Franz, German soccer player known as 'Der Kaiser'?

7 John, Australian yachtsman who achieved sailing immortality when he skippered Australia II to victory in the America's Cup in 1983?

8 Matt, US swimmer who won 5 gold medals at the 1988 Olympics?

9 Serge, Venezuelan-born French rugby full-back who scored 38 tries in 93 internationals?

10 Louison, French cyclist who was the first man to win the Tour de France three years in succession?

11 Jim, Cleveland Browns running back who later turned to acting?

12 Richard (or Dick), the US ice skater who won gold medals at the 1948 and 1952 Winter Olympics?

13 Gordon, England goalkeeper in their 1966 World Cup winning team?

14 Maria, Brazilian tennis player who won the US Open four times and Wimbledon three times?

15 Jimmy, racing driver known as the 'Arizona Cowboy' he won the 1958 Indianapolis 500?

Answers 1 Baer 2 Baggio 3 Barna 4 Balas 5 Beamon 6 Beckenbauer 7 Bertrand 8 Biondi 9 Blanco 10 Bobet 11 Brown 12 Button 13 Banks 14 Bueno 15 Bryan

SPORTING GREATS

Quiz 3

All the answers begin with C.

1 Primo, Italian world heavyweight boxing champion known as the 'Ambling Alpi'

2 Georges, handsome French boxer, he was the first to attract women to the sport in significant numbers? He was world light-heavyweight champion and unsuccessfully challenged Jack Dempsey for the heavyweight title.

3 Vera, Czech gymnast who won 7 Olympic gold medals and was the most popular gymnast in the sport prior to Olga Korbut?

4 Fausto, Italian cyclist known as 'Il Campionissimo' who twice won the Tour de France?

5 Dennis, US yachtsman who virtually made the America's Cup his personal event during the 1980}s and 1990's?

6 Ty, legendary US baseball star?

7 Ron, Australian considered as possibly the best athlete never to have won an Olympic gold medal although he set 18 world records?

8 Julio Cesar, Mexican fighter who dominated world boxing for more than a decade, winning the first of his world titles in 1984?

9 Sebastian, British athlete who won the Olympic 1500 metres title in 1980 and 1984 and set world records for 800 metres, 1500 metres and the mile?

10 Eddie, Malaysian badminton player known as the 'mighty midget' and 'pocket rocket'?

11 Larry, tough Miami Dolphin full back who played in the Dolphins first two Superbowl victories?

12 Bob, although only 6 feet 1 inch tall he was the playmaker of the Boston Celtics basketball team of the 1950's?

13 Lorraine, the Australian swimmer who in 1956 became the first woman to break 5 minutes for the 400 metres?

14 Betty, US powerboat racer and grandmother who in the 1970s became one of the first women to challenge in what had become a macho male sport?

15 Henry, British heavyweight boxer who once sent Cassius Clay crashing to the canvas?

Answers 1 Carnera 2 Carpentier 3 Caslavska 4 Coppi 5 Conner 6 Cobb 7 Clarke 8 Chavez 9 Coe 10 Choong 11 Csonka 12 Cousy 13 Crapp 14 Cook 15 Cooper

SPORTING GREATS

Quiz 4

All the answers begin with D.

1   Real name Walder Pereira, he was a member of Brazil's soccer team in the 1954, 1958 and 1962 World Cups?

2   Roberto, legendary Panamanian boxer nicknamed 'Hands of Stone'?

3   John, US golfer who won the 1991 US PGA championship and the 1995 Open at St. Andrews and whose style has been described as 'grip it and rip it'?

4   Alexander, the Russian gymnast who won 8 medals at the 1980 Olympics?

5   Horst, a German, who although never a top-class sportsman, supplied kits and shoes to top teams and sports people and made the sports equipment firm Adidas world famous?

6   Harrison, US sprinter/hurdler who won Olympic gold medals in 1948 and 1952?

7   Bruce, US three-day event rider who was world champion in 1974 and 1978 and was a member of the winning US team at the 1976 and 1984 Olympics?

8   Klaus, Italian diver who won Olympic gold medals in 1968, 1972 and 1976?

9   Laura, British golfer who came to fame after winning the US Open in 1987?

10 First name of Davis, the man who founded tennis's Davis Cup?

11 Mary, US athlete who married British discus thrower Richard Slaney?

12 A famous grey racehorse, a British favourite who won the Cheltenham Gold Cup and a record four King George VI Chases?

13 Rick, US swimmer who was the first man to break the four-minute barrier for the 400 metres free-style and is also remembered as the first swimmer to be stripped of an Olympic gold medal for testing positive for a banned drug?

14 Not related, the surname of snooker legends Joe and Steve?

15 Jack, world heavyweight boxing champion known as the 'Manassa Mauler'?

SPORTING GREATS

Quiz 5

All the answers begin with G.

1 The surname of Gary and Paul, identical twins from Canada and superstars of Lacrosse's North American indoor league?

2 Dan, US racing driver who won four Formula One Grand Prix in the 1960s and despite never winning the Indianapolis 500 as a driver his Eagle cars won the race three times?

3 The name given to Manuel Francisco dos Santos, a member of Brazil's soccer team in the 1958 and 1962 World Cups?

4 Harry, US boxer who was the only man to beat Gene Tunney?

5 Sunil, Indian cricketer who scored a record number of 34 test match centuries?

6 Harold Edward, known as Red, early American footballer who helped to popularise the game in its coalescent days and was nicknamed 'The Galloping Ghost'?

7 Haile, phenomenal Ethiopian athlete who became the first man since Henry Rono to hold the 5000 metres and 10,000 metres world records simultaneously?

8 Shane, Australian swimmer who in 1972 became the first woman since the war to hold the world record for the 100, 200, 400, 800 and 1500 metres freestyle simultaneously?

9 Steffi, German tennis player who won all four Grand Slam tournaments and an Olympic gold medal in 1988?

10 Anton, the Dutch judo star who became the first heavyweight to beat the Japanese at the sport they invented?

11 Francisco, the Spanish soccer player who was the only man to play in all six of their European Cup triumphs in 1956, 1957, 1958, 1959, 1960 and 1966?

12 The only British horse to win the Cheltenham Gold Cup five times?

13 Lance, the West Indian cricketer who at one time held the record for the most wickets in test cricket?

14 Marc, multi-winning World Cup skier who represented Luxembourg?

15 Althea, US tennis player who won at Wimbledon in 1957 and 1958?

Answers 1 Gait 2 Gurney 3 Garrincha 4 Greb 5 Gavaskar 6 Grange 7 Gebrselassie 8 Gould 9 Graf 10 Geesink 11 Gento 12 Golden Miller 13 Gibbs 14 Girardelli 15 Gibson

SPORTING GREATS

Quiz 6

All the answers begin with H.

1   Walter, US golfer who won 11 major championships?

2   Named after a Titan in Greek mythology, which racehorse won the English Derby and St. Leger in 1933?

3   Gunder, Swedish athlete who in 1942 won all his 32 races at distances ranging from 800 to 5000 metres, breaking world records in nine of them?

4   Geoff, the Australian squash player who won the first ever world championship in 1976?

5   Rudy, the Indonesian thought by some to be the best ever badminton player?

6   Bobby, a Canadian ice hockey star with the Chicago Black Hawks and the first to score more than 50 goals in a season, he was known as 'The Golden Jet'?

7   Gordie, another Canadian-born ice hockey legend, he played in five different decades before retiring as a 52 year-old grandad?

8   Bob, US athlete who won the Olympic 100 metres title in 1964 and later achieved greater fame as a wide receiver for the Dallas Cowboys?

9   Lew, the Australian tennis player who won at Wimbledon in 1956 and 1957?

10 George, West Indian cricketer who in the 1930s was regarded as the 'Black Bradman'?

11 The surname of Graham and Damon, father and son who were both world motor racing champions?

12 Thomas, US boxer who won world titles at five different weights between 1980 and 1992 and whose nickname was the 'Hit Man'

13 John, US breast-stroke swimmer and fierce rival of Britain's David Wilkie. He set 12 world records for the breast-stroke between 1972 and 1976?

14 Nandor, member of the great Hungarian soccer team of the 1950's, he was the prototype of the deep-lying centre forward?

15 Eric, US sportsman who won all five Olympic speed skating gold medals in 1980 and was American professional cycling champion in 1985?

Answers 1 Hagen 2 Hyperion 3 Hagg 4 Hunt 5 Hartono 6 Hull 7 Howe 8 Hayes 9 Hoad 10 Headley 11 Hill 12 Hearns 13 Hencken 14 Hidegkuti 15 Heiden

SPORTING GREATS

Quiz 7

All the answers begin with K.

1   Duke, Hawaiian swimmer and surfer, he was Olympic 100 metres freestyle champion in 1912 and 1920 and played a major role in introducing the sport of surfing around the world?

2   Vladimir, the Russian athlete who won the Olympic 10,000 metres title in 1956 and broke the world record for the 5000 metres four times?

3   Pertti, the Finnish rower who won the single sculls at the Olympics three times in a row between 1976 and 1984?

4   Ladislav, Hungarian-born soccer player who played international football for Hungary, Czechoslovakia and Spain?

5   Stanley, the first of the great middleweight boxing champions, he also fought Jack Johnson for the heavyweight title and was shot dead in a dispute over a woman?

6   Julie, a gymnast of Olympic potential she was guided into horse racing by her mother and became the first woman jockey to win an American triple crown race when winning the 1993 Belmont Stakes?

7   Nelli, Russian gymnast who was world champion in 1979?

8   Ingrid, Norwegian athlete who has won world titles on the track, road and cross-country?

9   Marita, East German athlete who set 11 world records over 200 and 400 metres and lost only twice in one eight year period?

10 Jack, US tennis player who won at Wimbledon in 1947 and later started his own professional tennis 'circus'?

11 Ada, 6 feet tall Dutch swimmer who was a popular winner of the 200 metres butterfly at the 1968 Olympics?

12 Sandy, he was an overpowering pitcher for the Los Angles Dodgers baseball team during the 1960s?

13 Kip, athlete who in 1965 became the first Kenyan to set a world record?

14 Sean, scorer of eight goals during Britain's successful tournament in the 1988 Olympic hockey competition?

15 Don, famous US boxing promoter?

Answers 1 Kahanamoku 2 Kuts 3 Karpinnen 4 Kubala 5 Ketchel 6 Krone 7 Kim 8 Kristiansen 9 Koch 10 Kramer 11 Kok 12 Koufax 13 Keino 14 Kerly 15 King

SPORTING GREATS

Quiz 8

All the answers begin with L.

1   Surname of Rene and Catherine, he was a famous tennis player – one of the 'Four Musketeers' – and she was the first European golfer to win the US Open?

2   Michael, the Australian player who at one time held the record for scoring the most points in international rugby union?

3   Bernhard, German golfer who won the US Masters in 1985 and 1993?

4   Wayne, the highly successful US racehorse trainer who was the first to complete the US Triple Crown with two different horses and when he won the 1995 Belmont Stakes with Thunder Gulch he also became the first to win five straight Triple Crown races?

5   Larissa, Russian gymnast who won 18 Olympic medals between 1956 and 1964?

6   Nancy, US golfer who married baseball star Ray Knight?

7   'Champagne Tony', the US golfer who won the Open at St. Andrews in 1964?

8   Jonah, the massive New Zealand rugby union winger who was the star of the 1995 World Cup competition?

9   Suzanne, French tennis player who won at Wimbledon six times between 1919 and 1925?

10 Vince, legendary American football coach who guided the Green Bay Packers to back to back Superbowl victories in 1967/8?

11 The surname shared by the American boxers – Benny, the world lightweight champion from 1917 to 1925 – and Sugar Ray, the multi-world champion?

12 Bobby, the South African who won 11 tournaments in the US in the late 1940s and won the British Open four times between 1949 and 1957?

13 Walter, the Australian billiards player who conquered the games challenges so comprehensively that he made it unviable as a public entertainment?

14 Clive, cricketer who captained the West Indies in 76 of his 110 test matches?

15 Sonny, US boxer who defeated Floyd Patterson to win the world heavyweight title?

Answers 1 Lacoste 2 Lynagh 3 Langer 4 Lukas 5 Latynina 6 Lopez 7 Lema 8 Lomu 9 Lenglen 10 Lombardi 11 Leonard 12 Locke 13 Lindrum 14 Lloyd 15 Liston

SPORTING GREATS　　　　　　　　　　　　*Quiz 9*

All the answers begin with M.

1　Heather, the Australian squash player who was unbeaten between 1962 and her retirement in 1979?

2　Karen, South African swimmer who in 1965 broke the world record for the 110 yards backstroke at the tender age of 12 years 10 months and 25 days?

3　Herb, Jamaican athlete who had the distinction of competing in Olympic finals at 100, 200 and 400 metres, winning the silver medal in the 400 metres in 1948 and 1952?

4　Noureddine, Algerian athlete who broke the world records for the mile and 1500 metres?

5　Bruce, New Zealand racing driver who won his first Grand Prix at the age of 22 in 1959 and in 1966 formed his own racing team?

6　Carlos, Argentinian boxer who was world middleweight champion from 1970 to 1977?

7　Surname of Phil and Steve, the American twin brothers who finished first and second in the slalom event at the 1984 Olympics?

8　Eugenio, Italian bobsleigh driver who won 11 world titles?

9　Mickey, effective switch-hitter for the New York Yankees baseball team. In 1956 he came within 18 inches of becoming the first man to hit over the top of the Yankee Stadium?

10　Joe, outstanding quarterback who took the San Francisco 49ers to four victorious Superbowls?

11　Roland, outstanding East German swimmer who won the Olympic 100 and 200 metres backstroke titles in both 1968 and 1972?

12　Ivan, the New Zealander who was six times world speedway champion?

13　The name of the dog that put greyhound racing on the map in Britain, winning the Derby in 1929 and 1930 and winning 46 out of 61 races?

14　Francois, French racehorse trainer who was the first in Europe to have 200 horses in his care?

15　Bob, US decathlete who won the Olympic title aged 17 years 263 days in 1948. He retained his title in 1952?

SPORTING GREATS — Quiz 10

All the answers begin with P.

1 Laszlo, the Hungarian boxer who won Olympic gold medals in 1948, 1952 and 1956 and won the European middleweight title after turning professional?

2 Ferenc, another Hungarian, he was a member of their great national soccer team of the 1950s and had the nickname the 'Galloping Major'?

3 The legendary Brazilian soccer player whose real name is Edson Arantes do Nascimento?

4 Oleg, a Russian who along with his wife Ludmila Belousova won the Olympic pairs skating title in 1964 and 1968?

5 Willie, US boxer who was world featherweight champion in the 1940s and had four epic fights with another champion Sandy Saddler?

6 Alain, the Frenchman who was world motor racing champion four times?

7 Fred, world table tennis champion in 1929 he turned to tennis and won at Wimbledon three years in a row 1934-36?

8 The surname of the Russian athletes and sisters Tamara and Irina, Olympic gold medallists in the 1960s?

9 Michel, French soccer star who was voted European Footballer of the Year in three successive years 1983-85?

10 Mike, US long jumper who ended Carl Lewis's unbeaten run of 65 long jump competitions at the 1991 world championships breaking the world record in the process?

11 Jean, captain of the French rugby union team from 1953 to 1955, he was a drop goal expert, unusual for a forward and had the nickname 'Monsieur Rugby'?

12 Nelson, a Brazilian who won the world motor racing championship three times?

13 Nelson, another Brazilian, a popular show jumper who rather curiously won the European championship in 1966?

14 Alexander, Russian swimmer who won the 100 metres freestyle at the 1992 and 1996 Olympics?

15 Francois, South African captain when they won rugby union's World Cup in 1995?

Answers 1 Papp 2 Puskas 3 Pelé 4 Protopopov 5 Pep 6 Prost 7 Perry 8 Press 9 Platini 10 Powell 11 Prat 12 Piquet 13 Pessoa 14 Popov 15 Pienaar

HISTORY

General History

GENERAL HISTORY — General 1

1 Which city was the residence of Holy Roman Emperors from 1558 to 1806?

2 Name the Roman gladiator and rebel who led a revolt against the Roman Empire between 73 and 71 BC.

3 At the end of the 18th century, where did a man named Toussaint-L'Ouverture lead a rebellion?

4 Which country was ruled by Akbar the Great in the 16th century?

5 Who was appointed head of the Spanish Inquisition in 1483?

6 Name the Frenchman who was allied commander-in-chief in 1918 and directed the hammer blows that drove back the Germans to win the First World War.

7 Who was the Roman emperor at the time of the execution of St. Paul, circa 64 AD?

8 In which rather unusual place did representatives of France's Third Estate take the oath to form a national assembly on 20 June 1789, after being locked out of their normal assembly place?

9 Which city in northern Italy, said to have been founded by the Sabines, was the capital of the western Roman Empire from 402-476 AD and capital of the Ostrogoth kings from 476-526 AD?

10 What name is given to the period between Napoleon's return to France after his escape from Elba, until his final defeat at Waterloo?

11 Who was president of the USA throughout World War One?

12 The Treaty of Panmunjon ended which war?

13 The Virgin Islands of the United States, a territory in the West Indies, were bought by the USA in 1917 from which European country?

14 In 1940, who did Hitler make marshal of the Reich, or Reichmarshal, the first and only holder of that rank?

15 Who was the war commissar who led the Red Army to victory in the Russian civil war of 1918 to 1920?

Answers 1 Vienna 2 Spartacus 3 Haiti 4 India 5 Tomas de Torquemada 6 Marshal Ferdinand Foch 7 Nero 8 A tennis court 9 Ravenna 10 Hundred Days 11 Woodrow Wilson 12 Korean War 13 Denmark 14 Hermann Goering 15 Leon Trotsky

GENERAL HISTORY — *Women in History 1*

1 Mary Todd was the wife of which US President?
   a Jefferson
   b Grant
   c Cleveland
   d Lincoln

2 Who is reputed to have said: "If the people have no bread, let them eat cake"?
   a Anne Boleyn
   b Marie Antoinette
   c Madame Pompadour
   d Catherine the Great of Russia

3 Which tennis player was known as 'Little Miss Poker Face'?
   a Billie Jean King
   b Maureen Connoly
   c Martina Navratilova
   d Helen Wills Moody

4 In the Bible, who was the Hebrew prophetess who helped the Israelites conquer the Canaanites?
   a Esther
   b Haggith
   c Deborah
   d Judith

5 Which fashion designer said "There is time for work. And there is time for love. That leaves no other time"?
   a Mary Quant
   b Vivian Westwood
   c Denise Klahn
   d Coco Chanel

6 In which spacecraft did the first woman astronaut, Valentina Tereshkova, make her historic space journey?
   a Sputnik 2
   b Vostok 6
   c Mariner 3
   d Mars 1

7 Miriam "Ma" Fergusan was Governor of which state in the 1920s?
   a California
   b Kentucky
   c Texas
   d Colorado

8 In 1911 Marie Curie won the Nobel Prize for Chemistry for her discovery of which two elements?
   a Radium and promethium
   b Europium and francium
   c Radium and polonium
   d Radium and francium

9 What was achieved on 3 November 1965 by Mrs Lee Ann Breedlove of Los Angeles, California?
   a The greatest altitude attained by a woman
   b The fastest downhill speed by a woman on skis
   c The highest land speed recorded by a woman
   d The highest water speed recorded by a woman

10 Whose mistress was Carlotte Monti?
   a W.C. Fields
   b Charlie Chaplin
   c Mussolini
   d Enrico Caruso

Answers 1 d, **2** b, **3** d, **4** c, **5** d, **6** b, **7** c, **8** c, **9** c, **10** a.

GENERAL HISTORY   *Identify the Year 1*

1   England lose to the USA at soccer; swimmer Mark Spitz is born and Al Jolson dies?

2   Mount St. Helens erupts; Jesse Owens dies and Princess Beatrix becomes queen of the Netherlands on the abdication of her mother Queen Juliana?

3   Idi Amin seizes power in Uganda; Charles Manson is convicted of murder in the USA and Lee Trevino wins the Open at Royal Birkdale?

4   Abebe Bikila wins the Olympic marathon in bare feet; Playboy magazine is banned in the state of Connecticut and Tiros 1 the first meteorological satellite is launched?

5   The Sudan is declared an independent republic; Grace Kelly marries Prince Rainier III of Monaco and boxer Rocky Marciano announces his retirement from the ring?

6   Elvis Presley and his wife Priscilla are divorced; the US dollar is devalued by 10 per cent and a Libyan Boeing 727 is shot down by Israeli jets?

7   John Glenn becomes the first American to orbit the earth; Marilyn Monroe is found dead and New Zealander Peter Snell breaks the world record for the mile?

8   Ismail Azhari becomes the first Prime Minister of the Sudan; Marilyn Monroe marries Joe DiMaggio and the Boeing 707 makes it's maiden flight?

9   Actor Boris Karloff dies; the Boeing 747 makes it's first flight and the Mariner 6 is launched on it's journey to Mars?

10 The EEC recognise Croatia and Slovenia as independent states; Mike Tyson is sent to jail for rape and Marlene Dietrich dies?

11 Lyndon B. Johnson is sworn in as US president; Winston Churchill dies and Alexei Leonov becomes the first man to walk in space?

12 Former Israeli Prime Minister Golda Meir dies; Martina Navratilova wins at Wimbledon and the Turin Shroud goes on public display?

13 Russian spacecraft Lunik III photographs the moon; John McEnroe is born and Cecil B. de Mille dies?

14 Greece becomes the 10th member of the EEC; rock 'n' roller Bill Haley dies and Ronald Reagan is wounded in an assassination attempt?

15 Australian Prime Minister Menzies resigns after 16 years; silent movie star Buster Keaton dies and an unmanned US spacecraft lands on the moon?

Answers 1 1950 2 1980 3 1971 4 1960 5 1956 6 1973 7 1962 8 1954 9 1969 10 1992 11 1965 12 1978 13 1959 14 1981 15 1966

GENERAL HISTORY   *The Roaring Twenties 1*

1   Which film actor, noted for his daring athletic feats and expert swordsmanship, starred in 'Robin Hood' (1922), 'The Thief of Baghdad' (1924) and 'The Iron Mask' (1929)?

2   Who, in 1926, created Winnie-the-Pooh?

3   What was the professional name of Rodolpho Guglieni, who was born in Castellanteta, Italy in 1895 and died in New York in 1926?

4   In the 1920s Gene Tunney was a world champion in which sport?

5   Who, in 1921, wrote 'Women in Love'?

6   The American heiress Jennie Jerome, who died in 1921, was the mother of which leading 20th-century political figure?

7   Who, in 1924, wrote 'Rhapsody in Blue'?

8   Which principle, formulated in 1927 by Werner Heisenburg, was of great significance in the development of quantum mechanics?

9   At which sport did William (Bill) Tilden excel during the 1920s?

10 In 1925 F. Scott Fitzgerald completed which novel, regarded as his masterpiece, about the pursuit of success and collapse of the American dream?

11 Which film director formed the United Artists Corporation in 1920 with Douglas Fairbanks, Mary Pickford and Charlie Chaplin?

12 Who, in 1928, discovered penicillin?

13 Constantine I, who died in 1923, was king of which country?

14 Which Earl died in 1923, two months after opening the tomb of Tutankhamen?

15 Incorporated in 1927 as United Independent Broadcasters Inc., but now known as CBS; what do the initials CBS stand for?

Answers 1 Douglas Fairbanks 2 A.A. Milne 3 Rudoph Valentino 4 Boxing 5 D.H. Lawrence 6 Sir Winston Churchill 7 George Gershwin 8 The Uncertainty Principle 9 Tennis 10 The Great Gatsby 11 D.W.Griffith 12 Sir Alexander Fleming 13 Greece 14 Carnarvon 15 Colombia Broadcasting System

GENERAL HISTORY   *The Swinging Sixties 1*

1   Which rock guitarist had hits with 'Purple Haze' and 'The Wind Cries Mary' in the 1960s?

2   Which American actor starred in his first hit film 'Barefoot in the Park' in 1967?

3   In which country was Che Guevara shot dead in 1967?

4   Who was the Godfather of Soul whose 1968 hit record was 'Say It Loud, I'm Black and I'm Proud'?

5   Which black American leader was assassinated in 1965 while addressing a rally in New York City, by men allegedly connected with the Black Muslims?

6   Who, in 1961, wrote 'The Prime of Miss Jean Brodie'?

7   Which American World Motor Racing champion won the Daytona 500 stock-car event in 1957 and the Indianapolis 500 in 1969?

8   In which 1968 movie did Jane Fonda star as an erotic space maiden?

9   Hendrik Verwoerd, who was assassinated in 1966, was Prime Minister of which country?

10 Who, in 1964, wrote and recorded 'The Times They Are A-Changin''?

11 Who, in 1968, produced, directed and starred in 'The Green Berets'?

12 Which leader of the pop group The Who wrote the rock opera 'Tommy'?

13 Who was the original drummer with the Beatles whom Ringo Starr replaced in 1962?

14 Which rock band, formed in 1965, was fronted by its vocalist and lead guitarist Jerry Garcia?

15 In which sport was Jim Ryun a leading figure in the 1960s?

Answers 1 Jimi Hendrix 2 Robert Redford 3 Bolivia 4 James Brown 5 Malcolm X 6 Muriel Spark 7 Mario Andretti 8 Barbarella 9 South Africa 10 Bob Dylan 11 John Wayne 12 Pete Townsend 13 Pete Best 14 The Greatful Dead 15 Running (800/1500 metres)

GENERAL HISTORY — *Women in History 2*

1. For her biography of which American poet did Elizabeth Frank win a Pulitzer Prize in 1986?
   a Maxine Kumin
   b Louise Bogan
   c Sylvia Plath
   d Anna Sexton

2. Martha Dandridge married which President?
   a Warren G. Harding
   b Abraham Lincoln
   c George Washington
   d Thomas Jefferson

3. Born in Massachusetts 1793, died Philadelphia 1880, what cause did Lucretia Coffin Mott devote most of her life to?
   a Votes for women
   b Equal rights for women
   c Midwifery
   d Coeducation

4. In the 1960s, which designer created the mini skirt?
   a Mary Quant
   b Liz Claiborne
   c Sonia Terk Delauney
   d Coco Chanel

5. Whose mistress was Emma, Lady Hamilton?
   a The Duke of Wellington
   b Sir Walter Raleigh
   c Lord Nelson
   d Napoleon Bonaparte

6. Who has been the subject of literary works by Shakespeare, John Dryden and George Bernard Shaw?
   a Nell Gwynne
   b Delilah
   c Helen of Troy
   d Cleopatra

7. Who became the first woman in U.S. history to serve as chief of protocol (1976-77), in the administration of Gerald R. Ford?
   a Patricia Roberts Harris
   b Shirley Temple Black
   c Shirley Mount Hufstedier
   d Ann Dore Mclaughlin

8. How did Delilah betray Samson?
   a Accepted a bribe and poisoned his drink
   b She cut off his hair
   c By committing adultery and revealing his secret strength
   d By revealing his whereabouts to the Philistines

9. Which old time movie star was known as the `Queen of the Swashbucklers`?
   a Mary Pickford
   b Maureen O`Sullivan
   c Lilian Gish
   d Maureen O`Hara

10. In Greek mythology, which goddess was the wife of Zeus?
   a Hera
   b Leda
   c Diana
   d Phaedra

Answers 1 b, 2 c, 3 b, 4 a, 5 c, 6 d, 7 b, 8 b, 9 d, 10 a.

1   Baines was the middle name of which US president?

2   Which US president was, in 1841, the first to die in office as a result of catching pneumonia one month after his inauguration?

3   What is the name of Bill and Hillary Clinton's only child?

4   Which president and lifelong bachelor served one term from 1857-61 and tried unsuccessfully to stave off the crisis that led to the American Civil War?

5   Who was the first president of the United States?

6   Who succeeded to the presidency on the death of F.D.Roosevelt in April 1945?

7   Which US president was known as Old Hickory because of his toughness?

8   Who was the first Republican US president?

9   Who, in 1841, was the first vice-president to succeed to the office of president on the death of a president?

10   Robert J. Dole was vice-presidential candidate with which US president?

11   Which US president was in office when the Vietnam War ended?

12   On appointing which General and future US president to lead the Union forces in the Civil War in March 1864 did President Lincoln say: "I can't spare this man – he fights!"?

13   Who served as US Secretary of State under Presidents Nixon and Ford?

14   Chester Alan were the first names of which US president?

15   Which president had held office for only six months when the US stock market crashed in 1929?

Answers 1 Lyndon Johnson 2 William Henry Harrison 3 Chelsea 4 James Buchanan 5 George Washington 6 Harry S Truman 7 Andrew Jackson 8 Abraham Lincoln 9 John Tyler 10 Gerald R. Ford 11 Nixon 12 Ulysses S. Grant 13 Henry Kissinger 14 Arthur 15 Herbert Hoover

GENERAL HISTORY *The Roaring Twenties 2*

1   Which revolutionary leader died on 21 January 1924?

2   What piano style, a form of blues consisting of short bass patterns played over and over by the left hand, while the right hand played various rhythms, was developed in the 1920s?

3   The author, the 1st Baron Tweedsmuir, elected to the British House of Commons in 1927, was better known by what name?

4   Which exuberant American dance, originating in South Carolina, became a popular craze after it was featured in the musical 'Runnin' Wild' in 1923?

5   Who, in Germany, became chief of the Schutstaffel (SS) in 1929?

6   Which future American president was born in Plains Georgia on October 1, 1924?

7   Who was the author of 'Far From the Madding Crowd' who died on January 11, 1928?

8   Who, in 1926, composed the musical 'The Desert Song'?

9   Who, in 1925, took over a Chicago organisation dealing in illegal liquor, gambling and prostitution from his former gangster boss Johnny Torrio?

10 Who became a national figure in America in the 1920s when she appeared on Broadway in her plays 'Sex' (1926) and 'Diamond Lil' (1928)?

11 With whom ho did George Burns form a comedy team in 1923, and marry in 1926?

12 Which psychologist, who devised the term Intelligence Quotient (IQ) wrote 'The Stanford Achievement' test in 1923?

13 Who, in 1926, wrote 'The Murder of Roger Ackroyd'?

14 Who was the American frontier law enforcement officer who died in 1921, and is most famous for assisting Wyatt Earp in bringing law and order to Tombstone, Arizona in 1880-81?

15 Who, in 1920, was canonized by Pope Benedict XV, her traditional feast day being May 30?

Answers 1 Lenin 2 Boogie-woogie 3 John Buchan 4 Charleston 5 Heinrich Himmler 6 Jimmy Carter 7 Thomas Hardy 8 Sigmund Romberg 9 Al Capone 10 Mae West 11 Gracie Allen 12 Lewis Terman 13 Agatha Christie 14 Bat Masterson 15 Joan of Arc

GENERAL HISTORY — Women In History 3

1 Who was the American religious leader who founded the Christian Science movement?
a Anne Hutchinson
b Mary Baker Eddy
c Annie Besant
d Helen Keller

2 In 1979, Jane M. Byrne became the first woman elected mayor of which city?
a New York
b Pittsburg
c Chicago
d San Francisco

3 Of whom was Ethel Le Neve the mistress?
a Al Capone
b King George V of England
c English wife murderer Dr. Crippen
d British Prime Minister David Lloyd George

4 Who was the first wife of King Henry VIII of England, whom he divorced in 1533?
a Catherine Parr
b Catherine of Aragon
c Jane Seymour
d Anne of Cleves

5 By what name was the American businesswoman born Florence Nightingale Graham better known? She was famous for her beauty salons and cosmetics.
a Helena Rubenstein
b Mary Quant
c Elizabeth Arden
d Coco Chanel

6 In the Bible Elijah was driven from Israel by which of the following women?
a Salome
b Leah
c Jezebel
d Sarah

7 To what cause did Massachusetts-born Susan B. Anthony (1820-1906) dedicate her life?
a Woman's Suffrage
b Anthropology
c Welfare Reform
d The American indian

8 In 1985, Wilma Mankiller became first woman leader of which Indian nation?
a Creek
b Cherokee
c Choctaw
d Shawnee

9 Janet Reno was the first woman to be appointed to what position in U.S. Government?
a Secretary of State
b Postmaster General
c Attorney General
d Secretary of Defense

10 Who was born Jeanne Antoinette Poisson and lived in France from 1721-64?
a Saint Theresa of Lisieux
b Comtesse Du Barry
c Marquise de Montespan
d Madame Pompadour

Answers 1 b, 2 c, 3 c, 4 b, 5 c, 6 c, 7 a, 8 b, 9 c, 10 d.

GENERAL HISTORY — Identify the Year 2

1 US space probe Viking 1 lands on Mars; Italian Prime Minister Aldo Moro resigns and John Curry wins an Olympic ice skating gold medal?

2 Andy Warhol died; Cher is nominated for an Oscar for her role in Moonstruck and German student Mathias Rust lands his plane in Moscow's Red Square?

3 The Rev. Jim Jones led the mass suicide of over 900 of his followers in Guyana; China cuts all aid to Vietnam and Jomo Kenyatta dies?

4 Tom Watson win the Open at Troon; Sophia Loren is jailed for tax evasion and the Princess of Wales gives birth to a son, William?

5 The US Peace Corps is founded; movie star Gary Cooper dies and South Africa becomes a republic?

6 Martin Luther King is assassinated; Russian cosmonaut Yuri Gagarin dies in an air crash and South America gets first ever visit from a Pope?

7 Maureen Connolly wins at Wimbledon; Eva Peron dies and Elizabeth Taylor marries Michael Wilding?

8 Paul McCartney marries Linda Eastman; President De Gaulle of France resigns and Richard Nixon is sworn in as US president?

9 Boris Becker wins at Wimbledon; Ronald Reagan is sworn in for a second term of office as US president and a massive earthquake kills thousands in Mexico City?

10 Muhammad Ali is stripped of his world title; Anastasio Somoza is elected president of Nicaragua and 10,000 hippies rally in New York's Central Park?

11 The first H-bomb is successfully tested; American writer Sinclair Lewis dies and Greta Garbo becomes a US citizen?

12 The Soviet version of Concorde crashes at the Paris air show; the Miami Dolphins win the Superbowl and Edward G. Robinson dies?

13 David Niven dies; 63 people die in a fire in a Turin theatre and President Reagan announces the beginning of the 'Star Wars' programme?

14 Mahatma Gandhi is assassinated, Israel is established as a Jewish state and Andrew Lloyd Webber is born?

15 Nelson Mandela is sentenced to life imprisonment; film star Alan Ladd dies and Elizabeth Taylor marries Richard Burton?

Answers 1 1976 2 1987 3 1978 4 1982 5 1961 6 1968 7 1952 8 1969 9 1985 10 1967 11 1951 12 1973 13 1983 14 1948 15 1964

GENERAL HISTORY   *American Presidents 2*

1   Which American president won the Pulitzer Prize for his book 'Profiles in Courage'?

2   Which US president, whose ancestors lived in Germany, was born in Denison, Texas on October 14, 1890?

3   Who is the only US president who did not reside at the White House?

4   Which US president had a children's toy names after him?

5   Who was the second president of the United States?

6   In which decade of the 20th-century was Calvin Coolidge US president?

7   Which president was referred to by his supporters as 'The Little Magician'?

8   Lady Bird was the nickname of the wife of which US president?

9   Prior to becoming president, Jimmy Carter served as governor of which US state?

10   Millard was the first name of which US president, who served from 1850-53?

11   How was Eleanor Roosevelt, the wife of F.D.Roosevelt, related to President Theodore Roosevelt?

12   Spiro T.Agnew was vice-president to which US president?

13   Which US president abolished slavery?

14   In the 1840s John Plumbe became the first man to photograph a US president. Which president did he photograph?

15   Which US President was director of the Central Intelligence Agency (C.I.A.) from 1976-77?

Answers 1 John F. Kennedy 2 Dwight D. Eisenhower 3 George Washington 4 Theodore Roosevelt (teddy bear) 5 John Adams 6 The 1920s 7 Van Buran 8 Lyndon B. Johnson 9 Georgia 10 Fillmore 11 She was his niece 12 Nixon 13 Lincoln 14 James Knox Polk 15 George Bush I

GENERAL HISTORY — Women in History 4

1   Which of these writers was a woman ?
    a   Jean-Paul Sartre
    b   George Eliot
    c   W. D. Howells
    d   T. S. Eliot

2   Who said, on meeting Harriet Beecher Stowe: "So you're the little woman who wrote the book that made this great war"?
    a   Ulysses S. Grant
    b   Robert E. Lee
    c   Abraham Lincoln
    d   William T. Sherman

3   Who was the first wife of actor Mickey Rooney?
    a   Ava Gardner
    b   Judy Holiday
    c   Lana Turner
    d   Judy Garland

4   Who was Queen of England for just 9 days?
    a   Anne Boleyn
    b   The Duchess of Windsor
    c   Mary Queen of Scots
    d   Lady Jane Grey

5   Where was Joan of Arc burned at the stake?
    a   Rheims
    b   Paris
    c   Rouen
    d   Orleans

6   Who was the mother of Oedipus?
    a   Creusa
    b   Jocasta
    c   Penelope
    d   Andromeda

7   Who was born Margaretha Geertruida Zelle in 1876?
    a   Jenny Lind
    b   Colette
    c   Simone de Beauvoir
    d   Mata Hari

8   What first was achieved by Nellie Taylor Ross in 1925 ?
    a   First woman elected Governor of a State
    b   First woman candidate for President
    c   First woman elected to U.S. Senate
    d   First woman member of U.S. House of Representatives

9   Why was Sara Jane Moore in the news on Sept 22, 1975?
    a   She successfully reached the summit of Everest
    b   She attempted to assassinate Gerald R. Ford
    c   She walked solo across America from East to West
    d   She climbed into a pit containing 25 deadly rattlesnakes and lived to tell the tale

10   Who is said to have sewn the first American flag?
    a   Sally Ross
    b   Sally Rose
    c   Betsy Rose
    d   Betsy Ross

Answers 1 b, 2 c, 3 a, 4 d, 5 c, 6 b, 7 d, 8 a, 9 b, 10 d.

GENERAL HISTORY   General 2

1   Which nomadic people conquered China during the 16th and 17th centuries and established the Qing dynasty which ruled the country for some 250 years?

2   Who was Prime Minister of China from 1949 until his death in January 1976?

3   Which Italian monastery was the scene of bitter fighting in 1944?

4   In 1940, who signed an armistice with Hitler that allowed a third of France to remain unoccupied and set up a government at Vichy?

5   The third battle of Ypres in 1917 is also known by the name of which village captured by the Canadians?

6   Genseric, or Gaiseric, was a fifth century king of which Germanic tribe?

7   What name is given to the massacre of French Huguenots on the night of 24/25 August 1572?

8   Also known as the battle of Arbela, which battle of 331 BC saw the forces of Alexander the Great defeat a much larger Persian army and decide the fate of the Persian Empire?

9   Name the mountain pass which gave it's name to the battle of 321 BC where the Samnites defeated and captured a Roman army who acknowledged defeat by passing under a yoke of Samnite spears, a unique disgrace.

10 A signatory to the Declaration of Independence, he was the first vice-president of the USA. Name him.

11 During which war was the naval battle of Navarino fought in 1827?

12 After seeing the heavy casualties of which battle of 1859 did Henri Dunant campaign for the establishment of the Red Cross?

13 Which town, the capital of the Vaucluse department of France, was the residence of seven successive Popes during the 14th century?

14 What first name was shared by the father and son who were the first two emperors of Brazil?

15 Which battle of the Second World War took place between 23 October and 5 November 1942?

Answers 1 Manchu 2 Chou En-Lai 3 Monte Cassino 4 Marshal Henri Philippe Petain 5 Passchendaele 6 The Vandals 7 St. Bartholomew's Day Massacre 8 Gaugamela 9 Caudine Forks 10 John Adams 11 War of Greek Independence 12 Solferino 13 Avignon 14 Pedro 15 El Alamein

GENERAL HISTORY — *Women in History 5*

1 Who was called 'The Virgin Queen'
   a Queen Isabella I of Spain
   b Queen Elizabeth I of England
   c Catherine the Great of Russia
   d Mary Queen of Scots

2 Who was the lover, then wife of the French philosopher Peter Abelard?
   a Cressida
   b Thisbe
   c Heloise
   d Clytemnestra

3 Born in Massachusetts in 1874, for what did Amy Lawrence Lowell achieve fame?
   a Historical novels
   b Poetry
   c Sculpture
   d Tennis

4 What was the real name of writer George Eliot?
   a Isabel James
   b Anne Hurst
   c Mary Ann Evans
   d Mary Eleanor Freeman

5 Which American first lady said: "The First Lady is an unpaid public servant elected by one person – her husband"?
   a Eleanor Roosevelt
   b Pat Nixon
   c Jaqueline Kennedy
   d Lady Bird Johnson

6 How is Sophie Fredericke Auguste von Anhalt-Zerbst better known?
   a Catherine the Great of Russia
   b Saint Bernadette
   c Joan of Arc
   d Marie Antoinette

7 What first in the US was achieved by Sandra Day O'Conner in July 1981?
   a First woman candidate for Vice-President
   b First woman astronaut to walk in space
   c First woman admiral of U.S. Navy
   d First woman member of U.S. Supreme Court

8 The followers of which King captured the Sabine women?
   a Stephen
   b Romulus
   c Croesus
   d Tamerlane

9 Who is the patron saint of Paris?
   a Saint Cecilia
   b Saint Genevieve
   c Saint Helena
   d Saint Joan of Arc

10 In Greek mythology, who was the nymph who was changed into a laurel tree?
   a Daphne
   b Ariadne
   c Minerva
   d Bellona

Answers 1 b, 2 c, 3 b, 4 c, 5 d, 6 a, 7 d, 8 b, 9 b, 10 a.

GENERAL HISTORY — *Battles*

1 At which battle of 490 BC during the Greek-Persian wars did the Athenians under Miltiades defeat the Persians?

2 Name the battle of the American War of Independence, fought on 17 June 1775 at Charlestown near Boston, where the British, led by General Howe, won a costly victory?

3 In 1854, an armed battle took place between gold miners and government troops at Ballarat in Australia. The miners stockaded themselves into a goldfield which gave it's name to this clash. By what name is this skirmish known?

4 Which battle was fought on 25 October 1415?

5 And which battle was fought on 18 June 1815?

6 Who led his army to defeat the Romans at the battle of Cannae in 216 BC?

7 What is the name of the stream which gave it's name to two battles of the American Civil War, the first in July 1861, the second in August 1862?

8 Which battle, fought between 1 and 3 July 1863 was said to be the turning point of the American Civil War?

9 Fought in September 1854, the battle of the Alma River took place during which war?

10 What was the name of the escarpment in France successfully stormed by the Canadian Corps of the British army in 1917?

11 'Operation Market Garden' was the code name for which major conflict of World War Two?

12 Name the victorious commander at the battle of the Nile in 1798?

13 Who commanded German forces at the Battle of the Bulge during World War Two?

14 Name the battle of 1757 in which Robert Clive's victory over the Nawab of Bengal made possible Britain's acquisition of Bengal?

15 Which port in the Italian region of Campania was the scene of heavy fighting following major allied landings in September 1943?

Answers 1 Marathon 2 Bunker Hill 3 The Eureka Stockade 4 Agincourt 5 Waterloo 6 Hannibal 7 Bull 8 Gettysburg 9 Crimean War 10 Vimy Ridge 11 Battle of Arnhem 12 Horatio Nelson 13 Karl Von Rundstedt 14 Plassey 15 Salerno

GENERAL HISTORY   *American Presidents 3*

1 Zachary was the first name of which US president?

2 Which US president was played by Henry Grace in the 1962 movie 'The Longest Day'?

3 Which US president in his inaugural address said: "Ask not what your country can do for you; ask what you can do for your country"?

4 Who was US president during the Iran-Contra Affair?

5 Which US president was the author of the 'Declaration of Independence'?

6 In which year in the 1970s did a burglary take place on June 17 at the Watergate office complex in Washington DC, which led to the eventual resignation of President Nixon?

7 Which President was called 'the Father of the Constitution'?

8 Who assassinated President Lincoln on April 15, 1865?

9 Who was the 14th President of the United States, who, on his way to his inauguration witnessed his 11-year-old son's death in a train mishap?

10 Who was the Texas billionaire who finished third behind Bill Clinton and George Bush I in the 1992 US elections?

11 Which US president invented the folding bed and swivel chair?

12 Which US president was assassinated by Charles Jules Guiteau in July, 1881?

13 In which state was Bill Clinton born?

14 Which US president once told a 5-year-old boy, Franklin Delano Roosevelt: "Son, I hope you never become President of the United States"?

15 Name the 31st President of the United States who was the first president born west of the Mississippi River and was, with Richard Nixon, one of only two Quaker presidents

Answers 1 Taylor 2 Eisenhower 3 J. F. Kennedy 4 Ronald Reagan 5 Thomas Jefferson 6 1972 7 James Madison 8 John Wilkes Booth 9 Franklin Pierce 10 H.Ross Perot 11 Thomas Jefferson 12 James Garfield 13 Arkansas 14 Grover Cleveland 15 Herbert Hoover

GENERAL HISTORY — *Women in History 6*

1 Of whom was Clara Petacci the mistress?
   a Mussolini
   b Dr. Crippen
   c Hitler
   d Idi Amin

2 Apart from Anne Boleyn, which other of his wives did Henry VIII of England have executed?
   a Jane Seymour
   b Catherine Parr
   c Catherine Howard
   d Catherine of Aragon

3 Mamie Geneva Doud was the wife of which U.S. President?
   a Coolidge
   b Hoover
   c Taft
   d Eisenhower

4 What first was achieved by Dr. Kathryn D. Sullivan in 1984?
   a First woman to successfully carry out a heart transplant operation
   b First woman astronaut to walk in space
   c First woman to to go over Niagara Falls in a barrel
   d First woman to abseil down the Empire State Building

5 Who, in 1907, was the first woman to receive the Order of Merit?
   a Florence Nightingale
   b Marie Curie
   c Jenny Lind
   d Emmeline Pankhurst

6 Who, in Greek mythology has a name meaning 'all gifts'?
   a Ariadne
   b Eurydice
   c Pandora
   d Electra

7 The record breaking stunt woman and racing car driver Kitty O`Neil once said: "A handicap is not a defeat, but a challenge to conquer". To what handicap was she referring?
   a She was deaf
   b She had only partial vision
   c She was a polio sufferer
   d She had lost part of her left leg in an accident as a child

8 Who was the Spanish queen who financed the voyage to the New World by Christopher Colombus?
   a Maria-Theresa
   b Anna
   c Maria
   d Isabella

9 Which woman is the subject of an opera by Richard Strauss?
   a Helen of Troy
   b Salome
   c Jezebel
   d Aphrodite

10 In which field did Maria Montessori gain eminence?
   a Physics
   b Aviation
   c Writing
   d Education

Answers 1 a, **2** c, **3** d, **4** b, **5** a, **6** c, **7** a, **8** d, **9** b, **10** d.

GENERAL HISTORY — *General 3*

1 During which war was the battle of Fontenoy fought in 1745?

2 Against the forces of which country did the Ethiopians win the battle of Adowa in 1896?

3 What were the names of the two semi-legendary Jutish brothers, said to have led the first band of Germanic invaders to Britain?

4 The neutrality of which sea was agreed at the Treaty of Paris in 1856?

5 Which military town was the scene of the first uprising of the Indian Mutiny in 1857?

6 Name the Pope who inspired the first Crusade of 1095 to 1099.

7 Which French monk rallied an army of 20,000 peasants during the first Crusade but was badly beaten by the Turks at Nicaea?

8 What is the name of the mountainous region which was incorporated in Czechoslovakia in 1919 but the Munich Agreement of 1938 permitted German occupation of the area?

9 Which French Duchy was ruled by Philip the Bold and Philip the Good?

10 What popular name was given to the German counter-offensive in the Ardennes in December 1944?

11 Stretching some 90 miles and named after a German commander, what name was given to the defensive barrier that formed part of the Western Front during World War One?

12 What was the name of Cesare Borgia's infamous sister who became notorious, quite unfairly, for wantonness, vice and crime?

13 By what name were members of the religious order of knighthood, Poor Knights of Christ and of the Temple of Solomon, more commonly known?

14 Which navigator and explorer, after whom a river and a bay were named, was cast adrift by his mutinous crew in what is now north-east Canada in 1611 and was never seen again?

15 Name the 12th century sultan of Egypt and Syria who was the famous adversary of king Richard I during the Crusades.

Answers 1 War of Austrian Succession 2 Italy 3 Hengist and Horsa 4 Black Sea 5 Meerut 6 Urban II 7 Peter the Hermit 8 Sudetenland 9 Burgundy 10 Battle of the Bulge 11 Hindenburg Line 12 Lucrezia 13 Templars or Knights Templars 14 Henry Hudson 15 Saladin

GENERAL HISTORY — *Women in History 7*

1 By what name is Catherine II of Russia better known?
   a The Terrible
   b The Wise
   c The Conqueror
   d The Great

2 In which country was Marie Antoinette born?
   a Austria
   b Germany
   c France
   d Belgium

3 What, in 1914, was created by a West Virginian Miss Anna Jarvis?
   a Anniversary cards
   b The first team of cheerleaders
   c Mother's Day
   d Airmail envelopes

4 What famous song was written by Julie Ward Howe?
   a Marching Through Georgia
   b The Battle Hymn of the Republic
   c Dixie
   d Happy Birthday

5 What first was achieved by Elizabeth Blackwell?
   a The first female member of Congress
   b America's first female attorney
   c The first woman medical doctor in the United States
   d The first female prospector to strike gold

6 Bess Wallace was the wife of which American President ?
   a Woodrow Wilson
   b Harry Truman
   c Calvin Coolidge
   d Grover Cleveland

7 Which Saint was the mother of John the Baptist?
   a Saint Hilary
   b Saint Anne
   c Saint Cecilia
   d Saint Elizabeth

8 What was the original name of the `Oprah Winfrey` show?
   a Talkback Chicago
   b Have Your Say
   c A.M. Chicago
   d Chicago Today

9 In what field did Jaqueline Cochran achieve spectacular success?
   a Aviation
   b War Correspondence
   c Horseshoe Pitching
   d Ice Skating

10 Belle Gertrude Elion was a pioneer in the fight against which disease?
   a Smallpox
   b Leukemia
   c Diphtheria
   d Leprosy

Answers 1 d, **2** a, **3** c, **4** b, **5** c, **6** b, **7** d, **8** c, **9** a, **10** b.

GENERAL HISTORY   *Identify the Year 3*

1   Fred Astaire dies; the Philippines hold their first democratic elections for 16 years and Dennis Conner skippers Stars And Stripes to victory in the America's Cup?

2   'Buffalo Bill' Cody dies; John F. Kennedy is born and the US officially enter the First World War?

3   Congress is broadcast for the first time on TV in the US; Henry Ford dies and Elton John is born?

4   Nazi war criminal Adolf Eichmann is executed; Martin Luther King is jailed for leading an illegal march and Brazil win football's World Cup?

5   Martina Navratilova wins her 5th Wimbledon singles title; Desmond Tutu wins the Nobel Peace Prize and Johnny Weissmuller dies?

6   Former Soviet leader Nikita Khruschev dies; Baltimore Colts win the Superbowl and Apollo 14 and 15 space missions are launched?

7   Maureen Connolly wins at Wimbledon; Eisenhower is inaugurated as US president and the Marilyn Monroe movie 'Gentlemen Prefer Blondes' is released?

8   Russia invades Czechoslovakia; Arthur Ashe becomes the first black tennis player to win the US Open and Jackie Kennedy marries Aristotle Onassis?

9   Pablo Picasso dies; building of the Sears Tower in Chicago is completed and Juan Peron becomes president of Argentina after nearly 20 years in exile?

10   Spain and Portugal join the EEC; Swedish Prime Minister Olaf Palme is assassinated and Prince Andrew marries Sarah Ferguson?

11   Woodrow Wilson is elected US president; Stockholm hosts the Olympic Games and Scott reaches the South Pole to find that Amundsen has beaten him to it?

12   Michael Jackson is born; Elvis Presley begins his US army service and Iceland extends fishing limits to 12 miles?

13   US introduce 45 and 33.$\frac{1}{3}$ rpm records; Newfoundland becomes Canada's 10th province and Meryl Streep is born?

14   Evonne Goolagong wins at Wimbledon; Winnie Mandela is jailed for a year and women are given the vote in Switzerland?

15   The film 'Indiana Jones And The Temple Of Doom' is released; Richard Burton dies and the first Virgin Atlantic flight leaves Gatwick for New York?

Answers 1 1987 2 1917 3 1947 4 1962 5 1984 6 1971 7 1953 8 1968 9 1973 10 1986 11 1912 12 1958 13 1949 14 1971 15 1984

GENERAL HISTORY — *Great Military Leaders*

1 Name the king of Sweden who displayed military genius during the Thirty Years' War.

2 Which Spanish conquistador destroyed the Aztec capital of Tenochtitlan in 1521?

3 The illegitimate son of Augustus II, which French soldier showed splendid tactical skill during the War of Austrian Succession?

4 Who was the foremost US military figure between the Revolution and the Civil War? He held the rank of general in three wars and was the unsuccessful Whig candidate for president in 1852.

5 Name the Vietnamese military leader, an expert in conventional and guerrilla warfare, whose tactics led to the Viet Minh victory over the French and an end to French colonialism, and later to the North Vietnamese victory over South Vietnam and the US.

6 Which US soldier commanded II Corps in Tunisia and Sicily in 1943, in 1944 he commanded US troops at the Normandy invasion and later led the US 12th Army through France?

7 Who was commander-in-chief of the American forces which inflicted notable defeats on the British army at Trenton and Princeton in 1777?

8 A Zulu chief from 1816 until his death in 1828, he made the Zulu nation the strongest in southern Africa and set the period of warfare called the Mfecane in motion. Name him.

9 One of the US Navy's foremost strategists, who commanded the US Pacific fleet from 1941 to 1945?

10 Name the military leader who successfully defended Finland against greatly superior Soviet forces in 1939. He was president of Finland from 1944 to 1946.

11 Which US air strategist advocated long and successfully for a separate air force ranking equally with the army and navy? In 1944 he was made general of the army, and on the creation of the United States Air Force as an independent service in 1947 he was the first to hold the rank of general of the air force. .

12 Name the Japanese naval commander whose destruction of the Russian fleet in the battle of Tsushima Strait in 1905 ensured Japan's victory in the Russo-Japanese War.

Answers 1 Gustavus Adolphus 2 Hernan Cortes 3 Maurice, Comte de Saxe 4 Winfield Scott 5 Vo Nguyen Giap 6 Omar Bradley 7 George Washington 8 Shaka 9 Chester Nimitz 10 Carl Gustav Mannerheim 11 Henry Harley 'Hap' Arnold 12 Heihachiro Togo

GENERAL HISTORY   *Assassinations 1*

1   Name the king of Macedonia, father of Alexander the Great, who was assassinated in 336 BC?

2   The German king Albert I was killed in 1308 by his nephew who was known as John the... what?

3   Which king of France was assassinated by a fanatical Roman Catholic named Francois Ravaillac in 1610. Was it Henry I, Henry II, Henry III or Henry IV?

4   The French general Jean-Baptiste Kleber was killed by a Turkish fanatic in which African city?

5   Which Russian emperor was mortally wounded by a bomb in 1881?

6   Stabbed by an anarchist in 1894, Sadi Carnot was president of which country?

7   US president James Garfield died from his injuries after being shot. Where was he shot, was it in a hotel, at a railway station or in a theatre?

8   In which city did Leon Czolgosz shoot and fatally wound US president William McKinley?

9   Which hero of the Irish struggle for independence was killed in an ambush in 1922?

10 After agreeing to retire from politics, which Mexican revolutionary was killed in 1923?

11 Killed by a bullet intended for president-elect Franklin D. Roosevelt in 1933, Anton Cermak was the mayor of which US city?

12 In which French city were French foreign minister Jean Louis Barthou and King Alexander I of Yugoslavia assassinated in 1934?

13 Name the governor of Louisiana and US senator who was killed by Carl Austin Weiss in 1935.

14 Which famous person was killed by Nathuram Godse?

15 In which city was the Swedish humanitarian and diplomat Count Folke Bernadotte killed along with UN observer Andre-Pierre Serot in 1948?

Answers 1 Philip II 2 Parricide 3 Henry IV 4 Cairo 5 Alexander II 6 France 7 Railway station 8 Buffalo 9 Michael Collins 10 Pancho Villa 11 Chicago 12 Marseille 13 Huey Long 14 Mahatma Gandhi 15 Jerusalem

GENERAL HISTORY — General 4

1 Which political leader and Zulu chief and opponent of apartheid was awarded the Nobel Peace Prize in 1960?

2 Name this minister of Louis XIV of France. He reformed taxation, built roads and canals and largely created a French navy. He was a lavish patron of the arts and sciences but his cold personality earned him the nickname Le Nord (the North).

3 Which 14 year-old boy met the rebel Kentish peasants at Smithfield in 1381?

4 Which saint and Cappadocian father was the brother of Gregory of Nyssa?

5 What name did Camillo Borghese adopt when he became Pope in 1605?

6 The Ruriks and Romanovs were ruling dynasties in which country?

7 Which famous paediatrician ran for the US presidency in 1972 and the vice-presidency in 1976?

8 Robert Kennedy was senator of which US state?

9 25 April is ANZAC Day. Where, on that day in 1915, did the Anzac forces land?

10 In which battle of 8 January 1815 did US forces led by Andrew Jackson defeat the British?

11 In which of the Punic Wars did the battle of Zama in 202 BC take place – first, second or third?

12 Henry the Navigator was responsible for the colonisation of Madeira and the Azores in the 15th century. What was his nationality?

13 The naval fleet of which country was defeated off Cape Matapan in 1941?

14 In which decade of the 19th century was Albert Einstein born?

15 Maximilian was offered the crown of which country by France and was emperor of that country from 1864 until his execution in 1867?

Answers 1 Albert Luthuli 2 Jean-Baptiste Colbert 3 Richard II 4 St. Basil 5 Paul 6 Russia 7 Dr. Benjamin Spock 8 New York 9 Gallipoli 10 Battle of New Orleans 11 Second 12 Portuguese 13 Italy 14 1870s 15 Mexico

GENERAL HISTORY — Identify the Year 4

1 Willy Brandt is elected Chancellor of West Germany; Samuel Beckett wins the Nobel prize for Literature and Golda Meir becomes Israeli Prime Minister?

2 Princess Grace of Monaco dies after a car crash; Iran invades Iraq and Italy win football's World Cup?

3 Althea Gibson wins at Wimbledon; Humphrey Bogart dies and Caroline, the first child of Princess Grace of Monaco is born?

4 Nat 'King' Cole dies; Madame Vaucher becomes the first woman to climb the Matterhorn and New York is blacked out by power cuts?

5 Victor Borge is born; at least 200,000 die in Italian earthquake and Bleriot makes the first flight across the English channel?

6 Bjorn Borg wins Wimbledon for the fifth time; Steve McQueen dies and Bani Sadr becomes Iran's first president?

7 'Only Yesterday' was a hit on both sides of the Atlantic for the Carpenters; the Suez Canal re-opens to international traffic after 8 years and Spain's leader Franco dies?

8 Martin Luther King makes his famous 'I have a dream' speech; the Boeing 727 makes it's first test flight and Alcatraz prison is closed?

9 Nelson Mandela is released from prison; Ayrton Senna is Formula One world champion and Iraq invades Kuwait?

10 Rock Hudson dies; Jose Sarney becomes Brazil's first civilian president for 21 years and Reagan and Gorbachev meet in Geneva?

11 Elton John's 'Rocket Man' is a hit on both sides of the Atlantic; the Winter Olympics are held in Sapporo and astronauts from Apollo 16 walk on the moon?

12 The liner Queen Mary arrives in Long Beach to be used as a floating hotel; Mrs. Gandhi re-elected Prime Minister of India and Vivien Leigh dies?

13 The first Miss World contest is held; Randolph Turpin beats Sugar Ray Robinson and king Leopold III of Belgium abdicates?

14 The World Health Organisation is established, Babe Ruth dies and Queen Wilhelmina of the Netherlands abdicates?

15 Groucho Marx dies; Gary Gilmore is executed by firing squad and the ban on Shakespeare is lifted in China?

Answers 1 1969 2 1982 3 1957 4 1965 5 1909 6 1980 7 1975 8 1963 9 1990 10 1985 11 1972 12 1967 13 1951 14 1948 15 1977

GENERAL HISTORY — *Women in History 8*

1   About whom did Shakespeare write: "Age
cannot wither her, nor custom stale her
infinite variety"?
  a   Portia
  b   Cleopatra
  c   His own wife, Ann Hathaway
  d   Juliet

2   Who said: "Europe will never be like
America. Europe is a product of history.
America is a product of philosophy"?
  a   Barbara Bush
  b   Barbara Walters
  c   Eleanor Roosevelt
  d   Margaret Thatcher

3   What in 1647 did a wealthy Maryland
landowner, Margaret Brent, unsuccessfully
try to secure in the USA?
  a   Equal opportunities for women
  b   Votes for women
  c   Land rights for women
  d   Property right for women

4   Which sport was dominated by Alice
Marble from 1936-1940?
  a   Golf
  b   Tennis
  c   Badminton
  d   Hockey

5   As whom is Maria Eva Duearte better
known as?
  a   Madonna
  b   Oprah Winfrey
  c   Eva Peron
  d   Carmen Miranda

6   Which Saint claimed that the Virgin Mary
had imported miraculous powers of healing
to a spring in Lourdes?
  a   Barbara
  b   Catherine
  c   Bernadette
  d   Maria Goretti

7   Which writer wrote her 'Hospital Sketches'
while serving as a nurse during the
American Civil War?
  a   Margaret Mitchel
  b   Edith Wharton
  c   Louisa May Alcott
  d   Harriet Beecher Stowe

8   In the Bible, who was the Phoenician
princess and wife of Ahab?
  a   Judith
  b   Naomi
  c   Rachel
  d   Jezebel

9   Who was the first woman to win a Nobel
Prize?
  a   Pearl Buck
  b   Emily Green Balch
  c   Maria Goeppert-Mayer
  d   Marie Curie

10   Of what was Margaret Sanger (1883-1966)
a pioneer?
  a   Penal reform
  b   Civil right
  c   Birth control
  d   Euthanasia

Answers 1 b, 2 d, 3 b, 4 b, 5 c, 6 c, 7 c, 8 d, 9 d, 10 c.

GENERAL HISTORY   *Exploration & Discovery*

1 Whose 18th century exploration of Alaska prepared the way for a Russian foothold on the North American continent?

2 Which 16th century Spanish soldier was the first to explore the river Amazon?

3 Which Norse explorer is regarded by some to be the first European to reach the shores of North America?

4 Name the 19th century French naturalist who alerted the West to the ruins of Angkor, capital of the ancient Khmer civilisation of Cambodia.

5 Which 20th century traveller has made several journeys of discovery, including sailing a leather boat across the Atlantic in the wake of St. Brendan the Navigator, captaining an Arab sailing ship from Muscat to China to investigate the legends of Sinbad the Sailor and steering the replica of a Bronze Age galley to seek the landfalls of Jason and the Argonauts and Ulysses?

6 Real name Elizabeth Cochrane, which US newspaper reporter became famous for her round the world trip which took 72 days in 1889/1890?

7 Thor Heyerdahl crossed the Atlantic twice in 1969/70 in papyrus boats. What name was given to both boats?

8 Which C is the Portuguese navigator frequently credited with having discovered Brazil?

9 Name the Dutch explorer whose 1615-16 expedition discovered a new route, the Drake passage, around the southern tip of South America, connecting the Atlantic Ocean with the Pacific.

10 Which king and queen of Spain were the patrons of Christopher Columbus?

11 Which English navigator discovered the Falkland Islands in 1592?

12 Name the Italian navigator and explorer for France who was the first European to sight New York and Narragansett Bays. He gave his name to a famous suspension bridge spanning New York harbour.

13 Which Spanish explorer and conquistador discovered the Mississippi river?

14 What nationality was Carsten Niebuhr who provided detailed and important information on Arabia during the 18th century?

15 Which Scottish explorer became known for his explorations of the river Niger?

Answers 1 Vitus Bering 2 Francisco de Orellana 3 Leif Eriksson 4 Henri Mouhot 5 Tim Severin 6 Nellie Bly 7 Ra 8 Cabral 9 Willem Schouten 10 Ferdinand and Isabella 11 John Davis 12 Giovanni Verrazano 13 Hernando de Soto 14 German 15 Mungo Park

GENERAL HISTORY — *Identify the Year 5*

1 Former US president Lyndon Johnson dies, thousands evacuated in Iceland as volcano erupts and Paul Getty's grandson is kidnapped?

2 The body of Stalin is removed from the mausoleum in Red Square, golfer Gary Player wins the US Masters and psychoanalyst Carl Jung dies?

3 King Farouk of Egypt abdicates, John Cobb is killed attempting to break the world water speed record and Jimmy Connors is born?

4 Al Capone dies, Truman becomes the first US president to make an official visit to Canada and Lord Mountbatten is appointed as India's last viceroy?

5 The supertanker Amoco Cadiz runs aground off Brittany, Russian UN official Arkady Shevchenko defects to the west and Argentina win football's World Cup?

6 US hostage David Jacobsen is freed after 18 months in Beirut, Mike Tyson wins the WBC heavyweight title and the Duchess of Windsor dies?

7 Malcolm X is shot dead, Gemini 6 and 7 spacecraft rendezvous in space and the Kinks song 'Tired Of Waiting For You' is a hit on both sides of the Atlantic?

8 Burt Reynolds is born, Hitler opens the first Volkswagen factory and Addis Ababa falls to Italian troops?

9 The army seizes power in Thailand, racing driver Niki Lauda suffers serious burns in a crash at the Nurburgring and Howard Hughes dies?

10 The winter Olympics are held in Lake Placid, Robert Mugabe is elected premier of Zimbabwe and Alfred Hitchcock dies?

11 The Commonwealth of Australia is formed, the composer Verdi dies and actor Clark Gable is born?

12 Hitler is imprisoned, the Le Mans 24-hour motor race is held for the first time and the Mexican revolutionary Pancho Villa is assassinated?

13 Tito becomes president of Yugoslavia, John F. Kennedy marries Jacqueline Bouvier and Winston Churchill wins the Nobel prize for literature?

14 Former US president Calvin Coolidge dies, Roman Polanski is born and British tennis player Fred Perry wins the first of his three US championships?

15 Canadian Prime Minister Pierre Trudeau resigns, singer Marvin Gaye is shot dead by his father and Brunei gained independence from Britain?

Answers 1 1973 2 1961 3 1952 4 1947 5 1978 6 1986 7 1965 8 1936 9 1976 10 1980 11 1901 12 1923 13 1953 14 1933 15 1984

GENERAL HISTORY   *The Swinging Sixties 2*

1   In the 1960s the US launched a series of meteorological satellites known as TIROS. What did TIROS stand for?

2   What was the location of French atom bomb tests in February 1960?

3   What nationality was golfer Kel Nagle, winner of the centenary Open at St. Andrews in 1960?

4   Syngman Rhee died in 1965. He had been the first president of which Asian country?

5   The film 'Something's Got To Give' was never completed because of the death of Marilyn Monroe. Who was to be the male lead opposite Monroe in that movie – Sammy Davis Jr., Peter Lawford, Dean Martin or Frank Sinatra?

6   Lon Nol was deputy premier, minister of defence and premier of which Asian country during the 1960s?

7   What was the nickname of Gerald Lloyd Kookson III played by Ed Byrnes in the TV series '77 Sunset Strip'?

8   A popular children's TV show in Britain during the 1960s, 'Tales From The Riverbank' was produced in which country?

9   Tom Mboya was assassinated in July 1969. He was a leading politician in which African country?

10 Which South American country suffered major earthquake damage on 21 May 1960?

11 Which US basketball team were NBA champions every year in the 1960s except 1967 when it was won by the Philadelphia 76ers?

12 Muhammad Ali, then known as Cassius Clay, had his first professional fight on 29 October 1960. It was against Tunney Hunsakar and took place in the city where he was born. Which city?

13 A moderator of the Second Vatican Council from 1962 to 1965 and instrumental in effecting liberal change in the Roman Catholic Church, what nationality was Cardinal Suenens – Belgian, Dutch or French?

14 In July 1960, Chad and the Central African Republic gained independence from which country?

15 In which year did Edward Kennedy become a US senator?

Answers 1 Television and Infra-red Observation Satellite 2 Sahara Desert 3 Australian 4 South Korea 5 Dean Martin 6 Cambodia 7 Kookie 8 Canada 9 Kenya 10 Chile 11 Boston Celtics 12 Louisville 13 Belgian 14 France 15 1962

20ᵗʰ Century History

20ᵀᴴ CENTURY HISTORY

Quiz 1

1   Which day did Franklin Delano Roosevelt say would live in infamy?
a   Dec 12, 1941
b   Dec 8, 1941
c   Dec 7, 1941
d   Dec 5, 1941

2   Which one of these is not a George Gershwin composition?
a   Porgy and Bess
b   On the Town
c   Rhapsody in Blue
d   An American in Paris

3   'And his mama cries' is a line from which Elvis Presley song?
a   In the Ghetto
b   Can't Help Falling in Love
c   Are You Lonesome Tonight
d   Love Me Tender

4   What was the profession of Rudolph Valentino after he arrived in New York City in 1913?
a   Barber
b   Singer
c   Fashion Model
d   Ballroom Dancer

5   In which country was Albert Einstein born?
a   America
b   Russia
c   Germany
d   Czechoslovakia

6   In which state did Thomas Alva Edison construct his experimentation and research laboratory, now known as the Edison National Historic Site?
a   Virginia
b   Connecticut
c   Pennsylvania
d   New Jersey

7   For his starring role in the film of which Shakespeare play did Laurence Olivier win the best actor Oscar award?
a   Richard III
b   Othello
c   Hamlet
d   Henry V

8   In which 1953 film did Marilyn Monroe star with Joseph Cotton and Jean Peters?
a   Niagara
b   How to Marry a Millionaire
c   River of No Return
d   We're Not Married

9   Which writer's biography is entitled 'In Memory Yet Green, In Joy Still Felt'?
a   John Steinbeck
b   Isaac Asimov
c   Norman Mailer
d   Truman Capote

10 What relation was Barbara Cartland to Princess Diana?
a   Great Aunt
b   Great Great Grandmother
c   Step Grandmother
d   Half-cousin

Answers 1 c, 2 b, 3 a, 4 d, 5 c, 6 d, 7 c, 8 a, 9 b, 10 c

20ᵀᴴ CENTURY HISTORY   *Quiz 2*

1   Queen Alexandra, who died in 1925, was the widow of which English king?

2   Born David Ivor Davies, who was the composer of 'The Dancing Years' who died in 1951?

3   Who brought out his autobiographical novel, 'Of Human Bondage', in 1915?

4   The first factory for which 'people's car' was opened by Adolf Hitler in 1936?

5   In which year in the first half of the 20th-century did Halley's comet visit earth?

6   Sergei Rachmaninov, who died in 1943, wrote two concertos for which instrument?

7   James F. Fixx died of a heart attack in 1984 doing something which he pioneered as a method of keeping fit. Can you say what he was doing when he died?

8   In 1904 which singer made his first American recording, 'La Donna e Mobile'?

9   Which US vocalist had a hit in 1958 with 'A Certain Smile'?

10   Danny Kaye, who died in 1987, worked tirelessly as an ambassador for which organisation?

11   Which fashionable hairstylist, along with Sharon Tate, was one of the victims of the Charles Manson killings in 1969?

12   Who was the American aviator who disappeared on the last half of her round-the-world flight from California in 1937?

13   Who was crowned emperor of Japan in 1928?

14   What subatomic particle was discovered by James Chadwick in 1932?

15   Which Norwegian was rewarded for his collaboration with the Nazis when they installed him as puppet Prime Minister of Norway following their invasion of that country in 1942?

Answers 1 Edward VII 2 Ivor Novello 3 Somerset Maugham 4 Volkswagen 5 1910 6 Piano 7 Jogging 8 Caruso 9 Johnny Mathis 10 UNICEF 11 Jay Sebring 12 Amelia Earhart 13 Hirohito 14 The Neutron 15 Vidkin Quisling

20ᵀᴴ CENTURY HISTORY

Quiz 3

1   What was Walt Disney's first feature-length cartoon ?
   a   Snow White and the Seven Dwarfs
   b   Pinocchio
   c   Fantasia
   d   Bambi

2   How was T. E. Lawrence (Lawrence of Arabia) killed in 1935?
   a   In a motorcycle accident
   b   Fighting for the Arabs against Turkish rule
   c   In a brawl in a London tavern
   d   When the plane he was piloting crashed

3   What was Elvis Presley's first record?
   a   Jailhouse Rock
   b   Are You Lonesome Tonight
   c   That`s All Right (Mama)
   d   Blue Suede Shoes

4   Who was the composer of such songs as 'Stardust' and 'Lazy Bones'?
   a   Jerome Kern
   b   George Gershwin
   c   Hoagy Carmichael
   d   Irving Berlin

5   At which Olympic Games did Bob Beaman smash the world long-jump record?
   a   Mexico City
   b   Munich
   c   Tokyo
   d   Rome

6   A jazz icon of the swing era and beyond, what did Gene Krupa play?
   a   Trombone
   b   Saxophone
   c   Drums
   d   Clarinet

7   Which American President was a former director of the CIA?
   a   Lyndon B. Johnson
   b   Gerald Ford
   c   George Bush
   d   Dwight D. Eisenhower

8   'The Painted Desert' (1931) was the first movie to feature which cinema icon?
   a   Errol Flynn
   b   Clark Gable
   c   Burt Lancaster
   d   Lassie

9   Which Russian-born, American engineer built his own helicopter in 1909 and the world`s first multi-engined aircraft in 1913?
   a   Werner von Braun
   b   Robert Goddard
   c   Ivan Jerome
   d   Igor Sikorsky

10 How old was Martin Luther King when he became the youngest man to win the Nobel Peace Prize in 1964?
   a   35
   b   37
   c   39
   d   40

Answers 1 a, 2 a, 3 c, 4 c, 5 a, 6 c, 7 c, 8 b, 9 d, 10 a.

20ᵀᴴ CENTURY HISTORY

1 In what category was Bertrand Russell awarded a Nobel Prize in 1950?

2 Whom did Mehmet Ali Agea attempt to assassinate on May 13 1981?

3 Which American president proposed a League of Nations in 1919?

4 Who did a Mrs Chaikovsky, who arrived in the United States in February 1928, claim she was?

5 The film 'Gigi', which premiered in 1956, was based on a story by which French writer?

6 Which former Monty Python star went 'Around the World in 80 Days' in 1989?

7 Which Brazilian racing driver was killed in 1994 during the San Marino Grand Prix?

8 What was Alfred Hitchcock's first sound film which opened in 1930?

9 In 1960, the publisher Penguin faced trial for planning to publish which book?

10 Who, in 1971, was found guilty of murdering Vietnamese civilians at Mylai in 1968?

11 At which castle was Prince Charles invested as Prince of Wales in 1969?

12 Which US male vocal group had a No.1 with 'Hangin' Tough' in 1990?

13 'I'm Wishing' was a song from which Walt Disney film which premiered in 1938?

14 Which World boxing title was won by Nigel Benn in 1996?

15 Which member of the British royal family was murdered by the IRA in 1979?

Answers 1 Literature 2 Pope John Paul II 3 Wilson 4 Anastasia (daughter of the murdered Tsar Nicholas and his wife Alexandra) 5 Colette 6 Michael Palin 7 Ayrton Senna 8 Blackmail 9 Lady Chatterley's Lover 10 Lieutenant William Calley 11 Caernarvon 12 New Kids on the Block 13 Snow White and the Seven Dwarfs 14 Middleweight 15 Lord Mountbatten

20ᵀᴴ CENTURY HISTORY

Quiz 5

1   Who is the dancer and choreographer, said to have pioneered modern dance in the US, who died in April 1993, aged 96?
   a   Doris Humphrey
   b   Hermes Pan
   c   Martha Graham
   d   Bob Fosse

2   Golda Meir was Prime Minister of which country from 1970-74?
   a   Pakistan
   b   Israel
   c   Lebanon
   d   Iceland

3   Which golfing icon said: "It is nothing new or original to say that golf is played one stroke at a time. But it took me years to realize it"?
   a   Ben Hogan
   b   Bobby Jones
   c   Jack Nicklaus
   d   Arnold Palmer

4   Which fashion designer is famous for his American styles such as the 'prairie look' and 'frontier fashion'?
   a   Pierre Balman
   b   Giorgio Armani
   c   Bob Mackie
   d   Ralph Lauren

5   Which movie great, who died in August 1987, directed such films as 'The Maltese Falcon' and 'The Treasure of Sierra Madre'?
   a   John Huston
   b   Otto Preminger
   c   Francis Ford Coppola
   d   Howard Hawkes

6   Why did Bob Dylan take two years out of music in 1966?
   a   He became disillusioned with the music scene
   b   He devoted himself entirely to the protest movement
   c   He joined the Army
   d   He had a motorcycle crash

7   Whose presidency was known as 'the businessman's administration'?
   a   Eisenhower
   b   Ford
   c   Hoover
   d   Coolidge

8   What was the name of the spacecraft that took the first man, Yuri Gagarin, into space?
   a   Luna 1
   b   Soyuz 1
   c   Vostok 1
   d   Sputnik 1

9   What was the meaning of Mahatma Ghandi's message 'Satyagraha'?
   a   Fast till death
   b   Free India
   c   God walk with you
   d   Non-violent protest

10 What was Alfred Hitchcock's first Hollywood film?
   a   Strangers on a Train
   b   Rebecca
   c   The Lady Vanishes
   d   Rear Window

Answers 1 c, 2 b, 3 b, 4 d, 5 a, 6 d, 7 a, 8 c, 9 d, 10 b.

1 How was King George V related to his enemy in World War I, Kaiser Wilhelm II?

2 For which film did Sissy Spacek win best actress Oscar in 1980?

3 Who was created Poet Laureate in 1984?

4 At which event did Abebe Bikila win the Gold Medal at both the 1960 and 1964 Olympics?

5 Who was the car manufacturer arrested on cocaine smuggling charges in 1982?

6 Who was the Democratic opponent whom Ronald Reagan defeated in the 1984 US presidential elections?

7 Trevor Nunn took over as director of which theatrical company from Peter Hall in 1968?

8 Which Egyptian king abdicated in 1952?

9 Who in 1957 said "Don't knock the rock"?

10 Which married couple starred in 'Who's Afraid of Virginia Woolf' in 1966?

11 Where, in Europe, did Charles Lindbergh land after flying the Atlantic solo in 1927?

12 The post-war labour politician Herbert Morrison was the grandfather of which recently disgraced politician and member of Tony Blair's cabinet?

13 Whose work, 'The First Man on the Moon' was published in 1902?

14 Who, in 1913, wrote: "conscience is the internal perception of a particular wish operating within us"?

15 In which German city did the Manchester United plane tragedy take place in 1958?

Answers 1 Nephew 2 Coal miner's Daughter 3 Ted Hughes 4 Marathon 5 John De Lorean 6 Walter Mondale 7 Royal Shakespeare Company 8 Farouk 9 Bill Haley 10 Richard Burton and Elizabeth Taylor 11 Paris 12 Peter Mandelson 13 H.C.Wells 14 Sigmund Freud 15 Munich

20ᵀᴴ CENTURY HISTORY
Quiz 7

1 Who became leader of the Palestine Liberation Organisation in 1969?

2 Which volcano in Washington state spectacularly exploded in 1980 resulting in the deaths of 57 people?

3 In which war did American forces battle in Pork Chop Hill?

4 In 1939, which two leaders signed a 'Pact of Steel' committing their nations to support each other in times of war?

5 What was the name of the Republic of Sri Lanka prior to 1972?

6 In America, who signed off from hosting 'The Tonight Show' in 1992 after almost 30 years?

7 In 1977, because of the Watergate scandal, who became the first US attorney general to serve prison time?

8 In which decade did Graham Greene publish 'The Quiet American' and Alan Sillitoe publish 'Saturday Night and Sunday Morning'?

9 In what year was Margaret Thatcher first elected Prime Minister in Britain?

10 Name the Queen's art expert who, in 1978, was disclosed as being the 'fourth man' following the defection of Burgess and MacLean in 1951?

11 What nationality was Sir Edmund Hillary who, with Sherpa Tenzing, was the first to reach the summit of Everest in 1953?

12 Who was the American businessman, aviator and film producer who died aged 71 in 1976, having spent his later years as an eccentric recluse?

13 In which country, in 1989 was opposition leader San Suu Kyi placed under house arrest for her outspoken attacks on the country's military rulers?

14 Which war ended in 1902 with the treaty of Vereeniging?

15 Who, in 1935, at Bonneville Salt Flats in Utah became the first man to exceed 300mph in an automobile?

Answers 1 Yassir Arafat 2 Mount St. Helens 3 The Korean War 4 Hitler and Mussolini 5 Ceylon 6 Johnny Carson 7 John Mitchell 8 1950s 9 1979 10 Sir Anthony Blunt 11 New Zealand 12 Howard Hughes 13 Myanmar (Burma) 14 The Boer War 15 Sir Malcolm Campbell

20ᵀᴴ CENTURY HISTORY

Quiz 8

1 Who was 'discovered' by Roger Vadim?
   a Marilyn Monroe
   b Rita Hayworth
   c Brigitte Bardot
   d Leslie Caron

2 Who became President of the Fifth Republic on Jan 8, 1959?
   a Charles De Gaulle
   b Nicolae Ceaucescu
   c Georges Clemenceau
   d Chou En-Lai

3 In the world's first ever recording, what nursery rhyme was recited by Thomas Edison?
   a Little Bo Peep
   b Humpty Dumpty
   c Mary Had a Little Lamb
   d Jack and Jill

4 Who premiered his symphony 'Black, Brown, And Beige' at Carnegie Hall on Jan 23, 1943?
   a Paul Whiteman
   b Dmitri Shostakovich
   c Duke Ellington
   d Count Basie

5 Who, in 1954, was awarded the Nobel prize for literature for his "mastery of the art of modern narration"?
   a Boris Pasternak
   b Jean-Paul Sartre
   c Samuel Beckett
   d Ernest Hemingway

6 Who was assassinated by Mark Chapman?
   a John Lennon
   b The mother of Martin Luther King
   c Huey Long
   d Robert Kennedy

7 Who did Joe Louis defeat to win his first world heavyweight title on June 22, 1938?
   a Tommy Farr
   b Jersey Joe Walcott
   c Arturo Godoy
   d Max Schmeling

8 Who was the youngest man ever to win a Nobel Peace prize?
   a Martin Luther King Jr
   b Albert Schweitzer
   c Lech Welesa
   d Lester Pearson

9 Which film stars famous last words were: "I should never have switched from Scotch to Martinis"?
   a James Stewart
   b Peter Sellers
   c Humphrey Bogart
   d Clark Gable

10 Who was President when America entered the First World War?
   a Taft
   b Harding
   c Wilson
   d Coolidge

Answers 1 c, 2 a, 3 c, 4 c, 5 d, 6 a, 7 d, 8 a, 9 c, 10 c.

20ᵀᴴ CENTURY HISTORY

Quiz 9

1   An Hungarian-born escapologist named Ernst Weiss died of a burst appendix on October 31, 1926. By what name was he better known?

2   In which decade was London's 'Crystal Palace' destroyed by fire?

3   Who said, in 1941: "our enemies have performed a brilliant feat of deception, perfectly timed and executed with great skill"?

4   Which two South African politicians jointly won the Nobel Peace Prize in 1993?

5   What was the name of Queen Elizabeth the Queen Mother when she married the Duke of York in 1923?

6   In a hit song of 1939, where was the washing going to be hung out?

7   In which town in England at the Iffley Road stadium did Roger Bannister become the first man to break the 4-minute mile?

8   The cellist Jacqeline du Pré, who died of multiple sclerosis was married to which pianist and conductor?

9   Which writer married Nora Barnacle in 1931?

10   Who was the Siberian seer and miracle worker who was murdered by Russian nobles in December 1916?

11   Who, in 1963 said: "let us not seek to satisfy our thirst for freedom by drinking from the cup of hatred and bitterness"?

12   Which West Indies cricketing hero was knighted in 1975?

13   What music, in 1922, was condemned by American churchmen as a return to the jungle?

14   Who was the author of 'Dr. Zhivago' who died in 1960?

15   In the World Cup victory by England over Germany in 1966, Geoff Hurst scored a hat-trick, but who scored England's other goal?

Answers 1 Harry Houdini 2 1930s (1936) 3 President F. D. Roosevelt about the bombing of Pearl Harbour 4 Nelson Mandela and Fredrick de Klerk 5 Lady Elizabeth Bowes-Lyon 6 On the Siegfried line 7 Oxford 8 Daniel Barenboim 9 James Joyce 10 Rasputin 11 Martin Luther King, in his 'I have a dream' speech 12 Sir Garfield Sobers 13 Jazz 14 Boris Pasternak 15 Martin Peters

20ᵀᴴ CENTURY HISTORY

Quiz 10

1   Where was Florence Nightingale born?
   a   London
   b   Florence
   c   Paris
   d   Chicago

2   'Maybelline' was the first recording of which rock and roll icon?
   a   Elvis Presley
   b   Little Richard
   c   Chuck Berry
   d   Bill Haley

3   Which fictional icon was said to have lost his virginity in Paris at the age of 16?
   a   Harry Lime
   b   James Bond
   c   Philip Marlowe
   d   J. R. Ewing

4   What country was the birthplace of Irving Berlin?
   a   Russia
   b   America
   c   Germany
   d   Poland

5   Out of his 20 major championships, how many times has Jack Nicklaus won the Masters at Augusta?
   a   Never
   b   Once
   c   4 times
   d   6 times

6   Who, in July, 1925, was the first actor to appear on the cover of 'Time' magazine?
   a   Douglas Fairbanks
   b   Rudolph Valentino
   c   Charlie Chaplin
   d   Lionel Barrymore

7   In which state was Henry Ford born in 1863, and die in 1947?
   a   Michigan
   b   Missouri
   c   Wisconsin
   d   Illinois

8   Which fashion designer achieved fame in 1947 with the 'New Look', and later designed the 'H' line and the 'A' line?
   a   Mary Quant
   b   Charles Worth
   c   Christian Dior
   d   Gabrielle (Coco) Chanel

9   Which icon of the cinema was born Issur Danielovitch Demsky?
   a   Kirk Douglas
   b   Burt Lancaster
   c   Danny Kaye
   d   Spencer Tracy

10   Indira Ghandi was the daughter of which Indian Prime Minister?
   a   Ghandi
   b   Desai
   c   Shastri
   d   Nehru

Answers 1 b, 2 c, 3 b, 4 a, 5 d, 6 c, 7 a, 8 c, 9 a, 10 d

20ᵀᴴ CENTURY HISTORY

Quiz 11

1   What magazine was founded by De Witt Wallace in 1922?

2   Which US male vocal group were singing about 'My Girl' in 1965 and 'Ball of Confusion' in 1970?

3   Which two countries signed a peace agreement at Camp David in 1978?

4   In which year in the UK was the Soccer Premier League formed?

5   The Saunders-Roe SRN1 made the first passenger journey of which vehicle in 1959?

6   From 1930-1971 what was the world's tallest building?

7   What important event took place in Britain on 15 February, 1971?

8   What were found near Qumran, Palestine by an Arab shepherd in 1947?

9   In 1969 a war between which two Central American countries was provoked by a football match?

10 From 1976-85 which team, Oxford or Cambridge, created the longest ever run of wins in the University Boat race?

11 Who, in 1929, wrote the best-seller 'Revolt in the Desert'?

12 Who ended a momentous broadcast in 1936 with the words: "God bless you all, God Save the King"?

13 Who in 1947 was Britain's last Viceroy to India?

14 What honour was bestowed on the island of Malta in 1942?

15 What was the nickname of Vincent Coll, a psychopathic gangster gunned down in a telephone booth in 1932?

Answers 1 Readers Digest 2 Temptation 3 Egypt and Israel 4 1993 5 Hovercraft 6 The Empire State Building 7 Decimalisation was introduced 8 The Dead Sea Scrolls 9 Honduras and El Salvador 10 Oxford 11 T.E.Lawrence 12 Edward VIII in his abdication speech 13 Lord Mountbatten 14 The George Cross 15 Mad Dog

20ᵗʰ CENTURY HISTORY — Quiz 12

1 What was the name of Andy Warhol's New York studio?
   a The Culture Warehouse
   b The Factory
   c Art Attack
   d Culture Club

2 When hailed as a genius, who retorted: "Genius is one percent inspiration and 99 percent perspiration"?
   a Albert Einstein
   b Marie Curie
   c Henry Ford
   d Thomas Edison

3 What was Dwight D.Eisenhower's slogan when he ran for president in 1952?
   a I like Ike
   b The peoples choice
   c America's choice
   d Ike to the White House

4 In which film did Greta Garbo speak the line: "I want to be alone"?
   a Grand Hotel
   b Queen Christina
   c Anna Karenina
   d Ninotchka

5 Apart from womanizing and producing films what was the other passion of Howard Hughes?
   a Golf
   b Aviation
   c Automobiles
   d Socializing

6 Hadley Richardson, Pauline Pfeiffer, Martha Gellhorn and Mary Welsh were all wives of:
   a F. Scott Fitzgerald
   b Mickey Rooney
   c Ernest Hemingway
   d Sam Goldwyn

7 In what year did Charles Lindbergh make his solo Atlantic crossing?
   a 1932
   b 1926
   c 1930
   d 1927

8 In the 1936 'Jesse Owens' Olympics' for which event below did Owens not win the gold medal?
   a 200 meters dash
   b Broad jump
   c 100 meters dash
   d 220 yards hurdles

9 Which baseball player was known as the "Sultan of Swat"?
   a Lou Gehrig
   b Wally Pipp
   c Babe Ruth
   d Joe DiMaggio

10 Who was the eldest son of the American heiress Jennie Jerome?
   a Harry Truman
   b William Randolph Hearst
   c Winston Churchill
   d Lyndon Baines Johnson

Answers 1 b, 2 d, 3 a, 4 a, 5 b, 6 c, 7 d, 8 d, 9 c, 10 c.

MISCELLANEOUS

MISCELLANEOUS 4 — Quiz 1

1   Name the US golfer who died in a freak flying accident in October 1999.
2   Wagga Wagga is a city in which Australian state?
3   By what name is the poem 'Casabianca', about the death of a ten year old boy and his father, a French navy captain, better known?
4   The Ardennes are a range of hills which extend through France, Belgium and which other country.
5   Presbyopia affects which part of the body?
6   Which 19th century British Prime Minister said: "We are part of the community of Europe, and we must do our duty as such"?
7   What nationality was the 17th century landscape painter, Meindert Hobbema?
8   Which American comedienne once said: "I don't work out. If God wanted us to bend over he'd put diamonds on the floor"?
9   An otoscope is a medical instrument used to examine which part of the body?
10 Which Pakistani cricketer is known as the 'Rawalpindi Express'?
11 In the TV series 'Happy Days', what was the surname of Richie and his parents Howard and Marion?
12 Which 20th century South American revolutionary once said: "In a revolution, one wins or dies"?
13 Following her performance in a 1960 film, which actress claims she has never had a shower since and even in a bath positions herself so she is facing the door?
14 The Bight of Bonny is an inlet of which ocean?
15 Which famous woman was born in Domremy, France in 1412?

Answers 1 Payne Stewart 2 New South Wales 3 The Boy Stood On The Burning Deck 4 Luxembourg 5 Eye 6 William Gladstone 7 Dutch 8 Joan Rivers 9 Ear 10 Shoaib Akhtar 11 Cunningham 12 Che Guevara 13 Janet Leigh 14 Atlantic 15 Joan of Arc

Quiz 2

1   Name the actress who played Helen Daniels in the Australian TV series 'Neighbours' who died aged 68 in 1999.

2   What sort of creature is a chickadee?

3   The site of a decisive battle in 1863 during the American Civil War, which city in Tennessee features in the title of a famous Glenn Miller tune?

4   What's the name of the muskrat who is cartoon character Deputy Dawg's sidekick?

5   Which female singer once said: "I have got little feet because nothing grows in the shade"?

6   Who wrote the novels 'Disclosure', 'Congo' and 'The Andromeda Strain'?

7   What name is given to the small bones which make up the spine?

8   French is the official language of the African republic of Guinea, but what is the official language of the republic known as Equatorial Guinea?

9   Which actor played horror film director James Whale in the 1999 movie 'Gods And Monsters'?

10 If you arrived at Flinders Street station and crossed the Yarra river to Queen Victoria Gardens, in which Australian city would you be?

11 With which male singer did Nancy Sinatra record the songs 'Jackson', 'Ladybird' and 'Did You Ever'?

12 Which contagious disease, found in animals and which can be transmitted to humans, is caused by the bacterium, *Bacillus anthracis*?

13 The German town of Wuppertal stands on which river?

14 In 1996, a humidor once owned by John F. Kennedy was sold at auction. What is usually kept in a humidor?

15 What was the first name of the founder of the Ferrari motor company?

Answers 1 Anne Haddy **2** Bird **3** Chattanooga **4** Muskie **5** Dolly Parton **6** Michael Crichton **7** Vertebrae **8** Spanish **9** Ian McKellen **10** Melbourne **11** Lee Hazlewood **12** Anthrax **13** Wupper **14** Cigars, cigarettes or tobacco **15** Enzo

Quiz 3

1   Which TV series ended episodes with words such as: "Goodnight John-Boy, Goodnight Grandpa, Goodnight Mary Ellen"?

2   Name the British frogman who disappeared in a famous incident of the 1950s while swimming around a Russian warship in Portsmouth harbour.

3   Tennis. In March 1999, who became the first male Spanish player to top the ATP Tour's world rankings since they began in 1973?

4   Developed around the 15th century and using music, dancing and themes from religious stories or myths, No or Noh, is classic drama performed in which country?

5   The Nobel prize winning poet Gabriela Mistral came from which South American country?

6   Name the town in Colombia, with the same name as a former Soviet republic, which was devastated by an earthquake in January 1999.

7   What type of creature is a lumpsucker?

8   Name the actor who appeared in the films 'Bonnie And Clyde', 'I Never Sang For My Father', 'Mississippi Burning', 'Unforgiven' and 'The Firm'.

9   The Primate of Australia is the Archbishop of which city?

10 Are polar bears native to the Arctic or Antarctic?

11 From which country did the Philippines gain independence in 1946?

12 In 1979, which 40 year-old Italian film star gave birth to a baby daughter just two months after she had become a grandmother?

13 If a motorcade is a procession of motor vehicles, what is a procession of people on horseback called?

14 In conventional chess notation, what letter represents the knight?

15 What was the model number given to the World War Two German fighter plane, manufactured by Messerschmitt, of which more than 33,000 were built?

Answers 1 The Waltons **2** Commander Lionel 'Buster' Crabb **3** Carlos Moya **4** Japan **5** Chile **6** Armenia **7** Fish **8** Gene Hackman **9** Melbourne **10** Arctic **11** USA **12** Claudia Cardinale **13** Cavalcade **14** N **15** ME 109

1 In February 1999, which unconventional British fashion designer unveiled her Red Label collection in New York?

2 Which outdoor athletics event is run over 25 laps of the track?

3 Frascati, Chianti and Barolo are all wines from which country?

4 What type of creature is a krait?

5 Traditionally divided into statics and dynamics, which branch of physics is the study of the motion of bodies and the forces acting on them?

6 What eight letter word beginning with Y is the name given to the skullcap worn by Orthodox male Jews at all times and by other Jewish men during prayer?

7 And what eight letter word beginning with K is the name given to the cotton headdress worn by Arab men?

8 The battle of Agincourt was fought on which saints' day?

9 Which 19th century social, political and economic theorist paraphrased an anarchist doctrine by writing: "From each according to his abilities, to each according to his needs"?

10 In 1923, Canadians Frederick Banting and John MacLeod shared the Nobel prize for Medicine for the discovery of what hormone?

11 The name of which element, atomic number 27, is derived from the German word for a goblin or imp?

12 And the name of which noble gas, discovered in 1898, is derived from the Greek word for hidden?

13 What is the official language of Liechtenstein?

14 Brazil in South America, Angola in Africa and Goa in Asia were all colonised by which European country?

15 In 1968, Bob Beamon famously set a world record in which athletics event that was to stand for 23 years?

Answers 1 Vivienne Westwood 2 10,000 metres 3 Italy 4 Snake 5 Mechanics 6 Yarmulke 7 Keffiyeh 8 St. Crispin 9 Karl Marx 10 Insulin 11 Cobalt 12 Krypton 13 German 14 Portugal 15 Long Jump

Quiz 5

1   Which Italian city's two leading football clubs are known as the 'red and blacks' and the 'black and blues'?

2   Baden-Powell founded the Boy Scouts, but which similar organisation was founded by Scottish businessman William Smith in 1883?

3   Spandau is a district of which city?

4   Pliny the Younger and Pliny the Elder were Roman writers. What relation was Pliny the Younger to Pliny the Elder?

5   What is the largest country in South America?

6   How many lives is a cat said to have?

7   Brown, spotted and striped are three species of which scavenging creature?

8   What year connects Napoleon's retreat from Moscow and a famous overture by Tchaikovsky?

9   Derived from the Greek word for 'over' or 'above', which prefix is used in composite words to mean excessive?

10 Which variety of cabbage is also called 'turnip cabbage'?

11 In which American state were the Chukwu octuplets born in December 1998?

12 Which city became the capital of Turkey in 1923?

13 What name was given to the 2,000 mile long trail undertaken by settlers in the 1840s which ran from Independence, Missouri to the Columbia River?

14 Which character has been played in films by Ralph Byrd, Morgan Conway and Warren Beatty?

15 What six letter word beginning with B is the name given to a piece of wood or metal used to secure a tarpaulin over a ship's hatch?

Answers 1 Milan 2 Boy's Brigade 3 Berlin 4 Nephew 5 Brazil 6 9 7 Hyena 8 1812 9 Hyper 10 Kohlrabi 11 Texas 12 Ankara 13 The Oregon Trail 14 Dick Tracy 15 Batten

MISCELLANEOUS 4 *Quiz 6*

1   Who died first – Queen Elizabeth I or William Shakespeare?

2   Only one 20th century US president was a graduate of the US Military Academy at West Point. Name him.

3   Name the notorious camp doctor at Auschwitz who was known as the 'Angel of Death'.

4   What type of creature is the Hawaiian honeycreeper?

5   Franglais is a mixture of which two languages?

6   Calamine is an ore of which metal?

7   Which pair complete the following sequence – Armstrong and Aldrin, Conrad and Bean, Shepard and Mitchell, Scott and Irwin, Young and Duke and…?

8   Rampart Street, Bourbon Street and Royal Street are famous streets in the French quarter of which US city?

9   Which bird of the family *Picadae*, chisels through tree barks with it's long straight bill in search of insects?

10 Known as the 'great white hope', which American heavyweight boxer of the1960s and early 1970s unsuccessfully challenged Joe Frazier and Jimmy Ellis for the world title and twice lost to Muhammad Ali in non-title fights?

11 In March 2001 the world's largest oil rig toppled over and collapsed into the Atlantic Ocean. It was situated off the coast of which South American country?

12 Which singer was killed in a plane crash along with Buddy Holly and the Big Bopper on 3 February 1959?

13 Of whom did Bette Midler once say: "A woman who pulled herself up by her bra straps"?

14 What's the name of the detective created by Leslie Charteris and known as 'The Saint'?

15 What type of basic incendiary device is named after a Russian politician?

Answers 1 Elizabeth I 2 Dwight D. Eisenhower 3 Josef Mengele 4 Bird 5 French and English 6 Zinc 7 Cernan and Schmitt (all men who have walked on the moon) 8 New Orleans 9 Woodpecker 10 Jerry Quarry 11 Brazil 12 Ritchie Valens 13 Madonna 14 Simon Templar 15 Molotov cocktail

MISCELLANEOUS 4 — Quiz 7

1 In 1999, who became the first quarterback in American Football to play in five Superbowls?

2 Which famous London square was once known as 'porridge island' because the squalid courtyards were filled with cheap eating houses?

3 In 1915, Japanese businessman Rokuji Hayakawa invented the first automatic propelling pencil. This pencil was marketed by the company Mr. Hayakawa founded in 1912 and which developed into a major electronics company. Which company?

4 In Australia, what do they call a pick-up truck, it being short for utility truck?

5 'Linger', 'Zombie' and 'Salvation' are all songs recorded by which group fronted by Dolores O'Riordan?

6 Name the thick steak cut from a fillet of beef which takes it's name from a French writer and statesman who lived from 1768 to 1848.

7 Which word beginning with A and derived from the Spanish for affection, describes an ardent supporter or devotee of a particular interest or hobby?

8 Snooker players Bob Chaperon, Alain Robidoux and Jim Wych all originate from which country?

9 Which sculpture is referred to in the Oxford Companion To Art as the 'best known of all ancient statues'?

10 Named after a character in Fellini's movie 'La Dolce Vita', what P is the name given to photographers who follow celebrities around, often specializing in candid shots?

11 Which is the only US state to have the word 'West' in it's name?

12 The American model Christie Brinkley was once married to which singer/songwriter?

13 What is the full name of AMPAS, the organisation responsible for the Oscars?

14 F is the chemical symbol for which highly reactive pale-yellow halogen gas?

15 Well known for his songs recorded by Meatloaf, who wrote the lyrics for the Andrew Lloyd Webber musical 'Whistle Down The Wind'?

Answers 1 John Elway 2 Trafalgar Square 3 Sharp 4 Ute 5 The Cranberries 6 Chateaubriand 7 Aficionado 8 Canada 9 Venus de Milo 10 Paparazzi 11 West Virginia 12 Billy Joel 13 Academy of Motion Picture(s) Arts and Sciences 14 Fluorine 15 Jim Steinman

1   Which London monument was officially re-opened by the Queen in October 1998 after extensive restoration?

2   What word is a hand at bridge or whist without trumps and is also a short section of sharp narrow bends formed by barriers or humps on a motor racing circuit?

3   According to the New Testament of the Bible, who said: "I am innocent of the blood of this just person"?

4   On 16 March 1986, which European country held a referendum on whether or not to join the United Nations and 75% of the voters said No?

5   Which common phrase, meaning 'the whole lot', comes from military jargon for the principal parts of a gun?

6   Which town in the Drome department of south-east France is famous for it's nougat?

7   Followers of which religion follow the Noble Eightfold Path?

8   What is the English name of the native American chief Tatanka Yotaka?

9   Name the American civil rights leader whose intervention helped to secure the release of three US servicemen from Yugoslavia in 1999.

10 Native to the Andes, what V is a hoofed animal which resembles a small camel and is valued for it's wool?

11 What sort of creature is a cockatiel?

12 In the TV series 'Star Trek: The Next Generation', what species was Lt. Worf?

13 'Secrets', 'The Ranch', 'Heartbeat', 'Full Circle', 'Daddy' and 'Kaleidoscope' are some of the works of which novelist dubbed the 'Queen of Romance'?

14 The forenames of Greek shipping magnate Onassis, the man who married Jacqueline Kennedy were the names of ancient philosophers. Aristotle was one, name the other?

15 In 1999, which TV cartoon series reached the cinema screen 'bigger, longer and uncut'?

MISCELLANEOUS 4   *Quiz 9*

1. Later to become world famous, which singer was a member of the prize-winning Italian Modena Choir at the renowned Llangollen music festival in 1955?

2. Which female singer won the awards for best new artist, best album, best R & B album, best R & B song and best R & B vocal performance at the 1999 Grammys?

3. Which is the nearest to Australia – New Zealand or Papua New Guinea?

4. Quoted in a 1999 book on blondes, which singer said: "I'm not offended by all the crude dumb-blonde jokes because I know I am not dumb. I also know I am not blonde"?

5. Which French word, the literal meaning being 'between the rib' refers to beefsteak cut from between the ribs?

6. Acre is a town and fishing port in which Middle Eastern country?

7. Mario Soares became president of which European country in 1986?

8. The Sea of Japan is a part of which ocean?

9. Who co-starred with Julia Roberts in the films 'Pretty Woman' and 'Runaway Bride'?

10. Which Beatles song features the lyrics 'I am the egg man'?

11. In geological terms, which of the following eras occurred most recently – Cenozoic, Mesozoic or Palaeozoic?

12. If you spend too much time squashed in an airline seat, you may possibly suffer DVT. What does DVT stand for?

13. Straddling the borders between Kazakhstan and Uzbekistan it was formerly the world's fourth largest body of inland water. It is now of great interest to scientists because of the remarkable shrinkage of it's area and volume during the second half of the 20th century. Name this body of water.

14. During which century did the battles of Trafalgar, Waterloo and Balaclava all take place?

15. If a Texan comes from Texas, what name is given to someone who comes from New York state?

Answers 1 Luciano Pavarotti 2 Lauryn Hill 3 Papua New Guinea 4 Dolly Parton 5 Entrecote 6 Israel 7 Portugal 8 Pacific 9 Richard Gere 10 I Am The Walrus 11 Cenozoic 12 Deep-vein thrombosis 13 Aral Sea 14 19th 15 New Yorker

MISCELLANEOUS 4

Quiz 10

1   According to historical researchers, which London landmark was Hitler planning to move to Berlin?

2   By what nickname is Jack Kervorkian, the American doctor and champion of euthanasia who was jailed in April 1999, popularly known?

3   Edmonton, Calgary and Medicine Hat are all places in which Canadian province?

4   Name the American author of 'The Scarlatti Inheritance', 'The Matarese Circle' and 'The Prometheus Deception' who died aged 73 in March 2001.

5   In which 1994 film does Samuel L. Jackson say these words: "The path of the righteous man is beset on all sides by the inequities of the selfish and the tyranny of evil men"?

6   The ski resort of Davos is in which country?

7   If you went on a scuba diving holiday to Hurghada, in which sea would you be?

8   Had he lived, Elvis Presley would have celebrated his 65th birthday in which year?

9   Who was East Germany's last communist leader, being in power when the Wall was opened up in 1989?

10 What is the English name of the native American chief Goyathlay whose name means 'one who yawns'?

11 Name the American author, she died in 1995, whose first and third novels 'Strangers On A Train' and 'The Talented Mr. Ripley' were adapted into films.

12 Kunte Kinte and Chicken George are characters in which Alex Haley novel?

13 According to the book of Genesis in the Bible, who was the hairiest of Isaac's twin sons when they were born – Esau or Jacob?

14 Cala Longa, Es Cana and Portinatx are all holiday resorts on which Mediterranean island?

15 Who won the US Masters golf championship in 1980, just four days after his 23rd birthday?

Answers 1 Nelson's Column 2 Dr. Death 3 Alberta 4 Robert Ludlum 5 Pulp Fiction 6 Switzerland 7 Red Sea 8 2000 9 Egon Krenz 10 Geronimo 11 Patricia Highsmith 12 Roots 13 Esau 14 Ibiza 15 Seve Ballesteros

1 In 1999, which British actress looking back on her career said: "I started off as a babe, became a bitch and now I'm playing an old bag"?

2 What F is a railway that runs up the side of a mountain, consisting of two cars at either end of a cable passing round a drive wheel at the summit?

3 Which Simon & Garfunkel song contains the line 'I'm sitting in a railway station, got a ticket for my destination'?

4 Set on a train, which 1985 action movie featured Jon Voight, Eric Roberts and Rebecca DeMornay?

5 The Danes, Jan Pedersen, Hans Nielsen, Erik Gundersen and Ole Olsen, have all been world champions in which sport?

6 The highest mountain on the continent of North America is Mount McKinlay. Which is the second highest?

7 In 1897, Charles Wilson devised an apparatus for tracking ionized particles. By what name is the apparatus commonly known?

8 In which country would you find a cluster of rock-cut temples known as the Ellora Caves?

9 In which river is the submerged islet of Philae, the former home of many ancient temples?

10 Derived from Hindi, what P is a strip of cloth worn around the leg from the ankle to the knee?

11 When Spanish TV bought the comedy series 'Fawlty Towers', the character of Manuel was changed to what nationality?

12 A stapedectomy is surgery carried out on which part of the body?

13 Named after the hotel where it was first served, which salad is traditionally made with apples, walnuts, celery and mayonnaise.

14 Name the husband of Julie Andrews who directed the 'Pink Panther' films.

15 Which American guitarist had a worldwide hit in 1968 with 'Classical Gas'?

Answers 1 Joan Collins 2 Funicular 3 Homeward Bound 4 Runaway Train 5 Speedway 6 Mount Logan 7 Cloud Chamber 8 India 9 Nile 10 Puttee 11 Italian 12 Ear 13 Waldorf Salad 14 Blake Edwards 15 Mason Williams

1   In 1887, which famous fictional character was described as follows: "Knowledge of literature – nil; knowledge of philosophy – nil; knowledge of chemistry – profound; knowledge of sensational literature – immense; he plays the violin well!"?

2   Tritium is a radioactive isotope of which gas?

3   Which country won the 1999 Rugby Union World Cup to become the first to win the competition twice?

4   The following lyrics are from which Elton John song: "If I were a sculptor, but then again no. Or a man who makes potions in a travelling show"?

5   Which actor played the young Obi-Wan Kenobi in the 1999 film 'Star Wars: Episode One – The Phantom Menace"?

6   Aioli is mayonnaise flavoured with what?

7   Which country is known as 'the land of the rising sun'?

8   According to Nicholas I of Russia, which two winter months were the 'two generals in whom Russia could always trust'?

9   Popular amongst followers of swing music in the 1930s, what Z was men's apparel consisting of baggy trousers caught in at the bottom, a long coat and flowing tie, all in vivid colours?

10   Which 1954 film musical starring Howard Keel was adapted from the Stephen Vincent Benet story 'Sobbin' Women'?

11   Which doctor has been played in movies by, amongst others, John Barrymore, Frederic March, Spencer Tracy and Ralph Bates?

12   What was built in Rome to commemorate the fall of Jerusalem in AD 70?

13   The name of which famous diamond means 'mountain of light'?

14   Which is the most northerly – the Panama Canal or the Suez Canal?

15   Which Empress was born in Granada, Spain in 1826, became a Frenchwoman by marriage and retired to England after the fall of the Empire in 1870?

Answers 1 Sherlock Holmes 2 Hydrogen 3 Australia 4 Your Song 5 Ewan McGregor 6 Garlic 7 Japan 8 January and February 9 Zoot-suit 10 Seven Brides For Seven Brothers 11 Dr. Jekyll 12 The Titus Arch 13 Koh-i-noor 14 Suez Canal 15 Eugenie

MISCELLANEOUS 4 — Quiz 13

1 Which famous literary Welshman once said of his country: "The Land Of My Fathers – and my fathers can have it"?

2 Which heavyweight boxer, known as the 'Easton Assassin', won his first 48 professional bouts, including 21 world title fights before losing his IBF title to Michael Spinks in 1985?

3 What is a female swan called?

4 The Isla Mas a Tierra, one of three volcanic islands of the Juan Fernandez islands, situated some 400 miles west of Valparaiso, Chile, was the inspiration for which famous novel?

5 Nilotic refers to which river?

6 Iosif Vissarionovich Dzhugashvili lived from 1879 to 1953 and was educated in a Theological Seminary. By what name was he better known?

7 What ornament of medieval architecture derives its name from the Old French word for 'throat' ?

8 In which Italian city would you find a university that was founded in 1222 and the Basilica of St. Anthony's?

9 What K is a short stick with a knobbed head used as a weapon by indigenous peoples of South Africa?

10 And what K is a Malaysian or Indonesian dagger with a wavy-edged blade?

11 De Gaulle was the first president of the 5th Republic of France. Who, from 1953 to 1959, was the last president of the French Fourth Republic?

12 What word for a powerful person in business was an archaic name given by foreigners to the Shogun of Japan?

13 In which century did the Seven Years' War between Prussia, Britain and Hanover on one side and France, Russia, Austria and Spain on the other, take place?

14 Who was the mother of the French kings Francis II, Charles IX and Henry III?

15 Which Greek philosopher is sometimes known as the Stagyrite after Stagira where he was born?

Answers 1 Dylan Thomas **2** Larry Holmes **3** Pen **4** Robinson Crusoe **5** Nile **6** Josef Stalin **7** Gargoyle **8** Padua **9** Knobkerrie **10** Kris **11** Rene Coty **12** Tycoon **13** 18th **14** Catherine de Medici **15** Aristotle

1 One of the most successful and prolific songwriters of pop music of recent times, she has written songs such as 'Starship's' 'Nothing's Gonna Stop Us Now', Cher's 'If I Could Turn Back Time' and the massive 'How Do I Live' which was a big hit for both Trisha Yearwood and LeAnn Rimes. Name her.

2 The name of which Mexican volcano means 'smoking mountain'?

3 The Golden Horn is a natural harbour serving which major city?

4 If you ordered 'rognons' in a restaurant, what would you be served with?

5 Derived from the Italian for a 'person who loves the arts', what D is someone who dabbles in a subject for enjoyment but without serious study?

6 Colcannon is an Irish or Scottish food dish consisting of which two ingredients boiled and mashed together?

7 Who led the American forces that defeated the British at the Battle of New Orleans in 1815?

8 Which 20th century French dramatist wrote plays about both Thomas a Becket and Joan of Arc?

9 What name was given to the treaty of 1929 which established the Vatican City as an independent state?

10 Which famous 18th century king of Prussia was known as the 'Philosopher of Sans Souci'?

11 If Atomic Number 1 is Hydrogen, what is Number 2?

12 Which US ballet dancer and choreographer who died in 1991 founded the School of Contemporary Dance in New York in 1927? Amongst her best known ballets are 'Primitive Mysteries', 'Appalachian Spring' and 'Acts Of Light'.

13 Which three countries signed a security treaty in 1951 known as the ANZUS Pact?

14 Which dissident group played a leading role in the upheaval, known as the 'Velvet Revolution', which ended communism in Czechoslovakia in 1989?

15 Played in a 1944 movie by Elizabeth Taylor, what is the name of the horse-loving young girl in Enid Bagnold's novel?

Answers 1 Diane Warren 2 Popocatepetl 3 Istanbul 4 Kidneys 5 Dilletante 6 Cabbage and Potato 7 Andrew Jackson 8 Jean Anouilh 9 Lateran treaty 10 Frederick (II) the Great 11 Helium 12 Martha Graham 13 Australia, New Zealand and USA 14 Charter 77 15 Velvet Brown

MISCELLANEOUS 4   Quiz 15

1   What C is a Yiddish word for shameless audacity?

2   Who supposedly said: "Father I cannot tell a lie. I did it with my little hatchet"?

3   Which arts movement was founded in Italy in 1909 by the poet Marinetti?

4   What M from the Sanskrit for 'great soul' is a holy person or sage?

5   Formed in Paris in 1888, which group of French artists took their name from the Hebrew word for 'prophets'?

6   Which writer who died in 1990, wrote the screenplay of the James Bond movie 'You Only Live Twice'?

7   What is the second longest river in South America after the Amazon?

8   It's name means 'The empty quarter' in English and it is the largest area of continuous sand in the world. In which country is it mostly situated?

9   Which US folk singer wrote the songs 'This Land Is Your Land' and 'So Long It's Been Good To Know You'?

10 According to the Gospel of St. Matthew in the Bible, what did John the Baptist feed on whilst in the wilderness?

11 What is the least number of sides a figure must have to be described as a polygon?

12 Although Davy Crockett is famously associated with the Alamo, the Texan defenders were commanded by Colonel James (Jim) Bowie and which other man?

13 The emblem of which christian organisation is a two-handed pitcher and torch?

14 The Trobriand or Kiriwina Islands are in which ocean?

15 Which US anthropologist wrote 'Coming Of Age In Samoa' and 'Growing Up In New Guinea'?

Answers 1 Chutzpah 2 George Washington 3 Futurism 4 Mahatma 5 Nabis 6 Roald Dahl 7 Parana 8 Saudi Arabia 9 Woody Guthrie 10 Locusts and wild honey 11 3 12 Colonel William B. Travis 13 Gideons International 14 Pacific 15 Margaret Mead

1   What did Robert Burns refer to as 'Great chieftain o' the pudding-race'?

2   And what did Burns refer to as 'Wee, sleekit, cow'rin, tim'rous beastie'?

3   What P is a small hammer with a rubber head used to test reflexes?

4   Meaning to cut the abdomen, or bowels, what S is another word for hara-kiri?

5   Which NASCAR racing legend, known as the 'Intimidator' was killed during the 2001 Daytona 500?

6   Who was Prime Minister of Rhodesia and Nyasaland from 1956 to 1963?

7   'Little Red Rooster' and 'I'm Your Hoochie Coochie Man' are just two songs written by which legendary Blues musician who died aged 76 in 1992?

8   Founded in 1912, which world famous communist newspaper finally ceased publication in July 1996?

9   Which world famous Parisian nightspot celebrated it's centenary in 1989?

10 In 1982, American Barney Clarke became the first person to receive a Jarvik 7. What's a Jarvik 7?

11 In March 2001, 54 year-old Jim Shekhdar became the first person to row unaided across which ocean?

12 Who was the last of the Inca emperors?

13 Which 20th century writer and poet once said: "My name is only an anagram of toilets"?

14 What does a depilator do?

15 Which cheese with a soft white exterior and a pale yellow interior comes from an area of France situated between the rivers Seine and Marne?

---

1   On 27 March 1992, upon which world famous structure did four members of Greenpeace stage a protest over nuclear testing?

2   Alcock and Brown completed the first non-stop flight across the Atlantic in 1919. Which one of them was killed in a flying accident later that year?

3   Since divorced, which actor did singer Paula Abdul marry in 1992?

4   Name the two men who wrote the hugely successful musicals 'Les Miserables' and 'Miss Saigon'.

5   A lustrum is a period of how many years?

6   To which country do the Antipodes Islands belong?

7   Played by John Karlen, what was the name of Mary Beth's husband in the TV series 'Cagney and Lacey'?

8   In 1985, which member of the Bee Gees married Dwina Murphy, who in the early 1990s was elected Patroness of the Druids?

9   With which sport do you associate Ireland's Joanna Morgan, American Julie Krone and Sweden's Suzanne Berenklint?

10 Written by John Parker, 'The Joker's Wild' is a biography of which Hollywood star?

11 Medellin, Cali and Cartagena are all cities in which South American country?

12 Which genetic disease is known by the initials CF?

13 What nationality was the explorer Vitus Jonassen Bering, after whom the Bering Sea was named?

14 Which order of monks take their name from Citeaux in France?

15 Pop Eye, Veil-Tail and Lionhead are species of which fish?

1   Drummer Rick Allen lost his left arm after a car accident on New Year's Eve 1984 but was able to resume his career with which heavy metal rock band?

2   Found in the Himalayas, what type of creature is a markhor?

3   Which film producer, responsible for many of the Laurel and Hardy classics, died aged 100 in 1992?

4   Because of it's humorous staccato quality, which woodwind instrument is often referred to by musicians as the 'clown of the orchestra'?

5   Fought in 1879, the battle of Isandhlwana took place during which war?

6   Which notorious Chicago bartender gave his name to any kind of drink which has a 'knockout' effect on the imbiber?

7   Which American jazz musician and songwriter wrote 'Honeysuckle Rose' and 'Ain't Misbehavin'?

8   Which white wine takes its name, literally meaning 'virgin's milk', from the convent in Worms where it was originally made?

9   Mons was the location of a famous battle in World War One. In which country is the town of Mons?

10 A German Shepherd dog appeared with Roy Rogers in several of his films. It had a rather appropriate name for western movies, what was it?

11 The American humorist and film star Will Rogers died in a plane crash in 1935. Which famous aviator piloted that plane and also died in the crash?

12 The powdered root of the Florentine iris, smelling of violets, is used in the manufacture of perfumes and medicines. What is it's name?

13 Which singer once said: "I live just like a monk– a monk with big red lips, short dresses and big hair"?

14 Which 'passage' were Baffin, Franklin and Frobisher all trying to find?

15 Cachalot is another name for which species of whale?

MISCELLANEOUS 4

Quiz 19

1 In November 1992, the historic Hofburg Palace was badly damaged by fire. In which European capital city is it?

2 And which Hollywood film studios were badly damaged by fire in November 1990?

3 What kind of creature is a wapiti?

4 If anaemia is a reduction in the number of red blood cells, what P is an increase of them?

5 Which popular song begins with the words 'The loveliness of Paris seems somehow sadly gay'?

6 When asked by Oprah Winfrey if he was a virgin, who replied: "How could you ask me that question? I'm a gentleman"?

7 What is the common name of the butterfly *Vanessa atalanta*?

8 According to the well known World War One song, the 'Mademoiselle' comes from which French town?

9 Soldiers used to carry 'sword and buckler' into battle. What was a buckler?

10 King Albert I died whilst mountain climbing in 1934. Of which lowland European country was he king?

11 Patrick Bergin and Kevin Costner both played which famous character in different films released in 1991?

12 What is the name of the vampire-hunting doctor who searches for Count Dracula in Bram Stoker's story?

13 A major factor in the build up to the Boer War, which invasion of the Transvaal by some 500 men in December 1895 ended ignominiously with them being captured. Named after the leader, by what name is this attack remembered?

14 Jessica Adams wrote the bestseller 'Single White E-mail'. Complete the title of the following novel of hers: 'Tom, Dick And .... '?

15 Name the port and resort situated at the southern extremity of Israel and at the head of the Gulf of Aqaba.

Answers 1 Vienna 2 Universal Studios 3 Deer 4 Polycythaemia 5 I Left My Heart In San Francisco 6 Michael Jackson 7 Red Admiral 8 Armentieres 9 Shield 10 Belgium 11 Robin Hood 12 Van Helsing 13 The Jameson Raid 14 Debbie Harry 15 Elat or Eilat

650

1   What is the common name of the plant *Polemonium caeruleum*?

2   What kind of creature is a boomslang?

3   In Conan Doyle's stories, what is the name of the Scotland Yard inspector with whom Sherlock Holmes often worked?

4   Name the American painter of portraits and everyday life whose controversial 'Gross Clinic' shows a surgeon operating.

5   How are Cuba, Hispaniola, Jamaica and Puerto Rico collectively known?

6   According to the Bible, chapter 17 of the First Book of Samuel, who 'had an helmet of brass upon his head, and was armed with a coat of mail; and the weight of the coat was five thousand shekels of brass'?

7   Louis, Mary and Richard were husband, wife and son who made important 20th century discoveries in Eastern Africa concerning origins of human beings. What is their surname?

8   Who was the supreme god in Babylonian mythology?

9   Popular in North America, what name is given to the rich soup which contains fish, clams, or corn with potatoes and onions which derives it's name from the French for 'large kettle'?

10 A devil's dozen is a gathering of how many witches?

11 Which 19th century French novelist wrote 'The Black Tulip'?

12 Which international organisation celebrated the 50th anniversary of it's foundation with a gathering of world leaders in New York on 24 October 1995?

13 What was the name of the land battle of July 1799 in which some 7,000 of Napoleon's men defeated an unruly Turkish force of some 18,000 men?

14 The Andaman and Nicobar Islands are a union territory of which country?

15 Name the French painter who developed pointillism, a technique where large scale paintings are built up from a series of tiny dots.

Answers 1 Jacob's Ladder 2 Snake 3 Lestrade 4 Thomas Eakins 5 Greater Antilles 6 Goliath 7 Leakey 8 Marduk 9 Chowder 10 13 11 Alexandre Dumas 12 United Nations 13 Battle of Aboukir 14 India 15 Georges Seurat

1   Immortalised in song, name the Cumberland farmer who lived from 1776 to 1854 and was a most enthusiastic huntsman who kept his own pack of hounds for more than 50 years.

2   Which female American impressionist painter was famous for her mother and child scenes, most notably her 'Woman And Child Driving'?

3   What name is given to the division of Oceania that contains amongst others, the Bismarck Archipelago, Solomon Islands, Vanuatu and Fiji?

4   With regard to Turkish food, what name is given to the rich cake consisting of thin layers of pastry filled with nuts and honey?

5   'The Burial Of Count Orgaz', painted in the late 16th century, is considered to be the masterpiece of which artist?

6   The inventor Thomas Alva Edison was born in a place in Ohio which has the same name as which Italian city?

7   And movie star Clark Gable was also born in Ohio, in a place which has the same name as which Spanish seaport?

8   What is the common name of the herb *Foeniculum vulgare*, which has a characteristic aniseed flavour?

9   And what is the common name of the herb *Artemisia dracunculus* used in salads and sauces and often used as an ingredient for tartare sauce?

10 Lara Antipova and Tania Gromeko are characters in which novel?

11 Which city in the Andalusian region of Spain is sometimes referred to as the 'Athens of the West'?

12 Name the German-born novelist who wrote the famous war novel 'All Quiet On The Western Front'.

13 Belgrade stands at the confluence of the Danube and which other river?

14 On which coast of Africa is Kenya situated – east or west?

15 In which TV series did Lloyd Bridges play Mike Nelson, a navy frogman turned undersea investigator?

Quiz 22

1 Which poet was a member of the Irish senate from 1922 to 1928?

2 According to the Bible, the Book of Judges chapter 20 verse 16, what was unusual about the 700 men of the tribe of Benjamin who fought the Israelites at Gibeah?

3 Named after a Trappist monastery in north-west France where it was first made, what is the name of the mild semi-hard whole-milk cheese with a flat-round shape?

4 Which writer was wounded at the battle of Lepanto in 1571 and in 1575 was captured by pirates and imprisoned in Algiers for five years?

5 Which Frenchman, who invented many recipes including Peach Melba, was known as 'The king of chefs and the chef of kings'?

6 Maxim de Winter and Mrs. Danvers are characters in which novel?

7 Which 16th century Italian artist whose name is derived from his birthplace Parma, painted 'Madonna With The Long Neck'?

8 Name the Japanese author of 'The Sailor Who Fell From Grace With The Sea' who shocked the world when he committed hara-kiri in 1970 in an attempt to rouse the nation to return to pre-war nationalist ideals.

9 A carillon is a set or collection of what?

10 Whom did Maria Elena Santiago marry in August 1958?

11 In 1956, Canadian diplomat Lester Pearson played a key role in settling which crisis that earned him the Nobel Peace Prize?

12 Which world famous self-help organisation was founded by William Wilson in Ohio in May 1935?

13 According to legend, vampires are killed by a stake through the heart. What kills a werewolf?

14 The islands of Hierro and Gomera belong to which island group?

15 By what name is the 15th century Florentine sculptor Donato de Nicolo di Betti Bardi commonly known?

Answers 1 W.B. Yeats 2 They were all left-handed 3 Port Salut 4 Miguel de Cervantes 5 Auguste Escoffier 6 Rebecca 7 Parmigianino (or Parmigiano) 8 Yukio Mishima 9 Bells 10 Buddy Holly 11 The Suez Crisis 12 Alcoholics Anonymous 13 Silver Bullet 14 Canary Islands 15 Donatello

1   Name the Roman governor of Britain circa 78 to 84 AD whose fleet circumnavigated Britain to discover it was an island.

2   A leading figure in the world of pop art, which American's works include 'Whaam'?

3   In 1935, the poet W. H. Auden became the son-in-law of which German writer?

4   Derived from the French for 'crunch', what C is a savoury cake, ball or roll of minced meat, fish or vegetables etc, fried in breadcrumbs?

5   In which Frank Sinatra song does an ant 'move a rubber tree plant'?

6   Which 1969 film musical tells the story of a widowed matchmaker who has designs on a wealthy grain merchant?

7   Which condiment is obtained from the perennial climbing vine *Piper nigrum*?

8   Before embarking on a singing career, who played Beth Brennan, later to be Beth Willis, in the Australian TV soap 'Neighbours'?

9   Which fish is dry cured and marinated in herbs in the Scandinavian dish gravadlax?

10 Which film actress once said: "Playing love scenes with Mickey Rourke is like kissing the inside of an ashtray"?

11 What is the common name of the owl *Tyto alba*? It has a heart-shaped face, long feathered legs and usually a reddish plumage with pale underparts.

12 The late Linda McCartney was born in the suburb of Scarsdale in which US city?

13 Which plant is also known as Jack-Go-To-Bed-At-Noon?

14 A string quartet consists of two violins, a cello and which other instrument?

15 Where, in July 1998, did Chek Lap Kok replace Kai Tak?

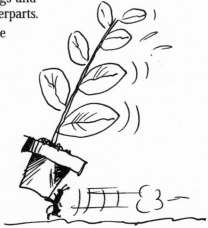

1 Name the English poet who died of wounds received whilst fighting the Spanish at Zutphen in 1586.

2 Erle Stanley Gardner created the fictional lawyer Perry Mason. What was the name of Mason's secretary?

3 And who was the private detective who helped Mason clear his client's names?

4 What nationality was the actor Chips Rafferty?

5 By what name is the tree *Cedrus libani* commonly known?

6 Brescia is a city in which European country?

7 Who married 52 year-old Graca Machel on 18 July 1998, the day of his 80th birthday?

8 Which Biblical warlike seafaring race gave their name to people who are indifferent to artistic and cultural values?

9 In area, which is the largest – Argentina or Spain?

10 What name is given to the person who rides the nearside horse of the leading horses in order to guide a team of horses drawing a coach?

11 Al Capone, Lester Piggott and Sophia Loren were all sent to prison for what offence?

12 Which former Beatle said of Alanis Morissette, who sang on his album "Vertical Man': "She's twenty four. I've got shoes older than her"?

13 Todor Zhivkov who died aged 86 in 1998 had been a former Communist leader of which country?

14 Zlata's Diary, a 1994 best-seller, was the story of a child's life in which war-torn city?

15 Which famous mountain is named after the engineer who completed a trigonometrical survey of the Indian sub-continent in 1841?

Answers 1 Sir Philip Sidney 2 Della Street 3 Paul Drake 4 Australian 5 Cedar of Lebanon 6 Italy 7 Nelson Mandela 8 Philistines 9 Argentina 10 Postilion 11 Tax evasion 12 Ringo Starr 13 Bulgaria 14 Sarajevo 15 Everest

1   Bred chiefly in the US, what type of creature is a Plymouth Rock?

2   BMI is a figure calculated by dividing a person's weight in kilograms by their height in metres squared. What does BMI stand for?

3   Which famous Australian beach gets it's name from an Aboriginal word meaning 'noise of tumbling waves'?

4   Name the female vocalist of the B-52's who sang on REM's hit 'Shiny Happy People'.

5   A three word slogan hung above the Wembley Live Aid concert stage. What were the words?

6   The breast of which creature goes into the food dish known as 'terrine de canard a l'orange'?

7   Which female singer married Norwegian shipping magnate Arne Naess in Geneva in 1986?

8   In literature, who is referred to as 'the Knight of the Sorrowful Countenance'?

9   Which of the Apostles was called the Canaanite and had the surname Zelotes?

10   In Greek mythology, what was the name of the king of Lydia who was punished for certain offences against the gods by being made to stand within reach of water and fruits that moved away whenever he tried to reach them?

11   During a performance of which Puccini opera would you hear the 'Humming Chorus' and the 'Flower Duet'?

12   What type of creature is an oryx?

13   In 1989, who succeeded Nicolae Ceaucescu as president of Romania?

14   Which small islet, lying between Italy and Corsica, is mentioned in the title of a famous novel by Alexandre Dumas?

15   How many orbits of the earth did Yuri Gagarin make during the first manned space flight in 1961?

Answers 1 Domestic fowl 2 Body Mass Index 3 Bondi Beach 4 Kate Pierson 5 Feed The World 6 Duck 7 Diana Ross 8 Don Quixote 9 Simon 10 Tantalus 11 Madame Butterfly 12 Antelope 13 Ion Iliescu 14 Monte Cristo 15 One

1 Which product was developed by American chemist Norman Larson in 1953 after 39 previous attempts had failed?

2 What sort of creature is a noctule?

3 Rolihlahla is the middle name of which former world leader?

4 Of which country is Gelderland a region?

5 What F is a desert fox of Africa and the Middle East?

6 What kind of creatures are classified as passerines and non-passerines?

7 Enlargement of the thyroid gland is caused by a deficiency of what?

8 What is the plural of ovum?

9 What's the name of the fictitious clergyman schoolmaster created by writer William Combe?

10 Which army won the two battles of Bull Run during the American Civil War? Was it the Confederate State forces or the Federal Government forces?

11 What T is a Russian vehicle drawn by three horses abreast?

12 Canuck is a slang name for a person from which country?

13 Founded in 1961, which human rights organisation was awarded the Nobel peace prize in 1977?

14 Which American golfer won the US Masters in 1958, 1960, 1962 and 1964?

15 What is the latin term which is abbreviated to RIP and in English translates as 'rest in peace'?

Answers 1 WD-40 2 Bat 3 Nelson Mandela 4 Netherlands 5 Fennec 6 Birds 7 Iodine 8 Ova 9 Dr. Syntax 10 Confederate State forces 11 Troika 12 Canada 13 Amnesty International 14 Arnold Palmer 15 Requiescat In Pace

MISCELLANEOUS 4   *Quiz 27*

1   Sydenham's chorea, or rheumatic chorea, affects which part of the body?

2   From which continent does the breed of dog known as the 'basenji' originate?

3   What kind of creature is a tope?

4   In which sport was American Scott Hamilton the world champion for four consecutive years, 1981 to 1984?

5   In 1914, the Germans defeated troops from which country at the battle of Tannenberg?

6   A type of short pointed beard, and a broad lace or linen collar with an edge deeply cut into large points, are named after which 17th century Flemish painter?

7   What B is a temporary encampment, as used by soldiers or mountaineers?

8   What type of material is guipure?

9   Which type of tangerine is named after a former province of Japan?

10 What is the common name of *Alca impennis,* a flightless seabird which became extinct during the 19th century?

11 In days gone by, which part of the body was beaten by a stick in the form of punishment known as bastinado?

12 During which century did the composer and pianist Frederic Chopin live and work?

13 The city of Tomsk stands on which river?

14 The flag of which Canadian province features the cross of St. Andrew?

15 Which of Shakespeare's plays was constructed from two stories – The Bond Of Flesh and The Casket Choice – both with long traditions in folklore?

Answers 1 Central nervous system 2 Africa 3 Shark 4 Ice skating 5 Russia 6 Van Dyck 7 Bivouac 8 Lace 9 Satsuma 10 Great Auk 11 Soles of the feet 12 19th 13 Tom 14 Nova Scotia 15 The Merchant Of Venice

1   In what state or condition would you be if you were described as being crapulous?

2   Meaning 'pungent spice', the standard spice mixture used in Indian cookery is known by what name?

3   Developed in Germany, which breed of dog is known as the 'grey ghost' because of the colour of it's coat?

4   And which breed of dog is named after a bay on the east coast of the USA?

5   The name of which type of pasta means 'little tongues'?

6   In the Muppet Show, Jim Henson provided the voice for which one of the two hecklers – Statler or Waldorf?

7   According to a famous novel, who had 'the smallest waist in the three Georgia counties'?

8   Which Nicaraguan group overthrew president Samoza in 1979 and governed the country until 1990?

9   Name the director of the movies 'Klute', 'Sophie's Choice' and 'Presumed Innocent' who died in a freak motoring accident in 1998 when another vehicle caused a metal pipe lying in the road to be thrown through his car's windshield.

10 In the Peanuts cartoon strip, what is the name of Charlie Brown's sister?

11 Which part of the body is affected by myositis?

12 Who wrote the novels 'The Ice House', 'The Dark Room' and 'The Sculptress'?

13 In which city is there a world famous zoo in the city's Tierpark?

14 Traditionally, what is the first event in an athletic decathlon?

15 And what is the decathlon's last event?

1   Name the group led by Abimael Guzman against which the Peruvian government fought a bitter civil war in the 1980s.

2   What name is shared by a range of mountains in eastern France and a French department whose capital is Epinal?

3   What type of creature is a colobus?

4   From the Arabic word for 'castle', by what name are the Moorish palaces or fortresses built in Spain known?

5   With which cartoon character do you associate the expression 'suffering succotash'?

6   And what is succotash?

7   Which European capital city is served by Ferihegy airport?

8   Which US novelist wrote 'From Here To Eternity' and 'The Thin Red Line'?

9   Who survived accusations of sexual harassment to be appointed to the US Supreme Court in 1991?

10   Switzerland is bordered by how many countries?

11   Which 20th century French composer's work 'Pacific 231' was an orchestral depiction of a steam locomotive?

12   The name of which type of pastry is derived from the Greek for 'leaf'?

13   In Jewish folklore she is a female demon and was the first wife of Adam. Name her.

14   Who succeeded Joseph Smith as leader of the Mormons and led the major migration to Salt Lake City?

15   In which US city was the famous Smithsonian Institute founded in 1846?

Answers 1 Sendero Luminoso or Shining Path 2 Vosges 3 Monkey 4 Alcazar 5 Sylvester 6 A food dish, usually consisting of beans and corn 7 Budapest 8 James Jones 9 Clarence Thomas 10 5 11 Arthur Honegger 12 Filo 13 Lilith 14 Brigham Young 15 Washington DC

1   Who or what is a 'vaquero'?

2   What name is given to the medical condition where a person stops breathing for a few seconds whilst sleeping?

3   Which creatures, there are two and four winged varieties, make up the *exocoetidae* family?

4   Indian statesman Mohammed Ali Jinnah was largely responsible for the creation of which country?

5   Formed in Paris in 1888, which group of French artists took their name from the Hebrew word for 'prophets'?

6   What kind of creature is a 'bobolink'?

7   Which is the longest river of the Iberian peninsula?

8   What is the common name of the star constellation Monoceros?

9   What one name is the name given to a different character in each of the following Shakespeare plays: 'The Two Gentlemen Of Verona', 'The Merchant Of Venice', 'Much Ado About Nothing', 'Twelfth Night' and 'The Tempest'?

10   Which 20th century American female poet used the pen name H.D?

11   King George Sound, Shark Bay and Spencer Gulf are all inlets of water around the coast of which country?

12   The request to a response to an invitation RSVP, comes from which language?

13   Herengracht, Keizersgracht and Prinsengracht are canals in which European city?

14   The Great Pyramid at Giza is the tomb of which Egyptian pharaoh?

15   The words 'democracy' and 'political' are derived from which language?

MISCELLANEOUS 4   Quiz 31

1   What is the literal meaning of the word 'asterisk'?

2   Which European capital city is served by Okecie airport?

3   What type of creature is an orb weaver?

4   Which American poet won the Pulitzer Prize four times between 1924 and 1943?

5   To which native American tribe do the Mescalero and Chiricahua belong?

6   Known for his glassware with frosted patterns in relief, which French Art Noveau glassmaker established his factory at Wingen-sur-Moder in 1920?

7   When completed in 1931, the main span of which New York bridge doubled the record for suspension bridges?

8   Which large retailer was founded in Arkansas by Sam Walton in 1962?

9   Barrel, Hedgehog, Cholla and Peyote are all types of which plant?

10 Derived from the Greek words for 'green' and 'leaf', what name is given to the pigment in plants responsible for the absorption of light energy during photosynthesis?

11 The Glyptothek is a sculpture museum in which German city?

12 What name was given to the area of the USA, extending through Kansas, Oklahoma, Texas, New Mexico and Colorado that was struck by a devastating drought during the 1930s?

13 What slogan used to advertise 'Wheaties' breakfast cereal in the US in the 1950s is also the title of a 1973 Kurt Vonnegut novel?

14 Which 19th century Belgian missionary, originally named Joseph De Veuster, was renowned for his work among the lepers on the Hawaiian island of Molokai?

15 What type of creature is a copperhead?

Answers 1 Small or little star 2 Warsaw 3 Spider 4 Robert Lee Frost 5 Apache 6 Rene Lalique 7 George Washington Bridge 8 Wal-Mart 9 Cactus 10 Chlorophyll 11 Munich 12 Dust Bowl 13 Breakfast Of Champions 14 Father Damien 15 Snake

1 Which group wrote and performed the soundtrack songs for the 1986 movie 'Highlander'?

2 Who was assassinated by the Nazis in his Vienna chancellery in 1934?

3 Which African capital city lies closest to the equator?

4 Name the Cherokee leader who developed their written language and after whom a species of tree is named.

5 Demetrius and Lysander are both in love with Hermia in which Shakespeare play?

6 On which sea is the Bulgarian port of Varna?

7 Who composed the musical piece 'Missa Solemnis'?

8 Which Italian astronomer discovered the so-called 'canals' of Mars and the asteroid Hesperia?

9 The play 'The Lower Depths' was written by which Russian novelist?

10 What does the *ptero* in pterodactyl and pterosaur mean?

11 Portoferraio is the chief town of which island in the Tyrrhenian Sea?

12 Which port, situated at the confluence of the Capibaribe and Beberibe rivers is known as the 'Venice of Brazil'?

13 Which fruit is obtained from the tree *Carica papaya*?

14 In the card game Piquet, how many cards are there in the pack?

15 If a turbot is a fish, what is a turbit?

Answers 1 Queen 2 Engelbert Dollfuss 3 Kampala 4 Sequoyah (or Sequoia) 5 A Midsummer Night's Dream 6 Black Sea 7 Beethoven 8 Giovanni Schiaparelli 9 Maksim Gorki 10 Winged 11 Elba 12 Recife 13 Papaw or pawpaw 14 32 15 Bird (type of pigeon)

1   Gondar was once the capital of which African country?

2   Lavinia and Martius are the children of which Shakespearean character?

3   Which fictitious 18th century German soldier is famous for his ridiculously exaggerated exploits?

4   Which 19th century French composer wrote the opera 'The Trojans'?

5   Black, White-headed, King, Egyptian and Griffon are all species of which carrion eating bird?

6   In which country was Sir Walter Scott's historical novel 'Quentin Durward' set?

7   Rich in antiquities, in which African country is the town of Wadi Halfa?

8   Who wrote the novel 'The Exorcist' which was adapted into a controversial film?

9   Grenada is the most southerly of which island group?

10   The name of which citrus-like fruit is derived from the Chinese for 'little golden orange'?

11   Established in March 1933, which was the first Nazi concentration camp?

12   Nineveh was the capital of which ancient kingdom?

13   Which Canadian-born American economist, author of 'The Affluent Society', was US ambassador to India from 1961 to 1963?

14   What type of creature is an anole?

15   Calabrese is an Italian variety of which vegetable?

Answers 1 Ethiopia 2 Titus Andronicus 3 Baron Munchausen 4 Hector Berlioz 5 Vulture 6 France 7 Sudan 8 William Peter Blatty 9 Windward Islands 10 Kumquat 11 Dachau 12 Assyria 13 John Kenneth Galbraith 14 Lizard 15 Broccoli

1   Spoken by Christopher Sly, 'I'll pheeze you, in faith' are the opening words of which Shakespeare play?

2   What type of creature is a hoopoe?

3   Although Genoese by birth, who was nicknamed 'Iberia's Pilot'?

4   Also known as pimento, the name of which widely used aromatic spice is derived from the fact that it combines the flavours of several different spices?

5   In which US state does the Daytona 500 motor race take place?

6   Which French astronomer gave his name to M numbers, used to catalogue galaxies, star clusters and nebulae?

7   Named after a line of latitude, which channel separates the Andaman and Nicobar Islands?

8   Actor Jack Nicholson was born in a place in New Jersey that has the same name as which planet?

9   Name the Scottish-born explorer who went to Canada in 1779 where, ten years later, he discovered the river that bears his name and who reputedly was the first European to cross the Rockies to the Pacific.

10 The dabchick belongs to which species of bird?

11 Which fruit does the tree *Punica granatum* yield?

12 And which fruit is obtained from the tropical tree *Mangifera indica*?

13 By what name is the flat, wingless insect *Cimex lectularius* more commonly known?

14 Which 20th century political leader, when dying, was told by his daughter that the noise outside his windows was the people who had come to say goodbye to him, is reputed to have said: "Why? Are they going somewhere?"?

15 By winning the 2001 Golf US Masters, who became the first golfer in history to hold all four 'major' titles at the same time, having won the US Open, British Open and USPGA in 2000?

Quiz 35

1   Which English navigator and hydrographer, who conducted a voyage of discovery to the South Seas in 1699/1700, has a town and archipelago in north-west Australia and a strait in New Guinea named after him?

2   Which Russian composer was born at Tikhvin in 1844?

3   The French composer Georges Bizet lived during which century?

4   What was the first name of the Spanish conquistador Pizarro?

5   In which European city was US astronaut Michael Collins born – London, Paris or Rome?

6   Derived from an Arabic word meaning sweat, what A is an alcoholic spirit made from the sap of a coco palm, sugar cane or rice?

7   Which Armenian city was severely damaged by an earthquake on 7 December 1988?

8   Krung Thep is the local name for which capital city?

9   Name the 19th century French philosopher known as the founder of sociology and positivism.

10 Where in Algeria did the French Foreign Legion have their headquarters until 1962?

11 And to which town near Marseille did they move their headquarters in 1962?

12 Who was assassinated at Manila airport on his return to the Philippines in August 1983?

13 Which former British athlete, a European champion at 400 metres in 1971, was jailed in the US for dealing in steroids?

14 With which creature do you associate the star constellation Cetus?

15 Name this Australian actress: she went to drama school with Mel Gibson; received awards in Australia and Britain for her role in the movie 'My Brilliant Career'; and was nominated for the Oscar for Best Actress for her role in 'A Passage To India'.

Answers 1 William Dampier 2 Nikolai Rimsky-Korsakov 3 19th 4 Francisco 5 Rome 6 Arrack 7 Leninakan 8 Bangkok 9 Auguste Comte 10 Sidi bel Abbes 11 Aubagne 12 Benigno Aquino 13 David Jenkins 14 Whale 15 Judy Davis

1 Which of Tchaikovsky's ballets features the 'Waltz of the Flowers'?
2 And in which century did Tchaikovsky live?
3 Which British composer wrote the musical pieces 'In A Monastery Garden' and 'In A Persian Market'?
4 Which variety of black grape is traditionally used to make Beaujolais wine?
5 Derived from the Spanish for 'rough' what name was given to a wild or half-tamed horse of the western US?
6 Kiev stands on which river?
7 How many stars are there on the flag of Australia?
8 And how many stars are there on the New Zealand flag?
9 Which European capital city was almost totally destroyed by an earthquake in 1755?
10 Which war was ended by the Treaty of Westphalia in 1648?
11 The famous Borromean Islands are in which Italian lake?
12 In which city would you find the famous street known as the Reeperbahn?
13 What is the name of the famous clinic in Budapest, well known for it's treatment of cerebral palsy and other diseases affecting the nervous system?
14 Baku lies on the shore of which sea?
15 What was the first name of Colt, the man who invented the revolver?

Answers 1 The Nutcracker 2 19th 3 Albert Ketelby 4 Gamay 5 Bronco 6 Dnieper 7 6 8 4 9 Lisbon 10 Thirty Years War 11 Maggiore 12 Hamburg 13 Peto Institute 14 Caspian 15 Samuel

1   In computing terms, what H is the term which refers to the arrival of a solution by trial and error or by loosely defined rules?

2   Which Italian conductor was the principal conductor of the London Symphony Orchestra from 1979 to 1988 and in 1989 became principal conductor of the Berlin Philharmonic?

3   In which country is Lake Tegernsee?

4   Who succeeded Rajiv Gandhi as leader of India in 1989?

5   What D is an Australian slang word for genuine or honest?

6   What M is a man who calls Muslims to prayer from the minaret of a mosque?

7   Which Australian 'supermodel' is known as 'The Body'?

8   In 1990, which Russian musician returned to the Soviet Union to perform 16 years after he had been stripped of his citizenship?

9   Also in 1990, in which American city did thieves dress as policemen and steal paintings worth millions of dollars?

10 What's the nationality of Annette Sergent, winner of the women's world cross-country championship in 1987 and 1989?

11 Of the Russian composers known as 'the Five', Borodin, Mussorgsky and Rimsky-Korsakov are probably the three best known. Name either of the other two.

12 Which town in Lombardy was the site of a decisive battle for Italian national independence in 1859? A dye was named in honour of the event.

13 In which European city did Madonna start her 'Drowned World' tour on 9 June 2001?

14 What is the collective name given to the group of islands that include Mauritius, Reunion and Rodrigues?

15 Which Israeli port lies at the foot of Mount Carmel?

1 In 1968, Enriqueta Basillio became the first woman in the history of the Olympic Games to do what?

2 Who played Christ in the 1973 movie version of 'Jesus Christ Superstar'?

3 The song 'Bibbidi Bobbidi Boo' is featured in which 1950 Disney animated film?

4 Which brittle grey-white metalloid was discovered by C. A. Winkler in 1886? Like gallium it is present in coal. Being a semi-conductor, it's most important use is in the electronics industry.

5 What name was given to the snake-like serpent in ancient Greek and Roman mythology whose glance could kill all living creatures except a cock and a weasel?

6 Who, in 1886, said: "All the world over, I will back the masses against the classes"?

7 In 1992, which American lost a multi-dollar advertising contract to promote the family image of an Italian food chain?

8 Who was the Prime Minister of New Zealand from 1975 to 1984?

9 Blue Wave, Preziosa and Kyushu are all varieties of which flowering shrub?

10 Which famous park, situated a couple of miles from the centre of Moscow was named after a Russian novelist?

11 In which of the 'Dirty Harry' movies did David Soul play a cop gone wrong?

12 Name the Spaniard who wrote and directed the 1972 movie 'The Discreet Charm Of The Bourgeoisie'.

13 Tennis. Which European country played in three Davis Cup finals between 1969 and 1972 and lost all three?

14 Kristi Yamaguchi won the 1991 world ice skating championship representing which country?

15 In Italy, is Naples situated to the north or south of Rome?

Answers 1 Light the Olympic flame 2 Ted Neeley 3 Cinderella 4 Germanium 5 Basilisk 6 Gladstone 7 Woody Allen 8 Robert Muldoon 9 Hydrangea 10 Gorky Park 11 Magnum Force 12 Luis Bunuel 13 Romania 14 USA 15 South

MISCELLANEOUS 4   Quiz 39

1 What's the surname of the brothers who are the benevolent merchants in Dickens' Nicholas Nickleby?

2 And with which 'brothers' do you associate the songs 'Listen To The Music' and 'What A Fool Believes'?

3 In which sport did Ireland's Michael Carruth win a gold medal at the 1992 Olympics?

4 Which American director made the film 'Rich And Famous' when he was 81 years old?

5 In 1951 which king of Egypt said: "There will soon be only five kings left – the kings of England, Diamonds, Hearts, Spades and Clubs"? He abdicated in 1952.

6 Which South American country won the first ever men's world basketball championships in 1950?

7 Which US trumpeter and bandleader, popular in the Big Band era, recorded a memorable version of 'The Flight Of The Bumble Bee' played on the trumpet?

8 Name the German theologian and opponent of Nazism who was executed at Flossenburg in 1945.

9 Living 20 million years ago, the remains of which genus of extinct ape were found in Kenya?

10 Which ferromagnetic material is an alloy of aluminium, nickel and cobalt?

11 The name of which small mammal appears in the title of a Shakespeare play?

2 In the TV comedy series 'The Addams Family' what was the name of Gomez's octopus which had the same name as an ancient Greek philosopher?

13 Centred around what is now Nova Scotia, what name was given to the North American Atlantic seaboard possessions of France in the 17th and 18th centuries?

14 Which novelist wrote 'When The Lion Feeds', 'The Diamond Hunters', 'River God' and 'Birds Of Prey'?

15 Who played Brandon Walsh in the US TV series Beverly Hills 90210?

13 Acadia 14 Wilbur Smith 15 Jason Priestley
7 Harry James 8 Dietrich Bonhoeffer 9 Proconsul 10 Alnico 11 Shrew 12 Aristotle
Answers 1 Cheeryble 2 Doobie Brothers 3 Boxing 4 George Cukor 5 Farouk 6 Argentina

1. In 1992, which popular British author published 'Every Living Thing', his first new novel for ten years?

2. Who was the female star of Charlie Chaplin's 1952 movie 'Limelight'?

3. From the Italian for 'little belly', what P is cured belly of pork?

4. In which 1961 Disney animated film did Rod Taylor provide the voice of Pongo?

5. What is the surname of Buffy in the TV series 'Buffy the Vampire Slayer'?

6. In which country was the 20th century philosopher Ludwig Wittgenstein born?

7. In Christian religion, what S is the word used to describe the appearance of wounds or scars on a human's body corresponding to those of Christ's body after the Crucifixion?

8. Hog-nosed, Amazonian, hooded, spotted and striped are all species of which New World carnivorous mammal of the weasel family?

9. Which is the second largest city in Syria after Damascus?

10. Who composed the following jazz classics: 'Night In Tunisia', 'Manteca', 'Con Alma' and 'Birks Works'?

11. What nationality was Ngaio Marsh, the writer who created Inspector Roderick Alleyn of Scotland Yard?

12. Eugenia Charles was Prime Minister of which Caribbean island during the 1980s and 1990s?

13. Skanderbeg Square is in which European capital city?

14. Kenyan-born athlete and 800 metres world record holder Wilson Kipketer represented which European country?

15. Named after a French missionary, which rare species of deer can now only be found in zoos, game reserves and private collections?

Answers 1 James Herriot 2 Claire Bloom 3 Pancetta 4 101 Dalmatians 5 Summers 6 Austria 7 Stigmata 8 Skunk 9 Aleppo 10 Dizzy Gillespie 11 New Zealander 12 Dominica 13 Tirana 14 Denmark 15 Pere David's deer

MISCELLANEOUS 4   Quiz 41

1   With regard to Queen Elizabeth II, what year comes next in the following sequence – 1948, 1950, 1960 and…?

2   Actor Jim Backus provided the voice for which popular cartoon character?

3   Which US state suffered considerable damage from the hurricane Iniki in September 1992?

4   According to the title of Del Shannon's 1960s hit, how many kinds of teardrops are there?

5   In 1979, who succeeded Ahmad Hassan al-Bakr to become his country's president?

6   Which Indian actress is also a best-selling writer of cookery books? She introduced James Ivory to Ismail Merchant.

7   The singer/musician Youssou N'Dour comes from which African country?

8   What surname is shared by Clyde, a famous West Indian cricketer and Derek, a West Indian playwright, poet and Nobel prize-winner?

9   Carinthia and Styria are provinces of which European country?

10 In Germany, what was the Abwehr?

11 By what name was the US B-52 bomber popularly known?

12 What is the name of the elephant created by French writer and illustrator Jean de Brunhoff?

13 Which US city was founded in 1701 by French trader Antoine de la Mothe Cadillac?

14 In which African city did Churchill, Roosevelt and Chinese nationalist leader Chiang Kai-shek have two meetings in November and December 1943 to discuss the Allies war policy in the Far East?

15 A slogan from a World War One poster showing a man obviously pondering how to answer the daughter on his knee was adapted for the title of which 1966 movie directed by Blake Edwards and starring James Coburn?

Answers 1 1964 (the years in which she gave birth to her children) 2 Mr. Magoo 3 Hawaii 4 Two 5 Saddam Hussein 6 Madhur Jaffrey 7 Senegal 8 Walcott 9 Austria 10 Military Intelligence Service 11 Stratofortress 12 Babar 13 Detroit 14 Cairo 15 What Did You Do In The War, Daddy

1   Who was the chairman of the royal commission that published a report on homosexuality and prostitution in Britain in 1957?

2   What are the indigenous orchestras of Java and Bali that consist of gongs, xylophones and drums, called?

3   In which sport was the Indian Geet Sethi world champion in 1992 and 1993?

4   Oscar Arias Sanchez was president of which Central American country from 1986 to 1990? In 1987 he was awarded the Nobel Peace Prize for his Central American peace plan.

5   In which European country was the American pop-art sculptor Claes Oldenburg born?

6   Which singer provided Daffy Duck's singing voice in Daffy Duck's Quackbusters. Was it Perry Como, Vic Damone or Mel Torme?

7   Popular in the 1940s, what were 'dagger-pointed goldies'?

8   Dainties is an American and Australian euphemism for what?

9   Which drug is known simply by the letter 'E'?

10 Which town in northwestern France was the site of a famous battle of 1944 when 50,000 Germans were encircled and taken prisoner and is also the birthplace of William the Conqueror?

11 Officers of which US organisation are known as G-men?

12 What Australian slang word for a silly person is also a type of cockatoo?

13 IBM is a leading computer manufacturer, what does IBM stand for?

14 In which city was Marie Curie born?

15 On narrowly surviving an attempted assassination in 1962 who said: "They really are bad shots'?

Answers 1 Lord Wolfenden 2 Gamelan 3 Billiards 4 Costa Rica 5 Sweden 6 Mel Torme 7 Shoes 8 Women's underwear 9 Ecstasy 10 Falaise 11 FBI 12 Galah 13 International Business Machines 14 Warsaw 15 Charles de Gaulle

1   Which port in the Republic of Ireland stands at the mouth of the River Lee?

2   Who's motto is *Legio Patria Nostra*?

3   What W is a Japanese plant with a thick green root which tastes like strong horseradish and is used in cookery?

4   And what C is a straight, close-fitting silk dress with a high neck worn by Chinese and Indonesian women?

5   In 1947, who became the first governor-general of Pakistan?

6   Belmopan is the capital of which Central American country?

7   'H' is drug abusers' slang for what?

8   Which unit of measurement used in radio astronomy is named after the man who invented the first radio telescope?

9   What is a kalimba? Is it an African dance, an African musical instrument or an African snake?

10 Which Italian actress is known as 'La Lollo'?

11 Mack the Knife is the villain of which opera?

12 What name was given to the boundary between northeast India and Tibet as agreed at the Simla convention in 1914?

13 Which 20th century Indian gave his name to a long narrow tailored jacket or tunic, buttoned down the centre with a high collar?

14 In the world of computing, what does OCR stand for?

15 In musical terms, what does R & B stand for?

Answers 1 Cork 2 French Foreign Legion 3 Wasabi 4 Cheongsam 5 Mohammed Jinnah 6 Belize 7 Heroin 8 Jansky 9 African musical instrument 10 Gina Lollobrigida 11 The Threepenny Opera 12 McMahon Line 13 Nehru 14 Optical Character Recognition 15 Rhythm and Blues

MISCELLANEOUS 4

1   After winning his fourth gold medal in 1996, which famous Olympian asked to be shot if he ever went near a boat again?

2   Bianca, former wife of Mick Jagger was born in which Central American country?

3   Silvery-coloured hair for women was popularised after which actress played the title role in the 1931 film 'Platinum Blonde'?

4   And from which Raymond Chandler novel does the following passage come: "it was a blond's. A blond to make a bishop kick a hole in a stained glass window"?

5   Derived from the Spanish word for sauce, which type of dance and dance music that is a mixture of Latin American music infused with jazz and rock, was popularised in New York in the mid-1970's?

6   A patented name for a public address system in the 1920s, which name has subsequently been applied to any form of public address system?

7   Desert Orangetio, Desert Green Hairstreak, Blue Copper and Tiger Swallowtail are all types of what?

8   The permanent headquarters of UNESCO are in which European city?

9   Name either of the two states of the USA who can be referred to as the 'Valentine State' because they were admitted as a state on 14 February, one in 1859, the other in 1912.

10 Which US record producer was famous for his 'Wall of Sound'?

11 Which US group had a hit on both sides of the Atlantic in 1958 with the song 'Yakety Yak'?

12 Which character has been played in films by Douglas Fairbanks, Tyrone Power, Guy Williams and Antonio Banderas?

13 Name the place in New Mexico where the first atomic bomb was exploded in 1945.

14 Name the large ravine near Kiev which was the site of a mass grave of an estimated 100,000 victims of Nazi extermination between 1941 and 1943.

15 'Cairo Fred' is a nickname given by the film industry to which actor?

Answers 1 Steve Redgrave 2 Nicaragua 3 Jean Harlow 4 Red 5 Salsa 6 Tannoy 7 Butterfly 8 Paris 9 Oregon and Arizona 10 Phil Spector 11 The Coasters 12 Zorro 13 Alamogordo 14 Babi Yar 15 Omar Sharif

1 "Ee, ain't it grand to be daft" was the catchphrase used by which Liverpool-born comedian who was popular in the 1940s and 1950s? He appeared in the 1950 film 'Up For The Cup'.

2 What A is a portable lamp for signalling in Morse code, named after it's inventor?

3 To which fellow actress was Lillian Gish referring when she said: "Her temperament reflected the rain and gloom of the long dark Swedish winters"?

4 What nationality was the neurologist Alois Alzheimer after whom the degenerative disease is named?

5 According to the old advertising slogan, what night of the week was 'A mami night'?

6 Which now deceased actor starred in the films 'National Lampoon's Animal House' and 'The Blues Brothers'?

7 AWACS is a radar and communications system. What does AWACS stand for?

8 With what do you associate the name of Cristobal Balenciaga?

9 'Bambi' is a Disney animated film classic. Who wrote the novel on which the film was based?

10 Name the peninsula in the Philippines which witnessed some of the fiercest fighting in the Pacific in World War Two and where, after surrendering in 1942, thousands of US troops died on a long 'death march'.

11 Scene of many armed clashes, the Bekaa Valley is in which Middle Eastern country?

12 Meaning 'fine period' which French term describes the period in Europe from the turn of the century to the start of the First World War in which the affluent lived in great comfort and style?

13 The Bismarck Sea is a section of which ocean?

14 With which TV sci-fi series do you associate the slogan 'to boldly go where no man has gone before'?

15 What B are the salt flats in Utah where several land speed records have been set?

Answers 1 Albert Modley 2 Aldis Lamp 3 Greta Garbo 4 German 5 Friday 6 John Belushi 7 Airborne Warning And Control System 8 Fashion 9 Felix Salten 10 Bataan 11 Lebanon 12 Belle Epoque 13 Pacific 14 Star Trek 15 Bonneville

MISCELLANEOUS 4

Quiz 46

1 Whose motto is 'Nation shall speak peace unto nation'?

2 What alternative name for a telephone came into vogue in the 1940s? It was the surname of the US actor who played the inventor of the telephone in the 1939 film 'The Alexander Graham Bell Story'.

3 What was the first name of Balmain, the designer who started his own fashion house in the 1930s?

4 Meaning 'may you live for ever', what was the battle cry of Japanese troops as they went into battle?

5 Basin Street, possibly the original home of jazz music, is in which US city?

6 Named after a US seismologist, what name is given to the zones in the earth's crust that are closely linked with earthquakes?

7 In which country is the village of Belmez, where in August 1971 unexplained ghostly faces appeared on the kitchen floor of a house?

8 Name the fictional US detective created in 1886 as the US counterpart of Sexton Blake.

9 What C is lumpy fatty tissue beneath the skin, especially of the thighs and buttocks?

10 What was the real first name of Guevara, the revolutionary known as 'Che'?

11 By what name was the popular bullfighter Manuel Benitez Perez, who was at the peak of his career in the 1960s, known?

12 Which six-year old starred in the 1935 film 'Curly Top', which was also a nickname she was known by?

13 What Y is the fictitious county in the US which is the setting for many of the novels and short stories of William Faulkner?

14 WAVES is the women's section of the US Naval Reserve. What does WAVES stand for?

15 The trade name of which synthetic polyester is derived from it's main constituents terephthalic acid and ethylene glycol?

Answers 1 BBC **2** Ameche **3** Pierre **4** Banzai **5** New Orleans **6** Benioff zone **7** Spain **8** Nick Carter **9** Cellulite **10** Ernesto **11** El Cordobes **12** Shirley Temple **13** Yoknapatawpha **14** Women Appointed for Voluntary Emergency Service **15** Terylene

MISCELLANEOUS 4

Quiz 47

1   In which Indian city were hundreds of demonstrators shot dead by British troops in April 1919?

2   Which archipelago of islands in the Atlantic gave their name to knee-length brightly coloured shorts?

3   A system of radar installations set up by America at Clear in Alaska, Thule in Greenland and Fylingdales in Yorkshire, what does BMEWS stand for?

4   What C is a form of dance that originated in France, essentially a form of the jitterbug it has been described as the 'dance equivalent to fast food'?

5   In 1923, Italian forces bombarded and held which Greek island in retaliation to the murder of Italian delegates, who were trying to define the Greek-Albanian border, by Greek soldiers?

6   'Cowabunga!' was a favourite expression of which sewer-living creatures?

7   What nickname was given to a band of European mercenaries who joined Congolese government forces in 1964 and whose exploits formed the basis of a film starring Roger Moore, Richard Burton and Richard Harris?

8   What's the pen name of the reclusive author of 'The Death Ship' and 'The Treasure Of The Sierra Madre'?

9   What S is another name for 'Bigfoot'?

10   What items were the subject of the 'Sperati forgeries' in 1942?

11   Which model of Citroen car with a two-horsepower engine was originally designed in the 1950s to provide French farmers with a practical and inexpensive vehicle?

12   Name the place in the Netherlands, near Utrecht, which was the home of Kaiser Wilhelm II from his exile in 1919 until his death there in 1941.

13   Austrian-Italian film star of the 1930s, Elissa Landi was known as the 'Empress of...'?

14   Also the name of a type of bird, what was the name of the suave detective created by Michael Arlen and played in films by George Sanders?

15   'Fatha' was the nickname of which jazz pianist and bandleader?

Answers 1 Amritsar 2 Bermuda 3 Ballistic Missile Early Warning System 4 Ceroc 5 Corfu 6 Teenage Mutant Ninja Turtles 7 Wild Geese 8 B. Traven 9 Sasquatch 10 Postage stamps 11 Deux-Chevaux or 2 CV 12 Doorn 13 Emotion 14 The Falcon 15 Earl Hines

1 By what name was the African country of Botswana known until 1966?

2 The name of which light machine gun is a blend of the name of the place in Czechoslovakia where it was originally made and the place in England where the British version was made?

3 What name was given to the bitter war fought between Bolivia and Paraguay in the 1930s?

4 Who was the divorced Roman Catholic hero of Evelyn Waugh's trilogy 'Sword Of Honour'?

5 The Spartacists were an extreme socialist group that flourished in which European country between 1916 and 1919?

6 Which town, 40 miles to the east of Cape Town is South Africa's second oldest settlement and was the main British military base during the Boer War?

7 What nickname was given to Daniel Cohn-Bendit, a West German student who led a students revolt in Paris in 1968?

8 What was the pseudonym adopted by the French artist and fashion designer Romain de Tirtoff?

9 A hero of early animated film cartoons, which cat 'kept on walking'?

10 What's the name of Flash Gordon's girlfriend?

11 Which catchphrase appeared at the end of Warner Brothers Merry Melodies cartoon series and was chosen by Mel Blanc, who had done so many of the characters voices, as his epitaph?

12 Which 20th century US president's family nickname was 'Dutch'? Other nicknames he was given were 'The Gipper' and the 'Great Rondini'.

13 Which Bobby McFerrin song was George Bush's unofficial theme song?

14 Height 1211 was one of the bloodiest battles of the Korean War. By what name is it more popularly known?

15 Which famous US TV chat show host was introduced with 'Here's Johnny'?

Answers 1 Bechuanaland 2 Bren-gun (from Brno and Enfield) 3 Chaco War 4 Guy Crouchback 5 Germany 6 Stellenbosch 7 Danny the Red 8 Erte 9 Felix 10 Dale Arden 11 That's All Folks 12 Ronald Reagan 13 Don't Worry Be Happy 14 Heartbreak Ridge 15 Johnny Carson

MISCELLANEOUS 4 — Quiz 49

1 Known by the colour of their shirts, what name was given to Hitler's Nazi stormtroopers?

2 Situated at the junction of Friedrichstrasse and Zimmerstrasse, what was the popular name of the checkpoint on the border between East and West Berlin?

3 The name of which extremely effective irritant gas is derived from the initials of its inventors?

4 Which British stage and screen actor was known as 'Sexy Rexy'?

5 Which 20th century US soldier was known as 'The Bear' and 'Stormin' Norman'?

6 Which US actor played a character called Andy Hardy in a series of films made between 1936 and 1946?

7 Husky was the code name for the Allied invasion of which Mediterranean island during World War Two?

8 What was the popular name for New York International airport before it was renamed John F. Kennedy International or JFK for short?

9 By what name is the mass execution of approximately 5000 Polish officers by Soviet secret service officers in a wood near Smolensk in 1940 known?

10 And what popular name is given to the countryside around Pnomh Penh dotted with the mass graves of Cambodians killed by the Khmer Rouge?

11 In which African country did the Lari massacre of 1953 take place?

12 Name the former Paris international airport, the airport where Charles Lindbergh landed in 1927 after the first solo crossing of the Atlantic.

13 Introduced in America by Roche Laboratories, what is the trade name of the tranquillizer chlordiazepoxide?

14 Minamata disease is a form of mercury poisoning named after a town in which country?

15 To whom was Cybill Shepherd referring when she said: "She had curves in places other women don't even have places"?

Answers 1 Brownshirts **2** Checkpoint Charlie **3** CS Gas (from Carson and Staughton) **4** Rex Harrison **5** Norman Schwarzkopf **6** Mickey Rooney **7** Sicily **8** Idlewild **9** Katyn massacre **10** Killing Fields **11** Kenya **12** Le Bourget **13** Librium **14** Japan **15** Marilyn Monroe

MISCELLANEOUS 4

1   The former capital of Castile, where did Franco set up his Nationalist government during the Spanish Civil War?

2   In Britain it is slang for a carpenter and in the US and Australia it is slang for a prostitute. What's the word?

3   What name was given to the German dive-bombers of the Second World War, especially the Junkers JU-87?

4   By what name was the US B-29 high altitude bomber popularly known?

5   Deep Thought is a supercomputer in which humorous 1979 sci-fi novel?

6   Which escapologist was known as the 'Handcuff King'?

7   Ijsselmeer is a shallow freshwater lake in which European country?

8   Name the mining village in Czechoslovakia that was destroyed in a reprisal attack by the Germans on 10 June 1942.

9   What was the name of the Japanese detective played by Peter Lorre in a series of films in the 1930s?

10 What name was given to the pair of interplanetry probes launched by the US in 1977?

11 What nationality is writer Peter Carey, known for his black humour in novels such as 'Bliss', 'Illywacker' and 'Oscar And Lucinda'?

12 What O is a hockey-like game or sport played underwater in swimming pools?

13 In July 1969 who said: "This is the greatest week in the history of the world since the Creation"?

14 By what other name is carbonyl chloride, a toxic gas having an odour like musty hay, and which first came into prominence when it was used during World War One, known?

15 The title of which 1971 Rod Stewart chart-topping album was originally a phrase used as a slogan for Doane's Backache Kidney Pills in the early years of the 20th century?

Answers 1 Burgos 2 Chippy 3 Stuka 4 Superfortress 5 The Hitch Hiker's Guide To The Galaxy 6 Harry Houdini 7 The Netherlands 8 Lidice 9 Mr Moto 10 Voyager (I and II) 11 Australian 12 Octopush 13 Richard Nixon 14 Phosgene 15 Every Picture Tells A Story

MISCELLANEOUS 4   *Quiz 51*

1　In 1927, which US president announced his decision not to stand for re-election with the characteristically short speech: 'I do not choose to run for president in 1928'?

2　Who would execute an 'Immelmann turn'?

3　Richard John Seddon, Prime Minister of New Zealand from 1893 to 1906 was known as 'King .....'?

4　The Knesset is the parliament of which country?

5　What's the name of the handsome hillbilly character of the long -running newspaper comic strip created by Al Capp in the 1930s which ran until Capp's retirement in 1977?

6　In 'Peter Pan', what is the name of the land where the Lost Boys live?

7　Which island is the largest of Japan's Ryukyu Islands and was the scene of bitter fighting during World War Two? It was not returned to Japan by the US until 1972.

8　Four words from the popular song 'As Time Goes By' are the title of which 1987 novel written by the American author Joyce Carol Oates?

9　Set in World War Two, who wrote the expansive two volume historical novel 'The Winds Of War' and 'War And Remembrance' which were adapted into a TV mini-series?

10　Lake Winnebago is in which US state?

11　Facing the front or the bow of a boat, is starboard to your left or right?

12　What T is the horizontal bar fitted to the head of a boat's rudder post and used for steering, and is an implement or machine for breaking up soil?

13　Whom did Maria Shriver, the niece of John F. Kennedy, marry in 1986?

14　Which king of France was 'St. Louis', regarded as the model medieval king; Louis II, Louis IX or Louis XII?

15　The River Nile flows into which sea?

1   What four letter word beginning with C is an Italian word used as a greeting or a farewell?

2   In 1980, who said: "If a woman like Eva Peron with no ideals can get that far, think how far I can go with all the ideals that I have"?

3   With regard to books, what does ISBN stand for?

4   A US boxer of the early 1900s and then one of America's top boxing referees, Ruby Goldstein was known as the 'Jewel of the…'?

5   Between 1936 and 1957 Jan Striker wrote 17 novels about which fictional hero of the American West?

6   Situated near Houston, Texas, a 570 feet high tapering monument commemorates which battle?

7   What does a demographer study?

8   Tortoiseshell is ornamental material obtained from the curved horny shields of which species of turtle?

9   The name of which famous Hawaiian beach means 'spurting water'?

10   The World War Two Japanese fighter plane the Zero was made by which company?

11   What S is the common name given to the venomous fish of shallow Indo-Pacific waters?

12   And what T is a dwelling of native Americans consisting of skins or cloth on a frame of poles?

13   Complete the title of this 1976 animated film featuring the voice of Dick Van Dyke; 'Tubby the…'?

14   Gander, one of North America's largest international airports is in which Canadian province?

15   What is a currycomb?

Answers 1 Ciao 2 Margaret Thatcher 3 International Standard Book Number 4 Ghetto 5 The Lone Ranger 6 Battle of San Jacinto 7 Human populations 8 Hawksbill 9 Waikiki 10 Mitsubishi 11 Stonefsh 12 Tepee 13 Tuba 14 Newfoundland 15 A device for grooming horses

Quiz 53

1 What was the pseudonym of the German agent Elyesa Bazna?

2 Name the comic-strip hero created by Alex Raymond in the 1930s who was played by Johnny Weismuller in a series of low-budget movies between 1948 and 1955 in which he was described as 'Tarzan with clothes'.

3 Which British singer, star of musicals such as 'Cats', 'Evita', 'Sunset Boulevard' and 'The King And I' is sometimes referred to as 'Leather Lungs'?

4 According to the Hans Christian Andersen story, who lived in the Ice Palace?

5 Who wrote the novels 'The Bridge Across Forever', 'Illusions' and 'Jonathan Livingston Seagull'?

6 Which actor appeared in the Disney films 'Blackbeard's Ghost' and 'One Of Our Dinosaurs Is Missing'?

7 What breed of dog is referred to as the 'Mexican hot water bottle' or 'Aztec Snack'?

8 What nationality is former tennis player Mats Wilander?

9 Who played private eye Matt Helm in four movies in the 1960s?

10 And who played Matt Helm in a US TV series in the mid-1970s?

11 One of the world's oldest sporting trophies, what was originally known as the Hundred Guinea Cup?

12 What was the name of the hospital featured in the US TV drama series 'St Elsewhere'?

13 And in which US city was St Elsewhere set?

14 Mexico staged soccer's World Cup finals in 1986. Which South American country was the original choice but had to drop out because it had neither the money or the facilities to host the event?

15 What K is a shrimplike crustacean that is food for whales?

Answers 1 Cicero **2** Jungle Jim **3** Elaine Paige **4** The Snow Queen **5** Richard Bach **6** Peter Ustinov **7** Chihuahua **8** Swedish **9** Dean Martin **10** Anthony Franciosa **11** America's Cup **12** St Eligius **13** Boston **14** Colombia **15** Krill

1   Name the nightclub in Boston where nearly 500 people were killed in a fire in 1942.

2   What code name used during the Watergate investigations was the same as the title of a Linda Lovelace film?

3   Which British show jumper became famous for his V-sign made at Hickstead in 1971?

4   From which Sammy Cahn song do the following lyrics come: 'Go together like a horse and carriage, This I tell ya brother, Ya can't have one without the other'?

5   Polish-born actress of the silent screen Pola Negri was known as the 'Magnificent...' what?

6   In which James Bond movie does 007 have a close encounter with a tarantula in his bed?

7   In which 1966 movie does Steve McQueen play a cynical sailor on a US gunboat on the Yangtze river?

8   What P is the family name of carnivorous marine mammals that include seals and walruses?

9   A stinkhorn is a type of what?

10 The guitar used in the Live Aid poster was in the shape of which continent?

11 Commemorating a battle, Motherland is a large statue in the figure of a woman on the outskirts of which Russian city?

12 Which American country singer was noted for his hobo persona and imitations of train sounds?

13 Which is the heaviest venomous snake found in Africa and has the longest fangs of any snake?

14 In hi-fi, what W is the loudspeaker which reproduces the low frequencies?

15 Found in waters stretching from Queensland to Malaysia, what is regarded as the most venomous jellyfish, with even a moderate sting causing death within minutes?

Answers 1 Coconut Grove **2** Deep Throat **3** Harvey Smith **4** Love And Marriage **5** Wildcat **6** Dr. No **7** The Sand Pebbles **8** Pinniped **9** Fungus **10** Africa **11** Volgograd (formerly Stalingrad) **12** Boxcar Willie **13** Gaboon or Gabon viper **14** Woofer **15** Sea wasp

MISCELLANEOUS 4 — Quiz 55

1   Darwin's, Leopard and Goliath are all species of which tail-less amphibian?

2   Derived from Spanish, what C describes parallel ranges of mountains?

3   What is the name of Dumbo's only friend, a mouse, in the famous Disney animated movie?

4   Paul Elvstrom was the first man to win individual gold medals at four successive Olympic Games. In which sport did he achieve this feat?

5   Which country is the setting for the 1975 film 'Picnic At Hanging Rock'?

6   Which US TV series featured the characters 'Boss' Hogg and Roscoe P. Coltrane?

7   Name the island which separates the Horseshoe Falls and the American Falls at Niagara.

8   What type of creature is a Gila Monster?

9   What H are the areas of high-pressure that encircle the earth around 30 to 35 degrees north and 30 to 35 degrees south?

10 Which US comedy duo starred in the 1952 movie 'Jumping Jacks'?

11 Known as 'Queen City' and 'Queen of the West', which is Ohio's third largest city after Cleveland and Columbus?

12 What's the name of the Flintstone's pet dinosaur?

13 Which park has been called the 'lungs of New York'?

14 What E is the term given to the location of objects by reflected sound, as used by dolphins and bats?

15 And what S is a lightweight horse-drawn carriage, as used in harness racing?

Answers 1 Frog 2 Cordillera 3 Timothy 4 Yachting 5 Australia 6 The Dukes of Hazzard 7 Goat Island 8 Lizard 9 Horse Latitudes 10 Dean Martin and Jerry Lewis 11 Cincinnati 12 Dino 13 Central Park 14 Echolocation 15 Sulky

1   What's the title of the 1983 film which told the story of Billy Mills, the Sioux Indian who won the 10,000 metres at the 1964 Olympics?

2   The German Axel Springer founded a business empire in which type of industry?

3   Name the volcanic mountain on the Indonesian island of Sumbawa which violently erupted in 1815.

4   Often found on beaches, by what name are the eggs of the fish, the skate, known?

5   Which spider constructs burrows in the ground and at the entrance builds a silken-hinged door?

6   According to Shirley Temple's song, what was the name of the 'good ship'?

7   In which US TV comedy series did Gary Coleman play a precocious child called Arnold?

8   What is the famous jockey Lester Piggot's middle name? Is it Keith, Kenneth or Kevin?

9   Which one of the Three Musketeers was known for his size and strength?

10   What is a water boatman?

11   What K is the local bird of paradise featured on the flag of Papua New Guinea?

12   Odontology is the scientific study of what?

13   Which birds belong to the family *Columbidae*?

14   What H is the cultivation of plants without soil, using specially prepared solutions of mineral salts?

15   Brunei is bordered by the South China Sea on the north and elsewhere by which Malaysian state?

Answers 1 Running Brave 2 Publishing 3 Tambora 4 Mermaid's purses 5 Trap-door spider 6 Lollipop 7 Different Strokes 8 Keith 9 Porthos 10 An insect 11 Kumul 12 Teeth 13 Pigeons and doves 14 Hydroponic 15 Sarawak

1 Published in 1977, the year before he died, whose last novel was the Booker prize winning 'Staying On'?

2 Where is the Mare Serenitatis to be found?

3 The Epcot Centre is in Florida. What does EPCOT stand for?

4 The Handlebar Club was formed especially for people with large what?

5 What name is given to the medical condition in which the ability of the blood to clot is severely reduced, causing severe bleeding from even the slightest injury?

6 Which specific part of the body is affected by *pyorrhoe alveolaris*?

7 By what name was the French novelist Amandine Aurore Lucie Dupin known?

8 Derived from German, what does the word 'ersatz' mean?

9 What A is a shady recess in a garden or a leafy glade shaded by trees?

10 Name the civil rights leader who in the 1980s became the first black man to make a serious bid for the US presidency.

11 David Scott, commander of Apollo 15, was the first man to do what on the moon?

12 What G is the word used to describe the moon when the illuminated part is greater than a semi-circle but less than a full circle?

13 And what C is the shell of a marine snail that was used as currency in parts of Africa and Asia?

14 What form of naval punishment involved dragging a person under the ship with ropes?

15 Where was Leonardo da Vinci born?

Answers 1 Paul Scott 2 On the moon 3 Experimental Prototype Community Of Tomorrow 4 Moustaches 5 Haemophilia 6 Gums 7 George Sand 8 Imitation or artificial 9 Arbour or arbor 10 Rev. Jesse Jackson 11 Drive a lunar vehicle or 'moon buggy' 12 Gibbous or gibbose 13 Cowrie 14 Keelhauling 15 Vinci

1   Which British poet and dramatist wrote a poem entitled 'Blackbird' and the play 'Abraham Lincoln'?

2   Which US cartoon animator was a descendant of Judge Roy Bean and Daniel Boone? He created Daffy Duck and Porky Pig and came up with Bugs Bunny's catchphrase 'What's Up Doc!'.

3   Also created by the man in question 2, what kind of creature is the cartoon character Chilly Willy?

4   Name the department store founded by the heroine of Barbara Taylor Bradford's heroine in the novel 'A Woman Of Substance'.

5   Created by Barry Humphries, what is the name of the drunken, slovenly Australian cultural attache, an associate of Dame Edna Everage?

6   What is the common name for the long-winged hawk *Pandion haliaetus* also known as the fish hawk?

7   Released in 1971, which Doors album features the song 'Riders On The Storm'?

8   In which Paris cemetery are Oscar Wilde, Chopin and Jim Morrison of the Doors all buried?

9   At just over 12,000 feet, Mount Timpanogos in Utah is the highest point of which mountain range, a segment of the Rocky Mountains?

10   What S is the oily secretion of the sebaceous glands that acts as a skin lubricant?

11   What G credited with various tonic and medicinal properties is sometimes referred to as 'man-root'?

12   Which Nat King Cole classic song combines 'chilli con carne and sparkling champagne'?

13   Osculation is the act of doing what?

14   Derived from German, what S is a straight high-speed downhill run on skis?

15   What name is shared by a lake in southeastern New South Wales in Australia and a lake in northeastern New York state?

MISCELLANEOUS 4 — Quiz 59

1 The British soldier Sir John Moore died in 1809 during which war?

2 If you went in a straight line from Paris to Vienna you would pass through which other country besides France and Austria?

3 What L is the name of the traditional Hawaiian garland of flowers?

4 Who, according to the hymn, go 'marching as to war'?

5 Who won the Pulitzer Prize for his 'Tales Of The South Pacific' upon which the musical South Pacific was based?

6 Mindanao is the second largest island of which island group?

7 What does the word 'glabrous' mean?

8 Resembling a hedgehog, what T is a mammal that is native to Madagascar and the Comoro Islands?

9 And what C is the crude preparation used by South American indians to poison their darts and arrows for hunting?

10 Biltmore Estate, with its vast house and gardens established by George Vanderbilt near Asheville, is in which US state?

11 Noctuid, peppered, plume, owlet and gypsy are all types of what?

12 She appeared in the 1961 movie West Side Story and has won all four major show business awards – Oscar, Emmy, Tony and Grammy. Name her.

13 Early hovercraft were known as ACV's. What did ACV stand for?

14 Hamlet said: "Nymph, in thy orisons be all my sins remember'd". What are orisons?

15 Mount Isa is a mining city in which Australian state?

Answers 1 Peninsular War 2 Germany 3 Lei 4 Christian soldiers 5 James Michener 6 Philippines 7 Without hair or smooth 8 Tenrec 9 Curare 10 North Carolina 11 Moth 12 Rita Moreno 13 Air Cushion Vehicle 14 Prayers 15 Queensland

MISCELLANEOUS 4 *Quiz 60*

1   Which one of the Mitford sisters, a known admirer of Hitler, committed suicide?

2   With which US comedian do you associate the comedy monologue recordings of a driving instructor and a conversation with Sir Walter Raleigh?

3   The entertainer and pianist Liberace often talked about his two favourite people – his mother and his brother. What was his brother's name?

4   What colour was the Rolls-Royce in the title of the 1964 movie starring Rex Harrison, George C. Scott and Ingrid Bergman?

5   What is the common name for the wood-boring beetle *Xestobium rufovillosum*?

6   Which actress was married to boxer Mike Tyson for a short period during 1988/9?

7   What is 'homiletics'?

8   What was the name of the amorous skunk with the French accent that featured in Warner Brothers cartoons?

9   What term can mean either a train pulled by two locomotives or a sporting event in which two games are played consecutively or back-to-back?

10 In which form of Olympic wrestling is the use of the legs prohibited and no holds below the hips are allowed?

11 In which US city would you find the American Museum of Natural History, one of the world's largest museums?

12 Released in 1984, the movie 'The Shooting Party' was the swan-song of which British-born actor who died that year?

13 Name the US nuclear chemist best known for his work on isolating and identifying elements heavier than uranium who had element 106 named in his honour.

14 The mature males of which ape are known as 'silverbacks'?

15 Which early heavyweight boxing champion, a symbol of the bareknuckle era, was known as 'The Great John L' or 'The Boston Strong Boy'?

Answers 1 Unity **2** Bob Newhart **3** George **4** Yellow **5** Deathwatch beetle **6** Robin Givens **7** The art of preaching or writing sermons **8** Pepe LePew **9** Double-header **10** Greco-Roman **11** New York **12** James Mason **13** Glenn T. Seaborg **14** Gorilla **15** John L. Sullivan

1   Elvis Presley set foot on British soil only once. Where, specifically?

2   Caterpillars have cylindrical bodies consisting of how many segments?

3   According to her song, what did Shirley Temple have 'in her soup'?

4   Father Francis Mulcahy was a chaplain in which TV series?

5   What double D is the name of the game where stones are thrown so that they skim on water?

6   What S is the name shared by a bird which has species known as black, African and Indian, and an insect also known as water strider or pond skater?

7   What year did Rudolf Nuryev obtain political asylum in Paris?

8   In the Disney animated film 'Dumbo', who is Dumbo's mother?

9   Which city was built as the operational base during construction of the Suez Canal and named after the then khedive of Egypt?

10 For a time, the poet Rainer Maria Rilke was the secretary of which French sculptor?

11 Which 19th century German composer's 'Opus 1 for Piano' is known as the 'Abegg Variations'?

12 In 1964, the German company Agfa merged with which Belgian company?

13 The name of which city and port in Argentina literally means 'white bay'?

14 In which country is there a state and city called Aguascalientes?

15 What is Royal Dux a type of?

Answers 1 Prestwick Airport **2** 13 **3** Animal crackers **4** M.A.S.H **5** Ducks and Drakes **6** Skimmer **7** 1961 **8** Mrs. Jumbo **9** Ismailia **10** Auguste Rodin **11** Robert Schumann **12** Gevaert **13** Bahia Blanca **14** Mexico **15** Porcelain

1   In Shakespeare's 'Macbeth', name the character whom Macbeth has murdered but whose ghost returns to haunt Macbeth in a scene which is a turning point of the play?

2   What C is the name of the high priest during the trial of Jesus?

3   Which city in Alaska was founded during a gold strike in 1902 and was named after the man who became the 26th vice-president of the USA and who was sometimes referred to as 'the last of America's log-cabin statesmen'?

4   Name the most famous radical group of the French Revolution who under Robespierre overthrew the Girondists and instituted the 'Reign of Terror'.

5   Situated in the northwest part of European Russia between Lake Ladoga and the White Sea, what is the second largest lake in Europe?

6   What name is given to the public holiday celebrated in the US and Canada on the first Monday in September?

7   Which composer's 'Symphony no. 35 in D major' is known as the 'Haffner Symphony'?

8   And which composer's 'Piano sonata no. 29 in B flat Opus 106' is known as the 'Hammerklavier Sonata'?

9   In the Old Testament of the Bible, which book comes between Proverbs and the Song Of Solomon?

10 Which I is the Australian rock band formed in 1980 who were originally called Flowers and released the albums 'Love In Motion' and 'Man Of Colours'?

11 Meaning 'House of Misfortune', what is the name of the chateau near Paris which became famous as the residence of the Empress Josephine?

12 What G is the bibulous giant who is the central character of a Rabelais satire?

13 In the Old Testament of the Bible, who is the mother-in-law of Ruth?

14 What K is the small shrine located near the centre of the Great Mosque in Mecca and considered by Muslims everywhere to be the most sacred spot on earth?

15 What name is shared by a city in Texas and the surname of the US vice-president from 1845 to 1849?

Answers 1 Banquo 2 Caiaphas 3 Fairbanks 4 Jacobins 5 Lake Onega 6 Labor Day 7 Mozart 8 Beethoven 9 Ecclesiastes 10 Icehouse 11 Malmaison 12 Gargantua 13 Naomi 14 Kaaba 15 Dallas

1 On which British racecourse is the Ebor Handicap run?

2 Known for it's aviation training school, in which US state is the city of Pensacola?

3 Which march by Johann Strauss the elder was named in honour of the veteran Austrian field-marshal who defeated the Sardinians at the battle of Custoza in 1848?

4 According to the title of Henry Williamson's book, what type of fish was 'Salar'?

5 Valladolid is a city in which country?

6 According to the Old Testament, which Z was the last king of Judah?

7 What type of transport is sometimes referred to as a 'blimp'?

8 The name of which Brazilian city means 'beautiful horizon'?

9 In which month is Dominion Day celebrated?

10 Upanayana is a ritual of initiation undergone by boys of which religion?

11 What A is the second brightest star in the constellation Perseus and also a computer language?

12 Which 18th century Italian violinist and composer wrote the 'Devil's Trill Sonata'?

13 The Flores Sea is part of which ocean?

14 The Wafd was a nationalist political party in which African country between 1923 and 1953?

15 What popular name is given to the executive committee of the Democratic Party in the US?

Answers 1 York 2 Florida 3 Radetzky March 4 Salmon 5 Spain 6 Zedekiah 7 Airship 8 Belo Horizonte 9 July (1st) 10 Hindu 11 Algol 12 Giuseppe Tartini 13 Pacific 14 Egypt 15 Tammany Hall

MISCELLANEOUS 4 *Quiz 64*

1   What G is the name of the former well-known London store which closed in 1972?

2   And what M is the well-known New York department store founded in 1858?

3   What single letter was the name of the American punk rock band formed in Los Angeles in 1977 and whose lead singer was called Exene Cervenka?

4   Grand Rapids is a city in which US state?

5   What H was the name of the wild elephant in Kipling's 'Jungle Book'?

6   KB are the oldest football club in which European country?

7   What was Ulysses S. Grant's real first name - Harvey, Henry or Hiram?

8   Found in Asia, the argali is the largest type of which creature found in the wild?

9   What is meant by the heraldic term 'sejant'?

10 What I is the name of Cymbeline's daughter in the Shakespeare play of the same name?

11 What shape is the pasta called farfalle?

12 And what shape is the pasta stelline?

13 'Planet earth is blue and there's nothing I can do' is a line from which David Bowie hit song?

14 In which New England state of the US is Casco Bay?

15 What Z is the name of a lake, a town and a canton in Switzerland?

Answers 1 Gamages 2 Macys 3 X 4 Michigan 5 Hathi 6 Denmark 7 Hiram 8 Sheep 9 Sitting 10 Imogen 11 Bows or butterflies wings 12 Star-shaped 13 Space Oddity 14 Maine 15 Zug

MISCELLANEOUS 4 — *Quiz 65*

1   In 2001, Benicio Del Toro won the Oscar for Best Supporting Actor for his performance in which film?

2   And for her performance in which film did Marcia Gay Harden win the Oscar for Best Supporting Actress?

3   And which film won the Oscar for Best Foreign Language Film in 2001?

4   The island of Lesbos lies nearest to the mainland of which country?

5   Name the 19th century Italian revolutionary who founded the movement known as 'Young Italy'?

6   What was the pseudonym of the French satirical writer Jacques Thibault who won the Nobel Prize for Literature in 1921?

7   Left Bower and Right Bower are terms used in which card game beginning with E?

8   What P is a card game for two players which uses the terms Quatorzes and Trios, Carte Blanche and Capot?

9   And what B is a card game for two players played with two packs of cards from which each 6, 5, 4, 3 and 2 have been removed?

10 'The Children's Hour' and 'Toys In The Attic' are plays written by which 20th century female US dramatist?

11 Which 20th century US president said: 'The best way to silence any friend of yours whom you know to be a fool, is to induce him to hire a hall'? Was it Richard Nixon, Theodore Roosevelt or Woodrow Wilson?

12 The children's book 'Emil And The Detectives' was written by which 20th century German writer?

13 What was the name of the arrogant but brilliant sleuth created by US writer S.S. Van Dine?

14 And which Irish writer created the character Inspector French of Scotland Yard?

15 Which US humorist and writer wrote 'The English are mentioned in the Bible: "Blessed are the meek, for they shall inherit the earth" '?

Answers 1 Traffic 2 Pollock 3 Crouching Tiger, Hidden Dragon 4 Turkey 5 Guiseppe Mazzini 6 Anatole France 7 Euchre 8 Piquet 9 Bezique 10 Lillian Hellman 11 Woodrow Wilson 12 Erich Kastner 13 Philo Vance 14 Freeman Wills Crofts 15 Mark Twain

MISCELLANEOUS 4

1 Derived from a Persian word for 'man-eating creature', what M is a mythical beast having the body of a lion, the face of a man and the sting of a scorpion?

2 And what M is the decimal part of a logarithm?

3 What was the first name of Putnam, the US general who distinguished himself at the Battle of Bunker Hill. Was it Isaac, Ishmail or Israel?

4 Who was the first man to sign the US Declaration of Independence? Was it Benjamin Franklin, John Hancock or Thomas Jefferson?

5 'Symphonie Espagnole' is the best-known work of which 19th century French composer?

6 In which decade of the 20th century was legal aid introduced in the UK?

7 What D is a common name for *seborrhoeic dermatitis*?

8 In which African country would you find the Ngorongoro Conservation Area?

9 And in which Canadian province would you find the Viking site known as L'Anse Aux Meadows?

10 One of the founders of surrealism, which French poet and essayist wrote the Manifesto of Surrealism?

11 Which secret agent and anti-hero first appeared in the 1961 novel 'Call For The Dead'?

12 What nationality was the 19th century philosopher and religious thinker Soren Kierkegaard?

13 What was the name of Thor's legendary hammer?

14 And what was the name of his spear?

15 Which of Shakespeare's plays opens with the following words spoken by Archidamus, a lord of Bohemia: 'If you shall chance, Camillo, to visit Bohemia'?

Answers 1 Manticore 2 Mantissa 3 Israel 4 John Hancock 5 Edouard Lalo 6 1940s 7 Dandruff 8 Tanzania 9 Newfoundland 10 Andre Breton 11 George Smiley 12 Danish 13 Mjollnir 14 Gungner 15 The Winter's Tale

1   The island of Salamis lies in which gulf of the Aegean Sea?

2   What C is the name of the first Old English Christian poet?

3   Paul Hindemith's opera 'The Harmony of the World' was based on the work of which German astronomer?

4   Which Australian-born US composer, pianist and conductor is best remembered for 'Country Gardens' and the orchestral work 'Molly On The Shore'?

5   What was the surname of the Flemish brothers Pol, Herman and Jehanequin who were the most famous of all Gothic illustrators?

6   In which European city is the Alte Pinakothek, an art gallery specializing in European painting from the Middle Ages to the late 18th century?

7   Gondar, or Gonder, was the capital of which African country from 1632 to 1855?

8   In which 1956 film comedy did Danny Kaye have several tongue-twisting lines including: "The pellet with the poison's in the flagon with the dragon; the vessel with the pestle has the brew that is true"?

9   What M is the surname of the man who was chief of the Prussian and German General Staff from 1858 to 1888 and his nephew who was chief of the German General Staff at the outbreak of World War One?

10 Name the woman who founded the American Red Cross.

11 What did the D stand for in the name of US President Franklin D. Roosevelt?

12 Name the French lawyer and politician who wrote the celebrated gastronomical work 'The Physiology of Taste'

13 The Horsehead nebula is in which star constellation?

14 What P is a canal and a type of hat?

15 What A is an organic base used to make drugs, dyes, explosives and plastics? It was first obtained in 1826 by the destructive distillation of indigo.

Answers 1 Saronic Gulf 2 Caedmon 3 Johann Kepler 4 Percy Granger 5 Limburg or Limbourg 6 Munich 7 Ethiopia 8 The Court Jester 9 Moltke 10 Clara Barton 11 Delano 12 Anthelme Brillat-Savarin 13 Orion 14 Panama 15 Aniline

1   According to Aristotle, what is 'the best provision for old age'?

2   In the northern part of which African country is there a strip of territory known as the Aozou Strip, which extends along the country's entire border with Libya?

3   What nationality was the composer Michael Praetorius?

4   And what nationality was the 19th century composer Franz Berwald?

5   Spica is the brightest star in which constellation?

6   The artists Murillo and Velazquez were both born in which Spanish city?

7   Who won the Nobel Prize for Literature in 1925 and in 1938 won an Oscar?

8   What nationality was Tadeusz Kosciusko, the patriot and statesman after whom Australia's highest mountain is named?

9   What H is a person or animal having both male and female sex organs?

10   Which Sicilian-born dramatist, novelist and short-story writer was awarded the Nobel Prize for Literature in 1934?

11   Also featuring Henry Winkler, which famous Hollywood star had his first major role in the 1974 movie 'The Lords Of Flatbush'?

12   How many Oscars did 'The Bridge On The River Kwai' win – 5, 6 or 7?

13   Which period preceded Picasso's Rose or Pink Period?

14   Lennie and George are the central characters of which John Steinbeck novel?

15   The name of which volcanic island off the southern coast of Iceland is derived from the name of the fire god of Icelandic mythology?

Answers 1 Education 2 Chad 3 German 4 Swedish 5 Virgo 6 Seville 7 George Bernard Shaw 8 Polish 9 Hermaphrodite 10 Luigi Pirandello 11 Sylvester Stallone 12 7 13 Blue period 14 Of Mice And Men 15 Surtsey

MISCELLANEOUS 4 — Quiz 69

1 Known as the 'New England mystic', which US poet wrote some 1700 poems, most of which were published after her death in 1886?

2 The two main regions of which European country are known as the Oesling and Bon Pays or Gutland?

3 The musette was a fashionable musical instrument in French court circles in the 17th and 18th centuries. What kind of instrument was it?

4 Which 1966 Roman Polanski movie was shot in and around Holy Island in Northumbria?

5 What nationality was the painter and printmaker James Ensor?

6 And what nationality was the 20th century painter Asger Jorn whose work was influenced by James Ensor and Paul Klee?

7 Which legendary Hollywood actress played Mrs. Van Schuyler in the 1978 movie 'Death On The Nile'?

8 What real surname is shared by Ethel Merman and Bob Dylan?

9 Which French actor/singer was born Shahnour Varenagh Aznavourian?

10 In which European city is the Schloss Schonbrunn Palace?

11 Which 1951 Disney animated film featured the song 'I'm Late'?

12 The TV series 'Happy Days' was set in which US city?

13 Nicknamed because of his height, with which sport do you associate Wee Willie Keeler?

14 What M is an epic Sanskrit poem made up of almost 100,000 couplets, it's length being about seven times the length of the 'Iliad' and the 'Odyssey' combined?

15 Born on 27 June 1880, who wrote several books despite being blind and deaf?

Answers 1 Emily Dickinson 2 Luxembourg 3 Bagpipe 4 Cul-De-Sac 5 Belgian 6 Danish 7 Bette Davis 8 Zimmerman 9 Charles Aznavour 10 Vienna 11 Alice In Wonderland 12 Milwaukee 13 Baseball 14 Mahabharata 15 Helen Keller

1 Which river flows through Salzburg?

2 What was the title of Ronald Reagan's last film? A 1964 thriller, it starred Lee Marvin and featured a young Angie Dickinson.

3 Which 16th century German artist left his early works unsigned, then signed with his initials LC and then later in his career used a 'winged serpent' as his identification?

4 The black swan originates from which continent?

5 What L is the name given to the large group of plants that are formed by the mutually beneficial association between fungi and algae?

6 Landrace, Duroc-Jersey, Poland China and Chester White are all types of which creature?

7 Which apostle was crucified on a cross described as X-shaped?

8 In the Gospel of St. Matthew, the birth of Jesus is told as: 'Behold, a virgin shall be with child, and shall bring forth a son, and they shall call his name ....' what?

9 In which month of 1938 did German troops enter Austria?

10 Name the Hungarian statesman and premier of the 1956 revolutionary government whose attempt to establish Hungary's independence from the Soviet Union cost him his life.

11 Bundini Brown was a flamboyant corner man for which world heavyweight boxing champion?

12 Name the city in northern Mexico, on the Rio Grande, that is an important point of entry into Mexico from the US and where a bullring attracts tourists.

13 What N is an Australian marsupial also known as a banded anteater?

14 Who was the oldest of the five Marx brothers?

15 And who was the youngest?

Answers 1 Salzach 2 The Killers 3 Lucas Cranach 4 Australia 5 Lichens 6 Pigs 7 Andrew 8 Emmanuel 9 March 10 Imre Nagy 11 Muhammad Ali 12 Nuevo Laredo 13 Numbat 14 Chico 15 Gummo

MISCELLANEOUS 4 — Quiz 71

1 Who directed the 1950s films 'A Streetcar Named Desire', 'Viva Zapata' and 'On The Waterfront'?

2 And which actor starred in those films?

3 According to local tradition, Augustus Toplady was inspired to write which hymn whilst sheltering from a storm in the Cheddar Gorge region of England?

4 In 2001, Canadian Gayl King made history by becoming the first woman to compete with men in the world championships of which sport?

5 The Faroe Islands are in which ocean?

6 Alberta is one of only two Canadian provinces not to have a saltwater coastline. Name the other.

7 Which country held the presidency of the EU from 1 January to 30 June 2001?

8 When asked if he liked children, who replied: "I do, if they are properly cooked"?

9 What colour of flag is the symbol of surrender?

10 Which famous indoor sports arena was opened in New York city in 1874? Undergoing several re-developments, the present arena was opened in 1968 on the site of the former Pennsylvania station.

11 In the Bible, which one of the twelve apostles is described as 'the son of Alphaeus'?

12 What N is another name for your *umbilicus*?

13 In November 2000, disgruntled fans of which king of bedroom soul' chanted: "Love god needs Viagra" as they stormed out of a concert in Sydney, Australia when he arrived late and didn't measure up to their expectations?

14 In 1995, which high-speed stage show promised '1600 legs and 3,500 taps per minute'?

15 What P is also known as a scaly anteater?

Answers 1 Elia Kazan 2 Marlon Brando 3 Rock of Ages 4 Darts 5 Atlantic 6 Saskatchewan 7 Sweden 8 W.C. Fields 9 White 10 Madison Square Garden 11 St. Matthew 12 Navel 13 Barry White 14 Riverdance 15 Pangolin

1 Which movie thriller, of which two versions were made, one in 1946 and one in 1978, featured the characters Eddie Mars and Philip Marlowe?

2 James Gleick wrote a biography entitled 'Genius'. Who was the subject?

3 Which great showman styled himself 'The Prince of Humbugs'?

4 Name the French actor and playwright who died after collapsing on stage during a performance of the play 'Le Malade Imaginaire'

5 In which country was the operatic soprano Adelina Patti born?

6 By the Treaty of Kiel in 1814, which country ceded Norway to Sweden?

7 What C is the SI unit of luminous intensity?

8 Name the 18th century Italian physicist who investigated the nature and effects of what he conceived to be electricity in animal tissue. His discoveries led to the invention of the voltaic pile, a kind of battery that makes possible a constant source of current electricity.

9 Which actress appeared in the 1990 film 'Mermaids' at the age of nine? She then played Wednesday Addams in the movie 'The Addams Family' and more recently appeared in 'The Opposite Of Sex' and 'Sleepy Hollow'.

10 In December 1999, Austrian parachutist Felix Baumgartner took base-jumping into a new dimension when he leapt from which 120 foot high statue in South America?

11 The name of which malt whisky is the Gaelic for 'glen of tranquility'?

12 What Z is the hill on which Jerusalem stands and is also a name sometimes given to Jerusalem?

13 Jacksonville, St. Petersburg and Hialeah are all cities in which US state?

14 In December 2000, which British actress was heavily fined by the American union, Screen Actors Guild, for crossing a picket line whilst shooting a commercial earlier in the year?

15 What C is the name given to a circle of light around a luminous body such as the moon, is a circular chandelier and is a long cigar with blunt ends?

Answers 1 The Big Sleep **2** American physicist Richard Feynman **3** Phineas T. Barnum **4** Moliere **5** Spain **6** Denmark **7** Candela **8** Luigi Galvani **9** Christina Ricci **10** The Statue of Christ, overlooking Rio de Janeiro **11** Glenmorangie **12** Zion **13** Florida **14** Elizabeth Hurley **15** Corona

1   During which century did the landscape gardener Lancelot 'Capability' Brown live and work?

2   On 28 November 2000, which European country passed a law to legalise euthanasia?

3   Which town in the Lazio region of Italy, a summer resort in Roman times, is famous for the remains of Hadrian's villa and the Renaissance Villa d'Este?

4   What is the common name for the infectious disease mononucleosis? Mainly affecting adolescents and young adults, it is caused by the Epstein-Barr virus and includes fever and a particularly sore throat amongst its symptoms.

5   What W is the name given to the piece of cloth that frames the face and was worn by women in the Middle Ages and is still worn by some nuns?

6   What is the common name of the non-venomous European snake *Natrix natrix*?

7   Riots erupted in which US city in 1992 after four white policemen were acquitted of beating black motorist Rodney King?

8   'Professional Widow', 'Cornflake Girl' and 'Pretty Good Year' are all songs recorded by which female US singer?

9   The choroid is a vascular membrane in which part of the body?

10   Name the only state of the USA whose name begins with D.

11   And the only one beginning with L?

12   Name either of the James Bond films, one released in 1977, the other in 1979, in which the villain Jaws appeared.

13   Who wrote the best-selling novels 'The Brethren', 'The Testament', 'The Street Lawyer' and 'The Partner'?

14   Prior to the start of the 2000 Olympics, a team official from which former Soviet republic was arrested after allegedly carrying human growth hormone, an illegal performance enhancer, into Sydney airport?

15   Which Canadian singer has had hits singing duets with Tina Turner, Bonnie Raitt, Barbra Streisand and Melanie C and also had a hit singing with Rod Stewart and Sting?

Answers 1 18th 2 Netherlands 3 Tivoli 4 Glandular fever (sometimes referred to as the kissing disease) 5 Wimple 6 Grass snake or water snake 7 Los Angeles 8 Tori Amos 9 Eye 10 Delaware 11 Louisiana 12 The Spy Who Loved Me or Moonraker 13 John Grisham 14 Uzbekistan 15 Bryan Adams